The Liturgy in Medieval England

This is the first comprehensive historical treatment of the Latin liturgy in medieval England. Richard W. Pfaff constructs a history of the worship carried out in churches – cathedral, monastic, or parish – primarily through the surviving manuscripts of service books, and sets this within the context of the wider political, ecclesiastical, and cultural history of the period. The main focus is on the mass and daily office, treated both chronologically and by type, the liturgies of each religious order and each secular "use" being studied individually. Furthermore, hagiographical and historiographical themes – respectively, which saints are prominent in a given witness and how the labors of scholars over the last century and a half have both furthered and, in some cases, impeded our understandings – are explored throughout. The book thus provides both a narrative account and a reference tool of permanent value.

Richard W. Pfaff is Professor Emeritus of History at the University of North Carolina, Chapel Hill. His numerous publications include *New Liturgical Feasts in Later Medieval England* (1970), *Montague Rhodes James* (1980), and *Liturgical Calendars, Saints, and Services in Medieval England* (1998). He is a Fellow of the Medieval Academy of America, the Society of Antiquaries of London, and the Royal Historical Society, and is a vice-president of the Henry Bradshaw Society.

The Liturgy in Medieval England

A History

Richard W. Pfaff

CAMBRIDGE
UNIVERSITY PRESS

CAMBRIDGE UNIVERSITY PRESS
Cambridge, New York, Melbourne, Madrid, Cape Town, Singapore,
São Paulo, Delhi

Cambridge University Press
The Edinburgh Building, Cambridge CB2 8RU, UK

Published in the United States of America by
Cambridge University Press, New York

www.cambridge.org
Information on this title: www.cambridge.org/9780521808477

First published 2009

Printed in the United Kingdom at the University Press, Cambridge

A catalogue record for this publication is available from the British Library

ISBN 978-0-521-80847-7 Hardback

To my grandchildren,
Andrew, Helen, and Edward

Contents

Preface

It may be helpful to the reader if some inadequacies obvious to the author of this book are acknowledged at the outset. The first has to do with its title, the justification for which is that it is more accurate than all conceivable alternatives – at least in expressing aspiration if not necessarily accomplishment. To call it *The Liturgical Books of Medieval England* would misrepresent what is attempted: a genuinely historical account of what can be known about the Latin liturgy as used in England during the middle ages, based primarily, but by no means exclusively, on evidence drawn from the surviving service books and fragments. A fuller explanation of this hope and what is involved in trying to fulfill it is provided in the Introduction. Here the reader is asked mainly to notice that the indefinite article is employed deliberately: what is offered here is *a*, with no pretence to being *the* definitive, history of the subject. But it is intended as a history, not as an inventory or conspectus of sources, nor as an introduction to an admittedly complex subject. If it were not palpably absurd, a more accurate title might be *An Essay on the History of Medieval England as seen through Liturgical Sources*.

The next inadequacy is apparent in the book's length: it is too short. Treatment of the announced subject in a single volume, even one with the generous word-limit allowed me by Cambridge University Press, has required the almost complete omission of three large areas: (1) nearly everything having to do with distinctively episcopal liturgies (ordinations, consecration of virgins and other special classes of people, confirmations, dedications of churches and their equipment, coronations) and the books, usually called pontificals, that contain them; (2) pastoral liturgies, sometimes termed occasional offices, such as the rites for baptism, marriage, visitation of the sick, and burial of the dead – along with the separate books, normatively called manuals, in which these rites are often put together; (3) the liturgical aspects implicit in collections of private devotions and, specially important for the later middle ages, in Books of Hours. Consideration of each of these three areas could well fill a separate volume (and indeed has done so, specially in the case of Books of Hours, intensively studied for their art-historical importance).

A third inadequacy involves approach rather than content: that the dimension of music is almost completely ignored. Where the musical aspect plays a prominent part in a liturgical manuscript, this is generally indicated, and the nature of the chant books that are considered – grad-uals, antiphonals, processionals, tropers – is kept at the forefront when they are discussed. Friends who are eminent musicologists have agreed that this exclusion is necessary, as a matter of space as well as (I con-fess) of insufficient expertise. Nonetheless, I am aware of it, and regret it. Certain factors that temper the regret at least mildly are alluded to briefly in the Introduction.

Less regrettable, perhaps, but equally glaring is the lack of attention paid to the dimension perhaps better encapsulated by the French phrase *sentiment religieuse* than by the English word "spirituality." Just as the present work does not pretend to delve into the psychological, socio-logical, or anthropological aspects of Christian worship, it aims also to steer clear of the primarily theological aspects. So there will be no discussion of eucharistic doctrine as such, nor of the growth of Marian piety, both of which have a marked reflex in liturgical expression, nor of individual cults, above all that of Corpus Christi; still less, of the development of para-liturgical devotions like the Rosary or the Stations of the Cross (which in any case are mainly features of post-medieval spirituality). The general assumption here is that practicioners of wor-ship in the middle ages were serious about what they did; but an effort is made to keep in mind that they were all also human beings, not angels. Such human characteristics as inattention, greed, family pride, and the desire to keep warm in frigid churches need therefore to be factored in to any attempt at understanding liturgical practice. Even if the obser-vation that all history is social history is a truism, it may be a valuable one to keep in mind as we attempt to deal with an area of activity that is no less human because it involves matters primarily characterized as "religious."

The length of this book (too long, it may be thought, as well as too short) requires a structure which, I believe, a glance at the table of contents will make plain. It requires, too, that each chapter be as self-contained as possible, even at the risk of a certain amount of repeti-tion. Recognizing that few will probably wade through every page here, I have attempted to cast each chapter so that it can be read separately (but not, ideally, in isolation) from other chapters. This means that the book is heavily cross-referenced, so that readers of one part understand where they need to go to follow a specific point. This is particularly true with respect to the many historiographical sections, discussions of the work of individual scholars from the past and (especially) of editions they have produced. These sections are meant to be a prominent feature of the present book, and I hope they will be found useful rather than tiresome. I hope also that readers will have a serious look at the Introduction before launching into any specific chapter. Much that is said there is *not* repeated elsewhere, especially the part headed "What the reader is presumed to know."

One such matter, but not appropriate to that section, requires a word of explanation here: Latin. As this book studies the Latin liturgy of medieval England, there is no feasible way that all traces of that language can be eliminated. Despite the current trend to provide translations of anything in Latin and other learned languages in even scholarly books, that is simply not possible in this case. Much of the Latin quoted here is formulaic – it would be ridiculous to supply "Lamb of God" whenever the *Agnus Dei* is mentioned – and in many cases a point at issue is established only by comparing the exact (Latin) wordings of prayer-formulas. In booklists, also (a source heavily mined), what counts is the way a book is described, whether as *vetus* or *imperfectus* or *sufficiens* or whatever. That said, much Latin is either paraphrased or translated; this is particularly true of any passages of Tacitean or Horatian difficulty. The aim is that any reader with a small amount of Latin, some familiarity with the liturgy in general, and a modicum of ingenuity can follow the discussion with little or no difficulty.

In a work primarily concerned with sources and source-editions, keeping abreast of secondary literature is, while never unimportant, not the highest priority. I hope nonetheless to have taken reasonable notice of articles and monographs published through 2006, plus a very few of 2007. An effort to retain some sort of balance in the amount of attention devoted to various periods and aspects has required not taking full account of the spate of publications which has appeared recently on the late tenth and eleventh centuries – as much, it seems, as on the twelfth and thirteenth centuries combined. A new flood of scholarship can be expected as a result of the most outstanding for our purposes of the several enterprises aimed at digitizing collections of medieval manuscripts: that of making generously available online the rich treasures of the Parker Library at Corpus Christi College, Cambridge (www.corpus. cam.ac.uk/parker). I have been unable to take full advantage of these electronic resources, but have had the incomparable benefit of being able to consult, in person and over more than four decades, all of the relevant manuscripts in that collection as well as the great majority of the other codices cited in this book.

Finally, a word about the total lack of illustrations. This is deliberate (as well as an economy), given the two alternatives. The first is to furnish the dozens, perhaps even hundreds, of reproductions of manuscript leaves that would be needed for there to be anything like a representative sample of the variety of sources on which this work depends. The second would be to provide a tiny selection – say, eight to twelve leaves – from, inevitably, the best known codices: treasures like the Lindisfarne gospels, benedictional of Æthelwold, St Albans psalter, Stowe breviary, Sherborne missal. This would be exactly counter-productive, in implying that these celebrated specimens (each one famous for its illustrations) are what this book is *really* about. If some of these do receive a good deal of attention here, it is because they contain a lot of pertinent information rather than because they are exceptionally beautiful.

Over the many years which this work has taken to complete I have received much help and encouragement, both from institutions and from individuals. Among the former, I am grateful for support in the form of multiple research grants from the University of North Carolina at Chapel Hill; of a fellowship at the National Humanities Center; of visiting fellowships at Magdalen College Oxford (an *alma mater* in many ways and for many years, going back to matriculation in 1957) and Magdalene College, Cambridge; and of a generous Emeritus Fellowship from the Andrew W. Mellon Foundation.

The assistance of librarians at the many libraries – over sixty in Britain alone – at which I have worked is by no means taken for granted; but to list them all (for many libraries, more than one) would be inexpressibly tedious. In all I have seen well over five hundred manuscripts in preparation for this book, as well as a great many printed books, early and modern. That translates into an immense amount of fetching, recording, and returning on the part of library staff members. I have received also a large amount of learned assistance from scholarly librarians, not least at many cathedrals; several are thanked at specific points in the footnotes.

Standing on the shoulders of other scholars is now a cliché, not to mention precarious. If I were to attempt to leap onto shoulders of any giants of the past, it would be those of the two scholars whose names appear most often on these pages: J(ohn) Wickham Legg (who died fifteen years before I was born) and Neil Ker (a cherished friend and mentor, who died in 1984). A reader who has any awareness of their achievement – to which might be added those of Edmund Bishop, M.R. James, and Dom David Knowles – should be well positioned to understand the kinds of approaches this book tries to take. A long alphabetical list of all those living colleagues to whom I owe gratitude would be as tedious as a list of librarians. Again, many are thanked in the footnotes, in connection with specific points, but a few more general obligations need to be spelled out here. With great generosity Nigel Morgan provided me with the early gift of a database he drew up (with the assistance of Nicholas Rogers) of all the English liturgical books in manuscript of which he could find any mention; he is modest about acknowledging the limitations of this database, and I hope that such use of it as I have made does not reflect adversely on either his generosity or his acumen. Brave souls who have read one or more entire chapters include George Hardin Brown, Barbara Harvey, Christopher (Drew) Jones, Sherry Reames, and Elizabeth Teviotdale; and Linda Voigts has ploughed valiantly through almost the entire typescript. I have prized their kind encouragement no less than their expertise, but they should not be held accountable for any of the numerous flaws that remain. Further encouragement has come, often at times of drooping confidence, from Margaret Bent, Sarah Foot, and Elizabeth Livingstone in Oxford; Eamon Duffy, Joan Greatrex, Rosamond McKitterick, Susan Rankin, and Tessa Webber in Cambridge; Brenda Bolton in St Albans; Nicolas Bell, Alan Thacker, and Christopher Roberts in London (whom I also thank for a great deal of hospitality as well as five decades of friendship); and here in Chapel Hill from Jaroslav Folda, Michael McVaugh, Francis Newton, and Janet Sorrentino. Two major boons were made possible by the Mellon Fellowship: the invaluable help of David Carlisle as a research assistant, and the superb indexing skills of Julia McVaugh. Anna Oxbury has been a wonderfully cooperative, as well as acute, copy-editor. A great debt is owed to Siegfried Wenzel for providing over many years a model of perseverance and exact scholarship, as well as an unfailing supply of both cheer and needed criticism; that this work would ever have been completed without his exhortations is doubtful.

A final word of thanks must go to my son David, who after reading drafts of several chapters suggested the four-word goal that I have kept prominently displayed on my desk: "comprehensive but not exhaustive." I shall be delighted if this book is thought even remotely to have achieved that goal.

Sigla and editorial conventions

Libraries

BL: London, British Library. B.m: Bibliothèque municipale. BN: Paris, Bibliothèque Nationale. Bodl.: Oxford, Bodleian Library. CCCC: Cambridge, Corpus Christi College. CUL: Cambridge, University Library. TCC: Cambridge, Trinity College. The abbreviation MS is not normally supplied after any of these, or where it reads cumbersomely.

Religious orders/institutes

Carm.: Carmelite. Carth.: Carthusian. Cist.: Cistercian. Clun.: Cluniac. OESA: Austin (Augustinian) friar. OFM: Franciscan. OP: Dominican. OSA (*or* Aug.): Augustinian canon. OSB (*or* Ben.): Benedictine.

In general, abbreviations are either conventional or obvious: brev. = breviary/*breviarium*; bull. = bulletin; cath. = cathedral; c. or col. = column; coll. = college; Fest. = Festschrift, followed by the name of the honoree (long explanatory subtitles are generally omitted); fol. = folio; fols = folios; jnl = journal; lib. = library; mm = millimetres; MS(S) = manuscript(s); p(p). = page(s); s(aec). = *saeculum* ["century"]; sacr. = sacramentary/*sacramentarium*; rev. = review (or *revue*); soc. = society; trans. = transactions. In measurements of MSS, height precedes width; size of written space, where known and useful, follows in brackets. Rectos of MS leaves have no special indication, versos are so specified (e.g., fol. 62v). Printed books of the late fifteenth and sixteenth century are usually designated by place of publication and year (e.g., Rouen 1506); the printer's name is given only if needed to avoid ambiguity or if specially relevant. The simple designation *Cat.* will always refer to the main catalogue of (Latin medieval) manuscripts in a particular collection, where possible as listed in P. M. Kristeller, *Latin Manuscript Books before 1600*, 4th edn by S. Krämer, Monumenta Germaniae historica, Hilfsmittel 13 (Berlin 1993).

Common Latin abbreviations are sometimes employed when devotional formulas are cited: dne, dns = *domine, dominus*; Dq = *Deus qui*; ds = *deus*; mis = *misericors*; omps = *omnipotens*; qs = *qu(a)esumus*. Two widely used prayer formulas are abbreviated as a whole: Osd = *omnipotens sempiterne deus*; per = *per dominum nostrum Iesum Christum*. All other abbreviations should be self-explanatory.

Wherever it is useful to suggest similarity or identity of wording, spellings have been normalized into forms most often found in printed texts (usually *v* for consonantal *u*, less consistently *e* for *ae* or *ę*). Punctuation and capitalization (especially in the case of proper nouns) have generally been modernized. The goal being to enable the reader to use this book in conjunction with the many tools available for liturgical study, especially collation tables, concordances, and indexes, pragmatic considerations have taken precedence over any desire for perfect consistency.

Bibliographical abbreviations

Basic reference tools, journals, and source collections.

AA. SS.: *Acta Sanctorum* (Antwerp, Brussels, etc., 1643–; cited by month and day).

ACC: Alcuin Club Collections (London 1899–).

Anal. Boll.: *Analecta Bollandiana* (Brussels 1882–).

ASE: *Anglo-Saxon England* (Cambridge 1972–).

BAA Conf. Trs: British Archaeological Association Conference Transactions 1978– [for 1975 conf.–]).

BHL: *Bibliotheca Hagiographica Latina*, 2 vols (Brussels 1898–1901); *Supplementum*, by H. Fros (1986).

Binns, *Dedications*: A. Binns, *Dedications of Monastic Houses in England and Wales 1066–1216* (Woodbridge 1989).

Biog. Reg. Oxf.: A. B. Emden, *A Biographical Register of the University of Oxford to 1500*, 3 vols (Oxford 1957–9).

Bishop, *Liturg. Hist.*: E. Bishop, *Liturgica Historica* (Oxford 1918).

C & S 1205–1313: *Councils & Synods, with other documents relating to the English Church*, II: *A.D. 1205–1313*, ed. F. M. Powicke and C. R. Cheney. 2 vols (Oxford 1964).

C & S 871–1204: *Councils & Synods, with other documents relating to the English Church*, I: *A.D. 871–1204*, ed. D. Whitelock, M. Brett, and C. N. L. Brooke. 2 vols (Oxford 1981).

CBMLC: Corpus of British Medieval Library Catalogues (London 1990–).

CCSL: Corpus Christianorum, Series Latina (Turnhout 1954–).

CLLA: K. Gamber, *Codices liturgici Latini antiquiores*, Spicilegii Friburgensis Subsidia 1. 2 vols (2nd, much expanded, edn, 1968, of 1st edn Fribourg 1963); *Suppl.* by B. Baroffio, SF Subs. 1A (1988).

CMCAS: N. R. Ker, *Catalogue of Manuscripts Containing Anglo-Saxon* (Oxford 1957).

Corp. Orat.: E. Moeller, J.-M. Clément, and B. Coppieters 't Wallant, eds. *Corpus orationum*. 10 vols. CCSL 160 (1992–97).

Eadwine Psalter: M. Gibson, T. A. Heslop, and R. W. Pfaff, eds. *The Eadwine Psalter: Text, Image and Monastic Culture in Twelfth-Century Canterbury* (London 1992).

Eph. Liturg.: *Ephemerides Liturgicae* (Rome 1887–).

Fasti 1066–1300: J. le Neve, *Fasti Ecclesiae Anglicanae 1066–1300*, new edn D. E. Greenway et al. (London 1968–).

Fasti 1300–1541: J. le Neve, *Fasti Ecclesiae Anglicanae 1300–1541*, new edn J. M. Horn et al. (London 1969–).

Harper, *Forms and Orders*: J. Harper, *The Forms and Orders of Western Liturgy from the Tenth to the Eighteenth Century: A Historical Introduction and Guide for Students and Musicians* (Oxford 1991).

Hartzell, *Cat. Music*: K. D. Hartzell, *Catalogue of Manuscripts Written or Owned in England up to 1200 Containing Music* (Woodbridge 2006).

HBS: Henry Bradshaw Society (London 1891–).

Heads Rel. Houses: *Heads of Religious Houses; England and Wales*, I: *940–1216*, ed. D. Knowles, C. N. L. Brooke, V.C.M. London (2nd edn); II: *1216–1377*, ed. D. M. Smith and V.C.M. London (both Cambridge 2001).

Hughes, *MMMO*: A(ndrew) Hughes, *Medieval Manuscripts for Mass and Office: a Guide to their Organization and Terminology* (Toronto 1982).

Kauffmann, *Romanesque MSS*: C. M. Kauffmann, *Romanesque Manuscripts 1066–1190*. SMIBI III (1975).

Knowles, *Mon. Order* or *MO*: D. Knowles, *The Monastic Order in England ... 940–1216*, 2nd edn (Cambridge 1963).

Knowles, *Rel. Orders* or *RO*: D. Knowles, *The Religious Orders in England*, 3 vols (Cambridge 1948–59).

Lapidge, *Litanies*: M. Lapidge, ed. *Anglo-Saxon Litanies of the Saints*. HBS 106 (1991).

Lapidge, *Swithun*: M. Lapidge, *The Cult of St Swithun* (Oxford 2003).

Learning and Literature: *Learning and Literature in Anglo-Saxon England* (Festschrift P. Clemoes), ed. M. Lapidge and H. Gneuss (Cambridge 1985).

Lincoln Cath. Stats: H. Bradshaw and C. Wordsworth, eds. *Statutes of Lincoln Cathedral*, 3 vols (Cambridge 1892–97).

Med. Rel. Houses: D. Knowles and R. N. Hadcock, *Medieval Religious Houses in England and Wales*, 2nd edn (London 1971).

MLGB: N. R. Ker, ed. *Medieval Libraries of Great Britain*, 2nd edn (London 1964).

MLGB Suppl.: A. G. Watson, ed. *Medieval Libraries of Great Britain. Supplement to the Second Edition* (London 1987).

MMBL: N. R. Ker, *Medieval Manuscripts in British Libraries*. 5 vols (Oxford 1971–92, vol. IV with A. J. Piper; vol. V, Index, by A. G. Watson et al., 2003).

Morgan, *Early Gothic MSS*: N. Morgan, *Early Gothic Manuscripts 1190–1285*. 2 vols. SMIBI IV (1982–88).

NMT: Nelson's Medieval Texts (Edinburgh 1949–65).

ODCC: F. L. Cross and E. A. Livingstone, eds. *The Oxford Dictionary of the Christian Church*, 3rd edn (Oxford 1997 [revised 2005]).

ODNB: H. C. G. Matthew and B. Harrison, eds. *Oxford Dictionary of National Biography*, 60 vols (Oxford 2004).

OMT: Oxford Medieval Texts (Oxford 1967–).

Oxf. Dict. Saints: D. H. Farmer, *The Oxford Dictionary of Saints* (Oxford 1978 [and several subsequent editions]).

PBE: [Pevsner] Buildings of England, founded by N. Pevsner (Harmondsworth 1951–, many vols now in 2nd edn). Cited by (pre-1974) county; related series for Buildings of Wales, Scotland, and Ireland are in progress.

Pfaff, *LCSSME*: R. W. Pfaff, *Liturgical Calendars, Saints, and Services in Medieval England* (Aldershot 1998).

Pfaff, ed. *Liturg. Bks ASE*: *Liturgical Books of Anglo-Saxon England*. OEN Subsidia 23 (Kalamazoo 1995).

Pfaff, *Med. Latin Liturgy*: *Medieval Latin Liturgy: a Select Bibliography*. Toronto Med. Bibliogs 9 (Toronto 1982).

Pfaff, *M. R. James*: *Montague Rhodes James* (London 1980).

Pfaff, *New Liturg. Feasts*: *New Liturgical Feasts in Later Medieval England* (Oxford 1970).

PL: Patrologia Latina, ed. J.-P. Migne. 221 vols (Paris 1844–64).

Rev. Bén.: *Revue Bénédictine* (Maredsous 1885–).

RS: Rerum Britannicarum medii aevi Scriptores/Chronicles and Memorials … ["Rolls Series"] 99 vols in 259 (London 1858–1911).

Salisbury 1066–1300: D. E. Greenway, ed. *Fasti 1066–1300*, IV: *Salisbury* (London 1991).

Sandler, *Gothic MSS*: L. F. Sandler, *Gothic Manuscripts 1285–1385*. 2 vols. SMIBI V (1986).

SCH: Studies in Church History (papers from Ecclesiastical History Society meetings; London, etc. 1964–).

Scott, *Later Gothic MSS*: K. Scott, *Later Gothic Manuscripts*. 2 vols. SMIBI VI (1996).

SMIBI: Survey of Manuscripts Illuminated in the British Isles, gen. ed. J. J. G. Alexander. 6 vols in 10 (London 1975–96).

SS: Surtees Society (York and London, etc. 1835–).

Sharpe, *Handlist*: R. Sharpe, *A Handlist of the Latin Writers of Great Britain and Ireland before 1540*, Pubs of the Jnl of Med. Latin 1 (Turnhout 1997).

Temple, *Anglo-Saxon MSS*: E. Temple, *Anglo-Saxon Manuscripts 900–1066.* SMIBI II (1976).

Tolhurst, *Eng. Mon. Brevs*: J. B. L. Tolhurst, *Introduction to English Monastic Breviaries*, vol. VI of his *Hyde Breviary* edn, HBS 80 (1942; repr. 1993).

Van Dijk, *Handlist*: S. J. P. van Dijk, *Handlist of the Latin Liturgical Manuscripts in the Bodleian Library.* 7 vols (typescript, in Duke Humfrey's Library [Bodleian], 1953).

VCH: Victoria History of the Counties of England (London and Oxford 1900–), followed by county and vol. number.

Vogel, *Sources*: C. Vogel, tr. and rev. W. G. Storey and N. K. Rasmussen, *Medieval Liturgy: an Introduction to the Sources* (Washington, DC, 1986).

Ward, *Pubs HBS*: A. Ward, *The Publications of the Henry Bradshaw Society: An Annotated Bibliography with Indexes.* Bibliotheca "Ephemerides Liturgicae" 67 = Inst. Liturg. Quarreriensia 1 (Rome 1972).

Watson, *BL Dated MSS*: A. G. Watson, *Catalogue of Dated and Datable MSS c. 700–1600 in… the British Library.* 2 vols (London 1979).

Webber, *Scribes and Scholars*: T. Webber, *Scribes and Scholars at Salisbury Cath. c. 1075–c. 1125* (Oxford 1992).

Wormald, *Eng. Kals*: F. Wormald, ed. *English Kalendars before A.D. 1100.* HBS 72 (1934).

Wormald, *Eng. Ben. Kals*: F. Wormald, ed. *English Benedictine Kalendars after A.D. 1100.* HBS 77, 81 (1939–46).

Editions of liturgical texts

Barking Ordinal: J. B. L. Tolhurst, ed. *The Ordinale and Customary of the Benedictine Nuns of Barking Abbey*, 2 vols. HBS 65–66 (1927–28).

Bec Missal: A(nselm) Hughes, ed. *The Bec Missal.* HBS 94 (1963).

Exeter Ordinal: J. N. Dalton, ed. *Ordinale Exon.* 4 vols. HBS 37, 38, 63, 79 (with G. H. Doble) (1909–39).

Fécamp Ordinal: D. Chadd, ed. *The Ordinal of the Abbey of the Trinity, Fécamp.* 2 vols. HBS 111–12 (1999, 2001).

Fulda Sacr.: G. Richter and A. Schönfelder, ed. *Sacramentarium Fuldense saeculi X* (Fulda 1912; repr. as HBS 101, 1980).

Hereford Breviary: W. H. Frere and L. E. G. Brown, eds. *The Hereford Breviary.* 3 vols. HBS 26, 40, 46 (1904–15).

Hereford Missal: W. G. Henderson, ed. *Missale ad usum percelebris ecclesiae Herfordensis* (Leeds 1874; repr. Farnborough 1969).

Hyde Breviary: J. B. L. Tolhurst, ed. *The Monastic Breviary of Hyde Abbey, Winchester.* 6 vols. HBS 69–71, 76, 78, 80 (1932–42).

Leofric Missal: N. Orchard, ed. *The Leofric Missal*. 2 vols. HBS 113–14 (2002).

Leofric Missal (Warren): F. E. Warren, ed. *The Leofric Missal* (Oxford 1883, repr. Farnborough 1968).

Lesnes Missal: P. Jebb, ed. *The Lesnes Missal*. HBS 95 (1964).

New Minster Missal: D. H. Turner, ed. *The Missal of the New Minster, Winchester*. HBS 93 (1962).

Regularis Concordia: T. Symons, ed. and tr., *Regularis Concordia ...*, NMT (1953).

Robert of Jumièges Missal: H. A. Wilson, ed. *The Missal of Robert of Jumièges*. HBS 11 (1894).

St Augustine's Missal: M. Rule, ed. *The Missal of St Augustine's Abbey, Canterbury* (Cambridge 1896).

Sarum Antiphonal: W. H. Frere, ed. *Antiphonale Sarisburiense*. 6 vols. Plainsong and Medieval Music Society (London 1901–5; repr. Farnborough 1966).

Sarum Breviary: F. Procter and C. Wordsworth, eds. *Breviarium ad usum insignis ecclesiae Sarum*. 3 vols (Cambridge 1879–86; repr. Farnborough 1970).

Sarum Gradual: W. H. Frere, ed. *Graduale Sarisburiense*. 2 vols. Plainsong and Medieval Music Society (London 1891–4; repr. Farnborough 1966).

Sarum Manual: A. J. Collins, ed. *Manuale ad usum percelebris ecclesiae Sarisburiensis*. HBS 91 (1960).

Sarum Missal (Dickinson) or *SMD*: F. H. Dickinson, ed. *Missale ad usum insignis et praeclarae ecclesiae Sarum* (Burntisland 1861–83).

Sarum Missal (Legg) or *SML*: J. W. Legg, ed. *The Sarum Missal Edited from Three Early Manuscripts* (Oxford 1916; repr. 1969).

Sarum Processional: W. G. Henderson, ed. *Processionale ad usum insignis ac praeclarae ecclesiae Sarum* (Leeds 1882; repr. Farnborough 1969).

Use of Sarum or *US*: W. H. Frere, ed. *The Use of Sarum, I: The Sarum Customs as set forth in the Consuetudinary and Customary*; II: *The Ordinal and Tonal*. 2 vols (Cambridge 1898–1901; repr. Farnborough 1969).

Westminster Missal or *WM*: J. W. Legg, ed. *Missale ad usum ecclesiae Westmonasteriensis*. 3 vols. HBS 1, 5, 12 (1891–97; repr. in one vol. Woodbridge 1999).

Winchcombe Sacr.: A. Davril, ed. *The Winchcombe Sacramentary*. HBS 109 (1995).

Worcester Antiphonal: L. McLachlan, ed. *Antiphonaire monastique, XIIIe siècle*. Paléographie Musicale, sér. 1, 12 (Tournai 1922).

Wulstan Portiforium: A(nselm) Hughes, ed. *The Portiforium of Saint Wulstan*. 2 vols. HBS 89–90 (1958–59).

York Breviary: S. W. Lawley, ed. *Breviarium ad usum insignis ecclesiae Eboracensis.* 2 vols. SS 71, 75 (1880–83).

York Manual and Processional: W. G. Henderson, ed. *Manuale et processionale ad usum insignis ecclesiae Eboracensis.* SS 63 (1875).

York Missal: W. G. Henderson, ed. *Missale ad usum insignis ecclesiae Eboracensis.* 2 vols. SS 59–60 (1874).

Nicknames for manuscripts frequently referred to

(For a full list of all manuscripts cited, see Index of Manuscripts, organized by libraries)

Æthelwold benedictional	BL Add. 49598
Abp Robt benedictional	Rouen, B.m. 369 (Y.7)
Arsenal missal [Legg's "A"]	Paris, Bibl. Arsenal 135
Bainbridge pontifical	CUL Ff.6.1
Barnwell antiphonal	CUL Mm.2.9
Beauchamp missal	Oxf., Trin 8
Bologna missal [Legg's "B"]	Bologna, Bibl. univ. 2565
Bosworth psalter	BL Add. 37517
Bury St Edmunds missal	Laon, B.m. 238
Caligula troper	BL Cott. Calig. A.xiv
Canterbury benedictional	BL Harley 2892
Cistercian missal	CUL Add. 4079
Coldingham breviary	BL Harley 4664
Cosin gradual	Durham UL, Cosin V.v.6
Crawford missal [Legg's "C"]	Manchester, JRUL lat. 24
Darley, Red Book of	CCCC 422
Durham collectar	Durham cath. A.IV.19
Durham missal	BL Harley 5289
Eadui psalter	BL Arundel 155
Eadwine psalter	TCC R.17.1
Ely breviary-missal	CUL Ii.4.20
Evesham pontifical	Bodl. Barlow 7
Exeter pontifical	BL Add. 28188
Exeter/preSarum missal	Exeter cath. 3515
Exeter/Sarum missal	Exeter cath. 3510
Gilbertine massbook	Lincoln cath. 115
Giso sacramentary	BL Cott. Vit. A.xviii
Gloucester antiphonal	Oxf., Jesus 10
Guisborough diurnal	Cbg., Sidney 62

Guisborough missal	BL Add 35285
Guisborough psalter	Bodl. Laud lat. 5
Hanley Castle missal	CUL Kk.2.6
Harley psalter	BL Harley 603
Haughmond gradual	Shrewsbury School 30
Hereford cath. breviary	Hereford cath. P.9.VII
Hyde breviary	Bodl. Rawl. liturg. e.1*
Kenilworth missal	Chichester cath. Med. 2
Lavington manual	Bodl. Lat. liturg. f.25
Leofric collectar	BL Harley 2961
Leofric missal	Bodl. 579
Leofric psalter	BL Harley 863
Lesnes missal	London, Vict. & Alb. 404
Lewes breviary-missal	Cbg., Fitzwilliam 369
Lyell processional	Bodl. Lyell 9
Lytlington missal	Westminster Abbey 37
Magdalen pontifical	Oxf., Magd. 226
Muchelney breviary	BL Add. 43405–6
New Minster missal	Le Havre, B.m. 330
Penwortham breviary	BL Add. 52359
Ramsey benedictional	BN lat. 987
Ramsey(?) pontifical	BL Cott. Vit. A.vii
Ranworth antiphonal	Ranworth, parish ch.
Rievaulx(?) missal	BL Add. 46203
Risby ordinal	BL Harley 1001
Robert of Jumièges missal	Rouen, B.m. 274 (Y.6)
Samson pontifical	CCCC 146
Sarum gradual (Frere)	BL Add. 12194
Sherborne missal	BL Add. 74326
Springfield antiphonal	CUL Add. 2602
St Albans breviary	BL Royal 2 A.x
St Albans gradual	BL Royal 2 B.iv
St Albans legendary	NY PML M.926
St Albans processional	Bodl. Laud misc. 4
St Albans missal	Bodl. Laud misc. 279
St Albans psalter	Hildesheim, parish ch.
St Albans sacramentary	Bodl. Rawl. liturg. c. 1
St Augustine's missal	CCCC 270
Stowe breviary	BL Stowe 12
Tewkesbury missal	CUL Gg.3.21
Tiptoft/Morris missal	NY, PML M.107
West Bedwyn gradual	CUL Add. 8333

Westminster missal	Westm. Abbey 37
Westminster pontifical	Bodl. Rawl. C.425
Winchcombe breviary	Valenciennes, B.m. 116
Winchcombe sacramentary	Orléans, B.m. 127 (105)
Winchester troper (Bodl)	Bodl. Bodley 775
Winchester troper (CCC)	CCCC 473
Worcester antiphonal	Worcester cath. F.160
Wulfstan portiforium	CCCC 391

1   Introduction

If a pictorial metaphor for the present book may be offered, it is that of a tapestry rather than a mosaic. A mosaic is characterized by clarity and coherence; if undamaged, it is a tidy whole. What we hope to trace here is never tidy, certainly never a static entity fixed in a framework: *the* medieval liturgy. There will always be loose threads and, all too often, faded patches, some of them scarcely recognizable. Indeed, we might best think of the picture we shall attempt to confect, of regular, formal public worship in England between about 600 and 1535, as a tapestry-in-progress. Because surprisingly little has been written towards the end here envisaged, of trying to get some idea of the history of the liturgy in medieval England as a whole, a bit of preliminary musing as to what can reasonably be expected from an attempt such as the present one – its shape and main emphases, along with its self-imposed limitations – may be helpful.

We know in a general way that Christian worship was carried on in England by those who professed that religion from the early seventh century on. Although we shall pay the most careful attention possible to that earliest period, our understanding of the details of worship during it will remain unavoidably exiguous for the early centuries, roughly up until the late tenth. From that time on, however, there survive considerable bodies of evidence, all of which need to be weighed and then balanced. Three such bodies are of the greatest importance, one of them indeed paramount.

The paramount evidence is that of the liturgical books themselves, in manuscript throughout our period, and exclusively so for all save the last sixty years or so (c. 1475–1535) when they are supplemented, and eventually supplanted, by printed books.[1] These service books, whether manuscript or printed, need to be studied the way other books are, mainly through such tools as palaeography, codicology, and scrutiny of

---

[1] The Latin service books printed c. 1554–57, during the reign of Mary Tudor, are not part of our concern.

medieval library lists. Also, as with most other medieval manuscripts, they have to be pondered with a continual awareness of how much has been lost. Tempting, and indeed necessary, as it will often be to regard a particular service book as in some way typical – that is, to extrapolate from it as representing wider usages of its genre, time, or place – we must try to keep in mind that our attempts to understand the extant books are inevitably incomplete because of other, lost, books which would have provided a broader context in which to regard them.[2]

The second major type of evidence can generally be called archaeological: the witness of the surviving places, whole or in ruins, where worship was carried on in medieval England. There are two challenges here, corresponding precisely to whether those places are currently whole (and, with a few exceptions, in use as churches) or ruinous.[3] With the latter the task is to try to build up, from whatever fragments survive and from literary and other types of indications, a tolerably complete picture of those places as they were used for worship during whatever span of years is under consideration. Sometimes this is relatively easy to do, as with Fountains Abbey in Yorkshire; at other times, as with Bury St Edmunds (not to mention totally lost or supplanted places like the late seventh-century Lindisfarne that produced the great Gospel book), it is extremely difficult. Equally obvious is the opposite challenge, to strip away the additions and alterations of four and a half centuries in an effort to try to understand, say, Salisbury cathedral as it was when completed in the mid-thirteenth century or the parish church at Tideswell in Derbyshire in the fourteenth or the minster church at Stow in Lincolnshire in the eleventh.

The third major category of evidence may be termed, collectively if a bit roughly, canonical – in, that is, its etymological meaning: having to do with rules. Among the "rules" to be noticed here are the enactments of synods (largely provincial but occasionally diocesan), instructions handed down by bishops, records of visitations, monastic rules and customaries, and the statutes of various collegiate churches and above all of the secular cathedrals.

There are of course other types of sources as well, among which the strictly literary (largely ignored here) may function as a kind of running

---

[2] An obvious instance is the magnificent Westminster missal (see chapter 6), which owing to its size may never have been used in public worship, but no other missals from that abbey survive.

[3] A few medieval churches are now used in other ways (notably several in Norwich, e.g., the Franciscan church, now an exhibition hall), and a handful are Roman Catholic, like St Etheldreda's, Ely Place, London; but the vast majority have for centuries been used for Anglican services.

sub-text. We shall also want to be aware of sources of biographical information; in some cases, like Hugh of Lincoln, we can have some idea of an historical figure as what may be called a liturgical person.[4] Narrative sources, like chronicles and histories, and some kinds of record evidence (notably, for the later period, wills) will have to be drawn on also. Modes of approaching these miscellaneous categories of sources need little in the way of detailed explanation, unlike the three main categories mentioned above, the study of each of which deserves somewhat more extensive, and individual, treatment. Such treatment is provided in the "Excursus on sources" at the end of this chapter; it can be skipped by readers already familiar with the information included there.

Some principles concerning evidence

In the light of what has been said above about the chief bodies of evidence, it seems natural that the main point of entrance will wherever possible be a service book or other manuscript (or early printed book) that bears primary witness to a liturgical observance. So it is important to stress here that evidence from such books is not to be used uncritically: the presence of a particular text or rubric or feast in a service book is not firm evidence for actual *use*, though of course we may infer a reasonable presumption. But liturgical texts may be written by enthusiasts trying to bring about a more elaborate worship than has been the case or to stress a particular cause, like a new feast, or approach, like greater reverence for the consecrated host. Or there may be service books which reflect the full practice of a great establishment but which have clearly been used in very modest circumstances at, say, small cells of religious houses or parish churches.

Given the caution required, therefore, it is necessary to establish some principles of understanding, or tests to be applied, if we are to have confidence as to what constitutes reliable evidence. These principles, applicable to particular features as well as to whole books, may be summarized as follows: (1) context; (2) likeliness of use; (3) uniqueness, as compared with widespread presence; (4) particular importance; (5) trouble, or how much work it costs a scribe to write whatever is under study.

1 "Context" is fairly obvious. Can a given liturgical book be set alongside others from the same scriptorium or intended for use in the

---

[4] See for example my "St Hugh as a Liturgical Person" (originally titled "The Liturgical Aspects"), in *De Cella in Saeculum*, ed. M. G. Sargent (Woodbridge 1989), pp. 17–27, repr. Pfaff, *LCSSME*.

same place? Are there meaningful points of comparison over a span of time? Are there other Premonstratensian books, for example, or other books from parish churches in the diocese of Worcester, or others written by the same identifiable scribe? The mutual reinforcing of books and texts in such ways adds greatly to what may be called the probability factor – how probable it is that a specific piece of putative evidence is really evidence for anything broader than itself.

2 "Likeliness of use" is also a self-explanatory criterion. How likely is it that a rite of infant baptism contained in the splendid massbook of a great monastery would ever be used? Or directions for a Rogation-tide perambulation to various churches in a village with only one? Or rubrics which presuppose a trained choir of boys as well as male clerks? Many, perhaps most, medieval liturgical books must have been used very selectively; part of our task is to try to recapture, by imagination, that selectivity.

3 "Uniqueness" refers to how rare a particular feature is in relation to other liturgical books besides the one we may be studying. An apparently unique text has to have been composed by someone, an apparently unique feast to have been established for some reason. The field of comparison, though not unlimited, is wide enough that – provided that we keep in mind the fortuitousness with which medieval manuscripts seem to have survived – something extremely unusual deserves to have attention paid to it for that very reason.

4 "Particular importance" is a different matter: particularly important to the scriptorium where the book is written or to the place of its intended or actual use. This criterion refers mainly to certain occasions within the liturgical year, not so much to its great days like Christmas and Easter as to those specific to individual places: feasts of dedication, feasts (especially translations of relics) of patron- or other closely possessed saints, and new feasts adopted with special enthusiasm, like Corpus Christi or the Name of Jesus.[5]

5 "Trouble" is the most pragmatic of these principles, but also the one that has to be applied with the greatest caution. In the abstract, it stands to reason that the more trouble a scribe goes to, especially in the matter of supplying music, the likelier it is that the feature

---

[5] As distinct from those which we may suspect were adopted chiefly out of obedience to canonical mandate, like the Transfiguration and Visitation or Winifred or Osmund; see pp. 539–42 and 437–41 below. M. Rubin's monograph, *Corpus Christi: the Eucharist in Late Medieval Culture* (Cambridge 1991), deals with many aspects of what becomes a highly popular feast, but the liturgical is not specially emphasized and English matters form only a small part of her story.

in question is seriously intended for use. The copying of liturgical books must have been an intensively laborious task, and we may well balance our basic caution, that appearance of something in a liturgical book does not necessarily guarantee its use, by remembering that every feature a scribe includes adds to the labor of producing the book.

Some concrete application of these principles will be encountered as we proceed: for example, the question of the usefulness of psalters as liturgical sources. Other explanations as to method will be offered as occasion requires, especially in the "Excursus on method in the comparison of liturgical texts" following chapter 4, and that on "Ascription of liturgical books to individual churches" (with Bury St Edmunds as the test case) after chapter 5. Explanations as to basic liturgical terms and information are a different matter; we turn now to what can reasonably be expected of the reader in the way of antecedent knowledge.

What the reader is presumed to know

The present work does not purport to provide either an introduction to Christian liturgy in general or a lexicon of liturgical, ecclesiastical, or codicological terms. Several reference works can among them serve those functions admirably, most notably the *Oxford Dictionary of the Christian Church*. Such matters aside, it is difficult, indeed possibly absurd, to try to specify everything that will *not* be spelled out in a work as long as this one, and that therefore the reader ought ideally to know already. But it may be helpful to readers to have it made clear that the following modicum of general information will be regarded as understood, or at least will not be explained beyond these six preliminary summaries.

1 The basic structure of the liturgical year, Advent through the season after Pentecost (or after Trinity Sunday), and the interplay of two elements: the annual but not regular cycle (mainly of Sundays) that changes each year according to when Easter falls, and the cycle of feasts with fixed dates (saints' days, mostly, but also the great occasions of Christmas and Epiphany). It will also be helpful to have in mind the dates of the most important of these fixed feasts: Stephen-John Evangelist-Holy Innocents (26–28 December), Purification (alias Candlemas, 2 February), Annunciation (25 March), John the Baptist (24 June), Peter and Paul (29 June), Laurence (10 August), Assumption of the Virgin Mary (15 August), her Nativity (8 September), All Saints (1 November), Martin (11 November),

Andrew (30 November); these are here singled out not as most important in an abstractly hagiographical sense but because of the degree to which they bulk large in the liturgical year.

2 The distinction between the proper of time, or temporale, and proper of saints, or sanctorale, in liturgical nomenclature and in liturgical books structured according to these sections. In brief, the temporale includes the annual cycle of Sundays, usually beginning either with Advent or (as often in the earlier middle ages and in some monastic usage) Christmas. The sanctorale, by contrast, includes most of the fixed-day feasts – except for Christmas to Epiphany, which is why Stephen-John Evangelist-Innocents were hyphenated above; they almost always appear in the temporale, as does, after 1173, Thomas Becket (29 December). Again, the sanctorale generally starts with Andrew.

3 The rough outlines of the structure of the mass and daily office.[6] Only a few potential confusions or ambiguities of terms need to be straightened out here. Unless otherwise specified, the night office will be referred to by the term commonly used in the high and later middle ages, "matins" (comprising either one or three nocturns), and the office following it, "lauds." On Sundays and important occasions the fullest office of matins in monastic use contains twelve lessons (each with a subsequent responsory), hence the term "feast of twelve lessons"; the corresponding number for secular use (and also for regular canons and many other groups of religious) is nine. In the mass liturgy the opening chant will generally be called "introit," although many of the sources use *officium* (which can be confusing to the unwary, especially on a closely written manuscript page). Similarly, the theme-prayer at the beginning of the mass will generally be termed "mass-collect," or merely "collect," although *oratio* is encountered just about as often as *collecta* in our sources. (The matter is further complicated by the fact that the three mass prayers that comprise a set, collect, secret and postcommunion, are sometimes referred to in modern works collectively as "mass orations.")[7] Other points of confusing nomenclature may arise with the "secret" prayer being sometimes called *super oblata* and the "postcommunion" being

---

[6] Two useful guides in this respect are those of John Harper, *The Forms and Orders of Western Liturgy from the Tenth to the Eighteenth Century: a Historical Introduction and Guide for Students and Musicians* (Oxford 1991), especially its Glossary, pp. 286–319; and Andrew Hughes, *Medieval Manuscripts for Mass and Office: a Guide to their Organization and Terminology* (Toronto 1982).

[7] As, most notably, in the ten-volume *Corpus Orationum*, ed. E. Moeller et al., CCSL 160/A-H, which covers all mass prayers (and no others).

termed *ad complendum*. Unless some significant point hinges on such distinction of nomenclature, the most familiar English terms – collect, secret, postcommunion – will be used.[8]

4   The names and definitions of the principal kinds of liturgical books, indicated below in small capitals. Those encountered most often for the mass fall into three groups. The prayers (both the fixed canon and the variable mass sets), proper prefaces, and mass-ordinary (the basic rite) are in the SACRAMENTARY; this comes to be supplanted by the MISSAL (or *missale plenum*), which contains the words of the chants and proper lessons as well. The chants themselves are mainly found in the GRADUAL (not to be confused with the service-element of that name, between the Epistle and Gospel), but elaborations of various kinds are sometimes encountered in a separate TROPER or SEQUENTIARY (rarely, PROSER). The lessons can be read from an EPISTLE BOOK and a GOSPEL BOOK (sometimes called EVANGELIARY) or GOSPEL LECTIONARY, the latter containing only the gospel pericopes, in liturgical order – or from the missal itself. (The selections of biblical lessons for a given occasion are collectively called "pericopes," things cut out [i.e., for reading at mass].)

5   Books for the daily office are somewhat more complicated. The most basic is the PSALTER, containing the totality of the psalms (in either biblical or liturgical order), the canticles used each day (the most important being the Benedictus at lauds and Magnificat at vespers, each with variable antiphons) or on specific days of the week, litany of saints, and sometimes a hymnal component. The officiant recites the collects, some variable and some fixed, at the different hours from the COLLECTAR, which contains also the variable short readings called *capitula*. The chants for the office, most notably antiphons for the psalms and canticles and the often long and complex responsories after each lesson at matins, are collected in the ANTIPHONAL. For the three main kinds of readings at matins several books can be used: a LECTIONARY for the biblical passages, HOMILIARY for the condensed sermons (mostly from the Fathers), and LEGENDARY or PASSIONAL for the excerpts from saints' lives; or all the readings may be contained in a single OFFICE LECTIONARY. The BREVIARY or PORTIFORIUM is the compendium of what is needed for all the daily offices for an entire year; it is often a fat book, and either extremely hard to read or divided into two seasonal halves (or both).

---

[8] In general, *secreta* and *postcommunio* is the usage of the Gelasian tradition, *super oblata* and *ad complendum* (or *completa*) that of the Gregorian. See further p. 56: "Excursus on the terms Gregorian and Gelasian as used here."

Occasionally the "day offices" – all those except matins, which is by far the longest – are collected into a DIURNAL.

6 Among the books for other kinds of services three are specially important. PROCESSIONALS are collections of the chants used at processions on important occasions, including the Rogation season just before Ascension Day. MANUALS are collections of rites such as baptism, marriage, visitation of the sick, and burial, all intended for pastoral use as needed (hence sometimes called "occasional offices"). Books distinctively for bishops are called PONTIFICALS (hence the name), and include such specifically episcopal services as confirmation, ordination, dedication of churches, coronation (but not always), and special blessings (those pronounced by the bishop after communion are sometimes collected into a separate volume called a BENEDICTIONAL). Despite the necessity of excluding systematic consideration of episcopal and pastoral rites, it will often be found necessary to refer to the books that contain them.

"Historiography": the previous study of the subject

In one of its meanings, "historiography" is too exalted a term for what we need to notice now: no grand theory of history will be enunciated, or even presupposed. But on a less exalted level, that of thinking about why particular students of history write what they write, there is one sizeable set of considerations to be kept in mind. Our subject is, to a degree, part of the larger history of religious thought and practice in England during the middle ages, and as such inevitably falls under the shadow of the religious controversies that have bulked large in historical writing about England since the sixteenth century. Happily, there has not been such a degree of *odium theologicum* involved in the study of English medieval liturgy as has characterized, say, the study of ecclesiology, but confessional considerations have played some part, and it would be naïve to pretend to be unaware of them – and in particular of the teleology implied by two events of the 1540s.

The first is the act of Convocation of Canterbury in 1543 mandating the Use of Sarum (specifically, the Sarum breviary), which had been employed increasingly throughout Britain during the later middle ages, as compulsory in the Southern Province: so that there was, albeit briefly, something very close to a uniform English "use" for the Latin liturgy within most of the realms then subject to the English monarch. The second is the emergence six years later of a different kind of single "use": of a liturgy, in English, ordered by Parliament in the (first) Act of Uniformity, which established the (1549) Book of Common Prayer as the official, and required, liturgy for all public worship in parish churches and cathedrals throughout the whole of England. And it is not unimportant that the liturgical books envisaged in both 1543 and 1549 (and of course thereafter) were printed ones, with every copy of a single printing thought of as identical. This has given rise to the implied, if not necessarily logical, teleology just referred to: that the "true" end of the centuries of Latin worship in England was the purified catholicism of the Book of Common Prayer. This teleology is itself an historiographical artefact of considerable, and very wide-ranging, importance; but it is articulated here precisely so that it can be subsequently ignored. Rather, we have to pay concrete attention to the nature of a renewed interest in medieval liturgy in nineteenth-century England.

In the religious history of that time and place the intertwined stories of Roman Catholic revival and of Anglican Tractarianism/Ritualism/ Anglo-Catholicism (and also the birth of Anglican religious orders), along with the emergence of medieval history as a subject of academic study at the universities, would provide enough material for a book on its own. This is not that book, but details that might form part of it will often appear in these pages. Indeed, one of the salient features of the present work is meant to be the attention paid to the historiographical (again, in the less grandiose sense of the word) context in which various cardinal pieces of liturgical scholarship have appeared. Several of the major sections will therefore include discussion of the way(s) the subject under consideration has been previously studied, and in these discussions a galaxy of scholars will be encountered: figures like Christopher Wordsworth, Dame Laurentia McLachlan, and Francis Wormald. For the moment, a mere sentence or two about each of a handful of the most eminent will suggest something of how personal considerations may be relevant to assessment of scholarly work in this field.

William MASKELL (c. 1814–90), one of the first scholars of the nineteenth century to devote himself to serious liturgical study, published two pioneering works, *The Ancient Liturgy of the Church of England* and *Monumenta Ritualia Ecclesiae Anglicanae* in 1844 and 1846 respectively; in 1850 he converted to the Roman church, and (aside from an expanded edition of the *Monumenta Ritualia* in 1882) made no more contributions of the magnitude of his earlier work. A lay amateur little known but often referred to in these pages, Francis Henry DICKINSON (1813–90), was a country gentleman, co-founder of Wells Theological College, and High Sheriff of Somerset. Having in 1850 published a careful *List of Printed Service Books according to the Ancient Use of the Church of England*, he then went on to produce the first modern edition of a medieval English service book: the *Missale ad usum insignis et praeclarae ecclesiae Sarum* which appeared in fascicles between 1861 and 1883 (see further p. 416). In marked contrast stands Edmund BISHOP (1846–1917): an obscure clerk by occupation, he published relatively little (his highly influential collected essays, *Liturgica Historica*, appeared only the year after his death), never studied at the ancient universities or held an academic position, and as a Roman Catholic layman felt himself to some extent distanced from the predominantly Anglican group of liturgical students whose work was to crystallize around the Henry Bradshaw Society; but the quality of his work and his influence were such that he now casts as large a shadow as any liturgical scholar of the period.[9] Henry Austin WILSON (1854–1927) was again almost exactly Edmund Bishop's opposite: an Anglican clergyman (and son of a bishop), lifelong Oxford don, and immensely productive editor of important liturgical texts (e.g., Gelasian Sacramentary, Gregorian Sacramentary, Missal of Robert of Jumièges, Magdalen Pontifical, Calendar of St Willibrord), mostly under Henry Bradshaw Society auspices.[10] Walter Howard FRERE (1863–1938), another High Anglican (Superior of the Community of the Resurrection and eventually Bishop of Truro), was a notable student of medieval music, especially chant, as well as of the English medieval uses.[11] The name that will appear most often in the present work is that of J(ohn) Wickham LEGG (1843–1921), an Anglican layman who retired early from a career of some eminence as a surgeon and became pre-eminent as a student of liturgical texts, editing the Westminster missal and the Sarum missal (in its early manuscript forms; Dickinson's edition had been made from the early printings).[12]

Legg was instrumental in a central development in the study of our subject: the founding in 1890 of the Henry Bradshaw Society "... for the editing of Rare Liturgical Texts."[13] It took its name to honor

---

[9] Nigel Abercrombie, *Edmund Bishop* (London 1959); on the HBS, see below.

[10] Details about all these editions will be given at the appropriate places. There is a brief entry on Wilson by the present writer in *ODNB* 59.559.

[11] C. S. Phillips, *Walter Howard Frere, Bishop of Truro, a memoir* (London 1947).

[12] A preliminary treatment of Legg's achievement is A. Ward and C. Johnson, "John Wickham Legg ...," *Eph. Liturg.* 97 (1983), 70–84; a full life is needed.

[13] The capitalization of the concluding words is still current on the front-title page of the Society's publications. The most complete information on what the Society has produced is Anthony Ward, *The Publications of the Henry Bradshaw Society: an Annotated Bibliography with Indexes.* Bibliotheca "Ephemerides Liturgicae" Subsidia 67 (Rome 1992), following the article by Ward and C. Johnson, "The Henry Bradshaw Society: Its Birth and First Decade, 1890–1900," *Eph. Liturg.* 104 (1990), pp. 187–200. The 1992 publication, current through vol. 106 (1991), is specially useful for its index of the manuscripts used in any of the HBS editions. There are also thumbnail summaries of the biographical facts about most of the editors of the Society's publications and a "Select Repertory of Manuscript Collections." HBS publications of the decade 1991–2000 are surveyed by Ward in *Eph. Liturg.* 115 (2001), pp. 82–94.

Henry Bradshaw (1831–86), a Cambridge polymath (most notably in the field of early printing) and University Librarian who had great influence on a number of fine scholars in the late nineteenth century. Growing interest in what was sometimes called "liturgiology" had in the last third of that century taken a somewhat more scholarly and less ecclesiological character, and although the early statement of purpose made plain that in the choice of texts to be printed by the Society preference would be "given to those which bear upon the history of the Book of Common Prayer or of the Church of England," it was equally explicit that the editions should be "on an historical and scientific basis." The first production, volume I (of three) of Legg's great edition of the Westminster missal (to be discussed at length in chapter 6; 1891), bore this out: the exhaustive nature of Legg's scholarship is as conspicuous as the centrality of Westminster Abbey to Anglicanism is obvious. Any degree of discernibly Anglican emphasis has long since receded, and the tally of the Society's publications now approaches 120 volumes.[14] More distinctively and enduringly Anglican is the Alcuin Club, founded in 1897 with a special concern for "the practical study of ceremonial, and the arrangements of churches, their furniture and ornaments, in accordance with the rubrics of the Book of Common Prayer." Despite what seems to be a narrow delimitation, its series of larger publications, called Collections, currently numbering over eighty volumes, includes several of prime importance for our purposes, like W. H. Frere's *Studies in Early Roman Liturgy* (in three volumes, 1930–35), which deal with early calendar and lectionary systems.[15]

A final historiographical current that must be noted is the influence of the Liturgical Movement (the customary capitals emphasize its distinctiveness). From its origins in Continental monastic circles about the end of the nineteenth century, it began to be heavily influential in England after World War I and was later a prime force in shaping the liturgical provisions enacted at the Second Vatican Council.[16] It has had powerful reflexes in modern liturgical scholarship as well as in liturgical praxis, and widely consulted works with titles like *The Study of Liturgy* and *The Church at Prayer* almost invariably reflect its approaches and values.[17] A prominent characteristic is a lack of interest

[14] In recent years, following a revitalization of the Society in the mid-1980s, many of the publications have been of pre-Conquest English sources.

[15] P. J. Jagger, *The Alcuin Club and its Publications 1897–1987: an Annotated Bibliography*, 2nd edn (London 1986).

[16] The literature on, and of, the Liturgical Movement, is vast; see, e.g., the entry in *ODCC*.

[17] Respectively, ed. C. Jones, G. Wainwright, and E. Yarnold (London and New York 1978, 2nd edn 1992); and ed. A. G. Martimort as the Eng. tr. (4 vols, Collegeville,

in, or even a positive devaluing of, the medieval, so it is necessary to be sensitive to this modern (i.e., mostly twentieth-century) development which in our time has come close to monopolizing the words "liturgy" and "liturgical."[18]

England and the Continent in medieval liturgy

It may appear that the present work is vitiated by being focused almost exclusively on England. To a degree such a charge can be dismissed out of hand: there is no less rationale for a history of the liturgy in medieval England than for the well known histories of monastic and religious orders in England or of English law in the middle ages.[19] Nonetheless, it must be acknowledged that a steady awareness of the main outlines, and often of detailed developments as well, of the liturgy on the Continent is essential if our picture is to be as full and accurate as possible.[20] To some extent we shall therefore need to notice Continental aspects as they have a bearing on our story, but always, and only, in passing.

What cannot be attempted at all is any treatment of the development of Christian liturgy in the West before the time of Gregory the Great (at whose instigation the Augustinian mission comes to Kent in 597).[21] Nor can we linger at Carolingian circles of liturgical reform and

---

MN 1986) of *L'Eglise en Prière* (4th edn Paris 1983). For bibliographic details and somewhat fuller discussion of the subject as a whole, see "The Study of Medieval Liturgy," the introduction to Pfaff, *LCSSME*, esp. pp. 8–11.

[18] As witness the International Consultations on Liturgy and the North American Academy of Liturgy, in both cases with little concern for the medieval. Recognizing this may help to allay confusion.

[19] D. Knowles, *The Monastic Order in England* (Cambridge 1940, 2nd edn 1963) and *The Religious Orders in England*, 3 vols (Cambridge 1948–59); F. Pollock and F. W. Maitland, *The History of English Law before the Time of Edward I* (Cambridge 1895, 2nd edn 1898; reissued 1968); and P. Wormald, *The Making of English Law: King Alfred to the Twelfth Century*, I: *Legislation and its Limits* (Oxford 1999).

[20] The most widely cited guide, and often referred to in these pages, is the translation and revision by W. G. Storey and N. K. Rasmussen of C. Vogel, *Medieval Liturgy: an Introduction to the Sources* (Washington, DC 1986; from *Introduction aux sources de l'histoire du culte chrétien du moyen âge* [Spoleto 1981]), immensely thorough in what it covers but highly partial in its selection of contents: it is weighted heavily towards the period before the 12th cent., and ignores the daily office almost entirely. More complete in coverage, if less comprehensive in detail, is E. Palazzo, *A History of Liturgical Books from the Beginning to the Thirteenth Century* (Collegeville, MN 1998; tr. M. Beaumont [the French original, Paris 1993, is titled *Le Moyen Age*]). Extremely influential, and strongly reflective of the modern Liturgical Movement, has been T. Klauser, *A Short History of the Western Liturgy: an Account and Some Reflections*, tr. J. Halliburton (Oxford 1979, with a complicated publication history that goes back to 1944).

[21] Three classic studies of early liturgy available in English are L. Duchesne, *Christian Worship, Its Origin and Evolution: a Study of the Latin Liturgy up to the Time of*

enthusiasm,[22] nor struggle through the heavy waters of the relationships of the main sacramentary families, Old Gelasian, Young (or Frankish, or Eighth-Century) Gelasian, pre-Hadrianic Gregorian, Hadrianic Gregorian (with or without its Supplement), late Gregorian, and fused Gregorian; an "Excursus on the terms Gelasian and Gregorian as used here" is provided after chapter 2.[23] Likewise, the emergence and eventual collections of *Ordines Romani* will have to be largely ignored.[24] The German-Roman pontifical (*PRG*), spreading from the mid-tenth century, will occupy our attention only as it bears on developments in England.[25] In the same way, the thirteenth-century "reform" of the liturgy of the papal chapel into what has come to be called the Modern Roman Liturgy (itself effected largely by an English Franciscan, Haymo of Faversham)[26] will have to be considered in the context only of English reflexes.

Charlemagne, tr. M. L. McClure (5th Eng. edn London 1919, from *Origines du culte chrétien*, first publ. 1889); J. H. Srawley, *The Early History of the Liturgy*, 2nd edn (Cambridge 1947, considerably revised from first edn 1913; eucharistic liturgy only); and J. Jungmann, *The Early Liturgy to the Time of Gregory the Great*, tr. F. A. Brunner (Notre Dame and London 1959). Closer to our purposes are G. G. Willis's two volumes of *Essays in Early Roman Liturgy* (ACC 46, 1964) and *Further Essays … (ACC 50, 1968)* and his posthumous *A History of Early Roman Liturgy to the Death of Pope Gregory the Great* (HBS Subsidia I, 1994).

[22] Among the numerous publications of Rosamond McKitterick, see in particular *The Frankish Church and the Carolingian Reforms, 789–895* (London 1977); among those of Donald Bullough, "Roman Books and Carolingian *renovatio*," and "Alcuin and the Kingdom of Heaven," both reprinted in his collected essays, *Carolingian Renewal: Sources and Heritage* (Manchester 1991), and also his posthumous *Alcuin: Achievement and Reputation* (Leiden 2004).

[23] Vogel, *Sources*, is a safe guide, if one not always easy to follow. The great classifier of these materials is K. Gamber, most notably in his *Codices liturgici Latini antiquiores*, Spicilegii Friburgensis Subsidia 1 (in 2 vols) (2nd, much expanded, edn Fribourg 1968), with a *Supplementum* by B. Baroffio et al. (Fribourg 1988). Also prolific, especially in the study of Gelasian materials, is A. Chavasse, much of whose work has latterly appeared in the periodical *Ecclesia Orans* (Rome). For details of the magnificent three-volume edition of the Gregorian by J. Deshusses and the three fine CCSL editions of leading specimens of Young Gelasian books (Angoulême, Gellone, and Phillipps *alias* "Augustodunensis") see the "Excursus on the terms Gregorian and Gelasian" after chapter 2. Some basic, and shaped, bibliographical help is offered, but only to about 1977, in my *Medieval Latin Liturgy*, Toronto Medieval Bibliographies 9 (Toronto 1982).

[24] Again, much guidance will be found in Vogel, *Sources*, but the great monument in this area is the five-volume edition of M. Andrieu, *Les* Ordines Romani *du haut moyen âge*, Spicilegium Sacrum Lovaniense 11, 23–4, 28–9 (Louvain, 1931, 1948–51, 1956–61).

[25] Best consulted in the magisterial edition of C. Vogel and R. Elze, *Le Pontifical romano-germanique du dixième siècle*, Studi e Testi 226–27, 269 (Rome 1963, 1972).

[26] S. J. P. van Dijk and J. H. Walker, *The Origins of the Modern Roman Liturgy* (London 1960); cf. van Dijk's edn, *Sources of the Modern Roman Liturgy: the Ordinals by Haymo of Faversham and Related Documents 1243–1307*, 2 vols (Leiden 1963; his edn of

Of course the whole question of the impact of the Norman Conquest, and especially of Lanfranc's Norman monasticism, will bulk large in the very center of our story. Overall, though, the contention underlying the present work is that there is a discreteness about the history of the liturgy in medieval England that makes it both intellectually and pragmatically possible to consider the subject in the dimensions implied by our title. Perhaps the best reply to a charge that, in the age of European Union dominance, this book seems inadequately "European" in focus, is that what is do-able should be preferred to an ideal solution that could probably not be carried out in practice – at least not by the present writer.

Two areas further excluded

As well as medieval liturgy on the Continent, there are (at least) two other large areas that this book has to ignore almost entirely, as being outside the realm of feasibility.[27] The first is music. Something was already said in the Preface about this exclusion; here it should be stated more emphatically that musical evidence is both so complex and so fitful that to try take it regularly into account would increase impossibly the length, and also the difficulty, of this work. Extremely technical, and often controverted, matters such as the palaeography of the neums or notes, the rate at which (and rhythm, if any, to which) they may have been sung, the numbers of singers involved, and the many other aspects of performance practice, are so numerous and often so hypothetical as to make a sensibly limited discussion of them unlikely. How truly this is the case is suggested above all by two factors: the fortuitous one of whether a given service book contains music (graduals and antiphonals do by definition, but by no means all missals and breviaries, nor other constituent books for the daily office like collectars); and the indeterminable one of how probable it seems that the music so contained would actually have been performed in services in whatever church the book in question seems to have belonged to. The musical dimension has to be kept constantly in mind, of course, and respected. That it is ignored here is a sign not of inattention but of recognition of necessary limitations.[28]

Haymo's *Ordinals* also appeared, anonymously owing to an editorial quarrel, as HBS 85, 1961).

[27] Other approaches are fascinating but would be more peripheral: the liturgy and English literature, for one (evidence from Chaucer or Langland, systematically pursued), or the liturgy and private devotion (the exclusion of Books of Hours being the glaring case here).

[28] An important recent resource is K. D. Hartzell, *Catalogue of Manuscripts Written or Owned in England up to 1200 Containing Music* (Woodbridge 2006); even at 700-plus

The other major aspect for the most part ignored is that of what are broadly termed episcopal and pastoral liturgies and the principal books that contained them: respectively, pontificals (with their integral but sometimes separated component, benedictionals) and manuals. Systematic treatment of the main services at which a bishop is the principal officiant and of those mainly entrusted to priests in pastoral roles would have overbalanced the present volume hopelessly.[29] Some of those individual stories have been traced already; others, and above all a concerted account of English pontificals, will have to be told on further occasions.

The excursuses

In addition to the considerable attention paid to the historiography (in the limited sense of the word, as discussed on p. 8) for each of the major topics taken up, five Excursuses are provided throughout this book; these need a word of special explanation. At a number of points in the course of our roughly chronological progress it has seemed useful to treat in a concentrated way certain matters that may be less comprehensible if noticed in a piecemeal or glancing fashion in more than one place. They tend to be (even) more severely technical than the material presented in the "narrative" chapters, and may be skipped, though possibly at some risk.

Each Excursus has been placed closest to the chapter to which it most closely relates, but each is also of wider application. The purpose of the first, following this Introduction, is to lay out the auxiliary tools for working with the three principal kinds of sources enumerated at its beginning, manuscripts, buildings, and canonical prescriptions; it is admittedly rudimentary in nature but should obviate the need for much chapter-by-chapter repetition. The next attempts to equip readers with what they need reasonably to know about the sometimes puzzling nomenclature of Gregorian, Gelasian, and "Young" Gelasian strands in early medieval liturgy, and also with a synoptic table showing in which strand individual saints' days first appear. Beginning in roughly the eleventh century, the period from which enough service books survive to make extensive comparisons possible, we shall often have to employ close textual criticism to establish certain points;

---

pages, full of wonderfully precise information, it covers only the period for which musical evidence is scanty in comparison with that in books from the 13th through the early 16th cen.

[29] I had hoped to include full treatment of at least one specimen rite of each kind – consecration of churches and marriage – but even this limited approach would require many thousands of words.

hence the Excursus "On method in the comparison of liturgical texts" is appended to the chapter on the Norman Conquest. The following chapters are heavily devoted to consideration of the evidence for each of a number of religious houses, and the next Excursus, "On ascription of individual books," tries to lay out the criteria by which certain manuscripts are assigned to individual churches, using the great monastery of Bury St Edmunds as the test case. Finally, at the end of the three chapters devoted to the liturgies of the various religious orders, a single Excursus on "Liturgical books from female religious houses" tries to survey the main service-book sources for that subject as a whole (evidence relating to specific houses for women, most conspicuously with the Bridgettines, is treated in course in several chapters).

Although the individual chapters are by no means devoid of technicalities, the Excursuses are deliberately stuffed with them – albeit laid out, as is the rest of the book, in narrative sentences. This approach is intended to make the matter contained in them somewhat more manageable than through a variety of charts and tables (save for the one about the Gelasian and Gregorian saints) and a proliferation of symbols. Some of the material in this book is likely to be found difficult, to be sure; nonetheless, the aim is that individual sections should be found reasonably readable – even, possibly, aloud.

Chronological sequence and the shape of this book

Any attempt to write history must respect chronological sequence as a primary mode of structure. Yet, since this book tries, within the narrow limits of its self-definition, to comprehend a span of time of nine-plus centuries, strict chronological progression would be as undesirable as it would be impossible. Even a century-by-century approach would be more artificial than useful. Of the three groups of sources mentioned above, only the canonical/legislative can almost always be dated with precision. Buildings are built and decorated over the course of decades or quarter- or even half-centuries, and then often re-built and re-decorated. Liturgical books and related sources occasionally have colophons or other indications of date, but for the vast number we have to rely either on termini – the presence, or absence, of a datable feature like a saint's feast or mention of a particular bishop – or on the evidence, always shaky without external corroboration, of handwriting.

Nonetheless, during the first third or so of the story we are trying to trace, moving in a steadily, if loosely, chronological fashion seems unavoidable. In the broad but somewhat hazy landscape of Anglo-Saxon England, the most noticeable features are bound to be the Augustinian mission and its immediate aftermath, the achievement of Theodore of Tarsus, Bede's monasteries, Alcuin's York, the centralizing force of the Alfredian dynasty, and the monastic revival under Æthelwold, Dunstan, and Oswald. These form an obvious chronological sequence, and it would be odd not to consider the period from roughly 600 to about 1000 in that way, with a point of division approximately at the beginning of recovery after the worst of the Viking incursions. The complications that arrive in the eleventh century, with the Norman Conquest rising from that landscape as something like the Matterhorn, also mandate more or less chronological treatment, although there seems adequate reason to consider the sources from the first two-thirds of the century in the chapter on liturgy in later Anglo-Saxon England, those from the last third in the following chapter.

From the twelfth century on, with the evidence vastly more abundant, it appears sensible to switch from a single to a double track: to separate the pursuit of the secular strand from that of the regular. It is the latter that seems to follow most naturally from consideration of the picture after the Norman Conquest, for the fullest fruits of Lanfranc's Anglo-Norman monasticism appear a century or so after his death, in houses like St Albans and Durham. The situation changes notably after 1215, when the Black Monk houses become organized into an entity fairly called the Order of St Benedict. By that time three other principal varieties of monastic life have emerged in England: Cluniac, Cistercian, and Carthusian. The discreteness of their stories justifies our tracing each one through to the end. A comparable phenomenon, though less clear-cut, is the emergence of bodies of canons regular, considered here under the broad headings of Augustinian, Premonstratensian, and Gilbertine. These, too, become "religious orders" after the regularizing legislation of the Fourth Lateran Council in 1215, made necessary above all by the appearance of yet another expression of the religious life, in the friar movement; this requires consideration of the four principal orders of friars in England, the Dominican, Franciscan, Carmelite, and Austin.

The second track to be followed after the Conquest is primarily, though by no means exclusively, that which begins in 1075 at what is now known as Old Sarum and flowers with the move to New Sarum – modern Salisbury – a century and a half later. That forms the basis for two sequential chapters, but before pursuing in a third the conclusion of the story of Sarum liturgy we divert our attention to Exeter, where in the mid-fourteenth century a splendid and extensive liturgical program, and one for which there is considerable documentation, was implemented. Having been made aware of secular liturgy at what seems its fullest elaboration, we then return to Sarum Use, to look at its final form and its spread throughout most of southern England. (The Latin term *usus*, capitalized here when Englished, is retained both because it is customary and because it is a convenient way of referring to the totality of liturgical practice in a given church; the meaningless distinction sometimes posited between "use" and "rite" is mostly ignored, and the two words are deployed almost interchangeably, although "rite" can also be used to refer to a specific service, like that of Palm Sunday.) The other two prominent secular Uses in England, those of York and Hereford, are treated in the next chapter, along with liturgy in three other major secular cathedrals, London, Lincoln, and (very briefly) Wells. The great predominance of evidence for these churches is late medieval, as is that for liturgy in parish churches, considered next. We conclude by noticing a few developments that mark the end of the story, just before the abolition of the Latin liturgy in England in 1549.

It should by now be obvious that chronology will provide only a skeletal framework rather than being consistently privileged (in the modern, and overused, sense of that word). The sole principle of consistency followed is to bring to the foreground whatever aspect seems the most telling at each stage. Occasionally this will be a short span of time, but much more often a person or, even oftener, a place will supply the primary focus of attention. Wherever possible, only those service books are considered that can reasonably be associated with a particular place. The amount of attention devoted to individual people may perhaps be surprising, but the assumption fundamental to this entire book is that specific liturgical practicioners – priests celebrating mass, monks and clerics of various kinds performing the daily office, bishops and deans enforcing liturgical change in their cathedrals and religious superiors in their houses – are as important for us to take into account as the liturgical texts they used; no less, that the scholars of the past century and a half who have studied these sources need to be seen in their contexts, human and academic. The hundreds of names and places that crowd the General Index are vital, not incidental, to our story.

These three co-ordinates – period, place, person – being constantly kept in mind as persistent background, we hunt our quarry with the aid of another three-fold formula: to look, as occasion requires and opportunity permits, for distinctive texts, distinctive saints, and distinctive rubrics. The pursuit of the distinctive (carried so far as to require occasional use of the admittedly ugly plural "distinctivenesses") becomes something like the salient element in the tapestry referred to at the beginning of this chapter. If the abrupt changes effected by the Reformations of the sixteenth century mark an end to work on that tapestry, the attempt to trace its lineaments and comprehend some of the details of its patterns remains fascinating and (so this book proposes) well worth the effort of students of history.

Excursus: on sources

Manuscripts and catalogues

To a large extent the study of manuscript service books utilizes the same resources, as it requires the same techniques, as for other medieval manuscripts of the "library" type (or, as it is sometimes put, "book hand" type, as distinct from archive or "court hand"). Fundamental to this study are catalogues of the manuscripts in the great public collections. These catalogues have been compiled over many decades and to widely different standards of detail and excellence, and it is not possible to enter onto a history of that subject here.[1] It is necessary only to make a few general remarks about the catalogues of the collections in the three great centers where these MSS are most heavily concentrated, and then to comment on a handful of enterprises of the past half-century

The three main places where liturgical manuscripts relating to England are concentrated are of course Cambridge, Oxford, and London. Chief among resources for studying manuscripts at Cambridge are M. R. James's catalogues of those at the Fitzwilliam Museum and (nearly) all the then extant colleges, published between 1895 and 1913.[2] For all their deficiencies and their outdatedness, they remain as a whole one of the most amazing feats in the history of the study of medieval manuscripts.[3] Even older, and much less adequate, are the descriptions published in the *Catalogue of the Manuscripts Preserved in the Library of the University of Cambridge* in six volumes between 1856 and 1867.

---

[1] The basic handlist (not a history) is P. O. Kristeller, *Latin Manuscript Books before 1600*, 4th edn by S. Krämer, Monumenta Germaniae historica, Hilfsmittel 13 (Berlin 1993), with *Ergänzungsband 2006* by S. Krämer and B. C. Arensmann, MGH, Hilfsmittel 23 (2007).

[2] Plus his catalogues of the medieval manuscripts in the Pepysian collection at Magdalene in 1923 and of the small collection at St Catharine's, published in 1925.

[3] A full discussion of these catalogues in the context of James's life as a whole will be found in my *Montague Rhodes James* (London 1980); the bibliography of his scholarly writings given there should be supplemented by that compiled by Nicholas Rogers in *The Legacy of M. R. James*, ed. Lynda Dennison (Donnington 2001), pp. 239–67.

Various schemes for supplementing or replacing these descriptions have been advanced over the years, most substantially by James himself, but none has reached publication stage.[4] There are summary notices of all "dated and datable" manuscripts in Cambridge in Pamela Robinson's volume in the international series devoted to manuscripts of that sort, and illuminated manuscripts in Cambridge – among which are some notable liturgical items – have been very fully treated in recent years.[5]

For the collections at Oxford richest in liturgical manuscripts the situation is even more fragmented. Those at the Bodleian (the University library), by far greater than those of the colleges, have been catalogued only sporadically – indeed, over a period of slightly more than three hundred years, if one goes back to the 1697 *Catalogus manuscriptorum Angliae* (to be discussed presently). By the mid-nineteenth century it was planned that detailed treatment would be supplied in the Quarto Catalogues, a large volume or volumes being devoted to each of a number of the main collections. Between 1854 and 1898 some nine volumes were published, but so much remained to be done that around 1890 it was decided that for the still uncatalogued manuscripts an enterprise much more restricted in scope was needed. The resulting *Summary Catalogue of Western Manuscripts in the Bodleian Library which have not hitherto been described in the Quarto Series* began to appear in 1895 and ended with introductory and index volumes (I and VII, respectively, of seven) in 1953.[6] The descriptions there are, however, often so summary as to be tantalizing, and it is fortunate that after World War II the Dutch Franciscan friar S. J. P. van Dijk compiled extensive typescript descriptions bound together in Duke Humfrey's library as "Handlist of the Latin Liturgical Manuscripts in the Bodleian Library" (seven volumes, 1953). With the Oxford colleges the picture is even more chaotic; for most, the basic descriptions are still those found in H. O. Coxe's two-volume catalogue published in 1852 – with the colleges treated in the chronological order of foundation.[7] It is, however, a happy development

---

[4] See my *M. R. James*, pp. 325–30. Some typescript descriptions by subsequent scholars, notably those of Jayne Ringrose, are kept in the Manuscripts Room of the UL.

[5] P. R. Robinson, *Catalogue of Dated and Datable Manuscripts c. 737–1600 in Cambridge Libraries*, 2 vols (Cambridge 1988); F. Wormald and P. M. Giles, *A Descriptive Catalogue of the Additional Illuminated Manuscripts in the Fitzwilliam Museum*, 2 vols (Cambridge 1982); M. Budny, *Insular, Anglo-Saxon, and Early Anglo-Norman Manuscript Art at Corpus Christi College, Cambridge*, 2 vols (Kalamazoo 1997); P. Binski and S. Panayotova, eds., *The Cambridge Illuminations* (London and Turnhout 2005).

[6] The dates of individual volumes in both Quarto and Summary Catalogue series are given in Kristeller, *Latin Manuscript Books* (as above).

[7] H. O. Coxe, *Catalogus codicum manuscriptorum qui in collegiis aulisque Oxoniensibus hodie adservantur*, 2 vols (Oxford 1852); vol. I (through Lincoln College) was reprinted by EP Publishing, Wakefield 1972, but not vol. II. Fortunately, van Dijk's handlist

that the medieval manuscripts in five Oxford colleges and one newly acquired collection at the Bodleian have in the last forty years received exemplary catalogues, and others are in progress.[8] And there are two further summary aids: Andrew Watson's volume for Oxford libraries (colleges as well as Bodleian) in the "dated and datable" series, and the three volumes by Otto Pächt and Jonathan Alexander on illuminated manuscripts in the Bodleian, plus one by Alexander and Elzbieta Temple for the colleges.[9]

The story of the cataloguing of the immense collections at the British Library is, as might be expected, yet more convoluted. Little more needs to be said here than that very few of the descriptions of its liturgical manuscripts published before about 1920 yield much information.[10] The stellar catalogue is that of the (Old) Royal collection published in four large folio volumes by G. F. Warner and J. P. Gilson in 1921. Its level of detail is unmatched by that of any other of the Library's catalogues, though the later descriptions of Additional MSS are increasingly adequate.[11] Here again one's best hope is often that a manuscript will have been found a place in the "dated and datable" volume for the Library, once more by Watson.[12] (Many of the BL catalogues are now on-line, but not yet those of the Cotton or Harleian collections; and an ambitious program of digitizing many of the illuminated manuscripts is underway.)

Of other collections in London the only one of liturgical interest which had been catalogued adequately prior to 1969 was that at Lambeth Palace, M. R. James's descriptions being published, belatedly, in

covers several colleges (Corpus Christi, Jesus, Lincoln, New College, Oriel, Trinity, and University) which at that point kept their manuscripts in the Bodleian.
[8] R. A. B. Mynors, *Cat. of the MSS of Balliol Coll, Oxf.* (Oxford 1963); A. C. de la Mare, *Cat. of the Colln. of Med. MSS bequeathed to the Bodl. Lib., Oxf. by James P. R. Lyell* (Oxford 1971); M. B. Parkes, *The Medieval MSS of Keble Coll., Oxf.* (London 1979); A. G. Watson, *A Descriptive Cat. of the Med. MSS of All Souls Coll., Oxf.* (Oxford 1997) and ... *of Exeter College* (Oxford 2000); R. Hanna, *A Descriptive Catalogue of the Western Medieval Manuscripts of St. John's College, Oxford* (Oxford 2002). Catalogues by R. M. Thomson of MSS at Merton and Corpus Christi are imminent.
[9] A.G. Watson, *Cat. of Dated and Datable MSS c. 435–1000 in Oxford Libraries*, 2 vols (Oxford 1984); O. Pächt and J. J. G. Alexander, *Illuminated MSS in the Bodl. Lib., Oxf.*, 3 vols (Oxford 1966–73; esp. III, *British, Irish, and Icelandic Schools*); Alexander and E. Temple, *Illum. MSS in the Oxf. Coll. Libs. ...* (Oxford 1985).
[10] This statement should be qualified with respect to the Harleian MSS, for which the four-volume catalogue by R. Nares et al., 1808–12, preserves some of the work of the great Humphrey Wanley, Harley's librarian a century earlier, as the collection was being assembled.
[11] This begins to be true from, roughly, the catalogue of those added between 1921 and 1925: not, however, published until 1950.
[12] A. G. Watson, *Cat. of Dated and Datable MSS c. 700–1600 in ... the British Library*, 2 vols (London 1979).

1930–32.[13] In 1969 there appeared the first volume of Neil Ker's great project, *Medieval Manuscripts in British Libraries*; it was devoted entirely to London. The aim of this enterprise was "to describe medieval manuscripts in collections hitherto uncatalogued or barely catalogued in print," which in practice meant mainly smaller collections.[14] For our purposes there were revealed noteworthy books at, conspicuously, St Paul's Cathedral, Sion College, and the Society of Antiquaries.[15]

This massive undertaking of Ker's was nearing completion by the time of his death in 1982, covering (always within its mission, as expressed above) libraries from Abbotsford to York in three further volumes; Alan Piper completed, and was to a large extent responsible for, volume IV.[16] It is not too much to say that the work has set a standard reflected in volumes like those of de la Mare, Parkes, and Watson already mentioned, and also the fine catalogues of Rodney Thomson on the important collections at Lincoln, Hereford, and Worcester cathedrals.[17]

In a sense Ker's *Medieval Manuscripts in British Libraries* brings full circle the noble plan of a number of late seventeenth-century scholars, notably Humphrey Wanley, for a kind of union catalogue (the term unknown then, of course) of medieval manuscripts in Britain, the fruit of which was the *Catalogus manuscriptorum Angliae*, which appeared in 1697 under the name of Edward Bernard, an eminent astronomer who merely supervised publication. The *CMA*, as it is widely known, was until the late nineteenth century the sole conspectus covering such a large area. The next attempt was the much more restricted, though still highly ambitious, effort of W. H. Frere in assembling

---

[13] This is often cited as by James and C. Jenkins; in fact, Jenkins's part consisted almost entirely of holding the enterprise up: see my *M. R. James*, pp. 281–3. Some account of *The MSS of Westminster Abbey* was published in 1909 by J. A. Robinson (then Dean) and James, but it inexplicably fails to cover the most important liturgical manuscript there, the Westminster missal.

[14] Preface to vol. I (Oxford 1969), p. v.

[15] Sion College has since been closed and its manuscripts moved to Lambeth Palace, and P. J. Willetts's *Cat. of MSS in the Soc. of Antiquaries of London* has appeared (Woodbridge 2000). An example of the effect of Ker's *MMBL* I is my investigation of St Paul's MS 1, published as "Bishop Baldock's Book, St Paul's Cathedral, and the Use of Sarum," in Pfaff, *LCSSME*, item XI.

[16] Volume II, *Abbotsford–Keele* (1977), III, *Lampeter–Oxford* (1983), IV, *Paisley–York* (1992); plus V, *Indexes and Addenda*, ed. I. C. Cunningham and A. G. Watson (2002).

[17] *Cat. of the MSS of Lincoln Cath. Chapter Library* (Woodbridge 1989); *Cat. of the MSS of Hereford Cath. Lib.*, with R. A. B. Mynors (whose name is first on the title page, though the bulk of the work is Thomson's; Woodbridge 1993); *Descr. Cat. of the Med. MSS in Worcester Cath. Lib.* (Woodbridge 2001). All the scholars mentioned in the above paragraph were pupils, colleagues, and/or friends of Ker's, as was the present writer.

a handlist – summary heading, dimensions, collation, brief outline of contents – of the liturgical manuscripts (at least, those containing any music) of Britain and Ireland in his *Bibliotheca Musico-liturgica*, which appeared in parts between 1894 and 1932.[18] In the late 1930s a group of young scholars – C. R. Cheney, Richard Hunt, J. R. Liddell, and Roger Mynors – headed by Neil Ker conceived a plan to work out the provenances of every manuscript, in any modern collection, which could be assigned to a medieval library: any assemblage of books belonging to an identifiable religious house, cathedral, college, or parish church. The first edition of the resulting *Medieval Libraries of Great Britain* appeared in 1941, with Ker's name on the title page as sole editor but with a long and fascinating preface by him stressing the collaborative nature of the work and explaining the principles by which ascriptions to individual libraries were decided on. The second, much expanded, edition came out in 1964, and a highly useful *Supplement*, edited by Andrew Watson, in 1987.[19]

In furtherance of the approach pioneered by Ker and his colleagues in the late 1930s, the Corpus of British Medieval Library Catalogues sponsored by the British Academy began to publish its substantial volumes in 1990.[20] These are, in almost equal proportions, massively useful in providing critical editions of all surviving lists of books, no matter how fragmentary, from British medieval libraries, and massively frustrating, in that they show vividly the discrepancy between the numbers of service books that once existed and the very small percentage that survive.[21] Another multi-volume enterprise often of great help in the study of liturgical manuscripts is the Survey of Manuscripts

---

[18] The subtitle is *A Descriptive Handlist of the Musical and Latin-Liturgical MSS of the Middle Ages preserved in the Libraries of Great Britain and Ireland*. Fascicles covering descriptions of MSS at Lambeth Palace and Oxford were gathered in vol. I (1901); those in II (1932) cover libraries in English cathedrals, Dublin, Edinburgh, and Cambridge (the British Library [then Museum] was left untouched). The two volumes, originally printed under the auspices of the Plainsong and Medieval Music Society, were reprinted by Georg Olms of Hildesheim in 1967.

[19] At the end of his original preface Ker remarked, "Dr M. R. James has been before us almost everywhere and his discoveries are on nearly every page of this book"; much the same could be said of Ker's preventing (in the Prayer Book sense) in the present work.

[20] There are to be eventually some seventeen volumes plus index. The main principle of organization is by religious order or affiliation, with individual volumes being devoted to a few very large libraries and some general thematic volumes, like the libraries of Scotland, towards the end.

[21] All the more striking because liturgical books were often not included in library lists, often being regarded as among church furnishings rather than as part of the book holdings of a particular house.

Illuminated in the British Isles, now complete, by six authors, all of them eminent art historians.[22] For manuscripts inadequately catalogued otherwise, especially, the descriptions in the volumes of this survey, though naturally fullest on the artistic side, can be of great value; also useful is that they treat manuscripts regardless of location, thus providing descriptions of numerous codices in Continental libraries.

Catalogues and other resources for the study of liturgical manuscripts in libraries outside England will on the whole be mentioned only as necessary with respect to individual books. There seem to be in such libraries fewer manuscripts relevant to our purposes than might have been expected, and those that do exist are widely scattered. Fortunately, because the preponderance of these are found in French libraries, they are for the most part dealt with in the detailed compendia of Victor Leroquais covering (each in two or more volumes) sacramentaries and missals, breviaries, psalters, and pontificals in the public libraries of France.[23] Amidst all the starts and stops in cataloguing of the manuscripts of the Bibliothèque Nationale in Paris, it is very helpful to have François Avril and Patricia Stirnemann's conspectus of illuminated manuscripts of Insular origin.[24] Only three other individual catalogues need to be named here as conspicuously useful for our purposes: one more by M. R. James, that for the foundation collection at the Pierpont Morgan Library in New York; Marvin Colker's for Trinity College Dublin; and Consuelo Dutschke's for the Huntington Library in California.[25]

In the present work references are given to catalogue descriptions only where they contain an exceptionally full or unusual level of detail. Physical data, especially size, have also been taken mainly from them, though in many cases the books have been measured afresh.

---

[22] Under the general editorship of J. J. G. Alexander, 6 vols in 10 (London 1975–96). The individual volumes are listed, under the authors' names, in the table of Bibliograpical Abbreviations.

[23] Respectively, 3 vols plus plates (Paris 1924), 5 vols plus plates (Paris 1934), 2 vols plus plates (Mâcon 1940–1), and 3 vols plus plates (Paris 1937). Not all important manuscripts are included; at least one, BN lat. 987 (the Ramsey benedictional) falls through the gap as being technically not a pontifical, although for pontifical – i.e., bishop's – use.

[24] *Manuscrits enluminés d'origine insulaire viie-xxe siècle* [in the BN] (Paris 1987).

[25] M. R. James, *Cat. of MSS from the Libraries of W. Morris et al … now in the Library of J. P. Morgan* (privately printed 1907); Marvin Colker, *Trinity College Dublin. Descr. Cat. of the Med. and Renaissance Latin MSS*, 2 vols (Aldershot 1991); C. W. Dutschke [et al.], *Guide to Med. and Renaissance MSS in the Huntington Library*, 2 vols (San Marino 1989).

Medieval English church buildings

The resources are excellent but not consistent; one needs to bear in mind both what in any given enterprise has been completed and strategies by which the gaps – sometimes surprisingly large – can be filled. No single guide exists that shows at a glance everything available.[26] There are general introductions to the Victoria County History[27] and the Pevsner Buildings of England series,[28] but it is necessary to keep up with the ongoing publications of those enterprises and a few others of a continuing sort.

The most important of these for our purposes are probably the transactions of British Archaeological Society conferences which for the past quarter century have met at, and concentrated on, a cathedral or the major buildings of a city or discrete region.[29] These are being complemented by a number of large collaborative volumes on, and usually sponsored by, individual cathedrals.[30] Finally, the Royal Commission

---

[26] Indispensable for certain kinds of serial publications, notably local history societies, is E. L. C. Mullins, *Texts and Calendars: an Analytical Guide to Serial Publications*, Roy. Hist. Soc. Guides and Handbooks 7 (London 1958), covering publications through 1956, with a second volume, for those of 1957–82, published in 1983. This lists, often with a summary note as to contents, publications of official bodies (notably the Rolls Series and the Royal Commissions on Historical Monuments), national societies (including the Alcuin Club and the Henry Bradshaw Society), and local societies (including the Surtees Society, under whose auspices editions of several North Country liturgical books were issued). But only record publications of those societies are covered, not local history journals such as *Archaeologia Aeliana* and *Archaeologia Cantiana*.

[27] R. B. Pugh, *The Victoria County History: General Introduction* (London 1970); but numerous volumes have appeared since then (the VCH is not included in Mullins, as above). Accounts of religious houses tend to be in the second volume for each county, and are often extremely detailed as to history as well as archaeology, but it should be remembered that the oldest volumes of the series came out early in the twentieth century.

[28] Bridget Cherry, *The Buildings of England, Ireland, Scotland and Wales: a Short History and Bibliography* (publ. in a limited edition for the Penguin Collectors Society, 1998). It is very difficult to keep track of the various revisions and new editions, especially when they tend to take account of the new county arrangements in force since 1974; in the present work reference will generally be made to the first edition for each county.

[29] The first, for the conference at Worcester in 1975, appeared in 1978 (no editor given), and contains the important paper by Nigel Morgan, "Psalter Illustration for the Diocese of Worcester in the Thirteenth Century," pp. 91–104. A few of the more recent volumes are devoted to relevant areas on the Continent, such as Anjou (27, 2003); in general, the emphasis is increasingly less on individual cathedrals.

[30] Esp. noteworthy with respect to the musical aspect here ignored are the chapters, both by Roger Bowers, on "Music and Worship to 1640" in *A History of Lincoln Minster*, ed. D. Owen (Cambridge 1994), pp. 47–76, and "The Liturgy of the Cathedral and its Music, c. 975–1642," in *A History of Canterbury Cathedral*, ed. P. Collinson, N. Ramsay, and M. Sparks (Oxford 1995), pp. 408–50.

on Historical Monuments produced, albeit at a stately pace, a number of "Inventories" of massive detail and great value.[31] (The Commission was formally disbanded as such at the end of 1999.)

Canonical materials for medieval England

The term "canonical materials" is used loosely here to refer to official acts of persons or corporate bodies recognized as having (or at least claiming to have) authority. Of the various kinds potentially useful for our purposes the most obvious one is the acts of church councils, whether national, provincial, or diocesan. Attempts to gather these together go back as far as the *Provinciale* of William Lyndwood (c. 1430), covering material from 1222 to 1416, but the first – and still the only – collection to cover the entire British middle ages is that primarily associated with David Wilkins, *Concilia Magnae Britanniae et Hiberniae*, published in four volumes in 1737.[32] The manifest inadequacies of that work, quickly recognized, led to a project launched by A. W. Haddan and the great historian William Stubbs to redo the medieval part of Wilkins; the outcome of this was the three large volumes (printed in four) of *Councils and Ecclesiastical Documents relating to Great Britain and Ireland*.[33] So expansive was this work that its 1700-plus pages manage to cover England only to 870 (but Cornwall to 1072), Wales to 1295, Scotland to 1188, and Ireland to c. 543![34] The foundation thus laid, a plan for the continuation for the rest of the middle ages was drawn up in the early 1930s, but its first fruit did not appear until 1964, and then out of sequence: two volumes, covering the period 1205–1313, of *Councils and Synods* edited by F. M. Powicke and C. R. Cheney.[35] The gap between

---

[31] In addition to the Inventories covering whole counties, sometimes in as many as five volumes (e.g., Dorset, 1951–75), among the last publications of the RCHMons were a few (somewhat) smaller, "partial" volumes like *The Churches of South-East Wiltshire* (1987) and monographs like Thomas Cocke and Peter Kidson, *Salisbury Cathedral: Perspectives on the Architectural History* (1993).

[32] On this, see D. C. Douglas, *English Scholars 1660–1730*, 2nd edn (London 1951), pp. 217–21.

[33] Oxford 1869–78. A reprint would be greatly welcome.

[34] Even so, one limitation was that "liturgies ... are omitted from our pages, with the small exception of certain ancient fragments, interesting historically as much as liturgically, and which also take up very little space" (Preface to I, p. xviii). The editors intended to go further: the Contents page for vol. II.ii claims to cover Ireland to 1175 and that for III to deal with England until 1066.

[35] The full title is *Councils and Synods with other documents relating to the English Church* (Oxford); vol. I covers 1205–65, vol. II 1265–1313. The two volumes total 1450 pages; nonetheless, several classes of documents have been excluded, including capitular statutes and documents dealing with the canonization of saints. The general introduction promised in the preface to vol. I never appeared.

"Haddan and Stubbs" and "Powicke and Cheney" was finally filled in 1981, with the appearance of two further volumes, for 871–1204, edited by Dorothy Whitelock, Martin Brett, and Christopher Brooke.[36] For the period after 1313 there is still, as far as overall *Concilia* go, only Wilkins.

There has, however, been great progress in the publication of bishops' registers, extant generally only from the later thirteenth century (the earliest is that of Hugh of Wells, bishop of Lincoln 1209–35, with documents from 1219 on) and extensively published, mostly under the auspices of the Canterbury and York Society.[37] Collections of miscellaneous episcopal *acta* for the period between 1066 and the inception of formal bishops' registers are being made available in an ambitious and fast-moving series sponsored by the British Academy.[38] Unfortunately, there is an amazingly small amount of information in either registers or *acta* concerning anything liturgical; one would scarcely think, perusing these episcopal documents, that bishops had any liturgical concerns whatever. Somewhat more informative are the results of visitations, whether by bishops, archdeacons, rural deans, or cathedral deans.[39]

Nor are papal documents much help. Papal letters and miscellaneous communications are occasionally useful in transmitting mandates having to do with the observance of feasts, and of course formal canonization establishes an at least theoretical celebration of the new saint liturgically; other direct papal influence on the history of liturgy in medieval England seems slight.[40]

Finally, documents issued by religious orders, especially the acts of general chapters once these are mandated uniformly by the Fourth Lateran Council of 1215, are occasionally helpful. Those for most groups will be noticed in the appropriate places; there should be

---

[36] The dividing point between the two volumes is 1066; again, some types of documents are omitted, including foundation charters and "texts, such as pontificals, concerned with ritual" (Preface, I.vii). The exemplary scholarship of the editors is not matched by the production, that being merely a rather faint reproduction of a typescript. Once more, there is no general introduction.

[37] These are summarily listed, with details of publication (under whatever auspices) to c. 1980, in D. M. Smith, *Guide to the Bishops' Registers of England and Wales*, Roy. Hist. Soc. Guides & Handbooks 11 (London 1981).

[38] The first volume to appear was *Lincoln 1067–1185*, ed. D. M. Smith (London 1980). The number of volumes currently exceeds thirty.

[39] For example, two volumes ed. by W. S(parrow) Simpson, *Visitations of Churches belonging to St Paul's Cathedral, 1249–1252* (in *Camden Miscellany* IX, = Camd. Soc. n.s. 53, 1895) and *in 1297 and 1458* (Camd. Soc. n.s. 55, also 1895).

[40] The main collection of such material is that of W. Holtzmann, *Papsturkunden in England*, Abh. der Gesellschaft der Wiss. zu Göttingen, phil.-hist. Kl., n.F. 25 (Berlin 1930–3), 3rd F. 14–15 (Berlin 1935–6), 3rd. F. 33 (Göttingen 1952).

mentioned here only those for the Benedictines, covering as they do a large number of houses and great variety of matters.[41] Likewise, statutes and other regulations for individual secular cathedrals, like those for Exeter, Lincoln, and Salisbury, will be noticed where they are relevant.[42]

---

[41] W. A. Pantin, ed. *Documents illustrating the activities of the General and Provincial Chapters of the English Black Monks 1215–1540*, 3 vols., Camden Soc. 3rd ser. 45, 47, 54 (London 1931–37).

[42] The work most notably of more than local application is the vast accumulation of documents, sometimes far beyond the range implied by the title, edited by H. Bradshaw and C. Wordsworth as *Lincoln Cathedral Statutes*, 3 vols (Cambridge 1892–7); on this, see p. 497.

2 Early Anglo-Saxon England: a partly traceable story

The difficulty of trying to begin our story at its chronological begin-ning, unavoidable if we are to pursue an historical rather than merely descriptive method, may be succinctly expressed by reminding our-selves of approaches taken in two of the greatest works ever to deal with England in the middle ages. The first approach is summed up in the often-quoted epigrammatic statement of Frederic William Maitland in explaining the title of his *Domesday Book and Beyond*: "Domesday Book appears to me, not indeed as the known, but as the knowable. The Beyond is still very dark: but the way to it lies through the Norman record. A result is given to us: the problem is to find cause and process."[1] The second is expressed in Dom David Knowles's explanation of why he began his *Monastic Order in England* no earlier than the mid-tenth century: that a continuous history of English Benedictine monasticism (his primary concern) is possible only from the time of Dunstan and his contemporaries because, despite the glowing witness of Bede, for the earlier period "the records of the times and places of which the Venerable Bede does not treat are in general so imperfect and of such questionable authenticity that an intensive critical and diplomatic inves-tigation by specialists must precede any fresh attempt to understand the conditions under which the monks lived."[2]

In matters liturgical as well as monastic much investigation of the "critical and diplomatic" sort has been accomplished in the sixty-plus years since Knowles wrote; but the partial and unsteady state of our knowledge of the liturgy in England before the so-called Monastic

---

[1] F. W. Maitland, *Domesday Book and Beyond: three Essays in the Early History of England* (Cambridge 1897), p. v.
[2] The full title is *The Monastic Order in England: a History of its Development from the Times of St Dunstan to the Fourth Lateran Council, 940–1216*; words quoted from 2nd edn (Cambridge 1963), p. xix. As the Preface to this second edition explains (p. xvi), when the first edition appeared in 1940 its subtitle carried the date 943, because Knowles thought that Dunstan had become abbot of Glastonbury in that year; a crit-ical charter moving the date back to 940 was published only subsequently.

Reform still compels a treatment of the earlier Anglo-Saxon centuries which looks heavily back from the "knowable" of the later tenth. Nonetheless, an attempt must be made to trace the story from, and not just back to, its earliest aspects. The amount of highly professional attention the subject has received during the last fifty years or so, combined with the general paucity of liturgical manuscripts from the earlier two thirds of this period (extending for our purposes over some five centuries, c. 600–1100), means that the approach of this chapter will be based somewhat more on the labors of other scholars and less on manuscript materials than will be the case elsewhere in this work.

Some historiography, c. 1643–c. 1900

Awareness of the liturgical dimension of early Anglo-Saxon England is evident as far back as the collections of material published in 1639 by Henry Spelman (1564?-1641)[3] and greatly expanded in the *Concilia* of David Wilkins (1685–1745) in four volumes, 1737. Something has been said already (p. 27) of the inadequacy of Wilkins's work and of the enterprise begun by A. W. Haddan and William Stubbs, *Councils and Synods* (1869–78), so expansive in conception that the material relating to Anglo-Saxon England reached only to 870. While they were issuing their collections F. E. Warren, as a relatively young scholar (born 1842), was preparing his masterly edition of the Leofric missal, which appeared in 1883. This composite, and complicated, massbook is in its original layer a Gregorian sacramentary made in Lotharingia c. 900, with English additions throughout the next century and a half; it will be considered at length in the next chapter (see p. 72). But it must be noticed here both because Warren's is the first full, "modern," edition of an Anglo-Saxon liturgical text and because his treatment of its earliest component stands at the beginning of systematic English attention to the complex problems connected with the study of the early Roman sacramentaries: attention that was to produce editions of the Gelasian sacramentary by H. A. Wilson in 1894 and the Leonine sacramentary by C. L. Feltoe two years later, with an edition by Wilson of the Gregorian sacramentary following in 1915.[4] (As the nomenclature of the principal Roman

---

[3] *Concilia, decreta, leges, constitutiones in re ecclesiarum orbis Britannici*, etc. (London 1639) – that is, vol. I, covering the period to the Norman Conquest, which was all that was published in his lifetime; a second volume, for the period after the Conquest, appeared only in 1664.

[4] Wilson's Gelasian edition was the starting point for Edmund Bishop's essay, "The Earliest Roman Mass Book (the *Gelasianum*)," in the 1894 *Dublin Review* (repr. Bishop, *Liturg. Hist.*, pp. 39–61).

sacramentary traditions will appear often on subsequent pages in this chapter and the next, the reader's attention is directed to the Excursus on p. 56, which aims to provide succinctly such minimal information about this immensely complex matter as will be needed here.)

It is worth pointing out here that this was pioneer scholarship. Even towards the end of the nineteenth century, study of liturgical texts of the kind that bear on the present subject was no more advanced on the Continent than in Great Britain. Léopold Delisle's path-breaking conspectus *Mémoire sur d'anciens sacramentaires* was published in 1886,[5] and a decade later a compendium of information about early massbooks in Italy was gathered in Adalbert Ebner's *Iter Italicum*.[6] But in, say, 1890 (the year in which the Henry Bradshaw Society was founded; see p. 10 above), for actual editions of texts students were still dependent on works published between 1642 and 1748: in Hugo Ménard's presentation of a late ninth-century massbook as *the* Gregorian sacramentary (1642); in the materials collected by G. M. Tommasi in *Codices Sacramentorum Nongentis Annis Vetustiores* (the first printings of the Gelasian sacramentary and of some key Gallican texts) and other works; and in collections made available by Jean Mabillon in his *Museum Italicum* (1687–9) and *De Liturgia Gallicana* (1695), and by L. A. Muratori's *Liturgia Romana vetus* (1748).[7] So when, for example, as a preliminary to preparing his edition of the Gelasian, Wilson put together his *Classified Index to the Leonine, Gelasian, and Gregorian Sacramentaries* (Cambridge 1892), it was perforce, as the subtitle reads, "According to the text of Muratori's *Liturgia Romana Vetus*." Not until 1918 did a Continental series of editions begin on anything like the scale of the HBS, which by then had produced some fifty-three volumes.[8] By the time the nineteenth century ended, the work of Warren, Wilson, and others of that pioneering generation had laid the foundation for Anglophone liturgical scholarship bearing – albeit perforce inconclusively – on the early centuries of what can reasonably be called English history.

Before 597

It is inevitable that any treatment of what becomes England should up to about 730 be colored by the overwhelming figure of Bede; his

---

[5] Published in the Mémoires de l'Academie des inscriptions et belles-lettres [Paris] 32, pt. 1, pp. 57–423.

[6] The full title is *Quellen und Forschungen zur Geschichte und Kunstgeschichte des Missale Romanum im Mittelalter* (Freiburg 1896; repr. Graz 1957).

[7] Several of these editions were reprinted, about 1850, in volumes 72 and 78 of Migne's *Patrologia Latina*, but with many errors and confusions introduced.

[8] Details of these two series are given in the Excursus below.

Historia Ecclesiastica Gentis Anglorum, in particular, has always been in the forefront of the consciousness of historians and other scholars who have dealt with the early Anglo-Saxon period.[9] So it is an admittedly "Bedan" approach to state that the history of Christian liturgy in England, as distinct from Britain, must begin concretely with the Gregorian mission of Augustine and his companions to Kent in 597. That said, we have to remind ourselves that such Christian worship as took place on the island during the previous three, possibly even four, centuries, is bound to have had some bearing (rather than, in most cases, direct influence) on the story we shall be trying to trace.

This bearing must have been of three main sorts. (1) Through interaction in the late fourth, fifth, and sixth centuries between those of the British population who were Christians and the Germanic pagans conventionally called Anglo-Saxons. (2) Through similar interactions with Christians of the type often termed Celtic: that is, those from what was to become Scotland (especially in its western parts, from the work of the shadowy Ninian in Galloway to Columba's establishment of a monastery at Iona in 563), and also from Wales. (3) Through interaction with Continental (Catholic) Christians, primarily in Frankland and most pointedly with Liudhard, bishop and chaplain to Queen Bertha of Kent, whose husband Ethelbert received the Gregorian missionaries in 597.

The witness of Bede to all these interactions is, as was just suggested, paramount, because of his immediacy in terms of both time and place, the vividness of his style, and the apparent reliability of his accounts. With respect to interaction between Anglo-Saxons and British Christians, however, Bede's dependence on the mid sixth-century British monk Gildas has probably had a negative effect: that is, in leading us to suppose that there was, as near as makes no difference, none. Precisely because Bede's famous sentence, "To other unspeakable crimes, which Gildas their own historian describes in doleful words, was added this crime, that they never preached the faith to the Saxons or Angles who inhabited Britain with them," serves as immediate prelude to his account of the Gregorian mission, total disjunction between British and what was to become Anglo-Saxon Christianity

---

[9] So, for example, William Bright's *Chapters of Early English Church History*, 3rd edn (Oxford 1897, revised and enlarged from 1st edn 1877) is confessedly a kind of extended gloss on Bede's account. The year 1897, as the 1300th anniversary of the landing of Augustine, was marked by the publication of the documents and essays edited by A. J. Mason as *The Mission of St Augustine to England according to the Original Documents* (Cambridge); the fourth essay ("Dissertation") was by the learned H. A. Wilson, "On some Liturgical Points relating to the Mission of St Augustine," pp. 235–52. Charles Plummer's great edition of Bede's *Opera historica* (2 vols) was published the previous year, 1896.

has generally been accepted.[10] That this cannot have been the case is shown by Bede's own account of the meeting somewhere in Worcestershire or Gloucestershire betweeen Augustine and "the bishops and teachers of the neighbouring British kingdom" (*proximae Brettonum prouinciae*) early in the seventh century, at which the question of a common effort to convert those who were still heathen is a fundamental part of the agenda (*HE* II.ii).[11] Although that meeting foundered, that it was held at such an early date in the conversion process of the Anglo-Saxons implies that there must have been a lot of acknowledged British Christian presence in areas where English settlement was in its first generation or two.[12]

In terms of our subject, however, this is no more than tantalizing; for we have next to no coherent sense as to how the early British Christians worshipped.[13] Nuggets here and there amount to no more than might have been expected. That one must always be aware of the brilliant filter of Bede's mind is shown by the following example. His account of the mass baptisms of many in the British army before its engagement with a combined force of Picts and Saxons (*HE* I.xx) specifies that these took place at Easter, Lent (*quadragesimae venerabiles dies*) being over. That baptism was often conferred at Easter is scarcely surprising, nor that the shout that discomfits the enemy should be that of Alleluia, appropriate to the day; but to postulate that the British bishops were in the early fifth century observing a forty-day Lent is somewhat more than can be established for that date.[14]

---

[10] H(istoria) E(cclesiastica) I.xxii; the translation is that of Bertram Colgrave in *Bede's Ecclesiastical History of the English People*, ed. Colgrave and R. A. B. Mynors, OMT (Oxford 1969), p. 69.

[11] Colgrave's translation here, p. 135, may mislead slightly by rendering *prouincia* as "kingdom."

[12] This is perhaps specially likely to have been the case in the western regions, where the people called Magonsætan and Hwicce settled: the area covered intensively by P. Sims-Williams, *Religion and Literature in Western England, 600–800*, Cbg. Studies in Anglo-Saxon England 3 (Cambridge 1990). Of the very earliest period he says, "The nature of seventh-century worship is scarcely open even to conjecture" (p. 273).

[13] Cf. C. Thomas, *Christianity in Roman Britain to AD 500* (London 1981), p. 83: "When we look at liturgy – set forms of wording for the Mass, for baptism and confirmation, marriage and burial, ordination, etc. – we have almost no information." He does offer the possibly instructive suggestion that "late Roman Christians in Britain spoke of the eucharistic service as *offerenda*," based on loan-words in British Celtic languages (p. 80). Much oblique information is available, for the whole of Britain and Ireland (and also Frankia), in A. Thacker and R. Sharpe, eds., *Local Saints and Local Churches in the Early Medieval West* (Oxford 2002), esp., for the topic under discussion, in Sharpe's paper "Martyrs and Local Saints in Late Antique Britain," pp. 75–154.

[14] It seems likely that the extension of the Lenten fast from thirty-six to forty days became common in the West no earlier than the beginning of the sixth century: P. Jounel in *The Liturgy and Time*, vol. IV of A. G. Martimort, gen. ed., *The Church at Prayer*, new edn (Eng tr. Collegeville, MN 1986, of Paris 1983 edn), p. 68.

Information about the second of the interactions that early Anglo-Saxon Christians would have encountered, those with the early Celtic church, is in some respects quite full, but trying to establish its influence on fledgling English Christianity (that is, its specifically liturgical influence) is almost as difficult as with British Christianity. Again, this is partly owing to Bede, in this case to his ambivalence about Irish and Scottish Christians. Several, notably Aidan and, more distantly, Ninian and Columba (*HE* III.iii–vi), are entirely praiseworthy, while Aidan's successors Finan and Colman are holy men but unsound about the dating of Easter (III.xxv), and Pictish Christians are converted to right thinking only by a long letter ghost-written by Bede himself in around 730 (V.xxi). Put rather crudely, for him either the losing side at the Synod of Whitby in 664 will become "Roman" in its worship or it will be tarred with the intransigency of Colman, who returned to Ireland rather than submit to the new order of things. Nonetheless that there must have been some two-way liturgical traffic is evident from so obvious an example as the Lindisfarne Gospels, which combine with the peerless Celtic illumination an Italian type of text and, most strikingly, a gospel lectionary that must come from Campania.[15]

As to the third source of immediate liturgical interaction with an Anglo-Saxon population on the eve of the Gregorian mission, the Frankish, we are both somewhat better informed and also not impeded by any animus from Bede. He is, it is true, not at all forthcoming about either Bishop Liudhard or Queen Bertha, both of whom receive no more than passing mention (I.xxv). But it seems likely that her practice of Christian faith was influential on her husband even before the Italian missionaries arrived; indeed, it has been suggested that Ethelbert may have been converted (in some sense, anyhow) in 595, two years before Augustine's arrival.[16] Now, virtually nothing is known about Liudhard save that he was a Frank; the worship he brought to Bertha's chapel (whether or not that should be understood as the church of St Martin in Canterbury, built in the early post-Roman period) would have been that which was familiar to Frankish churchmen of the late sixth century. That this would in its outlines have belonged to what is called generically the Gallican family is almost all that can be said for our purposes; how familiar or strange Queen Bertha thought the services

---

[15] This matter is discussed on p. 39, with facsimile editions and basic literature mentioned in note 24.

[16] J. M. Wallace-Hadrill, *Bede's Ecclesiastical History of the English People: a Historical Commentary* (Oxford 1988), p. 34, citing in particular I. Wood, *The Merovingian North Sea* (Alingsas 1983), p. 16.

conducted by Augustine and his band were must remain in the province of guesswork.[17]

The Augustinian mission

The concrete starting place is, inevitably, Bede's highly dramatic account of the initial meeting between Augustine and King Ethelbert of Kent, which takes place in the open air lest religious sorcery be inflicted on the king (I.xxv). At this first meeting the band of missionaries arrive carrying a silver processional cross and what is apparently an icon of Christ; and, on either this or a later occasion when they are clearly approaching the city of Canterbury (*ciuitati*: at that time, more likely a hamlet), they sing a text which Bede gives: "Deprecamur te, Domine, in omni misericordia tua, ut auferatur furor tuus et ira tua a ciuitate ista et de domo sancta tua, quoniam peccauimus. Alleluia." To beg that divine wrath be averted "from this city and from thy holy house" seems neither tactful nor specially relevant, and indeed this has been identified as one of the processional antiphons in a Gallican liturgy, that of Rogationtide, which was not imported to Rome until Carolingian times.[18] While that is undoubtedly true, it is worth remembering also that, according to some early biographers, Gregory the Great had begun, and recommended, the use of a seven-fold litany, from which the words quoted by Bede might have been taken – and that in any case Bede's work is completed well before Carolingian reforms begin.[19]

It certainly seems likely that the books Augustine brought with him were Roman rather than Gallican, though of course he could have picked up a supply of the latter during his trips through Frankland when travelling from Rome to Kent and, on at least one occasion, back to Arles. Precisely what kinds of Roman books – if indeed they were entire codices and not, as may well have been the case, *libelli*, pamphlets – can scarcely be answered in the present state of our knowledge.[20]

---

[17] The principal Gallican sources are discussed in Gamber, *CLLA*, pp. 153–93, but the vast majority are markedly later than the sixth century. Perhaps the closest similarity with what Liudhard might have used would be six leaves of a palimpsest sacramentary, now St Gall, Stiftsbibl. 908, probably from North Italy (*CLLA* no. 201); the famous "Masses of Mone" (seven masses, again from a palimpsest) are dated by Gamber to the 630s (*CLLA* no. 203).

[18] Colgrave, in Colgrave and Mynors, p. 76 n. 1, speculates that "Augustine may have learned the practice during his journey through Gaul." D. A. Bullough has remarked that the tradition of the singing of this chant "can hardly be regarded as historical": "Alcuin and the Kingdom of Heaven," in *Carolingian Essays*, ed. U-R. Blumenthal (Washington, DC 1983), pp. 1–69 at 6, n. 14.

[19] From, apparently, Paul the Deacon (died c. 799) on: PL 75.47.

[20] H. Ashworth answers the question "Did St Augustine Bring the 'Gregorianum' to England?," *Eph. Liturg.* 72 (1958), pp. 39–43, convincingly in the negative. Several

Again, the vividness and familiarity of Bede's text may mislead. When he says that the clerics sent to reinforce Augustine's original band in, presumably, 599 brought with them "all such things as were generally necessary for the worship and ministry of the church, such as sacred vessels, altar cloths and church ornaments, vestments for priests and clerks, relics of the holy apostles and martyrs, and very many manuscripts" (*codices plurimi*; I.xxix), we have to remember that this is precisely what the founding abbot of Wearmouth and Jarrow, Benedict Biscop, had in Bede's own lifetime demonstrably done; it seems possible that Bede is reading back a century or so activities understood to be essential to the establishment of the monasteries he knew.[21]

One of these *codices plurimi* may be identified, although to less purpose than might be hoped. It is widely held that the so-called St Augustine's gospels (now CCCC 286) was brought to Kent by that missionary.[22] The book, written in Italy in the sixth century, is much mutilated, and it is possible that some information of a liturgical sort (like the pericope lists in the Lindisfarne gospels, to be discussed presently) was originally present. As it stands, what we learn from it is mainly that a rather sumptuous gospelbook, with a good Vulgate text, appears inseparable from Christianity of the Roman strand as presented to an early Anglo-Saxon monarch. Whether the other circumstances of worship, which Bede tells us centered on the surviving fifth-century church of St Martin, were equally grand we do not know.

Having noticed something of the problem created by Bede's pre-eminence as a witness –the extent to which he accomplishes his goal of being *verax historicus* here as opposed to projecting the conditions of his Wearmouth-Jarrow back two or three generations – we may pose three general questions derived just from what his *History* says, and then observe ruefully how little evidence there is on which to base any kind of answer to the first two. (1) How long and how widely were whatever worship materials Augustine and his companions brought with

sensible short papers by Dom Ashworth bearing on the general subject are listed in his obituary notice in *Eph. Liturg.* 95 (1981), pp. 138–41.

[21] Here as elsewhere in the Colgrave translation the term *missarum sollemnia* is rendered "the solemn rites of the mass," as though something like the modern term "solemn mass" were meant; in fact, the phrase refers to the mass in general, as witness the title of J. A. Jungmann's deservedly famous work, *Missarum Sollemnia: Eine genetische Erklärung der römischen Messe* (many edns and trs since its first appearance, Vienna 1949).

[22] Of a large literature, see esp. R. Marsden, "The Gospels of St Augustine," in *St Augustine and the Conversion of England*, ed. R. Gameson (Stroud, Glos. 1999), pp. 285–312; mainly textual in approach. Marsden acknowledges the possibility that the book might have come in the wake of the Theodoran mission (see below) in the late 7th cent.

them used in the English kingdoms, given the failure of that mission in London and its narrow survival in Kent? (2) Did Paulinus take the same kinds of materials to Deira (southern Northumbria) in the 620s, and is there reason to think that they survived to any extent after the collapse of that mission following the death of Edwin in 632? (3) Are those known to, and used by, Wilfrid and Benedict Biscop in the time of Oswiu (reigned in Northumbria 642/54–670) and his immediate successors at all in the direct line of those of the previous two generations, or did these two ecclesiastical grandees bring back from their numerous trips to the Continent from c. 653 to 703 new strands of resources for worship? For that matter, were the worship patterns at Benedict Biscop's foundations at Wearmouth and Jarrow pretty much the same as those in the establishments headed at one time or another by Wilfrid (Ripon, York, Hexham) or markedly different – and if the latter, what is the source of the Wilfridian usages?

Such inklings as there may be to an answer for that third question will appear only as we approach the sophisticated ecclesiastical regimes of Northumbria in the late seventh and early eighth centuries. Before attempting that, however, we must just remind ourselves of the overall limiting factor in thinking about whatever liturgical materials must have been used in the Anglo-Saxon areas of Britain as they become (ostensibly) Christianized in the first two thirds or so of the seventh century: that almost no even remotely useful fragments, to say nothing of more substantial books, survive from before c. 670 for areas north of the English Channel, and, worse still, that there is south of it very little in the way of hard evidence for fixed structures of textual traditions – a cumbersome way of saying actual service books – at that time. Apart from a generalized source-pool of prayers which are being shaped throughout the seventh century into something like the earliest extant Continental massbooks (such as those noticed in the Excursus below; nothing of a remotely organized sort will be available for the daily office until a good deal later), what we have to work from concretely are a few bits of gospel-lectionary evidence, all from Northumbria and all dating from the period of Bede's lifetime (c. 670–735). That period also spans Theodore's work in England (669–90), which must be set alongside the lectionary evidence.

Gospel-lectionary evidence from the age of Theodore

It is hard to overstate the importance of the mission of the Greek monk Theodore of Tarsus, sent by pope Vitalian in 668 to be (arch)bishop of Canterbury.[23] Theodore, for some years resident in Rome, was accompanied on the trip by Benedict Biscop, who had been visiting there. Also to be of the party but held up for a year in Frankland was an elderly African monk, Hadrian, who had been abbot of a monastery near Naples, and who on his eventual arrival at Canterbury became head of the abbey there of SS Peter and Paul (later called St Augustine's), in succession to Benedict Biscop, who thereupon went on to found his houses at Jarrow and Wearmouth. These familiar facts, all made vivid in the pages of Bede, require repetition here because they frame the situation we now move on to, that of the last third of the seventh century and first third of the eighth. The questions raised above, of the interactions of the earliest proponents of Christianity among the Anglo-Saxons with British/Celtic, Gallican, and Old Roman influences, are – though by no means answered – given additional perspective and even complication by developments we have now to call to mind: the aftermath(s) of King Oswiu's decision at Whitby in 664 that Northumbria would follow Roman usage as urged by its champion Wilfrid; the worship patterns that Theodore and Hadrian can be supposed to have known, from their respective backgrounds of Asia Minor-plus-Constantinople-plus-Rome and Libya-plus-Naples; whatever the two men might have picked up during their lengthy journeys through Frankland; all that Benedict Biscop brought back to Northumbria from his five trips to Rome; and what English missionaries, from Southumbria as well as Northumbria, seem likely to have taken with them to the Continent between, say, 690, when Willibrord first went to Frisia, and the martyrdom of Boniface there in 753.

The first and best known of the pieces of gospel-lectionary evidence is that in the Lindisfarne gospels (probably written within twenty years or so of St Cuthbert's death in 687; BL Cotton Nero D.iv). This contains, among the introductory material for each of the four gospels, a list of the liturgical occasions for which pericopes are taken from that book – but in the biblical order in which the passages occur, and with no indication of precisely which passage is meant.[24] Within the text itself most

---

[23] This section owes a great deal to Michael Lapidge's discussion in the section "Liturgy" of his [and Bernhard Bischoff's] *Biblical Commentaries from the Canterbury School of Theodore and Hadrian*, Cambridge Studies in Anglo-Saxon England 10 (Cambridge 1994), pp. 155–72.

[24] There are two splendid facsimiles: *Evangeliorum Quattuor Codex Lindisfarnensis*, ed. T. J(ulian) Brown and many others, 2 vols (Olten and Lausanne 1956–60), and *The Lindisfarne Gospels*, with 2 vols of detailed description and commentary by M(ichelle) P. Brown (Lucerne 2002). The larger of the latter's accompanying volumes is published separately (including a paperback version) in the British Library Studies in

of these passages seem to be marked by colored initials surrounded by dots, but that device is used for some other passages as well and is not a consistently reliable guide.[25] The presence among the specified feasts of those of certain saints (most obviously, Januarius [Gennaro]) fixes the model to the general region of Campania.[26] (Closely related, but not quite identical, is the information in a more modest gospel book written in Northumbria in the first half of the eighth century, now BL Royal 1 B.vii, having most likely been copied from the same Campanian(?) exemplar as the Lindisfarne book.)[27]

The second such bit of evidence is provided by notes at the tops of the pages in a gospel lectionary brought from England – almost certainly, Wearmouth-Jarrow – by Burchard (Burgheard) to his new see at Würzburg in 743 (and still there: Würzburg, Univsbibl. M. p. th. f. 68). These notes, while reflecting the same basic liturgical model as the Lindisfarne book, are rather fuller and show also some clear Roman influence.[28] This influence is evident in the specification of pericopes for such distinctively Roman saints as Pancras, Marcellinus and Peter, Gregory, and Adrian (probably the Roman martyr venerated on 8 September), as well as a large number of Roman stational indications. Meaningful Roman stational liturgy would of course have been impossible at Wearmouth-Jarrow; we wonder, therefore, whether the saints' days mentioned were likely to be kept.

Another, very slender, thread of evidence may be the choice of titles for Bede's homilies, at least as they have come down to us. They suggest that the liturgical context in which he preached reflected definite Roman as well as possible Campanian influence. This needs to be stated cautiously, because in the extant manuscripts both the titles and the sequence of these homilies, which survive to a total number of fifty

Medieval Culture series as *The Lindisfarne Gospels: Society, Spirituality and the Scribe* (London and Toronto 2003). The liturgical aspect is discussed by Michelle Brown primarily on pp. 182–99, depending heavily on Julian Brown's discussion on pp. 34–43 of the 1960 commentary volume to the earlier facsimile.

[25] There are also a few rubrical indications in the *Capitula Lectionum* for each of the gospels.

[26] The wider term seems preferable to the more usually encountered "Neapolitan" or "Capuan": Lapidge provides a detailed discussion of the region and its churches in *Bibl. Comms.* (above, n. 23), pp. 92–120.

[27] Eight lines from the pericope list to John's Gospel (fol. 130v) are illustrated in *CLA* (*Codices Latini Antiquiores*, ed. E.A. Lowe, 12 vols, Oxford 1934–72), II (2nd edn, 1972), no. 213.

[28] The witness of this book was first made available, on the basis of a discovery by Edmund Bishop, by G. Morin, "Les Notes liturgiques de l'évangéliaire de Burchard," *Rev. Bén.* 10 (1893), pp. 113–26; there is a convenient table of these notes compared with the pericope indications in Lindisfarne and Roy. 1 B.vii in J. Chapman, *Notes on the Early History of the Vulgate Gospels* (Oxford 1908), pp. 52–63.

divided into two books, cannot necessarily be relied upon to reflect Bede's own usage.[29] That caution expressed, however, it may be significant that Lindisfarne and Burchard's *ieiunium* of John the Baptist is *vigilia* in Bede, as in Roman tradition, and that for the 27 December feast of John the Evangelist Bede lacks the characteristic title of Campanian tradition, *In adsumptione*. Such admittedly tiny details raise the possibility that such sacramentaries as may have "matched" the Roman-tradition gospel books to which Bede apparently had access (as well as those of the Neapolitan/Campanian/Capuan tradition witnessed to by the Lindisfarne book) were predominantly Gelasian.[30]

Northumbrian sacramentary tradition

In the absence of any such sacramentaries themselves, all that can be said is that it seems unlikely that a lectionary tradition (whether conveyed through a list or through an actual gospel book) would travel without, in some form, the complementary mass prayers and other formulas. The notion that the mass texts in use in England through at least much of the eighth century may have been of the Gelasian strand is buttressed by four surviving fragments from such books.[31] The first is a bifolium from what seems to be a sacramentary written in uncials in an apparently Anglo-Saxon hand, though its location and character are a matter of some dispute.[32] Used as flyleaves to a ninth-century *Lexicon Tironianum*, fol. 116 of BL Add. 37518 contains *Orationes matutin[ales et vespertinales]* and fol. 117 three gospel pericopes (John 14.7–14, Luke 24.49–53, Mark 16.15–24).[33] The size of the leaves, even cut down as

---

[29] See esp. the useful table of *Capitula Evangeliorum* comparing Bede with columns for Roman, Romano-Neapolitan, and Gallican usages in D. Hurst's edition of *Bedae Venerabilis Opera Homiletica*, CCSL 122 (1955), pp. ix–xvi. The two oldest manuscripts are both Continental and date from a hundred years or more after Bede's death: p. xvii.

[30] Another pointer in this direction is that Bede used *Theophania*, the consistent Gelasian wording for the commoner *Epiphania*.

[31] Attention was first called to them as a group in H. Gneuss's path-breaking treatment of "Liturgical Books in Anglo-Saxon England and their Old English Terminology," in *Learning and Literature in Anglo-Saxon England*, Fests. P. Clemoes, ed. M. Lapidge and Gneuss (Cambridge 1985), pp. 91–141 at 102. Other such fragments are extractable from Gneuss's subsequent *Handlist of Anglo-Saxon Manuscripts ... Written or Owned in England up to 1100*, Medieval Texts and Studies 241 (Tempe, AZ 2001).

[32] E. A. Lowe says "written doubtless in an Anglo-Saxon centre in England," *CLA*, II, no. 176. Sims-Williams, *Religion and Literature*, p. 285, calls it "Southern English"; Rosamond McKitterick, in a private communication of Jan. 2000, avers that "there is no way you could establish whether or not it was written in England or on the Continent."

[33] Fols 116, 117, 117v are reproduced in *CLA*, II, fol. 116v in New Palaeographical Soc., *Facsimiles of Ancient Manuscripts*, First Series I (1903), pl. 132. The text was first

they are, is c. 260 x 197 mm, which suggests an altar book more than a book of private devotion. Such sets of morning and evening prayers are commonly found towards the end of eighth- and ninth-century sacramentaries; all of the prayers here can be located in one or another Gelasian book, though the order of this set of eight (there may possibly have been more) does not correspond exactly to that of any surviving witness.

Too much must not be made to depend on this one fragment. In general, as Donald Bullough has said, it seems "perverse to doubt that the sacramentaries used in English churches in the late seventh and for much of the eighth century were of a type close to although by no means identical with the 'Gelasian' Sacramentary in Vat. Reg. Lat. 316" (i.e., the Old Gelasian).[34] That sacramentary is structured in three books, of which this fragment – if it is from a codex of this type – would have come in the third; and if so it must have been part of a substantial volume. It may indeed give us some idea of what a massbook near the beginning of our story looked like. We may, however, want to note that these two leaves are written (by several hands) in uncials, while all of the celebrated Gelasian massbook codices are in minuscule hands: as well as the Old Gelasian Vat. Reg. Lat. 316, the Phillipps, Angoulême, Gellone, St Gall 348, and Zurich Rh. 30 books (the latter five all being of the Young Gelasian strand).[35]

Further light may be shed by two other fragments. One, again probably part of a sacramentary, is fols 3–4 of BN lat. 9488, first brought to notice by H. M. Bannister in 1908.[36] These leaves belonged to what was clearly an altar-size book; even conspicuously cut, the pages measure c. 285 x 205 mm, and the hand is what Lowe called insular majuscule.[37] He dates the leaves no more closely than "saec. viii," and gives as the place of origin "Ireland or Northern England." Yitzhak Hen, however, in the context of trying to work out the liturgical practices St Willibrord may have taken with him to the Continent, and in particular to his

---

edited by A. Baumstark, "Ein altgelasianische Sakramentar-bruchstück in insularer Herkunft," *Jahrbuch für Liturgiewissenschaft* 7 (1927), pp. 130–36; his text, without any commentary, is reprinted as "Das Fragment Baumstark" in L.C. Mohlberg's Gelasian edition (see note 5 of the Excursus following this chapter), pp. 266–67.

[34] Bullough, "Alcuin and the Kingdom of Heaven," p. 12, n. 26.

[35] See in general B. Moreton, *The Eighth-Century Gelasian Sacramentary* (Oxford 1976), which, however, does not discuss this Add. 37518 fragment.

[36] "Liturgical Fragments, A: Anglo-Saxon Sacramentaries," *JTS* 9 (1908), pp. 398–411. Bannister sensibly noted that "The Anglo-Saxon script does not necessarily involve the book having been written either in or for England; it may, however, be conjectured that, even if it was written for a foreign house, it may very possibly have been copied from an English exemplar," p. 399.

[37] *CLA*, V (1950), no. 581. Bannister had termed the hand "large round half uncial."

foundation at Echternach, claims that palaeographical evidence proves the leaves to have been written in that abbey.[38] The contents come from the common of saints, with peculiarities that are identical to those of the Young Gelasian books, rather than the Old Gelasian; but there is also an episcopal benediction, which may suggest Gallican influence (such blessings are not common in the Gelasian tradition).

A textual though not physical fragment occurs in the celebrated Echternach manuscript of the "Martyrologium Hieronymianum" (BN lat. 10837); this contains, after its thirty-one martyrological folios and the almost equally celebrated Calendar of St Willibrord (treated below) and between sets of computistical tables for the years 722–59 and for 760–67, a mass for the vigil of the Ascension (fols 42v–43). Bannister, who published this discovery in the same 1908 article, called it "the earliest known specimen of a mass in Anglo-Saxon script," and ascribed it to the introduction of that vigil, apparently not in use earlier, for a brief period in the late eighth century.[39] Lowe called the hand "an expert and graceful pointed Anglo-Saxon minuscule," with the titles of the prayer "in a small uncial of an unmistakably Northumbrian type," though undoubtedly written at the great scriptorium at Echternach.[40]

A further complication is introduced by a pair of enigmatic phrases in the so-called Old English Martyology, a compilation of more or less narrative notices about the saints which has to be reconstructed from five fragmentary witnesses; the whole cannot be dated more firmly than the ninth century, but it relies heavily on Bede's martyrology and other eighth-century, as well as earlier, sources.[41] This contains eleven references to "the old sacramentary"/"older massbooks" and "the new sacramentary"/"newer massbooks."[42] The saints whose masses are ascribed to the older books are Priscus (1 June, actually

---

[38] Y. Hen, "The Liturgy of St Willibrord," *ASE* 26 (1997), pp. 41–62 at 55–57.

[39] Bannister, "Liturg. Frags.," pp. 406–11. His text was then printed in concise form by Mohlberg, *Gelasian Sacr.*, pp. 265–66, as "Das Fragment Bannister." That this was another Eighth-Century Gelasian touch was disputed by L. Eizenhöfer, "Zu Bannisters Echternacher Messformular für Vigil von Christi Himmelfahrt," in *Colligere Fragmenta: Festschrift Alban Dold*, ed. B. Fischer and V. Fiala (Beuron 1952), pp. 166–72; he found it to be basically Old Gelasian with two formulas that appear in the Leonine tradition as well; see also Hen (above), p. 58.

[40] *CLA*, V (1950), no. 606b.

[41] Lapidge, *Bibl. Comms*, p. 161, argues that the text was not composed until after c. 800 because of the inclusion of the feast of All Saints which dates only from about that time; but it should be remembered that the nucleus may well be earlier. His summary notice in the *Blackwell Encyclopaedia of Anglo-Saxon England*, ed. Lapidge et al. (Oxford 1999), pp. 303–4, gives the basic facts; the standard edition is by G. Kotzor, *Das altenglische Martyrologium*, 2 vols, Bayerische Akad. der Wiss., Philos.-Hist. Kl., Abh. N.F. 88/1–2 (Munich 1981).

[42] Listed in Kotzor's edition, I.258*–59*.

the dedication feast of a church), Nicander, Magnus, Rufus, Priscus again (1 September, main feast), Quintus, Sinotus, and Lupulus; to the newer books, Nicomedes (1 June, like the first Priscus), Agapitus, and Sabina. H. A. Wilson argued in 1902 that the obvious explanation for this distinction was that "old" referred to Gelasian books, "new" to Gregorian.[43] (The vexed question as to whether the latter are likelier to have come into England in the ninth or the tenth century will be discussed in the next chapter.) But Nicander, Quintus, Sinotus, and Lupulus are not Gelasian saints; whereas, as Lapidge points out, all seven "old sacramentary" saints have Campanian/Capuan connections and therefore the most economical explanation is that the "old" mass-book referred to is "certainly of Campanian, and possibly of Capuan, origin."[44] All of the three "new massbook" saints, Nicomedes, Agapitus, and Sabina, are in the Young Gelasian books, Agapitus being both Old Gelasian and Gregorian.

So there is ample reason to suppose that Roman (probably Gelasian) as well as Campanian massbooks may have been available in eighth-century Northumbria. About Southumbria we have, as is true in so many aspects, markedly less information. If by the mid-eighth century we can envisage a somewhat developed liturgical regime at the establishments which can be tied to such evidence as we have been able to review, this amounts to not much more than the Northumbrian houses at Lindisfarne, Ripon, Hexham, Wearmouth, Jarrow, and very likely Whitby (Streoneshalch) plus the cathedral at York (to be discussed presently); the two churches at Canterbury, monastic (eventually called St Augustine's) and cathedral (which became monastic only in the late tenth century); and, without much doubt, Lichfield and Worcester. For the rest we must resort to extrapolation and supposition: it is natural to presume that there *must* have been organized worship at, say, Bardney (where the monks were ambivalent about receiving Oswald's bones), Nursling (where Boniface was apparently trained), Malmesbury (where Aldhelm, educated at least in part at Canterbury, became abbot in 675), Reculver (because it is such a grand ruin), and Brixworth (because it is such a grand church, basically of the seventh century, though subsequently much altered): but only because of those parenthetical associations, not through anything like direct evidence. For patterns of worship at

---

[43] "English Mass-Books in the Ninth Century," *JTS* 3 (1902), pp. 429–33, on the basis of the then recent edition by G. Herzfeld, *An Old English Martyrology*, Early Eng. Text Soc. o.s. 116 (London 1900).

[44] Lapidge, *Bibl. Comms*, p. 162.

lesser places – what went on at, say, Escomb or Bradwell-on-Sea – we have next to no idea. (The little that may be gleaned about putative worship at secular "minsters," is treated on p. 63 below.) Canonical material may be of some help.

The canons of "Clofesho," 747

At Theodore's council at Hertford in 670 an annual council of, presumably, the entire English church was mandated, to be held at *Clofesho* (the site remains undetermined).[45] How often such gatherings in fact took place, and how extensively they were attended, aside, the meeting in 747 is well known as having produced a detailed set of canons, one throughout which the theme of "Roman-ness" sounds loud and clear. Of the thirty canons, seven in the middle form a bloc that sheds direct light on matters broadly liturgical.[46] They mandate (canon 12) that priests should sing the services (*sancta*) in church "simplici voce et modesta"; and that there should be kept faithfully the following: (canon 13) great feasts and feasts of martyrs; (14) Sundays, with special reverence; (15) the seven canonical hours; (16) the Greater Litany (that of April 25th, instituted by Gregory the Great) as well as the Lesser Litanies on the three days before the Ascension; (17) the feast days of Gregory and of Augustine of Canterbury; (18) the Ember weeks of the fourth, seventh, and tenth months (by old Roman reckoning; now June, September, December, the Lenten Ember Days being ignored). These have been studied expansively by Catherine Cubitt in one of the most substantial contributions in recent years to the subject, and the discussion here is much indebted to her work.[47]

The *leitmotif* of these canons is "according to the model of the Roman church." Baptism, mass, liturgical singing ("in cantilenae modo") should all be performed "juxta exemplar videlicet quod scriptum de Romana habemus Ecclesia" (canon 13); saints' days kept "juxta martyrologium ejusdem Romanae Ecclesiae" (also 13); only such material used in the divine office "quod Romanae Ecclesiae consuetudo permittit" (15); the Greater Litany and Rogation days followed "juxta

---

[45] Bede, *HE* IV.5. Various suggestions as to the location are assessed in the useful overview by S. Keynes, *The Councils of Clofesho*, Vaughan Papers no. 38 (Leicester 1994), at pp. 14–17.

[46] Canons 12–18, as printed by Haddan and Stubbs (p. 27 above), III.362–76. Of some relevance also is the prolix and confusing canon 27, "De sanctae psalmodiae utilitate," though it is not clear whether the intended context is liturgical or private prayer

[47] C. Cubitt, *Anglo-Saxon Church Councils c. 650–850* (London 1995), ch. 5, "The liturgical provisions of the Council of *Clofesho* (747)," pp. 125–47.

ritum Romanae Ecclesiae" (16); the Ember seasons celebrated, without variation, "secundum exemplar, quod juxta ritum Romanae Ecclesiae descriptum habemus" (18). The obvious question is, does this repeated insistence on Roman rite and custom (*consuetudo*) corroborate the existence of what we would think of as Roman service books in England, possibly as contrasted with non-Roman books from the Continent like those of a Campanian strand; or is this merely a generalized recognition of the "Roman-ness" which had triumphed, mainly over "Celtic-ness," through various means of transmission, above all the agencies of Theodore and Hadrian and Benedict Biscop?

Reviewing several of the fragments that have been considered here, albeit from a somewhat different angle, Cubitt speaks of a "mixed liturgy" in eighth-century England, combining non-Roman (both Gallican and Celtic) with Roman practices.[48] The most substantial evidence she deploys in support of such a characterization is four collections of private prayers (three surviving complete and one in bits), from the late eighth or early ninth century, three of them copied in Mercia. The "multi-cultural" nature of books of that genre has been recognized since the pioneer analysis by Edmund Bishop of Roman, Irish, Gallican, and Spanish strands in the best known of these, the Book of Cerne.[49] But private prayers, no matter how widespread, are not necessarily used liturgically.

This is not to contest Cubitt's fundamental assertion that "Anglo-Saxon liturgy both north and south of the Humber shows signs of non-Roman practices." Rather, it is to raise here a key issue (not directly addressed by her, being not quite central to her purpose): whether the detailed and centralizing force of these decrees aims at a kind of liturgical uniformity among all the fifteen(?) dioceses whose bishops were in theory meant to be at *Clofesho* in 747 (as opposed to recognition of need for a general tightening-up of sloppy practices such as the melodramatic roaring ["saecularium poetarum modo"] that seems to be aimed at in canon 12); and if so, whether the direction of such uniformity was to be exclusively and self-consciously Romeward – which of course still leaves open the question of how such a phrase as "Romanae Ecclesiae consuetudo" would be understood. Some light on this may come from the north.

---

[48] Enumerated and succinctly discussed in Cubitt, *Councils*, pp. 130–32.
[49] E. Bishop, "Liturgical Note'" in A. B. Kuypers' edition of *The Prayer Book of Ædeluald, the Bishop, commonly called The Book of Cerne* (Cambridge 1902), pp. 234–83. See now also M. P. Brown, *The Book of Cerne: Prayer, Patronage and Power in Ninth-Century England* (London 1996), esp. pp. 136–43.

York: archbishop Egbert

Contemporary with the 747 meeting at *Clofesho* is welcome evidence from the province of York in the time of its archbishop Egbert (Ecgberht; bishop from 732 and archbishop from 735, when the see was made primatial, until his death in 766). This is a statement in the prologue to the document, to be sure of vexed authenticity, known as his *Poenitentiale*.[50] The author, warming to his subject, enumerates the *arma* which a cleric ought to have before being ordained to the priesthood: "id est psalterium, lectionarium, antefonarium, missalem, baptisterium, martyrlogium [*sic*], in anno circuli ad predicationem cum bonis operibus." Are six discrete books to be understood here? The word *missalem* seems highly problematic, and *baptisterium* appears to be unique.[51] The order "psalterium, lectionariun, antefonarium" suggests the books necessary for full performance of the divine office, save that a collectar would also be needed, for the texts of, at least, the prayers and capitula. On balance, it appears that this Egbertine list is of only dubious value to our quest, and that we cannot infer with confidence that newly ordained priests were ideally to be armed with a handful of (personally-owned) service books: an ideal which, if realized, would have meant the existence in the mid-eighth century of a great multitude of such books – and perhaps a corresponding rate of at least fragmentary survival?

To Egbert belongs also, if a work called *Dialogus ecclesiasticae institutionis* is authentically his, the statement that Augustine brought with him two key books from Gregory himself, books from which it was clear how the Ember weeks ought to be calculated: "ut noster didascalus beatus Gregorius, in suo antiphonario et missali libro, per pedagogum nostrum beatum Augustinum transmisit ordinatum et rescriptum."[52] The expression "in missali libro" is odd: while the noun *missale* or

---

[50] Whether any part of this work should be ascribed to him, and if so how much, cannot be debated here. The text, as printed in Haddan and Stubbs III.416–31 at 417, seems to be accepted, cautiously, by E. Dekkers, *Clavis Patrum Latinorum*, 3rd edn (Steenbrugge 1995), no. 1887, as well as by R. Sharpe, *Handlist*, no. 251.

[51] For *baptisterium*, see *Dictionary of Medieval Latin from British Sources*, I (Oxford 1975), p. 180. Gneuss's 1985 article (n. 31), p. 97, sidesteps the question of authenticity, observing that the list "appears at any rate in Anglo-Saxon copies of the Penitential from the tenth century onwards." The comma should probably not be understood after *martyr[o]logium*.

[52] Haddan and Stubbs, III.411–12. Their text was taken from the sole witness, BL Cott. Vit. A.xii, a composite MS of which fols 4v–8 contain this text, at the beginning of a section of a largely computistical sort by Scribe viii of the new establishment at Old Sarum, as identified by T. Webber, *Scribes and Scholars*, pp. 144–45.

missalis is encountered fairly often from the ninth century on, mentions from the previous century are, as noted above, rare (is this in fact the earliest?); it seems possible that it is an attempt to express the exact equivalent of our modern compound word "massbook." As for *antiphonarium* – when applied to a collection of mass chants, as must be the case here (Ember weeks have no impact on the daily office) – the fact that this usage dates from more than a century earlier than the only one of the six oldest such books (none of them English) to contain the word in its title gives pause.[53] It does not look as though great weight should be put on this small bit of evidence from the mid-eighth century, and in any case Egbert, if it is he, does not assert that the massbook brought by Augustine was what we would call a Gregorian sacramentary, only that one connected with Gregory's name contains instructions about Ember Days.

York: Alcuin

The mid-point of the eighth century – the period of *Clofesho* 747 and of archbishop Egbert (whether or not either of the documents ascribed to him is genuine) – is about the time that Alcuin (735–804) was beginning to be educated in the nascent cathedral school at York. Testimony drawn from Alcuin is relevant on two levels, separable intellectually, if not always in practice: that of his liturgical experience at York before he left there for residence in Frankia in 786, and that of his liturgical work at the Carolingian court and at his abbey in Tours, where he died in 804. Whereas it was the latter level which was to become widely influential throughout the West, it is the former that mainly concerns us here. The most incisive analysis remains that of Donald Bullough, who, while acknowledging that "Evidence for the forms of liturgical observance and worship in which Alcuin had been brought up at York [is] ... shadowy and uncertain," derives a surprising amount of information from one section of the (possibly dubious) *Libri IV de laude Dei*.[54]

---

[53] The six are edited by R.-J. Hesbert, *Antiphonale Missarum Sextuplex* (Rome 1935); the oldest, from Mont-Blandin (now Brussels, Bibl. roy. 10127–10144, fols 90–115), dates from c. 800: see also Vogel, *Sources*, p. 359.

[54] D. A. Bullough, "Alcuin and the Kingdom of Heaven" (note 18 above), pp. 4–8. The *Libri IV de laude Dei* is unpublished as a whole; the antiphonary texts cited by Bullough are printed in the learned presentation by R. Constantinescu, "Alcuin et les 'Libelli precum' de l'époque carolingienne," *Revue d'histoire de la spiritualité* 50 (1974), pp. 17–56, at 38–51. Sharpe, *Handlist*, p. 45, classifies it as "doubtful." A full edition is adumbrated in D. Ganz, "Le *De Laude Dei* d'Alcuin," in *Alcuin, de York à Tours*, ed. P. Depreux and B. Judic, *Annales de Bretagne des Pays de l'Ouest* 11.3 (2004), pp. 387–91.

Among the most striking points identified by Bullough are "a unique antiphon from the Christmas Eve or Christmas Day office which (it has been suggested) reflects Rome's anti-Monothelite stand in the time of Wilfrid and John"; possibly the earliest reference to the inclusion of compline in a secular rather than monastic context; evidence for the importation of a set of Epiphany-tide antiphons of Greek origin, via mid-eighth-century Rome; a set of non-Roman antiphons for Rogationtide which must "belong to an earlier phase of Gallican influence"; a set of ten "O" antiphons for the last days of Advent, one of which may be unique to England and reflected in the Old English "Advent Lyric 7"; and a group of Marian antiphons which "point to a well-developed and largely unsuspected cult of the Virgin, with an unmistakable doctrinal basis, in the northern English church in which Alcuin spent his adolescence and early manhood."

These rather subtle points all pertain to the office (it seems unlikely that there was any radical disparity between the mass liturgy Alcuin knew at York and that at Bede's monasteries). Here the distinction between monastic and secular forms, obvious already in references in the Rule of Benedict, implies that the community of clerks at York Minster would have to have received materials from some other source than a Northumbrian monastery. Possibilities include either resources brought from Rome by John, archcantor of St Peter's basilica and abbot of St Martin's monastery, during his stay in Northern England in 680 (Bede, *HE* IV.xviii) or texts from whatever (presumably secular) community was staffing the cathedral at Canterbury. As to the latter, one can only guess. Concerning the former, the natural emphasis in Bede's account is on John's instructions to the cantors of Wearmouth and "almost all the monasteries in the kingdom," but it does not seem impossible that he could have passed on some knowledge of the "urban" (= secular) office liturgy at Rome as well.

Testimony drawn, however tentatively, from *De laude Dei* may, then, give clues to that secular office liturgy in eighth-century Northumbria. Bullough, in the large, posthumous book that apparently represents his final thoughts about Alcuin, has concluded that "we have here a personal reflection of the public worship and private study of Alcuin's York years."[55] It should be stressed that the *De laude Dei* is a florilegium, not by any means a service book, or even a commentary on the liturgy.

---

[55] *Alcuin: Achievement and Reputation* (Leiden and Boston 2004), p. 177. Bullough died in 2002, without having been able to check all the bibliographical references himself (and the second volume of what was meant to be a two-volume work will not appear). The book is rooted in his 1980 Ford Lectures at Oxford, the liturgical gist of which appeared soon thereafter as the article mentioned above ("Alcuin and the Kingdom

Bullough places it in the general context of devotional handbooks, often called *libelli precum*, like the better known and roughly contemporary Book of Cerne (above, p. 46). Used as a quarry, and supplemented by Alcuin's numerous letters, it provides snippets of information like those mentioned above, or like the fact that he seems, while at York anyhow, to know the Romanum version of the psalms. They can be used for our purposes only inferentially; Bullough speaks of their "eclectic character" as reflecting "Alcuin's experience of the liturgy in the first two-thirds of his life," but what that liturgy was as a whole we can speak of only in terms either of very small, if suggestive, textual details or of a generalized impression. And that impression is of a plethora of individual sources rather than of a single coherent systematic regime of worship like that assumed by Amalarius at Metz slightly later, around 830. One example will have to suffice here. In a letter Alcuin quotes, almost incidentally (the topic is the gender of the word *rubus*), a line from a hymn that he characterizes as "Ambrosius in hymno paschali," but that, rather than being by Ambrose, seems to originate in Ireland. This leads Bullough to infer that "The form of Alcuin's citation makes it likely that it [the hymn] was also part of the Easter Night liturgy in eighth-century York, although if so a distinctive one, at a time when the *Exultet* was presumably unknown there."[56]

To complement the bitty nature of the information discernible about liturgy at York minster in Alcuin's time is his own description of the building toward the end of his long poem (1,685 hexameters) entitled *Versus de patribus regibus et sanctis Euboricensis ecclesiae*.[57] He records in particular the building achievements of his patron, archbishop Ælberht (767–78): a splendidly adorned altar of St Paul in the cathedral and then, even more magnificently, an entire basilica next to it, dedicated to Holy Wisdom and containing the astonishing number of thirty altars.[58] This one reference is slim evidence on which to postulate anything like regular liturgical use of thirty altars. The statement may, however, help to make sense of Alcuin's response to a request of c. 800 from the then archbishop, Eanbald II, for advice about the arrangement of *missalis*

of Heaven"). It often refutes, and largely supplants, G. Ellard, *Master Alcuin, Liturgist* (Chicago 1956).

[56] *Alcuin*, p. 200. Bullough states that the hymn appears earliest in the late 7th-cent. Bangor antiphonary, headed "Ymnum quando caeria [sic: the Paschal candle] benedicitur": ed. F. E. Warren, HBS 10 (1895), p. 11.

[57] Ed. and tr. P. Godman, *The Bishops, Kings, and Saints of York*, OMT (1982); he proposes a date of 792/3 rather than the previously assumed 780–82.

[58] Lines 1488–1520; Alcuin's (and Ælberht's?) adjective characterizing *sophia* is *alma* rather than *sancta*. Discussed by Bullough, *Alcuin*, pp. 320–22; he points out that neither archaeological nor later textual evidence for the building exists.

libelli: that there had been at York "plenty of the larger sacramentaries of the old usage" which could serve as guides.[59] Possibly Ælberht did endow his basilica with a plethora of massbooks suitable for so many altars; possibly also the community contained enough priests to do justice to them. We simply do not know; the Vikings in the ninth century will have destroyed many books in the course of establishing their ascendancy at York.

Whether if all the tiny bits of information we can gather concerning liturgy in Alcuin's York were put together in a more systematic way there would emerge a coherent and elaborate liturgical regime at York is a question to keep – open – in the backs of our minds as we consider a different kind of approach, this time not to the secular but to the monastic office. Curiosity there inevitably leads first to Benedict Biscop's houses at Wearmouth and Jarrow, like York victims of the Viking incursions.[60]

The monastic office

It is certainly reasonable to suppose that at least after Archcantor John's mission to Wearmouth in 680 (above, p. 49) the daily office was carefully observed there, and subsequently at Jarrow also. Of possible relevance is the story told, in the (anonymous) *Lives of the Abbots*, of abbot Ceolfrith's decision, when only he and one small boy (commonly taken to be Bede himself) survive a visitation of plague at the newly founded house at Jarrow, that, their former practice having been suspended ("intermisso ritu priori"), "they should, except at vespers and matins, recite their psalms without antiphons. And when this had been done with many tears and lamentations on his part, for the space of a week, he could not bear it any longer, but decreed that the psalms, with their antiphons, should be restored according to the order of the regular course."[61] Whether this means that the antiphons would thenceforth be used also at the night office is not clear; in any case, a plentiful supply of antiphons, and therefore presumably of texts containing them, is to be understood. Indeed, Bede states that John's teaching ranged beyond singing and reading to keeping the liturgical year, with instructions for

---

[59] Alcuin, *Epist.* 226, cited in *Alcuin*, p. 204, with comments not specially relevant here.

[60] R. Cramp in *Blackwell Encyclopaedia ASE*, p. 326: "There is no evidence for occupation on these sites after the mid-ninth century."

[61] The translation is that of Charles Plummer in the introduction (p. xii) to the edition of this work, included in his *Venerabilis Bedae Opera Historica*, 2 vols (Oxford 1896); the Latin is on I.393.

the latter that were written down and widely circulated.[62] How widely, we wonder, and with what fullness of detail?

More broadly, Wearmouth and Jarrow aside, how extensively can we suppose a fully developed office was observed in early Anglo-Saxon monastic houses? Éamonn Ó Carragáin, in a series of publications centering on the iconography of the Ruthwell and Bewcastle crosses, has posited for the (monastic) community at Ruthwell the capacity for sophisticated liturgy, especially during Holy Week.[63] The existence of the community itself, for which there is no hard evidence, has to be presumed. Paul Meyvaert has suggested the possibility of "monks from the Lindisfarne communities ... moving into new territories" and that "It seems safe to assert that the Ruthwell cross was conceived by a Northumbrian monk, brought up in the Lindisfarne tradition, who was familiar with the works of Bede."[64] Whether such a community would have known recent developments in the Good Friday Adoration ceremony or have celebrated the Marian feasts of Annunciation, Purification, Assumption, and Nativity coming into Roman use around 700, as Ó Carragáin maintains, may be left open questions. No textual evidence that would help us decide survives.

To be sure, "harder" witness for the liturgy of the office in the eighth century, such as might be provided by service books, is all but nonexistent. Sarah Foot, in her recent, rich study of early Anglo-Saxon monastic life, stresses the possibility of a large amount of diversity in the way the office was observed.[65] The largest piece of evidence for actual texts is a fragment of only a few leaves (in Ushaw College, MS XVIII.B.1.2) which, according to Ian Doyle, contains readings very

[62] *HE* IV.18: "ea quae totius anni circulus in celebratione dierum festorum poscebat etiam litteris mandando, quae hactenus in monasterio seruata a multis iam sunt circumquaque transcripta" (Colgrave and Mynors, p. 388).

[63] Notably in his 1994 Jarrow Lecture, *The City of Rome and the World of Bede*, in "The Necessary Distance: *Imitatio Romae* and the Ruthwell Cross," in *Northumbria's Golden Age*, ed. J. Hawkes and S. Mills (Stroud, Glos. 1999), pp. 191–203, and above all in *Ritual and the Rood: Liturgical Images and the Old English Poems of the* Dream of the Rood *Tradition* (London 2005). This last is an ambitious and impressive work, and I am aware, dubious as I am about its basic premise, that I may have given his argument less stress than it deserves.

[64] P. Meyvaert, "A New Perspective on the Ruthwell Cross: Ecclesia and Vita Monastica," in *The Ruthwell Cross: Papers from the Colloquium ... Princeton University 1989*, ed. B. Cassidy (Princeton 1992), pp. 95–166 at 163–64. Would this familiarity have included a Campanian lectionary pattern as described above (p. 40)?

[65] S. Foot, *Monastic Life in Anglo-Saxon England, c. 600–900* (Cambridge 2006): "we know little about the details of the form of the office in England in this period, because of the lack of surviving office books" (p. 192). The book is primarily concerned with the organizational and financial aspects of her subject, with brief sections touching on the liturgy on pp. 191–207.

likely from Christmas Matins and thus offers "a glimpse of the divine office performed at Lindisfarne or one of the other earliest Northumbrian monasteries."[66]

More substantial but not quite conclusively liturgical is the celebrated Vespasian psalter (now BL Cott. Vesp. A.i), made probably at the Canterbury monastic community, later called St Augustine's, in the second quarter of the eighth century. Justly famed for its illustration – above all, the full-page depiction of David surrounded by musicians and scribes – as well as for its later (ninth-century) Old English interlinear gloss, the book's liturgical dimension has been largely ignored. Its text is the Romanum version, not surprisingly, and the canticles that follow the psalms are the normal "Roman" set: a variable canticle at lauds each day, then, invariably, the *Benedicite* for matins, *Benedictus* for lauds, and *Magnificat* for vespers. James Mearns, in his old but still standard work on canticles in general, expressed puzzlement as to why the *Nunc dimittis* was not included.[67] The answer is clear and instructive: that since the canticle has never been part of the monastic form of compline, its absence here shows that the Canterbury monks' office c. 725 is the monastic, not the secular, one.[68] That so apparently obvious a point is worth making is an indication of how rudimentary our knowledge still is.

Towards the ninth and tenth centuries

While such scraps as those contained in the two previous paragraphs suggest how frustratingly little evidence there is for monastic liturgy, it is still more than we know at present about a subject the importance of which is as clear as evidence concerning it is murky: that of the minsters. Such evidence as can be brought to bear on the subject is, as well as highly inferential, largely later. For this reason discussion of the topic (as well as an attempt at definition of "minster") will be taken up in the next chapter, on liturgy in later Anglo-Saxon England.

---

[66] A. I. Doyle, "A Fragment of an Eighth-Century Northumbrian Office Book," in *Words, Texts, and Manuscripts: Studies ... to H. Gneuss*, ed. M. Korhammer (Cambridge 1992), pp. 11–27, at 21. The readings are from Isaiah and short extracts from two of Augustine's sermons.

[67] J. Mearns, *The Canticles of the Christian Church Eastern and Western* (Cambridge 1914), p. 52; he notes, "even in the 11th century, when the Te Deum and the Quicumque vult were added it was still left out."

[68] There is, however, no sign of the "monastic canticles" for use at matins on Sundays and great feasts. The Romanum text is also found in a psalter of about the same period but written in Northumbria, now Berlin, Deutsche Staatsbibliothek, Hamilton 553, but only the variable canticles at lauds are provided, not those repeated daily.

Although any distinction between "earlier" and "later" is in a sense purely artificial, in the present case it does reflect a difference in both the quantity and the variety of the evidence that can be reviewed. For the earlier period, dominated, as we have seen amply, by the phenomenon of Bede, it is hard to get much beyond Canterbury in the time of Augustine and then three quarters of a century later in that of Theodore and Hadrian; Wearmouth and Jarrow under Benedict Biscop and his immediate successors; York in the time of Egbert and Alcuin; and by inference a few more places like Ruthwell and (shadowily) wherever the mandates of *Clofesho* in 747 were extensively implemented. By contrast, from the late ninth century on there is a good deal more to be considered.

By way of transition between the two chapters we can frame a simple question: when in 857 king Æthelwulf of Wessex stopped, on his way back from spending a year at Rome, at the court of Charles the Bald to woo Charles's daughter, did he find the use of Gregorian books there (as was undoubtedly the case) strangely at variance with what he had left behind in England?[69] If so, might this have been an occasion for the introduction of the "new" (*sc.* to England) book mentioned in the "Old English Martyrology"? In facing such a question it is necessary to remember that we are not trying to engage in an elaborate classification of sacramentaries such as Gamber, Deshusses, and others have done, but rather to keep the focus on concrete situations that ask for, even if we cannot supply, concrete answers.

One such situation, implied by the scenario just sketched, is the possiblity that, if "new" Gregorian books did come into England in Æthelwulf's wake, massbooks that had been in use in at any rate Southumbria were suddenly at variance with what the royal chapel was using. (An apparent rebellion against Æthelwulf on his return left him as sub-king – to his son Æthelbald, the chief rebel – in the southeastern areas of Kent, Sussex, and Surrey; which provides a possible channel of transmission of the new kinds of books to, most obviously, Canterbury.) Another has to do with the foundation of religious houses by Æthelwulf's youngest son and eventual successor, Alfred, and his immediate family: were places like Athelney and Shaftesbury and the New and Nuns' Minsters at Winchester going to be supplied with massbooks that were organized differently, and to a degree contained different saints' feasts, from those in use at, say, Winchester Old Minster and Sherborne and Worcester? Even before the great resurgence of monastic establishments in the third quarter of the tenth century – by which time it is quite clear

---

[69] *Anglo-Saxon Chronicle*, ad an. 855–58.

that Gregorian books are becoming the norm – was it the case that the Gregorian seemed the "newer" in the sense that the more up-to-date establishments would aspire to have them?

Phrases like "more up-to-date" inevitably imply that what is older is obsolescent. In the present chapter we have moved (sometimes crabwise and sometimes, it must seem, at a snail's pace) from something like Maitland's "Beyond" to, if not the knowable, at least the partly traceable. Beginning the next chapter with yet a further instance of the "unknowable," the one connected with minsters (as explained above), is not meant to dishearten the reader. Rather, it is to face squarely a feature of the Anglo-Saxon church the importance of which has just in the past twenty years or so become clear – even if its liturgical aspects are not.

SUPPLEMENTARY NOTE: Although, as explained in the Preface (p. xv), it has not been possible to take account of literature published after, at the latest, 2007, I particularly regret not having been able to incorporate the findings of one work relevant to chapters 2 and 3: Rebecca Rushforth, *Saints in English Kalendars before A.D. 1100*, HBS 117 (2008, though ostensibly "issued to members for the year 2005"). Her extensive introduction and synoptic tables of saints deserve to be widely consulted.

Excursus: on the terms Gregorian and Gelasian as used here

The Gregorian books are so named, since at least the time of Charlemagne, after the pope whose pontificate (590–604) provides our precise starting point, Gregory I – which does not necessarily mean, of course, that he had anything do to with the actual construction of such books – and represent a basically papal tradition: in theory, for the liturgy of the mass as celebrated by the pope in Rome.[1] Whatever earlier nuclei there may have been, perhaps going back to the pontificate of Honorius I (625–38), no form of a Gregorian massbook seems to be recoverable, even by extrapolation, until early in the last quarter of the seventh century, c. 675: the one known as Paduensis.[2] The best known Gregorian book, moreover, dates from roughly a century later: the Hadrianum, named from Pope Hadrian I, who in about 790 sent such a book to Frankland at the request of Charlemagne. Not adequate to that ruler's grand hopes and purposes, it was soon furnished with an extensive Supplement, confected by either Alcuin or (more likely)

---

[1] The third of the trio of Roman sacramentary traditions, the so-called Leonine, is scarcely relevant to our concerns. Closer to a collection of *libelli* than to an organized massbook, it exists only in a single, early 7th-cent. manuscript long in the cathedral library at Verona (MS 85, formerly lxxx). There are modern editions by C. L. Feltoe, *Sacramentarium Leonianum* (Cambridge 1896) and L. C. Mohlberg, *Sacramentarium Veronense*, Rerum Ecclesiasticarum Documenta, series maior: Fontes 1 (Rome 1956); see also the study by D. M. Hope, *The Leonine Sacramentary* (Oxford 1971). The book has, of course, many formulas in common with those of other traditions as well as a few that are unique. Its misleading nickname (the eponymous Leo is the pope who died in 461) appears only in 1735. The ambitious RED enterprise, from the Pontifical Institute of St Anselm in Rome and under the guiding spirit of L. C. Mohlberg, includes among the thirteen volumes in its Fontes series the now standard editions of the (Old) Gelasian sacramentary and three Gallican massbooks as well as the "Leonine."

[2] Padua, Bibl. capit. MS D.47: K. [=L.C.] Mohlberg, ed. *Die älteste erreichbare Gestalt des Liber Sacramentorum anni circuli der römischen Kirche*, LQF 11/12 (Münster 1927). The MS itself is of the mid-9th cent.; see Vogel, *Sources*, pp. 92–97. LQF combines two originally separate series, both published at Münster (for the Abt-Herwegen Institut at Maria Laach) from 1918: source editions in Liturgiegeschichtliche Quellen and monographs in Liturgiegeschichtliche Forschungen; in recent years the proportion of editions has been quite small.

Benedict of Aniane; this is signalled by a celebrated preface always referred to by its opening word, *Hucusque*. The Hadrianum itself has not survived, but several copies do: the earliest, made around 812, at Cambrai.[3] Further copies proliferated and ramified throughout the ninth and tenth centuries, and these, intermixed with Gelasian elements, eventually become the main stock of Roman-derived massbooks throughout northern Europe, including England.[4]

Gelasian books – the ascription to Pope Gelasius I (d. 496) goes back to at least the ninth century – seem to represent a tradition that is predominantly presbyteral: again in theory, for the use of presbyters in charge of the great non-papal churches in Rome. What is termed the "Old Gelasian" survives entire only in one manuscript, which, although probably written at the nunnery of Chelles in central Frankland about 750, seems to be based on Roman usages of seventy-five or more years before that date.[5] Such features as are unique may therefore be ascribeable to the mid-seventh century, if not earlier. Books of a generally Gelasian family come to proliferate in the later eighth century, hence the term "Eighth-Century" or "Young" Gelasian sacramentary, an adaptation, or version, of the "Old" Gelasian. The surviving Young Gelasian books, heavily influenced by Frankish usages, are quite numerous.[6]

A certain core of saints for whom masses are included is common to all these strands, but considerable quantities are distinctive to the (Old) Gelasian and others to the Gregorian, while the Young Gelasian books

---

[3] That MS (Cambrai 164, formerly 159) and two MSS in the Vatican Library, Reg. lat. 337 and Ottob. 313, were presented in a composite edition by H. A. Wilson as early as 1915, as *The Gregorian Sacramentary under Charles the Great* (HBS 49), the Cambrai MS more directly by H. Lietzmann as *Das Sacramentarium Gregorianum nach dem Aachener Urexemplar*, LQF 3 (1921).

[4] The great edition, one of the monuments of modern liturgical scholarship, is that of J. Deshusses, *Le Sacramentaire grégorien, ses principales formes d'après les anciens manuscrits*, 3 vols. Spicilegium Friburgense 16, 24, 28 (Fribourg 1971–82). Those of Wilson and Lietzmann are sometimes easier to move about in.

[5] H. A. Wilson's pioneer modern edition, *The Gelasian Sacramentary* (Oxford 1894), is still highly serviceable, though now cited less often than that published by L. C. Mohlberg under the title *Liber sacramentorum Romanae aeclesiae ordinis anni circuli*, RED 4, 2nd edn (Rome 1968). The MS is Vat. Reg. lat. 316.

[6] On the entire subject, the fullest general guide is probably still Vogel, *Sources*, pp. 61–134, but it is by no means easy to work through. The Old Gelasian tradition and related matters have been treated exhaustively by A. Chavasse in a long series of publications, many of them gathered in his *Le sacramentaire dans le groupe dit "Gélasiens du VIIIe siècle,"* 2 vols (Steenbrugge 1984). B. Moreton, *The Eighth-Century Gelasian Sacramentary: a Study in Tradition* (Oxford 1976), though still helpful, appeared before the CCSL editions of three of the main Young Gelasian representatives: the Gellone (BN lat. 12048), by A. Dumas and J. Deshusses, 2 vols (159, 159A, 1981); Angoulême (BN lat. 816), by P. Saint-Roch (159C, 1987); and Phillipps (*alias* Augustodunensis; Berlin, Deutsche Staatsbibl. lat. 105), by O. Heiming (159B, 1984).

include a number of Gregorian saints, and contain other variations. The most succinct way to show the complex nature of the conflated "Roman" sanctorale which is reflected in the majority of massbooks used (in England and elsewhere) after about the tenth century may be in the form of a list with distinguishing features for each strand. This list is not intended to be a scientific conspectus of the main witnesses; rather, a quick reference guide, in roughly calendarial order, as to the primary affinites of each "sacramentary" saint's feast likely to be met with in this book.

KEY (a symbol applies to all names following it):
CAPITALS: both Gelasian and Gregorian
CAPS ITALIC: both, but notable differences in spelling or order
#: Gelasian (Old)
†: Gregorian
§: Young Gelasian (with a few exceptions; see note at end of list)

#THEOPHANIA/ †EPIPHANIA 6.i
FELIX 'IN PINCIS' 14.i
MARCELLUS 16.i
†Prisca 18.i
#Sebastian; Maria, Martha, Audifax, Abacuc 19.i
FABIAN 20.i; †Sebastian 20.i
AGNES (#DE PASSIONE / †NATALE) 21.i
†Vincent 22.i
§Emerentiana & Macharius 23.i
§Conversion of Paul 25.i
§Proiectus 25.i
AGNES (#DE NATALE / †NATALE SECUNDO) 28.i

#PURIFICATIO / †YPAPANTI / § Symeon 2.ii
AGATHA 5.ii
#Soteris 10.ii
§Zoticus, Iacinctus, Irenaeus 10.ii
VALENTINUS; #Vitalis, Felicula; w. §Zeno 14.ii
#Juliana 16.ii
§Cathedra Petri 22.ii

#Perpetua & Felicity 7.iii
†Gregory 12.iii
ANNUNTIATIO 25.iii
§Leo pope 11.iv

#Euphemia 13.iv
†Tiburtius & Valerian 14.iv
†George 23.iv
†Vitalis 28.iv

PHILIP & JAMES 1.v
#Juvenal 3.v
†Alexander, Eventius, Theodulus 3.v
#Invention of Cross 3.v
†John at Latin Gate 6.v
†Gordianus & Epimachus 10.v
PANCRAS; #Nereus, Achilleus 12.v
†Maria ad Martyres 13.v
†Urban 25.v
§Primus & Felicianus 28.v

†Nicomedes (Dedication) 1.vi
#*PETER &MARCELLINUS* / †*MARCELLINUS PETER* 2.vi
#Cyrinus, Nabor, Nazarius; w. §Basilides 12.vi
#Vitus 15.vi
MARCUS & MARCELLIANUS 18.vi
#*GERVASE & PROTASE* / †*PROTASE & GERVASE 19*.vi
JOHN BAPTIST 24.vi
JOHN & PAUL 26.vi
†Leo 28.vi
PETER & PAUL 29.vi
PAUL (ALONE) 30.vi

†Processus & Martinian 2.vii
†Seven Brothers 10.vii
§Benedict 11.vii
§James 25.vii
#*SIMPLICIUS, FAUSTINUS, B(V)EATRIX* / †*F., S., B., Felix* 29.vii
ABDON & SENNEN 30.vii

#Machabees 1.viii
†Peter ad vincula 1.viii
†Stephen pope 2.viii
#*SIXTUS* / †*XYSTUS* 6.viii
†Felicissimus & Agapitus 6.viii
#Donatus 7.viii
†Cyriacus 8.viii
LAURENCE 10.viii

Tiburtius 11.viii
Hippolytus 13.viii
†Eusebius 14.viii
Assumptio Mariae 15.viii
Agapitus 18.viii
#Magnus 19.viii
†Timotheus 22.viii
§Bartholomew 24.viii
#Rufus 27.viii
Hermes 28.viii
§Augustine 28.viii
†Sabina 29.viii
#Passion John Baptist 29.viii
†Felix & Adauctus 30.viii

#Priscus 1.ix
Nativity of Mary 8.ix
§Adrian 8.ix
#Gorgonius 9.ix
†Protus & Iacintus 11.ix
Exaltation of Cross 14.ix
Cornelius & Cyprian 14.ix
†Nicomedes(Natale) 15.ix
†Euphemia 16.ix
†Lucia & Geminianus 16.ix
§Matthew 21.ix
§Mauricius, Exuperius, Candidus, Victor, Innocent, Vitalis
    22.ix
Cosmas & Damian 27.ix
Michael (Dedication) 29.ix

#Marcellus & Apuleius 7.x
†Marcus pope 7.x
†Callistus 14.x
†Luke 18.x
§Amand 26.x
§Symon & Jude 28.x
§Caesarius 1.xi
Quatuor coronati 8.xi
†Theodore 9.xi
†Menna 11.xi
†Martin 11.xi
Cecilia 22.xi

CLEMENT 23.xi
FELICITY 23.xi
†Chrysogonus 24.xi
SATURNINUS, #Crisantus, Maurus, Daria 29.xi
ANDREW 30.xi

§Damasus 11.xii
†Lucia 13.xii
#Thomas 21.xii
NATALE DOMINI 25.xii
STEPHEN 26.xii
JOHN EVANGELIST 27.xii
INNOCENTS 28.xii
†Silvester 31.xii

Note: YOUNG GELASIANS include almost all of the OLD GELASIAN saints and most of the GREGORIAN. There is some variation among YOUNG GELASIANS that is not material here, as these few examples show. ANGOULÊME has an Ebartius (Eparchius, Cybar), a local monk-hermit, on 1 July, Martin at 3 July (often called his Translation or Ordination feast) as well as at 11 November, an a Hilary (Helarius, bishop) on 1 November as well as Caesarius. GELLONE has Jerome at 30 September and Mary and Martha instead of Marius, Martha, Audifax, Abacuc on 19 January (as does Phillipps), but omits Conversion of Paul 25 January. PHILLIPPS has Albinus at 1 March, Maurilius at 13 September, and the martyrs Agnes, Lucius, and Victor at 19 October.

Noteworthy among the innumerable feasts not found in any of these Roman sacramentary traditions are Matthias 24 February, Mark (evangelist) 25 April, Barnabas 11 June, and All Saints 1 November.

3   Later Anglo-Saxon: liturgy for England

The working definition of "Later Anglo-Saxon" used here stops for
most purposes in about 1050, despite the now widely-accepted periodization that extends it to as late as 1100.[1] Although the year 1066
is for us by no means without significance (clearly much in the way of
decisive change begins because of the outcome of the battle of Hastings), to posit a clear break then would be specious; but extending the
period under consideration here to the end of the century risks being
too broad. Certain topics, most notably the work of Lanfranc and the
fresh start made possible by the move of the west-Wessex cathedral
site from Sherborne to (Old) Sarum around 1075, must sensibly be
treated in chapters devoted to matters sequential to the Norman Conquest. In general, evidence from the fourth, and even third, quarter
of the eleventh century – of which there is quite a lot, above all for
the liturgical program of Leofric of Exeter – will be treated later. The
present chapter will concentrate only on matters that may contribute
to our understanding of the liturgy in what is clearly "pre-Conquest"
England.[2]

At the beginning of the period the picture of that liturgy is at best
sketchy. The generalization that we have, as near as makes no difference, no knowledge of organized monastic life for men in the two or

---

[1] This more expansive periodization is reflected in Helmut Gneuss's highly valuable
*Handlist of Anglo-Saxon Manuscripts: a List of Manuscripts and Manuscript Fragments
Written or Owned in England up to 1100*, Medieval and Renaissance Texts and Studies
241 (Tempe, AZ 2001).

[2] The most important contributions to the rather scanty literature on the subject as a
whole include C. Hohler, "Some Service-books of the Later Saxon Church," in *Tenth-
Century Studies: Essays in Commemoration of the Millennium of the Council of Winches-
ter and Regularis concordia* (Chichester 1975), ed. D. Parsons, pp. 60–83 and 217–27;
M. McC. Gatch, "The Office in Late Anglo-Saxon Monasticism," in *Learning and
Literature*, pp. 341–62; and, among the numerous publications of D. N. Dumville,
"On the Dating of Some Late Anglo-Saxon Liturgical Manuscripts," *Trans. Cbg. Bib-
liog. Soc.* 10 (1991), pp. 40–57; *Liturgy and the Ecclesiastical History of Late Anglo-Saxon
England: Four Studies* (Woodbridge 1992); and *English Caroline Script and Monastic
History: Studies in Benedictinism, A.D. 950–1030* (Woodbridge 1993).

three decades on either side of the year 900, though much shaken by recent scholarship, still applies as regards the liturgy, and information about such women's houses as we have is tantalizing rather than conclusive.[3] This seems to be largely true also of liturgy in the cathedrals at the same period; we shall have to work hard to extract the maximum of information from no more than a handful of pieces of evidence. It seems likely that monarchs of the self-consciousness of Alfred, Edward the Elder, and Athelstan would have had what it may not be misleadingly grand to term "court chapels," but about the rites used in them there is again precious little information. And for what will be eventually recognized as parish churches, nascent towards the end of this period, there is almost nothing – and not much more for the aspect with which we shall begin, that of the minsters: of, that is, those that survived the Danish depredations.

Liturgy in minster churches

The greater understanding of minster churches which is an outstanding achievement in Anglo-Saxon studies of the last thirty years or so requires us to try to be as fully aware of them as centers of sacramental activity as we should like to be of the cathedral establishments and the putative chapel(s) of the Wessex (and perhaps other) monarchs. John Blair, in his numerous studies on the subject, has developed a wide range of criteria for minster status, one that encompasses establishments that are sometimes monasteries (however defined), sometimes regional baptismal or "mother" churches, sometimes headquarters (or sub-headquarters) of a diocese.[4] In the present work the definition will be narrowed, in a slightly arbitrary and certainly debatable way, to indicate a church perceived to be a kind of ecclesiastical center for an area in one or more of the following senses: (1) as having an understood status – at the time, even if we do not so understand it – as the

[3] For male houses, Knowles, *Mon. Order*, pp. 31–36 and 695; cf. *Med. Rel. Houses*, p. 11: "Thus at the beginning of the tenth century regular monastic life was wholly extinct in England." Concerning female houses Sarah Foot has extracted the maximum of information in *Veiled Women: the Disappearance of Nuns from Anglo-Saxon England*, 2 vols (Aldershot 2000). A number of nunneries were founded in the later years of Alfred's reign and early in Edward's, notably Shaftesbury, Wilton, Winchester ("Nunnaminster"), and Romsey: *Med. Rel. Houses*, pp. 251–69.

[4] Most fully in his *The Church in Anglo-Saxon Society* (Oxford 2005); pp. 527–29 list his many publications on the subject. See also the collections of essays edited by him as *Minsters and Parish Churches: the Local Church in Transition, 950–1200*, Oxford Univ. Comm. for Archaeology Monograph 17 (Oxford 1988) and, with Richard Sharpe, as *Pastoral Care before the Parish* (Leicester 1992).

only church of that sort in a somewhat discrete region; (2) as possessing certain rights of baptism and burial, even if these were sometimes more theoretical than actual; and (3) as being served by clergy, usually more than one, who cannot be defined primarily as monks living according to the Rule of Benedict or some similar regime.

This threefold functional approach aims to get around the problems surrounding the multiple shadings of the word *monasterium* in Anglo-Saxon England.[5] As a negative, it might be observed that because we do not associate with minster churches, as delimited here, anything like a scriptorium, there are not likely to turn up in this context the sorts of fragments from eighth-century service books noticed in the previous chapter as ascribed to Northumbrian monasteries or Continental writing centers influenced by them. This, of course, raises such questions as where minster churches would have obtained their written resources for worship; to what extent these resources would have differed from whatever was being used in establishments with their own scriptoria; and indeed to what extent many minsters would have had codices as distinct from *libelli*.

Awareness of the phenomenon of minsters adds, then, a dimension to our earlier awareness of liturgy in monastic and cathedral churches (it must be kept in mind that all cathedrals were "secular" until 964 when Winchester became monastic, to be followed by Worcester and Canterbury and eventually by half a dozen or so other English cathedrals; with liturgical consequences to be taken up presently); for anything like a detailed picture of liturgy in parish churches we shall have to wait at least three centuries. In minsters, as in cathedrals, the office liturgy would have been that of the non-monastic form most often termed "secular" but called occasionally "urban" – despite the latter's being an extremely odd appellation for a place like the great minster church at Stow in distinctly rural Lincolnshire.

Although Blair argues convincingly for the existence of individual minsters as early as the seventh century, the reason for considering the subject in the present chapter is that there is next to no evidence as to liturgy in them until the late ninth. Even then, there seems to be no liturgical book extant that can with confidence be assigned to use in a late Anglo-Saxon minster church. The best we can do is to consider here two books that *might* plausibly have had such a context, one relevant to

---

[5] For some idea of the complexities involved, see. S. Foot, "Anglo-Saxon Minsters: a Review of Terminology," *Pastoral Care before the Parish*, pp. 212–25; and for a quick overview, Blair's entry "Parochial Organization" in *The Blackwell Encyclopaedia of Anglo-Saxon England*, ed. M. Lapidge et al. (Oxford 1999), pp. 356–58.

the daily office and one to the celebration of mass. The manuscript known as the Durham collectar (Durham Cathedral A.IV.19) seems to offer the first substantial piece of evidence that we have from anything like a service book for the first third or so of the tenth century: sixty-one folios (of eighty-eight; the remaining twenty-seven will be noticed later) mostly dating from the late ninth or early tenth century. This portion contains a large number of collects, along with a smaller body of capitula, for both temporale and (separately) sanctorale: all of these deriving, according to its latest editor, Alicia Corrêa, "from various sacramentary traditions, the main impetus being the mixed Gregorian-Gelasian of the ninth century."[6] She posits the possibility that the putative Continental exemplar (as distinct from the manuscript now at Durham) may have come first to the New Minster, perhaps brought by Grimbald of St Bertin who arrived there c. 888; and suggests that this material, which clearly presupposes a fully articulated system of the hours of prayer, is particularly appropriate to a secular community, which was the case when the New Minster was founded at Winchester c. 900. In any case the book was originally written, presumably for liturgical use, in southern (probably southwestern) England, though no English saints are included in the sanctorale. Our interest here centers on whatever use it had there in the years until 970, when it was given to bishop Ælfsige of Chester-le-Street, the headquarters at that point of the community of St Cuthbert.[7]

The structure of this collectar, at least as it has survived, is odd. The temporale section runs from Epiphany through the Greater Litany (25 April). The sanctorale begins with the three post-Christmas feasts and Silvester (all more commonly found in the temporale) and continues with Felix *in pincis* (14 January) through Thomas (21 December). Then comes a common of saints, and finally a considerable section of blessings and other rites that would largely be particular to a bishop. Except

---

[6] A. Corrêa, ed. *The Durham Collectar*, HBS 107 (1992), with splendid collation tables; cf. her summary description in Pfaff, ed. *Liturg. Bks ASE*, pp. 48–49. Facsimile edn by T. J. Brown under the title *The Durham Ritual*, Early English Manuscripts in Facsimile 16 (Copenhagen 1969). The earlier edition by U. Lindelöf, *Rituale Ecclesiae Dunelmensis: the Durham Collectar*, SS 140 (1927) includes the Old English gloss (see next note).

[7] According to a colophon to the material added later that year by Aldred, the provost of the community and the celebrated glossator of the Lindisfarne gospels, Ælfsige received the book (but from whom?) at Oakley Down in Dorset on 10 Aug. 970: G. Bonner, "St Cuthbert at Chester-le-Street," in *St Cuthbert, his Cult and his Community to A.D. 1200*, ed. Bonner, D. Rollason, and C. Stancliffe (Woodbridge 1989), pp. 387–95 at 393. Oakley is the name of a hamlet a mile from Wimborne Minster, where at least the female religious survived from what was from the early 8th cent. a double house; if so, might Wimborne have been the original home for this manuscript? Further potential importance of Wimborne is discussed on p. 383.

for the period between 6 January and 25 April, therefore, an officiant would need access to another book containing forms for the temporale, though for the sanctorale only forms for such English saints as might be wanted would have been necessary.

Slender as this is as an indication of anything like a resource for office liturgy in a minster church, evidence for mass liturgy is even slighter. It comes a century or so later than the collectar, and in a document which is not a service book by any stretch of definition. The margins of an eleventh-century copy of the Old English Bede (the vernacular translation of his *History*; now CCCC 41) contain an extensive collection of liturgical formulas, mainly for the use of the celebrant at mass but also including some office and manual material; there are also charms and other vernacular texts. The contents give no hint as to a putative place of use; but a suggestion that it might have been compiled by a priest serving a minster was made by Christopher Hohler in a review of Raymond Grant's partial edition of this manuscript.[8] Hohler ingeniously posited a cleric, probably in the diocese of Wells, who "was told to bring his liturgical books up to date by a reforming bishop," most likely Dudoc (1033–61). Some of the material copied into this manuscript, including the charms and what Hohler called "superstitious items which ought not to be there" among the manual formulas, causes one to wonder whether that is an accurate suggestion. In any case this witness, though of limited value, points to a model that was not influenced by monastic reform (the office material among the marginalia is for the secular form of Sunday matins in nine lessons). Valuable corroboration comes from two vernacular documents, each known by a slightly misleading title, by the two giants of Old English prose around the year 1000: Wulfstan the Homilist and Ælfric (star pupil of Æthelwold and abbot of Eynsham 1005–c. 1010; his instructions to the monks there are treated in a subsequent section).

Prescriptions for secular clergy: Wulfstan and Ælfric

At some time in the first decade of the eleventh century Wulfstan, bishop of London 996–1002 and archbishop of York 1002–23 (as well

---

[8] R. J. S. Grant, ed., *Cambridge, Corpus Christi College MS 41: the Loricas and the Missal*, Costerus n.s. 17 (Amsterdam 1978); reviewed by Hohler in *Medium Aevum* 49 (1980), pp. 275–78. Five years earlier Hohler had called these entries "the most valuable record surviving of office chants from the period": "Some Service-books" (note 2 above), p. 72. Although it came into the possession of Leofric, bishop of Exeter, in the third quarter of the eleventh century, its marginalia do not seem relevant to his liturgical work, and will be ignored when that comes under discussion.

as holding the see of Worcester 1002–16), issued a set of instructions to clergy now called "Wulfstan's Canons of Edgar": an admittedly clumsy phrase that acknowledges both the ascription to King Edgar (d. 975) in the heading of one of the two principal manuscripts and the fact, established by Karl Jost in 1932, that the author of the anonymous work was Wulfstan, the great law-code maker of Cnut's reign as well as prelate.[9] It is in some respects a backward-looking document, drawing on earlier canonical sources (some of them Carolingian) and addressing problems that might have been encountered by, or among, minster priests at any time during the previous two or even three centuries – such as that "no dog nor horse [should] come within the churchyard, still less a pig, as far as one can prevent it" (clause 26). Among the prescriptions relevant to our concerns is that a priest should not celebrate mass without a book, "but the canon is to be before his eyes" (clause 32); that priests should preach every Sunday (52; probably a counsel of perfection); and that there should be uniformity about feast- and fast-days, so that all should "be equally advanced over the course of the year in church services" (48, 50).

Almost simultaneous with Wulfstan's "Canons" is a long epistle by Ælfric known as his "First Old English Pastoral Letter for Wulfstan."[10] It was commissioned by the latter, addressed to "you priests," and rendered into the vernacular, because "not all of you can understand the Latin" in which it was originally composed. We need not concern ourselves as to how purely Ælfrician the text is (some of the manuscripts show signs of revision and addition by Wulfstan); our purpose is well enough served by noticing, in particular, the prescription about service books: in modern translation:

You must be equipped with books as befits your order. A mass-priest must have a missal and a book of the epistles, and a hymn-book and a reading-book and a psalter and a manual and a penitential and a computus; and they are to be well corrected; and clean mass-vestments for Christ's service. And on Sunday nocturns and festival nocturns you must always sing nine responses, along with nine lessons.[11]

⁹ R. Fowler, ed. *Wulfstan's Canons of Edgar*, Early Eng. Text. Soc., orig. ser. 266 (1972), with parallel printing of the two main, and slightly divergent, MSS, CCCC 201 and Bodl. Junius 121; cf. Jost's "Einige Wulfstantexte und ihre Quellen," *Anglia* 56 (1932), pp. 265–315. The most convenient text, with facing translation, is in *C & S 871–1204*, I.313–38, from which the passages quoted here are taken.

¹⁰ Most fully edited by B. Fehr, *Die Hirtenbriefe Ælfrics* (Hamburg 1914, repr. with supplementary intro. by P. Clemoes, Darmstadt 1966); cited here from the edn and tr. in *C & S*, I.255–302.

¹¹ *C & S*, I.291. An almost identical list occurs in Ælfric's slightly earlier (c. 994?) "Pastoral Letter for Wulfsige III," bishop of Sherborne and therefore a neighbor when

This echoes clearly the list of six service books mandated in the *Poenitentiale* that may or may not be by Egbert, archbishop of York in the mid-eighth century: "psalterium, lectionarium, antefonarium, missalem, baptisterium, martyrlogium [*sic*]" (discussed above, p. 47). But Ælfric's list is in the vernacular – and hence a prime source for Helmut Gneuss's important treatment of the nomenclature of liturgical books in Anglo-Saxon England[12] – and also probably more realistic in specifying that the books are to be well corrected (*gerihte*): very likely what was happening when large chunks of *liturgica* were copied into the margins of the Old English Bede just noticed. This is worth emphasizing because this prescription is unquestionably directed to secular clergy whose bishop Wulfstan was, many of whom would have been serving minsters. Where and how they are to acquire these books is no more addressed by Ælfric than it had been by "Egbert." This remains a major puzzle for us. For the moment we can go no farther in this direction, but must shift our attention to a matter alluded to in Ælfric's prescription about uniformity in keeping feast- and fast-days: evidence from the early calendars, beginning with the curious genre of the metrical calendar. We notice it first in a document related to the glamorous court of King Athelstan.

Athelstan's books and the metrical calendar

The emergence of the Wessex royal family as monarchs of England (by one definition or another) during the reigns of Alfred (871–99), Edward the Elder (899–924), and Athelstan (924–39) is marked by increased Continental contacts, especially with the north of France, Flanders/Lotharingia, and Brittany. The previous chapter ended with a notice of a concrete point of contact, that of the visit of Alfred's father Æthelwulf to the court of Charles the Bald, and in the present chapter influence from St Bertin and Arras, both in greater Flanders, will bulk large. Particularly striking among the numerous foreign churchmen who are known to have visited Athelstan's splendid court are several Bretons, the importance of whom is stressed by David Dumville: "The presence of Breton clergy and Breton liturgical books (both perhaps accompanying some of their saints' relics) will have ensured the introduction of

Ælfric was a monk at Cerne, 987–1005: *C & S*, I.201–26 at 207. There is a good deal in this letter about the rites of the *Triduum sacrum*, but it is cast in the first person plural and specifies a cantor (usually a monastic term), so may not be relevant to the secular contexts under discussion.

12 H. Gneuss, "Liturgical Books in Anglo-Saxon England and their Old English Terminology," in *Learning and Literature*, pp. 91–141.

Breton Church-music and musical notation."[13] He speaks further of manuscripts imported in Athelstan's reign as testifying to "a concern to reestablish basic christian observance, education, and discipline, in their concentration on psalter and gospels, ecclesiastical canons, *grammatica*, and *liturgica*";[14] but of books in the latter category there is little trace.

Such books (at least six) as can be connected in one way or another with Athelstan have been intensively studied by Simon Keynes.[15] They include three gospel books, all written on the Continent (and all now in the British Library), given by that monarch to English churches: Cotton Tiberius A.ii, to Canterbury Christ Church; Royal 1 A.xviii, to Canterbury St Augustine's; and Cotton Otho B.ix, to Chester-le-Street, probably in 934.[16] The third of these would be of the greatest interest to us had it not been badly burned in the 1731 Cottonian fire, for it contained a capitulary list, presumably reflecting the usages of the church in Brittany where it was written; this, transferred to, and possibly used at, Chester-le-Street (whence it passed to Durham on the community's move there at the end of the tenth century) would have been a most precious piece of information.[17]

Among the three further books that Keynes calls "other manuscripts associated with king Athelstan" is a psalter, BL Cott. Galba A.xviii, often referred to as the Athelstan Psalter: a sobriquet awarded on the basis of what he has termed "the slenderest of evidence," namely an inscription to that effect written by the cleric who owned the book in 1542. To this ninth-century book, both written and supplemented on the Continent before it came to England, was added, presumably in Wessex, material summarized by Keynes as "a metrical calendar (with other computistical material), ...at least five miniatures ..., [and] at a slightly later date, probably towards the middle of the tenth century, a collection of prayers, followed by a sequence of Greek texts, was added at the end."[18]

---

[13] On Athelstan's reign in general, see D. N. Dumville, *Wessex and England from Alfred to Edgar: Six Essays on Political, Cultural, and Ecclesiastical Revival* (Woodbridge 1992), ch. iv: "Between Alfred the Great and Edgar the Peaceable: Æthelstan, First King of England," pp. 141–72, esp. pp. 156–67, at 157.

[14] Dumville, p. 162.

[15] S. Keynes, "King Athelstan's Books," in *Learning and Literature*, pp. 143–201 and pl. i–xvi.

[16] There is also the Irish pocket gospel book, the MacDurnan Gospels, now Lambeth Palace MS 1370, not reasonably to be regarded as a liturgical book because of its size; treated by Keynes on pp. 153–59.

[17] Only twelve fragments remain, so Keynes's analysis is perforce based on the accounts in the catalogues of Thomas Smith in 1696 and Humfrey Wanley in 1705.

[18] Keynes, p. 194.

Of these English additions, the most potentially useful to us is the metrical calendar, which is probably the earliest of four that are extant in tenth- and eleventh-century manuscripts. Taken together, the four show that the calendar of this Galba psalter (as it should perhaps be termed, given the slimness of any possible connection to Athelstan) is, far from being a *unicum*, one witness to a text that had some popularity in later Anglo-Saxon England. First presented in a mid-nineteenth-century, quite imperfect, edition by Edward Hampson, the text replicated in the Galba book is now generally known as MCH, the metrical calendar of Hampson.[19] It should be stressed that the inclusion of particular saints in metrical calendars does not guarantee that they are liturgically celebrated, any more than mention in a martyrology does. That said, there is reason to look more closely at the Galba calendar and especially at its possible relationship to the earliest extant English non-metrical calendar.

The metrical calendar as a genre, and specifically its appearance in the Galba psalter, was noticed by Edmund Bishop, obliquely but trenchantly, as far back as 1916.[20] Generally approving earlier suggestions that the author of the calendar may have been an Irishman perhaps working in Alfred's court (the two "contemporary" figures included are Alfred, who died in 899, and his wife Eahlswith, who died probably in 902), Bishop maintained that nonetheless "internal evidence shows that the author of the metrical calendar used a Missal, or the calendar of a Missal, just such as might be expected to be found in – to have been brought to – England and the court at Winchester in Alfred's day." The genre was then taken up more systematically by André Wilmart, who in 1934 investigated its earliest appearance in England, in the so-called Metrical Calendar of York (MCY); he placed authorship in the circle of Alcuin.[21] Returning to the subject and extrapolating from the contents of the four witnesses mentioned above, Michael Lapidge has suggested that "in the early tenth century a continental redaction of MCY apparently travelled back to England and served as a point of departure for a more ambitious metrical calendar by a poet who was arguably active in Anglo-Saxon England."[22] Was this poet also, in any meaningful sense, a liturgist?

---

[19] It has now been studied expertly by P. McGurk, "The Metrical Calendar of Hampson," *Anal. Boll.* 104 (1986), pp. 79–125. Hampson's edition appeared in his *Medii Aevi Kalendarium*, 2 vols (London 1841), I.393–420.

[20] E. Bishop, "On the Origin of the Feast of the Conception of the Blesssed Virgin," in *Liturg. Hist.*, pp. 238–49, reprinted as it originally appeared in *Downside Review*, 1886, but with a supplementary note, pp. 250–59, written c. 1916, "The 'Irish Origins' of the Feast of the Conception." It is this note which is relevant here.

[21] A. Wilmart, "Un témoin anglo-saxon du calendrier métrique d'York," *Rev. Bén.* 46 (1934), pp. 41–69.

[22] M. Lapidge, "A Tenth-Century Metrical Calendar from Ramsey," *Rev. Bén.* 94 (1984), pp. 326–69 at 342.

That is, can evidence from the metrical calendar in the Galba psalter tell us anything reliable about a (the?) sanctorale in England in, say, the first quarter of the tenth century – as Bishop thought was the case? The Galba calendar contains some 365 lines, with a saint for most days, compared with 82 saints in MCY; so there has been a vast inflation. The inclusion of some of those 82 was, Wilmart thought, owing to their appearance in massbooks, of either the Gelasian (Old or Eighth-Century) or Gregorian strands, while others seemed to have a strongly martyrological cast. He paid no detailed attention to the English saints, save to note that they reinforced his location of the calendar as originating around York at the time of Alcuin. These saints have an undeniably northern character – Cuthbert, Egbert, Wilfrid (I), Wilfrid II ([arch] bishop of York, d. 744), John of Beverley, Tatberht (friend of Wilfrid I and his successor as abbot of Ripon), Bosa, the Hewalds, Paulinus.[23] The appearance of Boniface and perhaps of (a) Thecla hints at a possible southern and/or German missionary element also. (This Thecla, here placed at 17 November, may be the English nun, probably from Wimborne, who accompanied Lioba to Germany, under the influence of Boniface, became abbess of two houses there, and has some liturgical commemoration, but on October 15th.)[24]

Though difficult to express intelligibly, there seems discernible here, if not a pattern, at least a strand of three threads. The earliest, that of the MCY, suggests the development of what might be called a north-English sanctorale by at least the end of the eighth century. The second would be represented by Bishop's "Missal ... such as might be expected to be found in – to have been brought to – England and the court at Winchester in Alfred's day," evident now in the metrical calendar in the Galba psalter and the three related ones. A third thread may be postulated when, some time in the tenth century, there appeared in southern England the only ninth-century English calendar that, as such, seems to survive: one attached to a computistical manuscript datable to the span 867–92 (now Bodl. Digby 63). Apparently written in Northumbria, this calendar was, according to David Dumville, at Winchester by the end of the tenth century.[25]

---

[23] The omission of Acca (d. 740) could conceivably be a reflection of his being driven from his see at York in 732, for reasons still obscure.

[24] On the English Thecla, see *AA. SS. Oct.* VII (1845), pp. 59–64. The day of the better known Thecla, an (apocryphal) second-century virgin, is Sept. 23rd.

[25] Dumville, *Liturgy and the Eccles. Hist.*, pp. 105-6; ed. Wormald, *Eng. Kals*, pp. 1–13. The appearance of the Thecla, whoever she is, on 17 Nov., may connect the (early tenth-century) Galba metrical calendar with the ninth-century Digby 63 calendar. A Thecla appears on this day in only four other calendars before 1100 (and in none thereafter), all of which are southern or western; in the north, Nov. 17th comes

Although the Digby 63 calendar appears in a "scientific" rather than liturgical context, we may fairly ask what a cleric who encountered it in Southumbria would have made not only of its many odd inclusions (like a bishop Augustine on November 16th) but, in particular, of the cross marks placed next to some thirty-two feasts. Some of these go to the obvious great feasts, like Epiphany, Purification, Martin, and all the apostles.[26] Notable among the others are Cuthbert, Wilfrid, John of Beverley, Oswald (all four connected mainly with the north), Gregory the Great, and Augustine of Canterbury. The crosses are clearly meant to signal feasts of special importance, in an age before anything like the "grading" of feasts exists. It seems possible to relate the distinction implied by these crosses to that of the appearance of "F" and "S" next to certain feasts in the calendar of the most famous Anglo-Saxon mass-book, the Leofric missal. To grasp the implication of this will require us to embark on a somewhat extended discussion of that book. Before undertaking that, however, we may just notice that, save two or three peculiarities on either side, each feast marked in Digby with a cross has an "F" next to it in the Leofric missal's calendar.[27]

The Leofric missal: its first component (= "A")

The fame of the Leofric missal (Bodl. Bodley 579) goes back at least to 1883, when F. E. Warren published his edition, a work that (as noticed above, p. 31) was both pioneering and, for its time, exemplary. Until recently a kind of consensus, based mainly on Warren's analysis, had emerged about the book's three main components. Its chief points were that the nucleus of the codex, which Warren named "Leofric A," was a Gregorian sacramentary written in northeast France (probably around Arras) some time before about 900; that it came early in the

---

increasingly to be devoted to Hilda of Whitby. The four are Salisbury Cath. 150 (perhaps from Shaftesbury), Bodl. Bodley 579 (the Leofric missal, its calendar being apparently from Glastonbury: see below), CUL Kk.v.32 (also probably from Glastonbury; followed by Anianus of Orleans), and Bodl. Hatton 113 (Worcester; again with Anianus, who here comes first): all printed in Wormald, *Eng. Kals.*

[26] Including both "Mathiani" (Matthias) at 24 Feb. and "Mathei" (Matthew) at 21 Sept., and also an odd "Apostolorum Iacobi et Albini" at 22 June: the latter is clearly Alban, misspelled or confused with the Frankish Albinus (Aubin, 1 March), but who is the extra James (both the Greater on 25 July and the Lesser, on 1 May with Philip, are present)? The Purification is called "Ypapanti," normally a Gregorian characteristic.

[27] Digby has crosses also against Wilfrid (24 Apr.), Oswald (5 Aug.) and the odd James-and-Albinus in the note above, and lacks one against John the Baptist, almost certainly by inadvertence; the Leofric calendar marks as "F" also Guthlac (11 Apr.), and – not strictly relevant here – the Greater Litany (25 Apr.) and Ascension (as 5 May).

tenth century to England, where it was supplemented by a calendar (widely agreed to be that of Glastonbury) and related computistical matter ("Leofric B"), the latter notable for its four full-page drawings; and that when the book migrated further, to Exeter in the episcopate of the eponymous Leofric, 1050–72, further additions ("Leofric C") were made, not as a group but on blank spaces and in the margins.[28]

This hitherto "mainstream" opinion will have to be largely revised if the positions advanced by Nicholas Orchard in the massively detailed introduction to his recent edition of the Leofric missal come to be generally accepted.[29] The most fundamental of these positions is that this massbook was in its original form written in England for Plegmund, archbishop of Canterbury from 890 to 923. If the Plegmund theory, as it can be called for brevity, is correct, among its corollaries is a picture of church life during the period of his episcopacy as relatively vigorous in southern England. It will not be possible here to recapitulate more than a very few of Orchard's arguments. They rely primarily on close textual comparisons with a large number of Continental texts, and are summarized in a lengthy concluding sentence as to the "Englishness" of Leofric A: "It contains an English *ordo* for Ash Wednesday; numerous formulae that never figure in the numerous French and Lotharingian sacramentaries that have come down to us, but which appear regularly in service books written in England ...; it has an English pontifical and Coronation Order; part of an English service of exorcism and baptism; and it places St Mark's day on the 18th of May."[30]

His locating it emphatically as a bishop's, indeed an archbishop's, book intensifies curiosity in two directions. One direction is to wonder to what extent the mass liturgy at the archbishop's cathedral in Plegmund's time could have been carried out according to the book's prescriptions. The main scribe of A is pretty clearly not English, and the model(s) he is working from – something like the Hadrianic Gregorian with the (Benedict of Aniane) Supplement and a good deal of "Young Gelasian" influence – is likely to have been a Continental one (although behind it may well lurk, as Orchard demonstrates, various English bits of influence, the most clearly discernible being, not surprisingly, that of Alcuin). Here the chant tags, summarized by Orchard as "the incipits of the sung parts of numerous masses [that] were written in A's margins

---

[28] This consensus is summarized in slightly greater detail in Pfaff, *Liturg. Bks ASE*, 11–14.

[29] N. Orchard, ed. *The Leofric Missal*, 2 vols, HBS 113–14 (2002). See also the extremely detailed description of the entire contents in Hartzell, *Cat. Music* (2006), pp. 400–27.

[30] Orchard, I.131.

by the original scribe, presumably with a view to helping the celebrant follow what the choir were doing, or at least what they were supposed to be doing, at given times," may offer a clue.[31] We are of course not dealing with anything like a plenary missal, where the chant texts are expected to be inserted in their proper places in each mass. That the original (Leofric A) scribe has gone to the trouble of supplying marginal chant tags for many, but by no means all, of the masses suggests that the book's user actively wanted the help they provide in following the musical parts of the service.[32] They detract from the attractiveness of the page, and the reason for including them can only have been practical.

A second point of special interest if this is an archbishop's book arises from its *ordo* for the dedication of a (new) church (fol. 283v). Here Orchard makes much of the second proper preface which reads in part "praecipue cum huius basilicę pręsul adscitus, uenerabilis andreas oblator existat," arguing from it that the mass could have been drawn up for the dedication of the cathedral at Wells and that "Plegmund, who will have officiated at the ceremony, simply had his scribe work into the book a copy of the *ordo* drawn up for the day."[33] It is of course possible, but by no means proven, that Plegmund made the journey from Canterbury to Wells for that purpose; equally, however, we should note that this preface is the second of three from which the officiant could choose, the first stressing the priesthood of Melchisedek, the third the patronage of more than one saint. This raises the alternative possibility that Plegmund (if indeed our book was written for him) expected to be consecrating a variety of churches with a consequent variety of dedications.[34] This possibility is strengthened by an incident pointed out

---

[31] Orchard, I.125. These can be seen clearly in the digitized presentation of this manuscript, e.g. on fol. 73, First Sunday after Epiphany: http://image.ox.ac.uk/images/bodleian/bodl579/73r.jpg.

[32] Orchard, I.127, points out that "as far as A is concerned, cues were not added to the pontifical sections of the book," where the chant texts tend to be embedded as integral to the bishop-celebrant's part.

[33] Orchard, I.83. It is a bit hard to imagine what Orchard envisages here: a *libellus*, perhaps, by its nature not likely to survive long? There is the additional question as to whether this *ordo*, and in particular these prefaces, are part of scribe A's original model, in which case they cannot have been copied from an original at Wells. There is no codicological discreteness about the quire (fols 278r–85v) containing this section, according to the collation of E. M. Drage (see p. 130), printed by Orchard, I.13–14. The Latin is murky: is it the officiating bishop (*presul*) who is meant to be the offerer (*oblator*), or the apostle Andrew?

[34] The Lanalet pontifical (Rouen, B.m. 368[A.27]), most likely written for Lyfing, bishop of Wells c. 999–1013, uses the first of the three (the "Melchizedek preface"), not the one that mentions Wells's patron saint, Andrew: ed. G. H. Doble, *Pontificale Lanaletense*, HBS 74 (1937), p. 26.

by Nicholas Brooks: Plegmund's dedication of a tower at Winchester (New Minster?) in 908, an act that "would normally have been the diocesan's work [and] was presumably made necessary by the death of Bishop Denewulf in that year."[35]

The second strand of the Leofric missal (= "B")

Any possible connection with Wells apart, we shall tentatively follow Orchard in regarding "Leofric A" as constituting a massbook used by archbishop Plegmund in the first quarter of the tenth century. Next we must look at the additions and alterations made, also as it seems at Canterbury, in the fifty or sixty years after his death: those collectively referred to as "Leofric B." These, if palaeographical analysis is correct (some caution is always wise, especially where date-ranges become as narrow as a quarter-century), were made variously in the second, third, and fourth quarters of the tenth century. Orchard contends that the book must have remained at Canterbury through the episcopate of Dunstan (959–88), and suggests that "It may even be that some of the new material was written by the archbishops themselves."[36] The first group was written by a total of ten scribes, all English, who added material largely of a pontifical sort. The most telling of these may be what he calls some additions and alterations to A's forms for the consecration of bishops; four of the scribes contribute bits to this section, a level of busy-ness that Orchard relates to "the relatively large number of bishops appointed in Wulfhelm's time [c. 926–41]: well over a dozen."[37]

The additions of the third quarter of the century are noteworthy in a pair of respects. One is in the provision of a blessing for a king, "Benedic domine hunc clementissimum regem," which both has distinctively English variants as against a "Young Gelasian" parallel and is somewhat longer than it is in subsequent English pontificals. The

---

[35] N. Brooks, *The Early History of the Church of Canterbury* (Leicester 1984), p. 214. A. Wareham on Pleg(e)mund in *ODNB*, 44.574–75, stresses his establishment of four new sees between 909 and 918, at Crediton, Ramsbury, and Sherborne as well as Wells.

[36] Orchard, I.132.

[37] It is slightly confusing that he assigns to these ten scribes alphabetical sigla A–J, to four scribes working in the third quarter of the century the lower-case letters a–d (p. 151), and to eleven working in probably the final quarter the Roman numerals i–xi (pp. 156–57); they are all scribes in "Leofric B," which he always denotes, as also A and C, by the use of italics. He continues, "that most of these consecrations took place in the 930s accords well with the palaeography of the new material," while acknowledging that much work remains to be done in identifying the work of these scribes in other English books; I.134–35.

other consists of alterations in the last half of the Easter Eve *Exultet* and particularly in its closing formula, from words that can no longer be read to "et archi episcopo nostro atque rege nostro."[38]

It is the additions of the last quarter of the tenth century that are the most famous sections of the entire book, and have also attracted the largest amount of scholarly attention. These (fols 38–58) include the calendar and related computistical matter, which form the most important section in terms of illustration. Again, Nicholas Orchard's concise summary as to why this material should have been added to the book deserves to be quoted in full:

First, the incorporation of a new calendar and practical computus, not to mention the supplement of saints' masses incorporated later on in the volume, suggest that *A* was still regarded as being a useful, working book; and second, that certain changes in liturgical practice had taken place at Canterbury by the last quarter of the tenth century. One cannot help but think that these changes were largely introduced by Dunstan. Indeed, as we shall see, *B*'s calendar seems to have been based on a sacramentary brought by the new archbishop to Canterbury from Glastonbury, where he had formerly been abbot. (I.157)

There cannot be laid out here the elaborate and detailed comparative analyses, above all with the roughly contemporary (c. 1000) calendar of a splendid codex called the Bosworth psalter (BL Add. 37517), necessary to substantiate generalizations about the "Leofric B" calendar. Tentative conclusions from such analyses (not solely Orchard's) may include the following. (1) There is unquestionably a relationship between those two calendars, one put to the fore by the prominence of anything Edmund Bishop wrote – in this case, in a monograph on Bosworth which appeared in 1908.[39] (2) The Bosworth calendar is quite clearly that of Canterbury St Augustine's. (3) Both bear witness to direct influence from Glastonbury, influence which it would be natural (but not necessaily inevitable) to relate to Dunstan, once abbot there and subsequently, after briefly holding the sees of Worcester and London, archbishop at Canterbury. Furthermore, Glastonbury – the

---

[38] Orchard, I.151-54, and II.171. In speculating as to what the original ("Leofric A") wording was in relation to the altered phrase, he seems to overlook the possibility that what is different about the alteration is the mention of the king in the singular, a circumstance which for England makes particular sense in exactly this period. But, as far as I know, there are no earlier English texts of the *Exultet* with which this can be compared.

[39] E. Bishop and F. A. Gasquet, *The Bosworth Psalter: an Account of a Manuscript formerly belonging to O. Turville-Petre Esq. of Bosworth Hall now Addit. MS 37517 at the British Museum* (London 1908). Bishop's chapter on the calendar and the related Addenda take up more than two-thirds of the volume. Gasquet's share was minimal.

major monastic house for which the least amount of liturgical evidence survives – is near Wells, three bishops of which became archbishops of Canterbury in the second and third quarters of the tenth century.

To posit from this, however, that the calendar in "Leofric B" is "based on the sanctoral of a sacramentary from Glastonbury," as Orchard does, seems to be a jump rather than an inevitable conclusion.[40] In the first place, it requires acceptance of the further assumption (yet to be examined) that there is a major change in the sanctorale at Canterbury cathedral after 1012, when Ælfheah, previously bishop of Winchester, becomes archbishop and Winchester influence comes to predominate. Secondly, it supposes that Dunstan regarded Glastonbury as somehow more normative than Canterbury: that he was willing to discard the saints' days calendar implicit in the sanctorale of "Leofric A" in favor not of whatever was in use at his cathedral in the 960s or even later but of a somewhat earlier Glastonbury calendar. Thirdly, it postulates the existence of an English sacramentary-with-calendar: an entity which, if it did exist, would be the earliest such book known to us.

These are sizeable assumptions. The reason for identifying and querying each of them is that they seem to imply that Dunstan was less influenced by developments at the Æthelwoldian monastic (re)-foundations at Abingdon (c. 954), Ely (970), and above all Winchester Old Minster (964) – developments which must be heavily reflected in the *Regularis Concordia* (to be discussed next, and abbreviated *RC*) – than by the traditions of the house he had left by the mid-950s. This is not the place to argue the relative contributions of Æthelwold and Dunstan to the monastic revival, nor to try to work out exactly when Christ Church became a monastic house (and precisely what is meant in that case). Rather, towards pursuit of our narrative agenda we must now remove the spotlight from the Leofric missal (it will be returned to when "Leofric C" comes into view at the end of the next chapter) and instead look at the *RC* and evidence related to it – above all at the great benedictional made for Æthelwold – and eventually at a presumably "Æthelwoldian" massbook that offers the most helpful comparison to what Dunstan might have used at Canterbury by the end of his tenure there: the so-called Robert of Jumièges missal, likely to have been written at either Ely or Peterborough (like Ely, an Æthelwoldian refoundation).

---

[40] Orchard, I.204, where he suggests also that a similar calendar "had also been adopted at London and Worcester: for Dunstan had been inaugurated as bishop of both sees in 959" (more likely, 957).

The *Regularis Concordia*

It is of course Æthelwold's presence that bulks largest in the *Regularis Concordia*, promulgated at the meeting of English abbots in 970 (or possibly 972) known as the Synod of Winchester.[41] Although the standard edition of the *RC* is in substance over half a century old, the millennial anniversaries of that Synod and of the death of Æthelwold in 984, followed by distinguished work from Michael Lapidge, Christopher Jones, and Lucia Kornexl, have kept the subject to the fore of scholarly attention.[42] It may be most efficient to look directly at the document itself before attempting some assessment of its influence and, more broadly, of that of its likeliest principal author, bishop Æthelwold.

The heading "Foreword to the harmony of the rule" (*pro[o]emium regularis concordiae*), in one of the two extant manuscripts, makes plain that it is meant to apply to the monks and nuns of the entire *natio anglica* (defined succinctly enough as that over which Edgar reigned as king): "Anglicae nationis monachorum sanctimonialiumque." In theory, every monastic house in the kingdom was to be covered by the agreement, the female establishments no less than the male.[43] It is possible that the latter point helps to explain why the document pays so much less attention to the mass than to the office and to special

---

[41] For general background on the monastic revival in England, Knowles, *Mon. Order*, ch. iii, and the pieces collected in D. Parsons, ed. *Tenth-Century Studies: Essays in Commemoration of the Millennium of the Council of Winchester and* Regularis Concordia (London and Chichester 1975) are still the best starting places. See also M. Gretsch, *The Intellectual Foundations of the English Benedictine Reform*, Cbg. Studs. in Anglo-Saxon England 25 (Cambridge 1999), where the approach is mainly philological.

[42] T. Symons, ed. and tr., *Regularis Concordia ...*, NMT (1953); this was reprinted, with text revised by S. Spath, critical apparatus by M. Wegener, and *apparatus explicativum* by K. Hallinger, in *Consuetudinum saeculi X/XI/XII monumenta non-Cluniacensia*, Corpus Consuetudinum Monasticarum 7/3 (Siegburg 1984), pp. 61–147; cf. Hallinger's discussion of the manuscript tradition in CCM 7/1, *Introductiones*, pp. 153–67, with a revision and condensation of parts i-ii of Symons's Introduction, pp. 373–93. See also B. Yorke, ed. *Bishop Æthelwold: His Career and Influence* (Woodbridge 1988); M. Lapidge and M. Winterbottom, eds. *Wulfstan of Winchester, The Life of St Æthelwold*, OMT (1991), esp. Lapidge's introductory section on "Æthelwold and the Liturgy," pp. lx–lxxxv; L. Kornexl, "The Regularis Concordia and its Old English Gloss," *ASE* 24 (1995), pp. 95–130. Kornexl's Munich dissertation, *Die Regularis Concordia und ihre altenglische Interlinearversion. Mit Einleitung und Kommentar* (Munich 1993), provides rich commentary and a more recent edition of the Latin text while retaining the paragraph numbers of Symons's. For C. A. Jones's edition of *Ælfric's Letter to the Monks of Eynsham* see next section; literature on the Benedictional of Æthelwold will also be noticed separately.

[43] It should be noted that the heading is given in only the younger of the two surviving manuscripts, BL Cott. Tib. A.iii, s.xi². The older, Cott. Faustina B.iii, s. xᵉˣ, begins with the first line of the Proem, "Gloriosus etenim Eadgarus." On adaptations, esp. those for female use, see numerous articles by J. Hill, notably "The 'Regularis Concordia' and its Latin and Old English Reflexes," *Rev. Bén.* 101 (1991), pp. 299–315.

rites for great occasions; but of course it is also true that the mass is less distinctive in monastic liturgy (i.e., less different from secular uses) than is the office. In any case, there is much in the document that will not apply to women; *fratres* is used commonly, *sorores* and similar terms not at all. The rather lengthy Proem is concerned with monastic matters other than liturgical, but the twelve chapters that form the body of the text are mostly but not exclusively concerned with liturgical detail.

The first of these twelve chapters gives general prescriptions for the office and for behavior in choir. Particularly interesting is the awareness shown of the secular (or "Roman") office, for example in the suggestion (section 20) that older monks might use *horae canonicae*, quite apart from choir observance, as a way of concentrating the mind before entering the church; this of course raises the question of where texts for such offices might have come from.[44] Again, when the monks are performing their daily quota of manual labor they are meant to be singing the "canonici cursus et psalterii" (sect. 25), and the secular office is to be used for the most sacred seasons of the *Triduum sacrum* and Easter week (sect. 37ff. and 50).[45] How reasonable would it have been to suppose that in all English religious houses access to both forms of the daily office would have been feasible? The problem is complicated by the fact that these prescriptions are themselves not distinctively English.[46]

The sections devoted to the rites of Holy Week and Easter are, not surprisingly, the longest and most detailed in the document. It is here, too, that the "dramatic" character that has become the document's principal claim to fame is most clearly seen. A certain self-consciousness is evident, as in the passage describing the night office of Maundy Thursday – frequently, but not in the *RC*, called *Tenebrae* – which records how (in Symons's translation) "in churches of certain religious men, a practice has grown up whereby compunction of soul is aroused

[44] One possibility that can be neither disproved nor dismissed would involve the texts that had been used by the canons who had been expelled from the Old Minster in 963: did they perhaps leave whatever service books they had behind?

[45] E.g., on Maundy Thursday, "nocturnale officium agatur secundum quod in antiphonario habetur" (p. 36), the implication being that the word *antiphonarium* connotes the secular office – and that an English monastic house was expected to possess one.

[46] Investigation of Continental sources for the *RC* began with a series of articles by Symons published in the *Downside Review*, esp. in vol. 59 (1941), pp. 14–36, 143–70, and 264–89; summarized on pp. xlv–l of his 1953 edition. When he was at work the principal resource available to him for comparative purposes was B. Albers, ed. *Consuetudines Monasticae*, 5 vols (Stuttgart, Vienna, Monte Cassino, 1905–12); it was only in 1963 that the great Corpus Consuetudinum Monasticarum series was begun under the editorship of K. Hallinger.

by means of the outward representation of that which is spiritual."[47] This aspect, most famously displayed in the *Quem quaeritis* ceremony of Easter matins (sect. 51), has given rise to much literature, and not a little controversy, as to the relationship between the *RC* and the origins of medieval European drama – controversy that will be strictly side-stepped here.[48]

Almost as well known are the major accretions to the daily office of the supplementary Offices of the Dead (nocturns, lauds, and vespers) and of All Saints (lauds and vespers only), and the equally time-consuming specifications of the *Trina oratio* and of prayers for the king and royal family. The Offices of the Dead and All Saints do not of course have their beginning in England; monastic developments at Cluny and in Lotharingia had supplied these.[49] The *Trina oratio*, a series of psalms and collects set out in a threefold structure and said at three points (which varied somewhat at different times of year) throughout the monastic day also has Continental antecedents.[50] What seems distinctively English are the prayers for the king, queen, and (sometimes) benefactors, which were to be said after every hour except prime; the same persons are mentioned also in the *Trina oratio* and often at the Morrow Mass.

Another practice that looks to be distinctively English is referred to in a way that manifests a self-consciousness about earlier practices. This is the ringing of the bells at Christmas after nocturns and vespers as well as mass, "as is the custom (*usus*) among the people of this country (*huius patriae*)." This is described as one of the honest customs (*mores*) which we learned from, literally, the practice of older persons (*veterum usu*) and should not abandon.[51] We would of course dearly

---

[47] Sect. 37: "in quorundam religiosorum ecclesiis quiddam fieri quod ad animarum compunctionem spiritalis rei indicium exorsum est." *Viri religiosi* always seems to refer to secular canons.

[48] A recent and extensive treatment of this aspect is M. B. Bedingfield, *The Dramatic Liturgy of Anglo-Saxon England* (Woodbridge 2002); cf. my review in *The Medieval Review* (electronic journal), 03.05.07. O. B. Hardison, *Christian Rite and Christian Drama in the Middle Ages* (Baltimore 1965) marked an important earlier stage in the discussion.

[49] Dom Symons weighed the aspects of the *RC* clearly traceable to each of those two strands and concluded that "it looks as though the customs of Ghent, indirectly discernible in the Concordia through Lotharingian parallels, had specially commended themselves to the English" (p. li). Dunstan had spent time at Ghent in mid-century. The considerable influence of Fleury, which Æthelwold knew, is evident through its late 10th-cent. customary, as redacted by Thierry of Amorbach: ed. A. Davril and C. Donnat in Corpus Cons. Mon. 7/3 (above, note 42), pp. 7–60.

[50] The collects are given in full, along with incipits of the psalms, in sections 16 and 27; these are in practice all to be recited from memory.

[51] Symons's rendering of *veterum* as "our fathers before us" is more a gloss than a translation, but the sense of this section (32) is clear enough.

like to know whose English *usus,* whether that of a religious house or ascribed to particular *veteres,* is alluded to here. Possibly also peculiarly English is what may constitute a suggestion that the monks, save those in a conscious state of sin or weakness, should receive communion daily, though the language here is not prescriptive (sect. 23: that they should not hesitate, *non renuant,* rather than that they should definitely do it). Even more surprising is the implication of the previous sentence, that after terce the bells should ring "fidelem aduocantes plebem [ad] missam." Dom David Knowles took this as indicating that "the people will assist at the chief Mass on Sundays and feasts,"[52] but if so it is a markedly casual reference to a practice for which there is little evidence otherwise. Still, the suggestion is specially appealing because it is on Sundays and great feasts that the magnificent book primarily associated with Æthelwold, the benedictional that goes by his name, would have been used by that bishop.

Æthelwold's benedictional

Of all English medieval service books of monumental quality, the one that has attracted scholarly attention for the longest time is the benedictional of Æthelwold (now BL Add. 49598, but owned by the Duke of Devonshire from around 1720 until 1957). As far back as 1832 John Gage (later Rokewode), a prominent figure in the Society of Antiquaries of London, published in its series *Archaeologia* what he called "A Dissertation [which, at 117 quarto pages, it certainly is] on St Æthelwold's Benedictional, an illuminated MS of the tenth century, in the library of his Grace the Duke of Devonshire."[53] The thirty-two engravings supplied there began a steady tradition of publishing some, or all, of

---

[52] *Mon. Order,* p. 44. Apparently the Old English glossator understood it that way, rendering *plebem* as *folc*: Kornexl (note 42 above), p. 38. Perhaps it would be wise to view the phrase with caution, keeping in mind Knowles's observation on p. 43 that the entire document, "though at first glance logically planned, abounds in repetitions, dropped threads, and paragraphs which appear to have been inserted without reference to the sequence of ideas ... ." It should be noted that although in the second edition of this work, 1963, he was able to mention the 1953 NMT edition of the *RC,* his references to the document continue to use the section numbers of the edition by Clement Reyner (Douai 1626), as reprinted in vol. I of the Caley-Ellis-Bandinel edition of Dugdale's *Monasticon Anglicanum* (1817), which Knowles had had to use for his first edition, 1940.

[53] *Archaeologia* 24 (1832), pp. 1–117. Gage's "Dissertation'" was followed, pp. 118–36, by a briefer treatment of a late 10th-cent. pontifical closely related, artistically and textually, to Æthelwold's benedictional: the mis-called *Benedictional of Archbishop Robert* (Rouen, B.m. 369/Y.7), edited under that title by H. A. Wilson, HBS 24, 1903.

the twenty-eight full-page illustrations; it is only fairly recently that extensive attention has been paid to the text.[54]

The book is celebrated not only for its illustrations, which mark the high point of the "Winchester School of Illumination," but also for the prefatory Latin poem supplied by the monk-scribe Godeman, who describes how bishop Æthelwold ordered the sumptuous decoration, and for the fact that it is datable to 971–84. The manuscript does not survive entire; probably twelve full-page miniatures have been lost at its beginning, as well as individual leaves for, apparently, Holy Innocents, the Nativity of the Virgin, and Michael.[55] Blessings for each of these feasts survive, however, and it seems fair to use the selection of occasions for which there are blessings as a kind of index to the principal feasts in the "massbook of Æthelwold" – which, of course, we do not possess. The arrangement seems instructive: temporale from Advent through the Sundays after Epiphany, then sanctorale from Sebastian (20 January) through Ambrose (4 April); then temporale again, from Septuagesima through the Sundays after Pentecost (with interruptions after Easter II for Tiburtius and Valerian, 14 April, and Invention of Cross, 3 May); finally sanctorale from Etheldreda, 23 June, through Thomas, 21 December, and common of saints. There are only thirty-three sanctorale feasts, and the gap between 3 May and 22 June implies that blessings for the feasts of, notably, Augustine of Canterbury, Alban, and Barnabas were, if used at all, taken from the common (Cuthbert and Oswald are also conspicuously absent). Swithun and Etheldreda are the only English saints, and the "ringers" are Vedast (6 February) and Tiburtius-and-Valerian. The appearance of the latter pair, without the Maximus who sometimes accompanies them, seems inexplicable, though it may help to date the book to 973.[56] The inclusion

---

[54] A Roxburghe Club facsimile, in monotone, was published by G. F. Warner and H. A. Wilson in 1910, and eight colored plates, with brief but incisive discussion, by F. Wormald, *The Benedictional of St Ethelwold* [*sic*], in the Faber Library of Illuminated MSS series (London 1959); but it was not until 2001, with the Folio Society/British Library's full color facsimile introduced by Andrew Prescott, that the complete MS became widely available. Prescott's discussion is heavily relied on here, as is the monograph by R. Deshman, *The Benedictional of Æthelwold* (Princeton 1995). There is a vast literature on the book, mostly of an art-historical sort.

[55] It is possible that the missing miniatures at the beginning would have clinched a putative connection between this scheme of illustration and that of the English additions to the Galba A.xviii psalter discussed above (p. 70): Wormald, *Ben. of St. Eth.*, p. 12.

[56] Their feast day, 14 Apr., is likely to be celebrated only in a year when Easter falls between 23 March and 6 Apr., but Ambrose is ruled out, as falling within Easter week, when Easter occurs after the 27th. The 27th was the date in both 970 and 981, the 26th in 965, and the 23rd in 973 and 984 (the year of Æthelwold's death); it looks as though the book may have been prepared for use in 973, the first realistic year after the translation of Swithun two years earlier. Deshman has argued for 973 in connection with the splendid coronation of Edgar in that year (*Ben. of Æ.*, pp. 260–61).

of Vedast, patron saint of Arras, speaks to north French influence; Lapidge states that, as a consequence of Æthelwold's importing monks from nearby Corbie to teach chant at his re-founded house at Abingdon, veneration of Vedast (in particular) "is a characteristic feature of liturgical books from the Winchester of his episcopacy."[57]

Andrew Prescott has traced the source of each blessing as either Gregorian, Gelasian, or Gallican (the use of an episcopal blessing at communion was originally Frankish, not employed at Rome), with a considerable number that appear to be purely English.[58] These strands are not cleanly separable; nonetheless it seems possible to infer that the massbook corresponding to Æthelwold's benedictional was of a somewhat more mixed ("fused," as sometimes expressed) Gregorian-Gelasian type than the more purely Gregorian "Leofric A" (enhanced by "B") missal.[59]

Whatever the case there, it does look as though the benedictional was put together with an eye to its being applicable to something like the "Anglica natio monachorum sanctimonialiumque" adduced in the *RC*'s proem. At the same time, the book is strongly personalized: it is conceivable that the miniature of a bishop pronouncing a benediction at the dedication of an imposing church, fol. 118v, is meant to depict Æthelwold, and it seems highly likely that he composed the blessings for Swithun and Etheldreda himself. Swithun is of course a basic figure in Winchester tradition, and his cult can serve jointly with the slightly later one of Æthelwold to clarify our whole sense of that tradition.

Swithun, Æthelwold, and the Winchester tropers

A massive work by Michael Lapidge, published in 2003 and titled simply *The Cult of St Swithun*, attempts to compile a complete dossier of all sources related to that cult, primarily those of earlier than 1100 but

[57] Intro. to *Wulfstan, Life of St Æthelwold* (note 42 above), p. lxvi, where he cites the presence of a mass for Vedast as evidence that fragments from a dismembered MS now (mostly) in Oslo belonged to a Winchester missal slightly later than Æthelwold's episcopate. For further remarks on the cult of Vedast, see V. Ortenberg, *The English Church and the Continent in the Tenth and Eleventh Centuries* (Oxford 1992), pp. 34–35.

[58] Facsimile edn, pp. 20–22; cf. his full and important study, "The Text of the Benedictional of St Æthelwold," in Yorke, ed., *Bishop Æthelwold*, pp. 119–47; it contains a number of considerations that our having to prescind from distinctively episcopal liturgy (as explained on p. 15) prevents us from taking up.

[59] Prescott, "Text," p. 127, states that the blessings in Leofric were drawn from the benedictional supplied, probably by Benedict of Aniane, to the *Hadrianum* Gregorian sacramentary (see p. 56 above). Lapidge points out sensibly that "manuscript benedictionals vary enormously one from the other, with the result that it is difficult to trace relationships except in broad outline": *Wulfstan, Life of St Æthelwold*, p. lxxx.

taking into account relevant later material as well.[60] The basic facts about the saint are few and of no great importance: he was bishop of Winchester from 852 to 863, and died on July 2nd of the latter year. Originally buried in a conspicuous tomb outside the west door of the Old Minster, his remains were translated by Æthelwold, with great ceremony, to a shrine inside it on July 15th, 971. This shrine in turn became a focal point in the rebuilding of the cathedral church, which was dedicated anew, again by Æthelwold, in 980. Whether because of the concurrence on July 2nd of the medium-important feast of Processus and Martinian or for some other reason, the Translation feast came to be more heavily emphasized than the Deposition, and indeed has become in popular imagination St Swithun's day *simpliciter*: heavy rain on that day portends forty subsequent days of deluge.

It is odd, then, that Æthelwold's benedictional contains blessings only for Swithun's Deposition, not the Translation. Lapidge suggests, as a possible explanation, that the book was designed (probably by Æthelwold himself) prior to the latter occasion.[61] We know a bit about the Translation liturgy through the florid *Narratio metrica* of the saint by the Old Minster's cantor, or precentor, Wulfstan; he describes performance of, but gives no texts for, the office (vespers, matins, lauds) prior to the actual ceremony.[62] Wulfstan's work was based on an earlier one, perhaps written quite soon after the event and in rhyming prose (but without any liturgical description), by the Frankish monk Lantfred, who spent some time at the Old Minster. An early text of both works survives in BL Royal 15 C.vii, and in this the first part of Lantfred's work has been marked for reading in eight lessons (out of twelve; hence, for monastic use). The date of this manuscript is c. 1000, and it seems to have been written at Winchester.

Æthelwold came to have two feasts as well. His death on 1 August 984 was followed twelve years later by a solemn translation of his remains into the choir of the Old Minster on 10 September. Of the two days, that on 1 August, though shared inconveniently with the feast of Peter's Chains (*Ad vincula*) and sometimes with the Holy Maccabees as well,

[60] Winchester Studies 4.ii ("vol. 4" is in all to be a three-volume treatment of "The Anglo-Saxon Minsters of Winchester," of which the other two have not yet appeared); Lapidge's volume has contributions by three other scholars, of which Susan Rankin's "St Swithun in Medieval Liturgical Music," pp. 191–213, is material here.

[61] Lapidge, *Swithun*, p. 88. If this should be the case, and if the point about the inclusion of Tiburtius and Valerian (above, note 56) holds water, the book could have been produced for use in 970 (Easter 27 March) or even 965 (Easter 26 March).

[62] Text and translation in Lapidge, *Swithun*, pp. 372–551, at 454–61. Wulfstan's main source was the somewhat earlier, prose *Translatio et miracula S. Swithuni* by the Frankish monk Lantfred, but that contains no liturgical description (pp. 252–333).

comes to be much the more widely observed, with that on 10 September largely confined to Winchester itself.

The importance of the cults of Swithun and Æthelwold is plainly seen in the two manuscripts that share the sobriquet Winchester troper. Both were probably written at Winchester: the earlier, here specified as the Corpus Winchester troper (CCCC 473), has recently been dated by Susan Rankin to the 1020s–1030s.[63] The other (Bodl. Bodley 775), occasionally called the Æthelred troper, dates from the mid-eleventh century but is heavily dependent on something like the earlier manuscript.

The Corpus troper is arranged in a somewhat jumbled way. It contains various kinds of tropes for both of Swithun's feasts, Deposition and Translation, and for the Deposition (but not Translation) of Æthelwold. This may indicate that the contents list, at any rate, was drawn up before 996, even if the codex itself is somewhat later.[64] That the same "cantor Wulfstan" who wrote the first part of the *Vita Æthelwoldi* should have been, as is probable, the author of "all or a good number of the English pieces," as Elizabeth Teviotdale asserts, implies an important role for him in liturgical organization at the Old Minster in the generation following Æthelwold's death.[65] A similar role seems to have been played at a smaller house of Æthelwoldian affiliation by one of the cardinal figures in Old English literature, Ælfric.

Ælfric's instructions for the monks at Eynsham; the influence of Amalarius

As we have seen, the *Regularis Concordia* is not meant to be anything like a service book, and the information it supplies for our purposes

---

[63] In her facsimile edition, with extensive introduction, *The Winchester Troper*, Early Eng. Church Music 50 (London 2007), p. xi. Her presentation largely supplants the "modern" edition by the scholar who in effect discovered the work, W. H. Frere, *The Winchester Troper, from MSS of the Xth and XIth centuries, with other documents illustrating the history of tropes in England and France*, HBS 8 (1894). The contents are listed clearly and definitively in Hartzell, *Cat. Music*, pp. 88–109, and the tropes edited usefully in A. E. Planchart, *The Repertory of Tropes at Winchester*, 2 vols (Princeton 1977).

[64] Hartzell agrees with Rankin in dating at the second quarter of the 11th cent., whereas D. Hiley maintains (as does Lapidge) c. 1000: *Western Chant: a Handbook* (Oxford 1993), p. 583. Hiley also points out that a considerable number of the pieces do not survive the Norman Conquest.

[65] E. Teviotdale, "Tropers," in Pfaff, ed. *Liturg. Bks ASE*, pp. 39–44, at 41. She observes that the Bodl. 775 book "might better be termed a *cantatorium* (i.e., a cantor's book) than a troper, for it contains virtually all of the genres of chant customarily sung by the cantor rather than the choir at mass."

is often exiguous and sometimes non-existent (there is nothing at all about the sanctorale envisaged, for example); in addition, it is markedly lacking in coherence and tightness of organization. Certainly as useful for our purposes is the adaptation of it – part copy, part abridgement, part augmentation – composed by the celebrated Ælfric of Eynsham: his letter (as it is always called; CCCC 265) to the monks at Eynsham, whose abbot he was. For this we have the great advantage of the recent edition by Christopher Jones, with a detailed and splendid commentary which is one of the prime tools for the study of many of the matters considered in this chapter.[66]

Ælfric begins his letter to the monks of the recently founded and almost certainly small house at Eynsham in Oxfordshire – its foundation charter may date from 1005 and he died around 1010 – by stating his intention of putting in writing a few things concerning the book of customs (*de libro consuetudinum*) which St Æthelwold assembled (*collegit*: which is incidentally the strongest direct evidence that Æthelwold was regarded as the primary author of the *RC*). This is not, however, to be a mere copy of the *RC*: some things have been omitted as too strict (or grand? – *districtionem tante obseruantiae*) for Eynsham and some matter from Amalarius, to be noticed shortly, has been added.

In content Ælfric's treatise is potentially a strong witness to monastic liturgy in a small, modestly endowed house at the beginning of the eleventh century. But the cautious "potentially" is necessary because he nowhere provides details specific to that house (not even its dedication, which we do not know) and because his inclusion of one or two points that cannot be relevant to it must raise some doubt as to the relevance of everything else; again, this is not a service book, although he does supply rather more incipits than does the *RC*. Clearly irrelevant is his treatment of the Maundy Thursday chrism mass (section 39), which as an exclusively episcopal liturgy would be pertinent only to a cathedral establishment, like Winchester Old Minster. The allusion to infant baptisms at the Easter Vigil (*Infantes, quando baptizantur*, sect. 46), which would seem to suggest a practice surprising in a monastic house, is at best of doubtful relevance and may reflect nothing more

---

[66] C. A. Jones, *Ælfric's Letter to the Monks of Eynsham*, Cbg. Studs. in Anglo-Saxon England 24 (Cambridge 1998). This supplants the previous edition by Mary Bateson published as an appendix to *Computus Rolls of the Obedientiaries of St Swithun's Priory, Winchester*, ed. G. W. Kitchin, Hampshire Rec. Soc., s.n. (1892), pp. 171–98, under the title *Excerpta ex institutionibus monasticis Æthelwoldi ... compilata in usum fratrum Egneshamnensium per Ælfricum abbatem* (the heading in CCCC 265, the sole MS), as well as the more recent edition of H. Nocent in *Consuetudinum Saec. X/XI/XII Monumenta Non-Cluniacensia*, ed. K. Hallinger, Corpus Cons. Mon. 7/3 (Siegburg 1984), pp. 149–85.

than an uncritical adaptation of a passage from Amalarius.[67] Of the most distinctive features in the *RC*, the *Letter* retains the *Trina oratio* and prayers for the king,[68] as well as the emphasis on use of the secular offices at certain seasons such as the Triduum.

Some of the divergences are as striking as the agreements. In the *Letter* there is no specification of daily communion for the monks, no implication of a lay congregation at mass, no chasubles prescribed for deacon and subdeacon during Lent, no *Quem quaeritis* ceremony at Easter. In addition, Ælfric includes some material lacking in *RC*: instructions for the repetition of Sunday masses after Pentecost in years when, owing to an early Easter, the stock of propers has run short; insistence on three nocturns at matins during the summer, when the Rule of Benedict permits only one; and a long section on the office lectionary, which shows some dependence on the early eighth-century document known as *Ordo Romanus XIIIA*.[69] One tiny point of potential importance arises when, having given incipits for the first set of lessons and collects for the Vigil of Pentecost, Ælfric's comment that "cetera [viz, the second to fourth set, or perhaps more] sicut in missali habentur": is this an indication that Eynsham's massbook was what is now usually distinguished as *missale plenum* rather than a sacramentary?[70]

The added matter specifed in Ælfric's preface is "some points [*aliqua*] from the book of the priest Amalarius": his massive *Liber officialis*, composed in various recensions in the 820s and 830s. The presence of Amalarius in late tenth- and eleventh-century England extends beyond use of his work in Ælfric's treatise. Although expositions of and commentaries on the liturgy cannot be included as a direct part of our story, they obviously influence liturgical practice as well as reflecting it, and Amalarius is probably the most influential of those commentators for our purposes. Paths by which his work came into England have been traced by, in particular, David Dumville and Christopher Jones.[71] A primary route seems to have been from Brittany, most likely through refugees, mentioned above, at the courts of Edward the Elder

---

[67] The reference is given by Jones, p. 200. On the obscure and vexed history of the house, see his Introduction, pp. 5–17.

[68] The queen is not included in the prayers, however, as she is in *RC*; could this possibly be a reflection of the unpopularity of Emma Ælfgifu, whose reeve, the Norman Hugh, was thought to have been responsible for allowing Danes to destroy the *burh* of Exeter (*Anglo-Saxon Chronicle*, ad 1003)?

[69] See the esp. important discussion in Jones's commentary, pp. 217–21.

[70] Sect. 51; a point about which Jones is uncharacteristically silent.

[71] Dumville, *Liturgy and the Eccles. Hist.*, pp. 116, 135–6; Jones, *Ælfric's Letter, passim*; and esp. his monograph, *A Lost Work by Amalarius of Metz. Interpolations in Salisbury*,

and Athelstan. This is almost certainly the source of an abridgement of the third edition of Amalarius's massive *Liber officialis* known as the *Retractatio prima*, of which a copy was made as early as the 930s at St Augustine's, Canterbury.[72] This *Retractatio*, itself in two books, has seemed to be the only form in which Amalarius's *magnum opus* was known in pre-Conquest England. Ælfric's references do not always correspond with the mainstream text of this abridgement, however, and Jones has worked out that a variant version must have been known in England. Furthermore, this variant version, apparently best preserved in Salisbury Cathedral MS 154, turns out to contain "interpolations" so extensive that they bear witness to what Jones demonstrates convincingly can fairly be termed a "lost work" of Amalarius's, composed around 815. The bulk of the new material, mainly concerned with the *Triduum sacrum* and the daily office, includes some ceremonial details like the use of incense at the office and the distribution of candles at baptism. Overall, the contents are more important for a fuller understanding of Amalarius and his work than of the liturgy in eleventh-century England as such. Nonetheless, the fact that this "lost work" was being copied at (Old) Salisbury, in the precocious scriptorium at the new foundation towards the end of the century, and indeed that it is known *in extenso* (as distinct from Ælfric's allusions) only from that manuscript, provides a salutary caution against any blithe supposition that the Norman Conquest is going to constitute a complete watershed in matters liturgical.[73] A similar caution arises from consideration of our final witness to the Æthelwoldian tradition, one named after the Norman archbishop of Canterbury who might, had the story of the 1050s turned out differently, have crowned the next monarch after Edward the Confessor.

From an Æthelwoldian house: the Missal of Robert of Jumièges

This witness is the massbook compiled probably at either Ely or Peterborough in the early eleventh century and known, unhelpfully, as the

---

Cathedral Library MS 154, Henry Bradshaw Society Subsidia 2 (2001), with text and translation.

[72] TCC B.11.2 (241). The standard edition of *Liber officialis* is vol. II of J. M. Hanssens, *Amalarii episcopi opera liturgica omnia*, 3 vols., Studi e Testi 138–40 (Rome 1948–50). There is currently no edition of the *Retractatio*, but D. N. Dumville is understood to have one in hand.

[73] The Salisbury MS was written mostly by Teresa Webber's Scribe iii, who worked also on the pontifical, BL Cott. Tib. C.i, discussed in chapter 10 below, and on the Wiltshire Geld Accounts bound with the Exon Domesday codex at Exeter cathedral: Webber, *Scribes and Scholars*, pp. 13 and 152–53.

Missal of Robert of Jumièges.[74] That nickname, as well as the fact that the manuscript has long resided in the Bibliothèque publique at Rouen (MS Y.6 [274]), arises from its ownership in the middle of the century by the Norman Robert Champart, appointed by Edward the Confessor as Archbishop of Canterbury in 1051 and ejected the next year during the successful coup of the Godwin family after their short-lived exile. Having previously been abbot of Jumièges, Robert became bishop of London in 1044, and, according to an inscription on the last leaf of this decidedly English book, while in that office he gave it to the monks of his former house. It may say something about the prestige of reformed English monasticism that a Norman monk-bishop came to possess (it is not known how) a massbook of the previous generation owned by an English bishop who was most likely himself a monk.[75] The book is tall and thin (342 x 220 mm) and decorated with thirteen (probably sixteen originally) full-page miniatures and much other ornamentation, all in the style of the Winchester School, of which it is indeed one of the great monuments.[76] That it is monastic in origin is plain from the inclusion of a dozen prayers to be said in various parts of a monastery; that it is, equally, designed for episcopal use, is shown from the pontifical elements provided for reconciling penitents, making clerics, and blessing virgins and widows. It is hard to believe that such a sumptuous book was not made for a specific person, as Æthelwold's benedictional clearly was, but no obvious candidate suggests himself. Arguments in favor of either Ely or Peterborough are not conclusive (neither house was a cathedral priory at that time, both being in the rather amorphous diocese of Dorchester); and the preponderant opinion about dating points to the first fifteen years or so of the century.[77]

Perhaps because H. A. Wilson's fine edition is over a century old, the contents of the Robert of Jumièges book have not been as well integrated into our awareness of the subject under discussion as its importance demands. How far there may lie behind it a Continental model

---

[74] Edited by H. A. Wilson, *The Missal of Robert of Jumièges*, HBS 11 (1896). The calendar was printed again, along with that of Bodl. Hatton 113 (the Wulfstan homiliary) by I. Atkins, "An Investigation of two Anglo-Saxon Kalendars," *Archaeologia* 78 (1928), pp. 219–54; F. Wormald cited the latter study as his rationale for not including the Robert of Jumièges calendar in his *Eng. Kals* (p. vi) – although he gave it a number (15) and reprinted the Wulfstan calendar as no. 16!

[75] This simple statement seems worth uttering in the light of the commonplace that the monk-bishops of the early eleventh century were mostly succeeded by secular clergy from the Continent: see, e.g., F. Barlow, *The English Church 1000–1066: a Constitutional History*, 2nd edn (London 1979), ch. i.4, esp. pp. 62–68.

[76] Temple, *Anglo-Saxon MSS*, no. 72 and ills. 237–40; she dates the book c. 1020.

[77] A summary of the relevant evidence as to place of origin and date is in Pfaff, *Liturg. Bks ASE*, pp. 15–19.

is less to the point than whether it can fairly be taken to represent Æthelwoldian tradition, both Ely and Peterborough being among his (re-)foundations. That is, does this codex provide further clues to the notional Æthelwoldian massbook we speculated about earlier? (We note that a separate benedictional, such as Æthelwold had, is implied by the absence of episcopal blessings from the Robert of Jumièges book.)

Its overall structure and contents show the book to be fundamentally a late Gregorian sacramentary with many Young Gelasian traces and with the Benedict of Aniane Supplement thoroughly integrated. Analysis of the saints who have proper masses in the sanctorale, of the (somewhat discrepant) singling out of feasts for special treatment in the calendar, of special invocations in the litany, and of a few other places at which specific saints are mentioned, points almost equally to Ely and Peterborough, with Winchester (Old Minster) also somewhat plausible.[78] On blank leaves before the calendar the original scribe has copied mass-forms for Guthlac, Edward the Martyr (both Deposition and Translation), Botulf, Alban, and Kenelm – all of whom had been in the calendar but not the original sanctorale. Each of these masses has a proper preface (which is not always the case with masses in the sanctorale); those for Guthlac and for both masses for Edward seem to be unique, while that for Alban appears only in "Leofric C" (which is somewhat later; see p. 73). It looks as though these masses may represent concerted original liturgical composition, on the part either of this scribe or of someone who instructed him. The same scribe wrote, integrally as it seems, some eighteen rubrics in Old English for ministration to the sick, in the context of the *Missa pro infirmis* (why here, and here alone, in the manuscript, is the vernacular used?).[79]

This scribe wrote as well all or part of four notable gospel books, of which three look to be connected with Canterbury, the fourth probably with Peterborough.[80] Some clarity as to the nature of this often puzzling massbook may emerge if this scribe is ever identified; if he could be shown to have moved from Peterborough to Canterbury, as seems not inconceivable, he might have taken the book with him, or written

[78] The most detailed anaylsis is that of C. Hohler, "Les Saints insulaires dans le missel de l'Archevêque Robert," in *Jumièges: Congrés scientifique du XIIIe centenaire*, 2 vols (Rouen 1955), I. 293–303 [in English].

[79] In Wilson's edn, pp. 286–95, and pl. xiv, illustrating fol. 207; studied by M.-M. Dubois, "Les Rubriques en Vieil Anglais," *Jumièges* (as above), I.305–8.

[80] Respectively, TCC B.10.4 ("Trinity gospels"), of which he wrote all; parts of BL Royal 1 D.ix and BL Loan 11 ("Kederminster gospels"), both attributed to Christ Church c. 1020; and Copenhagen, Roy. Lib. G.K.S. 10, 2°, a slightly earlier book possibly written at Peterborough: Temple, *Anglo-Saxon MSS*, nos. 65, 70, 71, and 47.

it for presentation to an archbishop such as Æthelnoth (1020–38) or even the king.[81] That fine service books were sometimes written for, so to speak, export is plain from the story in William of Malmesbury's *Vita Wulfstani* (concerning which more will be said, p. 128) about the sacramentary and psalter that (St) Wulfstan's teacher at Peterborough, Earnwig (later abbot there, 1041–52), illuminated and presented to King Cnut and Queen Emma.[82] Cnut gave that sacramentary to the German imperial court at Cologne (whence it was returned, amazingly, and became Wulfstan's possession), but there is no reason to think that this is a unique case, and it may be relevant that Cnut showed Æthelnoth several signs of conspicuous favor.

Æthelnoth and the Christ Church, Canterbury benedictional

The most outstanding ecclesiastical event at Canterbury during Æthelnoth's tenure there was the translation on 8 June 1023 of relics of the martyred archbishop Ælfheah (slaughtered by drunken Danes on 19 April 1012) from their temporary resting place in London to the newly prepared shrine beside the high altar of the cathedral. The feasts of his death and his translation are useful dating-points for several eleventh-century documents, e.g., the Eadui psalter (BL Arundel 155), the calendar of which contains the former event and not the latter, and thus (since it is clearly a Christ Church book) is datable to 1012–23. Cnut, in his post-coronation guise as a great Englishman and protector of the church, was much involved with Christ Church, in ways connected with its prize scribe Eadui Basan as well as with Æthelnoth, who had been monk and dean there.[83] We have just seen that it is conceivable that the

---

[81] Such an explanation might account for the fact that Dunstan is missing from the calendar, which comes at the beginning of the codex and was presumably written first, whereas the sanctorale contains a proper mass, with preface and two *Ad vesperum* prayers and headed in gold like thirty-four other feasts of major importance. Astonishingly, these propers seem peculiar to the Robert of Jumièges book. The question of movement of monks, in theory vowed to stability at their original houses, to other abbeys needs study; pointed here is the case of Æthelnoth, who had begun as a monk of Glastonbury before joining the cathedral priory at Christ Church.

[82] *William of Malmesbury, Saints' Lives*, ed. and tr. M. Winterbottom and R. M. Thomson, OMT (2002), p. 16. T. A. Heslop, "The Production of De Luxe Manuscripts and the Patronage of King Cnut and Queen Emma," *ASE* 19 (1990), pp. 151–95 at 159–62, muses on similarities between Wulfstan's (now lost) book and the Robert of Jumièges missal.

[83] See Brooks, *Early Hist. Cant.*, pp. 287–96; and my article "Eadui Basan, 'Scriptorum Princeps'?" in *England in the Eleventh Century*, ed. C. Hicks (Stamford 1992), pp. 267–83, repr. Pfaff, *LCSSME*.

Robert of Jumièges massbook was at Canterbury in that archbishop's time. That aside, no other direct witness to mass- or office-liturgy there survives; this is odd, because at least three distinctively episcopal books made at Christ Church in this period are extant.[84] Although they cannot be considered here in detail, we do need at this point to notice the one known as the Canterbury benedictional (BL Harley 2892), made there around 1030.[85]

In the introduction to his 1917 edition of this benedictional R. M. Woolley commented mainly on the blessings for individual saints, some eighty in number, and reconstructed a calendar of the days on which the special blessings were to be pronounced. This gives us an idea of the most important saints' feasts in liturgies at Christ Church after 1023 – Ælfheah's Translation feast is prominent – and before whatever changes come about in the wake of the Norman Conquest. Besides Ælfheah, Dunstan, and of course Augustine, the saints distinctive to Christ Church are those whose relics had come there in the recent past: Blaise, Austroberta, Salvius, Audoen, perhaps Bartholomew and (problematically: there were other claimants to the same bones) Mildred.[86] Ælfheah had been bishop of Winchester before being translated to Canterbury, and Winchester tradition is certainly apparent: Swithun (the 2 July feast), Æthelwold, Birinus; probably Ætheldrytha, from Æthelwoldian Ely, should be counted here. The most intriguing inclusions are blessings for the Presentation (21 November) and Conception (8 December) of Mary, which may reflect Winchester influence but seem equally likely to be original to Canterbury.[87] The book contains several other *ordines*: the rites for Ash Wednesday, Palm Sunday (at some length), Maundy Thursday, and Candlemas. One of these, the Maundy Thursday blessing of oils, was recopied, with only slight changes, on the first sixteen folios of the present codex (codicologically self-contained, two quires of eight) in an astonishingly large hand, the letters being seven to eleven millimeters in height as compared

---

[84] Three are pontificals, now known as Anderson (BL Add. 57337), Claudius II (BL Cott. Claud. A.iii, fols 9–18, 87–105; ed. D. H. Turner, *The Claudius Pontificals*, HBS 97, 1971), and Corpus-Canterbury (CCCC 44), still unedited; the fourth is the benedictional under discussion.

[85] R. M. Woolley, ed. *The Canterbury Benedictional*, HBS 51 (1917; repr. Woodbridge 1995).

[86] Summarized in Pfaff, "The Calendar," in *Eadwine Psalter*, pp. 66, 67n, 69, 71, 77.

[87] E. Bishop, "On the Origins of the Feast of the Conception," *Liturg. Hist.*, pp. 238–59; Pfaff, *New Liturg. Feasts*, pp. 103–15; M. Clayton, *The Cult of the Virgin Mary in Anglo-Saxon England*, Cbg. Studs. in Anglo-Saxon England 2 (Cambridge 1990), pp. 42–47, 85–88. Most distinctive here is the term *Presentatio*; Winchester-related sources seem always to use *Oblatio*.

with four to seven in the rest of the book. The likeliest explanation would seem to be an archbishop's failing eyesight, and it is tempting to relate this to the fact that in the last four years of his episcopate Æthelnoth was (had to be?) assisted by his eventual successor Eadsige, as a *chorepiscopus*.[88] The recopied section does not quite extend to the end of the Chrism mass, and it is possible that other quires were written, or at least intended, in the same giant script. In any case, a rubric within that mass makes plain that the book was very likely part of a pontifical.[89]

All the evidence considered in the last several sections testifies to liturgy in monastic settings: those of Winchester Old Minster, Eynsham, Ely *or* Peterborough, and Canterbury Christ Church (the latter certainly monastic after about 1000). A handful of other witnesses from massbooks of the same sort could be adduced: the so-called Winchcombe sacramentary (Orléans, B.m. 127 [105]), almost but not quite certainly written for that abbey; four quires from a missal, made probably at the Old Minster, now at Worcester cathedral (F.173); perhaps a substantial fragment of thirteen bifolia pasted inside the binding leather of the twelfth-century survey known as the Winton Domesday (now London, Society of Antiquaries 154*; it may have been written in Brittany and possibly used at Winchester Nunnaminster); a plenary missal, but lacking everything before Easter Friday, definitely from Winchester New Minster and perhaps of the 1070s (Le Havre, B.m. 330); and a sacramentary written in the 1090s, and subsequently much altered and added to, for Canterbury St Augustine's (CCCC 270).[90] (The dates of the last two of these compel us to consider them at some length in the next chapter.) But all are in a sense variations on a theme, and rather than considering each individually we had better now turn attention to whatever connection can be established between this rich monastic context and possible secular use.

[88] Brooks, *Early History*, p. 258 and n.

[89] "Postmodum duo cantores altiboando incipiant letanias ut supra in dedicatione ęcclesię continentur": fol. 71 (edn p. 38) and, in the recopied section, fol. 8; Woolley did not print this section, supplying instead a list of the slight variants, pp. xi–xii.

[90] Each of these is treated in my chapter on massbooks in Pfaff, *Liturg. Bks. ASE*, pp. 14–32. Three have been edited: by A. Davril, *The Winchcombe Sacramentary*, HBS 109 (1995); D. H. Turner, *The Missal of the New Minster*, HBS 93 (1962); and M. Rule, *The Missal of St Augustine's, Canterbury* (Cambridge 1896; the lengthy introduction is wildly eccentric). The Worcester fragments were presented by F. E. Warren, "An Anglo-Saxon Missal at Worcester," *The Academy* 28 (1885), pp. 394–95, and the Winton Domesday leaves by F. Wormald, "Fragments of a Tenth-Century Sacramentary," in *Winchester in the Early Middle Ages*, ed. M. Biddle, Winchester Studies 1 (Oxford 1976), pp. 541–49.

The Red Book of Darley: extrapolation to a possibly secular context

Such a connection might be hoped for in the enigmatic, and still unedited, codex known as the Red Book of Darley (CCCC 422). The nickname is the least puzzling thing about the book: it arises from a sixteenth-century inscription on the last pages, "The rede boke of darleye in the peake in darbyshire." There was scant monastic presence in Derbyshire in the eleventh century and nothing at all at Darley (until a small Augustinian house was founded in the mid-twelfth century): hence the hope, by default, that the book witnesses to secular use. It is certainly substantial, with some 544 pages (the book is paginated, not foliated) of eleventh-century liturgical material, to which a further sixteen pages of *liturgica* were added in the twelfth century – which is probably also when the first thirteen leaves, a mid-tenth-century copy of both the prose and verse forms of the dialogues *Solomon and Saturn*, were supplied to make the present composite book. The main section consists of paschal tables for 1061–96 (making a date in the 1060s likely), a calendar, a large part of a rather eccentric sacramentary, material for occasional and miscellaneous offices (notably ordeals and exorcisms), and a highly selective supply of daily offices.[91]

These contents are fitful, yet the physical presentation is impressive and some of the illustration elaborate. As it stands, the sacramentary section begins in the middle of the mass *ordo*, with two illustrations of art-historical importance. A highly unusual (indeed, unique?) combination of saints is included in the *Communicantes* section of the canon: Hilary, Martin, Benedict, Gregory, Augustine, Amand, and a thoroughly puzzling Caurentius (seemingly not a miswriting of Laurentius, who appears several names earlier). There is neither temporale nor

---

[91] The fullest description is that of M. Budny, *Insular, Anglo-Saxon, and Early Anglo-Norman Manuscript Art at Corpus Christi College, Cambridge: an Illustrated Catalogue*, 2 vols (Kalamazoo 1997), I.645–66, where each of the illustrations – to calendar and tables, important Christ in mandorla and Crucifixion depictions at the canon (both illustrated in color, vol II, pl. xii), and nearly two hundred other initials – is described separately; five text pages are reproduced in II, ills. 604–8. The mass-book contents are treated (by me) in Pfaff, ed. *Liturg. Bks ASE*, pp. 21–24, the office material (by A. Corrêa) on pp. 56–57. Recently Helen Gittos has used the MS as her main witness while studying "Is there any evidence for the Liturgy of Parish Churches in Late Anglo-Saxon England? The Red Book of Darley and the Status of Old English," in *Pastoral Care in Late Anglo-Saxon England*, ed. F. Tinti (Woodbridge 2005), pp. 63–82. She emphasizes mainly the vernacular element in the baptismal rite, especially appropriate here because, as she points out, "Darley's material for the occasional offices is the most substantial that survives in any pre-Conquest book" (p. 69). The entire MS is now online through the Stanford-Parker [Corpus Christi] Library website.

sanctorale as such, only an exceptionally extensive common of saints and a long series of votive masses, followed by masses for two saints on specific days, Olaf of Norway (martyred in 1030) for 29 July and Nicholas on 6 December.[92] For some masses full forms are given, for others only the celebrant's prayers.[93] There are strong indications of South English monastic influence, but they are not conclusive for any one house: the presence of a daily votive mass for Swithun suggests an Old Minster origin; emphasis in the calendar on Wulfsige (III, bishop of Sherborne c. 993–1002) points to Sherborne; while the New Minster seems implied by capitalization in the litany only of Grimbald, its first head. And the office material includes, besides the lengthy services of the *Triduum sacrum* (for which, as we have seen, the secular form is used by monks), the Office of the Dead and the common of saints in the twelve-lesson – and therefore monastic – form of matins, and with some notation.

These factors make it hard to suppose what might otherwise seem probable, that the book is intended as a liturgical vade mecum, perhaps for a monk-missionary (itself an anomaly in the eleventh century?). Mildred Budny's characterization of the book as "a portable service book ... . One of the few surviving Anglo-Saxon liturgical manuscripts of various types to combine different types of service books, participating in the development of the breviary in its full form," makes it seem a bit more coherent than looks to be the case. She raises the possibility that the presence of a mass of St Helen in the added final quire is related to the establishment of the small Augustinian house at Darley, the original dedication of which may have been to Helen.[94] But (as has not previously been noticed) the lessons at matins in the two sanctorale offices of that same final quire are in number four for Alexander, Eventius, and Theodolus, and eight for the Invention of the Cross – both feasts fall on May 3rd – thus adding up to a feast of twelve lessons; so again the context of the additional material must be monastic, not canonical.[95] In short, tempted as we are by the Derbyshire provenance to suppose

---

[92] I have expanded on the implication of the inclusion of both Caurentius and Olaf in *Liturg. Bks ASE*.

[93] Gittos, p. 69, corrects my earlier statement that in the full masses epistle lessons are provided but only tags for gospel lessons, so that a separate gospel book would have been needed; sometimes, as she points out, it is the other way round. This intensifies the puzzle.

[94] Binns, *Dedications*, p. 131, lays out the difficulty of being firm about the house's dedication.

[95] Budny (as above), p. 648, straightening out a confusion in C. Hohler, "The Red Book of Darley," *Nordiskt Kollokvium II i latinsk Liturgiforskning* (Stockholm 1972), pp. 39–47.

that this book was used in that county in the eleventh century, there is no convincing reason to do so. This dead, or at least inconclusive, end, may cause us to ponder a wider problem, whether we are bemoaning the lack of a kind of evidence that seldom, if ever, existed.

How widely was the secular office observed in late Anglo-Saxon England?

A major difficulty in looking for evidence for secular liturgy is that if a service book pertains to the mass there are unlikely to be telling differences between a monastic and a secular book, whereas with material pertaining to the office – where the difference is plain enough if the matter at hand comes from a Sunday or great feast (save for those days on which the secular office was used in the monastic rite: a further complication) – the question of where such material might have been used if secular poses a real difficulty. For example, some clues as to liturgy in minster churches, a matter raised at the beginning of this chapter, might be discernible in the five folios and three fragments that form the flyleaves of a thirteenth-century cartulary of Muchelney abbey in Somerset (BL Add. 56488) and are all that survive of a mid(?)-eleventh century breviary. The book to which these leaves belonged may or may not be monastic; Alicia Corrêa, who has studied them briefly, could find no stronger indication from their contents than that there seems to be no break between matins and lauds, which is a likely indication of secular practice.[96] But that is a slender thread indeed.

Lacking anything more substantial, one is tempted to consider the possibility that English secular clergy in the tenth and eleventh centuries tended not to perform the daily office unless in the few large communities, mainly cathedrals, that remained secular after the Æthelwoldian reforms; or indeed, the even more radical possibility that the secular clerks who are replaced by monks in the communities at the Old Minster in 964, and subsequently at the New Minster and Chertsey and Milton and eventually Christ Church and Worcester (and perhaps other places as well), did not keep the office either, and that this is part of the gravamen that justifies their expulsion. The passage in Wulfstan the Cantor's life of Æthelwold (and repeated in Ælfric's abridged life) which provides the *locus classicus* for the deficiencies of the ejected canons at the Old Minster includes the accusation that not a few disdained to celebrate *missas suo ordine*.[97] Quite apart from the ambiguity of *suo ordine* (does it

---

[96] "Daily Office Books," in Pfaff, ed. *Liturg. Bks. ASE*, pp. 58–60.

[97] *Wulfstan, Life of St Æthelwold* (above, n. 42), p. 30 (cap. 16). The editors, Winterbottom and Lapidge, print as an appendix Ælfric's *Life*, where the same words appear

refer to a fixed rota or to priestly obligation?), two inferences might be drawn from this: that if the peccant clerics scorned even to say mass, it would seem highly unlikely that they would be scrupulous about the office; and (or?) that Wulfstan might have intended the word *missas* to include all the regular services, offices as well as mass.[98]

An obvious test may be the appearance of canticles in psalters. Caution has to be exercised here, because the question of the extent to which psalters can be regarded as evidence of liturgical practice is a difficult one: any sensible answer will vary from case to case, depending partly on the date of the manuscript in question and partly on its size and sumptuousness. Probably it is safe to assume that, while the presence of canticles in a given psalter is not proof of liturgical use, their absence is a strong indication that the book is not so intended. The most succinct summary of the contents and character of all extant psalters produced or used in England before 1100 is that of Phillip Pulsiano, who enumerates (1) four "written in England in the pre-Reform period," (2) eighteen of the later tenth and eleventh centuries, and (3) six brought to England at that same time.[99] Of those in the directly relevant group (2), all save three or four seem to have a monastic origin. Of those that might be secular, one (BL Harley 863) is part of Leofric's liturgical program at Exeter, to be discussed in the next chapter; two (Bodl. Laud lat. 81, almost a miniature book, and BN lat. 8824) are described merely as "of unknown English origin" and could be monastic in character; one, the Salisbury psalter (Salisbury cathedral, MS 150) might conceivably be secular but seems more likely to have been written at the nunnery at Shaftesbury. So there is no clear example of a psalter that comes unambiguously out of a secular context save possibly Harley 863. The distinctive "monastic canticles" – sets of three to be used at great occasions in Benedictine houses – are present only in the Bosworth (BL Add. 37517) and Eadui (BL Arundel 155) psalters, but in the latter are a twelfth-century addition.

So evidence from psalters does not offer much help towards the basic question as to how widely or regularly the secular office was performed. In Ælfric's first Old English letter to Wulfstan (above, p. 67), a detailed enumeration of the work of the first four General Councils (through

---

(cap. 12; p. 75). In the next chapter in both lives, the wicked canons are depicted as singing the communio at the end of mass on the first Saturday in Lent; so even these hagiographers acknowledge that the sacrament was being celebrated at some times by the despised clerics.

[98] This may not be as far-fetched as it seems; the Rule of Benedict, esp. cap. 17, uses *missae* in ways that apply to the concluding prayers of the office: see note 40 in J. McCann's parallel text edn of the *Rule* (London 1952).

[99] "Psalters," in Pfaff, ed. *Liturg. Bks, ASE*, pp. 61–85, esp. 81–84.

Chalcedon, 451) is followed by a list, first in Latin then in English, of the hours, as having supposedly been established by those synods; this concludes with the injunction that "You must sing these canonical hours with much care, daily in church, in praise of our Lord, and likewise celebrate mass."[100] There is no suggestion that the daily office is any kind of innovation. Nonetheless, it remains striking that no shred of evidence seems to exist for the office at this period for the cathedral establishments at London, Hereford, Wells, Dorchester, Ramsbury, Selsey, Rochester, Elmham, Lichfield, York, or Durham (moved from Chester-le-Street, 995).[101] This dry listing of all the cathedrals staffed by secular clergy in, say, 1000 brings home what may otherwise not appear obvious: that a burden of proof lies with the assumption that the office *was* regularly performed in such communities.[102] The closest we can come to certainty is with the new cathedral foundation at Exeter under its first bishop (1050–72), the energetic bibliophile and liturgist Leofric.

Towards (inevitably) Lanfranc and the Anglo-Norman regime

Although Leofric's liturgical work could suitably be included in the present chapter, it fits somewhat better into the next (and echoes of it will be heard in the work of a succcessor as bishop of Exeter some three hundred years later; see chapter 12). A similar transitional aspect characterizes three other episcopates that begin between 1050 and 1061 and last well into the reign of William the Conqueror or beyond: those of Giso at Wells (1061–88), Ealdred at York (1061–69, but earlier at Worcester 1044–62), and Wulfstan at Worcester (1062–95). Consideration – again, in the next chapter – of evidence connected with each may help, at least in a small way, to balance the abundant evidence available for the monastic regimes. It remains true, however, that throughout the eleventh century (and indeed beyond) even the greatest secular churches are ill documented liturgically. Just as has been the present chapter, the

---

[100] *C & S 871–1204*, I.276.

[101] There is not even, to the best of my knowledge, any direct evidence for the performance of the office at Canterbury Christ Church before it becomes monastic (when, is a matter of some dispute, but by c. 1025 anyhow). Rochester and Durham become monastic only after the Norman Conquest.

[102] Even the appearance in calendars of major feasts graded with indications of the telltale nine or twelve lessons is not available for this period; the practice of extensive grading seems to begin no earlier than the twelfth century. The numbers sometimes placed in the margins of saints' lives, indicating division into lessons at matins, are almost always impossible to date.

next will be heavily weighted towards those monastic establishments for which there survive documents that enable us to get some substantial sense of the materials out of which worship was conducted. The most important of these is a set of regulations, the so-called *Monastic Constitutions*, issued by the Conqueror's new archbishop of Canterbury, Lanfranc – with whom any consideration of the English church after the Norman Conquest must begin.

A note on gospel books

An avenue of exploration not systematically pursued in the present work is that offered by gospel books. Although they have been intensively worked on, the major contributions have all had a thrust oblique to our primary concerns. Five may be mentioned here. In 1907 Stephan Beissel studied pericope-lists of various kinds up through about the year 1000, in pursuit of (as his subtitle makes plain) the history of gospel books in the first half of the middle ages.[103] His work adduces almost no manuscripts relevant to England save the Lindisfarne gospels (discussed above, p. 39). A few more such manuscripts are included in W. H. Frere's investigation of the Roman gospel lectionary, one of the three volumes of his *Studies in Early Roman Liturgy*. The thrust is therefore early, and his avowed purpose is to trace what he thought was "a fairly clear line of historical development which emerges from a study of the Gospel-books, though details remain obscure."[104] The typology he developed for this purpose is elaborate and complicated, and the book is correspondingly difficult to use. A comparable enterprise is that of Theodor Klauser, who mentions hundreds of manuscripts, some of them quite late, towards his goal of tracing the "oldest history" of what again he defines in the singular as *the* Roman gospel-lectionary tradition.[105] The entire approach – primarily, the establishment of typologies and regional traditions – is summed up in an extensive section of Cyrille Vogel's *Sources*, often referred to in these pages. Little is discernible about England, save that it is generally assigned to the

[103] S. Beissel, *Entstehung der Perikopen des römischen Messbuches, zur Geschichte der Evangelienbücher in der ersten hälfte des Mittelalters* (Freiburg 1907; repr. Rome 1967).

[104] W. H. Frere, *The Roman Gospel-Lectionary*, ACC 30 (1934), p. iv. Vol. I of his *Studies* is *The Kalendar*, ACC 28 (1930), vol. III *The Roman Epistle-Lectionary*, ACC 32 (1935).

[105] T. Klauser, *Das römische Capitulare Evangeliorum: Texte und Untersuchungen zu seiner ältesten Geschichte*, Liturgiewissenschaftliche Quellen und Forschungen 28 (Münster 1935, corrected and supplemented edn 1972. The title page reads "I. Typen," but no second volume appeared).

Roman tradition.[106] Directly focused on England is a massive study of Ursula Lenker, directed in the first instance at vernacular (West Saxon dialect) gospel-versions but containing a great deal of information about Latin evangeliaries as well.[107] Like the other works mentioned, it tends to regard lectionary systems as self-contained entities. While it is certainly true that pericope lists can be assembled and studied synthetically, the results are somewhat desiccated when divorced from the fuller considerations the present book tries to keep juggling.

---

[106] Vogel, *Sources*, pp. 291–355; this covers epistle as well as gospel readings. A most useful catalogue-study is P. McGurk, *Latin Gospel Books from A.D. 400 to A.D. 800* (Paris and Brussels 1961); its temporal limits rule out much use here.

[107] U. Lenker, *Die westsächsische Evangelienversion und die Perikopenordnungen im angelsächsischen England*, Münchener Universitäts-Schriften, Texte und Untersuchungen zur Englischen Philologie 20 (Munich 1997).

4   The Norman Conquest: cross fertilizations

It would be unreasonable to suppose that what is conventionally known as the Norman Conquest, beginning (just barely) with William I's victory at Hastings on 14 October 1066, made an immediate and decisive difference in the practice of the liturgy throughout England. It would be equally unreasonable to maintain that by, say, the deaths of William II in August of 1100 or of Anselm in April of 1109 the overall picture of the liturgy in England showed no marked influence as a consequence of ecclesiastical developments connected with the new regime. The present chapter will attempt to sketch a picture characterized by something of a balance between the "English" aspects predominant in the previous chapter and marks of the new Norman presence. First, though, it may be useful to indicate the picture's dimensions.

In structural terms, the number of provinces and dioceses did not change from what it had been in 1065. York continued as an archbishopric, even though its province contained only itself and Durham (which became monastic in 1083). Canterbury continued to have twelve suffragan sees, but there were six changes in location: Dorchester to Lincoln in 1072, Selsey to Chichester in 1075, Lichfield to Chester in 1075 (eventually to Coventry, 1102), Sherborne (incorporating Ramsbury) to Salisbury ("Old Sarum") in 1078, Wells to Bath in 1088, Elmham to Thetford in about 1091 and thence to Norwich in 1095.[1] The English phenomenon of the monastic cathedral, unknown in Normandy, survived, and indeed grew stronger with the addition of Bath and Norwich, and also of Rochester (which became monastic around 1080) and eventually of both Coventry and the newly founded (1109) see of Ely.[2]

---

[1] The sees continuing in the old locations are London, Winchester, Worcester, Hereford, Rochester, and Exeter (only from 1050). A clear account of these changes, and excellent overview, is F. Barlow, *The English Church 1066–1154* (London 1979), esp. pp. 29–53.

[2] By 1110, therefore, the number of monastic cathedrals was nine, of secular seven. The only subsequent alterations are the establishment of the Augustinian house at Carlisle as the center of a bishopric in 1133 and of dual episcopal seats at Coventry-and-Lichfield in 1228 and Bath-and-Wells c. 1245.

There was, however, a conspicuous proliferation of religious houses. At least half a dozen major Benedictine houses were founded: in the South, at Battle in Sussex (1067, the Conqueror's penance after Hastings); in the North, at York (St Mary's), Selby, and, as just mentioned, Durham; in the West, at Shrewsbury; in East Anglia, at Norwich (the new cathedral priory). In the last quarter of the century Cluniac monasticism came into England with the establishment of several substantial houses.[3] (The great period for the proliferation of Augustinian houses was to be the first quarter of the twelfth century, of Cistercians the second quarter.)

In ethos as well as structure, something of a balance may be discerned in the contrast between the legacy of the "English" past and the immediacy of the "Norman" presence. But the contrast must not be too glaringly drawn. Even if one posits a continuing grandeur to the Æthelwoldian-Dunstanian tradition, the preponderance of those figures and of subsidiary figures like Oswald of Worcester or Ælfric of Eynsham or Wulfstan of York was tempered in mid-century by, most notably, Lotharingian churchmen of the stamp of Leofric of Exeter and Giso of Wells, as well as by some Frenchmen of whom Robert of Jumièges is a notable example. If the obvious concrete starting point for this chapter is the work of Lanfranc, we must keep in mind that he did not enter on a liturgical *tabula rasa*; in no sense is he the Norman equivalent of Augustine of Canterbury in the early 600s.

The work of Lanfranc

Lanfranc, since 1063 abbot of St Stephen's, Caen, was consecrated archbishop of Canterbury on August 29th, 1070; his predecessor, the (perhaps unwarrantedly) notorious Stigand, had been deposed the previous April. All of the new archbishop's other activities, ecclesiastical, political, and intellectual, aside, he faced two challenges of a broadly liturgical sort.[4] The first had to do with the rebuilding of his cathedral, which had burned, virtually to the ground, in 1067. If, as appears to be

---

[3] See p. 243. Relevant to the present work will be those at Lewes, Much Wenlock, Bermondsey, Castle Acre, and Pontefract, all founded between 1077 and 1090. When the important abbey at Reading was refounded by Henry I in 1121 it was largely, though not officially, Cluniac.

[4] Two outstanding monographs and two excellent editions make Lanfranc an attractive object of study: Margaret Gibson, *Lanfranc of Bec* (Oxford 1978); H. E. J. Cowdrey, *Lanfranc: Scholar, Monk, and Archbishop* (Oxford 2003); *The Letters of Lanfranc*, ed. and tr. H. Clover and M. Gibson, OMT (1979); *The Monastic Constitutions of Lanfranc*, ed. and tr. D. Knowles, revised edn by C. N. L. Brooke, OMT (2002). Knowles's original edition was a NMT volume, Edinburgh 1951; this was reprinted, with fuller

the case, he was consecrated there, it must have been in what is described as "a temporary shed within the blackened ruins";[5] although, according to the *Acta Lanfranci*, less than four months later Thomas of Bayeux, archbishop-elect of York, was examined by Lanfranc "ante altare Christi," the usual designation for the high altar at Canterbury.[6] In any case, the broad statement that the new cathedral was built according to Lanfranc's specifications and modelled on the Romanesque churches of Normandy (above all, on St Stephen's, under construction at the same time), seems generally accurate, as does the seven-year building chronology according to which the new building was consecrated on October 4th, 1077. The "westwork" which the late Anglo-Saxon building almost certainly had was not replicated in the new design; everything in Lanfranc's church seems to have faced east.

Lanfranc's involvement in the building of the new cathedral was but one of his many responsibilities. As primate – "of all England," as the title eventually became after settlement of the long and vexed "Primacy Struggle" with the archbishops of York – he would have been at least aware of, if not actively involved in, attempts to secure the higher standard of liturgical observance that had been expressed in canons probably promulgated at the legatine Council of Winchester in April of 1070, four months before his consecration.[7] These sixteen canons, of which only the capitula survive, include prohibitions against (6) celebrations of the mass using ale or even water rather than wine, (16) the use of brass(?) chalices, (5) altars not made of stone, (7) baptisms outside of the traditional times of Easter and Pentecost save in cases of mortal danger, (4) ordinations outside of the Ember seasons. But they also inveigh against ordination *per symoniacam heresim* and against clerics who do not live *caste*: the twin insistences on prelatial elections free from secular interference and on clerical celibacy being those that in the 1070s mark the Gregorian reform program. These canons should therefore not be seen as proof positive of a lax, even decayed, English church (there are some parallels in canons of contemporary Continental councils); that we are meant to assume that the notional priest who says mass with a wooden altar and ale in a brass chalice is almost certainly not living in

---

apparatus, as *Decreta Lanfranci*, in the series Corpus Consuetudinum Monasticarum 3 (Siegburg 1967; bound with 4, *Consuetudines Beccenses*, ed. M. P. Dickson).

[5] F. Woodman, *The Architectural History of Canterbury Cathedral* (London 1981), p. 27, with no source-reference, and I can find no contemporary source for the statement.

[6] Gibson, p. 213: a late 11th-cent. addition to the Parker MS (CCCC 173) of the *Anglo-Saxon Chronicle*, ed. C. Plummer, *Two of the Saxon Chronicles Parallel* (Oxford 1892), I.288, cf. J. Bately, *The Anglo-Saxon Chronicle, a Collaborative Edition*, 3: *MS A* (Cambridge 1986), pp. 84–100.

[7] Printed *C & S 871–1204*, II.575–76.

celibacy and has been ordained by a bishop chosen and invested by the monarch is a picture too tidily tendentious to be wholly convincing.

In any case, the councils at which Lanfranc presided himself seem to have been more concerned with matters structural (like the moving of diocesan centers) and disciplinary (mainly clerical marriage) than liturgical. Only at the first, at Winchester in April 1072, was much attention paid to anything like ordinary secular liturgy: the first two of its fourteen canons deal with the circumstances of infant baptism; the ninth prescribes that every priest should say three masses *pro rege* (all other clerics are to say *unum psalterium*, as part of a campaign against the resistance – here called treason, *proditio* – of the sort that had been widespread in England during the previous months); and the final four clarify what seem to be tiny details about the scheduling of Ember days and three feast days in the late spring and summer.[8]

Two of these last four canons are instructive, however. Canon 11 provides that if the feast of Augustine [of Canterbury], May 26th, should fall on the vigil of Pentecost it should be celebrated the previous day. This was a situation that was about to occur and that would recur in six years (and all years when Easter falls on April 8th). An editorial footnote in *Councils and Synods* states, "Just such arrangements are forbidden in C[ouncil]. of Rouen (1072), c. 23." So it looks as though someone is making a point here about the importance of a distinctively English feast – and it is hard to suppose that Lanfranc did not at least concur. Less clear is the point of the final canon, which specifies that Bartholomew should be celebrated on the feast day of St Audoen, August 24th, *transmarino mare*, in accord with practice across the sea. Bartholomew had appeared in pre-1100 English calendars most often on the 25th and Audoen on the 24th, and this seems to have been the case at Christ Church, which by the late eleventh century claimed to possess important relics of both saints: and which in turn makes it improbable that the intent of this canon is that Audoen's feast is to be in effect suppressed in England. *Transmarino mare* must in any case refer to Normandy, and it could scarcely be supposed that the Duke of Normandy's archbishop should be complicit in diminishing the importance of Audoen (the great saint of Rouen), in favor of Bartholomew.[9]

---

[8] Printed *C & S 871–1204*, II.605–7. The rule about the Ember days got summarized in five lines of Latin verse ascribed to Lanfranc in the computistical tables of a late 12th-cent. psalter written by a priest named Simon and containing a Christ Church calendar; it belonged not long thereafter to the Bedfordshire nunnery at Harrold (formerly Bristol, Baptist College, MS Z.c.23, sold in 1976 and now in private hands); the verses are printed by Gibson, *Lanfranc*, p. 241, with translation and discussion on p. 143.

[9] M. Brett, "A Collection of Anglo-Norman Councils," *Jnl Eccles. Hist.* 26 (1975), pp. 301–8 at 303–4, noting that the commonest practice in pre-1100 England was

Such matters inevitably bring up the vexed question of Lanfranc's attitude towards, and therefore treatment of, certain English saints and above all his predecessor Ælfheah (known in Norman times as Alphege or Elphege). Our concern must be not with the large questions of cultural and political accommodation, and the relationship between the two, but rather with the aspect of liturgical observance. Here it seems possible to state that the evidence of the surviving calendars and sanctorales from roughly seventy years on each side of Lanfranc's accession provides no convincing reason to suppose that he engaged in anything like a deliberate removal of the liturgical commemoration of Anglo-Saxon saints as such.[10] Indeed, in the key case of Ælfheah he seems to have magnified the cult, charging the precentor at Christ Church, Osbern, to write a now-lost liturgical *historia* with music (at which Osbern was skilled) as well as the prose *vita et miracula* which has survived.[11] Some changes there were, to be sure. Insofar as one can generalize, it is for example unlikely that the Conception of John the Baptist (24 August), widely observed in Anglo-Saxon England, will be found after the Conquest, nor the Ordination of Gregory (I) on March 29th or 30th rather than on the eventually common date of September 3rd;[12] or that commemoration of some of the obscurer Anglo-Saxon holy persons dear to one or two localities only would survive. But such changes are scarcely evidence for a purge of the sanctorale of the old regime – not to mention the anterior question of whether any such thing as *the* Anglo-Saxon calendar would have been recognized, by Lanfranc or any other Continental churchman, as a discrete entity.

to observe Audoen on the 24th and Bartholomew on the 25th, argues that the new canon would place both feasts on the same day, as is witnessed by Osbern the Chanter, recounting a miracle of St Dunstan at Canterbury in 1089. This still does not explain what purpose would be served by piling both feasts onto the 24th and leaving the 25th vacant.

[10] As I have documented in "Lanfranc's Supposed Purge of the Anglo-Saxon Calendar," in *Warriors and Churchmen in the High Middle Ages*, Festschrift Karl Leyser, ed. T. Reuter (London 1992), pp. 95–108; repr. Pfaff, *LCSSME*, no. III. In an important paper a few years later J. Rubenstein, "Liturgy against History: the Competing Visions of Lanfranc and Eadmer of Canterbury," *Speculum* 74 (1999), pp. 279–309, stresses Lanfranc's de-emphasizing of saints' relics – a quite separate matter from their feasts. The whole question is taken up in a broad context by Hugh M. Thomas, *The English and the Normans: Ethnic Hostility, Assimilation, and Identity 1066–c. 1220* (Oxford 2003), esp. pp. 286–91, where an extensive literature of the previous decade is reviewed.

[11] J. Rubenstein, "The Life and Writings of Osbern of Canterbury," in *Canterbury and the Norman Conquest: Churches, Saints and Scholars 1066–1109*, ed. R. Eales and R. Sharpe (London 1995), pp. 27–40 at 31.

[12] P. A. Hayward, "Gregory the Great as 'Apostle of the English' in Post-Conquest Canterbury," *Jnl Eccles. Hist.* 55 (2004), pp. 19–55, esp. 28–32.

Lanfranc's *Constitutions*

Our knowledge of Lanfranc's concerns about the conduct of public worship must be derived almost entirely from his *Constitutions*, completed perhaps by 1077 and probably before 1080.[13] There is no title in any of the early manuscripts, and the ready application of the commonly applied qualifying adjective "monastic" rather begs an important question: whether it is only the monastic regime with which Lanfranc is concerned or whether he may have been thinking on a somewhat more national scale.[14] There are a couple of indications that the latter possibility is not entirely to be ruled out. In the section (5) on the first Sunday in Advent he specifies the vesture of those singing the invitatory at matins as being "duo fratres in albis, in sede episcopali in cappis," going on to point out that wherever the "ordo monachorum, qui hic describitur" mandates the wearing of albs during the office, in cathedrals the practice is to use copes ("in sede episcopali institutum est esse in cappis"). Of course Lanfranc would have known that in 1077 three of the grandest cathedral establishments were monastic (Winchester and Worcester, in addition to his own), and that he distinguishes the *ordo monachorum* as having one practice and those *in sede episcopali* as having another implies that to some degree he does have all the greater churches in England in mind.[15] This is reinforced by the passage in section 46 where it is noted that at the Easter vigil the "hymn" *Inventor rutili* is sung by two boys "in sede episcopali," but presumably not in monasteries.[16]

Nonetheless, it is clear that the *Constitutions* are applicable primarily to monastic contexts – in the plural, rather than just the usages of Christ Church. Indeed, something of a plurality of practices is recognized, including a few irrelevant to Lanfranc's own house. As part of the reception of a distinguished visitor (*aliqua persona*) a chant is sung "de sancto in cuius honore fundata est ecclesia": a provision not applicable

---

[13] The argument for 1077 is laid out extensively and cogently by Brooke in the revision of Knowles's edn of *Mon. Consts*, pp. xxviii–xxxv; Cowdrey, *Lanfranc*, p. 155 suggests a few years later.

[14] Brooke discusses the headings and titles the work has been given in his Introduction, pp. xliiiff., and shows that the title sometimes used, *Decreta Lanfranci*, has no warrant; it was confected by Clement Reyner in the *editio princeps* of 1626, part of his *Apostolatus Bendictinorum in Anglia*.

[15] A. W. Klukas, "The Architectural Implications of the *Decreta Lanfranci*," *Anglo-Norman Studies* 6 (1984), pp. 136–71, provides a valuable conspectus of ground plans for a variety of buildings that may well reflect Lanfrancian influence.

[16] Knowles's note (*Consts.*, p. 67) refers to the late 14th-cent. Westminster missal (below, p. 227), where the rubric calls for *duobus fratribus* (*WM*, II.578) – that abbey not having cathedral status.

in a church dedicated to Christ, as Canterbury cathedral was.[17] The practice he is prescribing has the procession with the new fire as part of the Easter eve ceremonies, but he recognizes that the same procession is held in "plurima monachorum cenobia" on Maundy Thursday and Good Friday as well, in which case the rod or staff with the candle is borne by the sacrist on the first day, the prior on the second, and the abbot on the third.[18] There is no indication that Lanfranc regards this kind of variation as undesirable, but in the same section he implies that some houses are recognized as more normative than others. The case in point is a certain level of austerity in the otherwise festive mass of the Easter vigil: to have no candles at the Gospel procession, no offertory or Agnus Dei or communion chant, is the practice "in almost all the principal monasteries of greater authority (*maioris auctoritatis*) in our time"; but in some monasteries "of no small repute" (*non improbande auctoritatis*) this is carried further, and lights are not used even as the celebrant goes to the altar. The principles by which Lanfranc distinguishes "greater" from "not disreputable" (*non improbanda*) authority are not spelled out. One obvious possibility is connected with the extent of his awareness of monastic customs apart from those in Normandy. His modern editors point out several instances in which his prescriptions follow Cluny usage more closely than that of Bec, but this is not invariably true, and in any case there is the problem that authoritative sources for the customs of both houses postdate the *Constitutions*.[19]

Perhaps the safest conclusion is that Lanfranc is trying to combine personal predilection with awareness of a variety of circumstances which the users of his provisions might encounter. The latter aspect comes through clearly in his specifying that on Good Friday if there are some clerics or lay people (*laici*), who wish to join in the adoration of the cross, it should be carried to a place outside the monastic choir where they can do so more fittingly (*aptius*). But while such a variety of circumstances seems to be accepted, there is also a suggestion that something close to a single use is desirable in some respects. This is particularly true in the virtual mass ordinary which is put in the section (77) on feasts of twelve lessons (without explanation as to what, if anything, in the practices described is specific to such feasts). It seems reasonable to take this section as representing an outline of the mass *ordo* preferred by Lanfranc. Notably peculiar here is the provision that

---

[17] A point made in Brooke's note (p. 106).
[18] Sections 46–49, pp. 66–69.
[19] In Brooke's succinct summarizing words "The loss of Lanfranc's sources in the precise form he knew makes all deductions from his use of them very tentative," p. xli.

at the beginning of the service the celebrant carries the missal (the word *missale* is used throughout for the celebrant's massbook; the subdeacon carries the gospel book, the deacon apparently nothing) and puts it on the altar, whereas at its end the deacon carries the book out, followed by the celebrant.[20] There seems to be something matter-of-fact about the celebrant's carrying the book in himself, and this may perhaps be congruent with a rather surprising sparseness about the occasions at which the Nicene Creed is to be used: never at the morrow mass, and at the high mass only on Sundays, the great temporale occasions of Christmas, Circumcision, Epiphany, Easter, Ascension, and Pentecost, and from the sanctorale just feasts of the Virgin and of apostles, plus the Dedication feast and All Saints. This means that, of the seventeen solemnities ranked by Lanfranc just below his five *festivitates principales* (Christmas, Easter, Pentecost, Assumption, and the *festivitas loci*), the Creed would not be used on those of Gregory the Great, Alphege, Augustine of Canterbury, Translation of Benedict, or Michael – nor apparently at the *festivitas loci*.[21] Such spareness seems to contrast with the sumptuousness of the provisions about vestments, above all of copes, prescribed in almost dizzying (and perhaps improbable) numbers for various great occasions.[22]

Dissemination of the *Constitutions*

The questions of how widely, deliberately, and prescriptively Lanfranc's *Constitutions* were disseminated are central to the present chapter. The evidence is of three kinds: the prefatory letter stating Lanfranc's intentions, the witness of two of the early manuscripts, and indications from tradition and inference. The author's intentions are laid out in the letter which forms the initial section of the *Constitutions* and is addressed to Prior Henry (a monk of Bec, brought over to head the community at Canterbury in the mid-1070s) and the other monks of Christ Church. In it Lanfranc makes plain both his multiple sources and his own divergence from or elaboration of them where he thinks it advisable, and also

---

[20] Sect. 77, p. 102. Also notable here is the provision that after the choir has been censed the thurifer censes the sick (*infirmis*) who are *extra chorum*; we would expect their worship to be in the infirmary chapel, at least in larger houses.

[21] Sect. 80 (p. 104). Of the sixteen feasts specified as being of the third rank (sect. 73, p. 96), the Creed would be omitted on masses for Vincent, Invention of the Cross, Laurence, Augustine (of Hippo), and Martin – and Decollation of John the Baptist, unless that counts as a feast of an apostle.

[22] In particular the great processional cope "with silver bells around the fringe and a topaz clasp set with amethysts," tr. Gibson, *Lanfranc*, p. 166, from the 1321 inventory of Christ Church treasures, ed. J. W. Legg and W. H. St J. Hope, *Inventories of Christchurch, Canterbury* (London 1902), pp. 50–57.

the likelihood, even the desirability, that there will be some diversity of practice elsewhere. And he stresses that some of his prescriptions, in particular those about the ranking of certain feasts, are to be seen as specific to his own, primatial church.

Although there is no suggestion in the language of this prefatory letter that Lanfranc expected his prescriptions to be adopted in other monastic houses, let alone that they should become uniform throughout England, we have seen some indications in the various sections that he was thinking of a wider audience than just the monks of Christ Church. John Cowdrey points out that "Lanfranc avoided, perhaps deliberately, topographical references that tied his constitutions closely to Canterbury," and speculates that he "may from the start have wished his constitutions to be available for use by other monasteries; his concern for the cathedral priory at Rochester and for the St Albans of his nephew Paul springs to mind."[23]

Both those instances will be considered presently, but first there should be noticed the most solid piece of evidence for deliberate transmission: that one of the two oldest manuscripts of the work was written, in the first half of the 1090s, by Eadmer (eventually to be better known as the biographer of Anselm) and another monk of Christ Church, and given by William of St Calais, second Norman bishop of Durham, to the monastic community he had established there in 1083 (still at Durham Cathedral Library B.IV.24). The other components of that codex, a calendar (really a register of obits), martyrology, chapter-house gospel lectionary, and Rule of Benedict (followed by an Old English version), suggest strongly that the *Constitutions* were to be regarded at Durham as having normative force.[24] A second early manuscript, now Hereford Cathedral Library P.V.1, belonged to the Prior Henry to whom the prefatory letter is addressed and who became abbot of Battle in 1096 and died in 1102. Brooke suggests that "It could be that he commissioned it after his move to Battle; but it seems perhaps most likely that he took it with him."[25]

---

[23] Cowdrey, *Lanfranc*, p. 159.
[24] The MS is described briefly by Brooke, p. xliv, and treated extensively in two articles in *Anglo-Norman Durham 1093–1193*, ed. D. Rollason, M. Harvey, and M. Prestwich (Woodbridge 1994): A. Piper, "The Durham Cantor's Book," pp. 79–92, and M. Gullick, "The Scribes of the Durham Cantor's Book," pp. 93–109, mainly about the scribe of the martyrology; for Gullick's identification of the scribe of fols 47v to 67v as Eadmer, see "The Scribal Work of Eadmer of Canterbury to 1109," *Archaeologia Cantiana* 118 (1998), pp. 173–89 at 183, with pl. IV showing the work of both scribes of the *Constitutions*. Gullick shows also that Eadmer wrote copies of episcopal professions and of papal letters for Lanfranc between 1086 and 1089 (pp. 181–82).
[25] Brooke, p. xlv; on p. 96, n. b, he points out that the erasure of Martin's name among the feasts of the third rank in this MS must reflect the higher dignity that feast would

As for indications from tradition and inference, various kinds of less direct evidence have led scholars to ascribe "observance" (Knowles) or "adoption" (Barlow) of Lanfranc's document also at Rochester, St Augustine's, Worcester, Evesham, Westminster, perhaps Eynsham, and above all St Albans (and thence to Crowland).[26] Its use at Rochester is a matter of inference only, monks having been introduced as the cathedral chapter there by Lanfranc in 1080. St Augustine's offers a possibly similar situation, after Scotland, monk of Mont Saint-Michel, had been put in as abbot in 1070; complications there will be looked at presently. Direct bearing of the *Constitutions* on Worcester, Evesham, and Westminster is more inferential still and can be ignored here. It is the case of St Albans that may prove the most instructive for us. Its *Gesta Abbatum* records that abbot Paul (1077–93; Lanfranc's nephew) brought with him *Consuetudines Lanfranci*, with the implication that they were papally approved.[27] A key question will be whether we can discern any direct presence of Lanfranc's work in the twelfth-century witnesses to liturgy at St Albans; these will be considered in detail in the next chapter. For the moment, attention must shift from Lanfranc and the houses where his influence is the most palpable to two great abbeys from which there survives evidence contemporary with the episcopate of Lanfranc but which do not seem to have fallen within his orbit.

Winchester New Minster and its missal

The first is the New Minster at Winchester (to be relocated, and renamed Hyde Abbey, in 1110). Its *missale plenum*, now Le Havre, Bibl. mun. 330, is for the extant parts the fullest surviving massbook from before 1100 used in England, but it lacks everything before the Friday after Easter in the temporale and after the votive mass of the Cross.[28] The consequent absence of a calendar and (probably) litany of saints makes dating the book more closely than the last third of the eleventh century extremely difficult, but a clue may exist in the prominence given to Denis and his companions (the October 9th feast has both vigil and octave, and there is also an Invention feast on April 22nd). By the twelfth century

---

have had at Battle, which was dedicated to Martin: a strong indication that Henry's book was being used there.

[26] Knowles, *Mon. Order*, pp. 123–24; Barlow, *Eng. Ch. 1066–1154*, p. 189.

[27] Knowles, *MO*, p. 123, n. 4, is cautious about the passage in Matthew Paris's *Hist. Anglorum* that lies behind the *Gesta Abbatum* account: "Some of the above phrases have the ring of anachronism, in particular the reference to papal approval."

[28] D. H. Turner, ed. *The Missal of the New Minster, Winchester*, HBS 93 (1962); cf. Pfaff, *Liturg. Bks ASE*, pp. 28–30.

the house owned relics of those saints, which it had not possessed in the 1020s, and it seems likeliest that they came in the abbacy of Riwallon (about whom little is known), 1072–88.[29] But the sanctorale also includes masses for no fewer than twenty "English" saints' feasts: not only those from Winchester (Birinus, Swithun, Æthelwold, plus the New Minster's own Grimbald and Judoc) but also a full complement from Ely (Etheldreda, Eormenhilda, Sexburga), and Alphege; the texts for six of these masses appear to be unique to this book.

Furthermore, the scribe of the missal was at home writing English, for his hand is found also in the Stowe psalter (BL Stowe 2, with continuous interlinear gloss) and in a collection of Old English homilies (CUL Ii.4.6).[30] There are as well clear Continental affinities; analysis by the missal's modern editor, Derek Turner, showed that the Alleluia verses are largely identical with those from Corbie and St Denis, whereas little if any clear Norman influence is discernible. In a time when the proportion of proper prefaces for individual saints' masses was beginning to decline in favor of prefaces taken from the common of saints, it is noteworthy that this book contains something like 158 proper prefaces, a few of them extremely long.[31] This fact, like the presence of the new masses for six English saints, gives weight to Turner's suggestion that the book "may have been designed as a standard liturgical book for the monastery for which it was written, a book to which reference could be made, or from which other books could be copied."[32] This possibility makes it all the more tantalizing that no further clue seems available as to a possible designer of this book; whoever he was, the person had an informed interest in the liturgy no less keen than Lanfranc's, and seems to have felt no discernible weight of the latter's *Constitutions*.[33] Nor does the book manifest any sign of tension between English and Norman elements; this was not to be the case at Glastonbury.

---

[29] The previous abbot, Wulfric, had been deposed in 1072, and the succeeding one was a Lotharingian and father of the quondam-notorious Herbert Losinga, eventually the first bishop of Norwich.

[30] T. A. M. Bishop, *English Caroline Minuscule* (Oxford 1971), p. xv, n. 2.

[31] It would be a potentially profitable exercise to chase all of these through the *Corpus Praefationum* (see p. 151 below) and then to trace similarities to the prefaces in other contemporary books.

[32] Turner's "Introduction," p. xxvi.

[33] Independence of Lanfrancian influence is evident in two small details of nomenclature. The 11 July *Translatio* of Benedict, one of Lanfranc's seventeen very great feasts, is in the New Minster book headed only *Natale*, exactly like the 12 March feast; and the *Decollatio* of John the Baptist, among Lanfranc's feasts of third rank, is in New Minster *Passio*. By contrast, the St Augustine's missal of the 1090s (see p. 113) follows Lanfranc in both cases.

Glastonbury and the disaster of 1083

Any assessment of the situation at Glastonbury – here, as throughout the whole of the present work, the most major house about which the smallest amount of liturgical information is available – will be skewed by the horrifiedly melodramatic account given in a number of more or less contemporary chronicles of the attack by "Frenchmen" on its helpless monks some time in 1083. The best known is that in the only version of the *Anglo-Saxon Chronicle* surviving for the years after 1073, the *Peterborough Chronicle*, which ascribes the cause of the discord to unspecified misgovernment of the Glastonbury monks by their abbot Thurstan (c. 1077[?]–96, formerly a monk of Caen).[34] But three of the other seven narrative accounts of this episode compiled within sixty years or so of 1083 indicate that the breaking point was a liturgical/musical quarrel: Thurstan's insistence on replacing the monks' familiar brand of Gregorian chant with that of "William of Fécamp."[35] Among the three, the most detailed is the highly colored later narrative of William of Malmesbury (died c. 1143), in his *De antiquitate Glastonie ecclesie*. His wording is instructive: that the incident took place in the context of the removal by Thurstan of "many ancient and favored customs" in favor of "certain practices according to the custom of his own country" – practices that were resisted by the monks as foreign-bred, *alienigenae*.[36]

This episode is not susceptible of simple interpretation. Supplementing the most obvious approach, that the chant question is simply the back-breaking straw amidst much other unsettlement in the wake of an abrasive new abbot, is the fact that at Glastonbury there had been

[34] *Anglo-Saxon Chronicle* (E), *ad* 1083: Cecily Clark, ed. *The Peterborough Chronicle 1070–1154*, 2nd edn (Oxford 1970), p. 7, with commentary on p. 71.

[35] Knowles, *Mon. Order*, p. 555, points out that the language about the conflict between the two kinds of chant seems to go back to earlier stages of the Worcester tradition (the chronicle formerly attributed to the monk Florence but now known to be by John of Worcester: Sharpe, *Handlist*, p. 116), put into writing by an author who "had no very precise notion of the point at issue." The episode has been treated extensively, with concentration on the musical aspect, by D. Hiley, "Thurstan of Caen and Plainchant at Glastonbury: Musicological Reflections on the Norman Conquest," *Proc. British Academy* 72 (1986), pp. 57–90; he shows that the William in question is William of Dijon, reformer of chant used at Fécamp, Jumièges, and other Norman houses, but not at Bec, from which Thurstan had come. No chant sources from Bec seem to have survived.

[36] Ed. and tr. by John Scott as *The Early History of Glastonbury* (Woodbridge 1981), cap. 78, p. 156. This is a textually difficult work, bearing signs of extensive interpolation from the "Florence of Worcester" tradition, but that does not affect the basic point here: that only William of Malmesbury specifies "foreignness" as the root of the problem.

only two abbots in the fifty-five years before Thurstan, so there may have been an unusual degree of conservatism there. Its musical tradition may also have been a point of special sensitivity, since it is not unlikely that it was strongly linked to Dunstan, whose musical expertise (and gift of an organ to the monastery) are stressed by William of Malmesbury.[37] A key question is the degree to which the traditionalist conservatism evident at Glastonbury was replicated in other monastic houses; and whether, if at all widespread, it was in conflict with what seems to be the considerable centralizing tendency of Lanfranc's *Constitutions*.[38] Unfortunately, the latter says very little about chant while the Glastonbury episode is (ostensibly, anyhow) about nothing else. Liturgical conservatism of a somewhat different kind is clearly evident in the next house at which we look, St Augustine's at Canterbury.

St Augustine's, Canterbury

With the sacramentary of St Augustine's (CCCC 270) we reach the latest of the eleventh-century books called into witness for this chapter.[39] It can be dated with unusual precision. The mass on fol. 117 for the Translation of Augustine and six more of the house's seventh-century abbots refers to a happening on 13 September 1091, and the bulk of the original book is in the hand of a scribe who has been identified as writing in at least half a dozen other manuscripts.[40] And at the end of the book (fol. 171v) he has written three additional masses, the first being for the fourth Sunday after the octave of Epiphany (Epiphany V), which would be required in any year when Easter falls on April 15th or later; the original temporale had provided for only three Sundays after the octave, but a mass for the fourth would have been needed in 1093,

---

[37] William of Malmesbury, *Vita Dunstani*, in *Saints' Lives*, ed. and tr. M. Winterbottom and R. M. Thomson, OMT (Oxford 2002), i.4 and ii.10 (pp. 178, 258).

[38] Knowles's conclusion (*Mon. Order*, p. 555) may be unduly sanguine: "There is no record of similar disturbances elsewhere, and it is probable that the English monasteries in general were left to continue in their inherited traditions; a community is particularly tenacious in such matters."

[39] Mis-called *The Missal of St Augustine's Abbey Canterbury* in the edition by Martin Rule (Cambridge 1896), which must still be used, although his introductory "monograph," heavily devoted to proving that the book was a direct copy of that which Gregory the Great gave to Augustine of Canterbury in 596, is best ignored. The MS is treated in great detail in M. Budny, *Insular, Anglo-Saxon, and Early Anglo-Norman Manuscript Art at Corpus Christi College, Cambridge: An Illustrated Catalogue*, 2 vols (Kalamazoo 1997), no. 48: I.693–704, including description of 124 initials, and II.pl. 642–75 and col. pl. XIV.

[40] Listed in Budny, p. 694, mostly from work by T. A. M. Bishop; she characterizes the scribe, who is active as late as 1110, as "of pronounced Anglo-Saxon training" (p. 689).

when Easter was to fall on April 17th – the only time it fell after the 15th in the decade of the 1090s. So it looks as though the book was complete, or virtually so, by 1093.[41]

The importance of the 1093 *terminus a quo* lies not only in its exactness but because it means that the book must have been written under the auspices of a new regime, installed after the *putsch* in 1087 when, following the death of the popular abbot Scotland (or Scolland), Lanfranc's imposition of Wido or Guy, a Norman monk (of Christ Church?), provoked several episodes of fierce resistance. The final outburst ended, soon after Lanfranc's death in late May 1089, with the dispersal of the dissident monks and their replacement by twenty-four monks from Christ Church.[42] We do not know what percentage of the house the number imposed on it represented, but it is reasonably clear that the massbook under consideration was written for use by a community many of whom had not been there very long (and who had certainly been living under the regime of Lanfranc's *Constitutions*). Its marked character as a St Augustine's book is therefore all the more striking.

It is striking not only because whatever tension existed between Christ Church and St Augustine's is a factor in the preceding story but also because of the textual conservatism that marks this massbook. Granted that we have little to compare it with directly, we still note with some surprise such details as the plethora of proper prefaces, the omission of Vedast from the feast that saint shares with Remigius and Germanus on October 1st, and the provision of masses for each of the first seven abbot-(arch)bishops of Canterbury. The last point stands in opposition to the absence of many of the more obvious Anglo-Saxon saints, Oswald, Etheldreda, Edward the Martyr, and the entire Winchester

---

[41] The third added mass is "Pro rege et regina populoque Christiano," in which each of the prayers mentions *regina* separately from *rex*. This has sometimes been taken as requiring a date after Nov. 1100, when Henry I, who had unexpectedly succeeded his unmarried brother William Rufus four months earlier, married Edith of Scotland; but the prayers are the same as those in the (later) coronation mass for a queen and in a votive mass for the royal family: respectively, *Westminster Missal*, II.714–21 (the secret and postcommunion are both the second of two, *Alia*) and *Sarum Missal (Legg)*, p. 398, so this does not seem decisive. Could these prayers have been used at the coronation of Matilda, William the Conqueror's queen, in 1068?

[42] Summarized in Knowles, *Mon. Order*, p. 116, where Wido is called a monk of Christ Church, but a monk of St Augustine's (from Thomas of Elmham, himself from that house and writing in the fifteenth century) in *Heads Rel. Houses*, I.36. Cowdrey, *Lanfranc*, p. 168, states that Wido "may have been, though this cannot be demonstrated, a monk of Christ Church." The point, which is not trivial, is not mentioned in the original account, the *Acta Lanfranci* annexed to MS A of the *Anglo-Saxon Chronicle* (as above, note 6); but cf. P. A. Hayward's recent caution about this source, "Some reflections on the historical value of the so-called *Acta Lanfranci*," *Historical Research* 77 (2004), pp. 140–60.

quintet of Birinus, Swithun, Æthelwold, Judoc, and Grimbald. The sanctorale has therefore a very strong southeastern English flavor: Mildred, Alban, Edmund, Dunstan, *Alfegus* (at the end, almost as an afterthought: see below), as well as the St Augustine's saints.

How much independence the liturgical authorities at St Augustine's – presumably the abbot, prior, and precentor, and perhaps others – felt from Christ Church as CCCC 270 was being written is not an easy matter to work out. In at least one case there is a marked discrepancy from Lanfranc's prescriptions. He specifies that on Good Friday, after the veneration of the cross, the Reserved Sacrament is brought to the high altar by a deacon, to whom it is handed by the officiating priest who has just censed it; whereas in the St Augustine's book the rubric prescribes two priests.[43]

We need to note also an apparent ambivalence about two distinctively Christ Church feasts, both eventually included though each is strikingly out of its correct place. In the common of saints the heading of prayers for a mass *In ordinatione* has been altered to read *beati Gregorii papae*, and his name specified in the collect; this is the commemoration of the Ordination of Gregory, 3 September.[44] The question here is whether its inclusion represents pressure from the new regime. Paul Hayward has proposed that the monks of St Augustine's undertook a campaign to promote their patron as *apostolus Anglorum*, a distinction that had by long custom belonged to Gregory the Great and that therefore reflected glory on the cathedral establishment.[45] He argues, largely on the basis of charter evidence, that the campaign probably began in mid-century, and that it was (after a seeming hiatus of a couple of decades) "taken up by the Norman abbots, Scolland (1072–87) and Guy (1087–1093 × 1106)." It is not made clear why these Normans (Scolland had been a monk at Mont St Michel; Guy's previous pre-Canterbury house, if any, is not known) should have been so keen to advance Augustine's reputation, save that the nose of the abbey they successively headed was out of joint.

The other feast about which notable ambivalence is discernible is that of Alphege. His mass was not included in the original design for the St Augustine's book, for it is the second among the three masses supplied by the original scribe at the end (fol. 171v): "De sancto Alfego

---

[43] Lanfranc, *Constitutions*, cap. 43 (OMT edn, p. 62); *St Augustine's Missal*, p. 39. This is the only ceremonial rubric in that entire massbook.

[44] Rule edn, p. 130. The feast is added to the calendars of the Leofric missal in the 11th cent. and the Wulfstan Portiforium (below, p. 126) in the 12th; otherwise it seems to appear in Christ Church documents only.

[45] Hayward, "Gregory the Great" (note 12 above), esp. pp. 28–32, at 31.

archiepiscopo," with a proper preface and, in full, epistle lesson from Maccabees and gospel from John. Each of its three prayers differs from the set in the only eleventh-century points of comparison, the New Minster and "Giso" books (the latter still to be considered, p. 124), and each prayer agrees with – and apparently only with – the set in a fourteenth-century Durham missal which reflects heavy Christ Church influence (see p. 120); so it is reasonable to suppose that these are the Christ Church prayers, imported into a book in which the mass for Alphege did not have a place in the original sanctorale.[46] Here, then, are two important points of conformity with what we imagine the post-Conquest liturgy of Christ Church to have been; at the same time, that neither was included in the original design of CCCC 270 must cast doubt on the claim that this massbook is "the earliest surviving copy of Lanfranc's version of the Bec sacramentary."[47]

Whatever the case, the book did not remain static. Extensive alterations and additions in the twelfth and thirteenth centuries both show it being turned into something like a missal and indicate dissatisfaction with some of the textual details of the 1090s. The most notable example may be that of the mass of the abbey's most distinctive feast, that of Augustine himself, emphasized by one of the finest initials in the book (fol. 92v). In the margin next to the secret the supplementing hand has written the same prayer as in the (later) Durham missal, one that speaks of Augustine merely as confessor and bishop rather than, as in the original prayer, "our father." Following the secret is an erasure of thirteen lines representing a lengthy proper preface (which may well have been unique to this book); then next to the original post-communion a marginal alternative is again supplied, once more as in Durham and omitting mention of Augustine as *Anglorum apostolus*.[48] A similar alteration, but one which is unlikely to have had any special

---

[46] Martin Rule tied himself into knots about what looks to be the correction of the word *meritis* in the secret to the *martyris* which the sense demands, arguing from this that "the two readings [were] derived from the very book on which Archbishop Lanfranc was working when it occurred to him to reconsider his doubt as to the claim of St Elfege to the crown of martyrdom," and that by the time the postcommunion's *ac martyre tuo* had been reached, his doubt had been resolved by Anselm (p. 157, n. 2). There is in fact a good deal of instability in Alphege's mass prayers: Legg's textual "Notes" in *WM* III (see Excursus at the end of this chapter) show that Westminster and Sarum had independent sets and that Giso's prayers were shared by Sherborne and (of special note given its relationship to Lanfranc's program) St Albans.

[47] N. Orchard, "The Bosworth Psalter and the St Augustine's Missal," in *Canterbury and the Norman Conquest* (n. 11 above), pp. 87–94. He maintains also that "an early version of Lanfranc's sacramentary – perhaps a book that had been resolved for the dedication of the cathedral in 1077 – underlies Corpus 270" (p. 93).

[48] Budny, pl. 663 shows fol. 92v. Of note also is the mass for Mellitus (fol. 86; her pl. 661), where an alternative collect has been written in the margin, replacing the

relevance to St Augustine's, is in the mass prayers for St Hermes (fol. 114v), where a different secret is supplied in the margin. Finally, we may note the faint marginal note at the mass for St Bartholomew (fol. 113) instructing the scribe to copy the postcommunion from the common of saints; the marginal words were then erased, presumably after the present text of the prayer was written.[49] This, beginning *Votiva domine*, is indeed the prayer given in the common of an apostle on fol. 139v. Some trace is also discernible of an original "S," the letter which begins the two proper postcommunions that are used in all other English sources.

It seems reasonably clear, then, that the thrust of the changes to this book in the decades after it was written is in the direction of suppressing "proper" elements, in mass prayers as well as prefaces, even in the cases of some of the house's most distinctive saints. That there are no twelfth- or thirteenth-century St Augustine's massbooks through which this tendency could be traced is all the more unfortunate because there is a wealth of hagiographical information for that house, all of it dating from after 1091. T. A. Heslop has suggested that the episode of Wido and intrusion of Christ Church monks "might help explain why there is a small clutch of broadly liturgical manuscripts extant from St Augustine's dating from the two decades following 1090: it was only at that stage that its liturgy was significantly reformed."[50] This suggestion is roughly congruent with what we have seen with the massbook.

The manuscripts in question are a passional (BL Arundel 92), homiliary (BL Harley 652), and martyrology (BL Cott. Vit. C.xii). We must also notice here the work of Goscelin, whose monastic career took him from St Bertin's in Flanders through a variety of English establishments, as a kind of wandering hagiographer, and who ended up at St Augustine's around 1090, remaining there and eventually holding the office of precentor, presumably until his death some time after 1114.[51]

---

elegant allusion to the saint's name, "melliflua tuae gratiae repleat dulcedo," with bland language suitable to the common.

[49] Rule, p. 106 n. 2, rendered as "Si placet scribe post-communionem de communi quia non est oratio plena." Rule expresses thanks to a colleague for help in "reading the all but illegible relic of this pencilled memorandum"; Linne Mooney has kindly scrutinized the writing afresh, and confirms this reading.

[50] T. A. Heslop, "The Canterbury Calendars and the Norman Conquest," in *Canterbury and the Norman Conquest* (above, n. 11), pp. 53–85, at 67: an important paper for this entire chapter, although (as he explains on p. 68) he and I differ in both our approaches to this subject and our conclusions.

[51] His works are listed in Sharpe, *Handlist*, pp. 151–54, and discussed by F. Barlow in an appendix to his edn of *The Life of King Edward who rests at Westminster*, NMT (London 1962; 2nd edn, as OMT, 1992), pp. 91–111. The entry in *ODCC*³ is also exceptionally helpful.

The saints' lives and masses ascribed to him (sometimes contestedly) are so numerous and varied that we must be careful not to let his prolixity overwhelm his potential, if limited, usefulness to the present chapter. Richard Sharpe has proposed that Goscelin was invited to St Augustine's by its new abbot, Wido, in the context of preparation for the translation of its saints which was to take place in 1091.[52] He suggests also that the proper liturgical texts for the cult at St Augustine's of St Mildreth (Mildred) – two major occasions, Deposition on 13 July and a Translation (much disputed) on 18 May – which survive in BL Harley 3908, fols 43–50v, were composed by Goscelin. These consist of eight lessons (monastic use for a great feast), a notated *historia* containing the antiphons and responsories for the office, and mass forms. A couple of references in Goscelin's other works seem to be to this liturgy, and it is not unlikely that he wrote the music as well as the texts.

Can Lanfranc's liturgy be inferred?

This survey of information available about the liturgy, largely of the mass, of these three establishments – Winchester New Minster, Glastonbury, St Augustine's – may, along with our awareness of the almost certain presence of the *Constitutions* at Durham and St Albans, enable us to proceed by inference to some sense of the actual mass (and office) liturgy that might have been used at Christ Church during the latter years of Lanfranc's tenure there. First, we must notice two blanket statements that have been made on the subject. In 1956 Christopher Hohler, studying the liturgies used for Cuthbert's feasts at Durham, spoke of the forms for the Deposition feast as having been "taken over, along with the rest of the Canterbury missal as revised by Lanfranc, by William of St Calais" (second Anglo-Norman bishop of Durham, 1081–96).[53] That implied entity, "the Canterbury missal as revised by Lanfranc," seems to be the object of the second statement, that published in 1995 by Nicholas Orchard, who, having called the St Augustine's book "the earliest surviving copy of Lanfranc's version of the Bec sacramentary" (as noted above), goes on to say that "the only other copy that survives complete is embedded in the late fourteenth-century missal from Durham Cathedral, now BL, MS Harley 5289."[54]

---

[52] R. Sharpe, "Goscelin's St Augustine and St Mildreth: Hagiography and Liturgy in Context," *JTS* n.s. 41 (1990), pp. 502–16.

[53] C. Hohler, "The Durham Services in Honour of St Cuthbert," in *The Relics of St Cuthbert*, ed. C. F. Battiscombe (Oxford 1956), pp. 155–91 at 157.

[54] "The Bosworth Psalter and the St Augustine's Missal" (note 47 above), p. 88, cf. 93. It is not clear whether he regards the "Lanfranc's sacramentary" which was among the books that, according to him, the two dozen Christ Church monks took with

We have, then, two obvious if tricky points for comparison, the St Augustine's book of the last decade of the eleventh century and the Durham missal: the latter, however, of the fourteenth century, perhaps third quarter (its dating is discussed on p. 183). One additional point must be brought in to complete a rough structure for a kind of triangulation, a massbook from Bec, datable to around 1265, now BN lat. 1105.[55] The temporale up until Epiphany is missing, as are the first two months of the calendar. Its original design is not that of a missal, for it lacks both ordinary and canon; this leads the modern editor, Anselm Hughes, to suggest that it might have been intended as either a dignitary's book or a reference volume for the precentor. He is candid about the perils of using it alongside Lanfranc's *Constitutions*, not only because of the gap in dates but also because of a revision that the Bec customs underwent in the late twelfth century. Of the four instances he cites "in which the Constitutions and the Bec Missal agree over details which are not normally found in the English mediaeval uses, at least those in secular cathedrals," three concern rather inconclusive details of the Good Friday rite.[56] The fourth, however, is quite telling: Lanfranc's provision (sect. 52) that on Low Sunday the introit of the morrow mass should be *Quasimodo geniti* and of the high mass *Resurrexi*. This peculiarity is shared by Durham in the fourteenth century, St Albans in the fourteenth century (that section of its twelfth-century sacramentary [see p. 158] is missing), and Bec in the mid-thirteenth century – but *not* by St Augustine's in the late eleventh. Does this divergence indicate that the latter house had a version of Lanfranc's book that antedated the *Constitutions* – or is it possible that that document and his sacramentary (not, as such, extant) were not always in accord?[57]

---

them to the dissident house in 1089 as being identical with the "early version of Lanfranc's sacramentary" that he says "underlies" CCCC 270.

[55] A(nselm) Hughes, ed. *The Bec Missal*, HBS 94 (1963).

[56] Hughes, pp. vii–viii; he mentions five, but the first arises from his misreading of Sunday before Advent as the fourth Sunday of that season.

[57] Brooke, in his introduction to the revised edition of *Mon. Consts*, p. xlii, repeats Orchard's opinions about Lanfranc's sacramentary, based on some commonality among the St Augustine's, Bec, and Durham books, to which Orchard added the fragment (26 fols) of a mid-12th-cent. missal (now Canterbury Cath. Add. 127/24, here misprinted as 124/14) as being from St Gregory's, Canterbury, the collegiate church (later an Augustinian priory) founded by Lanfranc in, probably, 1084. Much depends on interpretation of the phrase "sanctorum tuorum Gregorii, Augustini, Ædburgis, atque Mildrithe" (all four in capitals) as being among the saints whose relics were in *that* church (*ista ecclesia*) in the fragmentary missal's mass for the commemoration of relics (*MMBL*, II.319). St Augustine's would have claimed to possess relics of the last three and St Gregory's of the first, third, and fourth, but it is hard to believe that it could with a straight face claim a relic of Gregory. In any case, not enough survives of the book to make it a material witness in our quest.

Trying to make inferences as to Lanfranc's massbook from the slender evidence of the *Constitutions* alone is impossible, and only occasionally possible if the tri- or quadr-angulating witnesses are brought into play. Perhaps the most convincing case concerns the lessons at the Easter Vigil. For each lesson-segment there are normally three elements, the lesson itself (Creation, Crossing of Red Sea, and so on), a choral response called the tract (this does not usually occur after the first lesson), and a collect. A full missal will contain all three elements, a gradual only the tracts, and a sacramentary only the collects; but, as these elements tend to travel in sets, it is usually possible to infer from the existence of one element what its corresponding elements were. The variable factor is how many such lesson-tract-collect segments are prescribed, the number varying from twelve (in, for example, the original strand of the Leofric missal) to four, which becomes commonest. Five is an unusual number, so when we find that to be the case in all three witnesses noticed above, St Albans, Bec, and Durham, and in that from St Augustine's as well, and note that where elements of the five lesson-sets can be compared they are virtually identical, it seems highly likely that they are reflecting a common source: one which it seems safe to suppose either is common also to the massbook Lanfranc used or may conceivably be that book itself.

Two other, rather major, tests may be applied. Both concern masses for key occasions in the sanctorale, the Deposition feast of Cuthbert on March 20th (his Translation feast, September 4th, is less instructive) and the Ordination of Gregory on September 3rd. The latter stands at the center of the study, referred to above (p. 115), by Paul Hayward, who contends that it was magnified by the monks of Christ Church as their response to claims being put forward in the late eleventh century by St Augustine's that their patron should be hailed as *Apostolus Anglorum* rather than Gregory, as had tended to be the case since Bede's time. Part of this magnification consisted of moving the feast from the awkward March 29th or 30th date which it had in many Anglo-Saxon calendars to the more convenient time in early September, and all the mass forms we have for the feast appear as for the new date. It is therefore striking that Lanfranc, who ranks Gregory's main (March 12th) feast among the fifteen second in solemnity only to the five greatest, ignores the Ordination feast even among the sixteen of "third dignity" (sects. 66, 73). The possibilities are either that he did not think it an occasion of great import, or that he came to do so only after the *Constitutions* were compiled – or, of course, that the magnification of the feast came after his death entirely. If this development does take place during his lifetime but after around 1077–80, however, it is even more striking that the mass sets for the feast in the St Augustine's, St Albans, and Durham books differ completely; and even more so that the fourteenth-century "Burnt Breviary" from Christ Church (see p. 242) contains a still different collect at first vespers (which usually is the same as the collect of the mass). It is hard to believe that one of these three sets, or four if the "Burnt Breviary" is included, does not represent that used at Christ Church under Lanfranc; which one, looks to be impossible to state.[58]

The test offered by the prayers for Cuthbert's Deposition feast, March 20th, is even more complex. As noted above, Hohler's sweeping dictum about the prayers for this mass in the Durham missal implies that a book he calls "the Canterbury missal" existed before 1070, that Lanfranc somehow revised it, and that a copy of it was taken by William of St Calais to Durham, where its presence is heavily evident in the Harley 5289 Durham missal. The first two of these implications are central to the present argument, and Cuthbert is likely to be a good case in point simply because he can have been of no special interest to Lanfranc; nor is there likely to have been any Norman tradition or custom pertaining to the saint of which he would have been aware.

The tradition of forms for Cuthbert's mass likely to have been used at Canterbury apparently begins with the mass set in Leofric "B," the component of that book supplied there in the last three quarters of the tenth century; this appears also in the St Augustine's, St Albans (twelfth- as well as fourteenth-century codices), and Durham books.[59] In all of these the collect begins "Omnipotens sempiterne Deus, qui in meritis sancti Cuthberti pontificis." A significant variant appears as early as c. 975, in a sacramentary from Fulda (see p. xxiii above): *sacerdotis* in place of *pontificis*. That this is not merely a Continental reading, de-emphasizing Cuthbert's episcopal role, is shown by its appearance in the Robert of Jumièges book and also in the "portiforium" used by Wulfstan of Worcester, third quarter of the eleventh century (CCCC 391; p. 126).

---

[58] It is a weakness of Hayward's argument that it is drawn almost entirely from calendars and largely ignores the mass texts themselves. He does mention the St Augustine's set (p. 55 and n.), and points out that the annotator whose near-contemporary hand appears frequently has written at the foot of fol. 116 (between the masses for Priscus, Sept. 1st, and the Nativity of Mary on the 8th) "De ordinatione sancti gregorii require in ordinatione sancti martini" (July 3rd), followed by a fragmentary pencilled note that seems to contain part of the usual introit for a confessor-bishop, which of course would suit both Martin and Gregory. I doubt that anyone thought the prayers for what is really Martin's translation feast would be suitable for Gregory.

[59] N. Orchard, "A Note on the Masses for St Cuthbert," *Rev. Bén.* 105 (1995), pp. 79–98, at 79, states that "the mass for Cuthbert was added with other material at Exeter in Leofric's episcopate (1050–72)" – the section usually called Leofric "C" – but this is obviously a slip, for in his edition of the Leofric missal (II.380) Orchard assigns the mass to a late-tenth-century scribe (= "B").

The Canterbury benedictional of c. 1030 (BL Harley 2892; see p. 92) contains two three-part blessings for the feast, both of which appear to have been composed there. The first seems to show up otherwise only in the Westminster missal. The second appears also both in the earlier section of a pontifical likely to have been made at Canterbury (CCCC 146, nicknamed "Samson" after the bishop of Worcester who owned it c. 1100) and in the section of blessings for saints' days added, probably at Canterbury, to the so-called Ramsey benedictional (BN lat. 987) of the early eleventh century.[60] Its presence in a benedictional of the late twelfth or early thirteenth century, BL Cott. Tib. B.iii, is a key point in the present argument. This is a composite volume, beginning with a calendar clearly that of Christ Church (Ordination feasts for Dunstan and Alphege the clinching points) before 1220, followed by a benedictional which must be that of Durham: it contains blessings for only two English saints, Oswald (martyr) and Cuthbert. For the latter there is a blessing for the Translation (fol. 112), headed *In natale* and distinguished by a fancy initial, as well as that for the Deposition (fol. 95), identical with the second blessing in the Canterbury benedictional.[61] This point, quite apart from similarities in mass prayers, strengthens the argument for transmission of liturgical texts from Canterbury to post-Conquest Durham.

Does it therefore also strengthen the possibility of inferring from later texts the nature of regular liturgical worship at Lanfranc's Canterbury? If the pre-1070 "Canterbury missal" posited by Hohler looked either like the Robert of Jumièges book of roughly half a century earlier, or like the New Minster missal possibly written during the 1070s, or like the St Augustine's massbook of the 1090s, it would most likely have contained an extensive group of proper prefaces, as do all three of those – and as later missals tend not to have. All have, for example, prefaces for Cuthbert: but they are three different prefaces.[62] Which, if any, is likeliest to be Lanfrancian?

---

[60] *Canterbury Benedictional*, p. 89, Samson benedictional, p. 249 (of the MS); for the Ramsey benedictional, A. Prescott, "The Structure of English Pre-Conquest Benedictionals," *Brit. Lib. Jnl.* 13 (1987), pp. 118–58 at 152; cf. Pfaff, *Liturg. Bks ASE*, pp. 95–96 and 90–91.

[61] Calendar printed Wormald, *Eng. Ben. Kals*, I.63; the benedictional is unedited and has been little noticed, save in the apparatus to Hohler's article, with siglum Duβ and its date stated merely as "12th cent." (p. 160). The MS is disbound and the leaves separately mounted, so collation is impossible, nor is there any way of telling when the various parts were put together. There are further contents, including some in English verse. An inscription on fol. 11 speaks of the repair of psalters c. 1500, mentioning two priors of Durham of the period 1449–1517. It has not been combed for the *Corpus Benedictionum Pontificalium* (p. 151 below).

[62] That in the St Augustine's book appears also in a mid-12th-cent. collection of Cuthbert devotions in TCC O.3.55 (1227), fol. 50. Its date is somewhere around 1130:

Another possible strand of Anglo-Norman monastic tradition

Despite a resolve not to dwell on the question of Lanfranc's alleged "purging" of Anglo-Saxon saints, it has seemed necessary to concentrate somewhat on forms, and therefore feasts, of a pre-Norman type simply because they offer the clearest opportunity for focusing on what is inevitably the major question in a liturgical as well as more broadly historical assessment of the effects of the Norman Conquest: continuity versus disruption. Basing our evidence where possible on surviving manuscripts, in accordance with the overall thrust of the present work, we see that one clear statement is possible and that one large question must remain in the air. The clear statement is that there was no drastic change in the basic patterns of regular worship, nor in the texts according to which that worship was conducted.

But the question as to the extent to which English monasticism (and, to a large extent, the English church) became "Normanized" must remain largely unresolved. The key difficulty here has to do with the spread and authoritativeness of Lanfranc's *Constitutions*, a matter discussed earlier. Clearly some houses conducted their business, including liturgical business, heavily under its influence. But it does not follow that what was true at Durham, St Albans, Battle, probably St Augustine's, and possibly other places such as Westminster, necessarily obtained throughout the kingdom. The greatest obstacle to clearer understanding is the absence of evidence from the cathedral priory at Winchester, the house at which the effects of Æthelwold's *Regularis concordia* should have been most palpable. Failing that, the New Minster missal may offer the best clues. As was noticed earlier, a clear sign of the new regime probably to be connected with the abbacy of Riwallon (1072–88) is the prominence of feasts relating to St Denis. On the other hand, that among the twenty feasts for English saints are separate occasions for each of the three from Ely must represent continuity with the Æthelwoldian tradition. Indeed, might it be posited that the appearance of the most important of these saints, Etheldreda, serves as a litmus test? Her main feast, June 23rd, is absent from the St Augustine's and St Albans books for which Canterbury tradition is posited, but present in those from Peterborough/Ely (Robert of Jumièges) and New Minster.[63]

---

either no later than that, according to the opinion of Teresa Webber, or within thirty years thereafter, according to Michael Gullick; I thank both for their opinions.

[63] Two remarks by the HBS editor, D. H. Turner, are apposite: that he found it very plausible "that the *antiphonarium* in it, in arrangement at least, derives from Corbie by way of Abingdon," and that he was inclined to wonder whether the sacramentary underlying Le Havre 330 "was something proper in England to the New Minster, Winchester. If so, do the peculiarities in it possibly antedate the reforms of

Whether the strand that we can term roughly "Lanfrancian" comes to predominate in the twelfth century and later is a question that can recede into the background until we take up monastic liturgy again and look at the rich evidence from, in particular, St Albans in the twelfth century. First, though, we have to turn to secular liturgy, for which there are indications for (probably) Wells, (perhaps) Worcester, and – the one major program of secular liturgy for that period of which there is abundant evidence – Exeter.

Wells(?): the Giso sacramentary

For another look at the phenomenon of liturgical change during the years that can sensibly be understood as comprising the Norman Conquest we must ponder one of the more substantial of the few bits of evidence for liturgy in a secular context in eleventh-century England: the massbook often said to be connected with Giso, bishop of Wells (BL Cott. Vit. A.xviii). The connection with Giso, whose episcopate at Wells from 1061 to 1088 spans most of the years under consideration in the present chapter, is, to be sure, slim; it was first made by Edmund Bishop, who in 1908 wrote cautiously of its calendar that "the probable, perhaps only admissible, conclusion is that in V [his siglum for this manuscript] we have the calendar of the church of Wells under the 'Lorrainer' Giso."[64] That in itself would not make it "his" book; but it is clearly a bishop's book: the massbook proper is succeeded by a benedictional and an extensive Maundy Thursday *ordo* including the episcopal blessing of oils. Much remains to be investigated in this book, which has never been edited, but the following points seem material. It is at heart a sacramentary, not a missal. The *ordo missae* comes at the beginning, and pecularities in its contents as well as its placing lead to the suspicion that the book may have been designed not for regular liturgical use but rather as a repository of materials relating to the mass, the sorts of things one can suppose would have been needed by a Lotharingian churchman who entered his see facing a considerable job of restoring fabric (as well as revenues) for his cathedral and instituting

St. Ethelwold and survive them?" (both on p. xxvi of his Introduction). Also striking here is the presence of a mass for Ethelbert, king and martyr, an extremely rare occasion found only(?) at Westminster abbey, which claimed to possess his head, St Paul's cathedral nearby (see p. 487), and Hereford cathedral, where he was the patron saint.

[64] E. Bishop, *The Bosworth Psalter* (London 1908), p. 164. The calendar is printed in Wormald, *Eng. Kals*, no. 8, and the book as a whole discussed in Pfaff, *Liturg. Bks ASE*, pp. 19–21, from which some of the wording in the following paragraphs is taken.

some sort of canonical life there.[65] If this analysis is correct, it points to a date at the beginning of Giso's lengthy episcopate, and we have no way of knowing whether he used it (if at all) in the years after 1066.

The sanctorale contains some twenty-three masses relating to "English" saints, including Ælfeachus: all the usual suspects, with a heavy dose of Winchester influence (Birinus, Grimbald, and two masses each for Swithun and Æthelwold) and a clearly discernible Glastonbury presence (Aidan and a translation feast for Cuthbert: relics of the two being part of its tradition from the early tenth century; probably Patrick as well).[66] Furthermore, the calendar contains not only all of the "English" entries (save, puzzlingly, Æthelwold and Willibrord), but also, still in the original hand, Judoc (Translation feast 9 January as well as the commoner 13 December), Chad, Edmund, and above all Congar (27 November, distinctively Somerset) – as well as Valerius 29 January, Ansbert 9 February, Gertrude 17 March (after Patrick), Richarius (Riquier) 26 April, Desiderius 23 May, Remaclus and Mansuetus 3 September, Marsus 4 October, Benedicta 8 October, Gangolf 12 October, Lupus 15 October, Hubert 3 November, and Servulus 23 December It would be well beyond the limit of the space feasible here to identify all of these figures (some of whom are extremely obscure and/or problematic) and to analyze the appearances a few of them make in Anglo-Saxon litanies and other hagiographical sources. Taken in the aggregate, this odd mixture of English and (mostly) North French saints in the original calendar can perhaps best be explained on the supposition that it reflects an attempt to combine Wells tradition in the mid-eleventh century with a group of Continental saints important to the new bishop.

Given this very full original calendar, how might the numerous additions to it, almost all made in the eleventh century, be explained?[67] The obvious point to notice is that they are by no means all Continental. Most striking are four connected with a major abbey not in the diocese of Wells, Evesham: Wistan (albeit on the unusual date of 1 January, not the usual 1 June), Egwin 2 January, Odulf 12 June, Credan 19 August. The absence among this group of a saint apparently unique to English calendars, Canute of Denmark, martyred (sic) in 1086 and his cult papally approved in 1101, suggests a terminus ad quem for these additions.[68]

[65] The fullest treatment of Giso's episcopate is S. Keynes, "Giso, Bishop of Wells (1061–88)," *Anglo-Norman Studies* 19 (1997), pp. 203–71, of which only 251–53 are devoted to this book.

[66] The mass prayers for these are printed in Warren's edition of the *Leofric Missal* (1883), pp. 303–7.

[67] Kenelm, 17 July, is added in probably the 13th cent.

[68] Wormald, *Eng. Ben. Kals*, II.23, explains the connection in his discussion of Evesham calendars. The most obscure of all the additions is probably Candidus (sic; of Lucius,

Other additions of Englishmen include Guthlac 11 April, Erkenwald 30 April, and Wilfrid 12 October. That on 15 October, of the Sens archbishop Wulfram/Wulfran, to whom the notable church at Grantham in Lincolnshire is uniquely (in England) dedicated, rouses special curiosity (see p. 360 for more on him). Also of note are three additions that look like nods to the Norman political regime: the Translation of Rouen's most celebrated bishop Audoen/Ouen 5 April (in addition to his main feast, 24 August, after Bartholomew), another seventh-century bishop, Romanus 23 October (the soldier-martyr of that name is added at 9 August), and on the previous day its first bishop Maelonus/Mellon. There might be a similar reason for the addition of Patavius, the fourth-century bishop of LeMans, on 24 July. And is it conceivable that the addition of Syrus, first bishop of Pavia, at 8 December reflects the story of a eucharistic miracle connected with him which was added to the *De corpore et sanguine Christi* of Paschasius Radbertus, alluded to prominently in the controversy between Berengar of Tours and Lanfranc, whose native city Pavia was?[69]

Because Edmund Bishop's suggestion that this book may have been Giso's depended wholly on calendar entries, it is surprising that he does not seem to have noticed the concentration of Evesham saints among the additions. A possible explanation for this element is that some time after the death of the redoubtable Æthelwig, abbot of Evesham 1058–77, the book passed into the hands of his successor, Walter (1077–1104), formerly a monk of Caen and, if an amusing anecdote preserved by William of Malmesbury is factual, a familiar there of Gundulf (later bishop of Rochester) and Lanfranc.[70] That would leave the book in a monastic context, whereas our concern at the moment is purely secular.

Wulfstan of Worcester and his *portiforium*

The reverse phenomenon – a book from a monastic setting that seems adaptable to use in a secular context also – may be represented by a curious manuscript about which we have a lot of information but which is ultimately not fully comprehensible. The *portiforium* (generically an omnibus office-book, here a kind of collectar-plus) that almost certainly belonged to Wulfstan, bishop of Worcester, 1062–95 (now CCCC 391)

Rogatus, Cassian, and Candida) 1 Dec., who seems to have undergone a sex-change as well has having escaped the notice of the Bollandists.

[69] See the references in Gibson, *Lanfranc of Bec*, p. 74, n. 1.

[70] *Gesta Pontificum Anglorum*, I.lxxii.12–14, ed. and tr. M. Winterbottom, OMT (2007), p. 218.

is well known but extremely difficult to use, not least because of the piecemeal way it has been edited.[71] It has been succinctly described by Alicia Corrêa as "by far the most comprehensive representative of the breviary to survive from Anglo-Saxon England."[72] But it is still a long way from being a complete breviary, for, as she continues, "It provides for all of the day offices throughout the liturgical year and contains many (but not all) of the required liturgical formulae, both ferial and proper. The night offices of matins and lauds and a fuller office of first and second vespers are given only in a second set of the Common of the Saints." Indeed, the contents seem oddly jumbled as well as partial, but there is an explanation that makes better sense of them than that the book is either a proto-breviary or, as Mildred Budny has termed it, a "liturgical miscellany."[73] This is, that the book was designed for Wulfstan's use as he went round his diocèse, presiding at hours-services that would most often not be the night office.

To prove that this explanation is correct would require an investigation of monographic length. Here the following points seem to permit at least tentative acceptance of it. Wulfstan, though educated in monastic schools at Evesham and Peterborough, began his clerical career as a secular priest, entering the monastery at Worcester only when he was about thirty. In 1062, after seven years as prior there, he became bishop on Ealdred's translation to York, and, as well as being extremely long-lived, seems to have been the Anglo-Saxon churchman most trusted by the Conqueror in the 1070s and 1080s. A key question for us is when in his episcopate he might have acquired his *portiforium*. The manuscript seems datable to 1064–69, with 1064 or 1065 the likeliest times – if so, still during the reign of the Confessor, and early in Wulfstan's

---

[71] Edited in a partial and confusing manner by A(nselm) Hughes, *The Portiforium of St Wulstan*, 2 vols, HBS 89–90 (1958–60). (Hughes's spelling omits the medial "f," which is here restored in keeping with current usage.) The deficiency of this edition is owing partly to the inclusion of a "full abstract" of the collectar section of this hefty (724 pages; not foliated) codex as an appendix to the edition by E. S. Dewick and W. H. Frere of *The Leofric Collectar* (BL Harley 2961), discussed on p. 132 below; here in vol. II (1921), pp. xvii–xix, 501–85, followed by a full printing of "The contents of Wulfstan apart from the collectar," 587–613. The latter section includes the calendar, in parallel columns with those of four other Worcester-related documents, and litany. The calendar has also been printed by Wormald, *Eng. Kals*, pp. 211–23, but without its obits; the litany by Lapidge, *Litanies*, pp. 115–19 (almost all of the saints in the original litany were overwritten in the 12th cent.). Even as late as the M. R. James catalogue of CCC MSS (1912) it was known as "Portiforium Oswaldi," having been so headed in the 16th cent. The most comprehensible description is now Hartzell's extensive enumeration of contents, *Cat. Music*, pp. 53–66.

[72] A. Corrêa in Pfaff, ed. *Liturg. Bks ASE*, p. 57.

[73] Budny, *Manuscript Art at CCCC*, I.629–44, at 629. Plates 596–603 of vol. II show six pages roughly full-size and two openings reduced.

episcopate.[74] The book is clearly intended for use in a monastic context. It includes the "monastic canticles" on the occasions when they were used (Sundays, the seasons of Advent, Christmastide, Lent, and Eastertide, and great feasts), and all the offices on days when they would have been sung are of twelve lessons. There are very few ceremonial rubrics, but one preceding Maundy Thursday in the collectar uses the monastic term *fratres* – though to be sure in a cathedral context: enough bread must be consecrated for all the faithful (*fidelibus*) wishing to communicate on the next day.

The collectar is complete for the temporale, but for the sanctorale only nineteen feasts have full forms. Eighteen of these are unremarkable, but one stands out glaringly: Lambert, on 17 September. A possible explanation for the odd prominence of this seventh-century bishop of Maastricht (but buried at Liège) is that Lambert was the name taken by, or given to, Cnut on his baptism, the precise year of which is unknown. Lambert appears regularly in Anglo-Saxon calendars, as in the one here, but with no signs of special importance. It is tempting to relate his prominence here to the story in the *Vita Wulfstani* of William of Malmesbury, itself a translation from the lost Old English life by Coleman, Wulfstan's chancellor. This describes how a teacher of Wulfstan's at Peterborough, Earnwig (later its abbot, 1042–52), illuminated a sacramentary and psalter, entrusting their safekeeping to his pupil; the finished products were then given to Cnut and Emma, to the young Wulfstan's great distress. But during the embassy of Ealdred to the German imperial court at Cologne (where the books had been sent by Cnut) in 1054–55, the two books were produced and given to the English bishop, who on returning home presented them to his then new prior – thus fulfilling an angelic promise to the young Wulfstan many years earlier.[75] We do not know what happened to those books, and inevitably wonder whether they remained (possibly in use) at Worcester during Wulfstan's time as bishop there. More will be said about the office-forms for Lambert when the Leofric collectar is discussed below.[76] Here we note just that its presence, as one of eighteen specially

---

[74] P. R. Robinson, *Catalogue of Dated and Datable MSS c. 737–1600 in Cambridge Libraries*, 2 vols (Cambridge 1988), no. 157.

[75] *Vita Wulfstani*, bk. I, cap. 4–5 and 9, in *William of Malmesbury, Saints' Lives*, ed. M. Winterbottom and R. M. Thomson, OMT (Oxford 2002), pp. 16, 40. T. A. Heslop, "De luxe manuscripts and the patronage of King Cnut and Queen Emma," *ASE* 19 (1990), pp. 151–95 at 160, discussing this story, points out that the sacramentary must have been like (but cannot have been) the Robert of Jumièges missal (see p. 89 above).

[76] The antiphons to the canticles at first and second vespers and lauds differ in the two manuscripts, so neither can have been copied from the other.

singled-out feasts, must signify a particular interest either in that saint himself or in a baptismal namesake, as Cnut was.

After the section of eighteen full forms in the Wulfstan portiforium comes an extensive section of collects for specific saints – some 180 in all – from Silvester to the apostle Thomas. For each saint there are between one prayer and five, and the vast majority of figures in this sanctorale section appear also in the calendar (which, however, is much fuller). Present here but absent from the calendar are Botulf (17 June), Cuthburga (31 August, here spelled *Gutburga*; Paulinus in the calendar), Etheldreda (17 October, her Translation; her 23 June feast is present in both), Birstan (4 November), and the Octave of Birinus (10 December, Eulalia in the calendar). Botulf and Etheldreda are prominent mainly in the East of England, Cuthburga in Dorset (see p. 382), Birstan and Birinus around Winchester, so it is unlikely that all five of these discrepancies have the same, or indeed any, explanation; but, as it is more laborious to write out a collect than to place an entry in a calendar, each is probably meant to have been used by the owner of the book.

The elaborate David portrait and facing Beatus page (pp. 24–25) and the strong initials to the psalms and many of the prayers indicate that ownership by a dignitary is intended, while the extensive provision of neums for the antiphons in the collectar suggests that the book was meant for practical purposes, not display. The long section of private prayers (pp. 581–618), many of them couched in the first person singular, contains two important vernacular components. The first, after a lengthy *Oratio sancti Gregorii* and headed *Anglice*, is an extensive prayer for forgiveness. The second (pp. 611–18), headed *aliae orationes latine et anglice*, is a bilingual votive office of the Cross in which each Latin petition is followed by its English equivalent.[77] Although neither of these vernacular elements is unique to this book, their placement here, between the psalter and the collectar, implies use. In all, this volume, though enigmatic, may show us an eleventh-century bishop as a liturgical person with a vividness comparable to that provided by Lanfranc's *Constitutions*, if not quite as full as that derivable for the figure who is considered next, Leofric.

The liturgical program of Leofric at Exeter, 1050–72

Leofric, born of a substantial family in the West of England or Cornwall but brought up in Lotharingia (it is not known why), attracted there the

---

[77] Both are summarized, with references to late 19th-cent. editions, in Ker, *CMCAS*, no. 67.

notice of Edward who, upon becoming king in 1042, appointed him a royal chaplain. In 1046 he was given the dioceses of both Crediton (for, at that point, Devon) and St Germans (for Cornwall); when, four years later, he moved his episcopal seat to Exeter, amalgamation of the two dioceses appears to have been a *fait accompli*. Soon after his arrival at the new headquarters city he seems to have shut down the small monastery in its center and established his cathedral chapter as a body of secular canons, in theory following the Rule of Chrodegang.[78] A notable feature of it seems to have been an active scriptorium, studied intensively by Elaine Drage in her 1978 doctoral thesis.[79] A precise chronology of Leofric's activity in the twenty-two years of his episcopate there cannot be established; we have to work back from what survives of his liturgical and literary efforts, and forward from what he claimed, towards the end of his life, had been the dismal state of ecclesiastical equipment at Exeter in 1050. The latter is represented most vividly (if not necessarily accurately) by an inventory in Old English of church lands, goods, and books, drawn up for Leofric between 1069 and 1072. This document avers, in Patrick Conner's translation, that "when he took charge of the minster, he did not find any more books except one capitulary and one very old nocturnal antiphoner, and one epistolary, and two very old and worn-out office lectionaries, and one worn set of mass-vestments."[80] As Conner has pointed out, this must be an exaggeration, though something would depend on what is meant by *þam minstre* (that at Crediton, or what remained from the monastery at Exeter – the dedication of which, to St Peter, became that of the new cathedral?).

Whatever the degree of tendentiousness in that report, the contrast with what is listed as existing in Leofric's church c. 1070 is immense. All the literary titles aside – when he died Leofric left some sixty-six books as the foundation of the cathedral library, including the Exeter Book, the unspeakably precious codex of Old English poetry which is his greatest claim to renown – the liturgical books alone number thirty-one.[81] That

---

[78] F. Barlow, "Leofric and his Times," in the volume of commemorative essays he edited, *Leofric of Exeter* (Exeter 1972), pp. 1–16, is still the fullest account in print of Leofric's career, but pays next to no attention to his liturgical interests. It is possible that Leofric's copy of the *Regula canonicorum* survives in CCCC 191.

[79] E. M. Drage, "Bishop Leofric and the Exeter Cathedral Chapter 1050–1072: A Reassessment of the Manuscript Evidence" (unpublished Oxford D.Phil. thesis, 1978); much scholarly work on the subject during recent decades has depended heavily on this thesis, as does the present discussion.

[80] P. Conner, *Anglo-Saxon Exeter: a Tenth-Century Cultural History* (Woodbridge 1993), pp. 226–35, where the inventory is discussed and printed, with parallel translation.

[81] They are listed in convenient tabular form in S. Rankin, "From memory to record: Musical notations in manuscripts from Exeter," *ASE* 13 (1984), pp. 97–112 at 101; discussed by M. Lapidge, "Surviving booklists from Anglo-Saxon England," in *Learning and Literature*, pp. 33–90 at 65–69.

many of these are given Old English rather than Latin titles is a valuable resource in itself, but makes it difficult to derive a sense of how complete a liturgical collection is represented.[82] "Two great ornamented gospel-books" are listed among the furnishings rather than in the section on the service books, which in turn contains a few non-liturgical titles, including the Exeter Book itself. In a general way there seem to be sufficient books for mass – only two *fulle mæssebec*, however, one of which is almost certainly the Leofric missal – and office, though that there are only two Gallicanum psalters (plus one Romanum) suggests either that it was performed by a very small group of clerics or that there were other copies of the psalms which somehow Leofric did not regard as "his." Also listed are a martyrology and and the apparently disproportionate number of four benedictionals (one *deorwyrðe* "precious," and three "others").[83]

What can be identified with reasonable certainty as surviving forms a striking trove of books, each of a different kind – missal, psalter, collectar, and pontifical-with-benedictional. The latter is most likely to be BL Add. 28188, which contains a complete benedictional as well as (fragmentarily, but seventy-six folios' worth) pontifical material. Its scribes have been identified with some in Leofric's scriptorium.[84] Andrew Prescott's analysis of the contents of the 170 blessings shows that many of them appear to be original compositions, forming what he calls "one of the largest groups of new blessings produced in the Middle Ages."[85] Despite all this originality, heavy Winchester influence is discernible, a fact recognized by Edmund Bishop as long ago as 1886.[86] It would be no surprise if Leofric had turned to Winchester for extensive help, despite its monastic nature. How extensive the Winchester influence was might be more ascertainable if another pontifical probably owned by Leofric, BL Cott. Vit. A.vii, had not been so badly damaged in the 1731 Cottonian fire. Parts of 112 folios survive, but many are illegible or can be read only with the aid of cold light.[87] An argument,

[82] H. Gneuss has relied heavily on this list in his "Liturgical books in Anglo-Saxon England and their Old English terminology," in the same volume, pp. 91–141.

[83] See Conner, *Anglo-Saxon Exeter*, p. 232, n. 34, for possible identification of two of these; Rankin, "Musical notations," p. 101, suggests that *bletsingboc* here might have included pontificals; it is also possible that they might have been *libelli*, written seasonally as required by the bishop.

[84] T. A. M. Bishop, "Notes on Cambridge MSS, part iii: MSS connected with Exeter," *Trans. Cbg. Bibliog. Soc.* 2.ii (1955), pp. 192–99 at 193.

[85] A. Prescott, "The Structure of English Pre-Conquest Benedictionals," p. 130.

[86] Bishop, *Liturg. Hist.*, p. 240 (the 1916 printing left the original version of thirty years earlier unchanged).

[87] The most complete enumeration of contents is again that in Hartzell, *Cat. Music*, pp. 265–70.

based on the saints in the litanies, for Ramsey abbey as the book's place
of origin seems weak in the light of identification of two of its scribes as
those of other Leofrician books, one being among those writing in the
"C" part of his eponymous missal.[88] The litanies in Add. 28188 almost
certainly derive from those in Vit. A.vii, but with added saints, above
all Sativola (Sidwell), that provide an unmistakeably Exeter stamp. Neither of these pontificals is at all *deorwyrðe* physically, and notation was
never supplied in Add. 28188, though the text was spaced for it. Leofric's more precious pontifical book(s) must have perished.

Leofrician books for the office: collectar and psalter

Among the books to which Leofric's name is attached are two that,
though not strictly complementary, together furnish a more vivid
sense of developing office liturgy in eleventh-century England than
we get anywhere else. The book called *collectaneum* in Leofric's inventory is almost certainly what is now called the Leofric collectar, BL
Harley 2961. The somewhat imprecise term "collectar" tends to dis-
guise the fact that, as Alicia Corrêa has put it, this book "represents
a dramatic improvement in structure and contents over the earlier
collectars ... .[it] is a fully developed office collectar, and there is very
little difference in the arrangement of any given office between it and
early breviaries. It contains three new features: the inclusion of psalmody and choral material, the latter being written out in full for major
feasts; the assignment of each group of liturgical formulae to a particular office; and the arrrangement of all office texts in the order in
which they are celebrated."[89] The two volumes of the modern edition
are not easy to use. E. S. Dewick's presentation of the text appeared,
in a bulky quarto volume, in 1914, but the introduction not until 1921,
four years after Dewick's death and so described as "completed from
the papers of" by W. H. Frere; and in fact this second volume touches
on the Leofric book only insofar as it sheds light on the Wulfstan
portiforium, a partial edition of which (by Frere) is then supplied.[90]

[88] T. A. M. Bishop, *Eng. Caroline Minuscule*, p. 24, n. 1. The section containing the
litanies which include distinctively Ramsey saints was written by a third hand, not
necessarily that of an Exeter scribe: Drage thesis, p. 365.

[89] A. Corrêa in Pfaff, ed. *Liturg. Bks ASE*, p. 51.

[90] The full titles are illuminating: *The Leofric Collectar (Harl. MS 2961) with an Appendix containing a Litany and Prayers from Harl. MS 863*, HBS 45 (1914), and *The Leofric Collectar compared with the Collectar of St Wulfstan, together with kindred documents
of Exeter and Worcester*, HBS 56 (1921). The (very) partial edition of the Wulfstan
book helps to explain the inadequacy of the subsequent HBS edition of it, by Anselm
Hughes, HBS 89–90 (1956, 1960): above, p. 127.

Here we need to try to understand the Harley 2961 collectar in its Leofrician context, for it was written entirely at Exeter and by four scribes working there.[91]

In his [bracketed] contribution to Dewick's introduction, Frere pointed to the inclusion of three feasts, Mary Magdalen, Olaf, and Lambert, as directing our attention "to quite other quarters."[92] Oddly, he did not go on to state what these "other quarters" might be, save for observing that the forms for Lambert were as those in a Liège breviary of 1497, with which he had found many cases of correspondence. The Leofric collectar provides offices for only a small number of sanctorale occasions, all integrated into their proper liturgical places.[93] The late eleventh-century popularity of Mary Magdalen is a familiar enough phenomenon that the appearance of the feast here is not specially note-worthy; Lambert and Olaf are, however, another matter. There seems to be a connection between Olaf, the king of Norway "martyred" in 1030, and Exeter: most likely through the establishment of a church of that dedication in Exeter by Earl Godwin's Danish wife Gytha, marked by a grant of land in 1063 which is preserved in a thirteenth-century document.[94] Although this is not the only recognition of Olaf in south-west England, the donation here by a Dane whose husband owed his preferment to King Cnut (Cnut's sister Estrith married Gytha's brother Ulf; their son, Swein Estrithson, was king of Denmark in 1063) brings us close to the puzzle of the prominence of St Lambert: Cnut's baptismal name, as explained above (p. 128).

---

[91] Most of the book was written by a scribe whose hand, according to T. A. M. Bishop ("Notes, pt iii: Exeter," p. 193) "could be classified with the 'Exeter' style only by so diluting the criteria as to make the term unmeaning. The MS suggests that the standards of the scriptorium were not exacting; although a liturgical work, and not without some wretched attempts at decoration, it is badly written on very badly pre-pared parchment." This judgment may be thought a bit waspish. The scribe of the final parts of the book, fols 234–56v, writes better. This fourth scribe also wrote part of Harley 863 (the psalter to be discussed presently), the third scribe bits of that MS and also of the Add. 28188 pontifical: Watson, *BL Dated MSS*, no. 718 and pl. 44. Ten folios are illustrated on twelve plates in vol. I of the HBS edition.

[92] *Leofric Collectar*, II.xii.

[93] Besides the three post-Christmas feasts, those of the Purification, Annunciation, and Invention of the Cross, all roughly integrated into temporale locations; then, in a block after Trinity Sunday, John the Baptist, Peter and Paul, Paul, Octave of Apos-tles, Mary Magdalen, Olaf, Peter's Chains, Assumption, Nativity of Mary, Exaltation of the Cross, Lambert bishop and martyr, Michael, All Saints, Martin, and Andrew.

[94] P. Sawyer, *Anglo-Saxon Charters: an Annotated List and Bibliography* (London 1968), no. 1037 (with comment that Dorothy Whitelock in a personal communication had expressed doubts about authenticity). See also B. Dickins, "The Cult of S. Olave in the British Isles," *Saga-Book of the Viking Society* 12 (1937–45), pp. 53–80 at 56; on p. 69 he notes that in 1070–71 William I gave it to the monks of his new foundation at Battle, who established a small priory of St Nicholas next to it.

Now whereas the office for Olaf is found only in the Leofric book, there is one for Lambert also in the Wulfstan portiforium, discussed earlier in this chapter.[95] Its office is clearly related, but not absolutely identical, to that in the Leofric collectar, the main difference being that in the latter the antiphons for Magnificat and Benedictus are flowery and highly literary. It looks as though the parts where Leofric differs from Wulfstan are taken from the office for Lambert very likely composed in the tenth century by Stephen of Liège.[96] Lambert comes to be widely included in various English uses, but his cultus in the eleventh century is apparently confined to the western part: Leofric's Exeter, Wulfstan's (diocese of) Worcester, Giso's Wells (if Cott. Vit. A.xviii is correctly ascribed to him; p. 124), with corroboration in the twelfth century from the Glastonbury collectar (p. 179) and in the late fourteenth from the Sherborne missal (p. 236). The curious thing is that there is no mass for him in the "C" additions to the massbook, to which we will turn presently.

At first glance the psalter, now BL Harley 863, made at Exeter in Leofric's time, might seem to require only perfunctory notice, but it contains three major, if somewhat oblique, points of interest – one indeed connected with a frustration. The frustration is that the original calendar is missing, having been replaced by one of the late twelfth or (less likely) early thirteenth century.[97] The replacement is, however, valuable in showing that the book was still being used, if not necessarily liturgically, at Exeter both then, and, as numerous additions prove, later. A few among the many differences between the calendar of the Leofric missal as completed with its "C" component and the present Harley 863 calendar are Harley's changing of C's Mary and Martha to Marius, Martha, Audifax, and Habbacuc at January 19th, and supplying of Petroc June 4th, Mildred on July 13th, the Two Ewalds on October 3rd, Rumwold on November 3rd, Birstan (Beornstan) on the 4th, and Birinus on December 3rd; while many of the more exotic entries in the missal's

---

[95] *Wulstan Portiforium*, ed. Hughes, I.108. Both this and the Leofric office have different collects for each of first vespers, lauds, terce, sext, none, and second vespers.

[96] The question of Stephen's authorship is vexed. A reconstructed text is printed in A. Auda, *L'école-musicale liégeois au Xe siècle. Étienne de Liège*, Acad. Royale de Belgique, Classe des Beaux-Arts 2.i (Brussels 1923), pp. 187–97; in the preceding discussion he makes a good deal of the appearance of the office in Harley 2961 as evidence for Stephen's authorship, but he does not appear to have seen either the MS or the HBS edition and relies entirely on earlier scholarship in French. A brief but more reliable treatment is in Corrêa, *Durham Collectar*, pp. 15–18.

[97] The date range given by Watson, *BL Dated MSS*, no. 638, is 1173–1220; his pl. 102 illustrates the late 12th-cent. January page, pl. 43 one of the canticles, written by the 11th-cent. Exeter scribe who also wrote in Add. 28188, Vit. A.vii, and Harley 2961.

calendar are absent. Later additions to the psalter's calendar include the Exeter Feast of Relics (22 May), Kieran (Ciaran; 5 March), Sativola (1 August), and Francis (4 October). The strong Exeter character of the first three of these causes one to wonder whether the book had been elsewhere than at the cathedral when the late twelfth-century calendar was written but was subsequently returned to it.

The litany (original) in Harley 863 is so overblown that it invites floundering; Michael Lapidge calls it an "act of scholarly compilation rather than of local devotion."[98] There are some 123 martyrs (of whom Olaf is the last, Lambert nineteen places above him), 102 confessors, and 64 virgins (with Anna and Katherine added in a slightly later hand). The last three confessors are *Leo* [space of 4 mm] *ix* (the Roman numerals look to be in the original hand; if so, the reforming pope who died in 1054); Bardo, archbishop of Mainz and a member of Leo's circle (d. 1053); and a Simon. This last is probably the Palestinian hermit Sym(e)on, who became part of the circle of Poppo, archbishop of Trier, and died as a hermit there in 1035.[99] The sequence Leo IX, Bardo, Simon, none of whom is found in any other pre-1100 English litany, seems to point to Leofric, whose moving of his see center to Exeter was accomplished with Leo's aid and who is likely to have been familiar with leading figures of the Reform movement.

The matter of greatest interest in this psalter is a feature that points towards the development of the full breviary even more clearly than does the arrangement of offices in the Harley 2961 collectar. This feature, identified only recently and still not adequately studied, is the presence of what seems to be a kind of "sample week" between the usual contents of a psalter (psalms, canticles, litany, miscellaneous prayers) and the Office of the Dead.[100] It looks superficially like a week

---

[98] Lapidge, *Litanies*, p. 74; the litany is printed on pp. 193–202.

[99] This is the figure guessed at by Edmund Bishop, with his usual shrewdness, in *The Bosworth Psalter*, p. 163; see subsequently M. Coens, "Un document inédit sur le culte de S Syméon," *Anal. Boll.* 68 (1950), pp. 181–96. An alternative is a ninth-century monk of Reichenau called Symeon Achivus, "qui et Bardo ante vocatus" according to a *Vita* from that abbey, ed. by T. Klüppel and W. Berschin, "Vita Symeonis Achivi," in *Die Abtei Reichenau*, ed. H. Maurer (Sigmaringen 1974), pp. 115–24. A further but inconvenient possibility is Simon of Crespy or Crépi (or sometimes Valois), famous for declaring a *mariage blanche* on his wedding night, and for subsequently becoming a monk influential in Gregorian circles. But this Simon did not die until 1082, which would make identification of the Harley 863 psalter with one of the two in Leofric's inventory of c. 1070, strongly buttressed palaeographically, impossible.

[100] I coined the term in a paper, "Bishop Baldock's Book, St Paul's Cathedral, and the Use of Sarum," in *LCSSME* (1998), no. XI, and amplified the idea in "The 'Sample Week' in the Medieval Latin Divine Office," in *Continuity and Change in Christian*

in the most ordinary part of the temporale, possibly the second Sunday after the Epiphany, roughly the point at which things liturgical return to "normal" after the Advent and post-Christmas excitements. The nine lessons for the Sunday would work, just, but the three for each following weekday will not: those for the first two days are from Romans 2 (also used for the first six on Sunday), but those for the last two days – the leaves that would have contained Wednesday and almost all of Thursday are missing – are extra-biblical, apparently from a treatise on the immutability of God.[101] A partial parallel has been found in the Wulfstan portiforium and a more extensive one in a psalter-plus of about 1200.[102] Depending on when in the date-range of the Wulfstan book, 1062–95, it was actually written, the appearance of this "sample week" in the Leofric psalter may turn out to be the pioneering experiment in putting together a kind of template for the office in ordinary time: a format which could be repeated week after week, with variable formulas, throughout the entire temporale. The "sample week" section begins on fol. 117, line 15; on line 7 of 117v a second hand takes over, one which wrote also fols 234–56v (hymns and sequences) of the collectar.[103] The whole thing intensifies curiosity as to whose is the active liturgical intelligence at Exeter: is it Leofric's? To pursue this further we must attend to the "C" section of the famous missal.

Leofric missal "C"

The material added during Leofric's ownership is summed up by Nicholas Orchard succinctly as "by and large on new gatherings; four at the front of the book; one in the middle (a single sheet and a bifolium); and five at the end … . A series of marginal cues for the Lessons and Gospels to be read at mass were added to the cues for chant already provided; musical notation was supplied for pieces both old and

Worship, ed. R. W. Swanson, SCH 35 (1999), pp. 78–88, some words from which are repeated here.

[101] The commentary seems, however improbably, to be the reworking of some of Gregory the Great's *Moralia in Iob* by a 7th-cent. Spanish bishop Taio of Saragossa in his *Liber sententiarum* (PL 80.731). The Sunday office is neumed throughout; this section of Harley 863 has, understandably, puzzled Rankin, "Musical notations," p. 102.

[102] *Wulstan Portiforium*, II.48–62. The "psalter-plus" is the Baldock book referred to above, St Paul's Cathedral MS 1; its "sample week" is more subtly presented than those in the Leofric or Wulfstan books (treated on pp. 82–84 of the 1999 article; cf. pp. 87–88 for discussion of a "quasi-sample week" in the St Albans breviary, BL Royal 2 A.x).

[103] The change in hands was pointed out by Drage, "Bishop Leofric," p. 367.

new; prayers were modified and corrected by erasure, marginal annotation and interlinear addition throughout; and entries for a variety of Lotharingian (and other) saints ... added to B's calendar."[104]

All of these additions and alterations look to make the book, some century and a half old when Leofric would have encountered it, usable in his time and place. The inscription on fol. 1v recording his donation stresses that he is giving the book "ad utilitatem successorum suorum," and it is from this standpoint that the book as he left it will be most useful to us. Drage's analysis of the palaeography suggests involvement by at least eleven hands, of which that of scribe 1 is probably Leofric's own. Most notable among that scribe's marginal contributions may be his supplying of a new rota of lessons, tracts, and collects for the Vigils of Easter and Pentecost. This is a next to impossibly complicated subject in its permutations and combinations, but it is clear that Leofric wished to have the texts for those great services brought into line with those that become mainstream from the late eleventh century on, and that to do this he had access to sources that we cannot trace precisely.[105] Other material probably written by Leofric includes a large number of votive masses. Specially noteworthy here is a set of prayers for a "Missa propria pro episcopo" most likely composed by Leofric himself; the bishop of Exeter is mentioned in all three prayers, with language – like "me famulum tuum .ill. [= fill in the blank with the current bishop's name]" – which makes explicit his hope that it will be used by his successors.[106]

This and other new material is written on three new gatherings (fols 18–37v) inserted before the calendar and its associated computus matter. The liturgical additions to the calendar seem to be of a mixed character and are written by several scribes, presumably at a variety of times.[107] Those that could not have been in "B's" calendar are Edward the Martyr (killed in 978, but it was not until 1008 that a law of Ethelred mandated his feast throughout England), Dunstan (died 988), and Ælpheagus (as spelled here; martyred 1012). The only other new English figure is Eormenhilda, and there are three British saints: David, Maglorius (Magloire/Malo), and Winwaloe. None of

[104] *Leofric Missal*, I.206.
[105] A key witness here would be the New Minster missal, but it lacks everything before Easter Friday. The "old" system in Leofric "A" is found also in the Winchcombe sacramentary and otherwise, according to Legg's 1897 apparatus ("Textual Notes"), in a late 15th-cent. printed Roman missal.
[106] *Leofric Missal*, II.52. The language of the prayers is verbose and flowery.
[107] Two additions seem merely to remedy oversights: both Peter *ad vincula* and Saturninus have masses in "A."

the additions to the calendar appears to have been written by Leofric himself, and they cannot all have been made under his direction, for one is his obit, on February 10th. Of the thirty-eight additions, sixteen are obits of persons who died as late as William the Conqueror, 1087 (there is also a notice of Leofric's ordination date, the same day as Ælfheah's martyrdom, April 19th). Three are of bishops: Eadulf, the first bishop of Crediton; Lyfing, Leofric's immediate predecessor; and – is this significant? – Ælfwine, bishop of Winchester (d. 1047, here entered on the correct day, August 29th). Cnut is also entered on his correct day, November 12th, but under his baptismal name: "Obitus Landberti piissimi regis." Three are women (the Matilda on September 22nd is not the Conqueror's wife, who died on November 2nd) and two are laymen, "Ordlaui laici" being so specified.[108]

Nothing survives of the building in which mass could have been celebrated with the Leofric missal on the altar. Our next extensive awareness of Exeter will be in the mid-fourteenth century, when a program connected with its great bishop John Grandisson (1327–69) was meant to be carried out in a magnificent building that does survive, the present cathedral. By contrast, the imagination required to visualize Leofric and his chapter of canons at worship can take us only so far, despite the existence of the pontifical, two books for the office, and missal that can with some confidence be connected with him. Nonetheless, it seems not unreasonable to suppose that the liturgical regime at which they hint may not have been greatly different from those at other major secular churches – Hereford, London, York, and (soon) Lincoln – for all of which the evidence is much later. But between the episcopates of Leofric and Grandisson such story of secular liturgy as we can put together must proceed largely not through Exeter but through Sarum channels. When we resume looking at secular liturgy, it will be at the new Norman establishment just east of Salisbury Plain. Before doing that, however, we need to follow the trail of monastic liturgy into the twelfth century.

A further attempt at monastic uniformity?

The title of our next chapter, "Monastic Liturgy, 1100–1215," implies a discreteness that is clearly justified by the latter date but may be somewhat dubious when applied to the former. As will be explained

---

[108] Drage, "Bishop Leofric," pp. 114–17, discusses the identity of some of those memorialized, but some of her identifications require revision, notably the idea that the Landbert on 12 Nov. was a king of the Romans who d. 998.

in detail later, the regularizing activities of the Fourth Lateran Council in 1215 led to the establishment of what can fairly be called "orders" as the normative principle of organization for religious. The resulting multiplicity of orders is taken up in chapters 6–8, of which chapter 6 deals with houses of the Benedictine Order – as it comes to be after, and because of, the 1215 Council. The year 1100 marks no such organizational watershed for the (at that point) independent abbeys of England, no attempt to create a centralized organization or congregation.

Nonetheless, it is possible to wonder whether there were no more attempts at any kind of liturgical regularization after that of Lanfranc in his *Constitutions* (itself a successor to the Æthelwoldian effort that resulted in the *Regularis concordia*). The beginning of a possible trail may be Christopher Jones's investigation of an enigmatic manuscript in the Bodleian, Wood empt. 4.[109] It is a composite book, the first twenty-four folios being all that concern us. In presentation it is far from splendid; to Jones's eye, "this ragged little booklet (or sheaf of loose leaves and slips, later bound), was a place to jot down monastic customs bit by bit, as they were met in two or more sources." The date could be any time in the middle two quarters of the twelfth century, and, frustratingly, "in some twenty-four folios filled with monastic customs, not a single liturgical or geographical clue points to any more exact location."[110]

It may be, of course, that to the various jotters (two primary and as many as five occasional scribes) the source of what they copied was of little relevance; "when found, make a note of" might have been their motto. It is also conceivable, however, that these are jottings from something like a text: that is, a collection of customs drawn up with an idea to uniformity of use. This possibility is raised by a few of the liturgical points, of which only a couple may be adduced here. Among the duties of the conversi is the quite complicated management of candelabra, the rules for which are laid down *ex consuetudine*: but does *consuetudo* here mean informally transmitted custom or does it imply something like a written *consuetudinarium*, the sort of thing that, at however many removes, might have been the source of this set of practices?[111] Again, on solemn feasts after communion a boy standing before the altar and holding the chalice genuflects, which is a signal for those in choir to do likewise; but, as is spelled out, throughout the whole of Lent this

---

[109] C. A. Jones, "Monastic Custom in Early Norman England: the Significance of Bodleian MS Wood empt. 4," *Rev. Bén.* 113 (2003), pp. 135–68 and 302–36.

[110] Part i, pp. 138, 140.

[111] Part ii (the edition), section 16 (p. 311). In the notes at the end of part ii Jones indicates the degree of dependence, or otherwise, or these jottings on known customaries, Continental or English.

cannot be done, because the boy will be behind the Lenten veil (save on Sundays and major feasts when, at least according to Lanfranc, the curtain is pulled back, thus making the boy visible): are we meant to understand this as what does happen in a large number of English houses, or as what should happen?[112]

Our closing question must then be, is such a practice being *de*scribed or, in whatever was the basic model for Wood empt. 4, *pre*scribed? If the former, we are mildly interested; if the latter, we have a large quantum of unsatistifed curiosity to repress. It seems unlikely that an attempt, presumably of the immediate post-Lanfrancian period, at some prescriptiveness in English monastic usages has left no other trace than this jumbled twelfth-century manuscript, but the possibility cannot be ruled out entirely. The story we take up now will be dominated initially by one great house, that at St Albans, and we shall be able to think about broader matters only at the end of the next chapter.

---

[112] Part ii, section 14 (p. 310); cf. Lanfranc, *Consts.*, sect 23.

Excursus: on method in the comparison of liturgical texts

As has been noted in the Introduction, towards the end of the nineteenth century several factors coalesced to make the comparative study of liturgical texts possible, at least in England. The most directly obvious is the availability by that time of a number of catalogues of manuscripts, however imperfect and incomplete, which made possible some sense of the range of (for example) missals available for textual comparison.[1] These include catalogues for the Harleian, Cotton, Sloane, Egerton, and early Additional (through 34526) manuscripts at the (then) British Museum; for the University Library manuscripts at Cambridge (albeit quirkily); the Quarto Catalogues for manuscripts at the Bodleian and H. O. Coxe's two volumes for the Oxford colleges; for French manuscripts, the first twenty-five volumes of the Quarto Series of the *Catalogue Général des Manuscrits des Bibliothèques Publiques des Départements*, providing at least rudimentary coverage for Rouen and Orléans, and, much more importantly, Léopold Delisle's *Mémoire sur d'anciens sacramentaires*.[2] Other factors that can here be only enumerated include the foundation of the Henry Bradshaw Society in 1890 (see p. 10); widespread peace in Europe and rather advanced mail and rail communications for roughly forty years after about 1875; and what seem to have been relatively low printing costs.[3]

J. W. Legg's 1897 "Notes"

Many of these elements are reflected in the publication in 1897 of the "Liturgical Introduction" that comes at the end of the third and final

---

[1] The year 1895 is specially noteworthy because it saw the publication of the first five of M. R. James's many catalogues and the beginning (with vol. III) of the Bodleian *Summary Catalogue*. See the "Excursus on sources" for further discussion of these and other catalogues.

[2] Devoted primarily but not exclusively to French MSS. Often cited as a separate publication, it is in fact Number 3 of Part I of the 32nd vol. of *Mémoires de l'Institut national de France*, published by the Académie des Inscriptions et Belles-Lettres.

[3] For further aspects of the general historiographical background, see pp. 8–12.

volume of John Wickham Legg's great edition of the Westminster missal (on the book itself, see p. 227), of which the first volume was the initial HBS publication. This "Introduction" amasses facts taken from a variety of published catalogues, relies on information supplied by scholars working on the Continent, and occupies a total of 223 closely printed pages, of which some 187 are what are modestly called "Notes": these being the first, and still most extensive, collection of comparative data concerning mass texts in medieval England. The frequency with which these data of Legg's are cited in, or otherwise underlie, the present work may give some idea of the importance of what he put together. For this reason, and because Legg's rather brusque way of presenting information is sometimes difficult to penetrate, it may be useful to provide a rather full explanation of the nature and limitations of his massive labors, as well as to connect them with other, more recent efforts of the same kind.

Legg collected and arranged information from some seventy sources, of which twenty were modern (1557–1889) collections, ten were Continental missals printed between 1490 and 1617, and three were early printed editions of the famous Roman sacramentaries.[4] Most of the rest were either English liturgical manuscripts or, in a few cases, modern editions of them or of their early printed versions.[5] Some of the latter are discussed in the appropriate places in the present work: W. G. Henderson's editions of the Hereford missal (1874), York missal (also 1874), "York" (*recte* Bainbridge) pontifical (1875), and Sarum manual as presented in his York manual edition (also 1875). Included as well are F. E. Warren's edition of the Irish missal now Corpus Christi College Oxford MS 282 (1879), G. H. Forbes's of the "Drummond" (Irish) missal (1882); and Warren's of the Leofric missal (1883).[6] It should be

---

[4] See the "Excursus on the terms Gelasian and Gregorian as used here," p. 56. The editions Legg cites are not the editions in current use (as indicated in that Excursus), but rather the Leonine, Gelasian, and Gregorian from Muratori's *Liturgia Romana Vetus* (1748), and also Ménard's 1642 edition of the "St Eligius" more-or-less Gregorian massbook (BN lat. 12051). The "Young Gelasian" Gellone is cited from the MS, BN lat. 12048. Legg's "Bobbio missal," Milan, Bibl. Ambros. D.84 inf., is a 10th/11th-cent. book (*CLLA* 1968, no. 1473), not the celebrated 8th-cent. codex of that name, BN lat. 13256; fortunately it is not often cited, so the confusion is minimal. An important aid to Legg's work was H. A. Wilson's *Classified Index to the Leonine, Gelasian and Gregorian Sacramentaries according to the text of Muratori* (Cambridge 1892).

[5] A few witnesses from Normandy are also included: "Rouen" refers to a 1499 printed missal (but with a parenthetical note to compare BL Add. 10048, which is a 12th-cent. sacramentary with pontifical elements); "Evreux" stands for BL Add. 26655, an early 14th-cent. missal, and "By" for a Bayeux missal printed at Rouen in 1501.

[6] The Notes frequently include reference to "Rossyln," but this does not appear in the list of Symbols at the beginning. What is meant is the Rosslyn missal, in 1897 in the process of being edited by H. J. Lawlor (it appeared in 1899 as HBS 15); from

noticed specially that the edition of the Sarum missal cited by Legg is that of F. H. Dickinson, 1861–83, made from the early printed books, not that from manuscripts of the later thirteenth–early fourteenth century which Legg was to publish in (but not until) 1916; so his siglum "S[arum]" always refers to the late versions of that central massbook.[7]

Twelve pre-1100 witnesses, most of them considered in the previous chapters, are cited. The five massbooks are, in addition to the Leofric, the Giso sacramentary (BL Cott. Vit. A.xviii), the Winchcombe sacramentary (Orléans, B.m. 127),[8] and, from modern printed editions, the Robert of Jumièges (as edited by H. A. Wilson 1896) and St Augustine's (as edited by M. Rule, also 1896) books. A further five sources containing pontifical material, in addition to that contained in three of the massbooks, are also cited: the Æthelwold benedictional (then belonging to the Duke of Devonshire, and cited only from John Gage's 1832 monograph), the "Egbert" pontifical (BN lat. 10575, from the imperfect edition of William Greenwell, 1853), the Canterbury benedictional (from the MS, BL Harley 2892), the Ramsey (sic) benedictional (from BN lat. 987), and Archbishop Robert benedictional (from Rouen, B.m. 369/ Y.7).[9] The *Regularis concordia*, which contains virtually nothing in the way of mass texts, is not mentioned, but Ælfric's *Letter to the Monks of Eynsham* is cited in the partial edition by M. Bateson (1892); and Lanfranc's *Constitutions* in the rare edition of Clement Reyner, 1626.[10]

the acknowldgement on p. 1441 it appears that Legg consulted the MS at its then home, the Advocates' Library in Edinburgh (now at the National Library of Scotland, Adv. 18.5.19). It is, in A. Ward's summary of Lawlor's view, a late 13th- or early 14th-cent. "English copy of an Irish exemplar in turn descended from a book belonging to the Benedictine nuns of St Werburgh, Chester, in the 12th century": *Pubs HBS*, p. 36.

[7] This is further complicated by occasional reference to two MS Sarum missals: "Morris," the early 14th-cent. book formerly belonging to William Morris (d. 1896), now New York, Pierpont Morgan Lib. M.107, and generally known as the Tiptoft missal (see p. 380); and [BL Add.] "11.414," a composite book of some complexity (see p. 502), taken by Legg as "as agreeing with Sarum, unless stated otherwise." There are also a few tantalizing references to the Arsenal (MS 135) missal in Paris which will become one of Legg's *Early [Sarum] Missals* in his 1916 edition; by that time, at least, he had secured complete rotographs of the MS (p. 8 of that edition). Further discussion of the editions of Dickinson and Legg will be found in chapters 13 and 10 respectively.

[8] The Winchcombe book (see p. 93) was known only in MS until A. Davril's edition, HBS 109 (1995); the Giso remains unedited, as we have seen.

[9] J. Gage, "A Dissertation on St Æthelwold's Benedictional," *Archaeologia* 24 (1832), pp. 1–117; W. Greenwell, *The Pontifical of Egbert*, SS 27 (1853); the Canterbury benedictional was to be edited by R. M. Woolley, HBS 51 (1917), the Robert benedictional by H. A. Wilson, HBS 24 (1903), and the Egbert pontifical re-edited by H. Banting, HBS 104 (1989). The Ramsey book remains unedited.

[10] For these superseded edns and modern ones that have replaced them, see respectively pp. 86 and 106.

The meat of Legg's comparative data lies in the manuscript English missals dating from the late twelfth to the early fifteenth century, the central one being the subject of his edition, the Westminster, alias Lytlington (c. 1385) missal. That his symbols are listed in alphabetical order makes it hard to see the chronological span of the information provided. In rough chronological order and with dating indications somewhat more precise than Legg's, these massbooks are (his sigla are in the first column):

Alb.*	Bodl. Rawl. liturg. c.1	s. xii$^{3/4?}$	St Albans
Harl. 1229	BL Harley 1229	c. 1200	Cistercian (Waverley?)
Exeter	Exeter Cath. 3510	s. xiii^2	Exeter cathedral
Twk.	CUL Gg.3.21	s. xiii^{ex}/xiv	Tewkesbury
Alb.	Bodl. Laud misc. 279	s. xiv$^{1/4}$	St Albans
Durh.	BL Harley 5289	s. xiv$^{1/2?}$	Durham
Whit.	Bodl. Rawl. liturg. b.1	s. xiv$^{3/4}$	Whitby
W.	Westm. Abbey 37	c. 1385	Westminster
Sherb.	BL Add. 74326	c. 1400	Sherborne
Abin.	Bodl. Digby 227	1460–1	Abingdon (+ Oxf., Trin. 75)

The immediately striking point is that with the exception of the Exeter missal these are all monastic books – not surprisingly, if one remembers that the data derived from them are meant to be textual notes illuminating an edition of the grand missal from Westminster abbey.[11] Given the extensiveness of what Legg has provided, though, it is almost inevitable that the user will combine the evidence from the manuscripts listed above with that taken from the mostly sixteenth-century printed editions of the Sarum, York, and Hereford missals and think that what is thereby offered is something like a conspectus of the variable mass texts found in medieval England, *simpliciter.*[12] There are

[11] In addition to the missal itself, Legg's edition includes almost the whole of Bodl. Rawl. liturg. e.10, a late 15th-cent. book of liturgical devotions almost certainly from Westminster (despite the "?" in *MLGB*): III.1303–84, referred to in the Notes merely as Rawl. The remaining part, the calendar, is printed in Wormald, *Eng. Ben. Kals*, II.
[12] Some reference to comparanda for such pontifical material as is contained in the Westminster missal, including its benedictional section, is supplied by information from

many potential traps in so supposing; and, though Legg's Notes are literally invaluable, they must also be used with critical vigilance.[13]

A practice case

This may be easily seen if we lay out the data offered for just one, relatively simple, pair of instances from Legg's Notes, with his abbreviations expanded: mass forms for the two feasts of the Cross, the Exaltation (14 September) and Invention (3 May). For the Exaltation five Epistle-incipits are given:

> *Videte qualibet litteris*: Westminster, York, Sherborne, "Cout." (Coutances missal, printed Rouen 1557), "Paris" (missal, printed there 1543).
> *Confido in vobis*: Sarum, Durham, St Albans [Laud misc. 279], "Chart." (Carthusian missal, printed Paris 1541).
> *In Christo habitat*: Hereford, Abingdon.
> *Christus factus est*: Whitby, Rouen (printed 1499), "Cisterc." (Cistercian missal, printed Paris 1617), "Dom." (Dominican missal, printed Venice 1504), "Rom." (Roman missal, Venice 1490).
> *Hoc sentite in vobis*: "CCCO" (Irish missal at Corpus Christi, Oxford), Rosslyn.

Taken baldly, this information is more bewildering than helpful. Six English Benedictine houses appear to have used four different Epistles, while each of the three secular uses employs a different one. At the feast of the Invention "all the uses" (Legg's term for complete agreement of witnesses) save the Roman 1490 book have the same Epistle, which makes it all the more striking that there should be such variety for the Exaltation. The graduals – called by Legg, quaintly, "Grails" – seem to be the other way round. There is only one for the Exaltation (though with some variation at the Alleluia verse), whereas for the Invention

---

"Ev"[esham] (Bodl. Barlow 7), "Magd." (Magd. Oxf. 226), "Pecham" (Exeter Cath. 3513, the Lacy pontifical, which seems to incorporate a benedictional ascribed to Pecham), [Bodl.] "Tanner 5," [BL Cott.] "Tib. B.iii," and "York Pont." (Bainbridge pontifical, CUL Ff.6.1), in addition to the Anglo-Saxon witnesses noticed above.

[13] Wariness is necessary especially with Legg's "Canterbury," used for nothing more substantial than "Lambeth MS 20, which has a few gospels to be read *in capitulo*." No date is given, but this is in fact an early 16th-cent. Christ Church martyrology, obituary, etc., of which fols 126–44 contain gospels in temporale and sanctorale order; Becket is not included, and the relevance of this section to Christ Church is not clear. Legg adds that Bodl. Rawl. C.168 is a Sarum missal (in fact, just a large fragment), given by Archbishop Warham to Canterbury cathedral.

no fewer than six texts are found: one shared by Westminster and all three English secular uses (and three of the printed Continental books), one shared by St Albans (early fourteenth century), St Augustine's (late eleventh), and Rouen (1499 printed), one used by Durham alone, and yet another by Sherborne.[14]

To enter, group, and analyze every variant listed by Legg would be beyond the stamina of any human being and might give a powerful computer a good workout. Those limitations aside, it is highly doubtful whether whatever patterns might emerge would be anything like conclusive. Too much is missing: the thousands of service books no longer extant, all the relevant details from each of which would have to be precisely dated and located for a truly reliable database, albeit one of inconceivable magnitude, to be constructed. Also missing, or incompletely understood, are too many elements of an extra-textual sort: such obvious things as music (where melodies memorized and ways of performing them are likely to have been as significant as whatever notation may survive), architecture (arrangements that made sense for a then extant text but that have long since been drastically altered or, as with many monastic churches, lost entirely), and personalities (the eccentric preferences of a bishop or precentor, largely obscured to us). Probably the most that can be hoped for is the emergence of some tentative patterns with a mild plausibility and the capacity to rule out certain kinds of possibilities – if X and Y differ in dozens of textual details, it is most unlikely that both had Z as their model.

Legg's provisional conclusions

That said, it would be wrong not to take account of the general conclusions that Legg drew from his textual analyses. These were drawn primarily from comparison of the secrets and postcommunions of masses in the temporale. He postulated that each of the witnesses described above represented a "use," and found that "By applying these texts of varying secrets and postcommons [*sic*], the English uses resolve themselves into two groups. One may be called the Sarum group, from the name of its most important member; and the other the Gregorian group from its kinship with the Gregorian Sacramentary."[15] The first group

---

[14] Legg here omits Sherborne (which has *Alleluia. Crucifixum surrexit a mortuis*). Furthermore, Westminster, Sarum, York, and Hereford each has a different Alleluia verse!

[15] *Westm. Missal*, III.1418. Although arguments of "liturgiologists" of the nineteenth century about the correct employment of the terms "use" and "rite" resulted in no agreed conclusion, this locution of Legg's is clearly misleading; it regards evidence drawn from the very numerous Sarum missals as analogous to, say, that of the Giso sacramentary or Tewkesbury missal, each of the latter two in their way *unica*.

included "Sarum, Westminster, St Albans, Abingdon, and Tewkesbury" (plus a sub-group of the "Irish," as he called them, missals, Rosslyn, Drummond, and Corpus). Into the Gregorian group were lumped – in this order, and with the same abbreviated references as those he used in his Notes – "York, Durham, Whitby, St Augustine's Canterbury, Sherborne, Leofric, Winchcombe, Robert of Jumièges, Vitellius, Rouen, Bayeux, Coutances, Evreux, Paris, Dominican, Cistercian, Charterhouse." (Hereford could not, he thought, be "definitely placed.") Looking for factors that would explain the grouping his textual evidence seemed to require, Legg confessed himself stumped, above all as to the key questions of "the source of the Sarum group" and "when it first appeared in England" – questions that (insofar as the premise behind them is valid) indeed remain to be answered.

Nor did Legg derive any more conclusive help from his comparison of the episcopal benedictions at mass in the Westminster book (present there because its abbot had, as a "mitred abbot," the right to pronounce such blessings) or of the special rites of Ash Wednesday, Palm Sunday, Maundy Thursday, Easter Vigil, and Candlemas.[16] For the sanctorale Legg found with the "old Gregorian festivals" the same independence in secrets and postcommunions – the "Sarum" group frequently differing from the Gregorian sacramentary texts – whereas for the "non-Gregorian saints" there seemed to be no discernible principle as to variation. Indeed, he remarks that for some English local saints and even for some universal ones (he instances Ambrose and Jerome) "each use would seem to have desired to have its own collect, secret and postcommon." In those words – "each use would seem to have desired" – lies the nub of the matter: in place of the abstract formulation of a "use desiring" particular texts, the historian must try to supply specific persons and dates. Towards such an end Legg's method is a vast help, of course, but, equally, it is drastically imperfect. What seems a treasure trove of comparative data turns out to be guarded by both a dragon of imprecision and a beguiling serpent of presumption, that of continuity.

Our presumption of continuity

An important problem of method is raised by the fragmentary nature of the extant evidence for our subject, in two respects. The first is the

---

16 The succeeding section of Legg's Introduction, his brief analysis of the coronation rite (pp. 1434–39), is slight in content, understandably so in the light of the more extensive investigations published in his *Three Coronation Orders*, HBS 19 (1900), and esp. by the simultaneous labors of his son, Leopold George Wickham Legg, published as *English Coronation Records* (London 1901).

fact that many more service books survive from the later middle ages than from earlier periods; the second, that for certain churches, especially those of religious houses, there may be witnesses – missals, for instance – written in widely separated centuries. Given these two considerations, how justified is the student in supposing continuity?

Difficulties arising from the preponderance of later over earlier evidence are compounded by the technological development that makes easy, and can be argued sometimes to have brought about, standardization: that of printing. The prime example of this is the way in which as service books of Sarum, York, and Hereford Uses come to be printed, their texts appear to be standardized; verbal variations in manuscripts of a certain strand seem – sometimes illusorily – to have been smoothed into uniformity. (There looks to be a large field of enquiry as to exactly how this happens; many frustrations must be expected.) The corrective is not to privilege manuscript over printed evidence automatically, which would be naïve, but rather to maintain a simple vigilance against the tendency to suppose that a text or rubric or occasion found in a later, especially printed, book can invariably be used to illuminate the liturgies of an earlier period.

The second problem, more complex, is well illustrated by the two St Albans mass books referred to by Legg in his Notes. As has been mentioned, one (Bodl. Rawl. liturg. c.1, quite imperfect) is of the third quarter of the twelfth century, the other (Bodl. Laud misc. 279) of probably the early fourteenth. It is the later, and fuller, book to which Legg assigned the siglum "Alb.," using an asterisk ("Alb.*") for the earlier. Here it is necesssary for the student to remember that each time "Alb." appears in the copious apparatus, this is evidence for liturgy at that house only in the age of Edward II, not necesssarily that of Henry II. Further, Legg's postulating of "Sarum, Westminster, and St Albans" as a group is based on texts of, respectively, the early sixteenth century (the numerous printed missals used by Dickinson in his edition), late fourteenth, and early fourteenth – and in the latter two cases, on a single manuscript as opposed to the multiple printed editions of the Sarum book. Is this, then, in effect a grouping of bananas generically considered, a specific strain of apple, and an equally specific strain of orange?

Of course there can be no blanket answer as to the degree of continuity in liturgical texts from, and for, the same church. A conservative position in the matter is illustrated by the observation of the musicologist David Hiley: "Working through large numbers of chant sources one is struck time and time again how faithfully manuscripts within the same melodic tradition will agree on seemingly insignificant melodic details ... . The scribes of the later sources do not, by and large, add or substract such notes on their own initiative. The written exemplar is respected."[17] If this is true with respect to tiny details of notation, it would seem likely to be true also of texts.

But to maintain such a conservative view exclusively is manifestly impossible, for it would mean ignoring the numerous additions, corrections, and supplements that liturgical manuscripts frequently possess. The many changes in the St Augustine's missal (CCCC 270), already discussed, are an obvious case in point, and witness to a dynamic rather than static view of the mass liturgy at that house in the early twelfth century. Another, alluded to again later in this work (p. 502), is BL Add. 11414, a more-or-less Sarum missal in which large sections of erasures and over-writings show a quite puzzling degree of liturgical free-spiritedness. Even if we permit the Norman Conquest to be regarded as something of a (limited) watershed for England, it cannot be the case that there were no significant changes in liturgical texts, beyond the adding of a certain number of new feasts, from the twelfth to the sixteenth century. We have therefore to be at least sceptical about statements like the following: "Lanfranc's sacramentary was certainly in circulation in the 1080s. The sacramentary embodied in the late fourteenth-century Durham Missal [BL Harley 5289; Legg's "Durh."] was probably sent north shortly after Bishop William Carilef replaced the seculars serving his cathedral with monks [1083]."[18] If such a statement can be substantiated, it can be only by indirect routes such as comparison and cross-checking with other liturgical books. Some tools for such comparisons, most of them not available to Legg, must now be looked at.

Collation tables, concordances, and *corpora*

The printing of extensive collation tables is a recent development in the editing of liturgical texts and has been made feasible by the existence of appropriate computer programs, especially spreadsheets. This aid is seen most clearly, and with greatest relevance to the present work, in several Henry Bradshaw Society publications since 1992. In that year Alicia Corrêa's edition of the Durham collectar (Durham Cath. A.iv.19) included tables that indicated in nine columns which of the 667 items in

---

[17] D. Hiley, "Thurstan of Caen and Plainchant at Glastonbury" (p. 112, n. 35), pp. 77–78.
[18] N. Orchard, "The Bosworth Psalter and the St Augustine's Missal" (p. 116, n. 47), p. 92.

the manuscript appeared in Gregorian (with sigla distinguishing four aspects) or Gelasian (similarly subdivided) sacramentaries, Leofric missal, Leofric collectar, Wulfstan portiforium, and several other, generally Continental, sources.[19] This enables the user to see at a glance that, for example, the eight collects for Epiphany in the Durham book are present in so many witnesses as not to be remarkable, while the single collect for Lucia occurs only in the Gellone ("Young Gelasian") massbook and Wulfstan portiforium, and one of the five capitula and one of the six prayers for Michael appear nowhere else and are therefore a matter of considerable interest. A similar set of tables has been provided by Nicholas Orchard in his edition of the Leofric missal. Here the six columns stand for slightly different sources depending on the section of Leofric "A" analyzed (temporale and sanctorale require one set, common of saints, votives, and prefatory material each a different set; the "B" and "C" components are not included), but the effect is the same.[20]

Because a collation table tends to rely heavily on incipits, that two prayers share opening formulas (on which most collation tables rely) may lead to the assumption that the two are identical – an assumption that comparison of the full texts of the prayers may show to be false or at least dubious. Some variants are of course to be ignored: almost certainly those in spelling, usually those in word order if fairly minor, sometimes those that add or omit words (addition of *sempiterne* in the middle of an *Omnipotens deus* opening, for example, or omission of an adverbial *suppliciter* or *humiliter*). In the final analysis individual judgment must be used in deciding what is significant.

A similar problem occurs with the related comparative tool of the concordance. These have been produced mainly with respect to the "Roman" sacramentaries. The outstanding example is the work of Jean Deshusses and Bénoit Darragon, in two large volumes, for what they term the "*Grandes Sacramentaires*" of the Roman tradition.[21] The first volume supplies both incipits and explicits (last two or three words, excluding closing clauses of the "per Jesum Christum ..." type) for 4,258 formulas

---

[19] A. Corrêa, ed. *The Durham Collectar*, HBS 107 (1992). As a collectar, this contains capitula as well as prayers (see p. 65); for the former, the table supplies reference to the appropriate repertory.

[20] N. Orchard, ed. *The Leofric Missal*, 2 vols, HBS 113–14 (2001), I.266–322. Other recent HBS volumes to contain such tables are A. Davril, ed. *The Winchcombe Sacramentary*, HBS 109 (1995), and Y. Hen, ed. *The Sacramentary of Echternach*, HBS 110 (1997), late ninth century (BN lat. 9433).

[21] J. Deshusses and B. Darragon, *Concordances et Tableaux pour l'Etude des Grandes Sacramentaires*, 2 vols, SF Subsidia 9–10 (Fribourg 1982), I: *Concordance des pièces*, II: *Tableaux synoptiques*.

in the "Roman" books conventionally called Leonine, (Old) Gelasian, Hadrianum Gregorian, Paduensis Gregorian, and Supplement to the Gregorian, and also the Young Gelasian Gellone and St Gall books; this is followed by *Tables de correspondance* for each. The second volume lays the information out in the order in which it is found in each of the main strands, with columns for each of the other witnesses.

This enables one to see at a glance that, for example, the *Nat. S. Leonis* on 28 June is purely Hadrianic-Gregorian. But this is only the starting point of the information we require, for here it is not the first and last words that are instructive, but rather the insertion into the secret of the phrase "intercedente beato Leone," in place of "animae famuli tui Leoni," in three of the Hadrianum manuscripts collated by Deshusses in his edition.[22] As will become apparent in the Case Study which follows, this variant in the middle of the prayer may offer a clue as to the transmission of Gregorian texts into England. Nor does the *Concordance des pièces*, covering as it does only the Roman sacramentary traditions, provide information about another important variant: that as well as the Hadrianic "Deus qui animae famuli tui" there is another postcommunion for the feast, beginning "Sumentes domine diuina misteria." Clearly we need also a fuller conspectus of possible sources or analogues; for this we must look at three sets of *corpora*.

Although editions of liturgical texts in the Corpus Christianorum Series Latina are limited to the three "Young Gelasian" volumes already noticed, the Angoulême, Gellone, and Phillipps books, a complementary enterprise has resulted in a trio of vast *corpora*: *Corpus Benedictionum Pontificalium*, edited by E. Moeller, in four volumes (CCSL 162–162C, 1971–79); *Corpus Praefationum*, also the work of Moeller, in five volumes (CCSL 161–161D, 1980–81), and *Corpus Orationum*, in ten volumes, edited by Moeller, M. Clément, and B. Coppieters 't Wallant (CCSL 160–160H plus 161, 1992–97). Each of these is drawn from an extremely wide variety of sources, most of them published editions. For the *Corpus Orationum*, the one immediately relevant to the present discussion, an astonishing 197 sources are listed, each with a siglum-abbreviation. They range in date from the sixth century (fragments related to the so-called Masses of Mone) to the mid-sixteenth (the 1554 printed Sarum missal, wrongly described in the sigla as "ed. princeps"),[23] but with a strong preponderance of early witnesses, as

---

[22] J. Deshusses, ed., *Le Sacramentaire grégorien ...*, 3 vols, Spicilegium Friburgenses 16, 24, 28 (1971–82), I.243.

[23] In effect, Dickinson's edition of Sarum (1861–83), from the printed missals; why the 1554, Marian-reaction version was singled out from the numerous printings represented in this edition is not explained. It is surprising, and for our purposes highly

befits the series; and equally broadly in space, over the whole of Europe. Information extracted from this enormous hoard must obviously be used with caution and discrimination.

Consulting it for the "variant" Sarum postcommunion for Leo, "Sumentes domine diuina misteria," we find reference only to "Sarum" [i.e., printed], Westminster [missal, c. 1385], and, in parentheses, St Albans [the early fourteenth-century book] – these three references being taken straight from Legg's Notes – plus two "Celtic" books that Legg included sporadically, both available in nineteenth-century printed editions: the Scottish Arbuthnott missal of 1491[24] and the Irish Drummond missal, the date of which is problematic but almost certainly before 1200.[25] In the Drummond book the prayer is found in the common of a confessor: which, as this is the oldest of these five witnesses, may be significant in suggesting that, for what is an occasion of minimal importance, a formula was taken from the common and made proper by the insertion of Leo's name – and which would itself raise a question as to what impetus might have brought that about.

In any case, how meaningful is it to argue from the fact that Drummond is, as an artefact, the oldest of these five? This variant postcommunion is also found in Legg's manuscript Sarum missals, and the gap between the earliest of these (the Crawford) and Drummond is only a century or less. All we know is that the prayer had been composed, worded generically as befits a common, by the time Drummond was written in the third quarter of the twelfth century, and has been assigned as proper to Leo by the third quarter of the thirteenth (Crawford's date). It remains the postcommunion for that saint in the fourteenth-century books of St Albans (early) and Westminster (late), and

inconvenient, that the makers of this *Corpus* did not include the Legg *Sarum Missal* edn of 1916 (reprinted in 1969) among their sources. Among English massbooks that are included are the St Augustine's (as "Cantuar."), Hereford, Leofric (in Warren's 1883 edn), Lesnes, Red Book of Darley (here miscalled "Derby"), Robert of Jumièges (obscurely disguised as "Gemm."), Rosslyn, Giso (under "Vitell."), Westminster, New Minster (under "Winch."), York (for details, see the list of nicknames for manuscripts at the beginning of this book). But this is somewhat misleading, because, as the "Bibliographie" makes plain but not the list of sigla, data from Darley, Giso, and [Bodl.] "Digby 39" (two masses for Birinus in a 12th-cent. Abingdon book) are limited to the selections printed in F. E. Warren's appendix to his edn of Leofric, pp. 271–75, 303–7, and 307.

24 A. P. and G. H. Forbes, eds, *Liber ecclesiae beati terrenani de Arbuthnott* (Burntisland 1864), from the MS, now Paisley, Renfrew Museum and Art Gallery, s.n.

25 G. H. Forbes, ed. *Missale Drummondiense: the Ancient Irish Missal in the Possession of the Baroness Willoughby de Eresby, Drummond Castle, Perthshire* (Edinburgh 1882). The manuscript is now New York, Pierpont Morgan Lib. 627, and includes a martyrology, ed. P. Ó Riain, *Four Irish Martyrologies*, HBS 115 (2002); he discusses the complex problem of its date on pp. 10–12.

is so employed in the late fifteenth-century Arbuthnott book as well as in the printed Sarum missals.

But what the historian most wants to know is, of course, what the earliest instances are, along with any other information that would make it possible to speculate how the prayer came to be so used. This means that as well as following the fortunes of the prayer text, we must look at the occasion to which it becomes attached. The following Case Study attempts to do this, by way of illustrating the strengths and weaknesses of the various methods employed in the tools noticed above and also of pursuing one detailed point – one of many thousand such points that the exhaustive kind of analyis referred to above might well turn up if *ars* and *vita* were both of indefinite duration.

Case study: the feast(s) of pope(s) Leo and the associated mass prayers

The name of Leo, often styled *papa*, appears at June 28th in eighteen of the twenty pre-1100 English calendars edited by Francis Wormald in 1934.[26] Leo's name appears at April 11th as well in fourteen, styled *papa* in all save two.[27] This slight discrepancy becomes marked after 1100. Each of thirty-five calendars consulted for this purpose includes a Leo in late June, but in April only five do.[28]

The Gregorian (Hadrianum) set of mass prayers for (a) Leo on June 28th – *Dq beatum Leonem, Annue (nobis) domine*, and *Dq animae famuli tui Leonis* – is found in massbooks of that strand on the Continent and in England. Among Continental books that include the set are the Echternach sacramentary of c. 895–900, Eligius sacramentary of the later ninth century, and Fulda sacramentary of c. 975.[29] The set appears

---

[26] Wormald, *Eng. Kals*. It is missing altogether only from the calendar in BL Cott. Vit. A.xii. The Leofric missal (Bodl. 579) gives "Fabiani Gordiani" for the 28th but "Pauli, Timothei, Leonis, et Albini confessoris [sic]" on the 30th; similarly, CUL Kk.v.32 has on the 28th "Sanctorum Fabiani, Gordiani, Sereni, Ereni," and on the 30th "Sancti Pauli, Timothei, Leonis."

[27] Wormald's nos. 1, 3, 8, 10–20. No. 1 (Bodl. Digby 63) has just "Sancti Leonis," no. 3 (BL Cott. Nero A.ii) "Cuthlaci confessoris et Leonis et Hilari," all the others have *pap(a)e*. None of the three calendars in the previous note has an Apr. 11th Leo.

[28] The Apr. 11th feast is found in calendars from Chertsey, Chester, and Crowland (all in Wormald's conspectus of nineteen post-Conquest Benedictine calendars [*Eng. Ben. Kals*]), and in those of the Bologna Univ. Lib. MS Sarum missal (Legg's "B") but not its sanctorale, and, quite puzzlingly, in the ordinal of the nuns of Barking, c. 1400 (ed. J. B. L. Tolhurst, HBS 65, 1927).

[29] Respectively, *The Sacramentary of Echternach*, ed. Y. Hen; "Eligius" Sacramentary, in the 1642 edn of H. Ménard as repr. in PL 78; and Richter and Schönfelder's 1912 edn of the Fulda Sacramentary (see p. xxiii), repr. as HBS 101, 1980.

also in Leofric missal "A," in origin apparently an early tenth-century Lotharingian book though perhaps written for English use or even in England (see p. 72).

The Young Gelasian books have another prayer-set, this one for an April 11th mass for a pope Leo: *Exaudi dne preces ... Leonis, Sancti Leonis confessoris tui,* and *Ds fidelium remunerator animarum.* This is a recycling of the Old Gelasian set for pope Marcellus (January 16th), with Leo's name substituted. Both this set and that for the June 28th feast are included in the Echternach sacramentary, which is primarily Gregorian but with strong (Young) Gelasian influences.[30] This is the case also with the Fulda book, but there the set for the June Leo is intercalated, as *alia,* with that for the vigil of Peter and Paul. Among English books the April 11th set is present in the early eleventh-century Robert of Jumièges massbook and in the Giso book (fol. 87v), but apparently only there; it is not in the New Minster nor St Augustine's missals, nor in the mid-twelfth-century St Albans massbook, Rawl. liturg. c.1 (see p. 158).

Who is or are the pope(s) Leo commemorated in these two feasts? It seems likelier that both the Gregorian June 28th and Young Gelasian April 11th are meant to commemorate Leo I than – although this is possible – that one is intended for him and the other for Leo II (pope 681–3). But Leo I is thought to have died on November 10th (his modern-day feast) in 461, and Leo II on July 3rd, 683; so how are the June and April dates come by? The *Liber pontificalis* account for Leo I states that he was buried on April 11th, which may indeed represent a first translation.[31] The same source is explicit that remains of Leo I were translated by Pope Sergius I (687–701) – but it does not specify a date.[32] The learned Duchesne's comment on this passage seems to hit at the center of the puzzle, but is offered without documentation: "La translation eut lieu le 28 juin 688. Son anniversaire est marqué dans les livres liturgiques grégoriens. Actuellement on fête à ce jour la mémoire de saint Léon II."[33] But the June 28th date must be seen in the light of

---

[30] The Echternach book has two collects (nos. 1076–79); see also Hen's Introduction, esp. pp. 32–38.

[31] This is the day under which he is entered in the Berne MS of the *Martyrologium Hieronymianum* and in the second recension of Bede's Martyrology (H. Quentin, *Les martyrologiques historiques du moyen âge*, Paris 1908, p. 50). For futher discussion of the date of Leo I's death, see T. Jalland, *The Life and Times of St Leo the Great* (London 1941), p. 418.

[32] L. Duchesne, ed. *Liber Pontificalis,* Bibl. des Ecoles françaises d'Athènes et de Rome, 2 vols (Rome 1886–92), I.375.

[33] Ibid., I.379. Likewise, in Duchesne's note on Leo's death he states that the Apr. 11th date is false and that the June 28th offered in *Mart. Hieron.* is the true date, but without giving reasons.

the *Liber pontificalis* statement that Leo II was buried at St Peter's on July 3rd.[34]

We confront next the fact that around the middle of the eleventh century the April 11th feast seems to have dropped largely, though not quite completely, out of use – certainly in England and apparently on the Continent as well; even mentions of it in calendars become rare, as the figure of five out of thirty-five consulted indicates. It is beyond the scope of this study to speculate as to whether this is a consequence of a more or less conscious elimination of some (Young) Gelasian elements as the much supplemented Gregorian strand comes to be supreme. Instead, we must concentrate on just two points, the interpolated secret prayer and the variant *Sumentes* postcommunion.

The three Gregorian books signalled by Deshusses, in the apparatus to his magnificent edition, as containing the phrase "intercedente beato Leone haec nobis," are his manuscripts (Q), the Rodradus sacramentary (BN lat. 12050, written in 853 by the priest Rodradus for the abbey of Corbie; *CLLA* no. 742); (S) a North French sacramentary of the third quarter of the ninth century (Cambrai, B.m. 162–163; no. 761); and a (T2) sacramentary-with-chants of the late ninth century, eventually at Noyon (Reims, B.m. 213; no. 1385). It was not to Deshusses' purpose to follow the tradition into the indefinite future, so there was no reason for him to have noticed the English books that include this interpolation. The earliest of these seems to be the Giso sacramentary, which also appears to be the latest book to have mass prayers for the April 11th feast. (The somewhat earlier Robert of Jumièges book, which also has both feasts, lacks the additional phrase.) The next in time, of extant witnesses, looks to be the St Albans massbook of perhaps a hundred years later (Bodl. Rawl. liturg. c.1, fol. 79). The same reading appears in Legg's manuscript Sarum missals, as noted above.

Are we therefore entitled to establish, at least for this one tiny detail, any link beyond the fortuitous between books of, roughly, the third quarters of three successive centuries, eleventh, twelfth, and thirteenth? Or to posit any influence on the part of one of the three Continental massbooks identified by Deshusses as possessing the telltale phrase? In this case, to rely solely on Legg's 1897 Notes, where the secret prayer is marked simply "all the uses" with no account taken of the interpolated phrase, would result in a seriously misleading impression.

The picture with the variant postcommunion is equally shadowy. Here Legg noticed not only that "Sumentes domine divina misteria" was shared by Sarum, Westminster, and "Alb" (by which he meant

---

[34] Ibid., I.360. This of course does not rule out his having died six days earlier.

St Albans' fourteenth-century missal, but it is in the twelfth-century book as well), but also that the Sherborne missal and Giso had yet a still different prayer at this point, "Sancti Leoni confessoris tui," one which he recognized as having been adapted from the Gelasian postcommunion for Marcellus. Textual peculiarities are frequently shared by Giso and Sherborne: a fact that requires detailed working out, especially because the former has not been edited and the text of the latter not even photographed. Here we notice merely the fact that they agree, and turn to wondering about the "Sumentes" prayer, which has no known antecedents: that is, as far as we can tell, the earliest witness to it is the St Albans book. Why should this one monastic massbook either preserve a prayer from some source obscure to us or offer a new one for what can never have been an important feast – one which, indeed, is generally subsumed into the mass of its concurrent occasion, the vigil of Peter and Paul?

To sum up: what can this investigation of the tiny puzzles of the dual dates for a/the feast of pope Leo, of the interpolated phrase in the secret of the mass prayers that come to predominate, and of the variant postcommunion that appears in a prominent strand of English massbooks, tell us about the overall question of method in this kind of liturgical study? Through the use of several of the aids described in the previous paragraphs we have elicited certain textual facts that enable us to assert, or more definitely prevent us from asserting, similarities, and sometimes to postulate affinities. This, we have seen, must always be done with due caution; similarities may point towards proof but can seldom establish it without other, corroborating evidence. In short, the comparative-textual method is irreplaceable but limited, in both scope and accuracy. We cannot operate without it, but it is unlikely ever to reveal a whole story.

5 Monastic liturgy, 1100–1215

The "long twelfth century" covered by this chapter is marked by date-limits that are not entirely perfunctory. By 1100 the *Constitutions* of Lanfranc (who died in 1089) had, as we saw in chapter 4, been disseminated to, at least, the monastic establishments at Durham, St Albans, Canterbury St Augustine's, and probably Rochester, Westminster, and a number of other places as well. But they were by no means prescriptive and did not form anything like a common customary for all Benedictine houses in England. Individual houses exercised varying degrees of liturgical independence, within a common framework (much of it shared, of course, by secular churches). This independence is, at least in theory, limited in 1215, when the program of Innocent III, expressed above all in the canons of the Fourth Lateran Council which met in that year, brought about the emergence of what can fairly be called the Benedictine order. (That said, the present chapter is concerned with "mainstream" Benedictine establishments only; the liturgies of other groups of more-or-less Benedictine monks – Cluniacs, Cistercians, and Carthusians – will be dealt with separately.)

Documentation for the study of the present subject is plentiful but irregular, as the example of just three monasteries shows. For one major house, St Albans, we have not only a number of surviving service books but also a rich historical tradition stretching from the work of Roger of Wendover and Matthew Paris in the thirteenth century to the fifteenth-century chronicles of Thomas Walsingham and John Whethamstede.[1] For another, Glastonbury, evidence from service books survives only in fragmentary leaves from a collectar (now in the library of Wells cathedral, with no shelf number; p. 179 below).[2] For a third, Malmesbury,

---

[1] For a quick overview of this tradition, see E. B. Graves, ed. *A Bibliography of English History to 1485* (Oxford 1975), p. 388 and the references there; for detailed discussion, the two vols of Antonia Gransden, *Historical Writing in England* I, *c. 550 to c. 1307* (London and Ithaca 1974), ch. 16, and II, *c. 1307 to the Early Sixteenth Century* (1982), chs 5 and 12.

[2] Treated in my article, "The Glastonbury Collectar"; see note 75 below.

there is nothing at all save the oblique witness of its great twelfth-century historian William.[3]

Aside from relatively numerous calendars, the bulk of service-book evidence available to us can be quickly summed up. For the mass, St Albans is in a class by itself, with three or four relevant books surviving from the twelfth century. The most important is a sacramentary; contemporary with this is a processional, while slightly later are a gradual-troper and another gradual. Those books will obviously provide our principal source. Other central documents for the mass will be a missal from Bury St Edmunds and a very early (partial) gradual from Durham. For the daily office we shall have to rely heavily on books approximating breviaries used at St Albans and Winchcombe (Gloucestershire), both of the mid-twelfth century. There seems to be no usable antiphonal.[4] Other kinds of evidence will of course be pressed into service as well, especially for Sherborne and Ely. But it is overwhelmingly the evidence from St Albans on which, with the aid of its medieval *Gesta Abbatum* and of formidable modern studies by K. D. Hartzell and Rodney Thomson, we have to base our treatment.[5] The following discussion, at times remorseless in its detail, could be replicated many times over if equally large bodies of evidence existed for other houses in this period.[6] The situation being what it is, however, it seems justifiable to devote roughly half the length of the present chapter to this one house.

The St Albans sacramentary and its textual puzzles

By far the fullest of the witnesses to mass liturgy at St Albans in the twelfth century is Bodl. Rawl. liturg. c.1: a "pure" sacramentary – that

---

[3] Some hints as to his liturgical ideas may be discernible through his selective abridgement of the *Liber officialis* of Amalarius: see my commentary and edition, "The *Abbreviatio Amalarii* of William of Malmesbury," *Rech. de Théologie ancienne et méd.* 47 (1980), pp. 77–113 and 48 (1981), pp. 128–71; repr. in Pfaff, *LCSSME*.

[4] The only 12th-cent. part of a sort of antiphonal used probably at Gloucester, now Oxford, Jesus College 10, is its calendar. It will be noticed further at the end of this chapter.

[5] The *Gesta Abbatum Monasterii Sancti Albani* is itself of the early 15th-cent. but draws heavily on the earlier St Albans historical tradition, above all Matthew Paris; ed. H. T. Riley, 3 vols, RS 28d (1867–9). It is fundamental to this chapter, as are K. D. Hartzell, "The Musical Repertory at St Albans, England, in the Twelfth Century," Ph.D. dissertation, Univ. of Rochester, 1970, and R. M. Thomson, *Manuscripts from St Albans Abbey 1066–1235*, 2 vols (Woodbridge 1982). The lecture by C. N. L. Brooke, "St Albans: the Great Abbey," in *Cathedral and City: St Albans Ancient and Modern*, ed. R. Runcie (London 1977), pp. 43–70, is full of concise and valuable information.

[6] Houses discussed at some length in the previous chapter or the next chapter are largely ignored here; this includes notably both Christ Church and St Augustine's at Canterbury, Hyde (formerly New Minster) at Winchester, Evesham, Norwich, Worcester, and Westminster.

is, containing the celebrant's mass prayers only – with one exception, that incipits for the introit verse and its psalm are supplied before the collect at each occasion.[7] A date around 1160 is sustainable for both palaeographical and contextual reasons.[8] We can use it to focus on the central question, posed in the previous chapter, of the diffusion of the Lanfrancian model and possible tension with other models in twelfth-century monastic houses. Analysis of some textual details led Hartzell to speculate, in 1970, that an Italian service book may have lain at the root of this St Albans sacramentary (his "SA") and that in any case "in choosing the text present in SA rather than that in the Gregorian books which made up the bulk of the Norman stock, St Albans early in its post-Conquest period turned away from the text which must have come with Paul of Caen and chose one foreign to the Norman heritage."[9] This is a bold claim, the full testing of which is not possible here; rather, we must see what light is shed by a look at each of the three co-ordinates of the method often followed in the present work: rubrics, texts, and saints.

In terms of rubrics, of which the sacramentary contains very few, two for Good Friday are virtually identical with the wording in Lanfranc's *Constitutions* (for example, in calling the two deacons involved *levite*), while one for the Easter Vigil bears strong similarities.[10] Considering what different kinds of documents these two are, the resemblances seem to point unmistakably to the copy of the *Constitutions* sent (according to Matthew Paris) to abbot Paul.[11] It is unfortunate that there are no further rubrics against which this presumption can be checked, though some might have been contained in the numerous leaves now missing.

Among these now missing leaves was apparently a calendar, for against the mass-collect for Germanus (31 July; fol. 90v) is a marginal note, "Require missam de sancto Germano post kalendare." (As it stands, the St Albans book begins on fol. 3 – the first two folios are

---

[7] See the detailed treatment in Hartzell, "Musical Repertory," I.35–73, including indications of the numerous lacunae, and an explanation (pp. 38–39) of the probable reason for F. Madan's (mis)dating of the MS to before 1115 in the Bodleian *Summary Cat.* III (1895), no. 15849, which in turn seems to have led Legg to the misleading "c. 1100" date offered in his 1897 "Notes."

[8] Thomson, *St Albans MSS*, I.110 sums up reasons for this dating.

[9] Hartzell, I.72; he acknowledges on p. 68 considerable help from, and agreement with, views transmitted to him (in letters) by Christopher Hohler, while stating that he came to suspect a possible Italian connection independently.

[10] Respectively, fols 25, 23v (which is dislocated and should come after 28), and 29. But in the mid-12th-cent. gradual (Bodl. Laud misc. 358, to be considered presently) the rite for the Adoration of the Cross adds to Lanfranc's (with which it otherwise agrees) the hymns *Crux fidelis* and *Pange lingua*.

[11] The passages from Matthew Paris are printed in the Knowles and Brooke edition (see p. 102 for details) of the *Constitutions*, p. xxxiv.

from a German sacramentary – with the mass for Stephen.) Germanus, important at St Albans because of his visit to the martyr's tomb in 429, appears also in what is in effect an implied rubric. This occurs in a slightly confused section after the fifth Sunday after Easter (called here the fourth after the Octave; fol. 31); this consists of antiphon tags and collects (only) for Michael, Peter, Stephen, Germanus, and Mary Magdalen, followed by the introit tag, mass set, and full texts of Epistle and Gospel (both with chant neums) for Rogation Monday. The five saints in question are, then, those to whom are dedicated the places where the procession of that day must have stopped.[12] This shows something of an expansion of Lanfranc's prescription, which involved procession from the cathedral to just one church.

Turning from rubrics to texts, we ask what it might be possible to determine from the wording of the prayers themselves, given that there are few prayer texts in the *Constitutions,* and that Legg's "Alb.[ans]" refers to a fourteenth-century book, Bodl. Laud misc. 279, rather than to the one under consideration, called by him "Alb.*" and included only exceptionally in his apparatus. If we have recourse to the later St Albans book, the presumption of continuity (see Excursus above, p. 147) leads us to suppose that, unless there is strong reason to the contrary, prayers for a specific and more or less standard occasion in a fourteenth-century massbook from a particular house were probably used there two centuries earlier. But this is by no means consistently the case. A pair of small details plunge us back into the thicket of Latin textual criticism.

As the postcommunion in the mass for the quite unimportant feast of Rufus, 27 August, the twelfth-century sacramentary has "Epularum tuarum alimento" (fol. 104) but the later (Laud misc. 279) book has a blander "Celestibus repleti" prayer which is also found, Legg's "Notes" tell us, in the fourteenth-century Durham and late eleventh-century St Augustine's books (while Sarum and Westminster each has a still different one). Now, "Epularum tuarum" is quite commonly found in English books: not, however, for Rufus but for the Invention of Stephen,

---

[12] This seems the likeliest explanation, but that there was some confusion at the time is shown by a marginal note on fol. 31v, still in a 12th-cent. hand, "Collecte que dicende sunt ad missas hiis tribus [the three Rogation Days] scilicet sanctorum Stephani, Michaelis, et Petri, Querantur in fine libri" – where they do not appear to be found, or at least to survive. The ancient parish churches in St Albans are indeed those of SS. Stephen, Michael, and Peter. There was apparently an oratory dedicated to Germanus from the mid-10th cent. (*Gesta Abbatum,* I.6), but it would be surprising to find anything comparable for Mary Magdalen that early. The mass for her in the sanctorale comes after that for Wandregisilus [Wandrille], the "older" saint on 22 July, which suggests that hers is a relatively new feast at St Albans in the mid-12th cent.

August 3rd.[13] The challenge here is to account both for the unusual, possibly unique, use of "Epularum" at this place in twelfth-century St Albans and for the change to the more common "Celestibus" by the early fourteenth century. To do this we must go back to a decade or so on either side of the year 1000.

The Invention of Stephen, although it commemorates a celebrated finding of his body (along with those of Nicodemus, Gamaliel, and Abibo) on, supposedly, December 4th, 415, is neither a Gelasian (Old or Young) nor Gregorian feast; indeed it is not clear when and/or how the occasion comes to be observed liturgically, and on August 3rd. The earliest evidence for it in England comes in the mass forms (prayers and chant tags, but not lesson tags) added to the Leofric missal in its "B" component. The prayers refer to Stephen alone, most notably in the collect, "Deus qui es sanctum corpus protomartyris (tui) Stephani ... iugem perseuerantiam." A second mass set, evident in the Robert of Jumièges and St Augustine's books, adds "et sanctorum Nichodemi, Gamalielis, atque Abibon ... de eorum societate gaudere." And a third, totally different set is found in three witnesses, Leofric "C," Giso, and New Minster; its collect begins "Deus qui ad celebrandum nobis honorabile ... in beati martyris et leuite Stephani inuentione."[14]

---

[13] *Corp. Orat.*, no. 2437; used as a postcommunion for Praeiectus in a Tewkesbury missal (CUL Gg.3.21; p. 215 below) and for Dionysius et al. in one from Whitby (Bodl. Rawl. liturg. b.1), otherwise only for the Invention of Stephen save in the (earlier) St Albans book.

[14] All these manuscripts are discussed in the previous chapter. Leofric "C" and the New Minster book contain tags for the chants and lessons which are totally different from those in the (13-cent.) Bec missal, although it has the same prayers (without the alternative postcommunion). Unfortunately, both Bec and New Minster books are missing the leaves containing Stephen's 26 Dec. feast, so we cannot compare the forms for that. The Wulfstan portiforium – which, it should be remembered, is not a massbook but a sort of collectar (see p. 126) – compounds the confusion by containing four prayers: the collect of the third set, then that of the second (as "Alia de eodem"), and as "Collecta unde supra" (the meaning of which is unclear) the *alia* postcommunion shared by the first and third, and finally an entirely new prayer, "Sacratissimum dne sancti martyris tui Stephani diem inuentione," of a rather flowery sort. See the table in Dewick and Frere, *Leofric Collectar* (p. 132 above), II.596, which shows that the homiliary (Bodl. Hatton 113) and passional (CCCC 9) ascribed to Worcester in Wulfstan's time are like the portiforium (in both calendar and sanctorale except for the second prayer) in celebrating only Stephen, whereas the early 13th-cent. calendar of a Worcester psalter (Oxf., Magd. 100) adds Nicodemus and Gamaliel, and the Worcester antiphonal, also 13th-cent., Abibo as well. The Crawford (Sarum) missal, contemporary with the Bec (which is almost certainly datable to 1265–72), confuses the matter further by containing for the Invention feast the collect of the second set and the secret and (first) postcommunion of the third, but cast in the plural. This is a peculiarity which is followed by the early 14th-cent. St Albans missal. A further complication is provided by the Arsenal (Sarum) missal of c. 1300, which has the collect as well as secret (for Stephen alone, however) of the third set but a quite

So there were, within less than a century, three sets of mass prayers current in England for this relatively new feast. St Albans has a fourth, one which combines the collect of the second set (with all four names) with the secret and postcommunion of the third. It does not seem possible, given the fortuitousness of source-survival, to come up with an indisputable explanation: a model now lost to us or a keen liturgical eye on the part of a St Albans monk, perhaps the precentor, seem equally likely. Nor is it clear why "Epularum tuarum" should serve as the postcommunion for Rufus as well as for the Invention of Stephen.

A second convoluted textual detail suggests that there was such an eagle-eyed liturgist active at the abbey around the end of the twelfth century. At that time a corrector supplied a new postcommunion for the feast of the obscure martyrs Timothy and Symphorian (August 22nd; fol. 101v). The old one, beginning "Sacro munere satiati," is also the prayer in the Sarum tradition and the Westminster missal, whereas the newer one, "Divini muneris largitate," is used almost everywhere else: so much Legg's "Notes" tell us. But behind these simple facts lies another complicated story. Masses for the Roman martyr Timothy and the Gallic martyr Symphorian (from Autun), both culted on the 22nd, came to be conflated. Timothy, a Gregorian saint, is alone in Leofric "A" but an Exeter scribe (the Leofric "C" campaign; see p. 136) added above the line both Symphorian's name and the necessary plurals; the postcommunion is "Divini muneris." The late tenth-century Winchcombe sacramentary has separate masses, with "Sacro munere" as the postcommunion for Symphorian, while its German contemporary the Fulda sacramentary alternates the mass forms for the two (including separate prefaces) under the heading of Timothy alone. In the late eleventh-century New Minster and St Augustine's missals Symphorian's name is simply slid into the prayers (and the heading) for Timothy.[15] What, then, can it signify that in the St Albans book of c. 1160 the postcommunion for Symphorian found a place alongside the collect and secret for Timothy, in all three cases with both names? And what can have been the exemplar against which the St Albans monk was checking that caused him to write the correction? Conclusive answers do not

---

different postcommunion, "Da nos prothomartyris tui S. hodierna inuencione." And the 14th-cent. Durham missal (BL Harley 5829) has still another postcommunion, "Quesumus domine salutaria [sic?] repleti mysteriis."

[15] Respectively, *Leofric Missal*, II.286, nos. 1657–60; *Winchcombe Sacr.*, nos. 1193–1200; *Fulda Sacr.*, nos. 1236–43. There are separate masses for the two in the late 10th-cent. French *Sacramentary of Ratoldus*, ed. N. Orchard, HBS 116 (2005), nos. 1678–80, with collect and postcommunion different from Winchcombe's; the opening of the collect, "Peculiari patroni festiuitatem," suggests that Ratoldus's may be the original mass set, perhaps from Autun (Symphorian as *patronus*).

seem available for either question, but the independence of attitude is clear enough.

Evidence from our third co-ordinate, saints – here, the selection of sanctorale occasions for which mass-forms are specified – provides only a small amount of light. The two outstanding features are the pointers to additions "in fine libri" of mass prayers for the Eleven Thousand Virgins (October 21st) and for the Transfiguration. A marginal note at the end of the mass for Romanus (October 23rd; fol. 118) reads "In natali undecim milium virginum require secundo folio ante gradale versus finem libri," followed by the introit tag and first words of the collect. (This is tantalizing: are we to understand that after the sacramentary proper ended there was as an integral part of this book a gradual section? There is no such section, nor such mass forms, at the book's end now.) The hand of the inscription looks somewhat later than those of the marginal references for the Transfiguration or for the Translation of Edward the Confessor (1163; fol. 116v). The mass collect mentioned is that used in the later St Albans and Westminster missals, but an earlier set of forms is found, in its proper sanctorale location, in the St Augustine's missal (and, as well, in Sarum, York, and Hereford books). So the feast was known in England by the end of the eleventh century and in a monastic context – one which there is reason to think is at that point strongly under Lanfrancian influence (see p. 114).[16] In another house supposedly under the same influence, Durham, the feast does not appear in a calendar of the first third of the twelfth century but is present in those of a late thirteenth-century breviary and a missal of the first half of the fourteenth century.[17] In the latter the mass prayers are the same as at St Augustine's. So the marginal collect-incipit in the St Albans sacramentary is the earliest witness to a tradition preserved in its fourteenth-century missal and also in use at Westminster c. 1385, and, a few years later, among the nuns of Barking.[18] Because the hand of the marginal cross-reference is somewhat later than that which signals the 1163 Translation of Edward the Confessor, we cannot suppose that it necessarily reflects the "invention" of the relics of those virgins,

---

[16] But it does not appear in two contemporary sources that reflect monastic usage also, the New Minster missal and the Wulfstan portiforium. And it is dropped in the later (from first half of the 13th cent. on) St Augustine's calendars collated by Wormald (*Eng. Ben. Kals*, I.61). It is present, expressed in a martyrological fashion, in the original calendar of the Giso sacramentary (1061–88?): "In colonia xi milium virginum" (Wormald, *Eng. Kals*, p. 109), but not its sanctorale.

[17] Respectively, Durham Cath., Hunter 100 (dated 1100–35), the Coldingham breviary (see p. 223; BL Harley 4664), and the Durham missal (BL Harley 5289); in the latter two it appears after Hilarion, abbot.

[18] *Westminster Missal*, II.980; *Barking Ordinal*, II.325.

headed by Ursula (who is not named in any of the English witnesses just alluded to), at Cologne in 1155. The presence of the Eleven Thousand Virgins at St Albans must, at least for the moment, be regarded as a curiosity.

More significant, probably, is the marginal reference to the feast of the Transfiguration, beside the old August 6th feast of Sixtus, Felicissimus, and Agapitus (fol. 95). Here the "in fine libri" indication can be followed up: on fol. 158 appears a mass set for the feast, beginning with the collect, "Deus qui hanc sacratissimam diem." Again, as with the Eleven Thousand Virgins, the St Albans collect is strikingly different from another, in this case one with powerful backing. In 1132 the feast was made compulsory for all Cluniac houses, largely under the influence of the great abbot Peter the Venerable, who compiled an office and mass which were certainly known in England.[19] The collect for his mass begins "Deus qui hodierna die." The full mass, available for example in a fifteenth-century missal from the Cluniac house at Pontefract (Cambridge, King's Coll. 31), is exactly replicated in the fourteenth-century Laud misc. 279 St Albans missal – except for the collect, which is still the one in Rawl. liturg. c.1. The feast continues to have been celebrated at St Albans, as well as at its cells in Tynemouth, Wymondham, and Belvoir, and in 1430 an altar with the dual dedication of Transfiguration and Visitation was dedicated at the abbey church. By that time somewhat more widespread awareness of the feast is discernible, although the marked increase in popularity comes only after a papal promulgation in 1457, following a defeat of the Turks at Belgrade the previous year, and it becomes a widely celebrated *novum festum*; but the mass collect used at St Albans seems never to appear again. Unlike its counterpart for the Eleven Thousand Virgins, this prayer is apparently unique to St Albans: who, we wonder, composed it, and why?

Another sanctorale figure whose presence may be notable is Taurinus, for whom a mass set is given, in the original hand, after that of the Roman martyr Tiburtius (fol. 98). Both saints are celebrated on the same day, August 11th, but there is no indication in the St Albans book that they are to be celebrated jointly (the next mass set is that of Hippolytus on the 13th). Taurinus was an early fifth-century bishop of Evreux in Normandy, whose relics were elevated there in 1158.[20] This is during the abbacy at St Albans of Robert de Gorron (1151–66), nephew of the abbot Geoffrey (to be considered presently),

[19] The evidence is laid out and discussed at length in Pfaff, *New Liturg. Feasts*, pp. 16–27.

[20] *AA. SS., Aug* II.650.

and a Norman by birth. Once more the textual evidence that might lay a trail is scarce. No mass set known is exactly like that of St Albans (in both twelfth-century sacramentary and fourteenth-century missal), of which the collect seems unique.[21] There is virtually no evidence for any cult of Taurinus in England before this, and it is tempting to connect his appearance in the book of about 1160 with the 1158 event – though no quite convincing way to do so.[22]

These details, none of them decisive or capable of full explanation, point to a considerable, and continuing, degree of what we may call liturgical curiosity at St Albans. If we could understand completely what is behind each of them, we would most likely gain a sense, not surprising, that a variety of influences and currents attracted the attention, and sometimes enthusiasm, of abbots, precentors, and other members of the community. The basic post-Conquest pattern may have been Lanfrancian, and there may have been a heavy dose of borrowing from a single Continental model, perhaps of an Italian sort as Hartzell suggested; but this one witness, the sacramentary of c. 1160, shows a variety and vitality that transcend dependence on any single source. The same is true also of the two chant books that in their different ways may be seen as complementing the sacramentary.

The two St Albans graduals and a processional

It may seem a surplus of riches to have extant two graduals from the same house and the same period: roughly, middle of the twelfth century, and therefore contemporary with the sacramentary just discussed at length. In fact, neither is quite as satisfactory as might be hoped. The more useful of the two, although the shorter, is Bodl. Laud misc. 358.[23] This contains, after an extensive series of Kyrie and Gloria chants, separate temporale and sanctorale sections. In the temporale of this gradual there is no provision for weekdays, even in Lent, whereas

---

[21] The Hereford missals, folding the prayers for Taurinus into the mass for Tiburtius as a *memoria*, have a different collect (one which was used in Normandy) but the same secret and postcommunion as the St Albans books: *Hereford Missal*, p. 300, cf. *WM* III.1579. Taurinus's feast appears in the Westminster missal (c. 1385); the abbot there from c. 1158 to 1173, Laurence, had been a monk of St Albans. All three prayers in Westminster's set appear to be unique.

[22] Taurinus is among the numerous additions to the Giso sacramentary calendar – additions so numerous and so apparently indiscriminate (p. 125 above) that it is hard to know what to make of them: Wormald, *Eng. Kals*, p. 107. At Hyde abbey there was after Tiburtius a combined *memoria* for Taurinus and Gaugericus (a 7th-cent. bishop of Cambrai-Arras) with yet a different, very bland, collect: *Hyde Brev.*, V, fol. 316.

[23] A detailed list of contents is provided by Hartzell, *Cat. Music*, pp. 472–80.

the sacramentary has incipit-tags for introits on those days: does this indicate that gradual texts were not chanted at the conventual mass on Lenten weekdays? The sanctorale contains full forms for the masses on some thirty-two feasts, the last being the Conception, mandated, as will be explained soon, by abbot Geoffrey (1119–46). There is nothing noteworthy about the selection of saints, which does not include forms for either Becket or the Invention of Amphibalus (25 June 1178).[24] A curious reversal of order appears in the common of saints, where that for Several Martyrs contains a reference back to the proper forms for Cosmas and Damian rather than, as is usual, the other way round.[25]

The other book, BL Royal 2 B.iv, is a gradual-troper – that is, with an extensive provision (fols 1–54) of farsed Kyries and Glorias, followed by a gradual that intermixes temporale and select sanctorale and, at the end, troped versions of the Sanctus and Agnus Dei.[26] There is some dislocation of leaves, and many are missing, including that which would have contained Alban's main feast; but the presence of forms for his Invention makes the ascription to that house sure. There are, however, three saints' feasts here that are lacking in the Laud misc. 358 gradual: those of Mark, John at the Latin Gate, and Nicholas. This may suggest that the Royal gradual is (slightly) the later of the two.

The Laud book contains at the Easter Vigil the hymn *Inventor rutili* that Lanfranc had specified was to be used "in sede episcopali": the episcopal chair that of course St Albans lacked. This leads Hartzell to ask whether the abbot of St Albans in effect considered himself a bishop; and Thomson connects the hymn's inclusion with a papal grant in about 1156 authorizing abbot Robert to use pontificalia (mitre, staff, and the like).[27] That grant did not, of course, establish the abbey as a cathedral (it was bitter enough for the diocesan, the bishop of Lincoln, to have to accede to its exemption from his control).[28] But it may

---

[24] Though it is not clear whether the *Amphibalus*, central to Alban's conversion, is orginally a priest or a priest's cloak (*amphibalus*), the 1178 Invention is of course predicated on its being the former.

[25] Also, Augustine is not included, which calls into doubt whether the fragments of a 12th-cent. antiphonal that form the first two leaves and contain parts of offices for Augustine as well as Gregory and Benedict originate at St Albans; they are also in a different hand from that of the gradual. Further details in Thomson, *St Albans MSS*, I.105.

[26] Contents detailed in Hartzell, *Cat. Music*, pp. 308–16. He discusses it from the musicological standpoint extensively in "Musical Rep.," I.179–230; pp. 179–81 compare the contents of the two graduals. The trope-texts are printed in W. H. Frere, *The Winchester Troper*, HBS 8 (1894), pp. 132–39; none seems to be proper to St Albans.

[27] Hartzell, "Musical Rep.," I.238; Thomson, *St Albans MSS*, I.47.

[28] The bull *Incomprehensibilis* is conveniently printed, with translation, in *Adrian IV: the English Pope*, ed. B. Bolton and A. J. Duggan (Aldershot 2003), pp. 312–19.

be possible to discern its effect in the use of the *Inventor rutili*: that is, as an expression of what might be called liturgical equality with any cathedral – possibly even Lanfranc's Canterbury.

Some further information about St Albans liturgy is available from the processional (Bodl. Laud misc. 4), which fortunately contains a fair number of rubrics.[29] It has long been said to have been written at St Albans for its cell at Tynemouth.[30] This is, however, unlikely to be correct, and the nickname used here for this book, the St Albans processional, is not misleading.[31] The book, dating from the third quarter of the twelfth century, has a claim to be "the oldest English monastic processional in existence."[32] It is a small volume, c. 117 x 80 mm, and therefore highly portable. S. J. P. van Dijk asserted, in his brief description of the manuscript, that it was intended as a cantor's book, and it does show signs of hard use.[33] It is, however, not adequate for the entire year: its temporale stops at Trinity Sunday and it includes no saints' days between Epiphany and Alban (22 June); so there may have been a complementary volume, or even two, of some sort.[34] Only eleven saints' days are included for the second half of the year, from Alban on, but even if the number of such days then on which there were processions was extremely limited, in the first half of the year they must have taken place on, at the least, the feasts of Andrew, Purification, Annunciation, and probably Gregory. It is also somewhat hard to believe that no

---

[29] Hartzell, *Cat. Music*, pp. 466–72.

[30] After a shaky early history, the house at Tynemouth was re-founded as a cell of St Albans, probably in the late 1080s, by Robert de Mowbray, earl of Northumberland, with the consent of Lanfranc, i.e., in the abbacy of Paul (1077–93). *Med. Rel. Houses*, p. 79, states that the cell had some thirty monks by 1090, which would make it as large as most medium-sized independent houses. The main source of information seems to be again the St Albans *Gesta Abbatum*.

[31] The ascription had been based on the fact that Oswin comes second among the martyrs (after Alban, who is in capitals) in the first Rogationtide litany (fol. 124) and in a second litany seems to be called "nostrum … patronum" (fol. 126v); in fact, the latter reads "Albanum vel Oswinum nostrum rogitemus corde patronum," which would make it possible to use the text in either house. Oswin does appear in two of the other four litanies in the book, in one of them doubled, but always after Alban. The telling detail is the omission of Oswin, Aug. 20th, in the select sanctorale, which starts with Alban (June 22nd) and in Aug. goes directly from Assumption (15th) to Decollation of John Baptist (29th). Also, there seem to have been no churches to which monks at Tynemouth could process, and the priory church had a quite different ground plan from that at St Albans (PBE *Northumberland*, p. 302).

[32] Hartzell, "Musical Repertory," I.118; his entire ch. iv (pp. 118–51) is devoted to this MS, the text of which is given, in summary form (mostly incipits), on pp. 31–41 of vol. II, and the notation of some musically interesting chants on 42–45.

[33] Van Dijk, *Handlist*, III.85. It is no. 85 in his Bodleian exhibition guide, *Latin Liturgical Manuscripts and Printed Books* (Oxford 1952); pl. v reproduces fols 85v–86.

[34] The book is lacking some leaves at the end, but these are unlikely to have been the missing saints' days.

processions were envisaged on any Sunday between Trinity (not in fact marked as a Sunday, but merely *De sancta trinitate*) and the beginning of Advent. In short, the cantor must have needed something besides this volume. Despite these gaps, there is, as Hartzell's careful analysis has shown, plenty in this book to reinforce our impression that liturgy at St Albans manifested both aspects of continuity with and points of difference from the regime envisaged in Lanfranc's *Constitutions*, even though that document supplies few textual or even rubrical details about processions.

One such point of difference connects us to the Rogation processions about which we drew inferences from the sacramentary. The processional offers separate litany-forms for each of the three days; they begin, respectively, *Humili prece*, *Suscipe deprecationem*, and *Ardua spes*. Only one litany is specified by Lanfranc, although he mentions a litany of saints earlier in the service, one that doubles the name of the saint to whom the church is dedicated – the church in question being that to which the procession has gone.[35] The Lanfrancian litany cannot therefore be the *Humili prece* of the Monday procession in Laud misc. 4, which is an elaborate metrical composition invoking the saints in some twenty strophes and ending with eleven Greek words.[36] That this is not solely a St Albans usage is shown by the presence of these three litanies in the Arsenal and Bologna Sarum missals of the late thirteenth century – books that, as we shall notice, often contain evidence of earlier practice even though they are, as manuscripts, dated somewhat later than the "standard" Crawford missal (see pp. 357 and 380).[37]

This last detail suggests a possibility of wider significance: the presence in secular liturgy of a non-Lanfrancian usage observed at a monastic house under general Lanfrancian influence. A Norman origin seems likely. As well as its appearances at Bec and Rouen (pointed out by Hartzell), the incipit *Humili prece* is specified for Rogation Tuesday in the ordinal of Fécamp abbey, but that is slightly later than the St Albans

---

[35] *Lanfranc's Monastic Constitutions*, ed. Knowles and Brooke, p. 76.
[36] Hartzell, II.40–41, prints the text; my transcription from the MS differs slightly. The martyrs are ALBAN (in capitals, with three strophes all to himself), Stephen, Linus, Clement, Anacletus, Sixtus, Alexander, Cornelius, Hippolytus, Vitus, Laurence, Modestus, Grisogonus, Cyriac, Boniface, Pancras, Paul, George, John; confessors Silvester, Damasus, Gregory, Ambrose, Hilary, Zeno, Maximus, Leo, Martin, Gildard, Cesarius, Eusebius, Benedict (a strophe to himself), Romanus (likewise), Paul, Antony, Macarius, Arsenius, Pachomius, Bede(!), Pafnucius, Medard, Libertinus, Basil, Jerome; virgins Felicitas, Eulalia, Verena, Petronilla, Perpetua, Agnes, Agatha, Cristina, Euprepia, Tecla, Eugenia, Eufemia, Regula, Bona.
[37] *SML*, p. 153.

manuscript.[38] In the absence of any more convincing choice, the special attention paid to Romanus, the bishop of Rouen who died in 640 – he is the only saint besides Benedict to have a strophe to himself (to Alban's three) – may point to Rouen as the place of origin for this intriguing litany.

Gestures towards shortening liturgy at St Albans

As a kind of corrective to the impression of elaboration and prolixity that some of the developments noticed above suggest – things like farsed chants of the ordinary and extensive Rogation processions – it is refreshing to note the attempt of abbot John de Cella (1195–1214) to limit the number of collects at mass to seven: as many as six mass sets (*oratio*, secret, and postcommunion) for votive and other purposes after the set for any particular day being quite enough (*propter sufficientiam*).[39] Is it significant that this section of the *Gesta* follows immediately one that records another of John's decisions, to limit the number of monks at the house to one hundred? Anything like that number, the majority of whom would probably have been priests, would strain the liturgical fabric of even the best equipped house, as well as its resources of other kinds; but it may be an improbably large figure.

In something of the same spirit the immediately preceding abbot, Warin (1183–95), had apparently tried to shorten the office somewhat.[40] This seems to have involved mainly those extra devotions like the *Psalmi familiares* that, originally accretions to the Benedictine office, came to be regarded as integral to it. The one example offered by the *Gesta Abbatum* within the office proper is Warin's rather drastic shortening of that for the Invention of Stephen on August 3rd: probably – although the author of the account does not state this – because of the length of the previous day's office for the Invention of Alban. If this is indeed the reason, it shows a nice sense of liturgical practicality. But the liturgy of the monastic office was always going to be complex and lengthy. It was no more possible then to celebrate it simply than it is now to apprehend it readily.

---

[38] D. Chadd, ed., *The Ordinal of the Abbey of the Holy Trinity Fécamp*, part i, HBS 111 (1999), pp. 271 (from an early 13th-cent. ordinal) and 367 (from an early 14th-cent. processional). The *litania cotidiana* from a collectar of the mid-12th cent. is printed on pp. 371–78, with variants from other MSS, and there is almost no similarity with the saints in the St Albans version of *Humili prece*.

[39] *Gesta Abbatum*, I.235. This kind of multiplication of mass prayers is a frequently encountered problem in the middle ages; seven seems to be the top number feasible.

[40] *Gesta Abbatum*, I.212–13.

Office liturgy at St Albans

It is therefore tempting, and would indeed be gratifying, to be able to say that the most vivid witness to the office in the twelfth century is the wondrous book that is widely known as, simply, *the* St Albans psalter.[41] The overwhelming experience of viewing each page online (as recent digitization of the manuscript makes possible) notwithstanding, there is little in its contents, even in the calendar and litany, that is informative about liturgy at the abbey; for it was made for the anchoress Christina of Markyate, most likely under the auspices of abbot Geoffrey (de) Gorron. Its fascinations (and peculiarities) of devotion seem for the most part unrelated to any evidence we have for the monks' liturgy.[42] For that we must turn instead to the only one of the genuinely liturgical St Albans books to be concerned with the office, BL Royal 2 A.x. This is not quite what it is widely called, a breviary.[43] Its contents show it to be a kind of expanded psalter with hymnal and collectar elements as well. Full offices are provided only for a specimen season of the proper of time: the first week following the first Sunday after Epiphany and the four Sundays thereafter – the "sample week" phenomenon discussed in the previous chapter (p. 135).[44] For the proper of saints there is even less, only the main feasts of the Virgin, and those not quite complete. There are also some special services (fols 126–45) and a full common of saints. Rodney Thomson summarizes it as "the sort of small-format book of which each monk would have had a copy when in choir," but this is hard to square with the contents.[45] Each

---

[41] Hildesheim, Dombibliothek, St Godehard MS 1. Of the vast literature, mostly art-historical, there needs to be mentioned here only the collaborative volume by O. Pächt, C. R. Dodwell, and F. Wormald, *The St Albans Psalter (Albani Psalter)* (London 1960) and the online presentation of the entire codex by Jane Geddes, www.abdn.ac.uk/~lib399/english/index.shtml (2003); cf. her semi-popular book, *The St Albans Psalter* (London 2005).

[42] In the psalter's calendar but not that of the Rawl. liturg. c. 1 sacramentary are Felix (of East Anglia) 8 March, Amalberga added (after the Seven Brothers) 10 July, Hilda 17 Nov., and "Tumulatio sancti Benedicti" 4 Dec. In the litany Alban, doubled, comes immediately after Stephen, but among the virgins "Ursula, Cordula, and their companions" are specified rather than the unnamed Eleven Thousand Virgins who were noticed as a marginal addition in the sacramentary.

[43] So termed in the catalogue of Royal MSS, *MLGB*, and Thomson. Hartzell (whose dissertation treats the book at length, I.74–117), recognizes that it is not a true breviary and calls it instead a portiforium – not precisely the accurate term either.

[44] Discussed in my "The 'Sample Week' in the Medieval Latin Divine Office," in *Continuity and Change in Christian Worship*, ed. R. N. Swanson, SCH 35 (1999), pp. 78–88 at 87–88; I concluded that apparently what began as a psalter-plus started to take on the character of a proto-breviary with the addition of these "template" services (and see above, p. 135).

[45] Thomson, *St Albans MSS*, I.38.

monk does not need an extensive provision of office collects, which are recited only by the officiant, whereas he does need a fuller supply of psalm- and canticle-texts than is given here. For almost all the psalms and the first two of the weekly canticles only as much of each verse is given as occupies a single line, and often a new verse is begun at the end of a line.[46] It looks as though this is something like an officiant's *aide-mémoire* volume.

Nonetheless it is greatly useful for our purposes. It witnesses to the liturgical reforms of Geoffrey (de) Gorron, abbot for the long and fruitful period 1119–46. Thomson's succinct but pregnant analysis of this should be quoted in full. He suggests that this book and several others which he thinks were also written in the 1140s testify to

a wholesale abandonment of both Bec custom (if St Albans had ever observed it) and the customs of Lanfranc, which we know the abbey had adopted in Abbot Paul's time. The stages by which this process was implemented cannot now be recovered ... . The sources of the new influences were various and drawn upon by Abbot Geoffrey in an eclectic fashion. Not all of the old ways were abandoned; St Albans continued to follow the Bec musical tradition. But among the new influences that of Italy is observable, the most notable instance being Geoffrey's introduction of the feast of the Immaculate Conception.[47]

Why Geoffrey wished to innovate is hidden from us; such details as we have concern mainly the grading of feasts. Geoffrey, who came from a noble family in Maine, is known to history chiefly through the story of his becoming a monk at St Albans as reparation for the loss through fire of several copes which he had borrowed from that house, apparently to use as costumes for a play in honor of St Catherine that he was directing at the school he headed in Dunstable.[48] The St Albans *Gesta abbatum*, in its generally approving notice of him, records among books he had made "a missal, adorned with gold, and another in two volumes ... and a precious psalter, similarly illuminated throughout with gold. And a book of blessings and episcopal services. Also a book containing exorcisms and a collectar."[49] It appears that none of these survives save perhaps the last, which could well be the Royal 2 A.x book under consideration.

---

[46] This is illustrated on pl. 84 of Thomson, *St Albans MSS*. The point was apparently to get every line about equal in length, thus preserving the tidy appearance, with initials alternately red and green and a two-line initial at the beginning of each psalm. That the practice was not undisputed is suggested by the fact that psalms civ–cx.2 are written in full with non-justified line endings.

[47] Thomson, I.38–39, with reference mainly to the *Gesta abbatum* and to Hartzell's dissertation.

[48] On this story, and Geoffrey's work in general, see Knowles, *MO*, pp. 187–89 and Thomson, I.20–22.

[49] *Gesta Abbatum*, I.93–94; Thomson's translation.

That this seems likely, and that the book has at least in part a reference aspect, is suggested by the contents of two sections. First, following the "specimen" temporale and sanctorale sections described above and an office of the Trinity (as a liturgical feast, probably new to St Albans at that point), come offices for the martyr-pope Alexander and for the Invention of the Cross, both observed on May 3rd, and for the Exaltation of the Cross and for Cornelius and Cyprian, both feasts being on September 14th. This looks like an attempt to straighten out difficulties caused by these concurrences, and it may be relevant that two of the five feasts ordered by Geoffrey to be upgraded are respectively the next major occasions: John at the Latin Gate, May 6th, and Matthew, September 21st. Secondly, after the lengthy common of saints come collects for Ambrose, Tiburtius et al., Alphege, George, Mark, Vitalis, and Philip & James: respectively, April 4th, 14th, 19th, 23rd, 25th, 28th, and May 1st; with, between George and Mark, a collect for any saint during Eastertide. This is clearly a discrete section designed to accommodate the saints of that season (only Guthlac, who is in the calendar at April 11th, seems ignored), sometimes regarded as falling into a discrete *tempore Paschali* category.[50]

What can be inferred more widely as to abbot Geoffrey's liturgical reforms from this book? His predecessor but one, Paul of Caen (1077–93; see p. 110), had supplied the house richly with liturgical books: the *Gesta abbatum* details "eight Psalters, a Collectar, an Epistolar, a book containing the Gospel pericopes for the year, two Gospel-books ornamented with gold, silver and gems, not to mention Ordinals, Customaries, Missals, Tropers, Collectars and other books."[51] The great church begun under Paul was not consecrated until 1115, four years before Geoffrey became abbot. The rise of St Albans to prominence among English abbeys was largely a post-Conquest phenomenon, and it seems likely that the number of fifty monks recorded in 1190 was reached only gradually.[52] Geoffrey's program of donations may have been partly in response to growth in numbers, partly an expression of increased splendor of the sort represented by the grand translation of Alban's body to a new shrine in 1129, on August 2nd, which was thenceforth an important feast at the abbey.

---

[50] Wormald's treatment of St Albans calendars in *Eng. Ben. Kals* is rather unsatisfactory. His base MS is Oxford, New College 358, a well decorated psalter of the third quarter of the 13th cent., of no great textual interest. The calendar of Royal A.x, the earliest surviving from St Albans, is collated as MS A; the other three collated do *not* include that of the Hildesheim "St Albans psalter."

[51] *Gesta abbatum*, I.57–58; Thomson's translation (I.13).

[52] *Med. Rel. Houses*, p. 75. This figure is hard to square with the limit, noticed above, of one hundred that abbot John de Cella is said to have imposed in 1200: *Gesta Abbatum*, I.234.

It was observed as we began to survey the St Albans service books that the fortuitous survival of several from that house would be the justification for such detailed treatment. The number of such books aside, the overall grandeur of St Albans – in wealth, saints, and magnificent building, as well as books – might, if no other house were considered, distort somewhat the impression of monastic liturgy that we are trying to obtain. It may therefore be a good idea to look now at evidence from a smaller and altogether more modest house, Winchcombe.

The daily office at Winchcombe

In contrast to the St Albans book just reviewed, the earliest surviving monastic breviary proper – that is, containing all the requisite components – used in England is a codex from Winchcombe (now Valenciennes, B.m. 116); indeed, it is the only one dating from the twelfth century.[53] It also includes what amounts to a select missal, so to deal with it as though it were simply a breviary is something of an oversimplification.[54] Features of its format suggest that it is not intended for performance of the office in choir, while the provision of missal elements – canon, numerous masses (in missal, not sacramentary, form) – would make it useful as a liturgical compendium for travelling, as would its compact size.[55] Whatever its precise nature, its value for our purposes lies not only in its age but in the chance survival of two older books also probably made, and possibly used, at Winchcombe: a late tenth-century sacramentary (now Orléans, B.m. 127 [105]) which seems to have gone to France within a few decades of being written, and a mid-eleventh-century psalter (often called the "Cambridge psalter," now CUL Ff.1.23) the litany of which – no calendar survives – points strongly to that house.[56] By using these two witnesses alongside

---

[53] The fullest description is still that of V. Leroquais, *Les Bréviaires manuscrits des bibliothèques publiques de France*, 5 vols (Paris 1934), II.283–85.

[54] As J. B. L. Tolhurst has done, using it as one of six sources on which he based his widely used *Introduction to the English Monastic Breviaries*, published as vol. VI of his edn of the *Hyde Breviary* (HBS 80, 1943), and reprinted separately by the HBS in 1993. Tolhurst's work is assessed more fully on p. 226.

[55] The dimensions are roughly 190 x 135 mm. As with the St Albans book just noticed, there is no psalter proper (where the ordinary of the office is usually located); only as much of each psalm-verse is written as fits a line in a tight, double-column format; the litany of saints is a mere list, without any of the usual *Or[ate]* indications; and the sanctorale is much more select than the calendar.

[56] The first is ed. A. Davril, *The Winchcombe Sacramentary*, HBS 109 (1995); cf. my remarks in *Liturg. Bks ASE*, pp. 14–15. The second is ed. in M. Lapidge, *Litanies*, no. 1; he observes, without further elaboration, that "the prominence given to St Kenelm has been thought to point to Winchcombe as the manuscript's place of origin, but other explanations of the prominence accorded to Kenelm are also possible"

the breviary we may be able to establish points of continuity with the liturgy of the house in pre-Norman times.

Winchcombe contrasts nicely with St Albans, in terms alike of obscurity of location (in a Gloucestershire village), size (roughly half the number of monks), wealth (perhaps a third as much revenue), and dimness of patron saint. The most distinctive detail for Winchcombe is emphasis on Kenelm, a Mercian prince whose death in the first quarter of the ninth century was, by the eleventh century anyhow, regarded as a martyrdom; and the possession of whose body was the crowning glory of the house at Winchcombe after its revival c. 970 under Oswald of Worcester. (Whether Kenelm is historical or fictitious is irrelevant for our purposes.) His legend and subsequent hagiography have been thoroughly studied by Rosalind Love, who prints the office for Kenelm from the Valenciennes manuscript.[57] Its lessons are drawn from a *Vita et miracula* possibly composed by, in Love's phrase, "the ubiquitous Flemish hagiographer Goscelin," who worked in the West Country between 1066 and 1075.[58] There is also a *Vita brevior*, which stands in an unclear relationship with the longer life and from which certain phrases, as Love points out, "seem to be echoed in the antiphons and responses" of the Winchcombe office. It looks as though the Kenelm office cannot have been of pre-Conquest composition, although from the late tenth century there was clearly a cult of Kenelm at Winchcombe.[59] This early cult is reflected in the sacramentary, which has a mass set for the saint, including a wordy proper preface and an *Ad*

(p. 62) – and, to be sure, the book is "Rejected" for Winchcombe in *MLGB*. The year after his *Litanies* volume appeared Lapidge proposed that the psalter should be assigned to Canterbury St Augustine's: "Abbot Germanus, Winchcombe, Ramsey, and the Cambridge Psalter," in *Words, Texts, and Manuscripts. Studies ... to Helmut Gneuss*, ed. M. Korhammer (Cambridge 1992), pp. 99–129: arguing in the same article that the sacramentary was written at Ramsey rather than Winchcombe. Points of comparison with the breviary discussed above make it likelier that the sacramentary and psalter are both Winchcombe products.

[57] R. Love, ed. and tr., *Three Eleventh-Century Anglo-Latin Saints' Lives*: Vita S. Birini, Vita et Miracula S. Kenelmi, *and* Vita S. Rumwoldi, OMT (1996), Appendix E (= pp. 130–34), without the twelve lessons, because they are taken verbatim from the *Vita brevior* which she has printed, from CCCC 367 with reference to the Valenciennes office, in the previous appendix (pp. 126–29). At least seven churches, all within 60 m of Winchcombe, were dedicated to Kenelm, including at a village with the Wodehouseian name of Upton Snodsbury (Worcs.).

[58] Love, p. xcvii; her detailed discussion concludes that "the evidence available at present falls just short of absolute proof and is open to debate, but the case for admitting this text into the canon of his works does seem quite strong" (p. ci).

[59] And apparently also at Worcester: the saint's death had taken place at Clent (near Kidderminster), briefly a dependency of the cathedral priory; but the evidence for a Worcester cult is not as clear as for Winchcombe.

vesperam prayer.[60] The entire set appears also in the slightly later Robert of Jumièges book, as the fifth of five mass sets for English saints at the very beginning of the codex.[61] The same three mass prayers for Kenelm survive in subsequent secular (Sarum and Hereford) and monastic (Westminster and Sherborne) missals, and the collect is that in the Valenciennes office (fol. 208).

In the missal section of the Valenciennes book the mass *De reliquiis* specifies Kenelm in all three prayers (fol. 32). In the litany he is listed as fifteenth among thirty-two martyrs, rather oddly placed between Sebastian and Valentine (whereas the other English figures, Alban, Edmund, and Oswald, are grouped together eleven places further down; fol. 25). This contrasts interestingly with the litany in the Ff.1.23 psalter, which puts Kenelm (in red, the only name so treated besides Peter's) just above those three.[62]

We have, then, in the twelfth-century Kenelm office the collect from a mass set used in the tenth century and lessons drawn from a life probably composed after the Norman Conquest had begun. (This life is also the source of the three lengthy lessons for Kenelm in the 1531 printed Sarum breviary, close to but not identical with the aggregate of the twelve lessons in the Winchcombe book.)[63] Instructive contrast is offered by the thirteenth-century breviary of Hyde abbey (on which, see p. 220), where Kenelm's feast is marked by three lessons and a different collect from that of the Winchcombe tradition.[64] The feast is not found in the missal of the New Minster (1070s?; see p. 110), Hyde's predecessor-foundation; the confector(s) of the Hyde book used as the office collect the second of the three prayers for Kenelm in the Wulfstan portiforium. This suggests a different route for, at any rate, a mass set, although the lessons are merely a radical boiling down of the *Vita*.

This book may be datable as precisely as the mid-1170s. The calendar contains, in the original hand, an obit on May 2nd for abbot Gervase, who died in 1171; but Becket's December 29th feast, which would have been widely observed after his canonization in 1173, is added in the same hand as his Translation, July 7th (1220). This places the book as

---

[60] *Winchcombe Sacr.*, nos. 1101–5.
[61] *Robert of Jumièges Missal*, pp. 6–7, with Winchcombe's *Ad vesperam* as an *alia* postcommunion.
[62] Lapidge, *Litanies*, p. 94. There is some indication that the original dedication of the 8th-cent. foundation was to Peter, though the principal dedicatee seem to have been Mary, with Kenelm's name added to hers only after the refoundation: Binns, *Dedications*, p. 89. Corroboration comes in the Valenciennes book's votive mass *Pro congregatione* (fol. 34), where Mary and Peter are the two saints named in the collect.
[63] *Sarum Breviary*, III.498.
[64] *Hyde Breviary*, IV, fol. 295.

an almost exact contemporary with several of those from St Albans. The same thing is true of a somewhat unusual source, a mid-twelfth-century cartulary of Sherborne abbey.

The Sherborne cartulary

Sherborne abbey is useful for our purposes in the present chapter because each of the three pieces of evidence we have about liturgy there, though widely separated in time, bears on the others. For the twelfth century, our current concern, there is the Sherborne cartulary, BL Add. 46487, the liturgical portion of which is limited but invaluable. Such information as can be extracted from it can be set beside the much fuller witness of the magnificent, indeed incomparable, Sherborne missal of around 1400 (BL Add. 74326; discussed on p. 236); and the sanctorale information from both compared with that in the calendar of the mid-eleventh-century massbook called the Red Book of Darley (CCCC 422; see p. 94) – a calendar which clearly has its origin in Sherborne. The saint whose presence is the most distinctive is Wul(f)sin, alias Wulfsige. (The latter is the preferred form of his name, but the former is that which appears in the three documents in question, and which will therefore be adopted here.)

Wulsin, already abbot of Westminster, came to Sherborne as bishop around 994 and a few years later effected the re-foundation of that house as a cathedral priory, on the model introduced at Winchester a generation earlier.[65] After his death on 8 January 1002 a feast day in his honor was observed at Sherborne, primarily, and with much less emphasis at Westminster and in a few other places. His name appears in capitals, and with the designation "F," which apparently denotes the highest-grade feasts, in the Sherborne/Darley calendar, probably datable to around 1060.[66]

As its name indicates, the Sherborne cartulary is mainly a collection of copies of charters that benefited, or could be altered to benefit, the

---

[65] As a bishop he would have needed a pontifical, and it is almost certain that he possessed the late 10th-cent. book, now BN lat. 943, known alternately as the Dunstan or the Sherborne pontifical. Wulsin may have been a protégé of Dunstan's: see J. Barrow in *ODNB*, 60.555–56 and, more fully, S. Keynes in *St Wulfsige and Sherborne: Essays to Celebrate the Millennium of the Benedictine Abbey 998–1998*, ed. K. Barker et al. (Bournemouth 2005), pp. 55–94. The same volume contains a translation by R. Love of Goscelin's life of Wulfsige, pp. 98–123.

[66] Wormald, *Eng. Kals*, p. 184. There seems also to have been a feast, July 13th, marking translations of Wulsin and Juthwara (a British virgin) that took place at Sherborne under Ægelward, abbot 1045–58 – probably towards the end of that time, for it does not appear in the Darley calendar.

abbey (as the house became in 1122, the bishopric having moved to Old Sarum in 1075–78). The present order of items is badly confused, but the original structure has been ascertained; it appears that the charter material came first, then the liturgical, and finally some miscellaneous documents. The liturgical section has been most plausibly explained by Francis Wormald as forming part of an abbot's book, including as it does gospels and collects that would be read by the abbot at the conclusion of matins on important occasions, plus the blessings at Candlemas, Ash Wednesday, Palm Sunday, and the *Triduum sacrum*. The manuscript is datable to 1146 or shortly thereafter, this precision made possible by its apparent origin as a kind of trophy of a victory the monks won over Jocelin, bishop of Salisbury, in that year. The story is a fascinating one but irrelevant to our purposes, save that, in Wormald's words, it explains "why this MS was written, and why it took the form, not of a chartulary, but of an altar book in which secular documents were included. It was to serve as an important weapon against any future attempts at interference by the bishop of Salisbury."[67] There are two splendid miniatures of evangelists.[68]

Although Wormald listed in detail all forty-one of the charter items, his account of the liturgical material was extremely summary, and additional information must be supplied here. The principal feasts for which gospels and collects are provided include the occasions from Christmas through Epiphany, Easter and the three days following, Pentecost and its next three days and octave (there is nothing for Ascension). Interspersed with these are the sanctorale occasions of Wulsin (January 8th), Purification, Annunciation, Mary Magdalen, Transfiguration, Laurence, Assumption, Nativity of Mary, Michael, Feast of Relics, All Saints, Martin, Andrew, Nicholas, and Conception. The forms supplied for these fifteen feasts (two leaves, almost certainly containing John the Baptist and Peter and Paul, are missing) are mostly unremarkable, but three or four should be noticed. The collect for Mary Magdalen is that found also in the three English secular uses rather than the one at Westminster, Durham, St Augustine's, and St Albans. That for the Transfiguration is the one popularized by Peter the Venerable's advocacy of the feast in 1132 (see p. 164), so its appearance here reflects quick circulation of that originally Cluniac influence. Inclusion of that feast in this select group, as also of those of Mary Magdalen, Nicholas, and the Conception, suggests a lively sense of emphasizing feasts newly

[67] F. Wormald, "The Sherborne 'Chartulary'," in *Fritz Saxl … Memorial Essays*, ed. D. J. Gordon (London 1957), pp. 101–19, at 109.
[68] That of St John is illustrated in M. Kauffmann, *Romanesque MSS*, ill. 155.

popular; any one would not be remarkable, but all four together are noteworthy.[69] Where the collects in the cartulary can be compared with those in the Sherborne missal, one distinctive point of continuity is that the missal's unusual collect for the Conception is the same as that in the cartulary.[70] (On the other hand, the Transfiguration is not present in the missal.) The cartulary's collect for Wulsin also reappears in the missal.

We might wish in particular to have some idea of who the Henry was who became abbot after, and as a consequence of, the controversy in 1146, but no information seems available. It is possible that the house remained something of a backwater after bishop Hereman moved his episcopal headquarters to Sarum around 1075. The prior at that point, Wulfric, lived until 1078, and was succeeded for the next twenty years by Ælfric, and he by Thurstan, prior until 1122 and thereafter (until at least 1139) abbot. The first two of those names are definitely, and the third possibly, English; is this reflected in the persistence in the Sherborne missal of around 1400 of such distinctively Anglo-Saxon feasts as Edwold (hermit of nearby Cerne), Ordination of Gregory, Translation of Æthelwold (as well as his main feast on August 1st), Conception of John the Baptist, Ordination of Swithun (as well as his July feast, with octave), and Oblation of the Virgin (under that title, rather than Presentation)?

Despite never being a very large or specially wealthy house, Sherborne seems to have flourished under the next abbot after Henry, Clement, in office from at least 1155 and perhaps for thirty years or more.[71] Although the church survived the Dissolution whole, being now the parish church of the town, the present fabric is mainly of the fifteenth century; but there is enough evidence of the Norman church to give an adequate idea of its splendor – not least, a Purbeck marble "portrait" head of Clement on his monument in the south aisle.[72] This makes all the more interesting the account at the end of the cartulary (in its original state; now fols 67–68) of donations made to the abbey by its sacristan, William of Thorncombe, brother of Clement.[73] A chapel dedicated in 1177 is referred to, but the hand is still of the twelfth

---

[69] Of these, only Mary Magdalen, in capitals, and Nicholas, in no way special, are in the Darley calendar.

[70] Of the witnesses included in Legg's 1897 "Notes," only the Whitby missal (Bodl. Rawl. liturg. b.1) and the "rogue" Sarum-like missal (BL Add. 11414: see p. 502) share this collect.

[71] *Heads Rel. Houses*, I.70.

[72] Pictured, wearing a braided beard, in PBE *Dorset* (1972), ill. 18.

[73] Printed as an appendix by Wormald, "Sherborne 'Chartulary'," pp. 118–19.

century. Thorncombe is a village northeast of Axminster and not far from Sherborne, so these are local figures, presumably with wealth behind them: for among William's gifts were two gospel books, a missal with silver and gold clasps, a great many vestments, altar and sanctuary hangings (including a "dossarium [curtain?] cum archa Noe" which one would dearly love to see), and something called a "pugilare Zacharie," which may provide evidence for communion in both kinds.[74]

Fragments of a Glastonbury collectar

As has been mentioned earlier, the disparity between the grandeur of a monastic house in the middle ages and the amount of evidence that survives for liturgical practice there is probably greatest in the case of Glastonbury. Pre-eminent alike in antiquity, size, wealth, and pride, it seems to have reached a kind of apogee in the third quarter of the twelfth century, during the reign as abbot from 1126 to 1171 of Henry of Blois, from 1129 simultaneously bishop of Winchester (and apparently once a monk of Cluny, as well as being a patron of the arts and, as King Stephen's brother, a major player in the political troubles of c. 1139–52). Henry's magnificence – he is in many ways comparable to Cardinal Wolsey in the sixteenth century – must be kept in mind as we try to assess the surviving fragments of the sole service book that seems to bear the stamp of Glastonbury, one almost certainly written during his abbacy.

These fragments – the remains of eight folios and two stubs – exist now as flyleaves in the *Liber Ruber*, one of the four large cartularies of, and at, Wells Cathedral; there are also bits of two folios pasted in as endpapers to its *Liber Fuscus*.[75] The *Liber Ruber* leaves include some of the temporale, the sanctorale from August 31st to October 28th, and some parts of the common of saints and Offices of the Dead and of the Virgin Mary. Of this material, that which is likeliest to be distinctive is the selection of saints and, to some extent, the texts of the collects (there

---

[74] W.-H. Maigne d'Arnis, *Lexicon manuale ad scriptores mediae et infimae latinitatis* (Paris 1866), col. 1823: "anciens instruments sacrés qu'on portait devant le prêtre quand la communion sous les deux espèces était en usage."

[75] This is explained in greater detail in my article, "The Glastonbury Collectar," in *Contexts of Medieval Art: Images, Objects and Ideas. Tribute to Nigel Morgan*, ed. J. Luxford and M. Michael (London 2009), pp. 31–38. The *Liber Fuscus* leaves, much harder to make out than those in the *Liber Ruber*, seem to be exclusively hymns and add little to our quest. The only previous study of these fragments was by Dom A. Watkin, "Fragment of a Twelfth-Century Collectarium in the Liber Albus [sic: this was incorrect] of Wells," *Downside Review*, n.s. 69 (1951), pp. 85–91. His tentative conclusions differed considerably from mine.

are, not surprisingly, no rubrics). The collocation of three sanctorale occasions points unmistakably to Glastonbury: the Translation of Æthelwold (once a monk of the house; 10 September), Translation of Aidan and Ceolfrith (their relics were thought to be there; 8 October), and Ordination of Dunstan (first abbot after its re-establishment in 940; 21 October). The major question is whether this is more fairly regarded as a book for services at the abbey or as in some sense a book personal to its abbot. That the latter is likelier is suggested by the appearance among the forty sanctorale occasions for September and October of such saints as Lazarus (along with Priscus, 1 September) and Piatus (1 October), who have no place in any of the four or five calendars that can reasonably be associated with Glastonbury.[76]

The book from which the fragments come was a fine though not sumptuous one, large enough (c. 290 x 190 mm) as to imply being held by an acolyte. A plausible hypothesis that takes into account both its nature as a book and the peculiarities of its contents is that it may have been compiled for use of the abbot as he peregrinated to the monastery's dependent churches. Yet the texts of those collects (and capitula) for occasions which were observed at the abbey – including all those in the temporale section – are likely to have been the ones used there, and to that (limited) extent we have for Glastonbury a witness comparable to that available for Sherborne through its cartulary.

Durham's Lanfrancian echoes

Evidence about liturgy at the great cathedral priory of Durham, though more plentiful than for Glastonbury, is markedly less than for the relatively obscure house at Sherborne. The most important witness from Durham is that offered by the early and partial chant book alluded to at the beginning of this chapter, the Cosin gradual (still at Durham, University Library, Cosin V.v.6), especially valuable here because there are indications that it was in continuous use, or at least under periodic revision, until at least the thirteenth century. The original book, carefully studied from the musicological standpoint by K. D. Hartzell, was written at Canterbury in the last quarter of the eleventh century and taken soon thereafter to Durham (where in 1083 the cathedral regime had

---

[76] In addition to those used by Watkin, including that of the "B" strand in the Leofric missal (p. 75 above), the calendar of a 15th-cent. psalter formerly at Upholland College in Lancashire, which Wormald, who edited it, thought witnessed to a 13th-cent. nucleus: "The Liturgical Calendar of Glastonbury Abbey," in *Festschrift Bernhard Bischoff*, ed. J. Autenrieth and F. Brunhölzl (Stuttgart 1971), pp. 325–45 (sold in 1987, present whereabouts not known).

been re-established as monastic; see p. 101).[77] The book itself is quite fine, though small (160 x 110 mm, cropped at the top); some obvious lacunae apart, it is either drastically incomplete or was to be complemented by another volume, for the sanctorale runs only from June 23rd to August 22nd, and there is no common of saints.[78]

Two notable features are an extensive Kyriale (chants for the ordinary of the mass, here with melismatic elaborations called *prosulae*), mostly in the original Canterbury hand, and eleven sequences, alias proses, added in a number of hands soon after the book arrived in Durham. The rationale for the choice of these sequences is clear only with those for Cuthbert, Oswald, and Aidan (the latter of which, *Alme concrepent*, may be unique); the one for Nicholas probably represents the new vogue for him after the 1087 translation at Bari, but there is no obvious reason why pieces for Vincent, Paul, the Exaltation of the Cross, and the Virgin (four) should be among those supplied. At various times in the twelfth and thirteenth centuries further bits were added, including a new sequence for Cuthbert; possibly as many as fifteen additional hands were involved. Hartzell suggests that the original scribe (responsible also for the notation) was probably a Norman – this would have been at Canterbury, presumably: the result being that the book "is written in a script and a notation that would have been familiar to the new bishop and to a Norman precentor."[79]

This is consonant with the nature of the book, which is more a reference-collection than a gradual to be used in a systematic way. Two aspects of its contents underline this. One is the presence of a full set of chants for the pontifical occasion of the dedication of a church, including cemetery, pavement, and bells, as though the cantor whose

---

[77] K. D. Hartzell, "An unknown English Benedictine gradual of the eleventh century," *ASE* 4 (1975), pp. 131–44. Plate IIIa illustrates fol. 40, actual size. His *Cat. Music*, pp. 168–81 lists the contents in detail (on p. 169 the first sequence listed, *Alme concrepent*, should be headed *De sancto Aidano* rather than Cuthbert, whose sequence comes next but one). Through the kindness of Ian Doyle, I have also been able to use an extensive typed description of the MS by Alan Piper, revised in 1990, which will appear in the yet-to-be-published catalogue of Durham Univ. Lib. MSS. The *Laudes regiae* on fols 19–21v have been ignored in the present discussion, in favor of a separate study.

[78] A surprising omission is the apostle James, whose feast is of the third rank in Lanfranc's *Constitutions*, just like Peter *ad vincula* and Laurence, both present here. Also present in this limited sanctorale section are Mary Magdalen (conspicuously unmentioned by Lanfranc), Processus and Martinian, Seven Brothers, Apollinaris, and Ciriac *et soc.*; but not pope Stephen and Invention of (protomartyr) Stephen, both of them feasts that might have been expected.

[79] Hartzell, "Unknown gradual," p. 140. On pp. 141–45 he provides a table of the chant forms in thirteen witnesses, mostly French, and argues therefrom for extensive Norman influence, perhaps directly from Bec.

book this was expected to accompany the bishop as he performed that rite throughout the diocese. The other is that each of the days of the week after the Octave of Pentecost (each weekday of which has chants assigned to it) is headed with the name of the votive mass often associated with that day: *De angelis* for Monday, *De sapientia* for Tuesday, and so on; this might be useful if an ordinary-time weekday were otherwise vacant.[80] (There is also an odd inconsistency between the styling *Epiphania* in the temporale and *Theophania* in the section later in the manuscript of antiphons for processions, which suggests a different ultimate source for the two sections.)

The "Norman precentor" who is likeliest to have used the Cosin gradual heavily is the historian Symeon. Almost certainly a Norman, he is thought to have come to Durham in 1091, and was active there, at least part of the time as precentor (or, as is often said in monastic usage, cantor) until about 1130. This is of course exactly the period of intensive construction of the incomparable church, 1093 to 1133. Symeon seems to have been present at the key event of the early twelfth century there, the translation of Cuthbert's remains in 1104 to a shrine behind the apse of the new choir.[81] A volume of monastic documents that has come to be known as the "Durham Cantor's book" (now Durham cath. B.IV.24) contains material which Michael Gullick has shown to be in Symeon's hand: a martyrology and a lectionary of gospel readings in chapter.[82] The martyrology (Usuard's) has been supplemented and altered considerably, and it is this additional hand that is Symeon's (he also copied there a letter written by bishop William of St Calais to his monks in 1091). Those alterations and marginal additions that can be dated to the early twelfth century are all of Insular saints, with one exception, and that an apparently inexplicable puzzle: Heribert, archbishop of Cologne at March 16th.[83] Many, but by no means all, of these are present in the oldest Durham calendar we

---

[80] At Friday there is space for words like *De cruce*, but no heading. This cursus is basically Alcuinian, but no particular continuity is being claimed here.

[81] Presumably on Sept. 4th (in 1104, a Sunday), the day widely observed as his Translation feast; curiously, the precise date does not seem to have been recorded in any surviving source.

[82] M. Gullick, "The Scribes of the Durham Cantor's Book ... and the Durham Martyrology Scribe," in *Anglo-Norman Durham*, ed. D. Rollason, M. Harvey, and M. Prestwich (Woodbridge 1994), pp. 93–109. The other main contents, all in English hands, include a strange calendar (no saints, just obits), Lanfranc's *Constitutions*, and both Latin and Old English texts of the Rule of Benedict. Gullick provides on p. 94 a useful list of all the contents.

[83] The additions are all given by A. Piper in "The Durham Cantor's Book," the article immediately preceding Gullick's, pp. 79–92, at 90–92. Three of the Insular saints are Irish: Brendan, Finbar, and Finnian. Heribert of Cologne died in 1031; founder of the abbey at Deutz.

have, that in the scientific collection of the first third (after 1104) of the twelfth century, now Durham Cathedral, Hunter 100: Benedict Biscop, Cuthbert and his Translation, Alphege, Dunstan, Bede, Swithun and his Translation, Boisil, Oswald, Aidan, Etheldreda, Edmund the Martyr.[84] It would be unreasonable to expect a Canterbury-written gradual of the end of the eleventh century to include forms for even Oswald (whose August 5th feast falls within the limited range of the surviving sanctorale-fragment) or other important northern saints; lacking them, however, the Cosin gradual would not have been of practical use at Durham.

To connect the one surviving Durham missal, BL Harley 5289, with the mass liturgy presupposed by the Cosin gradual of the late eleventh century, while keeping constantly in mind possible echoes of Lanfrancian prescriptions, requires some stretching of our principle of continuity. One verifiable aspect is pointed out by Hartzell: that the Alleluia verses for the Sundays after Easter and after Pentecost are exactly the same in the gradual and in this missal.[85] The missal dates from the middle of the fourteenth century and is a modest book, with no notation and very little illumination. It is emphatically not the sort of grand book that would have been used at the high altar, and in fact two inscriptions tell us that it belonged to one of the altars in the Nine Altars Chapel and that it had been procured by Prior John (Fossor). Fossor, who held office from 1341 to 1374, is said to have set in motion a program of repair (*reparari*) of all the priory's missals.[86] There are almost certainly some traces of Lanfranc; it is hard to imagine any other explanation for the direction that on Maundy Thursday the Gloria is sung only if the bishop officiates (fol. 161v), just as in the *Constitutions*. But there are plenty of rubrical indications that show independence, most explicitly in the provision that on vacant Thursdays in ordinary time the votive mass of St Cuthbert is celebrated "secundum consuetudinem dunelmensis ecclesie in or[dinali?]" (fol. 428), and references to other sources or books "secundum consuetudinem quorundam secularium" (can these "certain seculars" possibly be meant to refer to uages of the pre-1083 community?), or "ut in libro pontificali plenius continetur" (fols 164–65).

[84] Wormald, *Eng. Ben. Kals*, I.161–79, collated as MS A.

[85] Hartzell, "Unknown gradual," p. 140. The series in the missal is shown to be almost identical with that in the 13th-cent. Bec missal (ed. A[nselm] Hughes, HBS 94, 1963, p. xii), which strengthens the notion of direct Bec influence on Durham; there is somewhat more divergence from Bec in the St Augustine's and St Albans missals.

[86] According to the contemporary Durham chronicler William de Chambre, *Historiae Dunelmensis Scriptores tres*, ed. J. Raine, SS 9 (1839), p. 131.

A Bury St Edmunds missal

Bury St Edmunds is another major monastic house, comparable in splendor and wealth with Durham, from which less liturgical evidence survives than might be expected. What does exist is laid out in the following Excursus on Ascription of Manuscripts (pp. 192–99), where Bury is the test case. Here just one book must be looked at in the context of our survey of the evidence for monastic liturgy in the twelfth century: a missal now at Laon (B.m. 238) It has been there since the early thirteenth century (the reason is unknown), which explains why the original canon and ordinary have been replaced by that of the French cathedral. It has no calendar, but masses in the sanctorale for Edmund and Botulf and especially for the Translation of Iurmin (a seventh-century East Anglian princeling, translated to Bury 24 January 1095), point most conclusively to Bury.[87]

Rodney Thomson has proposed that the book was "produced locally, c. 1120," and this tentative dating may be reinforced by a peculiar wording in the Solemn Collects for Good Friday.[88] There the bidding of the prayer for the ruler begins "Oremus et pro christianissimo imperatore nostro," and the prayer itself asks God to look favorably "ad romanorum ... imperium" (fol. 66v). Now, Legg's textual "Notes" show that *imperatore* was widely used in this prayer in England, but with *romanorum* replaced by *christianum*, *christianorum*, or *anglorum* in all of his English witnesses save one.[89] Is it conceivable that the (nearly) unique use of *romanorum* in the Bury missal is an intentional allusion to the Emperor Henry V, whom Matilda, daughter of Henry I of England, married in

---

[87] Recently M. Lapidge, *The Cult of St Swithun* (Oxford 2003), p. 60, has revived the idea that this is a Winchester book, arguing that "the presence of Æthelwold and Birinus points unambiguously to Winchester as the point of the manuscript's origin. The fact that the manuscript does not in its present state contain mass sets for either of Swithun's feasts is probably to be explained by physical loss of leaves." But there is no lacuna where masses for either 2 or 15 July would come; and Lapidge does not mention the Translation of Iurmin. He posits that the well known trip of some canons of Laon to England in 1113, to collect funds for construction of the new cathedral there after a destructive fire, resulted in their being presented with this book during their visit to Winchester. It is not implausible that they visited Bury as well; if so, possibly some sort of connection was established.

[88] R. M. Thomson, "The Library of Bury St Edmunds in the eleventh and twelfth centuries," *Speculum* 47 (1972), pp. 617–45 at 643.

[89] *WM*, III.1470. That one is the Giso massbook (see p. 124), so named because of its putative connection with the Lotharingian Giso, bishop of Wells 1061–88. It should be kept in mind that Legg's apparatus covers only material he knew by 1897; and that the New Minster missal (published only in 1972) lacks everything until Easter Friday.

1110 and whose death in 1125 precipitated a long and turgid struggle for the imperial crown?[90]

It may be further possible to date the book to before 1129 or 1130, on the grounds that the feast of the Conception of the Virgin on December 8th is not included (nor is that of St Sab(b)a(s) three days earlier). Observance of the Conception had been vigorously championed by Anselm, abbot of Bury 1121–48, as previously of St Saba in Rome c. 1110–21 (and nephew of archbishop Anselm, who died in 1109). Edmund Bishop's argument, first advanced in 1886, that Anselm "of Bury" had been one of the feast's chief proponents and that observance of the Conception was officially sanctioned at a legatine council at London in 1129, seems ungainsayable in general; although the only record of such a decision, a Gloucester interpolation into a copy of a Worcester chronicle some seventy years after the fact, leaves some room for doubt.[91] Still, it seems overwhelmingly likely that abbot Anselm insisted on observance of that Marian feast from at least that year, and therefore this missal, which lacks it, was written before then.[92]

If, then, this missal can be firmly established as being that of Bury in the second or third decade of the twelfth century, it makes a valuable link between the massbook of St Augustine's (treated in the previous chapter, p. 113; datable to just after 1091, but being extensively revised in the succeeding decades) and that of St Albans dwelt on above, dating from around 1160. A detailed textual comparison of the three books is much to be desired; in the absence of that, a few clues derived from proper prefaces in the mass are instructive.[93] One clear example is at the Epiphany, where Bury has the same preface as St Augustine's and, before that, as the late tenth-century books from Winchcombe (above, p. 173)

[90] A brief study of the permutations and combinations of phraseology in this prayer in all possible witnesses, Continental as well as English, might be well worth undertaking.

[91] Bishop, *Liturg. Hist.*, pp. 238–59: "On the Origins of the Feast of the Conception of the Blessed Virgin Mary," including an important ten-page "Supplementary Note" added to the original text published in *Downside Review* in 1886. The words in question are "Ex auctoritate apostolica confirmata est festiuitas Conceptionis sancte Dei Genetricis Mariae": *The Chronicle of John of Worcester*, III, ed. and tr. P. McGurk, OMT (1998), pp. 188–89; cf. *C & S 871–1204*, I.750–52.

[92] The miracle story connected with the younger Anselm's devotion to this Marian feast is told in R. W. Southern, "The English Origins of the 'Miracles of the Virgin,'" *Med. and Ren. Studies* 4 (1958), pp. 176–216 at 191. The mention of the feast of St Saba in two later Bury documents (see p. 197 below) certainly suggests abbot Anselm's initiative.

[93] This is specially the case because Legg's Apparatus almost never includes prefaces, tends to ignore the 12th-cent. St Albans book in favor of its 14th-cent. missal (as explained above, p. 148), and was made in ignorance of the Bury book at Laon.

and, on the Continent, those of Fulda and abbot Ratoldus; more widely, it is of the "Young Gelasian" tradition.[94] In this Bury book (fol. 15) it has been crossed through (possibly at Laon?), but no alternative supplied. Another instance is the very lengthy proper preface for Maundy Thursday (fol. 63v), which has a similarly long ancestry including use at Winchcombe and St Augustine's, but which is almost never found after the mid-twelfth century. A third instance works out exactly the same way: a prolix preface for the Annunciation (fol. 115), found also at Winchcombe and at St Augustine's, but in the latter book erased, though so imperfectly as to leave traces that make the identification certain. It looks to be the case that the Bury missal is a textually conservative book.

It is particularly frustrating that we have no Bury service books dating from the abbacy of Samson, 1182–1211, whose "life" – the celebrated chronicle of Jocelin of Brakelond – gives such a vivid picture of the house for that period.[95] Even lacking that, it is cause for special regret that there seems no way of telling whether the last two textual items in the missal reflect putative practical use or whether they were merely taken from its model. One, the "ordo qualiter infantes catecizantur seu baptizantur" (fol. 161), looks realistic for two reasons: that the brief litany of saints has been "customized" to include Edmund and Botulf (the only English saints), and that there seems to have been a baptistery in the main church.[96] The other is the "ordo ad deponsandam mulierem" (fol. 165v), which raises the possibility that grand weddings might have been held in the monastic church – a matter about which Jocelin is not forthcoming.

Towards a synthetic view: Ely and Gloucester as concluding instances

The richness that may well be the salient impression left by twelfth-century monasticism in England – richness in magnificent buildings, sumptuous manuscripts, saintly and/or commanding figures, hagiographers, and above all historians – is borne out only partially by the surviving directly liturgical evidence. We feel certain that the worship

---

[94] The Old Gelasian has another text entirely, as does the Gregorian, which is found in Leofric "A" and eventually prevails throughout (the St Albans sacramentary lacks almost all prefaces, and the New Minster missal is defective until after Easter).

[95] *The Chronicle of Jocelin of Brakelond*, ed. and tr. H. E. Butler, NMT (London 1949).

[96] M. R. James, *On the Abbey of St Edmund at Bury*, ii: *the Church*, Cambridge Antiq. Soc. Octavo pubs. 28 (1895), p. 129: "at the south-west angle of the Church, under the chapel of S. Katherine."

must have been congruous with the splendor of the settings and of many of the extant books. How can that not have been the case in a milieu out of which came the Winchester Bible, the Westminster psalter, the Eadwine psalter (from Canterbury Christ Church), the choir of Norwich, the nave of Peterborough, the sculpture of the south portal at Malmesbury – to choose examples only from houses that have *not* been considered in the present chapter? Our impressions of this splendor are reinforced by a variety of narrative accounts, inventories of a more or less systematic sort, and miscellaneous anecdotes.

All three of these types of somewhat oblique witness are present in the *Liber Eliensis*, the chronicle *cum* hagiographical ragbag *cum* legal dossier compiled by an anonymous monk of Ely in, most likely, the late 1170s.[97] The first of its three books deals with the early history of the house and will not concern us here; book II covers the period from the restoration under Æthelwoldian influence through the Translation in 1106 of Etheldreda and her kinswomen into the new Norman abbey church; the final book takes up the story as the diocese of Ely is carved out of Lincoln in 1109, Hervey (formerly, and unsuccessfully, bishop of Bangor) being the first bishop. The compiler had access to extensive monastic archives now lost, and is extremely touchy about any diminishment of the abbey's property or possessions; so two lists he provides that are of special value to us may be either documentarily accurate or tendentiously exaggerated to underline the rapacity of, as he sees it, the house's enemies. Either way, they are useful.

The first list purports to be an inventory of what Ranulf Flambard, the notorious tool of William Rufus, found at the abbey on the death of abbot Simeon in 1093.[98] It includes a staggering number of crosses, reliquaries, gospel books, copes (46), albs (102), and the surprisingly precise number of 277 books, of which only the service books are specified: two benedictionals, nineteen missals, twelve graduals, eight lectionaries (*lectionales*, an unusual term), twenty-two psalters, nineteen antiphonals, and seven *breviarii*. As there were in both 1093 and 1108 supposedly seventy-two monks at Ely, we see at once either that many service books must not have been counted in this inventory or that there must have been a great deal of peering in an often dimly lit

---

[97] *Liber Eliensis*, ed. E. O. Blake, Camden Soc. 3rd ser. 92 (1962), and transl. Janet Fairweather (Woodbridge 2005). Her translation is keyed to Blake's book- and chapter-numbering, and is provided with fine indexes which make it much easier to use than the edition.

[98] Book II, ch. 139; the account is placed, and introduced, inconsistently in the two principal MSS, but there is little reason to doubt that it is the last decade of the 11th cent. that is reflected.

church to permit performance of the daily office if there was only one psalter for every three or four monks – or, of course that the attendance in choir was seldom anything like as large as the number of monks at the abbey. The second list records an inventory of the contents of the house's treasury roughly half a century later, during the episcopate of Nigel (1133–69). It contains much descriptive detail, especially about the shrines and altar adornments and also about the sixteen gospel books with precious, mostly jewelled, covers.[99] The more valuable vestments are enumerated with similar detail, as are various furnishings, but there is no mention of service books as such.

Although the sum of liturgical information extractable from the *Liber Eliensis* is disappointingly small – all the more so because there is only one service book from that house that is of any use to us (discussed in the next chapter, p. 224) – it does contain an unexpected and precious piece of information about a topic taken up at length in chapter 14 of this book, that of liturgy in parish settings. The church of the Holy Cross, which eventually lay almost flush against the northwest side of the monastic church, had a lay patron who gave it to an unscrupulous priest. The cleric in question was, for reasons unspecified, inimical to the monks, and manifested this enmity by refusing to announce to his congregation (*populo*) on a July Sunday that the important Ely feast of Saints Withburga and Sexburga (and sometimes Eormenhilda as well) was to fall in the forthcoming week.[100] Striking here is evidence both that it was usual for parish priests in the twelfth century to announce the important occasions of the forthcoming week and that the renegade felt some latitude in which feasts to select, or at least to omit.[101]

That anecdote may seem to contribute little to our understanding of monastic worship in the twelfth century, but it does underline a general point otherwise easy to overlook: that the liturgy in and of the great religious houses, far from being a self-contained phenomenon, both reflected and affected the wider contexts in which those houses

---

[99] Book III, ch. 50. Two other, small gospel books covered with silver are mentioned but not described. The earlier list included fourteen gospel books "large and small, ornamented with gold and silver."

[100] Book III, ch. 121; despite quiet remonstrations, he remained obdurate and, going from bad to worse, spent the next several days in rioting and wantonness; the story concludes, in an exceptionally unpleasant way, the following Sunday as he vests and tries to begin the mass.

[101] The episode is even more astonishing if, as appears likely, the "church" of the Holy Cross was at that time just an altar immediately west of the pulpitum in the monastic church itself, but there is some ambiguity about the name and location of what is clearly described as a parish church: see VCH *Cambridgeshire*, IV (2002), pp. 82–86.

existed. The connotations of the term "cloistered," possibly appropriate to Cistercian worship and certainly to that of the Carthusians (both groups are treated in the next chapter but one), are wrong when applied to most Benedictine establishments – hence the possibility of weddings at Bury St Edmunds, just raised. Ely was a small place (it has always vied with Wells as being the cathedral city with the smallest population), but even there, two parish churches, Holy Cross and St Mary's, lay within two hundred yards or so of the cathedral. While much of the monks' day-to-day routine of worship must have passed unremarked by the townspeople, not to mention those of the diocese at large, so imposing a liturgical presence cannot have been without effect in the wider community – nor the concerns of that community without reflection in the cathedral priory.

That is one of two observations with which this chapter can end. The other is suggested by the antiphonal (of sorts) compiled for St Peter's abbey, Gloucester in probably the third quarter of the twelfth century (now Oxford, Jesus College 10). Now only the calendar is of that date, the rest being of the thirteenth and, in two sections, fourteenth centuries. Its dimensions (200 x 140 mm) indicate that it was not big enough to be a choir antiphonal, and the contents are confined mainly to the day offices, with also a number of masses and some material for processions. About the middle of the thirteenth century it passed to the abbey's cell at Hereford, St Guthlac's, where further material was added.

Its interest for our purposes lies in trying to tease out from the original calendar – the sole document of that sort from Gloucester – some sense of what the abbey's distinctiveness of cultus might have been. This house, dating as properly monastic from about 1022, was one of the larger foundations in England: figures such as eighty monks in 1078 and one hundred in 1104 may seem suspiciously high, but the grandeur of their church, evident today especially in the surviving Norman nave of the present cathedral, suggests a very considerable establishment.[102] The commanding figure in the early post-Conquest story is Serlo, who (formerly a canon of Avranches) came from Mont St Michel to be abbot, 1072–1104. The abbots after him were almost all monks of Gloucester, the notable exception being the great Gilbert Foliot, 1139–48, who had been monk and prior at Cluny.[103] Francis Wormald, who printed the calendar of the antiphonal, pointed out that much influence from Mont St Michel was discernible, and also that a number of the calendar's unusual saints, especially among the additions, can

---

[102] *Med. Rel. Houses*, p. 66, gives the above numbers.
[103] *Heads Rel. Houses*, I.52 and II.47.

be "explained by the fact that they were the patron saints of rectories appropriated to the monastery at the time when the calendar was drawn up in its final form."[104] Examples of the latter are Gundleius (Gwynllyw) of Newport at 29 March and Paternus of Llanbadarn Fawr at 15 April. Owing to Mont St Michel influence are such unusual entries as Karaunus, 28 May, Paternus (of Avranches?), 23 September, Gerald of Aurillac, 13 October, and Basolus of Verzy (outside Reims), 15 October.[105] There are such a lot of subsequent alterations in the gradings that it is hard to ascertain exactly what the various classes of saints' feasts were at Gloucester in the twelfth century, but it looks as though the original twelve-lesson feasts included those of Audoen (25 August), Britius (Brice, 13 November) and Oswald of Worcester (his second Translation, c. 1086, 8 October); with the higher grade, *in cappis*, for the Dedication of St Michael in Monte Tumba (18 October) as well as the Conception. It is easy to understand the emphasis on the obvious saint of Serlo's monastery and of the diocese in which Gloucester lay, but not the exact reasons for the similar emphasis on Audoen of Rouen and Britius of Tours.

Nonetheless, these smidgeons of hagiographic detail lead us to our other concluding reflection, or rather question: how likely is it that many of the major monastic houses would have possessed an individual liturgical *consuetudo*? The question is complicated by the fact that the word is commonly used in the plural, *consuetudines*, to indicate the sort of customary that is relatively common, one which specifies offices, duties, and timetables but generally contains little in the way of directly liturgical prescription (some examples are discussed in chapter 6). In the absence of ordinals for these houses – sets of precise instructions as to which forms are used at which services on which occasions, and ideally which of the monastic personnel are to perform them – we have to use such sanctorale information as is available to get an idea of the liturgical *amour propre* of each. It seems probable that much of what is expressed in some contemporary documents as *usus* or *consuetudo* is largely a matter of its distinctive saints' feasts. If this is the case, we may close this consideration of monastic liturgy in, mainly, the twelfth century with the tentative recognition that, while an entity that we may call Benedictine liturgy does exist for this period, its expressions were

[104] Wormald, *Eng. Ben. Kals*, II.40.

[105] Wormald points out that they are all found in a 15th-cent. breviary from Mont St Michel (BN Nouv. acq. lat. 424). According to F. G. Holweck, *A Biographical Dictionary of the Saints* (St Louis and London 1924), p. 141, without further reference, the October date for Basolus was observed at Soissons, whereas Basolus's usual day was Nov. 26th, as at Reims and other places.

diverse enough that (putative Lanfrancian influence notwithstanding) independence would have seemed to the monks as salient a quality as uniformity.

This, of course, mirrors the constitutional situation in this period, when each Benedictine house that was not a dependent cell or an alien priory was structurally independent. When we take up the subject again, following the reforms mandated by the Fourth Lateran Council in 1215, the newly formalized interconnections among these houses will be a natural focus. Even then, we will do well to remember that each house has a place in its local context and some individuality in its expressions of worship.

Excursus: on ascription of liturgical books to specific churches

Bury St Edmunds as test case

Fundamental to this work is the capacity to ascribe an extant liturgical manuscript to a particular establishment, secular or monastic. A brief explanation as to how this is done – by what methods, with what degree of confidence, and at what risk – may be found useful, and may best be approached not so much through setting down abstract principles as through tracing one case study. For this purpose it seems desirable to choose an establishment for which, though there is a great deal of documentation in a number of respects, not many ascribable liturgical books have survived: the abbey of Bury St Edmunds, a twelfth-century missal from which was discussed a few pages ago.

Bury has the further advantage that its monastic past extends only to 1020, when King Cnut established monks there to replace the shadowy community of canons who had kept the shrine of St Edmund, the East Anglian royal martyr killed by the Danes on November 21st (the traditional date, anyhow), 869. The immediate source of its original monks seems to have been the Norfolk monastery at Holme St Benets, but as this had been (re)founded only in 1019, what would seem material is the founding impetus for that house: apparently Ely.[1] If this, which is certainly plausible, is true, we can hope for traces of the much better documented abbey of Ely in particular and of the Æthelwoldian sphere of influence in general.

Fortunately, surviving information about the Bury's library is as full as that about its liturgical books is scanty. The study of its library goes back to at least an 1895 monograph by M. R. James, and has continued

---

[1] The late 13th-cent. chronicle attributed to John of Oxnead, monk of Holme, states that Bury's first abbot, Ufi, had brought books from that house, of which he had been prior, with him. That both Holme and Bury received monks from Ely is stated by David Knowles (*Mon. Order*, p. 70), but without reference. Only one liturgical book is even doubtfully ascribed to Holme, a 14th-cent. psalter now at Douai, B.m. 171 (*MLGB*, p. 102).

with further studies by him and in particular by Rodney Thomson.[2] Recently, a good deal of attention has been paid to booklists, three of which contain some information about Bury in the first century or so of its existence.

Two of these lists, both in Old English, date from the second half of the eleventh century.[3] The first enumerates some nineteen service books "found" by abbot Leofstan (1044–65) when he entered on his office, either in the church or in the possession of (?; the verb is *hæfð*) six other named people – presumably monks, though this is not stated.[4] None of these books can now be identified as extant. The only point of wider relevance to liturgy at Bury is that the gradual that one Osketel had is called an *Ad te leuaui*, after the introit for the first Sunday in Advent: this is not unusual, but worth noticing because many eleventh-century service books begin with the masses of Christmas. This is the only chant book in the list, as compared with four *maesseboc*; whether any of the latter are full missals, as distinct from sacramentaries, is not clear. Later in the document it is recorded that a gift to the monks from Baldwin, the next abbot (1065–97), is to be paid half at the Nativity of Mary, partly at the feast of Dionysius (9 October) and partly at that of Nicholas (6 December). The latter is missing from the calendar of a Bury psalter of c. 1050 at the latest (to be discussed presently), so it can be inferred that Nicholas's feast came to be observed in the time of Baldwin, who would probably have selected that of Dionysius because he had been a monk at St Denis before coming to England.

The second list is little more than eleventh-century scrawls on the flyleaf of an eighth-century gospel book.[5] Its main point of interest lies in the inclusion, among the ten books which are liturgical out of the

---

[2] M. R. James, *On the Abbey of S Edmund at Bury, I: the Library; II: the Church*, Cambridge Antiquarian Soc., Octavo Pubs. 27 (1895); its "Appendix of Documents" (pp. 150–212) is still extremely useful, specially for its summary of the contents of the ordinal, BL Harley 2977, on pp. 183–86. Subsequently, see esp. James, "Bury St Edmunds Manuscripts," *Eng. Hist. Rev.* 41 (1926), pp. 251–60; R. M. Thomson, "The Library of Bury St Edmunds in the Eleventh and Twelfth Centuries," *Speculum* 47 (1972), pp. 617–45; and R. Sharpe in *English Benedictine Libraries: the Shorter Catalogues*, ed. Sharpe et al., CBMLC 4 (London 1996), pp. 43–98.

[3] Edited by M. Lapidge, "Surviving booklists from Anglo-Saxon England," in *Learning and Literature*, pp. 33–90 at 57–58 and 74–76; repr. in M. P. Richards, ed. *Anglo-Saxon Manuscripts: Basic Readings* (New York 1994), pp. 87–167.

[4] This comes in the middle of a quire (fols 106–9) inserted into a Latin and English copy of the Rule of Benedict (Oxford, Corpus Christi College 197) in an inventory of food-rents, gifts, and other possessions; the whole quire is printed in A. J. Robertson, ed. *Anglo-Saxon Charters* (Cambridge 1939), 192–201. As this is not really a library list it is not printed under Bury by Sharpe, who nonetheless discusses it briefly on p. 45.

[5] Printed by Sharpe, pp. 49–50, as well as Lapidge (see above). The gospel book is Bodl. Auct. D.2.14.

total fifteen, of two tropers; the second is described as "little," which makes it sound like one of the Winchester tropers of earlier in the century, handbook size for a cantor (see p. 85). Again, none can now be identified.

A booklist from the late twelfth century, much more substantial, includes, though not at all systematically, references to between fifteen and eighteen more or less liturgical books, none of which can be identified with certainty now.[6] Among these are seven missals (in one group of four and one of three), designated by the altar to which they were assigned, two graduals with troper elements, a breviary for guests and one for the infirmary, and two big antiphonals, one of them chained. Given that service books were not ordinarily included in medieval library lists, these must represent only a small fraction of what existed at one time or another.

When we turn to extant liturgical books, only at most half a dozen can be ascribed to Bury:

> "Bury psalter" (Rome, Vatican Lib., Reg. lat. 12), s. xi[med].
> "Bury missal" (Laon, B.m. 238), s. xii[med] or slightly earlier.
> Psalter-hymnal (*olim* Bury St Edmunds Grammar School), s. xv[in].[7]
> Offices of the Dead (BL Harley 5334), s. xiv or xv.
> Ordinal, alias Rituale (BL Harley 2977), s. xiv; Advent to 1 May only.
> Processional (*olim* Norwich Castle Mus. 158.926.4g), s. xv.[8]

There are also two customaries, not primarily liturgical in contents: BL Harley 1005, called *Liber albus*, c. 1234;[9] and BL Harley 2977 (with the ordinal, noted above), s. xiv. One celebrated codex sometimes spoken of as a Bury liturgical book is the heavily illustrated Life and Miracles of St Edmund (NY, Pierpont Morgan Library M.736) dated to about 1130;[10] but its sole liturgical contents are the office and hymns for St Edmund (pages 170–98).

---

[6] On the difficulty in understanding its arrangement, see Sharpe's edn, pp. 50–52.

[7] Now deposited in Bury St Edmunds, West Suffolk Record Office, E 5/9/408.7: so *MLGB Suppl.*, p. 5.

[8] Now at Norwich, Norfolk and Norwich Record Office, St Peter Hungate Museum, 158.926.4g(4): ibid.

[9] Edited by Antonia Gransden, *The Customary of the Benedictine Abbey of Bury St Edmunds in Suffolk*, HBS 99 (1973). This notices also the fragments of a slightly later copy of the customary in CUL Add. 6006.

[10] Kauffmann, *Romanesque MSS*, no. 34; some further literature is listed in the entry by the same author in *English Romanesque Art 1066–1200* (Hayward Gallery Exhibition catalogue, London 1984), no. 20. Almost as well known, but somewhat problematic

How each one of this small number of books comes to be assigned to Bury depends on a number of factors. The most succinct explanation of method in general is still that given in some eight pages by Neil Ker in the "Revised Preface" to *Medieval Libraries of Great Britain*.[11] Ker summarizes ways in which ascriptions are made by using the following categories: *ex libris* inscriptions, *ex dono* inscriptions, pressmarks, presence in medieval catalogues, script, and binding, along with contents, marginalia, and (his term) *liturgica*.[12] One category omitted as such is the hagiographical, probably because it is thought to be subsumed under the liturgical. But because the appearance or non-appearance of certain saints is very likely the most frequently adduced consideration in the assignment of provenance to liturgical books, it – more than any of Ker's categories – will have to be at the forefront of the present brief discussion, as we try to apply these principles to each of the few books listed above.

The one that will require lengthiest discussion is the Bury psalter, one of the great illustrated manuscripts of the eleventh century. The evidence for its ascription is overwhelmingly hagiographic, in calendar, litany, and devotional contents alike.[13] In its calendar we find prominent (in this case, in capitals) the Translations of Iurmin 24 January, of Botulf 25 February, and of Edmund himself on 30 March. Other feasts are in capitals as well, including Edmund's main feast (20 November), Translation of Etheldreda (17 October), Deposition of Swithun (2 July), and, conclusively, "Dedicatio Basilice Sancte Marie et Sancti Eadmundi" (18 October). In keeping with the prominence awarded to Swithun are a number of Winchester-related occasions, like the Translation of Æthelwold (10 September) as well as his 1 August feast, and reflecting Etheldreda's prominence are several East Anglian and Fenland worthies, some quite obscure like Herefrith of Thorney (27 February) and Cyneswitha and Cynesburga (6 March), conspicuous at both Peterborough and Thorney. Two figures who turn out to have East Anglian

---

in its connection with Bury in the 12th cent., is a copy of the four gospels, apparently of about 1140, with twelve pages of drawings, illustrating the life of Christ, made perhaps ten years earlier (Cambridge, Pembroke College 120): Kauffmann, *Rom. MSS*, no. 35, and in *Eng. Rom. Art*, no. 21. While there is good reason for believing that the drawings come from Bury, the text very likely does not, and in any case no liturgical data are included.

[11] *MLGB*, pp. xv–xxii.

[12] On pp. ix–x Ker explains the italic letters used to signal the kind of evidence on which ascriptions have been based.

[13] On its illustration, see esp. Temple, *Anglo-Saxon MSS*, no. 84 (with pls 262–64), with many bibliographical references. Its calendar is printed in Wormald, *Eng. Kals*, no. 19, its litany of saints in Lapidge, *Litanies*, no. XLV.

connections are Oswald *archipresul* on 28 February (Oswald bishop of Worcester, but also archbishop of York in plurality), who was the founding abbot of Ramsey, and Kenelm of Mercia (17 July), a primary saint at Winchcombe, itself restored by Oswald and colonized from Ramsey. These data, taken in the aggregate, would work for no other religious house. Absence of the Translation of Ælfheah/Alphege on 8 June 1023 is not conclusive as to date, nor is there any other occasion, after 1012 (the year of his death, here on 19 April and called *Necatio*), which provides a point for dating.

The psalter's litany of saints corroborates the emphases of the calendar almost exactly. It has Edmund doubled – i.e., "Sancte Eadmunde ora ii," the commonest indication of prominence in such litanies – among the martyrs and includes Ethelbert, another "martyred" East Anglian king (d. 794), and Kenelm. Doubled among confessors are Botulf and Iurmin, and that list includes Birinus, Swithun, Judoc, and Grimbald as well as Oswald (of Worcester). The list of twenty-one virgins contains nine Anglo-Saxon ladies among whom are the Ely-Peterborough quartet of Etheldreda and her three kinswomen (Withburga, Sexburga, and Eormenhilda), and also Tova, a hermit of Thorney.

A third source for ascription of this book is the content of some of the twenty-one private prayers at the end of the manuscript. These, printed by André Wilmart in 1930, include a "Specialis et precluis ad Christi militem Eadmundum oratio" (no. xii) and another prayer that refers to "confessorum tuorum Botulfi et Hiurmini" as well as to Edmund (no. xxi).[14] Wilmart argued for a date about 1050 for the book, on the ground that the dedication commemorated in the calendar occurred only in 1032 and that the translations of Botulf and Iurmin took place during the abbacy of Leofstan, 1044–65. Temple contends that the latter dating is not quite firm, and maintains that the illustrations point to a date in the early 1030s.[15] Either way, we have a sumptuous, pre-Conquest book full of hagiographical evidence that pins it unmistakably to Bury.

The firmness of that ascription then makes it possible to fix the missal of roughly a century later – from the early thirteenth century, as now, at Laon (B.m. 238) – as also a Bury book. Unlike the psalter, the missal has scarcely been studied at all (see the discussion of it in the previous chapter, pp. 184–86), and its ascription to Winchester in Leroquais'

---

[14] A. Wilmart, "The Prayers of the Bury Psalter," *Downside Review* 48 (1930), pp. 198–216.

[15] Temple, p. 101; she further points out that the MS "could hardly have been made at Bury since the new foundation was probably not organized in the second quarter of the 11th century for the production of richly decorated books."

standard conspectus laid a false trail for decades.[16] It has no calendar, but the presence in the sanctorale of Edmund, Botulf, Iurmin, and even Oswald of Worcester and Kenelm, establishes it clearly as belonging to the same house that possessed the psalter. Nothing else in the contents is conclusive; nonetheless, there can be little question that this is a missal, of probably the second quarter of the twelfth century, used then at Bury St Edmunds.

All four of the later books reinforce each other and give a cumulative, if not always perfectly clear, idea of the pattern of distinctive feasts and usages at this great monastic house. The presence of St Saba(s) seems conclusive in two.[17] As was mentioned previously, Anselm "of Bury" (nephew of St Anselm, who died in 1109) had been abbot of St Saba in Rome c. 1110–21 before coming to preside at Bury, 1121–48, and he seems to have introduced there the commemoration of the saint on December 5th. The fragmentary fourteenth-century ordinal contained in BL Harley 2977, which has many references to the church and relics at Bury, specifies a procession on *Festum S. Sabe* on that day.[18] Likewise, the mid-fifteenth-century processional now at Norwich is ascribable to Bury because it includes Saba in a select group of fewer than three dozen sanctorale occasions provided with processions.[19] Its litany of saints is in turn consonant with that of the early fifteenth-century psalter formerly at Bury St Edmunds Grammar School, which has Edmund doubled, Kenelm, Botulf doubled, Iurmin, all the possible East Anglian ladies, and two distinctive hymns for St Edmund (the calendar is contemporary with the rest of the book but not integral to it, being codicologically separate and indeed a Sarum calendar adapted to the diocese of Norwich).[20] The little Offices of the Dead volume also has a conclusive litany full of all the distinctive names, including Saba (as well as an *ex libris* inscription).[21]

---

[16] V. Leroquais, *Les sacramentaires et les missels manuscrits des bibliothèques publiques de France*. 3 vols plus plates (Paris 1924), no. 101: "Missel de Winchester à l'Usage de Laon." *MLGB*, rejecting it for Winchester, lists it under Bury only with a question mark – which is removed in the *Suppl.*, which adds s(cript) to the l(iturgical) of the 1964 edn.

[17] Of the numerous saints of that name, the one in question is the 5th-cent. Cappadocian monk, later abbot, who was a pillar of orthodoxy against the Monophysites.

[18] James, *The Library* (note 2 above), p. 183; the next leaf, which would doubtless have contained the Conception, is missing.

[19] *MMBL*. III.522–3. Edmund, Botolph, and Iurmin are also prominent in the litany.

[20] *MMBL*. II.218–19; the litany is printed at the end of the discussion in E. W. Dewick, "On a MS Psalter formerly belonging to the Abbey of Bury St Edmund's," *Archaeologia* 54 (1895), pp. 399–410 plus two plates. The only puzzle here is that the name of Saba is inserted by a later hand between the confessors Gregory and Nicholas.

[21] Inscription and details of litany are printed in James, pp. 89–90.

It is clear that our discussion of how these books can with confidence be ascribed to Bury has been to a large extent based on hagiographical evidence. Apart from a direct indication such as a colophon naming scribe and place of writing (extremely rare in liturgical books) or mention of the dedication of a church, such evidence is bound to be paramount.[22] This means, of course, that it must be used with due caution. Mere inclusion of a saint in a calendar means little, a prominent grading a good deal more. Inclusion in a litany may again be a matter of convention or of regional affiliation; how high up a saint appears in the appropriate category (martyr, confessor, virgin, occasionally monastics as a separate group) is more convincing, as is, obviously, the doubling of the petition for a given saint's intercession. Presence in the sanctorale is also worth a good deal, for it is unlikely that occasions are included in a sanctorale unless there is reasonable chance of their being observed; particularly is this the case where the relevant forms, whether for mass or for office, are proper to the saint and not merely taken from the common. In the hierarchy here implied, therefore, probably the highest rank would be given to the saint whose proper office is written out in full in a breviary, especially if that saint is a somewhat specialized figure likely to be honored supremely at only one foundation: an Edmund at Bury, Erkenwald at London, Etheldreda at Ely (to stick with only one letter of the alphabet).

It should go without saying that all of the main categories of evidence adduced by Ker in the work spoken of above operate with liturgical books no less than with other types. The temptation to try to ascribe liturgical manuscripts on the basis of hagiographical aspects alone is one that must be resisted; every pertinent type of information, including the archaeological and the purely bibliographical (especially the evidence of booklists) must be utilized wherever possible. Even such an unlikely source as the Pleas of the Crown may yield valuable information, like the account of the massive damage done in riots of the Bury townspeople against the abbey in 1327; this mentions that among the goods destroyed or stolen were twenty missals, twenty-four portiforia (breviaries), twelve Bibles, twenty psalters, and ten *Jornalia* (diurnals?), while from the abbot himself were taken ten graduals, twelve antiphonaries, and ten tropers.[23]

---

[22] The other paramount kind of evidence is that of textual comparison of individual elements like prayers or chant texts. In addition to what is said in the "Excursus on method in the comparison of liturgical texts," here it should just be noted that word-by-word comparisons of liturgical formulas to establish affinities are highly tricky, and that it is especially dangerous to rely solely on machine-produced analyses as anything like conclusive.

[23] James, p. 163. Even allowing for exaggeration, this prompts us to wonder why the abbot seems to have had charge of all the chant books – or were these not all?

The present book depends greatly on ascriptions of manuscripts to particular churches – ascriptions made according to the kinds of criteria discussed above. Although it is not feasible to supply for all churches treatment as detailed as that offered in the preceding paragraphs, in the case of at least each major establishment evidence of hagiographical, bibliographical, textual, economic, and political sorts is wherever possible taken into account. The model furnished by Ker's *Medieval Libraries of Great Britain* is as invaluable as it is unavoidable, but we need to supplement it by other approaches and above all to keep in mind that our purpose is not to explicate the history of libraries or even the history of individual books but rather – to the extent that this can be done – the history of the liturgy.

6   Benedictine liturgy after 1215

The title of this chapter should not mislead the reader into thinking that after 1215 (or possibly before) there was an entity clearly identifiable as *the* liturgy of the Benedictines. The specifically liturgical provisions of the Rule of St Benedict are almost entirely concerned with the daily office, and worship which was in accord with those provisions can fairly be called Benedictine worship. Agreement with the Rule was the single criterion that mattered, although, as has been frequently noticed in previous chapters, considerable accretions grew around the office in connection with various influential monastic regimes: for example, Cluny (incomparably the most important; see p. 243 for a discrete section on worship in Cluniac houses), Fleury, the Winchester of the *Regularis concordia*. But there was never a mechanism for absolute liturgical uniformity, as was to come to be the case with some later bodies, above all the friars, spearheaded by the Dominicans. Even after 1215, Benedictine abbeys remained for the most part autonomous, liturgically as well as in other ways.[1]

In November 1215 Pope Innocent III's Fourth Lateran Council promulgated two canons that in effect brought about the establishment or, better, the regularization, of something like an Order of St Benedict. Canon 12 mandated General Chapters, to be held at least every three years, for all those living according to any religious rule; and canon 13 forbade the establishment of new religious orders, specifically using the term *ordo*.[2] The result for the Black Monks was that they discovered

---

[1] Movements of reform that led to the establishment of groups of houses called Unions or Congregations are largely a Continental phenomenon of the 15th cent., with almost no expression in England.

[2] Note that in the titles of D. Knowles's great tetralogy the meaning of "order" shifts somewhat from the singular *The Monastic Order in England ... 940–1216*, encompassing all who followed the Rule of Benedict (Cluniacs, Cistercians, and even Carthusians as well as ordinary "Benedictines") to the plural *The Religious Orders in England*, of which vol. I covers c. 1216–1340. Many of the MSS discussed in this and other chapters are treated in a somewhat synoptic but focused monograph by Sally Elizabeth Roper, *Medieval Benedictine Liturgy: Studies in the Formations, Structure, and Content of*

they had all along been part of the *ordo* of St Benedict, a discovery that required the quick deployment of a mechanism by which annual General Chapters could be called and run.[3] The unit mandated by the Council for such Chapters was the ecclesiastical province, and the model was to be provided by the Cistercians, whose structure had been characterized by such gatherings from, apparently, their inception.[4]

General Chapters and customaries

Documents, sometimes extensive, survive for most of the Chapters held in England, beginning with the first, datable only to between September 1218 and July 1219.[5] These documents are not tidy accounts, however, meeting by meeting, but a miscellaneous collection gathered from sources as varied as monastic chronicles and cartularies. It is not even perfectly clear when and where each Chapter met; for this and other reasons, it is difficult to construct anything like a coherent picture of the liturgical enactments of the various Chapters, and information derived from them will have to be regarded as complementary to that of the extant service books and ordinals, which must remain the primary focus – with, in the present case, monastic customaries as important witnesses also.

General Chapters of the second half of the thirteenth century paid a good deal of attention to trying to shorten somewhat the liturgical burden of each day (two such attempts earlier at St Albans are discussed on p. 169). To mitigate the danger that the accretions of the tenth and eleventh centuries threatened the balance of the office, in the 1255

---

the *Monastic Votive Offce, c.950–1450* (NY and London 1993). The title is inaccurately broad, and the subtitle suggests more consistent coverage than is the case; nonetheless, a great deal of valuable information is provided, shaped around case sudies of the daily votive office, the commemorative office (mainly of Mary or of a few principal saints), and the votive Marian antiphon. There is no satisfactory way to integrate her approach, which is basically musicological, with that of the present work, but the absence of numerous references to her book should not be taken to imply a negative judgment.

[3] In England, anyhow, they seem most often to have referred to themselves as monks or houses *nigri ordinis*.

[4] For the parenthetical "apparently," see p. 248. Whatever the antiquity of the practice among the earliest Cistercians, by 1215 their annual General Chapters clearly provided the necessary model; indeed, canon 12 specifies that each of the earliest "Benedictine" Chapters should be guided by two Cistercian abbots.

[5] W. A. Pantin, ed. *Documents Illustrating the Activities of the General and Provincial Chapters of the English Black Monks 1215–1540*, 3 vols, Camden Soc. 3rd ser. 45, 47, 54 (1931–37). Volumes II and III pertain to the period from 1336, the year when a constitution of Pope Benedict XII, *Summi magistri*, decreed that there should be a single Chapter rather than separate Chapters for the provinces of Canterbury and York.

Chapter it was suggested that vespers and lauds of All Saints might be omitted (*intermittantur*), and, more generally, that in the interest of providing more time for study superiors should cut out (*resecare*) unspecified *superflua*.[6] In 1277 a more radical approach was taken, one that provoked opposition. Some twenty-five clauses of an extensive program of reform put forward then concern liturgical matters, the great predominance of them towards shortening.[7] Examples include omission of the *Gloria patri* after the fourth and eighth responses in feasts of twelve lessons; the option of reciting the Office of the Virgin outside of choir; and abridgement of prayers at the conclusion of sext and none. An interesting move towards uniformity is the suppression of the feast of the Translation of Benedict (July 11th), "at least until the Roman Curia should have been consulted," and the establishment of his Deposition (March 21st) as a *festum principale*, with the added provision that if it fell during Passiontide it would be transferred until after the octave of Easter.

That some would be unhappy with these reforms is allowed for: one provision tactfully states that "we do not wish or intend that because of the present mitigation of prolixity," monks should be deprived of the *debita solacia* of the office.[8] Nonetheless, resistance seems to have been strong enough that a year later, 1278, the chapter presidents issued a revised version containing numerous modifications of the proposed reforms, a notable one being the restoration of the *Quicunque vult* to recitation after prime daily rather than only on Sundays and great feasts as had been enacted.[9] At the same time, some tightening-up is ordered; in particular, that monk-priests should normally not let four consecutive days pass without celebrating mass.[10] Further progress towards shortening the office seems to have been made in the General Chapter meeting at Abingdon in 1279, at which reception of the efforts of the previous two years was strengthened.[11] Nonetheless, steps

---

[6] Pantin, *Documents*, I.55.

[7] Ibid., pp. 67–71.

[8] Ibid., p. 69. A set of eight petitions, probably of 1277–79, survives in the fragmentary BL Add. Charter 34035B (ibid., p. 106); they seek such things as restoration of the feast of Benedict's Translation.

[9] Ibid., pp. 94–100, at 98. Detailed comparison of the two versions would be a useful undertaking. The new provisions begin with a strikingly worded regulation that the chapter of the Rule read daily after the martyrology should be followed by a brief exposition "in vulgari seu gallico," English or French: the purpose being that better understanding would lead to better observance: "quatinus ipsa regula eo melius intelligatur ab omnibus, intellectaque servetur" (p. 95).

[10] Ibid., p. 99.

[11] Ibid., p. 103. Unfortunately a key passage, perhaps more than one leaf, is missing in the section headed "Sub titulo divino officio." Just before the missing section it is

towards removing accretive elements of devotion continued to be made: a Worcester annalist grumbles that, after the General Chapter in 1300 decreed that *preces prolixae* hitherto used should be omitted, even the Lord's Prayer was at risk.[12]

It is precisely during this period of considerable efforts towards extensive tidying-up of monastic liturgy for the "order" as a whole that some notable surviving documents of the kind generally called customaries were compiled for individual houses.[13] As has been noted earlier (p. 190), the terminology for the genre is somewhat imprecise. A theoretical distinction has sometime been made between a "customary," as being largely concerned with details of timetable including of course worship, and a "consuetudinary," concerned mainly with monastic office-holders and their duties; but the line is often blurred, and the whole issue complicated by the term "ordinal," sometimes used in monastic as well as secular contexts. For our purposes, the blanket term "customary" should suffice, but the geographical randomness of the extant customaries does present a problem. Of the two areas we shall need to concentrate on, those covered by the diocese of Worcester and the diocese of Norwich, there survive no customaries for Benedictine houses in the former, while that for the cathedral priory at Norwich contains such a lot of liturgical information that it is almost indistinguishable from an ordinal. It deserves, consequently, a large measure of our attention.

The Norwich customary

The Norwich customary (now CCCC 465) was drawn up for that cathedral priory under Roger (de) Skerning, prior 1257–66.[14] Roger was

---

provided that Matins of the Virgin should be said privately on feasts of twelve lessons, when the office would be unusually long.

[12] "Dubito quod futuris temporibus superfluum videbitur *Pater Noster*": ibid., p. 143; from the Worcester chronicle, printed in *Annales monastici*, ed. H. R. Luard, 5 vols, RS 36 (1864–69), IV.547.

[13] Related customaries from Canterbury St Augustine's and Westminster (for the latter, see p. 232), both rooted in the period 1259–83 though extant in later MSS, are in several ways fragmentary; ed. E. M. Thompson, *The Customary of the Benedictine Monastery of Saint Augustine, Canterbury, and Saint Peter, Westminster*, 2 vols, HBS 23, 28 (1902–4). The earliest, that for Bury St Edmunds, c. 1234, is largely devoid of information about the liturgy: ed. A. Gransden, *The Customary of the Benedictine Abbey of Bury St Edmunds in Suffolk*, HBS 99 (1973). That for York St Mary's, c. 1400, is full for the temporale but lacks information about the sanctorale entirely: ed. Abbess of Stanbrook [L. McLachlan] and J. B. L. Tolhurst, *The Ordinal and Customary of Saint Mary's, York*, 3 vols, HBS 73, 75, 84 (1936–37–51). For the Norwich customary, see next note.

[14] J. B. L. Tolhurst, ed., *The Customary of the Cathedral Priory Church of Norwich*, HBS 82 (1948).

probably a Norfolk man (perhaps from the village of Scarning), a monk of Norwich before becoming prior, and its bishop from 1266 until his death in 1278. The modern editor, J. B. L. Tolhurst, has shown that the customary itself must originally have been drawn up during Roger's priorate, probably in response to the completion of a new Lady Chapel; but its form in the surviving manuscript reflects some changes datable to 1279–88, which is also the date of the calendar with which it is prefaced.[15]

Both in its datability and in the stability implied by Roger's long career at the priory, the book offers a highly useful opportunity to look at the liturgy of an establishment at which it is generally understood that the usages of a specific Norman house, Fécamp, were the model.[16] It was from there that Herbert de Losinga, then its prior, came to England, first as abbot of Ramsey c. 1088 and, from 1091 until his death in 1119, as bishop of East Anglia. The see center was moved from Thetford (not monastic) to Norwich c. 1095, whereupon the new cathedral was begun and, around the turn of the century, monks imported. Where the first, and quite numerous (up to sixty?), monks came from is not clear; Rochester has been suggested, faintly, as a possible source. Whatever the case, some time in the decade after 1109 Bishop Herbert sent to his former abbey for a copy of its customs; his letter survives, but nothing of whatever was sent in response.[17] What is extant, and has been recently edited by David Chadd, is the ordinal of Fécamp, in a manuscript of probably the early thirteenth century.[18] This makes possible some degree of comparison with the Norwich customary of a generation or two later, although the level of detail will have to be strictly limited in the present discussion.

Fécamp, on the northern edge of middle Normandy, was among the monastic houses influenced by the reforms associated with its abbot from c. 1001–1028, William of Volpiano (alias of Dijon): reforms themselves based to some extent on the early customs of Cluny.[19] Chadd has called

---

[15] Tolhurst, pp. vi–vii. M. R. James in his catalogue of the Corpus MSS (II.396) had dated the book early 14th cent. There are at its end some memoranda, in four or five different hands, dating from c. 1280 to 1379.

[16] Stated succinctly by C. Harper-Bill in his *ODNB* account of Herbert of Losinga (34.469): "The liturgy introduced in the cathedral was that of Fécamp, the house of Herbert's profession, and, as the customs of Fécamp were themselves derived from Cluny, Norwich was drawn into one of the great reforming movements of the eleventh and early twelfth centuries."

[17] Tolhurst, p. xiv; text in R. Anstruther, ed. *Epistolae Herberti de Losinga*, Caxton Soc. 5 (1846), pp. 68–69.

[18] D. Chadd, ed., *The Ordinal of the Abbey of the Holy Trinity, Fécamp*, 2 vols, HBS 111–12 (1999–2002); the principal source is Fécamp, Musée de la Bénédictine, MS 186.

[19] Other houses similarly reformed include Mont St Michel and Fruttuaria. Passages concerning the conclusion of lauds on the feast of St Thomas the Apostle in documents

the Norwich customary "esssentially a directory of ceremonial, with excursions into other related aspects of the community's life, intended probably for the use of the master of ceremonies ... . What it does not do is to detail all constituent chants and prayers of a given service. It assumes the existence of such information in the various books used in choir, none of which has survived." He further cautions that there are enough discrepancies between what can be inferred of forms for certain feasts at Fécamp and Norwich as to "leave us unable to be categorical about the liturgical (strictly speaking) pedigree of our book."[20] To be sure, some key details of performance can be accounted for only by their resemblance to those in the houses influenced by William's reform, but on the whole the dependence of liturgy at Norwich in the reign of Henry III on that of Fécamp must be regarded as a heavily filtered rather than a direct one.

Comparison of the calendar that precedes the customary with that derivable from the Fécamp ordinal shows this most easily. The only entry in the Norwich document that looks to derive definitely from Fécamp is Taurinus on August 11th; but even there, such incipits as can be compared show that the service forms were by no means identical.[21] A similar lack of identity is evident with the feast of Edmund the Martyr (almost the only English figure in the Fécamp sanctorale), where the mass forms at the two houses were totally divergent. Considerable divergence is also observable in the forms for two feasts probably adopted in the early twelfth century, Leonard and the Conception; in both, a good deal of agreement might have been expected.

Overall, there developed at Norwich a set of distinctive feasts having nothing to do with Fécamp. One was absolutely peculiar to the priory – Little St William of Norwich, subject of the first Ritual Murder allegation, 1143 – and several were of a generally East Anglian sort: besides Edmund, Felix, Ethelbert the Martyr, Botulph, Etheldreda (two feasts), Neot, and Osyth.[22] The most distinctive saint in Norwich cathedral tradition, however, is not English (or British) but rather French: Bonitus, bishop of Clermont (now Clermont-Ferrand) in the Auvergne,

---

from those two, St Bénigne at Dijon, Fécamp, and Norwich are printed together in D. Chadd's article, "The Medieval Customary of the Cathedral Priory," in *Norwich Cathedral: Church, City and Diocese, 1096–1996*, ed. I. Atherton et al. (London and Rio Grande 1996), pp 314–24 at 323.

[20] Chadd, "Customary," pp. 319, 320.

[21] Taurinus was first bishop of Evreux, the abbey at which became subject to Fécamp in 1035; at the latter house there was also an Invention feast, Sept. 5th.

[22] Perhaps Helena, for whom there is a commemoration after Agapitus on Aug. 18th, should be added, as in legend the daughter of King Coel (cf. Colchester, in East Anglia though not in the diocese of Norwich). Some of the large literature on William is given in the entry on him in *ODCC*.

who died around 710; his feast day is January 15th. He was apparently unknown in England before 1066, and after that date known only at Norwich, owing almost certainly to Herbert of Losinga's devotion to him. The part of Herbert's story that is relevant here is the simony of which he was accused in connection with becoming bishop of East Anglia in 1091 (and with purchasing the abbacy of Winchester New Minster for his aged father) and which he repented publicly some three years later, the repentance taking the form of a journey to Rome to resign his see into the hands of the reforming pope Urban II. Herbert's decision brought him into conflict with William Rufus, who deprived him of the temporalities of the see, though he was soon restored by both pope and monarch.

It seems highly possible, though not provable from any documentary source, that on his way either to or from Rome he stopped at Clermont, where Bonitus's body lay, in a church dedicated to him. Herbert must have been struck by the similarity between his own case and that of the saint, who had also become a bishop uncanonically, resigned his see in repentance, and journeyed to Rome for absolution.[23] According to a thirteenth-century collection of Miracles of the Virgin, Herbert saw and touched at Clermont a chasuble given to Bonitus by Mary; this seems to be the kind of detail likelier to be reliable than to have been invented.[24] Bonitus continues to be present in such liturgical books as can be assigned to the priory: for example, in the calendar of a miscellaneous volume (of considerable liturgical interest; now CCCC 470) of around the turn of the twelfth century; in the litany for the commendation of a soul in a mid-thirteenth-century psalter (Ushaw, St Cuthbert's College 7); in the litany as well as calendar of a mid-fourteenth-century psalter (Wadham College, Oxford A.5.28); and in the calendar added c. 1325 to the celebrated Ormesby psalter (Bodl., Douce 366). The latter is a specially interesting case, because that vastly sumptuous book was originally intended to celebrate the grandeur of the Foliot and Bardolf families in East Anglia but fell into the hands of Robert Ormesby, monk of Norwich, who had the Norwich calendar and litany added and gave it to the priory, assigning it (so the inscription on the first leaf reads) specifically to the choir.

---

[23] A useful account of Bonitus's Translation in 723 and cult is in I. Wood, "Constructing Cults in Early Medieval France …," in *Local Saints and Local Churches in the Early Medieval West*, ed. A. Thacker and R. Sharpe (Oxford 2002), pp. 155–88 at 175–78.

[24] Available conveniently in H. Kjellman, *La deuxième collection anglo-normande des miracles de la Sainte-Vierge* (Paris 1922), pp. 158–65, printed primarily from BL Royal 20 B.xiv. The main, anonymous, *Vita Boniti* is ed. by B. Krusch, Monumenta Germaniae Historia, Scriptores rerum Merovingicarum 6 (1913), pp. 119–39.

Norwich, then, exhibits two points of special interest. First, that because it was a clearly post-Conquest foundation under an abbot-bishop from Normandy, any traces of "Englishness," in saints culted or in practices, cannot have been "residual"; a degree of self-consciousness in importing such observances can therefore be supposed. Second, that although its founding prelate clearly intended its liturgy to be modelled on that of his Norman house at Fécamp, specific traces of influence from it are surprisingly slight; it seems to have been Herbert's memory that was revered – his anniversary service to be held every July 23rd, the otherwise inexplicable persistence in Norwich calendars of his devotion to Bonitus – rather than his North French legacy.[25]

The result seems to have been a rich liturgical tradition: rich in books and in personnel. Several of the expenses for manuscripts entered in the Norwich Obedientiary Rolls refer to the purchase, decoration, (re)binding, or repair of liturgical books (or of psalters, whether or not strictly liturgical): twenty-three pence to an illuminator "pro salterio prioris et pro istorial" in 1291–92; four shillings for two graduals for dependent churches at Denham and "Hyndelueston" in 1304–5; forty shillings for a "legenda sanctorum" in 1314–15; two shillings and two pence for binding the prior's psalter the following year.[26]

Bishop Salmon's visitation of Norwich, 1308

In 1308, about the time of those entries, Bishop John Salmon executed a formal visitation, the record of which is, according to its modern editor, probably "the earliest record extant of a visitation of the Norwich Priory."[27] Salmon had been prior of Ely, and the stringency of his comments on the house at Norwich may shed light on the standards he brought with him. His main liturgical fault-finding was that too few of the monks (supposedly sixty in number) attended the offices; indeed, he records, probably with some exaggeration, that there were sometimes only seven or eight, and he attempts to mandate that two-thirds of the convent should always be present in choir. A related problem was that, because of the numerous obligations for private and votive masses,

[25] The anniversary liturgy is on pp. 151–52 of the Customary. An early 12th-cent. homiliary from Norwich, now CUL Ii.2.19, has three quires of Herbert's sermons added at the end. In both this and its companion MS, CUL Kk.4.13, many of the homilies are divided into lessons.

[26] N. R. Ker, "Medieval Manuscripts from Norwich Cathedral Priory," *Trans. Cambridge Bibliog. Soc.* 1 (1949–53), pp. 1–28; repr. in his *Books, Collectors and Libraries*, ed. A. G. Watson (London 1985), pp. 243–72.

[27] E. H. Carter, ed. *Studies in Norwich Cathedral History* (Norwich 1935), pp. 7–31 at 7.

monks were slipping off from the main conventual services. He noted also difficulties with such matters as punctuality (and towards that end ordered that a great clock be erected), too many lay people crowding into the Lady Chapel for the Lady mass, and the tattiness of some of the vestments – some of which also fit badly.

The most interesting of his instructions was that, to avoid an impression that there was any divergence in the way services were performed, "we ordain and order that the books on the various private altars in the said Church must be uniformly maintained [*uniform-iter ordinati*] and ordered on the same lines."[28] Salmon's instruction implies a considerable effort of comparison, correction, and where necessary replacement of massbooks, although the exact number of altars in the cathedral church at this period does not seem to be known.[29] It is extremely unfortunate that there appears to be nothing surviving from this program – indeed, no service book from Norwich cathedral at all, nor from the other important Benedictine house in the region, Holme (or Hulme) St Benets. (For evidence from Bury St Edmunds see p. 192.)

Bishops of Worcester and the Benedictine houses in their diocese

There are, by contrast, a handful of important service books from Benedictine houses in the diocese of Worcester, witnesses to be looked at alongside the activity of two of its most vigorous bishops, William de Blois, 1218–36, and Walter Cantilupe, 1237–66.[30] The diocese of Worcester had a richer collection of major Benedictine houses than any diocese in England: besides the cathedral priory, Evesham, Gloucester, Pershore, Tewkesbury, and Winchcombe (plus the substantial cell of Westminster at Great Malvern). Several books to be considered come from the priory itself (here called, unless otherwise qualified, simply "Worcester"), two from Evesham, and one from Tewkesbury. (Important evidence from Winchcombe, and a limited bit from Gloucester, were considered in chapter 5; nothing substantial survives for Great Malvern or Pershore.)

---

[28] Carter's translation, p. 28; the original is given on p. 22. *Ordinati* might better be rendered "laid out."

[29] I am grateful to Eric Fernie for assistance with trying to ascertain the number of such altars: which, surprisingly, it does not seem possible to do.

[30] There survive for the period useful chronicles for two houses in the diocese, Tewkes-bury, to 1263, and (less informative) Worcester itself, to 1377: both ed. H. R. Luard, *Annales monastici*, 5 vols, RS 36 (1864–69), in vols I and IV respectively.

In 1219 bishop William de Blois issued, in the spirit of Lateran IV, several instructions, primarily concerning obsequies; and in 1229 a long series of orders, mainly applicable to parochial contexts, about pastoral matters and about the equipment and decoration of churches.[31] The questions raised for the present chapter by William's orders, and more pointedly by those of Walter Cantilupe in the next reign, have to do with the degree to which reforming bishops expected their mandates to be observed in the religious houses within their dioceses. The matter is of course related somewhat to the complex and often vexed subject of monastic exemption from episcopal control in general, but as there were only six or seven abbeys in England that had such exemption completely – St Augustine's Canterbury, Westminster, Bury St Edmunds, St Albans, Evesham, Battle, and Malmesbury (the last three controvertedly) – the problem was a real one for the vast majority of monastic houses, despite whatever degrees of partial exemption they may have had.[32] Recognition of the problem is implied by the clause in the 1219 statutes insisting that on the death of an archdeacon certain rites should be performed "in qualibet ecclesia tam conventuali quam parochiali."[33]

Equally, Cantilupe's orders seem intended to apply to all churches in the diocese. His major set of diocesan rules (often called, as in *Councils and Synods*, "Synodal statutes"), 102 in number, seem to have been issued in 1240. One of the three extant manuscripts of them concludes with two folios of what C. R. Cheney in his edition headed "Liturgical observances in the diocese of Worcester, ?1220–66."[34] The first leaf, following immediately on the 102nd rule, is concerned with the biblical lectionary at matins, with a certain amount of expository rationalization. The second leaf begins with a list, in no way explained, of the eighteen double feasts observed "in ecclesia Salusbur[iense]," followed

---

[31] *C & S 1205–1313*, I.52–57 (the 1219 statutes) and 170–81 (those of 1229).

[32] A somewhat different account is given in Knowles, *MO*, p. 591 from that in C. R. Cheney, *Episcopal Visitation of Monasteries in the Thirteenth Century* (Manchester 1931), esp. p. 39. In any case a distinction may be made for our purposes between (1) episcopal visitation of a disciplinary and financial sort, (2) episcopal insistence on certain standards relating to worship (e.g., adequate frequency of renewal of the Reserved Sacrament), and (3) episcopal desire for uniformity of observance throughout the diocese (esp. concerning certain local feasts). The first is of little relevance here, and will detain us no further. The existence of new religious orders, above all of friars, complicates the matter further.

[33] *C & S 1205–1313*, I.54.

[34] The MS is BL Cott. Claud. A.viii, fols 212v–19, of which 218v–19rv form the liturgical appendix: *C & S 1205–1313*, I.294–325, at 321–25. It seems that Cheney's "?1220" should be "?1240." As he had earlier pointed out, all three MSS must be later than 1247, for they refer to the feast of St Edmund (Rich), canonized that year: *English Synodalia of the Thirteenth Century* (Oxford 1941, repr. 1967), p. 95.

by a paragraph as to those occasions on which the choir is "ruled" (i.e., by cantors in special ways).[35] There follow three lists of *festa ferianda* for the diocese of Worcester, those most distinctive being Wulfstan and Oswald and their Translation feasts. The first list details some thirty-seven occasions (plus all Sundays and the feast of dedication of each church) requiring complete abstention (*ex toto*) from work; the second, seven on which only ploughing can be done; the third, four feasts of female saints (Agnes, Margaret, Lucia, Agatha), meant to be holidays for women only.[36]

Little of this would have mattered to the monastic houses in the diocese; both Oswald and Wulfstan were notable monk-bishops, whose main feasts would have had high grade whether episcopally ordered or not. But that the monks are paying attention to Cantilupe's regularizations seems to be implied by the spate of monastic church dedications performed in 1239: Tewkesbury on May 3rd, and in the autumn its cell at Bristol (St James's), Gloucester, Winchcombe, Pershore, and Great Malvern.[37] The cathedral church itself had been (re)dedicated on June 7th, 1218, in conjunction with the translation of the body of Wulfstan (who had been canonized only in 1203), by bishop Silvester.[38] This points our attention in two directions, to liturgy at the cathedral and to the distinctive saints of that church and diocese.

The Worcester antiphonal

Between 1218 and 1247 an antiphonal was compiled for Worcester cathedral, where it is to this day (MS F.160). It has been characterized by John Harper as "perhaps the best-known medieval English monastic source" and "the most complete English source of monastic choral chant to have survived."[39] Despite this justified encomium, it is not an

---

[35] These two sections correspond, almost verbatim, to *Use of Sarum* (see p. 412), I.29–30 and 27 respectively. The feast most distinctively "Sarum" among those mentioned is Ald[h]elm (see p. 362).

[36] Clause 89 in two of the MSS also specified that for the new feasts of Dominic, Francis, and Edmund the Confessor, all of nine lessons, the work of the faithful laity should not be impeded (p. 318). That ploughing is allowed on Oswald's Translation feast, Apr. 15th, is reasonable, since between March 25th and May 6th six plough-days plus the intervening Sundays would already have been lost. The Worcester cathedral saints are considered below, p. 212.

[37] So the Tewkesbury annalist: *Annales Monastici* (note 30 above), I.112. In 1241 Tewkesbury's dedication feast was moved so as to coincide with the Assumption, but this was apparently felt to be impractical, for the calendar of its missal (below, p. 215) has, in firm red capitals, "Dedicatio ecclesie Theoks" at June 18th; cf. *Ann. Mon.* I.119.

[38] Silvester died six weeks later; he had been prior before becoming bishop in 1216.

[39] Harper, *Forms and Orders*, p. 232.

easy source to use, in part because of the confused condition of the manuscript and, in even larger part, because of the nature of the modern facsimile edition in which it is generally consulted and cited.[40] No editor's name appears on the title page, but it is an open secret that the scholar responsible was Dame Laurentia McLachlan of Stanbrook Abbey, one of the pioneers in England in the restoration of plainchant. Her splendid and extensive introduction (in French; with indexes, it runs to nearly two hundred pages) is, given her interests and the series in which the facsimile appeared, directed principally towards the musical aspects, but there is much of value to our purposes as well.[41]

The original book of c. 1230 consists of an office antiphonal proper (fols 1–99, temporale, and 182–284, sanctorale) complemented by a processional (100–15), calendar, psalter, hymnal, and collectar (in all, 147–81). This is followed by a mid-thirteenth-century gradual (287–354). In the middle of the book (116–45) were inserted in the fourteenth century office and mass forms for Corpus Christi, and in the fifteenth for the Visitation.[42] The result is, and in the late middle ages very likely was, a composite volume more suitable for reference than for performance. The sanctorale is rather selective, providing proper chants for only about thirty saints' feasts (plus vigils and octaves for some), with some tag-references to the common for others; so it is particularly useful to be able consult not only the calendar but also at the end an extensive list headed "Festorum series qua propria missa cuilibet festo assignatur" (fols 252–53; not printed in the facsimile). This can be used to corroborate the feasts covered in the antiphonal and slightly later gradual, and provides us with a kind of working sanctorale.

The distinctive Worcester cathedral (as separable from diocesan) feasts are easily discernible from this manuscript: Oswald (three, including an Ordination feast), Wulfstan (two), Egwin (bishop c. 700, two), and an inexplicable "Veneratio sanctae crucis" on February 6th (in the calendar as well as this mass-list, but not the antiphonal's sanctorale).

---

[40] *Antiphonaire monastique de Worcester,* Paléographie musicale 12 (Tournai 1922).

[41] According to the notice of her by L. Johns in *ODNB* 35.706, "From the rubrics in the Worcester antiphoner, she was able to reconstruct details of the medieval cathedral later confirmed by archaeology." No details are given.

[42] The clearest and most succinct description is that of R. M. Thomson, *Descriptive Cat. of the Med. MSS in Worcester Cathedral Library* (Cambridge 2001), pp. 108–9. The facsimile prints most but not all of this material; Harper, p. 232, indicates what has been omitted (in brief, almost everything save the temporale and sanctorale of the antiphonal, calendar, and hymnal). He also provides a useful table showing Dame Laurentia's considerable reordering. This helps some, but the facsimile remains regrettably difficult to use, not least because the folio numbers are seldom visible, though quite legible on the manuscript.

Others not specifically related to Worcester but by no means common include Wulsin (probably not the well known Wulfsige, abbot of Westminster and bishop of Sherborne, but the Wulfsin or Wilsin who was a local hermit primarily connected with Evesham: see below), Milburga, Guthlac, Ives (his *Inventio*, April 24th), John of Beverley, Ethelbert of East Anglia and Hereford, Bede, Gudwal, Edburga, Etheldreda, Mildred, Kenelm, Winifred, Paulinus, Wilfrid, Frideswide, Birinus, and Judoc. Also striking are the French saints Taurinus of Evreux (two feasts), Romanus of Rouen, and an almost baffling Vigor of Bayeux. Dame Laurentia associated Taurinus with Mauger, bishop 1200–12 and formerly dean of Evreux; Romanus with John of Coutances, bishop 1195–98, formerly dean of Rouen and donor of an arm of Rouen to his cathedral; and Vigor with either of the two first Anglo-Norman bishops, Samson (1096–1112) or Theulf (1115–23), albeit on rather vague grounds.[43]

The Worcester cathedral sanctorale

The plethora of hagiographical detail provided by calendar, sanctorale, and later list of feasts-with-masses in the antiphonal can be combined with several other Worcester documents to provide an unusually clear picture of the development of the cathedral priory's sanctorale over a long period and in an area which in several respects is thought to have retained overt manifestations of "continuity" after the Norman Conquest.[44] Three of these documents belong to the eleventh century and three to the thirteenth. The earlier evidence is provided by (1) Wulfstan's portiforium of c. 1065 (see p. 126), which has a calendar as well as an inferrable sanctorale; (2) the calendar prefixed to a homiliary, also of the third quarter of the eleventh century and now Bodl. Hatton 113; (3) a calendar similarly prefixed to the first volume (CCCC 9) of a mid-eleventh-century passional. For the thirteenth century there are (4) the antiphonal just discussed; (5) a slightly earlier psalter (perhap c. 1225; now Oxford, Magdalen College 100);[45] and (6) somewhat obliquely,

---

[43] *Antiphonaire*, p. 45. Is it possible that some of the appeal of Vigor was the similarity of the word to the (abbreviated) Latin form '(V)Vigorn.' used for cathedral, diocese, and bishop alike?

[44] In addition to the impact of Wulfstan – the only Anglo-Saxon to remain in high office for decades after 1066, as bishop 1062–95 – of particular relevance may be the work of the Worcester monk-scribe who wrote in the "Tremulous Hand": C. Franzen, *The Tremulous Hand of Worcester: a Study of Old English in the Thirteenth Century* (Oxford 1991), esp. pp. 183–94.

[45] Morgan, *Early Gothic MSS*, no. 49, sees a slight difference in the hand that entered the 1218 occasions in the calendar and suggests that the text itself slightly antedates

a psalter that in the first half of the thirteenth century had belonged to the church of St Helen in Worcester – a substantial establishment that, after much effort, had come to be recognized as belonging to the priory – though it passed subsequently to Exeter cathedral (now its MS 3508).[46] Collation of these six sources reveals no discernible overall reduction in the English/British saints included in the later calendars; some are lost (e.g., Cuthman, Eormenhilda, Boniface, Botulf), some gained (Wulfsin, Ives, Gudwal, Winifred).[47] The distinctively Anglo-Saxon Conception of John the Baptist disappears, but the Oblation of the Virgin, which has equally Anglo-Saxon roots (under that title; see p. 92) appears.

By contrast, the most distinctive feast at Worcester cathedral after the Conquest seems to be, its saint-bishops aside, that of St Anne. It is well known that this feast tends to become popular throughout England from the later fourteenth century on, but at Worcester a cult seems to have begun in the second quarter of the twelfth century.[48] The motivating impulse is attributed to Warin, prior in the 1130s, who asked Osbert of Clare, monk and sometime prior of Westminster, for a *legendum* of St Anne which could be used as lessons during matins: for, apparently, an already existing feast which bishop Simon (1125–50) told Osbert (who recounts this in his introductory letter) was kept at Worcester, and with an octave. There is no twelfth-century evidence against which to test this claim, but no reason to doubt it. Nonetheless, in the Magdalen 100 psalter, of about 1225 and firmly attributable to the cathedral, she is not in the calendar, though appearing first, doubled, among

---

that year. He notes also that obits of the parents of Prior Richard (1242–52) are entered at two places.

[46] This MS contains references, specially notable in light of the book's date, to the Saturday office of the Virgin "secundum quod canit Salesburiensis ecclesia atque Wellensis ecclesia ... et Herfordensis ecclesia" (fol. 133rv; see further p. 396). Its decoration is characterized as "crude" and "coarse" by N. Morgan, "Psalter Illustration for the Diocese of Worcester in the Thirteenth Century," *Med. Art and Archit. at Worc. Cath.*, BAA Conf. Trs. 1 (1978, for 1975), pp. 91–104; a study of only those calendars which "having no clear connection with any religious house could be called 'diocesan'" (p. 99).

[47] In 1921 W. H. Frere, completing E. S. Dewick's edition of *The Leofric Collectar* [see p. 132; BL Harley 2961] *compared with the Collectar of St Wulfstan*, HBS 56 (1921), pp. 587–600, printed in columnar form the four 11th-cent. witnesses (one column each for the portiforium's calendar and sanctorale, the calendar of Magd. 100, and that of the antiphonal. He alludes briefly to the St Helen's psalter calendar (p. 587). Somewhat relevant is a collectar, now Worcester Cath. MS Q.26, contemporary with the antiphonal, from which its contents look to have been copied.

[48] A. Wilmart, "Les compositions d'Osbert de Clare en l'honneur de sainte Anne," in his *Auteurs spirituels et textes dévots du moyen âge* (Paris 1932), pp. 261–86, repr. from *Annales de Bretagne* 37 (1925–26).

virgins in the litany. The Worcester annalist notes that in 1240 Bishop Cantilupe "celebravit synodum die Sanctae Annae," as though the reference was self-explanatory.[49] She is listed as *in cap(p)is* in the calendar of the antiphonal, with no mention of an octave, and further hymns were added for her in the fourteenth-century section.[50]

The continuity of what seems discernible as a distinctive hagiographical tradition at Worcester is evidenced by the addition, in the early fifteenth century, to a glossed psalter of the late twelfth (now Bodl. Bodley 862), a litany of saints that features Oswald and Wulstan as the first two confessors and, further down, (19) Edmund, (20) Egwin, (21) Vigor, (28) Gudwal, and finally (40) Bede; while among the thirty-five virgins Anne comes first. It also includes as ninth among the martyrs, between George and Alban, a Demetrius. The litany of the Wulfstan portiforium was heavily over-written in the first half of the twelfth century; in this form it has a Demetrius in exactly the same place – and again, Anne first among the virgins.[51] An addition was also made to the portiforium's calendar in the same period, of "Translatio Sancti Oswaldi archiepiscopi [all in capitals], et Sancti Demetrii martyris" at October 8th.[52] The same entry appears in the original calendar of the early thirteenth-century Magdalen 100 psalter, the litany of which has Anne first among virgins, as was noted above. The litany added to Bodley 862 appears to have been copied from that in Magdalen 100, which in turn is extremely close to the rewritten one in the Wulfstan portiforium.[53] Why Demetrius – *megalomartyr* of Thessalonica – should have been included at all is a mystery; what seems clear is that mentions of him begin in the twelfth century, the same period as do those of Anne.

Of course, the appearance of a saint in a calendar, let alone a litany, is no proof that that person will in fact be honored on his or her "day." The kind of hard evidence we need to assert actual liturgical observance is instead found in a source like the saints-with-masses list at the end of the antiphonal, already discussed – or like the only massbook

---

[49] *Ann. Mon.*, IV.432.
[50] In the sanctorale her feast is *in albis* (facsimile, p. 339), and the *in capis* (a higher grade than albs) of the calendar is over an erasure; there seems to have been an upgrading by the time of the calendar, which is slightly later than the body of the antiphonal.
[51] Lapidge, *Litanies*, p. 116; on p. 65 he remarks that this litany is not "in its present form, an Anglo-Saxon litany of the saints."
[52] Wormald, *Eng. Kals*, p. 221.
[53] Dame Laurentia comments (*Antiphonaire*, p. 46) on the appearance of Demetrius in the litanies of CCCC 391 and Bodl. 862 (she does not seem to have known Magd. 100) – and in the litany of the antiphonal (fol. 163v), which however her facsimile does not include!

surviving from any of the Worcestershire houses, the Tewkesbury missal, to be considered next.

Tewkesbury's bifurcated missal

Virtually the sole service-book evidence for medieval liturgy at Tewkesbury abbey is a missal, now CUL Gg.3.21. The provenance is clear: its dedication feast is entered in the calendar at June 18th, *in cappis* and with an octave. The missal's usefulness to us is limited by the facts that it is of two periods (of its 256 folios, 3–135 and 149–54 are of the thirteenth century, the remainder of the fourteenth), and that the sanctorale covers only from Andrew through 21 March; so this book must have been supplemented by two, perhaps three, volumes covering the rest of the year. The thirteenth-century section includes the calendar and most of the temporale, that of the fourteenth century the rest of the temporale, sanctorale, and common of saints. The calendar (in the thirteenth-century section, with many additions) is highly individual, full of obituary notices of the abbey's founders and benefactors, as well as of monarchs and prelates.[54] Edmund of Canterbury (canonized 1247) has been added to the calendar in a contemporary hand, which suggests a like terminus for that part of the book; but so has the Translation of Wulfstan (1218) which would have been of only moderate importance at Tewkesbury.

A key, but unanswerable, question is the extent to which the later section represents a mere copying of the earlier, as opposed to an importing of new texts. One detail in the common of saints points to a model from which at least that section must have been copied and seems to be unique: the forms at the end of the common for a mass "in translatione cuiuslibet sancti," followed by "in octava cuiuslibet sancti" (fol. 251v). Had this book been entirely purpose-written for Tewkesbury no such form would have been needed, for the house possessed no such saint. That it is copied from a more generic book is shown also by the rubric at the feast of Peter's Chair (fol. 203), "*Credo* non dicatur neque prefatio sed ubi altare dedicatum est in honore ipsius"; there does not seem to be evidence for a St Peter's altar at Tewkesbury, the main dedication of which was to St Mary.[55] Its monastic annals

---

[54] There is also a curious mention on Feb. 9th, as well as an Octave for the Purification (itself unusual), of a "Trelyai, ep. & conf."; this appears to be Teilo of Wales, whose day that is. He is not found in the sanctorale.

[55] The dedications of the various altars at Tewkesbury are both not known and related to vexed questions about the building's architectural history; these are discussed in several of the contributions to *Medieval Art and Architecture at Gloucester and Tewkesbury*,

speak of chapels dedicated to St Nicholas and St James in 1238; one wonders whether the latter may be connected with a note at the foot of fol. 188 of the missal, in the January part of the sanctorale, about a puzzling Translation of James (merely to the effect that its forms were to be those of the "other," July 25th feast).[56] The book has two feasts for Ambrose: his principal feast, April 4th, with a mass collect and postcommunion that seem to be unique (the secret is shared, with one small change in wording, with Abingdon and Sherborne), and on December 7th, coinciding with the Octave of Andrew, the fairly rare Ordination feast (fol. 184).[57] The absence of Richard of Chichester (April 3rd, just before this select sanctorale ends), canonized in 1262 and a native son of the Worcester diocese, suggests that the later section does replicate with some faithfulness part of the earlier book that was somehow lost.

The thirteenth-century evidence from Tewkesbury offers a clearer than usual indication that, perhaps contrary to what might be expected, there is often little connection between the relics possessed by a church and the saints' feasts celebrated in its liturgy. A Feast of Relics was established there from July 2nd, probably only around 1232; in that year it was decided that both day and night offices should be *De reliquiis* on that feast. In that year also a layman gave a considerable collection, including three bones of St Atheus, better known as Tathai, a sixth-century Welsh monastic founder buried at Caerwent, and in 1239 Isabella, countess of Gloucester, gave a large collection, including relics of Pantaleon, Damasus and (astonishingly) Elizabeth – none of whom finds a place in the calendar.[58]

Tewkesbury's early history is not rooted in the diocese of Worcester; it became an abbey proper only in 1102, having formerly been a cell of Cranborne, in Dorset (diocese of Sherborne, later Sarum), itself founded only about 980. In this respect Tewkesbury contrasts strongly with Evesham, the Anglo-Saxon origins of which go back to the early eighth century. Its surviving liturgical books reflect a wealthy and proud community.

BAA Conf. Trs. 7 (1985, for 1981), esp. R. K. Morris, "Early Gothic Architecture at Tewkesbury Abbey," pp. 93–98 at 94.

[56] The dedication of the chapels is noted in *Ann. Mon.*, I.111.

[57] Since the Westminster missal lacks the Dec. 7th feast, Legg did not include it in his collations.

[58] *Ann. Mon.* I.96, 113. Is the Elizabeth "virgin" in question the Hungarian queen-saint of that name (and mother of three children) who died only in 1231 and was canonized four years later; or Elizabeth of Schönau, the mystic nun who died in 1164 but was never formally canonized; or even the mother of John the Baptist, who like Elizabeth of Hungary (and St Anne) fails to qualify as a virgin?

Evesham and its several books

Of Benedictine houses not cathedral priories, Evesham stands out as having not only a long history but also a sense of *amour propre* almost comparable to that of St Albans or Bury St Edmunds. Its great founding figure was Egwin (or Ecgwine; d. 717?); its other saints Wi(g)stan and Odulf;[59] its notable literary figures prior Dominic (d. 1125) and especially prior and then abbot Thomas of Marlborough (or "Marleberge"; d. 1236). Thomas, in addition to compiling an extended account of the abbey's struggle for exemption from supervision by bishops of Worcester and of its protracted battle to get rid of a scandalous abbot – matters which take up a good deal of space in what is known as the Evesham Chronicle – acquired a number of books for it.[60] These are enumerated in a list compiled by a continuator of the Chronicle. Among them are some liturgical books that Thomas had made, apparently after he became prior (1218), including a *magnum breuiarium* and a *magnum psalterium*, both characterized as better than anything that had been there before, and a book "de grosa litera de ordine officii abbatis" from Candlemas to Pentecost. He also "inuenit omnia necessaria ad quatuor antiphonaria cum ipsis notariis, excepto quod fratres monasterii scripserunt ea"; is this a valuable reference to monks' copying their own service books, save for certain specialized parts entrusted to paid notaries?[61]

As it happens, there do survive from Evesham both a breviary and a psalter from the thirteenth century, though each is a bit later than those Thomas could have provided. The breviary, now Bodl. Barlow 41, dates from the third quarter of the century and covers only *pars*

---

[59] Wigstan was a 9th-cent. Mercian prince whose body was translated to Evesham in 1019, Odulf a 9th-cent. Dutch missionary to Frisia whose relics, stolen from there by Viking pirates and sold to a bishop of London who was also abbot of Evesham, were given to the abbey around 1040.

[60] *Thomas of Marlborough, History of the Abbey of Evesham*, ed. and tr. J. Sayers and L. Watkiss, OMT (2003); the full chronicle (to 1418, with continuations) ed. W. D. Macray, *Chronicon abbatiae de Evesham*, RS 29 (1863). The struggle over abbot Robert's removal is the subject of the entire chapter xix in Knowles, *MO*, pp. 331–45.

[61] Translated by Sayers and Watkiss as "He further provided everything needed for the writing of four antiphonals complete with musical notation (though the brethren of the monastery did the copying)," p. 493. The list is printed in *Eng. Ben. Libs: the Shorter Cats.*, ed. R. Sharpe et al., CBMLC 4 (1996), pp. 131–38, with important editorial comments by Sharpe; in a subsequent letter he shares my puzzlement about the order of the work: in an antiphonal, surely the chant has to be written first, then the words to fit. The principal MS source for the list is Bodl. Rawl. A.287, probably written in Thomas's lifetime; it contains also his renditions of the Lives of Odulf, Wistan, and Egwin, the latter marked in a 15th-cent. hand into twelve lessons suitable for reading at matins. There is also a list of late 14th-cent. bequests that includes a "Missale dimidii anni" valued at twenty marks, a pricey volume (ed. Sharpe, p. 139).

hiemalis, with the sanctorale running from Andrew through Alphege (19 April). It is of the type sometimes called a rubricated portable breviary, substantial but not very large (354 folios, outer measurements 175 x 105 mm), so it does not necessarily represent the fullness of the office at the abbey; the rubrics are not of a ceremonial sort but mostly about occurrence and concurrence. Several loose slips have been pasted in: one for David containing the collect, for example (at fol. 304). There are proper lessons for only a small number of saints; even some feasts of twelve lessons, like that of Guthlac, are given proper collects only. Because the sanctorale covers only the winter months, the calendar, printed by Wormald as his base manuscript for Evesham, has to be used to get some idea of the full round of saints' feasts observed throughout the year.[62] Unusual features include the Translation of Aldhelm on May 5th, observed (with three lessons) presumably because of a supposed connection with Egwin, who is said to have visited his tomb; a confessor Maximus (not Maximus the Confessor), three lessons at May 29th; Canute of Denmark, eight lessons on July 10th (murdered in 1086 at Odensee, where an abbey was founded ten years later with Evesham its mother house); Anne, twelve lessons at July 26th, as is not surprising in the diocese of Worcester (she is also first among virgins in the litany). An apparent peculiarity is that the August 19th feast of Credan, an eighth-century abbot whose relics had survived a test of authenticity by fire in 1077, is marked as only a commemoration, but an octave, *in albis*, is entered on the 26th; this is presumably because the 19th falls within the Octave of the Assumption (Mary was the co-dedicatee of the abbey, followed by Egwin).[63]

The breviary's calendar agrees almost entirely with that of the celebrated book, perhaps slightly earlier, known for its excellence of illustration simply as the Evesham Psalter (now BL Add. 44874).[64] Its iconography, the inclusion of an abbot in its famous full-page crucifixion miniature, and the addition of the arms of Richard Earl of Cornwall, brother of Henry III, have led Nigel Morgan to offer a dating of about 1255, and to suggest both that the abbot pictured may be Henry of Worcester (1256–63) and that the book might have been given to Earl Richard by way of placation after the battle of Evesham in August 1265, which ended with the death of Simon de Montfort

---

[62] Wormald, *Eng. Ben. Kals*, II.21–38.

[63] The story of the 1077 proof by fire is in Macray, *Chron. Evesham*, p. 323.

[64] May through August are lacking from its calendar. In general agreement also is the calendar of an early 14th-cent. psalter long in private hands and on loan to the British Museum, where Wormald collated it as MS C for the abbey; it has now passed to the Almonery Museum at Evesham (*MMBL*, II.799; I have not seen the MS).

and his subsequent burial at the abbey.[65] Its litany contains, as well as the distinctive Evesham saints noted above (even Maximus), a virgin called Venera towards the end of that category (the last six are Milburga, Edburga, Etheldreda, Hilda, Venera, and Brigid). She is otherwise unknown, and it may be suspected that "she" is in fact the first letters of the curious feast noted in the Worcester antiphonal's calendar at February 6th, "[In] veneratione sanctae crucis." If this should be true, it is a fascinating example of uncritical borrowing, as well as of the unwitting invention of a saint.

The fullest amount of liturgical information about Evesham comes from a book of the type that the present work must generally, for reasons of space, prescind from: a pontifical. It is an unusual kind of pontifical, however, in that, rather than belonging to a particular bishop for use wherever he functions episcopally, it is for a specific office in a specific place, that of the abbacy of Evesham around 1300. The book, now Bodl. Barlow 7, is indeed titled "Officium ecclesiasticum abbatum secundum usum Eveshamiensis monasterii," and the first two items specify on which feasts and to what extent the abbot is required to be involved in the divine office, matter not usual in a pontifical; in that respect the book is close to being a customary.[66] Its late nineteenth-century editor, H. A. Wilson, remarked that peculiarities of arrangement suggest that it "may have been made up of three separate parts, each of which ended with a small gathering," and this seems likely both in the way the contents are allocated and as a practical matter.[67] Certain "pontifical rights" – things like the capacity to bless vestments and to wear a mitre, hence "mitred abbot" – were granted to abbot Roger Norreys (the rogue treated at such length in the Evesham Chronicle) as early as 1192, and after Norreys's deposition some twenty years later a formal expression of how the new privileges were to be exercised in actual services may be the "de grosa litera librum de ordine officii abbatis" noticed above as among the good works of Thomas of Marlborough.

---

[65] Morgan, *Early Gothic MSS*, no. 111. Cf. the extensive description in BL *Cat. Add'l MSS 1936–45*, pp. 16–23, probably by D. H. Turner, author of "The Evesham Psalter," *Jnl. Warburg and Courtauld Insts.* 27 (1964), pp. 23–41.

[66] H. A. Wilson, ed. *Officium ecclesiasticum abbatum...*, HBS 6 (1893). The sole other English "abbatial pontifical" extant is Bodl. Rawlinson C.425, a book for abbots of Westminster of about the same period (early 14th cent.). It contains less of a "customary" sort and more pontifical elements proper, including a benedictional; partly ed. by Legg in *Westminster Missal* III (1897), four years after Wilson discussed it in his introduction to the Evesham book. Note that the text of Wilson's edition is columnated, not paginated, whereas the MS is paginated, not foliated.

[67] Wilson, pp. x–xi; he does not mention the corroborating fact that, as currently bound, the book is surprisingly heavy.

Wilson argued that this book, now lost, underlay most of the current Barlow 7 codex, which was written for John of Brockhampton, abbot 1282 to 1316.[68]

The sorts of "extra-pontifical" information that the book yields include a fairly detailed *ordo* for pontifical mass on the greatest occasions (called at Evesham the *vii festum*, a term subsequently borrowed at Worcester), a long account of the Maundy Thursday liturgy, and a good deal about the altars and shrines of the abbey, including the fact that the Candlemas rite at Evesham began not, as usual, at the high altar but in the crypt.[69] From this book, supplemented by the breviary (albeit for only part of the year) and psalter noted above, we get as great a sense of liturgical life in a Benedictine house in the late thirteenth century as we do for Norwich or any other house from which a full customary survives. Yet the breviary, having only a quarter of a year's sanctorale, is far less informative to us than the comparable, and well known, book from Hyde.

Hyde abbey: its breviary and its miracles

Of the few surviving English monastic breviaries that of Hyde abbey, c. 1300, is the best known, simply because its contents have been long available in an extensive (if difficult to use) modern edition by J. B. L. Tolhurst.[70] The manuscript source is twofold, Bodl. Rawl. liturg. e.1* (453 fols) and Bodl. Gough liturg. 8 (70 fols); the latter contains the calendar and psalter (of which some leaves are missing) with canticles, litany, and Office of the Dead. It is not absolutely clear that the two formed part of the same book, for the Gough manuscript is much more highly decorated than the Rawlinson.[71] But the contents of the two are

---

[68] Wilson., pp. xii–xv.

[69] Wilson's note on the latter, pp. 190–91, deserves special attention. In general the forty pages of notes to his edition are a trove of valuable, and often rarely encountered, information.

[70] J. B. L. Tolhurst, ed. *The Monastic Breviary of Hyde Abbey, Winchester*, 6 vols HBS 69–71, 76, 78, 80 (1932–42), abbreviated throughout the present work as Hyde Breviary. Vols I and II contain the temporale, III and IV the sanctorale, and V (issued before the previous two) the common of saints, calendar, litany, and Office of the Dead; the psalter is not printed at all. Only folio references are given, and there are no indexes. Vol. VI is Tolhurst's monographic *Introduction to English Monastic Breviaries* (repr. by HBS, 1993), a useful but often confusing (and confused) work; see the extensive review by A. Strittmatter in *Speculum* 26 (1951), pp. 411–17.

[71] Sandler, *Gothic MSS*, no. 64, remarks that the illustrations are "associated stylistically with the Queen Mary Psalter" (BL Royal 2 B.vii), perhaps the earliest datable work of that atelier. Twenty-six full-page miniatures of the life of Christ from another contemporary psalter were inserted, possibly in the 18th cent., and have nothing to do with the Hyde breviary as such: Sandler's no. 42.

exactly complementary, and they seem at one point to have been bound together; on balance, it is fair to regard them as a single book.

The breviary is datable almost certainly to the abbacy of Simon de Kaynings (or Canning), 1292–1304. By that time the efforts of various General Chapters towards shortening the office seem to be taking practical effect: here seen most notably in how short the lessons at matins tend to be. On Palm Sunday, for example, the tenth lesson is twenty-seven words long, the eleventh lesson, twenty-four.[72] Similarly, the four lessons of the first nocturn for the common of one martyr – one that would frequently be used – average twenty-eight words each. This shifts the balance of the night office markedly towards the responsories, which are not similarly abbreviated and which were, unlike the lessons, sung, sometimes protractedly.

Hyde abbey, of which almost nothing remains, was Winchester's New Minster until 1110, when the house moved to a new site just outside the city. We have often had occasion to notice the New Minster missal (Le Havre, B.m. 105) of the third quarter of the eleventh century. That book contains mass prayers for both feasts (Deposition 13 December, Translation 9 January) of Judoc, whose relics had been brought by Grimbald, founding figure at the New Minster (c. 900), himself honored on July 8th. The other two distinctive Hyde saints are both "datable" in terms of special emphasis laid on them: Valentine, whose head had been given to the abbey in 1041 (by the redoubtable Emma Ælfgifu, widow of both Æthelred II and Cnut and mother of Edward the Confessor) and whose February 14th feast has an octave in the breviary. So does that of Barnabas, at whose intercession miracles were supposedly wrought in the monastic church in 1182, an occurrence probably reflected in the rare *Revelatio* feast for him, December 12th.[73]

On feasts of particular interest at Hyde the lessons tend, not surprisingly, to be vastly longer; the twelve for Grimbald's July 8th feast give the impression of having provided what may be called, not facetiously, a good listen. His office was in all likelihood a local composition. The lessons for Valentine, a "universal," though not widely emphasized, saint are drawn from an older *passio* for the martyred Valentine who was a

---

[72] In all, lessons ix–xii are identical to lesson vii and the first half of viii in the 1531 Great Sarum breviary (*Sarum Brev.* I.dcclvii) – which does, admittedly, contain exceptionally long lessons, likely to have been abbreviated in practice; but the brief Hyde lessons cannot readily be lengthened.

[73] Tolhurst, p. xi. The Hyde chronicle, the so-called *Liber de Hyda* (ed. E. Edwards, RS 45, 1866), though compiled in the late 14th cent., extends only to 1123, so there seems to be no narrative account of the Barnabas miracles to supplement the account in the breviary (for which, see below).

priest of Rome rather than the one who was bishop of Terni; the latter, mentioned already in Bede's martyrology, was commemorated in late eleventh-century passionals used at Worcester and Salisbury, so the Hyde tradition clearly has a different source.[74] This *passio* occupies the first eight lessons, and there is no indication what the last four should be: presumably, the lessons in the common of saints from the homily of Gregory the Great on the gospel "Si quis post me venire," the tag for which is given (four lessons that again average fewer than twenty words each). Despite the fact that the calendar shows an octave, with twelve lessons, for Valentine, there is no indication of such an observance in the sanctorale.

The case with Barnabas is even more interesting, both because here the octave indicated in the calendar is observed and because some of the lessons within it refer to the 1182 miracles; we have therefore a rare instance of datable hagiographical composition, and for use in one place only.[75] The collect for him in the New Minster missal of c. 1070 is not repeated in the breviary, though both prayers are equally bland. The proper lessons for the feast itself are a shorter version of a *passio* known at Salisbury.[76] Eight lessons from the longer version are prescribed for the next day, but those for the following days consist entirely of recitals of the miracles at Hyde: three sets of three lessons, two sets of eight (one for the Sunday within the octave, one for the octave day, June 18th).[77] These are told at no great length or artifice, as with that of the mute adolescent who comes *a Vernone* (wherever that is; Verona?) to England in the hope of being cured through Becket's intercession but gets diverted to that of Barnabas at Hyde.

Even more instructive are the eight lessons provided for the feast, unique to Hyde, of the Revelation of Barnabas, December 12th, *in albis*. These recount the glories of the New Minster's foundation by Edward the Elder and of its collection of relics, among which had been those of Barnabas. These had been not much noticed until a

---

[74] The Terni Valentine's *passio* is *BHL* 8460, found in the Cotton-Corpus passional from Worcester (P. H. Zettel, "Ælfric's Hagiographical Sources and the Latin Legendary Preserved in B.L. MS Cotton Nero E.i + CCCC MS 9 and Other Manuscripts," Oxford D. Phil. thesis 1979, p. 17) and in the *olim*-Bodl. Fell 4 passional from Salisbury (now Salisbury Cath. 221; Webber, *Scribes and Scholars*, p. 155). Whether the two Valentines were originally the same person is irrelevant here.

[75] The obvious case of English datable hagiographical composition after the 11th cent. is that of Becket, but night offices which included lessons composed after 1173 or (for the Translation) 1220 were used in a variety of locations: see S. L. Reames, "Reconstructing a Thirteenth-Century Office for the Translation of Thomas Becket," *Speculum* 80 (2005), pp. 118–70.

[76] The short Hyde version is *BHL* 987, the longer *BHL* 985, found in Dublin, Trin. Coll. 174 (Webber, *Saints and Scholars*, p. 143).

[77] The sequence is interrupted by the twelve-lesson feast of Edburga, June 15th.

badly afflicted woman is told by the saint to go to Hyde and there venerate his relics. When, as a result, their power is realized, relics of two further saints are found: those of Apollinaris of Ravenna and a martyr Vincent (not specified as the famous deacon of that name), for both of whom the breviary has a *memoria* on that day.[78] There is no question of an octave here, for on the 13th comes the great Hyde feast of Judoc.

The monks of Hyde must have enjoyed hearing this annual account of their unique *revelatio* – and in some comfort, because in 1288, a few years before the breviary was written, Pope Nicholas IV had issued a faculty permitting them to wear lambskin caps during divine office in cold conditions, as certainly would have obtained on December 12th.[79] David Knowles characterized life at Hyde, at least in comparison with that at the often troubled cathedral priory at Winchester, as "tranquil."[80] Substantiation for such a judgment may be inferred from the articles issued by bishop John Stratford after he visited Hyde in 1325; among them were that "the attendance of all at the night and day offices was enjoined, and brothers in priest's orders were to celebrate daily."[81] Whether this indicates some laxity in the house (chess and the playing of dice were also forbidden, as was the wearing of silk cinctures) or a fairly new bishop (as Stratford was at the time) flexing his episcopal muscle, we have no way of knowing. But for Hyde the bits of contextual vividness available complement its widely known breviary, making it possible as well as necessary for us to pass more quickly in review the three other monastic breviaries roughly contemporary (no more than twenty-five years earlier) with it: books from Coldingham/Durham, Ely, and Muchelney. These form Tolhurst's principal *comparanda* in his edition of the Hyde book – though, as we shall see, none of the three is strictly comparable.

Office books at Coldingham/Durham, Ely, and Muchelney

The Durham breviary, made originally for the cell at Coldingham in Berwickshire (now BL Harley 4664), is so elaborately illuminated

---

[78] This is the only pairing of these two, or mention of this Apollinaris (whose feast is normally 23 July), that I have encountered, and seems to defy explanation save in connection with this story.

[79] *Calendar of Papal Letters*, ed. W. H. Bliss, I (1893; the multi-vol. series is ongoing), p. 492. How had such a small request made it into the papal offices?

[80] Knowles, *RO*, I.316.

[81] Summarized in VCH *Hampshire*, II.118, citing the introduction to *Liber de Hyda* (p. lxii) by Edwards, who cites the (still unpublished) register of Stratford.

that its character as a working service book may be doubted.[82] It looks to have passed to the mother house in the fifteenth century, and the presumption is that its text, written about 1270, corresponds extensively to that of the cathedral priory.[83] There are definite indications of awareness when practice differs from that of Durham; for example, at the end of the eight lessons for Cosmas and Damian (fol. 278v) a note, in the original hand, reads "Apud Coldingham tamen tres lectiones fiant de eis" (with no explanation; the feast has twelve lessons in the calendar of this book, as in all Durham calendars). Tolhurst pointed out a primitiveness of arrangement, in that the book "still has a separate hymnal, in this case with music, bound up in the middle of the volume, and the Matins canticles form a group by themselves following the psalter."[84] He did not, however, comment on what seems to be a peculiarity of the temporale after Pentecost, that it is truncated, offering provision for only something like twelve Sundays (rather than the usual twenty-five): an oddity that a later (fifteenth-century?) hand begins to try to correct in the margins of fol. 113v–25.

A bit of light on liturgy at the cathedral priory of Ely in the last quarter of the thirteenth century is shed by a rather curious book, usually described as a combined breviary-missal and now CUL Ii.4.20.[85] The "breviary" section (fols 1–138, 208–318) is no such thing; it lacks the psalter-element entirely. For most saints' feasts there is only a collect, sometimes with the gospel and a Magnificat antiphon – items the prior was likely to recite or intone – with full offices, notably for the saints specially connected to Ely. At the first Sunday after Trinity (so expressed) ten antiphons are given for Saturdays, with a rubric stating that if all ten cannot be used *ob brevitate temporis* the first two and last

---

[82] Morgan, *Early Gothic MSS*, no. 176. The monk-donor in the fine full-page Virgin and Child may have been one of the priors listed in D. E. R. Watt and N. F. Shead, ed. *The Heads of Religious Houses in Scotland*, Scottish Rec. Soc. n.s. 24 (Edinburgh 2001), p. 31, but no obvious name springs out.

[83] So F. Wormald collated (as MS B) its calendar in his edition of those of Durham; *Eng. Ben Kals*, I.161; and C. Hohler treated it as a relevant witness for "The Durham Services in honour of St Cuthbert," in *The Relics of St Cuthbert*, ed. C. F. Battiscombe (Oxford 1956), pp. 155–91, siglum *Dub*; his preferred date is mid-13th cent., somewhat earlier than that offered by other authorities.

[84] Tolhurst, *Eng. Mon. Brevs*, p. 2. In other parts of his (unindexed) book tabular treatment of various accretive elements to the office shows in what respects Coldingham/Durham practice agreed with or differed from the main English monastic tradition.

[85] The date, 15th cent., given in the printed catalogue of CUL MSS (and followed in *MLGB*), is plainly wrong. N. Morgan, *Early Gothic MSS*, II.38, notes a resemblance between what decoration survives in this Ely MS (which he describes as "almost certainly made locally" but does not treat as such) and the Charter of Cambridge University, dated 1291/2. The CUL catalogue also calls the book "secundum usum Sarum"! There is no calendar. See above, p. 187, for more on Ely.

three should be omitted, and that "you will find (*invenies*)" prayers with gospels after the *historiae* (fol. 115). The second-person singular implies, at least mildly, either that the user is not wholly familiar with this kind of book, as might be the case with a newly-chosen prior, or that such a placement is unusual. The leaf at the end of the temporale, fol. 138, contains twenty-two hexameters for specific feasts, including Corpus Christi (which is lacking from the temporale itself), Anne, and Thomas Becket ("Per Thomam Christe tibi placeat chorus iste / Mors Thome grata sit nobis vita beata").

The missal section is highly select, and interrupted by a separate quire (which may be out of place) containing the Office of the Dead and special commemorations of Peter and Etheldreda, the co-dedicatees of Ely. The sanctorale has only mass prayers for most saints, even some of those distinctive to Ely. A collect for Richard of Chichester (canonized 1262 but not widely included in monastic books) has been added at the end of the common of saints, just before the office-sanctorale begins. The ordinary and canon of the mass are included, though now much mutilated; it would have been possible for a prior to celebrate mass, using only this book (in its original state), on many occasions. Indeed, the book makes no sense except as a volume for the prior's use.

Another service book apparently written for the use of an abbot (or prior) is the Muchelney breviary, owned by J. Meade Falkner until 1932 and now BL Add. 43405 and 43406. It was known to Tolhurst when in Falkner's possession and used for textual variants from the Hyde breviary. Tolhurst assigned no more specific date than "thirteenth century," but the splendidly detailed description in the relevant BL catalogue (probably by D. H. Turner) calls it "late" in that century.[86] It is a large book (250 x 170 mm) but generally free of decoration. The reason for supposing it an abbot's book is the extensive inclusion, both on blank original leaves and on leaves added, of notes and documents relating to the abbey, some annotated in the hand of the abbot from 1522–32. The catalogue description observes that between this book (counting the two volumes as one) and the Hyde volume "there are wide differences of content and arrangement," and that it "appears similarly to lack any close liturgical relationship" with the Winchcombe or Coldingham books. Such peculiarities as we can identify may therefore be of special usefulness.

The first volume contains the temporale, plus a few additions or insertions. The most interesting is the inserted leaf (fol. 20) that gives a *pica* – detailed schedule for all parts of the liturgy on a given day – for the

---

[86] *Cat. of Additions to the MSS, 1931–1935* (1967), 132–37.

third week in Advent, with an additional note that when the "ordinale de la pyca" was complete for the day, there should be sung "in conuentu" (dormitory rather than chapter house?) *memoriae* of Benedict, Peter (the main dedicatee), and Mary. The following page contains a list of the Advent O-antiphons, with a rare eighth (between the usual seven and the optional "O Thome didyme" for December 21st), "O celorum domine." The second volume, mostly taken up with the psalter and sanctorale, begins with the calendar.[87] This includes a quartet of saints distinctive to Somerset, Edwold (12 August), Decuman (30 August), Congar (27 November), and Athelwin (14 September).[88] The most striking thing about the calendar is the interest it shows in the Franciscans. The original hand has written entries for Francis, styled simply *confessoris*, at October 4th, and, most unusually in England, for "Sancti Antonii confessoris ordinis fratrum minorum" at June 13th: Anthony of Padua, canonized in 1232.[89] These are likely to have been honorific rather than realistic entries, but their presence is nonetheless noteworthy. (The calendar is not graded, save for great occasions being colored red or blue.)

To some degree, as we have seen, points of hagiographical distinctiveness can be identified for each religious house; the sanctorales, let alone the calendars, of no two are identical. But there are also, obviously, many points of textual identity where individual saints are not concerned. How useful are these? One widely used criterion for classification of sources is the responsories (or "responds") in the Office of the Dead. This test, applied by Tolhurst, showed three groups of monasteries: Ely, Worcester, and three others in one; Muchelney, Winchester Old Minster, and four others in a second; Hyde, Norwich, Evesham, Winchcombe, and four others in a third.[90] His comparison of the "monastic canticles" (those used at the third nocturn on Sundays and special occasions), however, showed several, entirely different groupings.[91] Another criterion is the groupings within the common of saints, where one might have expected a high degree of commonalty. This test, performed by Anselm Hughes in connection with the Wulfstan

---

[87] Printed in Wormald, *Eng. Ben. Kals*, II.91–103; and earlier, with somewhat rambling commentary, by J. A. Robinson, "An Essay on Somerset Mediaeval Calendars," in *Muchelney Memoranda*, ed. B. Schofield, Somerset Record Society 42 (1929), pp. 128–39; also issued, and paginated, separately.

[88] Alias Egelwine or Ethelwin, supposed eponymous founder of the small abbey at Athelney. In the original calendar he is listed after the Exaltation of the Cross and the martyrs Cornelius and Cyprian; but a 16th-cent. hand has inserted at the 18th, over an erasure, "Sancti Athelwyni confessoris aput athelney."

[89] In the 15th cent. entries were added for Peter Martyr and Dominic.

[90] Tolhurst, *Eng. Mon. Brevs*, p. 110.

[91] Ibid., pp. 182–84.

portiforium with twice as many witnesses as Tolhurst had used, shows a similar lack of uniformity.[92] Nor is there stability in the textual groupings. Often the Muchelney book will have a unique reading, especially in a place where it seems of little intrinsic importance (and is for that reason likely to be significant): at the antiphon for none in the common of apostles, for example, where all other witnesses have "In patientia vestra" Muchelney has "Beati qui persecutionem." Other houses, perhaps especially Worcester, have similar uniquenesses. It is tempting to suppose that each such uniqueness has some bearing on the larger story but difficult-to-impossible to ascertain what that might be.

Even more than with mass texts, those used in the office show such an enormous amount of variation, much of it quite tiny, that it seems impossible within the limits of human comprehension (if not necessarily that of computer programs of gigantic subtlety) to draw up tidy lines of filiation, let alone anything like a convincing stemma. As Benedictine abbeys remain largely independent even after 1215, while retaining a common framework of adherence to the Rule, so the liturgy used in them continues to show a good deal of variation from house to house – and not just in the saints included – even after the Chapters General start to legislate in an overall way about liturgical matters. This is true not only of the thirteenth- and early fourteenth-century office book evidence we have latterly been considering, but also, as we shall now see, of such cardinal witnesses for liturgy in the later middle ages as the great missals of Westminster and Sherborne: books of immense individuality as well as of staggering sumptuousness.

Westminster abbey and the Westminster (or Lytlington) missal

The obvious starting point for our consideration of liturgy at Westminster abbey is introduced succinctly by J. W. Legg in the brief preface to his edition of its famous missal, published in three HBS volumes between 1891 and 1897 and so often referred to in these pages (see especially p. 234 for further discussion of the edition): "The first liturgical book named in the inventory of the vestry of Westminster Abbey, that was made in 1388, is 'unum bonum missale et grande ex dono quondam Nicholai Lytlington abbatis'."[93] A later inventory shows that it was still there about 1540, as the monastic foundation was being

---

[92] *Wulstan Portiforium*, II.x–xxv.
[93] *Westminster Missal*, I.v. The three volumes of the edition are mostly columnated, not paginated, except for III.1385–1731; the brief prefatory material to each volume has Roman pagination.

dissolved. The arms of Nicholas Lytlington, who was abbot from 1362 to 1386, appear several times, and details of the calendar as well as in the book's contents make plain that it was designed for the high altar at the abbey.

Not necessarily for *use* at the high altar, however, for as a single codex (it is now divided into two volumes, each of which is more comfortably carried by two persons than by one) it was enormously bulky, with pages sometimes stiff with decoration. Each of the many illuminations is enumerated by Lucy Freeman Sandler, whose description also includes details from the Abbot's Treasurer's roll of 1383–84 as to the very considerable payments made for materials, for the decoration (unfortunately none of the artists involved is named), and for the scribe – a layman, Thomas Preston, who lived at the abbey during the two years it took him to write the book.[94]

Lytlington, a member of the Despenser family, was something of a grandee, and part of our task, if we are to be able to use his missal at all as a way into the liturgy of the monks of Westminster, is to ignore the splendor of the book and the self-image of its eponymous abbot.[95] We have also, in accordance with our self-denying ordinance about pontifical liturgies, to ignore the coronation rite that takes up the central section (fols 205–23) of the book; the abbey was understood to be the coronation church unless special circumstances prevented this. The other main "pontifical" component will, however, require notice: an extensive benedictional containing the blessings at the time of communion pronounced by bishops and mitred abbots.[96] This section is

---

[94] Sandler, *Gothic MSS*, no. 150, the fullest description the manuscript has received in print. (There is a complete collation by Douglas East in a binder at the Abbey's Library.) The relevant section of the Treasurer's Roll is reproduced in the catalogue of the 1987 Royal Academy exhibition, *Age of Chivalry: Art in Plantagenet England 1200–1400*, ed. J. J. G. Alexander and P. Binski, p. 519. The musical notation was written by a specialist at the cost of an extra four shillings. In all, the expenses recorded come to some £32 16s; the sacrist's accounts note that in 1354–55 a missal made for the high altar cost, all in, £11 3s (Westm. Abbey Muniment 19623: information from Barbara Harvey, whose help has greatly strengthened the present section).

[95] His initials and coat of arms are sprinkled liberally throughout the book. B. Harvey, *Living and Dying in Medieval England* (Oxford 1993), p. 73, notes Lytlington's gift of twenty-four trenchers and twelve salt-cellars, each marked with his initials and the Despenser coronet, for the room in which some monks, in some circumstances, might eat meat.

[96] The last ten folios, 333–42 (*WM*, III.1187–1216), contain forms for the profession of monks, profession of nuns, blessing of widows, and veiling of women; did the abbot of Westminster preside also at the last three kinds of services, all for women only? This grand book could scarcely have been taken to the small nunnery at Kilburn, in some way dependent on the abbey, for such services; in any case, Kilburn had only five nuns in 1381: *Med. Rel. Houses*, p. 259.

useful to us in two ways: first, because it has (as including the blessings for the day) somewhat complete *ordines* for the great occasions of
Ash Wednesday, Maundy Thursday, Good Friday, the Easter Vigil, and
Candlemas; secondly, because the blessings for individual saints' feasts
give a good indication as to which of those was regarded as specially
important. The latter point leads us to consider certain aspects of the
Westminster sanctorale as it had developed by the time of the missal, to
which we shall eventually return.

Aside from the missal, only two books relevant here survive: a psalter
of c. 1200, celebrated for its illustration (now BL Royal 2 A.xxii), and
an abbatial pontifical of the early fourteenth century (now Bodl. Rawl.
C.425), both noticed briefly later.[97] Little information survives as to the
overall supply of service books, which must have been ample. The 1388
document mentioned above, despite being titled "An Inventory of the
Vestry," is overwhelmingly devoted to the ornaments of the altar and
its ministers, and specially to the magnificent pontificalia – mitres, cro-
ziers, and the like – for the use of the abbot.[98] Under the heading "De
Missalibus et aliis libris," it specifies only seventeen books: five missals;
one each of epistle and gospel books for daily use at the high altar (presumably undecorated); two pontificals ("benedictionales cum corona-
cione regum"); two collectars, one of them given by Lytlington; two
psalters, one of them apparently the Royal 2 A.xxii book just mentioned
and the other, *cum apocalipsi*, given by Henry III; a book for the blessing
of water at the beginning of the Sunday high mass (this must have been
a fairly utilitarian book, for it is kept in the custody of the four servants,
servientes, of the church); one for the blessing of the Paschal Candle and
other parts of the Easter Vigil; and two containing the lessons for that
service and for the Vigil of Pentecost. The next section gives details

---

[97] There is also a tiny (about 95 x 65 mm) miscellany of liturgical forms of the late
15th cent., now Bodl. Rawl. liturg. g.10. Legg printed the entire contents (*WM*,
III.1303–84) save, inexplicably, for the calendar. Fortunately, the latter was printed
by Wormald, but it is puzzling that he chose this as the base MS in his presentation
of Westminster calendars (*Eng. Ben. Kals*, II.57–74), collating the psalter as MS A
and the missal as B. It contains also a full litany of saints, commemorations including one for Edward the Confessor not likely to be found elsewhere, an extensive
series of *preces* for prime, a fairly full form for compline, and brief devotions, either
supplementary to or as a substitute for presence at the other daily offices. Its diminu-
tive size and correspondingly tiny handwriting mean that it is likeliest to have been
meant as a private liturgical vade mecum (perhaps, as Barbara Harvey has suggested
to me, for the use of a travelling obedientiary) rather than for use in formal worship
at the abbey.

[98] J. W. Legg, ed. "On an Inventory of the Vestry in Westminster Abbey, taken in 1388,"
Archaeologia 52 (1890), pp. 195–286, the service books at 233–35. Perhaps it was
because Legg was already at work on his edition of the missal that he devotes none of
his commentary to the books.

of a number of gospel books (*textus*), six of them particularly precious (though the sixth had been despoiled of its ornament by a thief, who seems to have left the book itself behind – a notable early example of book vandalism). There must have been many more than this small number of books, considering the size of the chapter – around fifty monks seems to have been the norm at that time – and the number of altars there must have been in that very large, if incomplete, church.[99]

Saints and abbots at Westminster

The psalter is, like the missal, famous for its illustration, but its interest for us lies mainly in its calendar, apparently the earliest for that house.[100] The calendar shows the expected magnification of Edward the Confessor, who was regarded as the house's (re)founder and had been canonized in 1161. Somewhat unexpected is the high grading, twelve lessons, for Milburga (23 February), while noteworthy but perhaps explainable is the appearance (21 April), also with twelve lessons, of Æthelwald, the eighth-century bishop of Lindisfarne whose body had supposedly been translated to Westminster at the instigation of King Edgar.[101] Another tenth-century translation included is that of Aldhelm, 5 May (by Dunstan, in 986, but not to Westminster), though at three lessons; his main feast, 23 May, is *in albis*. A curious connection with the city of London and its cathedral (see p. 491) is the appearance of Genesius, at three lessons, on 25 August. All four of these notably appearing saints provide succinct points of continuity, for they remain in the calendars of the missal and the Rawl. liturg. g.10 miscellany (the Rawl. C.425 pontifical has no calendar), with only a couple of alterations in grading.

Two instances of inflation in grading enable us to ascertain something about one of the ways liturgical change happened in a major

---

[99] Not included in this inventory are books in the Lady Chapel and in the Infirmary (St Katherine's) Chapel. Accounts for the latter show that in 1386–87 a missal was made at a cost of £4 0s 7d, probably as a benefaction from Lytlington, who in the same year paid twelve shillings to have its breviary rebound (Abbey Muniments 19370, information again from Barbara Harvey).

[100] The psalter's art-historical importance is shown by the extensiveness of the bibliography in Morgan, *Early Gothic MSS*, no. 2. Its calendar is printed in *Westminster Missal*, III.1385–96.

[101] The sole authority for this seems to be the *History of Westminster Abbey* compiled c. 1450 by John Flete, monk there; ed. J. A. Robinson (Cambridge 1909), p. 71. This is puzzling, because Æthelwald's remains are also reported to have been present along with Cuthbert's when the latter's coffin was opened at Durham in 1104: Symeon of Durham, *Capitula de miraculis et translationibus sancti Cuthberti*, ed. T. Arnold, *Symeoni Opera*, 2 vols, RS (1882–85), I.229–61.

religious house. The abbot during the time that the Westminster psalter is likeliest to have been made was Ralph Arundel, in office from late 1200 until he was deposed for high-handedness in 1214. His immediately preceding position was as prior of the small dependent cell at Hurley, but there is some reason to connect him with the monk of Christ Church of that name who had been something of a stormy petrel in the cathedral priory during the early years of the Becket controversy.[102] In an episode of some conflict with the monks of Westminster over control of certain manors, one of the points of negotiation was the request that the number of feasts magnified by the use of copes and processions (and consequently wine and special food at dinner) should be increased by those of Laurence, Vincent, Nicholas, and the Translation of Benedict.[103] Why these four, listed in the relevant charter in that order but respectively on 10 August, 22 January, 6 December, and 11 July, were chosen is not clear, but all are duly marked *in cappis* in the psalter's calendar. The abbot got control of the manors, the monks the enhanced-status feasts and concomitant fare.

A similar innovation was introduced by Ralph's successor, William de Humes (or de Hommet), formerly a monk of Caen and then prior of its alien cell at Frampton in Dorset. Given this background, it is hard to comprehend why he should have promoted the keeping of the Translation of Edmund the Martyr (i.e., of Bury St Edmunds) on April 29th, and as a major feast, with the special distinction of five copes.[104] So it remains in the calendar of Lytlington's missal, whereas the February 22nd feast of Chair of Peter, the abbey's dedicatee saint, has only four copes – an invidiousness that seems to have irritated Lytlington, for the final item in Flete's notice of him states that with the unanimous consent of the entire chapter the Cathedra Petri feast should henceforth be marked by five copes.[105] Edmund's main, November 20th, feast gets five copes as well, a distinction shared by only the Epiphany, three Marian feasts (Purification, Annunciation, and Nativity), John

---

[102] E. Mason, *Westminster Abbey and its People* c. 1050–c. 1216 (Woodbridge 1996), pp. 72–73, leans in favor of the identification, the chief obstacle to which is that abbot Ralph did not die until 1223.

[103] E. Mason and J. Bray, ed. *Westminster Abbey Charters 1066–c. 1214*, London Record Soc. 25 (1988), no. 345. The key manor was Benfleet, the income from which provided frequent, sometimes daily, pittances amounting to as much as an extra course (information from Barbara Harvey).

[104] Flete's *History of Westminster*, p. 102. Mason, *Westm. Abbey and its People*, p. 79, slips here, understandably, in stating that it was the Translation of Edward rather than Edmund, but refers usefully to a confraternity agreement between Westminster and Bury based on the mutual martyrdoms and kinship of their royal patrons.

[105] Flete, p. 137. As the missal is datable to c. 1385, this is likely to have been done in the last year of Lytlington's reign, 1386.

the Baptist, and the Feast of Relics.[106] These examples give some idea as to how inflation of sanctorale feasts occurs – more a matter of accrual than of a tidy and fixed set of observances, such as is suggested by a customary. Nonetheless, the one (partly) extant customary has to be taken into account.

The abbacy of Richard (of) Ware, 1258–83, saw the compilation of a Westminster customary, part of which survives, though in a highly imperfect and fragile state, as BL Cotton Otho C.xi, the manuscript itself being somewhat later than Ware's time.[107] As with most customaries (see p. 203 above), there is only indirect liturgical information, and what look from the original table of contents to be sections of the greatest interest to us appear to have been burnt indecipherable. Of what survives, three sections are of particular use. The first is those that specify the eight greatest and twenty-five slightly less great feasts on which pittances (extra dishes, "normally of superior quality," in Barbara Harvey's phrase) were allowed.[108] These generally correspond with the developments sketched above. A second comes in the description of the liturgical obligations of the gardener (*gardinarius*), where there are references to processions held *more antiquo* and to provisions about mass attendance at certain times that are being tightened from what they were *ex antiqua consuetudine*.[109] A similar distinction is implied in the third, a lengthy section about measures to be taken when certain problems occur during mass, above all with the consecrated bread and wine: specifically, what is to be done in case they are spilled, where a distinction is posited between *mos antiquitus* – that the minute an accident happens with the sacred species the board is struck and the whole convent summoned – and *usus modernus*, according to

---

[106] The only higher grade at Westminster was eight copes, used at Christmas, the Deposition and Translation feasts of Edward the Confessor, Peter and Paul, the Assumption, and All Saints. The Annunciation received the five-cope grading in the abbacy of Richard of Barking, 1222–46: Flete, p. 109.

[107] E. M. Thompson, ed. *Customary of the Benedictine Monasteries of Saint Augustine, Canterbury, and Saint Peter, Westminster*, 2 vols, HBS 23 (1902) and 28 (1904); that for Westminster is in vol. II, with a plate that shows how badly the MS was damaged in the 1731 Cottonian fire. The complete customary *may* be reflected in that for St Augustine's, the sole MS of which survives in a slightly better state in BL Cotton Faustina C.xii, probably written in the 1330s; see Thompson's explanation in the preface to vol. I. What is extant is so fraught with difficulties, however, that one must be cautious in trying to use it as hard evidence for Westminster.

[108] *Customary*, II.77–78; Harvey, *Living and Dying*, p. 10.

[109] *Customary*, II.90; B. Harvey, *The Obedientiaries of Westminster Abbey and their Financial Records c. 1275 to 1540*, Westminster Abbey Record Series 3 (Woodbridge 2002), p. xix, points out that the full range of obedientary positions is first recorded in Ware's customary.

which that practice is not followed.[110] The extensiveness, and date, of the liturgical changes implied in these cases seems to be not now ascertainable.

One big change that is both datable and dealt with in Ware's customary (cap. xii) has to do with completion of the abbey's Lady Chapel in 1245 (the old Chapel, of course, taken down in 1502 to allow the building of that of Henry VII).[111] The warden (*custos*) of the Chapel is an important obedientiary from the outset, and subsequently elaboration of services, equipment, and endowment-income seem to have proceeded apace. This is most notable in the establishment, at the end of the fourteenth century, of a professional choir for the Lady Chapel: six paid singing men and a master of the choir, as well as boys, the latter more likely from the abbey's almonry school than of oblate status.[112] The musical implications of this are considerable; here we can notice only the likelihood that the daily votive antiphon of the Virgin (the *Salve Regina* or seasonal alternatives) after compline may have come to be sung not in choir but in the Lady Chapel, with a probable increase in musical elaboration.[113]

Whether or not the decision to employ a paid master of the choir and singers was pushed mainly by Lytlington, it seems to have been taken in the last year or two of his abbacy, and is a grand gesture, made at the same time as his grand missal for the high altar was being finished. At Westminster all the tokens of grandeur – its building (that constructed under the sponsorship of Henry III, though completed in stages throughout the next four centuries), its royal patronage, its abbots, and its missal – seem of a piece. This may make it hard for us to connect the missal with the liturgical worship of a working Benedictine house: the thrust of the present chapter. Yet that is how our necessary reliance on the book, and on Legg's edition of it, directs us to try to use it.

---

[110] *Customary*, II.211–22, at 212. Provisions of this sort, usually termed *cautelae* ("cautions") of the mass, are often included in later missals: for example, *Sarum Missal (Dickinson)*, cols 651–56.

[111] *Customary*, II.91–93; B. Harvey, "The Monks of Westminster and the Old Lady Chapel," in *Westminster Abbey: the Lady Chapel of Henry VII*, ed. T. Tatton-Brown and R. Mortimer (Woodbridge 2003), pp. 5–31; she distinguishes this from the "old" Lady altar in a chapel outside the north transept façade and also from the more popular Lady altar in the nave.

[112] R. Bowers, "The Almonry Schools of the English Monasteries," in *Monasteries and Society in Medieval Britain*, ed. B. Thompson, Harlaxton Medieval Studies, n.s. 6 (Stamford 1999), pp. 177–222, at 208–9.

[113] Harvey, "Old Lady Chapel," p. 19. For the Marian antiphon's becoming a "public devotion" with the Dominicans, see p. 319.

The Westminster missal again: Legg's use of it

The way in which J. W. Legg's brave approach to the textual history of English medieval rites takes this missal as a kind of base manuscript has been discussed in the "Excursus on method in the comparison of liturgical texts" above (p. 141). For our present purposes, we have to turn Legg's method around and think about what may be specifically applicable to liturgy at Westminster (to its mass liturgy only, since there is next to no useful information about the daily office at the abbey). For example, in discussing sequences, a component of the mass liturgy in which there is commonly a great deal of variety, he singles out two, one for Peter's Chair and one for the Common of Several Apostles, as apparently unique to Westminster, and extrapolates, in something of a throw-away remark, "Doubtless some Westminster monk with a knack for making Latin verses was allowed to exercise his talent for the more popular festivals."[114] Curiosity is aroused by the words "some monk" and "was allowed": what can lie behind them? Both these sequences are indeed noteworthy. The mass for Peter's Chair had, as Legg further points out, a sequence only at Westminster; perhaps mercifully, he spares details of how excruciatingly bad it is.[115] Given the importance of the feast at Westminster, this may suggest composition by someone whose efforts, risible though they may have been, could not be refused: an abbot, perhaps? The other unique sequence, beginning "Hodie lux diei recolit athletas dei petrum paulum pariter," is entirely concerned with those two apostles, although there is in the sanctorale a proper sequence for the specific feast of each, but no sequence for the feasts of Philip and James or of Simon and Jude, the two occasions for which the common-of-saints category of *plurimorum apostolorum* makes sense. In effect, this sequence is useless. This somewhat trivial detail should warn us yet again against assuming that everything in a service book, even (or particularly?) in such a splendid and laborious book as this missal, can be made sense of.

For the most part, however, we must assume that the contents of the missal, no matter how splendidly laid out, stand in close relationship to what happened in the high masses (at least) at the abbey. To some extent this can be checked, by comparing the abbatial pontifical referred to earlier (Bodl. Rawl. liturg. C.425) with the missal for the

---

[114] *WM*, III.1413; Legg continues, "He has hardly, however risen above the level of mediaeval sequences in any case."

[115] *WM*, II.771. One excerpt illustrates its quality sufficiently: "Antiochenam fundat ecclesiam. / Et quam federat fraterno sanguine. / Romulus urbi collocato nomine. / Intulit rome crucis uictoriam."

important liturgies of Candlemas, Ash Wednesday, and the *Triduum sacrum*: services which, because of the presidency (actual or potential) of a bishop or mitred abbot, often appear in pontificals.[116] At the Easter Vigil the Westminster ceremony for kindling the New Fire and lighting the Paschal Candle concludes, after the singing of the *Inventor rutili* hymn, with an antiphon "Sicut exaltatus est serpens in heremo": a feature unique among Legg's eight comparanda. This is apparently a bit of imaginative liturgical practice, used at the abbey since at least the early fourteenth century, as its presence in the Rawlinson pontifical as well as in the missal indicates. This provides both a tantalizing glimpse of one of the great liturgies of the year and something of a dead end; we wonder what significance can be attached to it. Unlike the slight matter of the two unique sequences mentioned above (one of them unlikely to have been used, the other probably difficult to sing through while maintaining a straight face), this Vigil antiphon represents either a noteworthy decision or a baffling clue about whatever (lost) model this service at Westminster drew from.

One possibility is that it is an expression of a somewhat heightened liturgical sensibility centering on the most solemn seasons in ways that may be distinctive to Westminster. This is hinted at in the missal by the curious particoloring of the headings for collect, epistle, tract, and gospel for Passion Sunday, written in alternate red and blue letters rather than the consistent red of other headings (fol. 66v). And on the same day there is an unusual rubric at the communion chant: "Data pace hac die sacerdos incipiat communionem, *Hoc corpus quod pro uobis tradetur*" which is then taken up by the other ministers at the altar, "Hic calix novi testamenti," and so on. There is no mention of the choir, and no notation in this part of the book (fol. 67). The Passion Sunday mass is not relevant to the pontifical, but in general the rubrics there for Ash Wednesday and the *Triduum sacrum* are more substantial than those in the benedictional section of the missal. Both witness amply to the splendor and complexity of those high holy-day services, the pontifical corroborating, so to speak, the missal.

There is something of a tension between, on the one hand, using this missal as in some sense "typical" (in part simply because no other mass-book has had devoted to it the attention that Legg gave to this one) and,

---

[116] Legg's edition prints these services by collation with those in the missal. Note also his useful comparative tables of certain forms on those select occasions: "Of the Lessons, Tracts, and Collects of Easter Even, ... [and] Whitsun Eve, of the Forms used at the Blessing of the Palms, of the Service of Easter Even, of the Blessing of the Candles on the Feast of the Purification": *WM*, III.1414, 1416, 1427, 1429, and 1431 respectively.

on the other, regarding the uniqueness of Westminster as somehow more unique (despite the linguistic solecism) than that of any other religious house. The survival of the magnificent missal at its place of origin, and the use (of whatever kind) it actually got there for over a century and a half, have no parallel elsewhere. And we might remind ourselves that the years in which the book was being designed and made were highly charged politically: between the so-called Peasants' Revolt of 1381 and the ugly politics of the Lords Appellant-Merciless Parliament crisis in 1387–88 (many of the crucial episodes of which took place in the abbey precincts). These years were chronicled by a monk or, more likely, two monks from the abbey in an almost contemporary account that covers the period 1381–94. The chronicle records that Richard II participated in the procession, mass, and vespers at the abbey on the feast of Peter's Chair (22 February 1388: was the particularly silly sequence, discussed above, sung?) – two days after the condemnation by parliament and execution of Sir Nicholas Brembre, one of the hated royal favorites.[117] The Westminster missal would almost certainly have been on the high altar on that occasion.

There is something daunting about a masterpiece of bookmaking like the Westminster missal in itself, quite apart from its context(s). The same daunting quality adheres to a book of even greater decorative splendor, the Sherborne missal. The contexts of its creation and its location are of what might be termed a lower voltage than those at Westminster; and it may seem therefore a more useful case with which to conclude this chapter. Nonetheless, once we have looked at it, it will be hard to avoid alternately shaking our heads in amazement and scratching them in bewilderment.

The Sherborne missal

Sherborne abbey has come already under our notice (p. 176), in connection with its mid-twelfth-century cartulary which contains valuable liturgical information for that period. By the later fourteenth century it seems to have been an abbey of medium size in terms of both numbers (probably fifteen to twenty; the complement when it reached abbatial status in 1122 had been fifty) and income, which just before the Dissolution was less than a fifth of that of Westminster. In these circumstances it becomes all the more astonishing that, probably between 1396 and 1406, there should have been commissioned, and illustrated by a

[117] *The Westminster Chronicle 1381–1394*, ed. and trans. L. C. Hector and B. Harvey, OMT (1982), p. 314.

prominent artist, the missal (now BL Add. 74326) that, in Kathleen Scott's words, is "the unrivalled masterpiece of English book production in the fifteenth century."[118] Scott's, the most detailed description of the illustrations in print, treats most of the 632 "illustrative formats" (her phrase), but not the "possibly several thousand images connected with borders." Given this literally indescribable riot of decoration, it is particularly useful that there is a splendidly illustrated and highly accessible "popular," but thoroughly scholarly, monograph by Janet Backhouse, published three years after Scott's description.[119]

The missal's size is, like that of the comparable Westminster missal, almost overwhelming, some 535 by about 380 mm at present (and cropped at that); one stands to study it out of necessity as well as reverence.[120] Its immediate fortunes after the Dissolution are not clear, but it was in France from at least 1703 to 1797, then (by 1800) in the possession of the Duke of Northumberland, who kept it at Alnwick Castle until 1983, when Trustees of the then Duke placed it on indefinite loan (Loan MS 82) at the British Library; in 1998 the Library bought it. These details are necessary to underline the point that the book was not available for protracted "public" study until it arrived at the British Library. Indeed, it has still not been treated as have many other precious manuscripts: it has not even been filmed in its entirety (because, apparently, of its size as well as rarity), let alone edited. So we can be grateful that the one scholar who has treated it textually is the indispensable J. W. Legg, who was able to study it for a brief time at Alnwick in October of 1895 and who shortly thereafter published a curt set of "liturgical notes" on it, as well as its calendar and sequences (and a few other texts) from a select group of masses.[121] His time with the book also enabled him to include the siglum "Sherb." in the textual apparatus, so often referred to in these pages, in the final volume of his Westminster missal edition, 1897. This makes it possible to get at some of the prayer- (and, to a lesser extent, chant-) texts in the Sherborne missal, though

---

[118] Scott, *Later Gothic MSS*, no. 9 (pp. 45–67 and ills. 44–56, plus colored pl. I).

[119] J. Backhouse, *The Sherborne Missal* (London 1999); almost all of the 68 illustrations are in color, many of them full-page (though of necessity much smaller than the gigantic pages of the MS). Before that was published art-historical students had to rely on the selected illustrations in a Roxburghe Club facsimile, *The Sherborne Missal*, edited by J. A. Herbert (Oxford 1920).

[120] I am specially grateful to have been permitted to stand at it for some time, through the courtesy of Michelle Brown (then at the BL), with Janet Backhouse occasionally peering around my shoulder.

[121] J. W. Legg, "Liturgical Notes on the Sherborne Missal," *Trans. St Paul's Ecclesiological Soc.* 4.ii (1896), pp. 1–31. Note that then, and ever since, the MS has been paginated, not foliated.

only by comparison with, and only for masses contained in, the West-minster book. (There is no other liturgical evidence for Sherborne later than that in the mid-twelfth-century cartulary discussed above.)

A rare and noteworthy aspect of this book is that we know the name not only of the main scribe, as with Westminster, but also that of the artist who seems to have been responsible for the majority of the dec-oration: John Siferwas, somewhat improbably a Dominican friar (so he is depicted three times in the missal) whose work appears in two other fine manuscripts, both associated with southwest England.[122] The scribe, named in four colophons, was Jo[h]n Whas, most likely a monk of the house (he signs himself as *monachus* on page 352). The other two individual people identifiable, indeed prominent, in the manuscript are Richard Whitford, bishop of Salisbury (the diocese in which Sherborne lay) 1396–1407 – hence the date-frame suggested above – and, repre-sented at least sixteen times, either heraldically or by a "portrait" mini-ature, Robert Bruning, abbot 1385–1415.[123]

Hagiographical peculiarities at Sherborne

These personal and historical facts can serve to focus our attention on the task of seeing what light this book may shed on liturgy in an English Black Monk house in the later middle ages. The most obvious question may be to what extent this missal may have resembled others designed for steady use (as this one is clearly not; it is for only the most spe-cial occasions, if any), specifically at Sherborne. It is highly likely that any other such books would have contained masses for the abbey's two most distinctive saints: Wulsin, the founder-figure (above, p. 176), both his Deposition on January 8th and his Translation on April 28th; and, less comprehensibly, Juthwara, a British virgin-martyr (supposedly the sister of St Sativola or Sidwell of Exeter), whose relics arrived in Sher-borne in the bishopric of Ælfwold II, 1045–58, on July 13th. Among the less distinctive saints, one striking point is that when there is some disagreement between calendar and sanctorale, which is itself quite

---

[122] One is the now fragmentary Lovel lectionary (BL Harley 7026), made c. 1408, prob-ably for Glastonbury: Scott, *Later Gothic MSS*, no. 10. For a full study of the artist, see T. S. Tolley, "John Siferwas: the Study of an English Dominican Illuminator," Ph.D. diss., Univ. of East Anglia, 2 vols (1984). To complement his art-historical analysis, he uses the presence or absence of certain saints' feasts to establish an out-side dating frame "for the written contents" of 1386–1415 (I.108).

[123] He was succeeded as abbot by John Bruning, probably his brother, 1415–36; Robert seems to have died just before a ferocious quarrel with the townspeople that left the abbey church heavily damaged by fire (see p. 241). The vowels in the surname are rendered in several ways, often as *y*.

common, it is most often the sanctorale that is fuller; this is extremely uncommon. Ansbert of Rouen, for example, is missing from the calendar but has a mass in the sanctorale at the appropriate place for his February 9th feast day. Other examples include Sexburga (6 July), Hedda (of Winchester; 7 July), Pantaleon (28 July), and the Sherborne Feast of Relics (27 September).[124] The most unusual saint included may be Mamertus of Vienne, in both calendar (11 May) and sanctorale, and the most unusual calendarial styling is that for Michael's May 8th feast, here called *Adventus sancti Michaelis* (generally *in Monte Gargano*).[125] At October 8th in the calendar and the comparable place in the sanctorale there is a very odd coupling, of Demetrius, the great Greek military saint (here styled a bishop-martyr and in the miniature at the head of his mass depicted as, in Scott's characterization, an academic) and Iwi, the seventh-century disciple of Cuthbert whose remains came to be cherished at Wilton nunnery.[126]

Cuthburga, who turns out to be a significant saint in Sarum tradition (see p. 381), is nowhere found here even though the location of her cult center was at Wimborne Minster, just twenty or so miles away and in the same diocese. In fact, elements that point to Salisbury and its bishop seem to be played down, possibly as an expression of what Backhouse calls "the abbey's refusal to be regarded as forever inferior to the bishopric whose centre it once had been."[127] This may be the reason also that Aldhelm, who also becomes, rather unexpectedly, a key Sarum saint, is somewhat downplayed here, despite his having been the first bishop of Sherborne; his main feast (25 May) is of twelve lessons rather than in albs or copes as might have been expected, and no notice is taken of either of his Translations, though both days (5 May and

---

[124] These details are all taken from personal inspection. In Scott's generally praiseworthy description there are many inaccuracies in the account of saints, some of them seriously misleading; e.g., Babillus is given as Bathild (who appears in her proper place on p. 412), Felix *in pincis* (here depicted with a sensitive face) is conjectured to be "?Felice (or ?Felicity), as young woman, with fiery vessel," and Matthias is given as Matthew (the latter also in his proper place, p. 553).

[125] Both feasts of Michael (8 May as well as 29 Sept.) are among the occasions on which the Creed is used at mass (p. 360). Is this a reflection of the indulgence granted by Boniface IX in 1401 for visiting the abbey on the Annunciation or the feast (unspecified) of Michael, or the Sunday following it (VCH *Dorset*, II.66, citing *Cal. Papal Letters*, V.406)?

[126] We have seen above (p. 214) that Demetrius had some popularity in Worcester as far back as the Wulfstan portiforium. Curiously, there is a bishop Demetrius whose Coptic feast day is 8 or 9 Oct.: the patriarch of Alexandria who died, not a martyr, in 231.

[127] Backhouse, p. 45. As we saw earlier (p. 177), it was in connection with the abbey's successful resistance to encroachment by a 12th-cent. bishop of Sarum that the Sherborne cartulary seems to have been compiled.

3 October) are vacant in the calendar (his cult was the most intense at Malmesbury, where he was the first abbot).

By contrast the number and importance of Winchester-related feasts is striking: Swithun, Æthelwold, Birinus, Grimbald, Bertin, Hedda. This is most conspicuous in the presence of the very rare Ordination feast for Swithun (30 September) as well as those of his Deposition (in copes, with octave) and Translation (in albs). This may possibly be an important indication of continuity with Anglo-Saxon tradition as well – tradition reflected also in the mass for the Conception of John the Baptist, extremely rare by the early fifteenth century, and in that for the Oblation of the Virgin, under that title rather than Presentation. It seems likely that the *Vita* and *Miracula Sancti Swithuni* were composed, perhaps by the hagiographer Goscelin (see p. 117 above) during his stay at Sherborne.[128] Several of those miracles take place at a statue of Swithun set up in the (then) cathedral church at the instigation of Bishop Ælfwold (II) some time between 1045 and 1058, and there is reason to think that the image might still have been at the abbey at the Dissolution.[129]

Mass at Sherborne

After the rich, slightly exotic, hagiographical tradition evident in the missal, it is something of a relief to turn to the actual celebration of mass at – presumably – Sherborne. For the ordinary-and-canon section the book contains what looks to be set of very small but detailed illustrations of a priest occupied in the most central part of the mass. These head the successive paragraphs of the canon: the priest is seen at various points bowing (*se inclinans*), lifting his hands in prayer, spreading or joining his hands, holding the chalice and apparently making the sign of the cross over it, holding up the paten, and apparently (this one is hard to make out) washing his hands.[130] Though it is not possible to ascertain an exact order of priestly gestures to match the progress of the canon, there seems to be something like a sequence. It is conceivable that the beautiful chasubles and sumptuous altar frontals represent something

---

[128] He wrote there a life of Wulsin, printed by C. H. Talbot in *Rev. Bén.* 69 (1959), pp. 68–85; cf. P. Grosjean in *Anal. Boll.* 78 (1960), pp. 197–206.

[129] M. Lapidge, *The Cult of St Swithun* (Oxford 2003), esp. pp. 680–81, and many other references to Sherborne. It is strange that he omits any notice of the Ordination mass in its missal.

[130] These are not listed by Scott, who describes only initials that occupy more than three lines of writing. The two of these miniatures on the *Te igitur* page, at the *In primis* and *Memento domine* sections, are easily visible in the full-color reproduction of that page as fig. 42 of Backhouse.

of an idealization, but given that the book was commissioned by an abbot, written by a monk, and decorated largely by a friar, there would seem to be a fair quotient of reality checks against excessively fanciful depictions. Nor may it be unduly fanciful for us to suppose that these tiny pictures (would that they could be more widely reproduced) complement this complete missal, made for what is still an almost complete medieval church (albeit considerably altered after the 1436 fire), to allow us to come closer to "seeing" a mass at Sherborne than at any other religious house.[131]

Indeed, the entire book is shot through with reminders of the abbey. Features like the representations of each of the (supposed) twenty-five bishops of Sherborne, from the first, Aldhelm, to Hereman under whom the see center was moved to (Old) Sarum, as well as the numerous depictions of Abbot Bruning and of the interior of a grand church: all seem meant to express, and evoke, pride in the abbey and its heritage. Yet – is this paradox or pathos? – Sherborne could not remotely pretend to the grandeur, in antiquity, aspiration, buildings, or revenues, of a Glastonbury, a St Albans, a St Augustine's. When the staggering illustrative features not relevant to our concerns are taken into account, above all the birds which are perhaps the greatest of all the book's glories, we may be left wondering whether the realm of serviceability, or even of reality, has been abandoned in an overwhelming desire for splendor.[132]

We may therefore be left with a sense not only of the great amount of liturgical variety that characterized the English Benedictines (an aspect stressed as we finished surveying some monastic office books above) but also of some uneasiness as to the relationship between the sumptuousness of the Sherborne missal and whatever impressions we have formed of the worshipping life of the Black Monks. This is said not with censorious frowning at such conspicuous use of resources – even if Siferwas, as a friar, was paid no more than a minimum wage and Whas, as a monk of the house, labored as part of his life according to the Rule, the cost of the materials must have been very considerable – but in mild bewilderment lest the splendor of such a book skew our understanding. Given the absence of what must have been a fair number of workaday service books at Sherborne, it seems an open question whether

---

[131] Particularly valuable in this respect is the eight-line initial C at Corpus Christi, containing a miniature of a layman (admittedly, a king) receiving a large host from the priest, a housel cloth being stretched under the paten and host by two acolytes (p. 279; Backhouse, fig. 28).

[132] Eight of these birds are shown in a double-page opening in Backhouse, figs 44–51, each a different and identifiable species; of the forty-four depicted throughout the book, all save three are labelled with their names – in English (p. 41).

the survival of this one, literally marvellous, volume helps or hinders us in our attempt to grasp the history of the liturgy among the religious houses of high and late medieval England.

Addendum: The "Burnt Breviary" of Christ Church, Canterbury

A very considerable frustration in any effort to get some idea of the office liturgy in Benedictine houses in the thirteenth through early sixteenth centuries is the existence of what would have been a prime witness had it not been rendered ruinous: a breviary from the cathedral priory at Canterbury dating from the second half of the fourteenth century. This is the so-called "Burnt breviary," badly damaged by a fire in, probably, 1674; now Canterbury Cathedral Add. 6. What survives, kept in two boxes, is most of roughly 360 folios, in a condition summarized by Neil Ker this way: "Throughout, the last twelve out of thirty-six lines are preserved on each page more or less completely. Many leaves … have more text than this, but they rise to a point, so that on the few leaves where some part of the original first line remains it is no more than two or three letters wide."[133] Perusal of these during World War II enabled a prebendary of the cathedral, C. S. Phillips, to make such a transcript as was possible of the remains – or rather, an abridgement of a transcript, cued to, and many damaged parts supplied from, Tolhurst's edition of the Hyde breviary.[134] Occasionally readings are clear enough that they can be cited with some confidence, especially with the collects (an example is on p. 121 above). As things stand, however, there are too few points at which Phillips's transcript presents a text that seems at once reliable and comprehensible for us to attempt to use it in the present work; to do so would risk compounding with hesitations and conjectures what is already complex enough.

---

[133] *MMBL*, II.303–5. He points out also that the book had suffered some damage before it was burned; numerous leaves of presumed artistic value have been removed, and the offices of Becket.

[134] Phillips's handwritten transcript of c. 1944 now forms MS Add. 6* in the Cathedral Library. Conclusions drawn from protracted study of the remains were laid out on pp. 18–26 of his substantial pamphlet, *Canterbury Cathedral in the Middle Ages* (London 1949). The next year Christopher Hohler studied the fragments somewhat and made a transcript of the calendar, also kept at the cathedral. It seems possible that, with modern technological aids, more could be made now of these fragments, and conceivable that something like a hypothetical edition could be constructed, perhaps for on-line publication.

7 Other monastic orders

Cluniacs

There is a marked disconnect between the period during which the ten or so important Cluniac foundations in England were established and dates of the seven manuscript sources from which we might hope to get some idea as to their corporate worship. In one sense this should not trouble us much; patterns laid down in the customaries of the great age of Cluny itself, the abbacies of Odilo 994–1049 and Hugh 1049–1109, were meant to be normative in all the houses connected to it.[1] In another, however, it is troubling that for the expression of Benedictine monasticism most celebrated for elaborate liturgical practice – the reputation, largely deserved, of the Cluniacs – we draw a blank among English sources until at least the third quarter of the thirteenth century.

The earliest of the ten English houses referred to above was Lewes, 1077, the latest Bro(o)mholm, 1113; the others are Much Wenlock, Castle Acre, Bermondsey, Montacute, Pontefract, Northampton, Lenton, and Thetford.[2] The most extensive ruins are those at Acre, Wenlock, and Lewes. One liturgical book survives each from Lewes and Wenlock, none from Acre. For Pontefract both a breviary and a missal are extant, though of widely different dates. The remaining witnesses are scattered in type, date, and place of origin.[3] The two we consider first are of a type not previously discussed.

---

[1] Details of these are laid out clearly in Noreen Hunt, *Cluny under Saint Hugh* 1049–1109 (London 1967), pp. 11–13, but this was before the modern editions of K. Hallinger, *Consuetudines Cluniacensium antiquiores cum redactionibus derivatis*, Corpus Consuetudinum Monasticarum 7/2 (Siegburg 1983) and P. Dinter, *Liber tramitis aeui Odilonis abbatis*, CCM 10 (1980).

[2] Data from *Med. Rel. Houses*, pp. 96–103; there were some thirty-six such foundations in all.

[3] There is unfortunately no warrant for trying to supplement the scanty information from these houses with anything from Reading, the great Benedictine abbey (re)-founded by Henry I in 1121, though its first abbot came from Lewes and it showed Cluniac influence early on. There is a similar, but even looser, connection with

Breviary-missals: priors' books?

These, the oldest books to be noticed, are a pair of combined breviary-missals, both rather splendid and probably designed for the use of a prior. The first was written, mostly in the third quarter of the thirteenth century, for Lewes. It seems to have remained in England through at least the early fourteenth century, when a calendar and litany were added, both with English saints. By the late sixteenth century it was in France, where it stayed, latterly in the collection of Georges Moreau, until 1934, when it was bought for the Fitzwilliam Museum in Cambridge, now its MS 369.[4] Disentangling the various parts of this now complicated codex seems to yield the following pertinent facts. First, the temporale is unusual in having the offices for its occasions followed immediately by their masses; this is not true of the sanctorale, for which there are no masses. Second, the sanctorale contains offices for English as well as Cluniac saints, the former including the usual Anglo-Saxon figures but also Milburga (the saint of Much Wenlock) and the thirteenth-century recognitions of Wulfstan (canonized 1203), Translation of Becket, Edmund of Abingdon and his Translation (1250), and Richard of Chichester, the date of the latter's canonization, 1262, providing a *terminus a quo*.[5] Third, though some of these figures are missing from the early fourteenth-century calendar, it is still overtly Cluniac and unmistakably for Lewes (Pancras, to whom the house was dedicated, and Richard, bishop-saint of the diocese in which it was located, are each in gold, with twelve lessons), but with a surprising prominence for Wulfstan (eight lessons, blue). Fourth, the litany at the end of the psalter, also early fourteenth-century, ranks Dunstan, Edmund, Richard, and Wulfstan above the abbot-confessors Odo, Maiolus, Odilo, and Hugh, promotes Martial to the status of apostle, and concludes the virgins with Mildred, just after Milburga. A possible inference to be drawn is that the book was made for a prior of Lewes who had previously been at Wenlock; this fits John de Thifford (or "of Avignon"), prior there 1272–85, before becoming prior of Lewes, 1285–98.[6]

Faversham, founded by King Stephen in 1149 and colonized from Bermondsey; an early 15th-cent. martyrology from there is Bodl. Jones 9.

[4] Just before being put up for sale it was studied by V. Leroquais in a brief monograph, *Le Bréviaire-Missel du prieuré de Lewes* (Paris 1935), with eight facsimile pages. After arriving in Cambridge it was described by P. Giles and F. Wormald, *Cat. of the Additional MSS in Fitzwilliam Museum* (Cambridge 1982), pp. 370–74 and pl. 10; they give references to the old foliation, used by Leroquais, as well as to the current one.

[5] There are also two obscure saints of Beauvais, Geremarus (24 Sept.) and Justus (18 Oct.); can this reflect influence of the second prior of Lewes, Eustace of Beauvais, 1107–20 (*Heads of Rel. Houses*, I.119)?

[6] *Heads of Rel. Houses*, II.241, 234. This may be the *breviarium* singled out, along with a cape and a palfrey, as among the goods of the recently deceased John "of Avignon"

The other breviary-missal, now BL Add. 49363 (formerly Holkham Hall MS 39), seems to have been written in the 1280s.[7] The anonymous cataloguer (probably D. H. Turner) has suggested that the book was written "possibly for use when travelling, perhaps by a superior of the jurisdiction of La Charité-sur-Loire in England"; but the presence of an office for the Invention of Milburga (fol. 249) points so strongly towards Much Wenlock that it seems more probably to have been made for a prior of that house, most likely Henry de Bonville or Bonvillars, 1285 to at least 1305, maybe as late as 1320.[8] His appointment (after a period of financial instability under his predecessor John, who had gone to Lewes) may reflect the influence of Sir Otto de Grandis(s)on, an influential advisor to Edward I, and the new prior is reported to have been in high favor with the king; such favor is congruous with the splendor of the book.[9] Its fifteen historiated initials included one, now cut out, for the Transfiguration, which the Cluniacs seem to have celebrated earlier and more steadily than any other religious group.[10]

A distinction shared by this book and the Lewes codex is that these two manuscripts are apparently the earliest English witnesses for the rhymed office for Thomas Becket. The words to be sung, and apparently also the music, seem to have been written by Benedict of Peterborough in the mid-1170s, and it is more likely a matter of the survival of manuscripts than of significance that this office should be first known in this pair of Cluniac books of roughly a century later.[11] Only the Lewes book is noted, however – and that in a style, as a modern

---

that have not been restored following his death, as Cluniac regulation demanded, in a document apparently dated June 13th, 1298, printed in the confused collection of G. F. Duckett, *Charters and Records among the Archives of the Ancient Abbey of Cluni[sic] from 1066 to 1534*, 2 vols (privately printed at Lewes, 1888), I.112–13, ostensibly from documents in the Bibliothèque Nationale. A point of added interest is that it had been in the possession of the cantor, Robert "de Novati."

[7] The dating is suggested by Morgan, *Early Gothic MSS*, II.15, on the basis of its decoration being "a later product of the group of artists who produced the Bible, Princeton, University Library, MS Garrett 28," and is adopted in the detailed description in the BL *Catalogue of Additions to the Manuscripts 1956–65* (London 2000), pp. 62–65.

[8] *Heads of Rel. Houses*, II.241 (Much Wenlock) and II.221 (Bermondsey, of which he had previouly been prior). Both houses had originally been founded from La Charité.

[9] Rose Graham, "The history of the alien priory of Wenlock," *Jnl. of Brit. Archaeol. Assn.*, 3rd series 4 (1939), repr. separately as a Dept of Environment Official Handbook, 1965, at p. 17. For another instance of Otto's influence see p. 399.

[10] Pfaff, *New Liturg. Feasts*, pp. 17–23. It had been made obligatory for all Cluniac houses in 1132.

[11] The folios (105–7) of Fitzwilliam 369 containing the Becket office are reproduced, at almost full size, in K. B. Slocum, *Liturgies in Honour of Thomas Becket* (Toronto 2004), pp. 129–33; she bases her edition of the office, with transcription of the chant in modern notation, on this MS.

musicologist points out, of unusual elaborateness.[12] This brings into question the presumption that such a book was written for the use of the prior: of what use is the provision of extensive notation for a choir office in a book apparently designed with a view to portability? David Hiley has suggested that, in view of its minute script, the Lewes volume might have been used "as a *correctorium*, when the prior of Lewes visited other English Cluniac houses."[13] But only six of the English houses had been founded by Lewes, four of them always very small, and in any case the Cluniacs had no prescribed pattern of annual visitation of daughter houses like that of the Cistercians. We might do well eventually to expand the question and ask how realistic the notion of a portable noted breviary is likely to be. Who is meant to sing what with, or to, whom? But not at the moment; we must turn instead to a pair of more workaday books, this time from the same establishment.

Office and mass at Pontefract

The only house for which more than one service book survives is Pontefract. The first is an early fourteenth-century breviary, now Oxford, University College 101.[14] It went from Pontefract (the dedication of which is on 16 April in the calendar) to Monk Bretton by at least the fifteenth century, perhaps earlier. The additions that occupy the first twenty-four folios were presumably made there; these include lessons for the Translation of Mary Magdalen (to whom Monk Bretton was dedicated), congruous with the addition of that feast at March 19th to the calendar.[15] How and why the book got to Monk Bretton is a puzzle, for although it had begun in the 1150s as a dependency of Pontefract, around 1279 it left the Cluniac family and became an independent Benedictine house. The original (Pontefract) book contains an office for Milburga, who is also in the litany. Its office for the Transfiguration is noteworthy in that it seems to contain some interesting alterations to the office composed for the feast by Peter the Venerable around 1130, including what may be the first appearance of a new hymn, "Deus manens primordium." It appears that there may have been among the monks of Pontefract one with a flair for liturgical composition.[16] (This

[12] S. Holder, "The noted Cluniac breviary-missal of Lewes," *Jnl. Plainsong and Med. Music Soc.* 8 (1985), pp. 25–32, at 30.

[13] D. Hiley, *Western Plainchant: a Handbook* (Oxford 1993), p. 322.

[14] Dated by van Dijk, *Handlist*, II.266 to c. 1299–1315, the reasons for this not being stated. The date assigned by Hughes, *MMMO*, p. 395, is merely 13th cent.; he prints much reduced facsimile pages of fols 35v–37 and 75v–81, pp. 312–17.

[15] What translation is this meant to be? March 19th is a day that is almost always vacant in English calendars.

[16] Details in Pfaff, *New Liturg. Feasts*, p. 20.

possibility might be tested by a critical edition of the office for Milburga as it appears here and in the Lewes and Wenlock books.)

The other *liturgicum* surviving from Pontefract is a missal, now Cambridge, King's College 31.[17] This dates from the fifteenth century, with a (slightly later?) canon apparently having replaced the original one, which had perhaps worn out. The calendar contains an obit (23 March) and on the previous day what is styled as a feast for "S. Thome martiris comitis lancastrie," Thomas earl of Lancaster, the king's cousin and great rebel (or hero) executed at Pontefract in 1322. It retains the emphasis of the breviary on Milburga, who, the calendar states, is to be celebrated with twelve lessons and in albs if her feast (23 February) does not fall in Lent; she is also the only English saint in the very brief litany (fol. 190, three saints to a category).

Other Cluniac books

Although the Lewes and Wenlock breviary-missals are handsomely produced books, neither could be called sumptuous: an adjective that can definitely be applied to the Bromholm psalter originally written about 1310, now Bodl. Ashmole 1523. Illustrated by the artist of the Ormesby psalter (Bodl. Douce 366) and a colleague, it was meant to be much grander than it now is, for only five of the historiated initials survive. All that was finished at the original writing was the first two-thirds of the book, including the calendar; in the mid-fifteenth century nearly a hundred folios were added, supplying most of the canticles, litany, and hymnal (selected feasts only) – in order, Lucy Freeman Sandler contends, "to complete an unfinished manuscript probably already in the possession of the priory."[18] Why this relatively small priory, usually numbering ten to twenty monks, should have had such a splendid book given to it remains unexplained.

Unlike luxury psalters, manuals are generally rather plain books; this is the case with CUL Add. 3060, a manual of c. 1400 from the priory of St Andrew in Northampton.[19] Its offices are largely devoted to the sick, dying, and dead. Notable here is the degree of reference to Sarum practice; for example, at the commendation of souls, that a particular

---

[17] M. R. James, in his 1895 catalogue of the college's MSS, miscalls it "Missale Eboracense," even while printing details from the calendar which show that it must have been used at Pontefract.

[18] Sandler, *Gothic MSS*, no. 44.

[19] Its dedication is entered in the calendar at 28 March, the Translation of Andrew (9 May) has an octave, and there is a special prayer for the soul of Simon (de Liz, the founder, 1093) on fol. 33v. There are also octaves for Vincent (why?) and the Purification.

commendation is said "in ecclesia Sarum" only if the body is present (fol. 81v); the services for visitation of the sick and burial of the dead are almost identical with those of Sarum use.[20] Though the book's calendar is purely Cluniac, albeit with some English saints (notably Milburga, Guthlac, Botulf, Kenelm), it is clearly compiled with direct awareness of the Sarum manual.

A similar awareness seems evident in the final Cluniac book to require at least passing notice, a martyrology made for Bermondsey around the middle of the fifteenth century, now Bodl. Rawl. A.371. It has some Sarum rubrics at the beginning (fol. 1) and at the end of the martyrology an imperfect copy (cap. 12–59, out of some 70) of the Sarum customary.[21] The creeping "Sarumization" implied is not surprising, especially because English Cluniac houses had to break their French connections in the later stages of the Hundred Years War. Despite the splendor of some of the Cluniac ruins, in England the liturgical footprint of this Benedictine offshoot does not seem to have been particularly large. This will not be the case with the next group we consider, the Cistercians.

Cistercians

The vexed problems of the earliest Cistercian history – in particular, the degree to which its (ostensibly) oldest documents witness to the order's famously tight structure of annual General Chapters and regular visitation by the heads of mother houses of each of their daughter establishments – need not detain us to any great degree. The traditional account distinguished four cardinal stages: at the years 1098, when Robert of Molesme founded the house at Cîteaux in Burgundy; 1109, when the Englishman Stephen Harding (d. 1134) became abbot; 1112, when Bernard entered the house (starting that at Clairvaux three years later); and 1119, when Pope Calixtus II confirmed some form of the constitutional document called the *Carta Caritatis*. All of these predate the first English foundation, at Waverley in Surrey in 1128. There followed quickly Tintern in the Wye valley, Rievaulx and Fountains in Yorkshire 1132, Garendon in Leicestershire 1133.[22] Eventually there

---

[20] There are also references that presuppose a non-monastic context: e.g., fol. 88 "duo clerici de secunda forma," fol. 98 "duo excellentiores persone in capis sericis."

[21] It is consequently described, very briefly, in Frere, *Use of Sarum* I.lviii, as well as in van Dijk's *Handlist*, II.200. For the peculiarity of its entry for the Transfiguration and its possible connection with the legend of the "Rood of Bermondsey" see Pfaff, *New Liturg. Feasts*, pp. 121–22.

[22] This does not include the early houses of the order of Savigny, formally merged into the Cistercians in 1147. Notable among these are Furness in Lancashire (1123/27),

were over seventy houses of the order in England, mostly before 1152, when proliferation was supposedly stopped, and many of them quite small.[23] The facts about the English foundations are solid even if Constance Hoffman Berman's drastically revisionist account of the earliest documents, published in 2000, should come to be widely accepted.[24] David Knowles's narrative of the story of the early Cistercians and their settlements in England ranks among the most splendid sections of his great *Monastic Order*; although much scholarship has been published since its second edition (1963), his remains the finest introduction to this distinctive story.[25]

The main point that must be noticed here for the period before the first English houses come into being is the insistence of the supposedly earliest documents on a simplification of the liturgy, and in particular of the chant, from the elaborations that much monastic worship had undergone in the later tenth and eleventh centuries.[26] Even taking into account challenges to received opinion mounted for over half a century, we cannot begin elsewhere than by noting the language of cap. iv of the *Carta Caritatis* and by supposing that this represents the regime under which the earliest Cistercians in England went about their fundamental task of worship:

And inasmuch as we receive in our cloister all the monks of their [i.e., the other Cistercian] houses who come to us, and they likewise receive ours in theirs, so it seems good to us and in accordance with our will that they should maintain

Stratford Langthorn in Essex and Buildwas in Shropshire (both 1135), Buckfast in Devon (1136), and Byland in North Yorkshire (1138). To the extent that they come under our notice, it will be in the present chapter. For useful summary notes on each of the English Cistercian (including former Savigniac) houses, see Peter Fergusson, *Architecture of Solitude: Cistercian Abbeys in Twelfth-Century England* (Princeton 1984). Other statistics, including those for post-12th-cent. foundations, in *Med. Rel. Houses*, pp. 110–32 and (for Cistercian nuns) 271–77.

[23] A splendid resource on the English Cistercian houses in general, and specially on those in Yorkshire, is the electronic project sponsored by the University of Sheffield at http://cistercians.shef.ac.uk.

[24] C. H. Berman, *The Cistercian Evolution: the Invention of a Religious Order in Twelfth-Century Europe* (Philadelphia 2000). Her basic contention is that close study of the relevant documents shows that "a Cistercian Order was invented only in the 1160s, and not in 1110 as is usually thought" (p. 46). Among challenging reviews is that of Bruce Venarde in the electronic journal *H-France Review*: www.h-france.net/vol2reviews/venarde.html.

[25] *Mon. Order*, chs xii–xiv and xxxvii; see also Additional Note C in the second edition, on Cistercian origins, pp. 752–53.

[26] Several general introductions to Cistercian liturgy tend to range from the earliest days to the twentieth century: e.g., J. M. Canivez, "Le Rite Cistercien," *Eph. Liturg.* 63 (1949), pp. 276–311; A. A. King, *Liturgies of the Religious Orders* (London 1955), pp. 62–156; B. Lackner, "The Liturgy of Early Cîteaux," in *Studies in Med. Cist. Hist. pres. to J. F. O'Sullivan*, Cistercian Studies 13 (Spencer, MA 1971), pp. 1–34; L. J. Lekai, *The Cistercians: Ideals and Reality* (Kent, OH 1977), pp. 248–60.

the customary ceremonial, chants, and all books necessary for the canonical offices, both by day and by night, and for the mass, after the form of the customs and books of the new minster [Cîteaux], so that there be no discord in our worship, but that we may all dwell in one love and under one rule and with like customs.[27]

In theory this would mean that the service books used in Cistercian houses in England should be identical with those at Cîteaux. As there are extant no such books from English houses earlier than the late twelfth century, there is no exact way to test the theory. The general austerity of early Cistercian worship is witnessed to by one soaked in Benedictine liturgy, William of Malmesbury. In a rather lengthy account of Stephen Harding in his *Gesta Regum* (to which it is largely irrelevant), William provides one of the best known descriptions of the primitive Cistercian ethos, noting in particular that "The canonical hours they maintain without flinching [*indefesse*], adding nothing further [*nulla appenditia aditientes*] from outside sources except the Vigils of the Dead. In the divine office they normally use the chants and hymns of the Ambrosian rite, so far as they have been able to learn them from Milan."[28] But this work was basically completed in 1126, before any English houses were established, so again we cannot test the accuracy of William's account as it might have applied at, say, Kingswood in Gloucestershire, founded in 1139 (during his lifetime; he died c. 1143) and perhaps the closest Cistercian house to Malmesbury.

The three key manuscripts which contain supposedly "prototypical" data for authentic Cistercian liturgy are Trent, Bibl. communale 1711, a collection of regulations which may be a palimpsest containing two successive versions, Ljubljana (Laibach), Univ. 31, a copy of the *Consuetudines*, and Dijon, B.m. 114, purportedly an exemplar codex of about

---

[27] Eng. tr. from D. C. Douglas and D. Greenaway, ed. *Eng. Hist. Docs. 1042–1189*, 2nd edn (London 1981), pp. 738–42. The text is identical in both *Carta caritatis prior*, traditionally dated 1119, and *CC posterior*, 1165?, as printed in J.-B. Auberger, *L'Unanimité cistercienne primitive: mythe ou réalité* (Achel 1996), p. 329: "Et quia omnes monachos ipsorum ad nos venientes in claustro nostro recipimus, et ipsi similiter nostros in claustris suis, ideo opportunum nobis videtur et hoc etiam volumus, ut mores et cantum, et omnes libros ad horas diurnas et nocturnas et ad missas necessarios secundum formam morum et librorum novi monasterii possideant, quatinus in actibus nostris nulla sit discordia, sed una caritate, una regula similibusque vivamus moribus."

[28] William of Malmesbury, *Gesta Regum Anglorum*, ed. and tr. R. M. Thomson and M. Winterbottom, 2 vols, OMT (1998–99): I, *Text*, bk. IV, sect. 336 (pp. 580–83). Thomson, commenting on this passsage in vol. II, *Gen. Intro. and Commentary*, p. 291, mentions the possibility that William had been to North France and perhaps visited the abbey of L'Aumône.

1185.[29] Under the general name *Ecclesiastica officia*, all three contain sets of liturgical instructions presupposing these fifteen books, as listed on fol. 1v of the Dijon manuscript: breviary in three volumes (Advent to Easter, Easter to Advent, and a separate volume for the sanctorale), epistolary, gospel book, *missale* (in view of the previous two items and of the gradual that concludes the list, almost certainly what would more usually be called a sacramentary), *collectaneum*, calendar, *regula*, *consuetudines* (this and the previous book are of course not exclusively liturgical), psalter, *cantica de priuatis, dominicis, et festis diebus* ("monastic canticles"), *hymnarium*, antiphonary, *gradale*.[30] Again, the muddy waters surrounding the codicology and relative dating of these books (and several others related to them) can mostly be stepped around, because it is unlikely that any of the English service books now to be surveyed was written earlier than the 1185 date which seems sound enough for the Dijon exemplar.

The oldest English witnesses: four late twelfth-century missals

The extent to which English Cistercians followed to the letter the prescriptions about marching in lock step with the official books from Cîteaux is the focus of one of the very few treatments of the subject as it pertains to England, an article by David Chadd published in 1986.[31] He concentrates especially on four English Cistercian missals that survive for the period from c. 1185 to 1202: one from a northern house like Rievaulx or Fountains, one possibly from Waverley, one very likely from Buildwas, and one unplaced. The one probably from Buildwas is in particular concerned with the presence of certain English saints and with some variation in prayer-texts for their masses.[32]

---

[29] The dating questions are considered at length by Berman, *Cistercian Evolution*, pp. 51–68.

[30] D. Choisselet and P. Vernet, ed. *Les Ecclesiastica officia cisterciens du xiième siècle: Texte latin selon les MSS édités de Trente 1711, Ljubljana 31 et Dijon 114*, Documentation Cistercienne 22 (Reiningue 1989), including four facsimile pages in color: Dijon printed in full, with variants from the others.

[31] D. F. L. Chadd, "Liturgy and liturgical music: the limits of uniformity," in *Cistercian Art and Architecture in the British Isles*, ed. C. Norton and D. Park (Cambridge 1986), pp. 299–314.

[32] The only English saints, besides Becket, ever approved by the order's legislation are Cuthbert in 1226, for a commemoration, and Edmund of Abingdon (who like Becket had spent some exile-time at the Cistercian house at Pontigny) in 1247, for two conventual masses: see, most conveniently, the summary list in B. Backaert, "L'Evolution du calendrier cistercien," *Collectanea ordinis cisterciensium reformatorum* 13 (1951), pp. 108–27 at 119–22; earlier parts are in 12 (1950), pp. 81–94 and 302–16.

Another detail, not considered by Chadd, should, however, be noticed before we turn to those books: that according to "authentic" Cistercian tradition, enshrined in the Dijon 114 exemplar-codex, the temporale year begins with the Vigil of Christmas as is common in monastic usage, but that of the sanctorale with Stephen (so that the saints' feasts of 26 December through early January, elsewhere commonly found in the temporale, all appear in the sanctorale). This organizational point will provide us with another test of English fidelity to, or divergence from, that tradition.

The unplaced northern book, now BL Add. 46203, is a proper missal but of relatively small size (240 x 165 mm) and for only part of the year.[33] The temporale runs from the nineteenth Sunday after Pentecost through Quinquagesima Sunday, and the sanctorale from Michael (29 September, very roughly corresponding to the beginning of the temporale) through Agatha (5 February); it is in effect a *pars hiemalis*. It contains only ninety-seven folios (excluding flyleaves, two of which come from an early thirteenth-century Cistercian missal), and one wonders why it was worth having such a small missal made, most likely for private masses at a side altar, since it presupposes a *pars estivalis* which would have to include the same ordinary and votive masses as the winter volume. The post-Christmas saints' feasts are in the sanctorale, in the Cistercian way. It is not surprising to find as an original feature a mass for Becket, for whom the Cistercians had corporate affection (he had spent some of his exile in their house at Pontigny), and who was admitted to their calendar in 1185. The book is written with an eye to maximum economy, as is indicated by the note that on the ancient feast of the martyr Vincent, 22 January, "omnia sicut in festiuitate Sancti Thomae martyris." There is one surprising addition: on the verso of the last folio and in a hand of the first half of the thirteenth century, of mass prayers for Etheldreda, whose feast day, 23 June, falls outside the scope of the volume (it is totally improbable that her translation feast, 17 October, is meant).[34] There was no Cistercian house, male or

---

[33] The description in the *Cat. of Additions, 1946–50* (1979), pp. 14–15, probably by D. H. Turner, is unusually full. The missal passed from J. Meade Falkner's collection to that of Sir John Noble, whose letter of Jan. 1933 about it to C. H. St J. Hornby, the last private owner, is kept with the book. It is assigned to Fountains in *MLGB Suppl.* (1987), because of its binding; but that is of c. 1500 (the catalogue says "probably a trade binding"). More useful are the decorative motifs, described as northern English Cistercian in the catalogue and confirmed by Michael Gullick on personal inspection in 1999.

[34] The secret and postcommunion are as those in the Westminster missal of c. 1385 in Legg's comparative tables (see p. 141), but the collect, "Dq eximie castitatis," has not been otherwise encountered. Is there a possible link with the collect of the mass

female, in the diocese of Ely, so migration of the book to that area is not a possible explanation.

A notable contrast in size is provided by the missal possibly from Waverley, now BL Harley 1229. At roughly 335 x 245 mm, it is half again as big as the one just looked at, and was probably intended for use at the high altar. It is also somewhat later, the key dates being 1192, when the feast of St Malachy was ordered to be observed, and 1202, when new collects for St Bernard were mandated: Malachy is here in the original hand and in sequence at November 3rd, whereas the prayers for Bernard are added on a marginal tag (fol. 171). The suggestion about Waverley derives from the presence in mid-July of Swithun, a figure likely to appear in a Cistercian book only from a house in the diocese of Winchester, as Waverley was; no legislation of the order ever authorizes his cult. Another feature contrary to Cistercian custom is that the book, complete in covering the entire year, begins with the first Sunday of Advent. Something is missing from the beginning, for at Becket's feast (again in the sanctorale, following the feasts of 26–28 December) a marginal note reads "Require proprias collectas in principio libri" – and nothing is there.[35] The book is suitably plain, with no decoration and no music, with indications as to Creed and Gloria in excelsis in the margin. The apparently odd omission of Ash Wednesday and all the weekdays in Lent, even in Holy Week, is in keeping with "authentic" Cistercian custom.

The missal likely to have come from Buildwas, now CUL Add. 4079, survives in a highly imperfect state, with more than half its leaves missing.[36] Only fols 11–14 of the first 96 leaves are present, but what survives begins with mid-Advent III, which shows that the temporale here, like that in the Waverley volume, began with Advent rather than with Christmas Eve. Again this is an early divergence from authorized practice; the dating-range for the book is between 1185 (Becket) and 1202 (the new collects for Bernard, for which the user is instructed to see the end of the book, now missing).[37] Also divergent from the

prayers for Cuthburga, similar but not identical in wording, which have been added to the last folio of the Crawford Sarum missal (*SML*, p. 496)?

[35] The same thing happens at the end; on fol. 182 Lambert is marked as "fiat sicut de sancto Thoma archiep.," but here the reader is instructed to look "in fine libri" – again, nothing there.

[36] In accord with usual CUL practice, the missing leaves have been taken account of in the foliation; and, like the other Additional MSS, it is not yet covered in a printed catalogue, though a fine draft description is available in the Manuscripts Room.

[37] The question of the forms for Bernard is codicologically complicated; see Chadd, p. 311, n. 66. It is not possible to say where the sanctorale began; the surviving leaves begin 25 Jan. and end 18 Oct.

official norms is the inclusion, in the body of the text, of Chad and, as early additions, of Milburga ("omnia in die sancte marie magdalene") and of Winifred (in June, her translation feast on the 22nd, "sicut in die lucie").[38] This juxtaposition of saints points, in a Cistercian book, straight to Buildwas – an ascription supported by ample codicological evidence marshalled by Jennifer Sheppard in her study of the books from that house.[39] She records traces of a dozen or so page-markers, mostly of cord or thread, as well as of various repairs; clearly this is a book that was heavily used, and its size (the page, somewhat trimmed, still measures c. 310 x 210mm) and the presence of at least one major and numerous minor initials suggests that it may have been the principal missal of the house.

The missal about which no suggestion as to location has been offered, BL Add. 17431, can again be dated in the final quarter of the twelfth century. Of comparable size to the Buildwas book, it follows Cistercian practice in beginning the sanctorale with Stephen but diverges from it in starting the temporale with Advent.[40] As this is true also of both the missals just considered (and not ascertainable with Add. 46203 because its temporale runs from autumn to late spring), it can scarcely be accidental, and arouses curiosity as to links among the three; Waverley's mother house was L'Aumône and Byland was Savigniac in origin, so wherever Add. 17431 was used, this feature cannot have been a peculiarity of the filiation of these abbeys and must be regarded as English.

"Native" saints in English Cistercian liturgy

By the odd arbitrariness of manuscript survival, the only other English Cistercian missal that can be taken into account dates from more than

---

[38] There are also added, in various 13th-cent. hands, Cuthbert (approved 1226, all as for Chad), Dominic (1255), and Edward (in October, so this must be the Confessor, transl. 13 Oct. 1162, never approved by Cistercian legislation); also marginal directions to the (missing) end of the book for George, Barnabas, John and Paul, Margaret, and Lambert, of whom only George was not approved at some point between 1203 and 1260.

[39] J. M. Sheppard, *The Buildwas Books: Book Production, Acquisition and Use at an English Cistercian Monastery, 1165 – c. 1400*, Oxf. Bibliog. Soc. Pubs, 3rd ser., 2 (Oxford 1997), pp. 44–50 and fig. 14, illustrating fol. 124v. She dates the book early, 1175–80 (Becket's canonization in 1173 possibly explaining his presence at a date earlier than 1185).

[40] Its undeniably Cistercian character is clear from the presence of five or six small variations in the wording of the canon, as enumerated in the BL catalogue description of Add. 46203 (above, note 33). I am specially indebted to Nicolas Bell for help with details about this MS and for confirming that these variations in wording are found in German Cistercian books as well, and also to Janet Tierney Sorrentino for sharing with me her meticulous notes on this codex.

two centuries later than the four just considered: a mid-fifteenth-century book, now Stonyhurst College 2, of which all is missing after June 23rd in the sanctorale and twenty-five other leaves also. Unlike the other books, it contains a calendar (calendars are not meant to be part of the Cistercian missal as originally mandated). Its temporale begins in Advent rather than with the Vigil of Christmas, though the sanctorale starts with the post-Christmas saints in the "authentic" way. An aid to localization may be the obit for Henry Beaufort, bishop of Winchester, on the correct date April 11th (1447). This might point to Beaulieu (established 1204) or Netley (1239) as well as to Waverley.

It is also conceivable that it could have belonged to the newly founded (1437) Cistercian house of studies at Oxford, St Bernard's College. The calendar puts Erkenwald in red, along with Edmund the Confessor and Edmund the Martyr; saints in black include John of Beverley (7 May), Translation of Edmund (Confessor, 9 June), Translation of Richard of Chichester (16 June), and Alban (22 June). Of these four occasions, only the Translation of Edmund was approved for Cistercian use, but all four feature in the Sarum calendar by the mid-fifteenth century. This might help to explain the puzzling inclusion of a "Prefacio secundum usum Sarum," noted, on fols 149v–51v, after the canon, which itself follows the usual (Cistercian) prefaces. The rubric immediately after these "Sarum" prefaces begins "Si episcopus uel dominus abbas celebrauerit," followed by threefold episcopal blessings for fourteen occasions in the temporale, four in the sanctorale (ending with the Assumption, but then a leaf is missing), and some from the common, including blessings for a translation of relics and for "sponsi et sponse": did weddings ever take place in Cistercian churches? The force of these details, taken cumulatively, is to suggest that the maker of this book was aware of the possibility that a bishop who was familiar (only?) with the Sarum rite might be celebrating mass in the house which owned it. Neil Ker notes the peculiarity that the mass collects for twenty-one saints, all dealt with by cues, are entered in groups against the name of a principal or older saint whose forms theirs are to imitate ("omnia sicut in die ...").[41] These twenty-one include most of the English saints, but it is hard to say more because seven leaves are missing throughout the sanctorale. This is a very big book indeed, roughly 425 x 300 mm, and has many decorative initials and line-fillers: altogether a fine service book.

---

[41] *MMBL*, IV.370–72. The calendar also includes some "exotic" saints commemorated in earliest (c. 1130?) Cistercian traditon, like Sequanus abbot of Langres (d. c. 580) and Andochius and companions, 2nd-cent. martyrs of Autun, both in Sept.; also Columbanus on 21 Nov. There is no sign of these in the sanctorale.

The large question as to how to interpret the inclusion (intrusion?) of English and other non-authorized saints into books for English Cistercian houses takes particular point with two calendars connected with the nunnery at Tarrant Keynston in Dorset. One is a calendar of the second half of the thirteenth century joined to a psalter of the mid-fifteenth, now Stonyhurst College 9. It seems that the calendar originally belonged to another psalter, for on the first folio a thirteenth-century inscription states that "Hoc est psalterium beate marie super Tharente de dono domine Leticie de Kaynes": a descendant, as a card kept with the manuscript points out, of Ralph de Kaynes, the principal founder.[42] Only six months of the calendar survive, January–April and September–October, and it is not graded, so it is a dubious document as a guide to the nuns' worship. Nonetheless, we must be surprised at its nature. It is clearly not a Cistercian calendar, ignoring (for the months extant) such figures as William of Bourges, Julian of LeMans, Robert of Molesme, Peter Martyr, Lambert, and Francis, all of whom were mandated between 1193 and 1255. Instead, it draws on two, possibly three, kinds of sources. One is Continental, with exotic figures like Agapita, Eugenia, a Eufemia in April as well as in September, and Regina, all virgins, and a *Helena regina* on February 7th. The other is a wide range of clearly English saints, notably Milburga (in red), Guthlac, Erkenwald, Paulinus of York, and two feasts each for Cuthbert and Wilfrid. A separate source-strand may be represented by two feasts seldom found outside of Anglo-Saxon England, the Ordination of Gregory and the Conception of John the Baptist. This may in turn be connected with the entry, in red, for an *Inventio capitis Ioh. Bapt.* on February 27th.[43] The greatest hagiographical peculiarity is that on January 22nd, where after Vincent, the only entry in blue, come (another) Vincent, Orontius, and Victor, obscure martyrs connected with Embrun, in the Alpes de Provence.[44] Such an exotic collection of

---

[42] Her obit is entered at Jan. 16th. The detail about the card is not included in the description in *MMBL*, IV.381. *Med. Rel. Houses*, p. 276, explains that Ralph II de Kahaynes gave the site and endowments before 1228, the first abbess making her profession to Richard Poore, until that date bishop of Salisbury. It seems to have been a relatively large and wealthy house.

[43] This *Inventio* feast is contained in four pre-1100 English calendars, nos. 3, 15, 16, 17 in Wormald's *Eng. Kals.* Of these there are striking points of resemblance between the Stonyhurst 9 calendar and no. 3, BL Cott. Nero A.ii, which Wormald categorizes simply as "Wessex" and describes as representing "the early type of English kalendar containing many martyrological entries" (p. vi). On Nero A.ii see further p. 153 above. The *Inventio capitis* is in Bede's martyrology, and thence into those of Florus and Usuard, but on the 24th: J. Dubois, ed. *Le Martyrologe d'Usuard*, Subs. Hagiog. 40 (Brussels 1965), p. 186.

[44] Mentioned only in the Carolingian martyrologies of Florus and Adon: Dubois, p. 166.

saints should probably lead us to regard the calendar as pleasing to the antiquarian tastes of whoever wrote it rather than being of any practical use to the Tarrant Keynston nuns after they were given it.

A useful contrast is posed by a much later psalter-with-calendar, Bodl. Lyell 23, probably datable to the third quarter of the fifteenth century: Osmund, canonized 1456, is an original entry. Here the expected Cistercian saints are all present. On the other hand, a *passio* for St Margaret is supplied at the end of the book divided into nine lessons and therefore unsuitable for monastic use; and, as is pointed out in the catalogue of the Lyell manuscripts, a prayer *Pro abbatissa* at the end of the slightly later litany (otherwise missing) is an adaptation of a Sarum prayer for a bishop.[45]

Evidence for the office

These psalters aside, almost all the service-book evidence that we have for the office among the English Cistercians must be derived from one hymnal, one legendary, and one breviary (or nocturnal).[46] The hymnal, BL Harley 2951, dating from the later thirteenth century, shows a perhaps surprising amount of English influence, both in the saints of its calendar and in a key addition to the original, self-consciously pristine hymnal(s) of the order. As we have seen, its earliest documents stated that the hymns were to be *Ambrosiani*, and in pursuit of this goal sources in Milan were consulted in the time of Stephen Harding, but the resulting hymnal proved so unsatisfactory that an extensive revision was promulgated in 1147; this fixed a canon of just over fifty hymns, some of them subdivided.[47] Additions were meant to be strictly controlled, with only four or five cases sanctioned through the sixteenth century: hymns for Bernard, Corpus Christi, the Visitation, and Anne. Those for St Anne are supposed to be "Orbis exultans," "Clara diei gaudia," and "Lucis huius festa"; but in Harley 2951 they are "Ave mater Anna plena," "In Anne puerperio," and "Felix Anna pre aliis"

---

[45] A. C. de la Mare, *Catalogue of the Collection of Medieval Manuscripts ... James P. R. Lyell* (Oxford 1971), pp. 49–52. Van Dijk's *Handlist*, II.30, notes that the obits include one for Richard Poore.

[46] There are fragments of a 13th-cent. Cistercian breviary in Bodl. Lat. liturg. b.7, nos. 53–58: portions of the sanctorale from 22 Jan. to 25 March. This very small book (108 x 57 mm) was, van Dijk's *Handlist*, VI.276 points out, "bound along the upper edges so as to allow the book to be hung from the girdle." This means that it could have been read while travelling.

[47] A convenient summary in tabular form is in the appendix to M. B. Kaul, "Le psautier cistercien," *Collectanea Cist.* 13 (1951), pp. 257–72; other parts are 10 (1948), pp. 83–106 and 12 (1950), pp. 118–30. Texts edited by C. Waddell, *The Twelfth-Century Cistercian Hymnal*, 2 vols (Gethsemani 1984).

(fols 113v–15v) – which are to be the Sarum hymns for vespers, matins, and lauds respectively.[48] The calendar, in a different but contemporary hand and unmistakably Cistercian, has as additions several entries of saints approved in the 1250s and 1260s: Peter Martyr 1255, Francis at twelve lessons 1259, Margaret and also the Eleven Thousand Virgins 1260; so it probably dates from around 1250.[49] The obit at October 4th of a "Dionis. Abb," with a year that looks like 1280, must be of abbot Denis of Beaulieu, who died that year, and suggests strongly that the book belonged to that house.[50] It was founded only in 1203/4, so its stock of liturgical books must all have been still recent by the middle of the century. Assignment to Beaulieu, which is in the diocese of Winchester, would explain the addition of Swithun, at twelve lessons. Harder to explain but worthy of mention is the addition at August 4th, in a tiny hand, "anno domini mcclxv occisus est Symon de Monteforti" (the correct date for the battle of Evesham, at which he was killed).

Corroborative evidence may come from a book described variously as an office lectionary, legendary, or collection of saints lives; now Bodl. Rawl. C.440. It has been studied from a largely bibliographical standpoint by Joanna Proud, who dates it, as seems likely, mid to later thirteenth century.[51] She regards it as a volume for private reading, an inference that can be drawn from the inscription of fol. 1, the first page of the calendar prefixed to the volume. It explains that this *kalendarium* serves as a kind of finding-list for lives and passions of saints in some thirty-four different books (*diversis libris*), through an alphanumeric system of reference for the various codices – of which this one is G III, as large letters on the flyleaf indicate. The calendar contains references for 198 such entries.[52] But the calendar is apparently not integral to the original book, though roughly contemporary with it; as it is ungraded, the possibility of using it as a guide to liturgical practice in the house from which it came seems slight. Nonetheless, there are thought-provoking entries: Gundulph, bishop and confessor, on

---

[48] "Are to be" because evidence for an office of St Anne in English secular use is later that this MS.

[49] There is a note at June 17th about the appearance of Corpus Christi (not officially sanctioned by the Cistercians until 1318); it fell on that day in 1246, 1257, 1268, and then not again until 1318.

[50] He is the only possible Denis among Cistercian abbots: *Heads of Rel. Houses*, II.260.

[51] J. Proud, "Collections of Saints' Lives in the Thirteenth and Fourteenth Centuries: Interpreting the Manuscript Evidence," in *Lives in Print: Biography and the Book Trade*, ed. R. Myers, M. Harris, and G. Mandelbrote (London 2002), pp. 1–21.

[52] Proud supplies a facsimile of the January calendar page and a transcription of the June page, and lists in calendarial order the saints whose lives are ascribed to each of the thirty-four MSS.

March 8th (the famous Anglo-Norman bishop of Rochester of that name died in 1108 on the 7th, a date here occupied by Thomas Aquinas); "Odonis archepiscopi" on June 2nd, the day that archbishop of Canterbury died in 958, and Godric of Finchale on his correct death-day, May 21st (1170). There are also three separate texts for Becket and one (the latest chronologically) for Edmund Rich. Of the sixteen somewhat random passions that comprise the main body of the manuscript, only five or six are likely to have been read at matins (whether from this volume or not) in a Cistercian house: those for Gregory the Great, Philip and James, James the Great, Bartholomew, and Simon and Jude, and (after 1247) Edmund. So it seems safest to conclude that Rawl. C.440 was probably not used liturgically in the house to the library of which it bears such tantalizing witness – one of which the dedication feast was kept on July 19th, as the calendar states.

The breviary or (as Chadd calls it) nocturnal, now BL Burney 335, is a small, fat book (written space only 100 x 75 mm, 342 folios) that must have been meant for travelling, for it contains the Canon and other mass forms, together with a selection of votive masses. Its litany of saints is highly abbbreviated – only six each of apostles and martyrs, nine confessors, no virgins – and is noteworthy in having Edmund Rich third among the confessors. The calendar contains the northern saints William of York and Wilfrid, and must have been written after the wonderfully-spelled entry for March 7th, "Thome alkini," ordered for the Cistercians in 1329.[53]

One more book possibly bearing on the office must be glanced at: a psalter of about 1300, now CUL Add. 851, with a calendar originally Cistercian; the inclusion of Wulfstan of Worcester, rarely found in Cistercian calendars, and of two feasts for Richard of Chichester, a native of Wych in the diocese of Worcester, suggests that the book might have belonged to the house at Bordesley.[54] But by the fifteenth century it had passed to the parish church in Shotesham (Norfolk). There the distinctively Cistercian saints like Robert of Molesme, Peter of Tarentaise, and Malachy were crossed through and numerous additions made, including Osmund and the dedication of a new

---

[53] Chadd, "Liturgy and liturgical music," p. 312, posits the unexpected appearance of William of York, originally anathema to Cistercians, as a sign of acceptance of reparations he made to Fountains after the bitter quarrel of 1145–57 (Knowles, *MO*, p. 255). A highly unusual addition, very faint, is on Apr. 27th: Sitha or Zita, the Italian maidservant (d. 1278) whose cult was unofficial until 1696. A few other exotic figures occur, like Mammas of Caesarea on Aug. 17th.

[54] Or just conceivably a Cistercian nunnery like Whistones (Worcs.): the litany has twenty-four virgins, many more than any other category of saint, at least seven of whom are Anglo-Saxon (fol. 95).

church of St Botolph; there also Sarum antiphons for matins and vespers were added.[55] Why and how this book moved can only be wondered at, but it does look to have been used liturgically, unlike some other psalters.[56]

Two Cistercian booklists

These individual books, though the indispensable building blocks, do little to give an overall picture of worship in English Cistercian houses. A slight bit of complementary information may be garnered from two surviving library catalogues. The more important is the well known catalogue of Meaux in Yorkshire, written by Thomas Burton, its abbot 1396–99 and author of the invaluable *Chronicon de Meaux*.[57] Out of some 363 entries in the list, twenty-eight are of service books – sometimes in groups, so that the total number looks to be around 110. Not all of these were necessarily in use in the same period; notably, of the eight books specified as "Pro magno altari," where the "antiquum Missale" is contrasted to the first item on the list, "Missale nouum cum gradali et collectis tantum." There were also for the high altar two gospel books (one large and one small), two matching (*consimiles*) epistle books, a *collectaneum* – the distinctively Cistercian word – for terce and presumably the other little hours as well, and a *quaternus* containing the readings at the Easter and Pentecost Vigils and other matter. Indicated as *in choro* are six graduals, eight antiphonals with the responsories for the temporale, six similar books for the sanctorale, and two for the entire year but without responsories. There are also two *collectanea*, two *quaterni* of the litany, and two *psalteria*, thirty-eight small processionals plus five for the feast of Corpus Christi and the commendation of souls; a couple of *libelli* for the Good Friday *Improperium*, and two chant

---

[55] Noted by Jayne Ringrose of the University Library. There were four churches in Shotesham, of which St Martin and St Botolph are now in ruins: PBE *North-West and South Norfolk* (1962), p. 314.

[56] The very beautiful Hailes psalter (Wells Cathedral 5), given to that house in 1514 as a memorial benefaction and written by a named humanist scribe, contains no information relevant to Cistercian liturgy. It has psalter collects in the margins next to each psalm (as discussed briefly in the description in *MMBL*, IV.561), and the ferial canticles have an interlinear gloss in red, so the thrust is heavily devotional. Psalter collects (in the same, "Romana," series, but with interesting variations) appear also in a late 12th-cent. psalter from the Gloucestershire house of Kingswood, now Bristol, Public Library 12 (kept in an unbound condition; *MMBL*, II.207).

[57] D. N. Bell, ed. *The Libraries of the Cistercians, Gilbertines, and Premonstratensians*, CBMLC 3 (1992), pp. 34–82, esp. 37–39. The MS, BL Cott. Vit. C.vi, is also that of the *Chronicon*, ed. E. A. Bond, 3 vols, RS 43 (1866–68); it was written during the lifetime of Thomas, who in 1399 resigned the abbacy and went to live at Fountains, where he died in 1437.

books for burial rites.[58] The infirmary chapel is listed as having not only two "antiphonaria cum responsoriis et collectis," four legendaries (two each for temporale and sanctorale), and one psalter, but also "alia Psalteria, Portiforia, et Collectanea, in priuatis vsibus abbatis, officialium et monachorum." The numbers of books of the latter sort cannot, of course, be ascertained.

It is fortunate that figures survive as to the size of the convent during the years when this list was drawn up: twenty-eight monks, probably all choir monks, are recorded in 1393, twenty-seven in 1399.[59] The thirty-eight small processionals were thus more than could be used at once, but some might have been quite old, and there had been forty-two choir monks at Meaux before the Black Death (and as many as sixty in 1249). In addition to the high altar, there were five eastern chapels radiating off the ambulatory and two in each of the transepts, so more missals must have been needed than are recorded. Other items in the list were at least para-liturgical, like the four passionals (for January, February, July–August, and November–December), the "Psalterium unum cum oracionibus" kept in the cloister book-cupboard, or the final item on the list, "Oracionibus cum sermonibus, et alia," but no further mention of massbooks. So it is likely that this list, magnificently full as it is, is incomplete as regards liturgical texts.

An almost exactly contemporary inventory, that of the small house at Stoneleigh in Warwickshire dated 1386, records about two dozen books.[60] Service books are in fact the only volumes listed, and the inventory includes also a list of vestments, so we may assume that the compiler was seriously interested in the equipment for worship – the occasion for the inventory being the confirmation of a new abbot. The books listed for the office make good sense: six *antiphonaria integra* with responsories and four *antiphonaria minora*, presumably without them; two large legendaries *pro choro*, two psalters, one *hymnarium*, and three *collectanea* – one *pro choro*, one *pro tercia*, and one for the dead. By contrast, books for the mass are limited to four graduals and (separated from the other items by the vestments-list) one "missale pro harnesio Abbatis" – although why it should be described as part of the abbot's equipment (*harnesium*) is not clear.

---

[58] Two psalters seems a very small number; did the majority of the choir monks bring their own psalters with them? As there is no separate designation of hymnals, the hymns must have been included in the psalters, making for a body of material very difficult to keep entirely in memory.

[59] *Med. Rel. Houses*, p. 125. There are no visible remains, and the site is in private hands, but a fine summary of the building history, as detailed in the *Chronicon*, is available in Fergusson, *Architecture of Solitude*, pp. 133–36.

[60] Bell, *Libs. of Cistercians*, pp. 141–42; the document is Public Record Office MS E.154/1/41.

In marked contrast to the modesty of the arrangements at Stoneleigh is the magnificence of Rievaulx, alike in numbers and in architecture. So it is ironic that the quite full library list from Rievaulx dating from the end of the twelfth century includes among its 225 items no service books proper.[61] Its great days were those from the abbacy of Aelred (1147–67) through the second quarter of the thirteenth century, when the extension of the choir and presbytery provided ample space for the many monk-priests the house would have contained. We have no exact information as to how many this might have been, but something can be extrapolated from the expansion in the number of altars in the church: from six in Aelred's time to nine in the early thirteenth century and eventually a maximum of seventeen, a figure reached in 1325.[62] Peter Fergusson has supplied substantiation for the estimate that one of every three choir monks was a priest, but that would be true only from well into the thirteenth century, when private masses, whether votive or contractual (for the dead, as a condition of benefactions) proliferate. It is improbable that if in Aelred's time there were some 140 choir monks, there had to be accommodation for anything like fifty monk-priests.[63] Nonetheless, even then many more missals would have been needed, and a great many more half a century further on, than the single codex, among the few that survive, which could have belonged to Rievaulx, the BL Add. 46203 missal discussed above.

How uniform was English Cistercian liturgy?

The preponderance of evidence reviewed seems to suggest that the liturgical uniformity that was meant to characterize the Cistercian order was more strongly felt in spirit than executed in letter. While some distinctively Cistercian practices, like the small variations in the wording of the Canon (above, note 40), and saints, like Malachy and William of Bourges, appear to have been maintained, in at least three areas divergence from the official norms is obvious. The first, for which we have seen witnesses as early as the late twelfth century, is the structuring of missals so that the temporale begins on I Advent rather than the Vigil

---

[61] Ibid., pp. 89–121. No. 218, an *orationarium*, could be a possible exception, but is likelier to have been a collection of private prayers.

[62] P. Fergusson and S. Harrison, *Rievaulx Abbey: Community, Architecture, Memory* (New Haven and London 2000), pp. 164–66. By the early 14th cent. the house was considerably in debt, and after the Black Death its numbers never reached anything like the earlier figures.

[63] The widely-cited figure of 140 is taken from Walter Daniel's *Vita Ailredi*, ed. and tr. F. M. Powicke, NMT (London 1950), cap. 30 (and see in particular Powicke's note, p. 38); cf. Fergusson, p. 165.

of Christmas. A second is the fairly liberal inclusion of "unauthorized" English saints in Cistercian books; several cases have been noticed of this. It may be that the monks of whatever southern English house the Stonyhurst 2 missal belonged to (above, p. 255) duly commemorated (probably with a minimal *memoria* collect) such remote figures as Andochius or Sequanus, but it is much likelier that they prayed with attention the collects written carefully into the margin for such figures as Erkenwald, John of Beverley, and Richard, when those saints' days, familiar to the wider world of their society, occurred. That is a late missal, but the same is true with such entries, or early additions, as those for Etheldreda to the BL Add. 46203 or Winifred and Chad to the CUL Add. 4079 books.

A third aspect of "divergence" may be accounted for by either English taste or slackness (or possibly both); it is exemplified by complaints made in 1217 against the monks of the neighboring abbeys of Dore and Tintern that they were singing "three- and four-voice polyphony *more secularium.*"[64] That it was the abbots of the relatively nearby Flaxley (Gloucestershire) and Neath (Glamorgan) who made the denunciations suggests both that they had heard the abominable noise personally and that the practice was a matter of some regional notoriety. The abbot of Dore from at least 1213 to 1227 was the Adam to whom the typological treatise generally called *Pictor in carmine* is now ascribed, and who may have been the author also of a *Rudimenta musices* noted by the sixteenth-century bibliographer John Bale.[65] If the latter, tantalizing attribution should be correct, we would seem to have a clear example of an English Cistercian abbot engaged in creative artistic activity quite alien to the spirit of the Bernardine chant reform which is thought to be another characteristic of Cistercian practice. (This reform has not been mentioned here because there survive no English chant books of the order.)[66]

---

[64] Chadd, "Liturgy and Liturg. Music," p. 305; his source is J.-M. Canivez, *Statuta Capit. Gen. Ord. Cisterciensis*, Bibl. de Revue d'histoire ecclésiastique 9–14B, 8 vols (1933–41), I.472.

[65] Sharpe, *Handlist*, pp. 9–10; the reference to a *Rudimenta musices* is from C. H. Talbot, who wrote in 1958 that "I have found a copy of this treatise in Cambridge, but unfortunately have mislaid the reference"! The choir and transepts of Abbey Dore survive, in use as the parish church; the frequency with which recordings are made there testifies to its acoustic qualities. The work was mostly finished under abbot Adam's predecessor, Adam (I): Fergusson, *Architecture of Solitude*, pp. 94–100.

[66] The large, technical introduction is S. Marosszéki, "Les Origines du chant cistercien," *Analecta sacri ordinis Cisterciensis* 8 (1952), pp. 1–179; more accessible is C. Waddell, "The Origin and Early Evolution of the Cistercian Antiphonary: Reflections on Two Cistercian Chant Reforms," in *The Cistercian Spirit*, ed. M. B. Pennington, Cistercian Studies 3 (Washington, DC 1973), pp. 190–223.

It is possible, perhaps even likely, that surveys of the evidence for Cistercian liturgy in medieval Germany or Spain would notice similar degrees of divergence from the uniformity aimed at in the official documents of the order. All that can be said in the present work is that the extant books used in English houses seem, while remaining unquestionably Cistercian – that is, one is never in doubt as to whether a particular book is Cistercian or not – to share a number of the particularities manifested in books of other strands, both regular and secular, from England.

Carthusians

Such substantive knowledge of the liturgy as practiced by Carthusian monks in England in the middle ages as we may acquire comes almost entirely from the later middle ages; there will be little to detain us from the first two or three English houses. The first priory was at Witham in Somerset, founded by Henry II as part of his reconciliation with the church after the murder of Becket, in 1178–79.[67] Roughly two years later the king managed to induce the Burgundian monk Hugh of Avalon, whose reputation as an outstanding Carthusian had reached Henry's ears, to become its prior, a position he held until 1186, when he became bishop of Lincoln (died 1200, canonized 1220).[68] None of his successors as prior is particularly noteworthy, but a distinguished recruit arrived, with Hugh's complicity, in 1188: Adam, abbot of the Premonstratensian house at Dryburgh on the Scottish borders. He remained at Witham until his death, c. 1212, but the majority of his considerable literary work seems to date from his Premonstratensian days.[69]

Only one other Charterhouse was established in England in the next century and a half, Hinton, also in Somerset, between 1227 and 1232 (after an abortive beginning in Gloucestershire a bit earlier). The next foundation, at Beauvale in Nottinghamshire, was not made until 1343.

---

[67] E. M(argaret) Thompson, *The Carthusian Order in England* (London 1930) is, despite its age, still the fullest and most useful account of its subject in general, although she stated candidly that "With the Carthusian rite ... being inexperienced in liturgical matters, I have judged it wiser not to deal" (p. vii). See also Knowles, *Mon. Order*, pp. 375–91, and *Rel. Orders*, II.129–38.

[68] The incomparable source is Adam of Eynsham, *Magna Vita Sancti Hugonis*, ed. D. L. Douie, and (D.) H. Farmer, OMT, 2nd edn, 2 vols (1985). See also Henrietta Leyser's superb lecture, "Hugh the Carthusian," in *St Hugh of Lincoln*, ed. H. Mayr-Harting (Oxford 1987), pp. 1–18.

[69] J. Bulloch, *Adam of Dryburgh* (London 1958), esp. pp. 26–32 and 138–51, on Adam as a Carthusian. For other bibl. and a review of his writings, see Sharpe, *Handlist*, p. 10.

From 1371 till 1398, however, five new Charterhouses came into being: in order, London, Kingston-upon-Hull, Coventry, Axholme (Lincolnshire), and Mount Grace (Yorkshire North Riding). One more concludes the list, Henry V's magnificent foundation at Sheen in Surrey, 1414. With no more than nine houses, each of them small,[70] the Carthusians in England seem to have played only a limited part on its religious scene, save for the spiritual writers who are among the order's great distinctions and among whom Nicholas Love, prior of Mount Grace (d. c. 1423) and author of the vernacular *Myrrour of the blessed lyf of Jesu Christ*, enjoys a particular prominence.

Liturgy at the English Charterhouses

No sense of liturgical life at Mount Grace is available to complement its splendid remains, and the scant evidence we have from extant liturgical books and other sources is largely connected with London and Sheen. The Carthusian liturgy, probably modelled on that of the diocese of Grenoble (where the mother house, La Grande Chartreuse, lay), with some Cluniac elements as well, was marked by reticence and simplicity: reticence in the admission of feasts, though this loosened notably in the later middle ages, and simplicity in ceremonial. (It is disappointing that the wonderfully vivid *Magna Vita Sancti Hugonis* written by Adam of Eynsham, St Hugh's chaplain, includes so little about his hero's liturgical life as a Carthusian; the most that can be inferred is that Hugh was observant if in some respects surprisingly eccentric.)[71] The general Carthusian practice was that the choir monks gathered in the church on a daily basis only for the night office and vespers, and for the conventual mass on Sundays and feasts; the other offices were said, and indeed nearly the entire day spent, in the monk's own cell and adjacent kitchen garden. The detailed prescriptions of this twelfth-century liturgy and of its subsequent elaborations have been worked out in great, and often confusing, detail.[72]

---

[70] The usual complement of a Charterhouse was a prior and twelve choir monks, plus some *conversi* and a few others; London, Sheen, and Mount Grace were larger, London being a double house. The modern practice of calling Carthusian monks "Dom" may reach back to the later middle ages.

[71] My paper, "St Hugh as a Liturgical Person," in Pfaff, *LCSSME*, no IX (originally in *De Cella in Saeculum*, ed. M. G. Sargent [Woodbridge 1989], pp. 17–27), is an attempt to winkle out what can be inferred on the subject.

[72] Around 1970 James Hogg founded a series, Analecta Cartusiana, for the publication of sources of and literature on all things Carthusian. The fascicles of the series, numbered in a convoluted and inconsecutive way, have grown to include something like 200, most of them published by the Institut für Anglistik und Amerikanistik of the

Distinctive features of the order's worship throughout the later middle ages (and beyond) are, however, clear enough to enable us to see both how the English houses appear to have conformed to the official norms and the extent of variation from them that seems to have crept in. A clear example is offered by the only substantial witness to the mass liturgy of the English Charterhouses, a late fourteenth-century gradual, now BL Egerton 3267, which was clearly owned by the London house. It is a large book (395 x 255 mm overall), as would be expected, and the sanctorale is highly condensed (fols 98v–117, out of 129), with mere tags for most saints. These include Hugh of Grenoble, a major Carthusian benefactor (1 April), celebrated throughout the order, and the Carthusian Feast of Relics on 8 November, but also the specifically English Translation of Becket (7 July) and, probably to be expected, of Hugh of Lincoln (in 1280; 6 October). This gradual seems to have been in continuous use well into the sixteenth century, for there are marginal additions for Catherine of Siena (canonized 1461; 30 April) and the order's founder Bruno, for whose feast within it on 6 October (the day also of Hugh's Translation feast) papal permission was given in 1514. Additions of this sort were made not casually but, at least towards the end of the middle ages, in the context of an elaborate mechanism of *quaestiones* which in theory ensured liturgical control by the mother house.

Three detailed sources: the "Questions," a collectar, and a mass ordinary

Questions concerning new feasts and a host of other matters, mostly liturgical and some of them concerned with tiny points of detail, were regularly sent from England to the prior at La Grande Chartreuse, to whom the duty of handling such things had been delegated by the General Chapter of 1441; some replies are preserved, along with the questions, in parts of five manuscripts printed by Joseph Gribbin in 1999.[73] Three of the five are certainly, and the other two likely to be, from the London house. All five lists seem to be of the late fifteenth

University of Salzburg; they pose a nightmare for bibliographers of the few research libraries that try to amass complete sets. Hogg retired from editorial management in the late 1990s. Before the series began students often consulted the long and diffuse, but sometimes useful, account in A. A. King, *Liturgies of the Religious Orders* (London 1955), pp. 1–61.

[73] J. Gribbin, ed. *Liturgical and Miscellaneous Questions, Dubia and Supplications to La Grande Chartreuse from the English Carthusian Province in the Later Middle Ages*, Anal. Cartus. 100:32 (Salzburg 1999).

or early sixteenth century and appear among other Carthusian material. The most detailed is Bodl. Rawl. D.318, which contains 287 such questions, 51 of which do not occur in any other collections; Gonville and Caius College, Cambridge 732/771 has 252, 20 unique; BL Cotton Calig. A.ii has 98, 21 unique; Jesus College, Cambridge A.12 (12) has 48, 2 unique; PRO E315/490 has 11, 1 unique.[74] This adds up to a total of some 331 questions sent by one Charterhouse, albeit an important one, to the authorities at the mother house in a period of perhaps fifty years – a figure that may help to explain the testiness that marks some of their replies.

The questions cover several subjects, notably tiny matters of pronunciation (it is possible to suspect a liturgical fusspot or two among the monks); nonetheless, they are largely concerned with details of corporate worship. It would be a useful labor for someone to work through all 331 questions and to relate them wherever possible to each of the three relevant service books (excluding three psalters, to be treated presently) which are extant: the gradual from the London house already mentioned, a breviary or diurnal from the same house,[75] and an instructive collectar possibly from Sheen.[76] This last book, now Lincoln Cathedral 64, contains not only collects (though not capitula, as in earlier collectars) for temporale and sanctorale but also lengthy services for visitation of the sick and burial of the dead according to Carthusian usage and for the reception of distinguished persons and commemorations of benefactors. The signature(?) of "D. Iohannes Bromley de Shene," whose name appears in three other books which have been ascribed to that house, is at the foot of fol. 1, and this has led Rodney Thomson to assign this book to Sheen as well.[77] But two of the three are printed books, later than a probable date for the collectar, and Bromley was at Sheen as late as 1539, so his signature cannot be taken as hard evidence for use there.

The list of benefactors on fol. 58v details five occasions on which special devotions are required, in addition to the order's general

---

[74] Gribbin provides tables of concordance of the five MSS in an Appendix, but there is no index. Expanded descriptions of the MSS are on pp. xix–xxix. He dates the written material in the Gonville and Caius MS to 1526 and later; it has been added to a 1510 printed edition of the Carthusian statutes.

[75] Now Blackburn, Museum and Art Gallery 091.21195, of the mid-15th cent: *MMBL*, II.112–3 [not seen by me]. The BL *Cat. of Additions to MSS, 1936–45* (1970) p. 368, calls it a diurnal (in the description of Egerton 3267).

[76] Gribbin has done this to a limited extent in the very brief monograph published four years prior to his edition of the lists: *Aspects of Carthusian Liturgical Practice in Later Medieval England*, Anal. Cartus. 99:33 (Salzburg 1995), largely his Cambridge M. Phil. thesis; again there is no index, not even of MSS. An attempt here to cover all the questions systematically would totally unbalance the present work.

[77] R. M. Thomson, *Cat. Lincoln Cath. MSS*, pp. 45–6; so also *MLGB* and its *Suppl.*

commemoration on the feast of Stephen: a *tricennarium* each for Cardinal Talarandus [Talleyrand] de Périgord around St Antony's day (17 January), for Jeanne de Bourbon and her husband Charles [V] of France at the beginning of March, and for Amb[e]llard bishop of (St Jean de) Maurienne around St Mark's day (25 April); also mentioned but not named are the abbot of Cluny around St Luke's day (18 October) and, associated with him, the abbey (not abbot) of St Vaast in Arras. Talarandus de Périgord was *in commendam* Dean of York from 1343 until his death in 1364, while Queen Jeanne, donor of one hundred pounds, died in 1377; so neither could have been a benefactor to Sheen, founded only in 1414.

These same benefactors (but not St Vaast) are commemorated in a Carthusian mass ordinary, interesting but not particularly remarkable, contained among miscellaneous documents in BL Cotton Nero A.iii and published by J. W. Legg in 1904.[78] He dated the piece late fifteenth or early sixteenth century and declared himself unable to assign it to any particular Charterhouse; but the formula of profession in English that precedes the ordinary specifies Mary, John the Baptist, and All Saints, a composite dedication which applies only to Hinton (though folio 160, not printed by Legg, has a Latin profession-formula that mentions Mary and John only). It is tempting to think that this is part of the "Statuta vetera et noua que ipsemet scripsit" which John Whet(e)ham of the London house took to Hinton as part of a loan of ten books, both printed and manuscript (among the latter was a "librum de legendis multorum sanctorum" which he also wrote).[79] This sort of book-laden travel seems, perhaps surprisingly, to have been not uncommon among late medieval English Carthusians.

Other service books owned by English Charterhouses

Indeed, the movement of books from one Charterhouse to another, most often as loans from the better supplied houses to those less well

---

[78] J. W. Legg, ed. *Tracts on the Mass*, HBS 27 (1904), pp. 99–110, 246–48, with intro. note on p. xxiv. The ordinary occupies fols 130v-35, "De officio nudo quomodo agitur" (the "dry mass" that Carthusians sometimes celebrated in their own cells) fol. 156v, and detailed provisions for the commemoration of benefactors fols 156v–60. This material has been printed also by J. Hogg, "Further Liturgical Documents," in *Miscellanea Cartusiana* 3, Anal. Cartus. 42 (1978), pp. 70–101, 89–101 being a muddy facsimile of chant texts on fols 160v–65v and formulas for profession and graces on fol. 166.

[79] Printed in Thompson, *Carthusian Order*, p. 329, and with commentary by A. I. Doyle in *Syon Abbey with the Libraries of the Carthusians*, ed. V. Gillespie, CBMLC 9 (2001), pp. 622–24.

off, provides the majority of the scanty evidence for Carthusian library lists. One such list, dated 1500, enumerates fourteen volumes sent by the prior of the London house on loan to Coventry; these include a *Legenda sanctorum* starting with John & Paul (26 June, so clearly a *pars estivalis*), a breviary of the order, probably the edition printed in Venice in 1491, a psalter, and a book of exequies, each of which may have been either printed or manuscript. Similarly, in 1519 a London Carthusian took with him to Mount Grace, perhaps for an extended stay, a supply of warm clothing and some sixteen books, including a diurnal donated by Dame Elizabeth Saxby of Northampton ("a fayer writtne yornall": the inventory is in English), a psalter, offices of the dead, and "a boke wrytten conteynynge certeyn masses, with the canon of the Masse and a kalendar."[80] These "certeyn masses" would almost without doubt be those of the newly popular feasts of the Holy Name and Transfiguration (the Visitation having been accepted by the order a good deal earlier) and possibly that of Bruno.

Gifts like those noted in these lists sometimes included liturgical books of a secular type which might be altered to some degree. Such is the deluxe Sarum missal of the late fourteenth century (now New Haven, Beinecke Library 286) given to the London Charterhouse by Marmaduke Lumley, Bishop of Lincoln, who died in 1450 having been in that see for only nine months.[81] A possible reason for this is that an ancestor with the same name who was buried in the Charterhouse in 1399–1400 may have commissioned the volume (a later connection with the Lumley name is one George, who in 1535 tried to encourage the monks at Mount Grace and other northern houses to join the Pilgrimage of Grace).[82] A similar case is that of a late fourteenth-century psalter, probably an East Anglian production, which seems to have been given to a Carthusian house (now Claremont, California, Honnold Library, Crispin 5). To its calendar, which contains William of Norwich and the dedication of the cathedral there, the name of Hugh of Grenoble has been added and an obit for Thomas Stele, "patris Ioannis monachi huius domus": the *domus* in question very likely being Sheen, where a Dom John Style died in 1500.[83]

[80] Printed by Doyle, pp. 620–22 (Coventry) and 628 (Mount Grace).
[81] B. Shailor, *Cat. of the Med. and Renaissance MSS in the Beinecke Rare Book and Manuscript Library*, 3 vols (New Haven 1987), II.57–60; a full-page reproduction of fol. 42 is pl. 32 in her exhbition catalogue, *The Medieval Book* (New Haven 1988, repr. Toronto 1991).
[82] The suggestion about the donor was made by Kathleen Scott, as recorded in Shailor's catalogue; the George Lumley detail is in Thompson, p. 471.
[83] C. W. Dutschke and R. H. Rouse, *Med. and Renaissance MSS in Claremont Colleges* (San Marino 1986), pp. 21–22 and figs. 2–3: formerly owned by J. Meade Falkner [not

A more substantial adaptation, and altogether more interesting case, is that of Bodl. Lat. liturg. e.21, a psalter of the second half (third quarter?) of the fourteenth century, which may be French in origin but to which a Carthusian calendar and litany have been affixed. To the calendar (which now lacks the first two and last two months) what van Dijk calls a Continental hand has added a number of English saints like Alban, Etheldreda, Translation of Thomas, and Swithun, and also both the Visitation and Anne, which seems to date the additions after 1412.[84] The litany has been considerably rewritten to be unmistakably Carthusian, and at its conclusion at least one leaf, with details about the order of items at lauds, is written in what Ian Doyle has recognized as the hand of William Darker, a monk of Sheen around 1500.[85] Another well known monk-scribe at Sheen appears in a psalter, now Trinity College, Oxford 46: "orate pro anima domini Stephani Dodesham huius libri scriptoris" (fol. 167v). Dodesham went from Witham to Sheen around 1470, but was apparently writing for the larger abbey for many years before that time.[86] Both calendar and litany are unremarkably Carthusian; the main point of interest in the contents are the two lists at the end, just before his autograph: one of (pre-Conquest) kings of England "pro Christo martirizatorum," and the other of confessor kings.[87]

As with the Cistercians, the tension between the centralizing control exercised by the General Chapters and the points of individuality (not to say vagaries) of individual houses and even monks seems to be a salient feature of Carthusian liturgical life. Possibly our sense of this is somewhat skewed chronologically, for, as will have been obvious, the great

seen]. There is unfortunately no booklist of any kind for Sheen. An earlier instance is offered by Peterhouse, Cambridge 276, a psalter with no calendar but containing a litany in which the virgins are headed by St Anne, doubled, and the confessors by Hugh, also doubled, and which contains on fol. 1 a statement of ownership by the Charterhouse of St Anne at Coventry; save for the litany, there is nothing distinctively Carthusian about the book.

[84] Van Dijk, *Handlist* II.i.100, suggests a date-range of 1352–66 because of the presence in the original calendar of the Eleven Thousand Virgins, mandated by the General Chapter in 1352, whereas Bernard, whose name was ordered to be inserted in the litany in 1366, is an addition. A convenient summary, too late for van Dijk to use, is J. Hourlier and B. du Moustier, "Le Calendrier cartusien," *Etudes grégoriennes* 2 (1957), pp. 151–61, where the rationale for the dates 1411–12 is made plain.

[85] A. I. Doyle, "English Carthusian Books Not Yet Linked with a Charterhouse," in *A Miracle of Learning: Studies ... in honour of William O'Sullivan*, ed. T. Barnard, D. Ó Cróinín, and K. Simms (Aldershot 1998), pp. 122–36 at 124. Darker is known to have copied at least seven other MSS, enumerated in M. B. Parkes, *English Cursive Book Hands 1250–1500* (Oxford 1969), p. 8 for pl. 8 (ii).

[86] His large hand is reproduced, copying a vernacular text, in Parkes, pl. 6 (ii).

[87] Among the former are Oswyn, martyred at "Tynby in Wallia" rather than at Gilling in Yorkshire; among the latter, Constantine (baptized by Silvester) and Deonatus, "king of Cornwall and father of St Ursula."

preponderance of evidence for liturgy among the English Carthusians is from the fifteenth and, especially, early sixteenth centuries. Indeed, the topic could have been included in the last section, titled "The End of the Story," of our final chapter – a placement that would have been justified emotionally, at least, in light of the savagery with which Henry VIII had several of the monks of that order punished because of their obduracy in resisting his doctrine of royal supremacy. Nonetheless, we should remember that the Carthusians formed something of a liturgical presence in England from the time of Henry II's foundation at Witham, and it would be wrong for this brief consideration of them to give the impression that they were primarily a male equivalent to the (predominantly) female Bridgettines, in England a solely fifteenth- and sixteenth-century group. Instead, the Carthusians can serve as an apt bridge between the more extensive consideration it has been both necessary and possible to devote to the mainstream Benedictines on one side and on the other to the non-monastic religious orders, the next topic to be considered.

8   The non-monastic religious orders: canons regular

Augustinian canons

The amount of attention it will be necessary to devote to the canons regular may seem surprising, given the prevailing assumption that they normally used the liturgies of the diocese in which a given house was located. If this turns out to be generally the case, it must not prevent us from looking into the ways in which this very large, if initially somewhat amorphous, group of religious have influenced the story we are trying to trace.

The factors of size and amorphousness are interrelated. As Sir Richard Southern has demonstrated, people of a level under the great landed aristocracy could afford to endow foundations at the middling level that seems to have sufficed for Augustinians (in contrast to Benedictines); the result was that, in his words, "living under a modest Rule the canons performed modest services for men of moderate means and moderate needs."[1] The consequence in liturgical terms is that their worship is likely to have been in many respects very close to that of ordinary parish churches, with the added factor of participation by a regular religious community. Where this factor was substantial, as in the greater houses like Cirencester and Guisborough, the regular, community aspect would probably have predominated; where it was slight, as with the great number of smaller Augustinian houses, there must often have been close approximation to parochial worship. Indeed, we shall see that some key liturgical manuscripts have reasonably been ascribed to both regular houses and parish churches.

The total number of Augustinian (Black Canon) houses in England and Wales seems to have been somewhere between 150 and 175 for men and about two dozen for women.[2] As with other religious orders,

---

[1] R. W. Southern, *Western Society and the Church in the Middle Ages* (Harmondsworth 1970), pp. 241–50 at 247.

[2] *Med. Rel. Houses*, pp. 137–82; the practice there of including under the general heading of Augustinian Canons houses that belonged to sub-units ("congregations")

it cannot be assumed that the most important houses are always those for which the largest amount of liturgical evidence survives. The three wealthiest male houses at the time of the Dissolution were Cirencester, Merton, and Leicester, but other houses, notably those at Guisborough and Kenilworth, will bulk larger in these pages. Carlisle acquired cathedral status in 1133, a decade after its foundation; Bristol and Oxford St Frideswide's were both made cathedrals in 1540, as was in 1905 Southwark (with major alterations and additions, as at Bristol). At least six further houses function at present as major churches, Christchurch, Dorchester, Hexham, London St Bartholomew's, Waltham, and Worksop, and a handful of other parish churches incorporate medieval Augustinian remains into their structures. Of Augustinian nunneries, the London houses at Halliwell and Clerkenwell seem to have been the most prominent.

The overall number of Augustinian liturgical books that survive for study is striking, if scanty in relation to the number of houses. Among the nicknames used in the present work are found the Haughmond gradual, Kenilworth manual-missal, Lesnes missal, Oseney ordinal, and four books connected with Guisborough (a breviary, diurnal, missal, and psalter); the provenance of several dozen more can be identified. Fortunately, there also survives information about book holdings at some thirty-four Augustinian houses, albeit in two thirds of these cases only through the witness of John Leland c. 1536–40; but there are also substantial catalogues for the sizeable libraries at Leicester and Lanthony.[3] Inevitably it will be necessary to depend on those two catalogues heavily, despite the irony that no liturgical books are known to survive from Leicester and only two from Lanthony.

In Scotland there were seven substantial houses of this order, six of them founded between around 1120 (Scone) and 1144 (St Andrews, a cathedral priory).[4] A thirteenth-century ordinal from Holyrood,

---

generally known as Arrouasian, Victorine, or of the Holy Sepulchre has been followed here. In the present work "Augustinian" *simpliciter* will always refer to the Black Canons; Augustinian friars will be so specified, and called by the shorter form Austin for greater clarity. A much larger number of Augustinian Canon houses is given in C. H. Lawrence, *Medieval Monasticism* (London 1984), p. 141: "the largest religious institution in the country, with 274 houses, excluding alien priories, as against 219 Benedictine establishments," but no source is given for this figure.

[3] T. Webber and A. G. Watson, eds. *The Libraries of the Augustinian Canons*, CBMLC 6 (London 1998). The latter house, technically "Llanthony secunda," is customarily referred to with a single "l," to distinguish it from its mother house "Llanthony prima" in Monmouthshire.

[4] I. B. Cowan and D. E. Easson, *Medieval Religious Houses: Scotland*, 2nd edn (London 1976), pp. 88–99. The seven houses listed all had incomes ranging from £1,240 to £12,500 in 1561; these figures seem enormous, but the calculation is a complicated

mentioned presently, provides the most substantial liturgical evidence. In Ireland Augustinian houses became numerous, but they were often very small and in many cases were transmuted (apparently most often in the twelfth century) in a blurred way from establishments founded centuries earlier into communities of regular canons. For our limited purposes the only houses to be noted are two in Dublin, the cathedral priory of Holy Trinity, which became Augustinian c. 1163, and the priory (1177), then abbey (c. 1192), of St Thomas the Martyr, founded by Henry II.[5]

Of the surviving books thought to be Augustinian, only three are available in complete modern printed editions: the Barnwell antiphonal (CUL Mm.2.9), as the base manuscript for Frere's partial facsimile presentation of what he titled *Antiphonale Sarisburiense* (it will be argued below that this is probably not Augustinian and certainly not from Barnwell); the ordinal from Holyrood (Edinburgh, Holyrood House, s.n.), edited by F. C. Eeles in a rather rare Scottish antiquarian series; and the Lesnes missal (London, Victoria and Albert Mus. 404–1916), edited by Philip Jebb in a Henry Bradshaw Society volume.[6] In addition, the Oseney ordinal (Bodl. Rawl. 939), dating mainly from the later thirteenth century, has been edited and studied extensively by Timothy Meeson Morris in a 1999 Oxford doctoral thesis that represents much the most extensive study of Augustinian liturgy to date.[7] Morris's work will be heavily drawn on (and is gratefully acknowledged), but the approach here will be markedly different: not a close study of a single witness but an attempt to get at the subject starting with what can be supposed about its earliest stages and, putatively anyhow, its most distinctive points.[8]

---

one and in any case "Scots money was, by 1561, worth only one-fifth of the corresponding sterling": App. III, "The Income of the Scottish Religious Houses," by G. Donaldson (pp. 245–46).

[5] A. Gwynn and R. N. Hadcock, *Medieval Religious Houses: Ireland* (London 1970), pp. 146–200.

[6] W. H. Frere, ed. *Antiphonale Sarisburiense,* 6 vols, Plainsong and Medieval Music Society (London 1901–24; repr. Farnborough 1966); F. C. Eeles, ed. *The Holyrood Ordinale: a Scottish Version of a Directory of English Augustinian Canons, with Manual and Other Liturgical Forms,* Old Edinburgh Club 7 (Edinburgh 1914); P. Jebb, ed. *Missale de Lesnes,* HBS 95 (1964). See p. 285 for a fuller discussion of the Frere edition.

[7] Timothy Meeson Morris, "The Augustinian Use of Oseney Abbey: a Study of the Oseney Ordinal, Processional and Tonale ...," Oxford D.Phil. thesis, 1999. The thesis is in two vols but numbered consecutively; all references here are to vol. I unless otherwise specified. Morris's preferred spelling has been followed in discussing this source, but the abbey from which it comes is more commonly spelled Osney.

[8] The "Handlist of English Augustinian liturgical MSS," in Morris's thesis, pp. 136–42, includes some items which are only doubtfully Augustinian; on the other hand, he omits manuscripts belonging to Augustinian nunneries, and also any evidence from the Irish houses.

The problem of shadowy beginnings

The phenomenon of the Augustinian canons is from a liturgical stand-point particularly fascinating for England. No matter what criteria are used either to identify a specific establishment as Augustinian or to specify a date at which that can be said to be the case, it is clear that the earliest observance in England that can fairly be so labelled postdates the beginning of the Norman Conquest by about thirty years.[9] Put simply, where did the earliest Augustinians in England get the forms by which they worshipped? Here the thoroughly vexed question of Augustinian origins must be at least noticed.[10]

Three well-known cases can point the problem. All belong to what Janet Burton has called "a brief 'pre-Augustinian' period in England when, as on the continent, communities of clerics adopted a common life without using the Rule [sc. of Augustine]."[11] These are, in probable chronological order, the community of St Gregory in Canterbury, established by Lanfranc c. 1085 to serve the nearby hospital of St John Baptist; St Mary's in Huntingdon, apparently extant by 1092; and St Botolph's in Colchester, probably something like a secular college in 1095. St Gregory's has become clearly an Augustinian house by c. 1123–36, for charter evidence ascribes the institution of regular canons to archbishop William of Corbeil. Its Lanfrancian origin raises the natural question as to the effect that the founder's liturgical prescriptions (as manifested in his *Constitutions*, which are, however, designed expressly for Benedictine communities) might have had on its worship in at least the early years of its existence.[12]

The house at Huntingdon, of scant importance in itself, seems to have sent some clerics to colonize a similar establishment at St Giles's, Cambridge: which, albeit short-lived and almost totally obscure, may in turn stand in some relationship to the house at Barnwell, originally near

[9] Knowles and Hadcock express the matter cautiously: "The rule of the order of St Augustine, of regular canons, appears to have been first adopted in England at Colchester c. 1100 and definitely some time before 1106; priests and brethren living under some form of rule, and sometimes referred to as regular canons, occur at several places earlier, but they did not then belong to the Augustinian order" (*Med. Rel. Houses*, p. 137).

[10] The standard work on English aspects of the subject is still J. C. Dickinson, *The Origins of the Austin Canons and their Introduction into England* (London 1950); this pays almost no attention to liturgy. The most useful recent, but very brief, treatment is in J. Burton, *Monastic and Religious Orders in Britain, 1000–1300* (Cambridge 1994), pp. 43–56.

[11] Burton, p. 45.

[12] The foundation charter is printed in Dickinson, pp. 280–82, and in A. M. Woodcock, ed. *Cartulary of the Priory of St Gregory, Canterbury*, Camden Soc. third ser. 88 (1956), pp. 1–3. There are no liturgical provisions beyond the specification that holders of prebends should observe the night hours in their churches as well as the day hours.

the castle at Cambridge (as St Giles's had been). Although the formal foundation of Barnwell dates from 1112, when the priory was moved to its permanent site just east of Cambridge, it is conceivable that some liturgical practices in use at Huntingdon around, say, 1090 continued, via St Giles's, at Barnwell before it became formally Augustinian.[13]

Our third case, Colchester, often said to be the earliest Augustinian house in England, presents a similar situation: a secular community c. 1093, it adopts the Rule of Augustine some time in the next thirteen years, and by 1107 seems to have supplied the nucleus, including a first prior, for what is to become the great foundation in London, Holy Trinity Aldgate. Apparently nothing of a liturgical sort survives from either Colchester or Aldgate.[14]

What is apparently the oldest liturgical document for an English Augustinian house did not remain there long. This is a calendar for the priory at Hexham, founded (after antecedents going back to the late seventh century) in 1113, but by about the middle of the twelfth century the document (now Oxford, Corpus Christi College 134) was taken to nearby Tynemouth, the large cell of St Albans, and there altered to fit monastic usage and put at the head of a considerable body of material, mainly about Oswin, Tynemouth's principal saint. The original calendar was undoubtedly written for Hexham, with special emphasis on Andrew (its dedication) and feasts for bishops Alkmund and Acca as well as its founder-patron Wilfrid – but also an octave for Augustine's August 28th feast and his Translation on October 11th. The latter two are usually taken to be the most distinctive signs of Augustinian identity.[15] Another sign is when the gradings for the most important feasts are, as in the Hexham calendar, of nine lessons, the maximum in the

---

[13] That this may not have been the case at all, however, is suggested by the fact that Ives, the main saint of the Huntingdon region, finds no place in the late 13th-cent. Barnwell calendar (below, p. 286).

[14] The early 13th-cent. calendar that, with an elaborate cycle of prefatory pictures, is all that survives of a psalter bound with a late 15th-cent. Eusebius (Cambridge, Emmanuel Coll. 252), is from Chertsey abbey, as N. Morgan has recognized (*Early Gothic MSS* I, no. 52), not from Aldgate – although eventually it fetched up there, with obits of three priors added.

[15] That the Translation is missing from the calendar in, for example, the ambitiously illustrated early 13th-cent. psalter BL Arundel 157 is a strong reason for doubting the ascription (with query, to be sure) to St Frideswide's, Oxford, in *MLGB Suppl.*, p. 52; there Oct. 11th has only Ethelburga ("aelburge"), followed by Nicasius. But there are three feasts for Frideswide and a *memoria* for her in the Little Office that concludes the book, so some connection with Oxford is overwhelmingly likely. In the litany, where Peter is doubled, the confessors are headed by Augustine, but he is not among the twenty-nine saints for whom there is a *memoria*, whereas Augustine of Canterbury (14th in the litany) is. The point has some additional interest in that Nigel Morgan finds the minor decoration to be by the same artist as a psalter possibly

secular office (which all canons regular followed) rather than the twelve of the monastic office. For anything beyond calendar evidence, we have to turn to a somewhat enigmatic gradual.

The Haughmond gradual

Since there seems no way of addressing directly the forms used for worship in English Augustinian houses in the early or even middle twelfth century, can the problem of their liturgical origins be approached by some judicious back-reading? Of the more substantial witnesses, the earliest appears to be a gradual from Haughmond abbey in Shropshire, now Shrewsbury School MS 30.[16] The original codex dates from around 1175 and was clearly written for Haughmond, with the only English saint being Milburga (of nearby Wenlock); Becket is an early addition. It was still in, or was returned to, use in the fourteenth century, when masses for some ten English saints or their translations were added, including the West Country figures of Ethelbert of Hereford, Wulfhad, Thomas Cantilupe, and Translation of Winifred; also a number of "winter" sequences and other material like Corpus Christi. It seems to have spawned a related gradual for its daughter house at Ranton (or Ron[c]ton, Staffordshire), which became independent by 1247; this book, now BL Harley 622, is closely related to the Haughmond gradual, but its rubrics are less extensive.[17]

The Haughmond gradual contains, as well as the notated mass chants (stemmed notes on four-line staves), frequent, quite lengthy rubrics, many of which read as though taken from an ordinal.[18] These rubrics often use the word *abbas* (sometimes in capitals, possibly pointing to the raising of the priory to abbatial status c. 1155?), are in at least one place couched in the first person plural (*celebramus*, fol. 101), and several times employ the phrase *de sancto loci*.[19] Though unquestionably

from Haughmond, BL Harley 2905, and the Lesnes missal (treated presently): *Early Gothic MSS*, I, p. 73.

[16] Full description in *MMBL*, IV.317; incipits of chants are listed in Hartzell, *Cat. Music*, pp. 564–79. I am grateful to James Lawson, Taylor Librarian of the school, for facilitating the acquisition of a microfilm and for correspondence about the book.

[17] A special point of interest is a sequence for St Chad, beginning "Munde meritis puritate munde voces," on fol. 154v, at the end of the twenty-third Sunday after Pentecost.

[18] Morris, pp. 428–35 prints excerpts from this MS, and especially from the rubrics (up to fol. 101).

[19] A rubric on fol. 136 states that in "ordinary" time the high mass on Thursdays should be "de sancto loci. Apud nos de sancte iohanne evangelista": the dedication of Haughmond, unique among major English Augustinian houses. It has also the Feast

written for this house, then, the book as a whole looks to have its origin in a more general context.

Was this context Augustinian in origin? We note the lack of proper forms for the feast of Augustine (fol. 117), for which it is specified that the chant texts are to be taken from various sections of the common of saints: introit from that of one abbot, other forms from those for a confessor or for a martyr. The same is true of the forms for Augustine's Translation, October 13th (fol. 119), for all of which the common of a confessor seems to be the source; as well, Nigasius and his Companions share the day. Here, where we would expect the most distinctive forms, the lack of attention to these two feasts suggests that the model for this gradual may have been a secular book in which Augustine is of no great importance. There is, however, enough congruence between Haughmond's rubrics and those of the Oseney ordinal to imply something like an Augustinian liturgical program. The likelihood of this is emphasized in Morris's work on the latter book, which we must now consider.

The Oseney ordinal

This ordinal is part of a manuscript, Bodl. Rawl. C.939, which is a sort of liturgical *omnium gatherum*, apparently bound together in the fifteenth century. Its 251 folios include such items as a calendar (lacking January and February), an extensive obituary, the ordinal itself (fols 32–76v), a tonal, orders for processions, for reading in refectory, and for profession of new canons, and lists of good and bad days for bloodletting (in French as well as Latin).[20] The section concluding with a list of abbots of Oseney (fols 164v–65) is datable to 1288–97; most of the rest of the items seem to be of the late thirteenth century, but not as conclusively.[21] The calendar must be post-1280, for the Translation of Hugh (6 October of that year) is original. George has, very unusually, an octave, doubtless with reference to the nearby collegiate church (royal free chapel) of St George, granted to the abbey in 1149. Even more unusual is the inclusion of Rumwold, on 3 November.

---

of Relics on Aug. 8th, the same day as the calendar of the late 12th-cent. psalter BL Harley 2905, perhaps from Haughmond.

[20] S. J. P. van Dijk's exhibition catalogue, *Latin Liturgical MSS and Printed Books* (Oxford 1952), p. 49, calls this a miscellaneous volume. His *Handlist*, III.220, lists some thirty-three items. Morris provides an edition of, as well as the ordinal, the calendar, processional, and tonal, with extracts from some of the other items.

[21] A. G. Watson, *Cat. of Dated and Datable MSS c. 435–1600 in Oxford Libraries*, 2 vols (Oxford 1984), no. 678 and pl. 135.

The ordinal itself seems more properly to be, in Morris's words, "a commentary on and enlargement of an existing ordinal, which does not survive."[22] That is, it does not spell out everything that a complete ordinal would, either on the assumption that the canons would in many respects be operating from memory or, as Morris suggests, because it is designed to complement a more conventional ordinal, not extant. Whatever the case, it is somewhat hard to compare it with other ordinals or with a liturgical book proper, such as the Haughmond gradual. Above all, it seldom provides text-tags – as a proper ordinal often does – which could be laid alongside texts in other books. This makes its calendar details the prime material for our purposes, and its usefulness to us mainly comparative and corroborative, as the next two books we look at demonstrate.

Corroboration from Wigmore and "Hanley Castle" books

One of the service books which can be compared with the Oseney volume in this respect is a small, portable breviary of roughly the mid-thirteenth century, now Bodl. MS Bodley 547, with a calendar much augmented and containing numerous discrepancies from the sanctorale, itself consisting for most occasions of a collect only. The book was Augustinian from its beginning, and its calendar, at least, apparently from the west country, most likely Herefordshire. Original calendar entries include, all at nine lessons, Ethelbert of East Anglia and Hereford, David, Kyneburga (Cyniburg, of Gloucester; 25 June), Kenelm, and Thomas Becket, as well as the telltale octave for Augustine's main feast and his October Translation feast. The sanctorale begins with Silvester rather than Andrew, a sign of a marked conservatism. Conservative also is the Conception of John the Baptist, one of almost sixty feasts in the calendar but not the sanctorale – along with all of those mentioned above save the two feasts of Augustine. (Becket is missing from the post-Christmas part of the temporale.) The calendar, almost certainly copied from an older model, is full of English saints, whereas the sanctorale contains not a single one. Likewise, when additions were made to the calendar of such saints as Wulfstan, Blaise, Milburga, Oswald (of Worcester), John of Beverley, Translation of Becket, and Francis, it is clearly with no reference to the sanctorale. (There are a number of hands involved, all of roughly the same period.) The calendar is in a separate, preliminary quire, and the one that should have followed it, the beginning of the temporale, is lacking. The sanctorale

---

[22] Morris, p. 37.

itself is almost certainly Augustinian, though the quire the decisive criterion, the October Translation feast, would have come in is also missing.

This amount of detail is necessary because Morris, basing his analysis mainly on textual variants in the temporale like the second vespers of Easter, has noted enough points of identity with details in the Oseney ordinal to be emphatic that "No doubt this manuscript represents a similar use to the Oseney sources."[23] The Augustinian house to which the calendarial details point most forcefully is Wigmore (ignored by Morris, who instead canvasses possibilities of Haughmond or the small alien cell at Beckford, Glos.). This widens, therefore, the range of foundations putatively reflecting something like a common ordinal, to include one of the most prominent houses of the Victorine strain of Augustinians.

It may possibly be widened further, to include a missal which will be relevant also to our consideration of liturgy in parish churches (see p. 513), CUL Kk.2.6, commonly known as the Hanley Castle missal. The original core of the book was written in the early thirteenth, or possibly late twelfth, century, but in the fourteenth (probably second quarter) it came into the possession of another church and was at that point equipped with a new calendar and much additional material. That this was the parish church of Hanley Castle in Worcestershire is only a guess, based on an inscription in a late medieval hand (c. 1500?), identifying it as the "prystys bocke" of that church (fol. 133v). It is a big book, 310 x 220 mm, suitable for use at a high altar, and completely noted but with almost no rubrics or headings. According to Morris's rather brief analysis, the earlier part of the book "agrees in most respects with Oseney use ... [with] uniquely, an almost identical mass for St Augustine, differing only in the offertory."[24] This is a fairly strong point, given the instability of service texts for that eponymous saint (see below, p. 283), but on balance there are too few places where direct comparison is possible to say conclusively that the original nucleus of the Hanley Castle book has close affinities with Oseney. It is nonetheless possible that it began life in some Augustinian house, even if we cannot identify which one, and that, discarded as being out of date or worn out, it came to belong to a parish church where, suitably corrected and supplemented, it saw further use for a couple of centuries.

---

[23] Ibid., p. 120.

[24] Ibid., p. 123. "Oseney use" is his construction; I would prefer, more cautiously, "the Oseney MS."

Augustinian processions and processionals

Further perspective may be offered by two processionals, one clearly Augustinian but not ascribed to a specific house, the other from St Osyth (Chich) in Essex. The first, Bodl. Lyell 9, is at present dated no more precisely than "thirteenth century."[25] It is curiously, though perhaps pragmatically, organized by different types of material, including responsories for vespers (sometimes presented separately as a *vesperale*, an uncommon kind of book in England). The section of sequences, which runs continuously rather than being divided into temporale and sanctorale, contains nothing for either Becket or Corpus Christi.[26] The only outstandingly odd contents are single vespers antiphons for Tiburtius (the 11 August, not 14 November, saint) and for Britius (13 November). Aside from a doubling of Peter in the Rogation Monday and Tuesday litanies, the one prominent saint appears to be Michael who, like Augustine, has a complete set of seven vespers antiphons; this led Albinia de la Mare to suggest Breamore (Hampshire), one of the few Augustinian houses dedicated to Michael, as a possible home.[27] Morris cites three points, such as the order of chants at Candlemas, where this book agrees with the Oseney codex, but on the whole it should best be regarded as an independent witness.

Possibly more useful is the fifteenth-century processional from St Osyth, now Bodl. Laud misc. 329. Its most obvious feature of interest is an amazingly luxuriant Rogationtide litany, with fifty-seven martyrs and fifty each of confessors (including such exotic figures as Affrodolus[?] and Constantine) and virgins. The book lacks many leaves, and some gatherings have been bound in the wrong order, but enough can be straightened out to enable Morris to suggest that a "probable conclusion is that St Osyth's and Oseney's uses have a common origin."[28] If this is the case – the evidence is slim, and caution is advisable – and if such an origin can be posited also for the Haughmond gradual and the Wigmore (as it seems) breviary, the geographical spread involved,

---

[25] According to the detailed and masterful description by A. C. de la Mare in her *Catalogue of the Lyell MSS* (Oxford 1971), pp. 21–26; she anticipates Morris's work, noting that "In some cases it is possible to identify items by a comparison with the contemporary processional in the Augustinian ordinal from Oseney abbey ... . Our MS is generally fuller" (p. 21).

[26] The catalogue description misunderstands the continuity, positing a separate sanctorale beginning with John the Baptist; in fact, no Sundays after Trinity had proper sequences, and the feasts of Purification, Annunciation, and Invention of Cross are placed in the Advent to Trinity temporale.

[27] *Cat.*, p. 26. If the doubling of Peter is more significant, Dunstable would be a strong possibility.

[28] Morris, p. 126; pp. 180–83 lists the contents, including incipits for each chant.

from the Hereford–Shropshire region through Oxfordshire (Oseney) to Essex (St Osyth), hints at an extensive web of liturgical affinity. We must now ask whether less bland terms than "web" and "affinity" may be justified.

A possibly unified Augustinian use?

It is widely understood that there was no centralizing structure for houses of Augustinian canons until the mandate of the Fourth Lateran Council in 1215 forced all bodies of religious to develop mechanisms for meetings at least every three years of the heads of all houses of that particular group – which henceforth, and therefore, could reasonably be called a religious order. In the case of the Augustinians this took the form of General Chapters of such heads either separately for the provinces of Canterbury and York or, after 1341, as a single body.[29] Among the enactments of these Chapters can be found a few that suggest something of a push towards liturgical uniformity in the fourteenth century: as when in 1323 William de Melton, archbishop of York, wrote to the northern Chapter that "there were diversities in the Augustinian houses in the diocese which should be remedied ... in liturgical and other matters"; or when two years later a Chapter at Northampton debates whether Corpus Christi should be observed as a double or a major feast.[30]

Before 1215, however, any measure of liturgical uniformity would have consisted merely of one or both of two things: some commonality of texts and something like a common ordinal. Given that theirs was always a secular ("nine-lesson") rite, any search for a commonality of texts distinctive to these regular canons will have to concentrate on those which a secular church is unlikely to have employed – texts used at Northampton, say, but not at the cathedral church of the diocese in which it lay, Lincoln; at Bristol but not Wells; at Guisborough but not York. Because liturgical texts for secular churches in the twelfth century are virtually non-existent, such a search will be at best parlous and must be conducted with hesitant step. The clearest clues ought to be given by texts for the feasts of Augustine: principally his main feast on August 28th, secondarily its octave and the October 11th Translation feast. Because the only churches likely to have observed the Translation

---

[29] H. E. Salter lays out, in the introduction to his edition of the *Chapters of the Augustinian Canons*, Canterbury and York Soc. 29 (1922), the rocky beginnings of these Chapters and the difficulties of ascertaining what they enacted. What survives in the written records must be only a fraction of the total.

[30] *Aug. Chapters*, pp. xxii (Salter's paraphrase) and 12 respectively.

are, as we have seen, Augustinian, it is only the main feast for which enough texts survive to be instructive – hence the following test case.

Mass texts for the August 28th feast

There is surprising instability among the mass texts for Augustine's main feast. In particular, there seem to be two main traditions for the collect and much variation among the chant texts. One collect-tradition derives from the Eighth-Century Gelasian books and is found in at least four English witnesses spanning the eleventh century: the Winchcombe, Robert of Jumièges, New Minster, and Canterbury St Augustine's massbooks (all discussed in previous chapters). It shows up also, however in the Lesnes missal (Augustinian, of the Arrouasian strand; see p. 288) and in the use of York. It seems to be an adaptation of a more generalized prayer for a confessor bishop, with the saint's name inserted fairly far down in the prayer:

Adesto supplicationibus nostris omnipotens Deus et quibus fiduciam sperandae pietatis indulges intercedente beato Augustino confessore tuo atque pontifice, consuetae misericordiae tribue benignus effectum.[31]

The other prayer-tradition is, not surprisingly, roughly Gregorian; that is, it surfaces – for the first time? – in one of the later ninth-century Gregorian massbooks.[32] It is found in England apparently not before the eleventh-century additions to the Leofric missal (Leofric "C"), and thereafter in Sarum, Westminster, and Hereford missals and was used at, inter alia, Oseney. This prayer is clearly proper to Augustine; in the Sarum missals it reads,

Deus qui beatum Augustinum ecclesie tue in exponendis scripture sancte misteriis doctorem catholicum prouidisti; da nobis eius semper et doctrinis instrui et oracione fulciri.

Strikingly, among witnesses to this prayer, Sarum and the Hyde breviary (in its vespers collect, which is the same as at mass) refer to the saint simply as "doctorem catholicum," whereas the others term him "doctorem optimum et electum antistitem."[33]

---

[31] *Lesnes Missal*, p. 121; *York Missal*, II.92.
[32] Cambrai, B.m. 162–3, from St Vaast: Vogel, *Sources*, p. 103.
[33] *SML*, p. 313 (*Corpus Orationum* #1429). Tolhurst, *Hyde Breviary*, IV, fol. 331 notes that his comparative witnesses, "CEM" – the Coldingham breviary, Ely breviary-missal, and Muchelney breviary – all have the longer reading, as does the Westminster missal; so the Hyde peculiarity may be noteworthy. The Hereford missal substitutes *defendi* for *fulciri*; ed. Henderson, p. 315.

The other two mass prayers are quite stable, the sole variation being a distinctive postcommunion for Sarum.[34] But among the chant texts there is puzzling variety. In brief, while the three Augustinian witnesses under consideration here, Haughmond, Lesnes, and Oseney, have the same introit, "In medio ecclesiae" (shared also by York and Hereford; the New Minster, Sarum, and Westminster books have "Statuit ei dominus"), at the gradual there are four different texts, and at the alleluia four also. At the latter Haughmond and Oseney seem to agree, as also at the communio, while Lesnes differs; but at the offertory it is Lesnes and Oseney that agree, apparently against Haughmond.[35]

What all this suggests is, not surprisingly, that the emergence of Augustinian canons' self-identity is not matched by anything like a commonalty of liturgical texts, even for their ostensibly most distinctive figure. By the time there is enough evidence to make possible comparative study, the various houses seem to have drawn on a variety of sources, neither manifesting any uniformity, as the more-or-less contemporary Cistercians attempted to do, nor – despite the common statement to the contrary – necessarily following the uses of the dioceses in which they were located.

This can be seen also in the more difficult question of the office for Augustine. Morris speaks of "the usual Augustinian history" for the saint, characterized by the first responsory at matins, "Invenit se Augustinus," but the matter is not so simple.[36] At points where it is possible to make comparisons one can perhaps discern a basic body of texts, but again there is a striking amount of variation. The Barnwell antiphonal (see next section) gives all the chant texts "In natali beatissimi patris nostri Augustini episcopi," but gives no indication as to lessons.[37] Oseney contains tags for the service "In commemoratione sancti augustini" which looks to be the office for his main feast (this is also where information about its mass liturgy for this feast is found), again with no hint as to lessons. The 1531 Sarum breviary has a full set of nine lessons but all other forms are from the common of a confessor

---

[34] This purely general prayer, "Sumentes Domine salutaria sacramenta quaesumus ut eius nos tribuas subsequi documenta cuius celebramus gloriosa sollempnia" (*SML*, p. 314), does not seem to be replicated elsewhere.

[35] "Apparently," in that Haughmond's rubric is rather confused here (fol. 117); but what is clear is that Haughmond's texts are drawn only from the common of saints, or in one case from another proper: at the introit the wording is "Require Sancti Iohannis ante Portam Latinum" (6 May).

[36] Morris, p. 94. This office is not one of the three for the feast lised in A. Hughes, *Late Medieval Liturgical Offices: Texts. Resources for Electronic Research* (Toronto 1994), p. 114.

[37] *Sarum Antiphonal*, p. 501.

bishop, save for four capitula and the collect (identical with that in Sarum missals). These lessons are found also, in shorter form, in the Legenda compiled for Bishop Grandisson of Exeter, c. 1337, the Hyde breviary, the printed York breviary, and, vastly shortened, the printed Hereford breviary of the early sixteenth century.[38] In none of these non-Augustinian sources are there proper antiphons and responsories; in that sense, the "Invenit se Augustinus" set can be used as another test of the distinctively Augustinian.

Because the forms used by the canons of Barnwell are the fullest of those available, the discrepancies with Oseney – in places where the two can be compared – are noteworthy. At first vespers O's opening antiphon is "Simulabo," B's "Letare mater nostra;" the hymn in B is "Magne pater Augustine," in O "Iste confessor" (also in Sarum, York, Hereford, and Hyde); and the antiphon to Magnificat is "Adest dies celebris" in B to O's "Letare mater" (which was B's first antiphon to the psalms). At lauds, although the two share the same opening antiphon, "Post mortem matris," there is again divergence in hymn ("Ihesu redemptor" in O, "Cives caeli" in B) and antiphon to Benedictus ("Euge serve" in O, "In diebus illis obsessa" in B). Indeed, the Oseney office is so different from Barnwell's that we are prompted to ask whether the latter was in fact used by Augustinian canons.

Liturgy at Barnwell

In view of the comparative fullness of the Barnwell antiphonal and, even more, the fact that W. H. Frere many years ago published most of it with the somewhat unhelpful title *Antiphonale Sarisburiense: a reproduction in facsimile of a manuscript of the thirteenth century*, it is not surprising that the codex is a source of the first importance for our enquiries. The preliminary question must be, a source for what? Frere's interest was mainly in the chant, as the seventy-odd pages he devotes to minute analysis of those of each mode shows. His assignment of its home is almost offhand: "The MS is not strictly speaking of Sarum Use pure and simple, but it was written for an Augustinian House, probably St Giles Abbey, Barnwell, near Cambridge."[39] No evidence is offered for this ascription beyond the possible coincidence that there is a full office for Edmund of East Anglia and that a chapel dedicated to

---

[38] *Sarum Breviary*, III, c.739; *Legenda Exon.*, = vol. III of *Ordinale Exon.*, ed. J. N. Dalton, HBS 63 (1926), p. 324; *Hyde Breviary*, IV, fol. 331; *York Breviary*, II.510; *Hereford Breviary*, II.312.

[39] *Sarum Antiphonal*, p. 77.

Edmund was built at Barnwell about the time he dates the manuscript, second quarter of the thirteenth century.[40] That the codex comes from Barnwell has apparently been unquestioned since Frere concluded his Introduction in 1925, but there seem good reasons to challenge the ascription. The chief is that Giles, the main patron saint of the house, is in no way magnified: "*Sancti Egidii abbatis oratio* Deus qui hodierna die" is all that is given for him.[41] Secondly, the dedication of the church is in fact a double one, to Giles and Andrew;[42] and, while Andrew's main feast is of course present with a full, proper office, his secondary feast, the Translation on May 9th, is completely ignored – although in the Barnwell calendar with which its *Liber memorandorum* begins the feast is kept with six proper lessons, the other three being for the Translation of Nicholas the same day. Thirdly, there is widespread incongruity between the text of the antiphonal and this calendar which, like the rest of the *Liber*, seems to be datable to c. 1296.[43] The lack of agreement works in both directions; for example, Arnulph (18 July) is mentioned in the antiphonal but not the calendar, but the calendar has on July 8th both Grimbald and, at nine lessons, Withburga, neither being in the antiphonal. In brief, although the full office for Augustine that it contains can neither be overlooked or explained away, it seems impossible to continue ascribing Mm.2.9 to Barnwell: a house for which there is otherwise a good deal of useful information.

This information is derivable from the extensive compilation known in its modern edition as *Liber memorandorum ecclesie de Bernewelle* (BL Harley 3601), of which book VIII (of eight), headed "Libellus de obseruanciis regularibus," is a detailed customary of the house. The customary section was published in 1897 by J(ohn) W(illis) Clark, with the rest of the *Liber* appearing ten years later.[44] At the head of the latter is the calendar, datable, like the rest of the *Liber*, to the last years of the thirteenth century (it is this calendar, with Barnwell's dedication feast on April 21st and Commemoration of Relics on October 15th, which

[40] The source for this fact, the Barnwell *Liber memorandorum*, indicates that this chapel was dedicated in 1229: ed. J. W. Clark (see note 44 below), pp. 69, 223.

[41] *Sarum Antiphonal*, p. 518. It is possible that nine lessons were involved, for the rubric goes on to say that *medie lc.*, most likely to be expanded into the plural *lectiones*, were to be of St Priscus, who shares the day. In any case, no chant forms, or even tags, are indicated for Giles.

[42] Binns, *Dedications*, p. 119.

[43] Watson, *BL Dated MSS*, no. 772.

[44] The customary is entitled *The Observances in Use at the Augustinian Priory of S. Giles and S. Andrew at Barnwell, Cambridgeshire* (Cambridge 1897). It must constantly be used alongside Clark's edition of the *Liber memorandorum* (Cambridge 1907); ideally the two would have been produced the other way round.

proves it impossible that the antiphonal just discussed should have been used at Barnwell). Of the fifty-seven chapters into which the customary (*Obseruancie regulares*) is divided, roughly a dozen touch on the liturgical usages of the house. The precentor, who was also the librarian (*armarius*), had the chief responsibility for the ordering of services, with the sacrist responsible for the physical accoutrements of worship. The duties of the sub-sacrist, or *matricularius*, include supplying "live coals in iron dishes to warm the hands of those who minister at the altar" in winter.[45] Behavior in choir is carefully regulated, with provisions as detailed as what a brother is to do who, as he is preparing to celebrate a (private) mass, hears the bell ring for a particular hour (almost certainly prime): if he has already put on his stole he is to go ahead with the mass, but if not he abandons the mass and goes into choir for the office.[46] Barnwell was among the Augustinian houses that seem to have celebrated the Transfiguration well before the general spread of the feast, with the blessing of fruits (normally new grapes, long associated with the older feast on August 6th, St Sixtus) performed on that day.[47]

Chapter 23, "De diacono et subdiacono," is a virtual mass *ordo* for the house. Of particular interest is the deployment of books at the high mass: the gospel book (*textus*) is apparently used only on feast days, the missal alone being specified on other days – so presumably the gospel is read (*legit*; does the verb cover chanting at high mass?) from that book except on great occasions.[48] The special devotion called, by Amnon Linder, who has studied the subject intensively, the "Holy Land Clamor" seems to be present here, placed somewhat unusually after the Agnus Dei.[49] The *ordo* concludes with the human touch that the assisting ministers, who ought to remain vigilant lest the celebrant become suddenly ill or have a seizure, should not pass the time by bringing to the altar material for singing or private (spiritual?) reading, "librum

---

[45] *Observances*, p. 75.

[46] Ibid., p. 87.

[47] Other Augustinian evidence for observance of the Transfiguration is laid out in Pfaff, *New Liturg. Feasts*, pp. 26–27.

[48] That this is the correct interpretation is clear from further on in the chapter, where it is provided that the deacon reads the Gospel from a book (*librum*), but from a *textum* if it is a feast (p. 114). After announcing the Gospel he signs himself with the cross on forehead and chest, which entails holding the missal in one hand: by no means an easy thing to do with some very large missals used at high altars.

[49] A. Linder, *Raising Arms: Liturgy in the Struggle to Liberate Jerusalem in the Late Middle Ages* (Turnhout 2003); the Barnwell MS is not mentioned. The devotion consists in its simplest form of Ps. lxxix, *Deus venerunt*, followed by one or more versicles, responses, and collects, as in *SML*, pp. 209–10; at Barnwell all that is specified is the psalm and following prayer (p. 108), and the practice seems to be confined to the Morrow Mass.

aliquem in quo psallant uel studeant secum." Though it is frustrating that no missal survives from Barnwell, the provisions of its mass *ordo* might well serve for a book that is extant, the Lesnes missal.

Lesnes: the evolution of a missal

The fine massbook now at the Victoria and Albert Museum in London, MS 404–1916, is of special value in suggesting stages at which a splendidly decorated missal, almost certainly for the use of the abbot or at the least at the high altar, came into existence in a recently established house. Lesnes abbey was founded in 1178 by Richard de Lucy, Henry II's trusted Justiciar.[50] As such, Richard had played a large, and largely antagonistic, part in the Becket episode, and it seems to have been in expiation for this that the new house was dedicated to St Thomas. The founder died, having taken the canonical habit, in 1179, and some time within the next eighteen years Lesnes affiliated itself with the Arrouasian congregation of canons regular. The de Lucy family remained as patrons and their symbol, the lucy (pike), appears in several of the initials. It is probably owing to their patronage that the massbook is so lavishly illustrated, with twenty-seven historiated initials and much minor decoration; Nigel Morgan has suggested that the latter is by the same group of artists, apparently based at Oxford, who worked on a psalter perhaps from Haughmond and a sumptuous psalter sometimes assigned to St Frideswide's (both of them Augustinian houses).[51]

The book was edited in 1964 by Philip Jebb, whose introduction analyzes the component parts of the book this way.[52] The writing seems to have begun with the first of the two sanctorales that it contains (fols 113–49v), in sacramentary form – that is, with the mass prayers only. Here there are only three English saints, Augustine of Canterbury, Alban, and Edmund Martyr. The presence of Nicasius (of Reims; 14 December) may be noteworthy. Jebb, relying on notes left by J. B. L. Tolhurst after his death, dates this section to about 1200. It was followed by a temporale which supplies the choir parts (but not the lessons, so still not a *missale plenum*) as well as the celebrant's prayers and a second

---

[50] Sometimes spelled Lessness (and occasionally called Westwood), in Belvedere, technically West Kent but effectively in suburban London. There are surprisingly instructive ruins, excavated by A. W. Clapham in the early 20th cent., described in his short monograph, *Lesnes Abbey* (London 1915); cf. J. Newman's summary in PBE *West Kent and the Weald*, 2nd edn (1976), pp. 150–51.

[51] Respectively, BL Harley 2905 and BL Arundel 157. The former is not so assigned in *MLGB*, and the latter ascription is argued as doubtful in note 15 above; Morgan, *Early Gothic MSS*, I.73.

[52] P. Jebb, ed. *The Lesnes Missal*, HBS 95 (1964).

sanctorale, with *only* the choir texts (mostly just incipits). The latter is much fuller than the first sanctorale, so another book would have had to be used for the prayers on such occasions as Alphege, Botolph, Etheldreda, Erkenwald, Ethelburga, Dunstan, Mildred, Paulinus, Kenelm, and fifteen saints, or groups of saints, all but two of whom can be associated with the region of Arras. This leads Jebb to the natural conclusion that "this change came about at the time of the aggregation of Lesnes to the Congregation of Arrouaise"; precisely when that happened is, however, not clear beyond the fact that an abbot Fulk, who is in office in 1197 and apparently died in 1208, is mentioned in the Necrology of Arrouaise.[53] The calendar, apparently written last but before 1220, was considerably added to later, with only a handful of additional saints' masses.

In its final form the book would have been suitable for occasional abbatial or high-altar use, but would have to have been supplemented by others for most purposes. The rather confused organization aside, its most striking textual feature may be the *ordines* for Good Friday and the Easter Vigil, about both of which Jebb comments that they "differ so much from the Roman both in order and content" that they are given in full (whereas he normally provides only tags for forms that are identical with those in the Henry Bradshaw Society edition of the *Missale Romanum 1474*), but without offering any details. One such detail, glaringly noticeable, is the supplying on Good Friday of a prayer after the tract "Domine audivi," "Deus qui peccati veteris hereditariam ... sanctificatione portemus." This prayer, Old and Eighth-Century Gelasian in origin, was in widespread monastic usage, and seems to be what Lanfranc's *Constitutions* refer to as the "second collect" on that day.[54] Another is a variant reading in the collect after the second lesson in the Easter Vigil, where after the standard opening "Deus cuius antiqua miracula ... quesumus," the *ut* clause ("ut sicut priorem populum ab Egiptis maris transitu liberasti, ita hoc ad salutem gentium per aquas baptismatis opereris") is the reverse of the previous example, the Lesnes ending being Gregorian, whereas the more usual ending ("... in israeleticam dignitatem totius mundi transeat plenitudo"), Gelasian in origin, is found in monastic and secular usage alike.[55] The extensive rubrical details for these two services also deserve close analysis – for

---

[53] Jebb, pp. xvi and xx; *Heads Rel. Houses*, I.171.

[54] *Monastic Constitutions*, ed. Brooke and Knowles (above, p. 102), p. 60. *WM*, III.1469 lists massbooks where it is found, including Westminster and the Leofric missal (ed. Orchard, no. 783).

[55] The only instance I have found of the "baptismatis opereris" conclusion is in the late 10th-cent. Fulda sacramentary (see p. xxiii above), no. 702.

example, in specifying that the abbot will always be the celebrant at them.[56]

Guisborough: the fullest picture

The Yorkshire priory at Guisborough (also spelled Gisborough and, archaically, Gisburne) is the Augustinian house from which we have the most extensive survival of service books. Generously endowed by its founder Robert de Brus in, probably, 1119, and sustained by generations of the Brus (Bruce) family, it flourished until a great fire in 1289 destroyed the church, its contents, and many of its extensive collection of theological books.[57] The church was subsequently rebuilt, on an even larger scale, and despite financial difficulties connected with the Scottish wars of the 1320s, the number of canons in 1380 remained around twenty-six.

The four extant service books span the period of the fire and subsequent rebuilding. The nicknames by which, for the sake of brevity, they are known are in two cases slightly inaccurate: the Guisborough psalter (Bodl. Laud lat. 5), diurnal (Cambridge, Sidney Sussex 62), missal (BL Add. 32585; actually a missal-breviary), and breviary (Woolhampton, Douai Abbey 4, actually a breviary-missal). All save the breviary have a calendar; those of the missal and (by collation) of the psalter have been published by Francis Wormald.[58] The Add. 32585 missal-breviary

---

[56] A useful comparison with the Lesnes book is offered by an early 15th-cent. Augustinian missal, from the Victorine house at Bristol (and still at Bristol: Public Library 2), described at length by E. G. C. F. Atchley, "Notes on a Bristol MS Missal," in *Trans. St. Paul's Ecclesiol. Soc.* 4 (1896–1900), pp. 279–92; at the end he prints two sequences, part of the Good Friday *ordo*, and an unusual mass for St Cadoc. Atchley found considerable areas of agreement with a 1529 printed missal from St Victor in Paris, but also, not surprisingly, a good deal with Sarum texts and some with Hereford. The book lacks many leaves, including those that might have contained a calendar and everything after early May in the sanctorale, and is in any case a rather bare-bones missal, not including the blessings for Purification, Ash Wednesday, or Palm Sunday, which must therefore have been in another book – though clearly this one was used at Candlemas, for there is a large drop of wax at that service (fol. 147v). The Good Friday rubric does not mention the second collect that the Lesnes book has, nor are there similiarities with Lesnes otherwise.

[57] Walter of Guisborough (or of Hemingburgh), one of the canons, gives a contemporary account of the fire in his *Chronicle*, ed. H. Rothwell, Camden Soc. 3rd ser. 89 (1957), pp. 225–26; this is second in vividness only to Gervase's account of the fire at Christ Church, Canterbury, in 1174.

[58] F. Wormald, "A Liturgical Calendar from Guisborough Priory, with some obits," *Yorkshire Archaeol. Jnl.* 31 (1934), pp. 6–35. He noted the similarity between the diurnal's calendar and the other two (p. 6), but suggested that it possibly came from Kirkham; this was followed in *MLGB*, but the judgment was reversed in its *Suppl.*, where the MS is assigned, with query, to Guisborough.

is probably by a slight margin the oldest of the four. Its calendar was written by 1283, for the Translation of William of York is an (almost contemporary) addition, another being a note at May 16th about the 1289 fire, with the year specified. A notable feature of all three calendars is the presence on August 18th of Helena, *mater imperatoris* in missal and psalter, *regina* in diurnal.

The missal-breviary is very oddly structured, the missal component being quantitatively the lesser part. Excluding later insertions and additions, it begins with some eighty-five leaves of office chants for the temporale, then continues with the missal section (fols 107–67); calendar; psalter with canticles and litany; manual offices for baptism, marriage, visitation of the sick, and burial; office chants for the proper and common of saints; office lectionary, in sets of nine or three lessons, for temporale, sanctorale, and common; and processional. This variety of contents caused Christopher Hohler to term it a precentor's book.[59] If so, it would have been usable only by a precentor with excellent eyesight; the letters are sometimes only one to two millimeters high. The book's size, about 235 by 165 mm (but there has been some cropping) is congruous with such a purpose, but it is hard to see why a precentor would need the mass prayer-texts or the manual offices, save perhaps for reference purposes. The processional section includes responsories to be used at the washing of all the altars on Maundy Thursday, and thus provides the dedications for all of the nine subsidiary altars, three being for St Helena, Thomas (Becket), and Augustine.

In contrast to the relatively undecorated nature of that book is the striking decoration of its contemporary, the Laud lat. 5 psalter.[60] It is also to be dated after 1283, and includes an extensive hymnal. The litany agrees with that of Add. 35285 in doubling Peter (though the priory was dedicated to Mary) and in including Martial among the apostles. At the beginning is a list of days on which no work was to be done according to the use of York, and only the first few words of each verse are given for the canticles used most often, like the Magnificat. These small facts, plus the decoration of the volume and the entry in it of notes about benefactors as late as 1427, suggest that it may have been

---

[59] C. Hohler, "The Durham Services in honour of St Cuthbert," in *The Relics of St Cuthbert*, ed. C. Battiscombe (Oxford 1956), pp. 155–91 at 160; variants in its office for Cuthbert are given, under the siglum Gum(b) on pp. 184–87. He discusses the text of its mass for St John of Beverley in a note (in English) in L. Gjerløw, "Missaler brukt i Bjørgvins bispedømne fra misjonstiden til Nidarosordinariet," in *Bjørgvin Bispestol*, ed. P. Juvkam (Bergen 1970), pp. 73–115 at 96.

[60] Morgan, *Early Gothic MSS*, II, no. 175. There are two framed miniatures and space left for a third, which was to be an image of the Holy Face; also unusually early devotions to the Five Wounds.

the prior's own book – which would seem particularly suitable for the prior in whose time it was made, William of Middlesbrough, in office for forty years, 1281–1320.[61]

The latter feature, first words of each verse only, is applied also to the psalms in the Sidney Sussex 62 diurnal, a tiny (roughly 80 × 50 mm) and severely pragmatic book but nonetheless with, on many pages, good little initials and elaborate borders. It contains only those psalms (mainly cix on) and other forms used during the day hours; the greatest point of interest is at the end, after three blank leaves, a series of collects (fols 199–207) for some sixty saints, all save eight being the old "sacramentary" saints – and those not the most important: none for feasts of apostles or Mary, nor for such major figures as Agnes, Agatha, Gregory, Laurence, or Martin, but rather figures like Basilides, Hermes, and Sabina. The implication is that the user would have access to another book for greater feasts and would need this one only for the office in simple feasts and commemorations; again, this (along with the elegant decoration) suggests a book for the prior's use.[62]

The largest, and in some ways most interesting, of the Guisborough books is the breviary-missal now MS 4 at Douai Abbey outside Reading. Its structure is, like that of Add. 35285, complicated but, in contrast to the other book which seems to be something like a reference collection, this one is so lavish in its illustration that it must have been intended as a volume to be used – again, possibly by the prior? – at services or, less plausibly, as a showpiece. Many (most?) of the historiated initials have been cut out, but enough survive to have qualified the book for extensive description (mainly by Francis Wormald) as an appendix to a full-scale art-historical monograph devoted to the Tickhill psalter (New York, Pub. Lib., Spencer 26) and six related manuscripts, one being the Douai book.[63] The description by N. R. Ker published in 1977 quotes a letter from Robin Flower of the (then) British Museum that

---

[61] *Heads Rel. Houses*, II.384.

[62] The memorial of Archbishop Richard Scrope, "martyred" in 1405, entered on fol. 207v may also point in this direction; printed by M. R. James in his 1895 catalogue of the Sidney Sussex MSS, p. 45.

[63] The inclusion of this MS among the six was made by D. D. Egbert, *The Tickhill Psalter and Related Manuscripts* (New York 1940), pp. 205–8, with facs. of Douai 4, fols. 67, 133v, and 164; also discussion on pp. 109–11. But Sandler, *Gothic MSS*, II, no. 26, claims that the discovery of further related MSS shows that the Douai book should be removed from the Tickhill family. (It is surprising that the Douai MS is not treated as such in Sandler's work.) Spencer 26 has Augustinian connections also; according to a 15th-cent. flyleaf inscription, it was written by John Tickhill, who was prior of the Augustinian priory at Worksop (Notts., in the medieval diocese of York), 1303–14, but was removed from office. The book is unfinished, with neither calendar nor litany, and is not further relevant to our subject.

"The text of the antiphons, responds, and hymns in the Breviary; the whole of the Missal as far as it goes; and the Litany are in close agreement with the corresponding parts of Add. MS 35285, a Guisborough book of somewhat earlier date"; but Ker dates Douai 4 to the second half of thirteenth century, and it seems to be only the supposed relationship with the Tickhill psalter that would push the date into the early fourteenth.[64] As with Add. 35285 and the diurnal, there is a peculiarity of structure: this time, that the first item in the book, the temporale of the breviary, is interrupted after Easter V by a limited version of the common of saints and by proper offices or collects for the saints of May. The temporale then resumes, and is followed by a selection of masses, interrupted before Easter by noted proper prefaces and the canon (in all, fols 145–86v; these constitute four quires, according to Ker's collation); psalter with canticles and litany; Office of the Dead and burial service; sanctorale (without any saints for May) and common of saints of the breviary. The twenty-eight masses for specific occasions are given in consecutive order, from I Advent through Nicholas, with Corpus Christi between Trinity Sunday and John the Baptist.[65] There is no mass for Augustine, although he comes first among the confessors, and doubled, in the litany and has a full office of nine lessons for both his feasts in the breviary section; but a leaf is missing after fol. 171, where his mass would have come. The experiment of trying to put all the Paschaltide offices together, presumably in imitation of the Christmas season practice (which generally includes all saints from Stephen through January 13th) is highly unusual, and suggests a liturgical intelligence of some keenness. This is just one of the points that make Guisborough for our purposes the most interesting Augustinian house; but our survey may more usefully conclude by looking at a priory with which only one liturgical book is connected, Kenilworth.

Towards an hypothesis, through the Kenilworth missal-manual

The priory of Kenilworth was among Augustinian houses in no way exceptional, save perhaps in its modest prosperity. Founded in 1125 by Geoffrey de Clinton, the *curialis* of Henry I and sheriff of Warwickshire, the priory and the adjacent castle were testimony to his new-found importance. The endowment was apparently adequate for

---

[64] *MMBL*, II.413.
[65] Nicholas always falls after Advent I, of course, but concludes a sequence All Saints, Andrew, Katherine (herself out of order), Nicholas. Ker's description omits the Assumption, between Laurence and Exaltation of the Cross.

double the usual minimum component of thirteen canons, and it had two or three small dependent priories, including one at Stone in Staffordshire. The sole liturgical book from Kenilworth extant is a select missal with extensive manual section, now Chichester Cathedral MS 2. In physical appearance the book is attractive but unremarkable; its contents, however, turn out to be worth close analysis, for two reasons in particular.[66]

The first has to do with the inclusion, by himself and not in any sanctorale context, of Richard of Chichester, canonized in 1262 (the *terminus a quo* for the book, which cannot be much later). His mass – proper prayers but tags from the common for the rest – is written between the mass for the faithful departed and the prayers for five votives, with no indication of its being an addition or afterthought (fol. 45).[67] A possible explanation for his appearance, unusual in Augustinian books, is that his home town, Wych (now Droitwich) in Worcestershire was the site of an early Augustinian priory that moved in 1151 to Studley, about fifteen miles from Kenilworth, and that there may have been connections between the two houses, including conceivably some supplying of service books from Studley after the damage to Kenilworth priory following the protracted siege of the castle when it was held by the Montfortians in 1266. Textually, the striking thing about the mass is that its collect ("Deus qui ad declaranda sanctorum tuorum") is that transmitted by Richard's contemporary biographer, the Dominican friar Ralph (of) Bocking, according to whom the mass prayers had been composed by the pope, Urban IV, himself. Bocking died in 1270, so the tradition, whether based in fact or not, was a recent one when he recorded it. This makes it highly curious that the collect for Richard in other missals – not numerous but including the Lesnes book – in which his mass appears is almost without exception totally different ("Deus qui ecclesiam tuam meritis").[68]

[66] I have discussed it in some detail in "The Kenilworth Missal," in *Music and Medieval Manuscripts: Paleography and Performance: Essays dedicated to Andrew Hughes*, ed. J. Haines and R. Rosenfeld (Aldershot 2004), pp. 400–18.

[67] But this is the page on which Robert Baskett of Blandford Bryan in Dorset signed his name, in a flowing 18th-cent. hand, as well as on fol. 1: a fact that puzzled Peter Atkinson (formerly canon chancellor of Chichester; my thanks for cooperation are here stressed) as well as me. Was it Baskett who gave this book to the cathedral, knowing of the special interest there in Richard?

[68] The Westminster and later (printed) Sarum missals have the same collect as Lesnes; the only trace of the Bocking–Kenilworth seems to be in Hereford missals, all of a later date than the Chichester MS: see *Hereford Missal*, p. 250. Richard seems never to have been culted in the North.

The other noteworthy point about this book concerns its structure. The first lengthy item is the visitation of the sick (with a litany that includes Wulfhad, the local saint of Stone, among the martyrs, and among the confessors Richard, between Edmund Rich and Hugh of Lincoln), followed by the burial office and *ordines* for making catechumens and for baptizing a sick infant. Then, with no break or codicological distinction, comes the missal section (fols 25v–101, of a total 131), after which there is further manual material. The missal material is itself oddly organized: thirteen votive masses, then proper prefaces and (after a missing leaf, where there was presumably a crucifixion painting) the canon, thirteen sets of mass prayers for the dead and three further sets for "missa generalis pro fidelibus defunctis," the mass for Richard just described, and five further votives for those in various kinds of need. Finally there is a sequence of masses that, highly selectively, covers the year from Christmas to Thomas the Apostle.[69] Among the roughly three dozen sets (sometimes full mass forms, sometimes prayers only) the only temporale occasions are Christmas and the Sunday after it, Circumcision, Epiphany, Easter, Ascension, and Pentecost; no Corpus Christi or even Trinity Sunday. The only surprise among the rest, which include Translation of Augustine as well as his main feast, is Aldhelm, though it should also be noticed that the order of the two Edmunds, martyr (20 November) and archbishop (16 November), is reversed; it looks as though archbishop Edmund, canonized in 1247, was put into an already established sequence, but in the wrong place (we have already seen that a saint canonized fifteen years later is treated separately). That the book was carefully planned is shown by the way the epistle for Mary Magdalen is handled: in the mass itself (fol. 73v) there is a two-word tag and then, in red, "Require post commune sanctorum" – which is exactly where it appears (fol. 101rv), concluding a two-leaf quire and requiring a twenty-fifth line instead of the usual twenty-four.

With the new quire that begins on fol. 102 the manual material returns, with forms for weddings ("ad facienda sponsalia"),[70] blessing of pilgrims, reception and then profession of a novice (Kenilworth and

---

[69] Ker, *MMBL*, II.390, did not notice that these masses form a continuous sequence and divided them into the expected temporale and sanctorale categories; he also overlooked the masses for John the Evangelist and Aldhelm. That for Becket is undamaged.

[70] A fine initial of what is apparently a grotesque winged and beast-footed woman points to this rubric; it is the main (surviving) illustration in the book, and has been well reproduced in a postcard for sale at the cathedral – with an unfortunate caption, "Fourteenth-century Benedictine Missal"!

the Rule of Augustine are specified), excommunication and absolution from it, the usual blessings at Candlemas, Ash Wednesday, and Palm Sunday, reconciliation of penitents on Maundy Thursday, and the blessing of new fire on Easter Eve. Many of these items would be performed only by a religious superior, and it is thus clear that the book is designed for use by the prior (abbatial status was achieved only after 1439).[71] The original codex ends with the Office of the Dead, with music supplied later; and a final three folios, added in the fourteenth century, show that the book was still in use at Kenilworth then, for they contain special prayers for the anniversary of the house's founders.

The reason for dwelling on this book at some length and ending the present section with it is that, as it is almost exactly contemporary with the oldest of the three Sarum missals edited by J. W. Legg in 1916 and still most often taken as representing *the* Sarum missal (the Crawford missal, discussed several times elsewhere in this book), a few textual divergences between Kenilworth and Crawford books, and even more a handful of agreements between Kenilworth and another of Legg's three missals, the Arsenal, may provide a way back into the origins of a common mainstream from which both English Augustinian and proto-Sarum sources drew.

For the moment, what can be said by way of summary about the Augustinians is that there is no congruence of the three elements that we have seen make for distinctive liturgical identity, texts, saints, and rubrics. The aspect of saints is clear enough: most obviously in the case of the two occasions often referred to above, an octave for Augustine's August 28th feast and his Translation on October 11th, but also often in some special prominence given to the two feasts of the Cross, Invention and Exaltation and sometimes, by extension, to Helena as responsible for the former.[72] Such rubrics as there are in the books we have looked at naturally tend to be couched in terms appropriate to religious communities – phrases like "facta trina oratione," "prior in stallo suo," "conventus non discalciatus" – to a degree that suggests monastic customaries and ordinals as prime sources. Textually, however, it may turn out to be the case that Augustinian affinities are clearer with secular sources than with monastic. When the story of secular liturgy is taken up again, therefore, we shall have to go over some of the same ground as with the early Augustinian canons. But before attempting that, we

---

[71] The implication that he was able to absolve excommunicates seems surprising, but the (scanty) rubrics are all cast in an impersonal way, largely in the passive voice.

[72] Feasts of the Cross have not been pursued here because they are also, of course, prominent in many non-Augustinian contexts; but there is often some special elaboration in Augustinian books.

should review the liturgies of the two other important groups of canons regular in England, Premonstratensians and Gilbertines, and then of the four principal orders of friars.

Premonstratensian canons

Evidence for the liturgical usages of the English Premonstratensians is more sketchy than for any other well known group of religious. The order itself, begun by Norbert of Xanten at Prémontré in the Low Countries about 1120, came to be prominent in England by the early thirteenth century; Knowles has stated that "the most remarkable feature of the regular life in England between 1170 and 1216 was the multiplication of the abbeys of the White Canons of Prémontré."[73] The first to be founded was Newhouse (alias Newsham) in Lincolnshire about 1143. Among the best known are Welbeck (Nottinghamshire, 1153–54) and Halesowen (Worcestershire, 1215), and there are specially fine remains at Bayham (Sussex, by 1182), Leiston (Suffolk, 1182), and Titchfield (Hampshire, 1232). Titchfield was the last major foundation, and by that time there were some three dozen abbeys, most concentratedly in the midlands.[74] There were also half a dozen houses in Scotland, most of which seem to have been vastly richer than the richest English house: the income of the greatest, Dryburgh, is given in 1561 as £2210, that of Torre (Devon) in 1539, £396.[75]

Exactly how the earliest Premonstratensians worshipped before any settlement in England is not clear. A papal document of 1126–27 mandates that the general model was to be taken from that of the Augustinians (itself far from transparent, as we have seen), as exemplified in the anonymous *Ordo monasterii* of c. 1100.[76] In the next few years there

---

[73] Knowles, *Monastic Order*, p. 360. As well as White Canons, they are sometimes (but seldom in Britain) called Norbertines, the latter being the most often used current nomenclature for the order.

[74] There is a good, succinct modern discussion in Janet Burton, *Monastic and Religious Orders in Britain, 1000–1300* (Cambridge 1994), 56–60.

[75] D. E. Easson, *Medieval Religious Houses: Scotland* (London 1957), pp. 86–88; *Med. Rel. Houses* [England and Wales], 183–93 (and 283, Canonesses).

[76] The basic evidence is gathered in P. F. Lefèvre, *La Liturgie de Prémontré: Histoire, Formulaire, Chant et Cérémonial*, Bibliotheca analectorum Praemonstratensium 1 (Louvain 1957), which is largely a reworking of a long article in *Eph. Liturg.* in 1950; he had earlier edited the original ordinaries as *L'Ordinaire de Prémontré d'après manuscrits du XIIe et XIIIe siècles* (Louvain 1941). Lefèvre's work was therefore available to A. A. King for the chapter on the Premonstratensian Rite in his *Liturgies of the Religious Orders* (London 1955), pp. 157–234: which, like all of King's work, must be used cautiously. The few pages devoted to the liturgy in H. M. Colvin's standard monograph, *The White Canons in England* (Oxford 1951), pp. 256–72, address only liturgical obligations of the canons to founders and benefactors. Much more helpful

seems to have been a concerted attempt to fix distinctive and uniform usages for the new order. This was largely the work of Norbert's successor, Hugh of Fosses, who compiled an *Ordinarius*, now not extant as such, by 1131. This was replaced by another version towards the end of the twelfth century, but by that time many of the English houses had been founded and liturgical regimes established. In theory the regular Provincial Chapters provided for by the Premonstratensian constitution, like the Cistercian General Chapters, should have been a strong factor in ensuring liturgical uniformity, but all that we can say with confidence about the English White Canons c. 1200 is that their rite was secular rather than monastic. Information about their liturgical books comes almost entirely from three surviving booklists.

Booklist evidence

The oldest is a list of service books in the late twelfth-century library catalogue of Welbeck Abbey.[77] Unusually in such catalogues, the service books come first: two "pairs" of breviaries (so stated because each is divided into summer and winter volumes); a collectar; three missals; an epistolary and a gospel book, then a *Textus Argenteus* (presumably a more elaborate book than the preceding one); two *antiphonarii veteres* and two *novi*; four graduals *cum troperiis*, as well as four other chant books of a mixed sort; eight processionals, of which three had black covers, three white, and two red. At the end of the list are enumerated sixteen psalters, each particularized in some way: most of them assigned to specific canons, besides an old one "in which novices learn," and one written by brother Ralph "for common use." Brother Hugh de Suwelle wrote three of these psalters, his own containing capitula and *collationes* (the sense demands *collectae* or *orationes*?) and hymns throughout the year, as does one belonging to brother Martin. One seems to have belonged, or been allocated to, a woman (or was she possibly the donor?): "Psalterium quod domine Idonee de Blacwelle," with no further information. The scribe Ralph wrote not only the above-mentioned psalter but also the two "pairs" of breviaries and the abbey's "Missale magnum et plenarium"; while Hugh of Suwelle wrote a "missale parvum et plenarium" as well as the three psalters.

---

is the recent monograph by J. A. Gribbin, *The Premonstratensian Order in Late Medieval England* (Woodbridge 2001), ch. 4, "The English Premonstratensian Liturgy," pp. 101–31, but this, as the title indicates, is mostly devoted to the situation in the fifteenth century.

[77] D. N. Bell, ed. *The Libraries of the Cistercians, Gilbertines and Premonstratensians*, CBMLC 3 (1992), pp. 255–67.

Finally, there are two *Ordinaria*, of which one, written by brother Roger Pasturel, contained all the material for ministry to the sick and burial of the dead. So we know that at Welbeck, which seems always to have had in excess of twenty canons, at least three were engaged in the compiling and writing of liturgical books before the end of the twelfth century.

Since nothing is known of books at any of the three houses founded between 1143 and 1151, Newhouse, Alnwick, or Easby, Welbeck is the earliest Premonstratensian house about which we have any liturgical information. It was technically a daughter of Newhouse, but lay only a few miles from the Augustinian house at Worksop, the prior, sub-prior, and another canon of which are the first three witnesses in its formal (and slightly after the fact) foundation charter.[78] The next witness is "Hugh the canon, son of Sewale," and it is natural to wonder whether this is not the "Hug. de Suwell(e)" who wrote the missal and the three psalters; if so, he would have been one of the original canons at Welbeck, and we can imagine him as a senior figure possibly in charge of a scriptorium there.[79]

Whether this identification is correct or not, what would have been the model(s) for the books the library catalogue ascribes to him, or for the breviaries and great missal written by Ralph? To suppose that the models came from Newhouse pushes the question back by no more than a decade; where did the canons of Newhouse get *their* books? The best historian of the order in England, Howard Colvin, suggests that all thirteen of the canons required to start a new Premonstratensian colony came from its mother house, Licques, near Boulogne, itself a daughter of one of the three original Norbertine foundations.[80] This is likely to have been true of both Gerlo, first abbot of Newhouse, and Berengar, one of its original canons and first abbot of Welbeck. While it would certainly have been possible for them to have brought sets of liturgical books from the mother house, there is no way of proving this.

Two other extant Premonstratensian booklists mention service books. The next chronologically to the Welbeck list, albeit about a hundred years later, is that from the small house of St Radegund at Bradsole in Kent (near Dover). Despite its size – probably never more than thirteen

---

[78] A. H(amilton) Thompson, *The Premonstratensian Abbey of Welbeck* (London 1938), pp. 12–14 supplies a translation and some annotation; the original is printed in Dugdale's *Monasticon Anglicanum*, ed. J. Caley et al., VI.ii (1846), p. 873. Some account of the difficulty surrounding this charter is given in Colvin, *White Canons*, pp. 63–68.

[79] Bell, *Libraries*, p. 267, conjectures that the Suwell(e) may be the place of a similar name in Beds., Oxon., or Northants., but these all seem somewhat far afield for a mid-Notts. house.

[80] Colvin, *White Canons*, p. 49.

canons – its late thirteenth-century list witnesses to a surprisingly rich supply of such books; these include three antiphonals (one in two volumes) as well as one *de veteri usu*, five graduals and again one of the old use, three or four further chant books, sixteen processionals, fourteen psalters, seventeen diurnals, fifteen breviaries, two legendaries, two manuals, and something like fifteen missals, one being for the high altar (with two gospel books and an epistolary) and others for dependent chapels at nearby manors. Nine of the missals are described as "well worn within and without (*agende interius et exterius*)."[81] There was also, interestingly, a Franciscan missal *de usu fratrum minorum*. Here, then, there is evidence for a lively interest in having service books both in usable condition and up to date.

About another hundred years separates the Bradsole from the third relevant list, that in a splendidly extensive catalogue of the library at Titchfield dated September 29th 1400.[82] This one mentions liturgical books at the very end, mostly by a simple listing of kinds and numbers: eight antiphonals, five legendaries, eleven processionals, and so forth. As well as three *missalia perfecta* there were fourteen *missalia imperfecta* that were said to be worn out (*que dicuntur agende*). Of twelve portiforia, three are specified as *de usu Sar[isburiensi]*, which leads to curiosity as to what the other breviaries may have been thought to be.

Nothing can be extrapolated from the information in these three lists as to the contents of these books (save possibly the last detail mentioned), and specifically as to how fully they corresponded with Premonstratensian books from Continental houses, as opposed to being much like, say, English Augustinian books. There seem to be no distinctive saints of the order itself, at least not in the middle ages (Norbert was not canonized until 1582). It is not until the late fifteenth century that the picture for the Premonstratensians becomes slightly fuller through the records of a few Provincial Chapters and, most important, of the visitations of Richard Redman.[83]

---

[81] Printed by Bell, *Libraries*, pp. 161–78, from Bodl. Rawl. B. 336, a cartulary. The Latin is rather odd, but that seems to be the force of *agend[a]e* here, as in the Titchfield list in the next paragraph.

[82] The Titchfield catalogue is printed by Bell, with full discussion, pp. 180–254; the MS is BL Add. 70507. The abbey was richly endowed by its founder Peter des Roches, but fell on hard times after the Black Death: *Med. Rel. Houses*, p. 192, gives between six and eleven canons after 1400.

[83] The documents were edited by F. A. Gasquet as *Collectanea Anglo-Premonstratensia*, 3 vols, Camden Soc. 3rd ser. 6, 10, 12 (1904–6). The inaccuracies with which the edition is riddled have been pointed out several times, most notably on pp. 389–91 of Colvin's *White Canons* (1951), where 85 of the more serious are printed (out of a longer list deposited by him in the Bodleian Library). The visitation records have been used to good effect by Gribbin: see below.

Redman's visitations; the late fifteenth century

Richard Redman – the central figure in Joseph Gribbin's monograph published in 2001 (note 76 above) – became a canon at the Westmorland house of Shap and, probably in the mid-1450s, its abbot. Shortly thereafter, it seems, he was named Commissary-General of the abbot of Prémontré: in effect, the official visitor, the individual houses having gained exemption from episcopal visitation. This title, in itself highly controversial because another canon claimed the dignity also, was not to be Redman's only distinction; in 1471 he became bishop of St Asaph (retaining the abbacy of Shap), of Exeter in 1495, and of Ely in 1501; he died in 1505. The majority of his visitations took place in the last quarter of the fifteenth century. His activities as bishop, traced in detail by Gribbin, need not detain us, save to note that he remained serious about his vocation as a religious. This is clear both from the papal permission he secured that as a bishop he could continue to use the Premonstratensian liturgical office and from his efforts to beautify and elaborate his abbey church at Shap.[84] Among his contributions there was a repaving of the nave, which included circular processional markings carved on the floor to show where the canons were to stand at the beginning of the high mass after the Sunday liturgical procession.[85]

His visitations of individual houses complement the provisions of the Provincial Chapters. The latter tend to be concerned with the observance of feasts, among other non-liturgical matters, whereas Redman's admonitions are mostly about standards of liturgical performance. For example, the Provincial Chapter at Lincoln in 1476 mandates the feast of the Visitation (2 July) as a *principale festum triplex* (the highest grade among the Premonstratensians, to whom it is unique); and the Chapter held (probably) in 1483, place unknown, orders that the feasts of St Radegund (11 February), St Martha (here 27 July, as also in many York books, but more commonly the 29th), and St Anthony (17 January) should all be kept with nine lessons.[86] The placing of Radegund's feast in February rather than the somewhat more widespread, and more convenient, date of 13 August (itself generally given to Hippolytus) is specially odd and deserves looking into.

---

[84] Gribbin, p. 204, citing *Cal. of Entries in the Papal Registers rel. to Great Britain*, ed. W. H. Bliss, J. A. Twemlow, et al., 19 vols to date (London 1893–), XIII.2 [1955], pp. 797–98.

[85] Gribbin, p. 192, citing H. M. Colvin and R. Gilyard-Beer, *Shap Abbey* (London 1963), p. 8.

[86] *Collectanea Anglo-Prem.*, I.141, 152–53 respectively.

The extent to which such provisions were observed is evident through the visitation reports of Redman. In 1491 he orders the abbot of Alnwick to procure proper texts for Martha and the Visitation, and also the Feast of Relics, within a year.[87] Similar lacunae had been noted at Halesowen three years earlier.[88] He is aware of the tendency for secular practices to creep into what is supposed to be the distinctive liturgy of the order: in 1478 the canons of Eggleston are commanded to celebrate the daily office "secundum usum nostri ordinis," spurning all secular practices. One of these may have been the abuse (*quendam abusum*) of superfluous genuflection by the deacon and subdeacon at the elevation of the Host that the canons at Titchfield are admonished in the same year to eliminate.[89] But as well as fault-finding there is praise, as in 1482 for the abbot of Sulby, who has had made for his house "duos magnos codices, antiphonaria, unum in dextero choro et alterum in sinistro."[90]

Towards "Englishness"

These scanty glimpses into the late medieval liturgical life of the Premonstratensians in England are generally congruous with what is apparently their sole surviving book of a liturgical sort, though not a service book proper: a late fifteenth-century ordinal from the abbey of St Agatha at Easby in Yorkshire, now Jesus College, Cambridge Q.G.7 (55). It is of the *Pie* or *Pica* type of ordinal (see p. 427) rather than the kind that specifies usages in any detail, but it is valuable in providing a sense of the full round of a year's occasions at that house, as seen through the eyes of the compiler, John Tanfield, one of its canons.[91] Gribbin has used it to good effect to establish what we otherwise lack, an English Premonstratensian calendar that can be taken as representative for at least the later middle ages. He does this by combining data from the Easby ordinal with those from a curious calendar (now in the Escorial in Madrid) of probably the late fourteenth century which was

---

[87] *Coll.*, II.24.

[88] *Coll.*, II.251.

[89] *Coll.*, II.210, III.126, respectively; this problem was noticed in a number of other houses as well: Gribbin, pp. 114–15

[90] *Coll.*, III.108.

[91] The preface is printed in M. R. James's catalogue (1895), p. 87, but James was baffled by the owner's identification being worded as "canonici de skyrpnes"; this refers to the chapel of St Silvester at Skirpenbeck, Yorks., of which Tanfield was chaplain: Gribbin, p. 119. A possibly complementary witness is the "four and a half folios of a vernacular version of rubrics on the role of the deacon and subdeacon at mass" in BL Sloane 1584, fols 2–6, in the miscellany of John Gisborn, canon of Coverham: Gribbin, pp. 117–18, who suggests that "these rubrics seem to have been culled from the orders' customaries and ordinals."

originally Augustinian but was acquired by the White Canons house at West Dereham in Norfolk by about 1500 and adjusted to reflect Premonstratensian practice.[92] Although the two witnesses are by no means identical in contents, taken together they give some sense of what saints' days can be regarded as characteristic of the order (but not of course exclusively so): most notably Martha and Radegund, mentioned above, John of Beverley, Sitha, a high grading for Agatha, and the comparatively rare Conception of John the Baptist (24 September).[93]

Several of these occasions are seldom or never found on the Continent: besides John of Beverley and the Baptist's Conception, feasts like those of Kenelm and of the popular late medieval saints David and Chad; the Easby ordinal includes also a number of North Country figures. The overall sense one gets is of a liturgy that is coming to be more and more distinctively English. Whether or not the force of the circumstances that led in 1512 to the total separation of the English Premonstratensians from the order on the Continent is judged to have been inevitable or fortuitous and/or avoidable, it seems likely that by the beginning of the sixteenth century, at any rate, their liturgy would have struck an informed observer as one of the English "uses" more than as the extension of a tightly centralized Continental rite.[94]

Gilbertine canons (and nuns)

The extraordinary story of (St) Gilbert and the order of Sempringham established by him fits into our narrative in two primary contexts. The first is that of high medieval monastic orders of a self-consciously reformed type, above all the Cistercians, about whom a good deal has been said in the previous chapter. The second is that of liturgy for women religious – to complicate matters further, in double houses where the strictly monastic women's communities were the main component, while those of the male clergy, present so that they could provide priestly and other services, were conducted like establishments of canons regular. And that the main outlines of this rather convoluted picture should have been complete by the death in 1189 of the amazingly long-lived founder (Gilbert may have been born as early as 1083, when Lanfranc

---

[92] El Escorial MS Q.ii.6, fols 7–12; assigned to West Dereham in *MLGB Suppl.*, with a date of xiv^in which of course does not apply to that house's possession of it. I have not seen the MS myself.

[93] Gribbin, pp. 121–25.

[94] Colvin tended to argue for the influence of "incipient nationalism" as a factor in precipitating the break, a position disputed by Gribbin, pp. 211–12. There was an abortive attempt at a somewhat similar separation as early as 1432.

was in his prime, and died in 1189, when Francis was hearing romance stories at his mother's knee) gives an unusual chronological discreteness to what has to be teased out from the scanty extant sources.

Gilbert of Sempringham and his communities

Gilbert himself is quite well documented, for soon after his death materials began to be collected towards potential canonization. These materials, with the miraculous prevailing over the drily factual, were convincing enough that in 1202 Innocent III approved Gilbert's canonization, noteworthy in the history of that subject as the first clear case under the new procedures put in place at the conclusion of the quarter-century of activity spurred by the murder of Becket. Soon afterwards the entire dossier, including a *Vita* and the canonization proceedings, was formed into *The Book of St Gilbert*, available in the fine edition of Raymonde Foreville and Gillian Keir.[95]

The regime under which these communities lived and worshipped evolved with the twists of fortune of their early history.[96] The initial stage, around 1131, was that of a group of pious women in Sempringham (Lincolnshire) living corporately under the direction of their then parson, Gilbert; a group of serving-women, formalized as lay sisters, was soon added. The 1130s saw the first flush of Cistercian enthusiasm, and foundations, in the north of England, so it is not surprising that when the Sempringham group was established on a firmer basis and when a second house was established at nearby Haverholme, both in 1139, the model was supposed to be that of Cîteaux (although there were at that point no Cistercian nuns). Attempts at a more formal connection were aborted in 1147, when the Cistercian Chapter General declined Gilbert's request that these houses should become officially part of the order. It is apparently at that point that he brought in the mixed element, establishing first a male lay component of *conversi* like those of the Cistercians, then a clerical one which was to follow the Rule of Augustine. He founded also a handful of exclusively male houses, notably at Lincoln and Malton (North Yorkshire). Papal approval was given in 1148, although the form in which the Gilbertine Rule, called *Institutiones*, survives is a version dating from the early 1220s.

---

[95] R. Foreville and G. Keir, ed. and tr., *The Book of St Gilbert*, OMT (Oxford 1987); cf. Foreville's earlier work, *Un Procès de canonisation à l'aube du xiiie siècle* (Paris 1943).

[96] The pillars of the small amount of detailed work on the Gilbertines in general are Rose Graham, *St Gilbert of Sempringham and the Gilbertines* (London 1903) and, nearly a century later, Brian Golding, *Gilbert of Sempringham and the Gilbertine Order* (Oxford 1995). Neither pays any particular attention to the liturgy.

So the challenge is to try to get some sense of the worship of a religious group whose liturgy must have been complicated by this multiplex structure. The nuns, who by their rule should have had a monastic rite, depended for sacerdotal offices on men who were technically canons regular. In the purely male houses there was of course no problem, but for the mixed houses the difficulties must have been considerable. (For the lay-brothers and lay-sisters, sometimes in considerable numbers, the Gilbertine regime prescribed simple but defined liturgical obligations, mostly the recitation of fixed formulas.)

Some of the mixed houses seem to have been quite large. The Gilbertine *Institutiones* of c. 1185–90 stipulated what were meant to be maximum numbers of nuns and lay brothers, the latter number being usually half the former.[97] Watton at 140 nuns leads the list, followed by Chicksands, Sempringham, and Sixhills at 120; three houses at 100 and one each at 80 and at 60 complete it. Even allowing for both idealization and exaggeration, and for the fact that these figures apparently include both choir nuns and lay-sisters, the number of bodies, voices, and presumably books involved in the liturgy in these houses meant that its management was not an easy matter. (In the mixed houses the quotas of canons, all of whom seem to have been priests, varied between seven and thirteen, and these sorts of numbers obtained also for the all-male houses.) The site of the church at Watton was excavated in 1901, and the ground plan uncovered extends for something like 600 feet.[98]

In view of such numbers and dimensions, there must have been hundreds of service books used in these houses from the mid-twelfth century until the Dissolution. Of these, there survive in any completeness one massbook (itself a composite volume from different periods), one Bible with a calendar and select missal elements, and one ordinal. There are also a single leaf in one manuscript and an isolated two-leaf fragment, both of which contain parts of services for the feast of Gilbert (4 February); beyond that, apparently nothing. Fortunately, the pieces of solid evidence were mostly published, in 1921–22, by R. M. Woolley, and have been the subject of a recent doctoral dissertation by Janet Tierney Sorrentino.[99]

---

[97] These figures are taken from the lists in *Med. Rel. Houses*, pp. 194 and 197, where the point is made that these conveniently round numbers are idealizations and that the actual numbers seem unlikely to have reached these totals. Nonetheless, they are large; Golding, *Gilbert of Sempringham*, p. 144, helps to flesh them out: "In c. 1210 the maximum number of monks at St Albans was fixed at 100; at Catley, one of the least endowed and signficant of the Gilbertine houses, the total figure for monks and nuns was 95."

[98] Published in a fold-out plan in Graham, *St Gilbert*, and, to a much smaller scale, in Burton, *Mon. and Rel. Orders*, p. 151.

[99] R. M. Woolley, ed. *The Gilbertine Rite*, 2 vols, HBS 59–60 (1921–22); J. T. Sorrentino, "Choice Words: the Liturgy of the Order of Sempringham," diss. Univ. of

An early-stratum book and its supplementing

By far the earliest document is the mid-twelfth-century sacramentary which occupies fols 64–144 of Lincoln Cathedral MS 115 (A.5.5). Its dependence on Cistercian models is clear, above all in some of the saints' feasts to be observed: figures like Mamertus, Sequanus, Andochius, and Columbanus, all of whom are found in the first stages of Cistercian tradition. These are among the nearly seventy feasts grouped together on fols 65–66 as having forms from the common of saints.[100] The two leaves are as rich in the questions they raise as in their contents, for on them have been written two sets of additions: one containing five English saints (Cuthbert, Guthlac, Augustine, Etheldreda, Oswald [the martyr]), the other supplying a further twenty-five names of which nineteen are English (the others are Blaise, Cletus, Translations of Andrew and Nicholas, Margaret, Leonard, and Linus). R. M. Thomson, who dates the main hand mid-twelfth century (Woolley thought it somewhat later), describes the first set of additions as by "another twelfth-century hand" and characterizes that of the second set, which includes William of York (canonized in 1227), merely as "thirteenth century."[101]

That Becket and Gilbert are not included in either set of additions may help us to understand why the second part of the present composite volume (though first in order, fols 1–63) was supplied. The Cistercians observed the cult of Becket by at least 1185 (see p. 252), so his absence from the first set suggests that it was written before that date, and therefore prior to the death (and canonization) of Gilbert. But these two are prominent, along with Mary Magdalen, in the new part, written in what Thomson calls a mid-thirteenth-century hand. (Its dating limit may be something like 1247, for Edmund of Abingdon, canonized that year, is included in a slightly later hand.) This part consists of the great feasts of the temporale and sanctorale intercalated, beginning in the Cistercian way with the Vigil of Christmas (but contrary to Cistercian usage in having Stephen, John, Innocents, and Becket in the temporale rather than in the sanctorale) and ending with Pentecost. Then come fourteen masses for the greatest saints' feasts, from John the Baptist through Nicholas, followed by the common of saints and eight votive masses, with the last two of these as well as Edmund being in the post-1247 hand. Astonishing here is

North Carolina, 1999, much of which is summarized in her "In houses of nuns, in houses of canons: a liturgical dimension to double monasteries," *Jnl. of Medieval Hist.* 28 (2002), pp. 361–72.

[100] It is often said that early Cistercian books had no common of saints section, but Sorrentino, "Choice Words," pp. 64–65, gives reasons to doubt this.

[101] R. M. Thomson, *Cat. Lincoln Cath. MSS* (Woodbridge 1989), pp. 89–91.

the fact that, although chant texts and lessons are provided throughout this section, no prayers are given for the Vigil and feast of Christmas, Stephen, John, Innocents, Ascension, Pentecost, and all the feasts
from John the Baptist through the (original) votive masses with the
following exceptions: Translation of Becket (the prayers only, all else
as in the December feast), Mary Magdalen, Catherine, and Nicholas,
plus collects alone for Assumption and Nativity of the Virgin. (For the
slightly later additions of the last two votives and Edmund of Canterbury there are only the prayers.)[102]

This is extremely puzzling. Who would be able to use a massbook that
contained only chant texts and lessons for most of the occasions in it?
And why are prayer texts supplied for some occasions if not for all? It is
almost as though the scribe, having provided the complete mass forms
for Becket, realized that he should do the same thing for the following
feasts, and so wrote the prayers for Circumcision through Invention of
the Cross, only to lose his concentration and lapse back into omitting
the prayers for the rest of the book, save for the exceptions noted. If
it is sugggested that the prayers in the older part of the book are supposed to be still used, why repeat those from January until early May?
A possible explanation is that, although the older part of the book was
clearly meant to be used at the altar, the later part, presumably joined
to it in the thirteenth century, was not so intended: that it represents
rather a collection of materials which, combined with those in the first
part, could be the basis for a proper *missale plenum* as such a book would
have been understood by the mid-thirteenth century. Might this in fact
represent an effort to establish a kind of standard Gilbertine missal,
somewhat like the exemplar copies of the Cistercians – or, by roughly
the mid-thirteenth century, Dominicans (see p. 312)?[103]

An attempt at standardization?

Whether or not the later part of Lincoln Cath. 115 represents a desire for
establishment of something like type-books, an attempt of that sort may

---

[102] The second of those votives is a mass *De perseuerencia*, which acccording to Sorrentino's cogent analysis, "Choice Words," pp. 81–90, represents a lingering memory of
the celebrated "Revolt of the Lay Brothers of Sempringham," the subject of an article of that title by D. Knowles, *Eng. Hist. Rev.* 50 (1935), pp. 465–87; more recently,
Golding, *Gilbert*, pp. 40–51.

[103] There are several points of detail that cry out for close scrutiny, above all the supplying, in the older part, of a complete set of stational indications in the headings for
masses of the temporale from Septuagesima through Holy Week and for such other
occasions as are appointed in the Gregorian books. Another is the use of *Epiphania*
for the vigil, feast, and Sunday after, but *Theophania* for the following five Sundays
(and the existence of a mass for a sixth Sunday itself).

well lie behind the Bible with calendar and select-missal elements, now
St John's, Cambridge 239 (N.1), written probably in the third quarter
of the thirteenth century: a book that Woolley suggested represented
an attempt at "a norm or standard text of the Gilbertine Kalendar and
Mass services, and never intended for use at the altar."[104] The calendar
that prefaces the book is clearly Gilbertine, including some but not all
of the "old" Cistercian saints (e.g., Sequanus but not Andochius et al.),
a standard group of English feasts, among them Translation of Becket
(but not Wulfstan of Worcester), and two feasts for Gilbert, Deposition
on February 4th and Translation on October 13th (1202).[105] The abbreviated missal section occupies fols 381–88, part of a gathering of twelve
leaves, the first four of which conclude the Bible. There is no mass
ordinary as such; the missal section begins with proper prefaces and
canon and continues with seventeen masses for the greatest occasions
(temporale and sanctorale intermixed), votives, common of saints, and
masses for the dead.[106] We know of Dominican and Franciscan books
having this peculiar combination of Bible and select-missal, and such
a book is more or less comprehensible if used by an itinerant friar. The
only Gilbertine for whom something like St John's 239 would be usable
might be the Master, peregrinating on visitations to the houses of the
order, but even this is hard to imagine.

The much later ordinal, now Pembroke College, Cambridge 226,
helps (within limits) to flesh out a somewhat fuller picture. The book
is of the fifteenth century, with signs of heavy use; Woolley suspected
that it was a copy from an exemplar a good deal earlier, on the ground
that the information about Corpus Christi is written in a different hand
from the main one.[107] As the heading, "De ecclesiasticis officiis secundum ritus [sic] canonicorum ordinis de Semp. de festis mobilibus et
immobilibus," suggests, it is not specific to any one Gilbertine house.
For example, the section on Christmas Eve is headed "De officio in
nocte natalis domini in domibus monialium," and specifies that the
nuns are to read the Christmas Genealogy without priest or deacon
present, whereas the next section explains how the gospel is read at

---

[104] Woolley, *Gilb. Rite*, I.xvi. He suggested a date somewhat before 1265, because of the
inclusion on an end flyleaf of a prophecy (unfulfilled) by Joachim of Fiore concerning a return of Greek Christians to Roman obedience in that year, but Sorrentino
points out ("Choice Words," p. 34) that the hand of the leaf seems to be somewhat
later than the rest of the book.

[105] Printed, with comparative documents in columns, in Woolley, I.xxxvi–liv.

[106] The text is edited by collation (as "J") in Woolley, vol. II.

[107] Woolley, I.xxiv, but this is an unreliable test, as Sorrentino, "Choice Words,"
pp. 36–37, shows; there are, however, other indications of an early date for the exemplar, notably the absence of Hugh of Lincoln, canonized 1220.

the first mass of Christmas in houses of canons as well as of monks.[108] And the list of principal feasts includes, as well as both feasts of Gilbert, that of the local saint (*sanctus loci*). Steady awareness of the practical problems when male clergy deal with female religious is evident in such provisions as that on the first day of Lent the ashes are conferred on the nuns by a *maturus sacerdos* through the window (in the wall that divides the women's part of the church from the men's) at which they receive communion. There is also a fascinating section about the problems involved in giving Easter communion to *seculares*: problems such as estimating how many hosts would be required, preaching a suitable sermon, and concern that the wrong people – excommunicates, notorious criminals, parishioners elsewhere "nisi de licencia sui pastoris aut peregrinus fuerit" – might offer themselves to receive.[109]

This tiny hint that at least some Gilbertine establishments may have enjoyed a wider popularity can serve as a slight corrective to an impression of them as having little impact on the religious picture of medieval England as a whole. Gilbert never found a place in the Sarum calendar, even though his main feast day, February 4th, was otherwise vacant. His proper office, nine lessons with rhymed antiphons and responsories, seems to be fully available only on one leaf at the end of Bodl. Digby 36 (fol. 110), of the fifteenth century, the latest of the three manuscripts containing the full Gilbertian dossier. There is some dispute as to whether or not the codex was meant to be used liturgically, but no doubt that the office (at least in its main outlines) and the mass which follows it were so used.[110] The ordinal gives just enough details, mostly incipits, to make that plain. The later medieval York books include the feast, the breviaries with an abbreviated three-lesson office and the missals with forms drawn largely from the common of saints.[111] Such scant evidence as there is for liturgical usages of the vast diocese of Lincoln (see p. 496), where the order was the strongest, seems to reflect little or no Gilbertine influence.

---

[108] Woolley, I.11.

[109] This is in the context of the rites of Easter (I.45), and offers a rare set of detailed instructions for the communion of those who probably communicate only annually, ending "deinde cum magna cautella communicet uenientes . duo teneant manutergium inter ipsum et illos . et unus offerat illi singulos . et alter teneat uasculum cum uino aqua mixto ut inde bibant."

[110] Foreville thought it likely that the book was made for a rich lay patron, but Golding (*St Gilbert*, p. 453) refutes this opinion and argues convincingly for Gilbertine ownership; in any case the codex itself is certainly not a service book.

[111] *York Breviary*, II.186. The three lessons are an abridgement of the nine (themselves generally short) of Digby 36; everything else is taken from the common of a confessor. *York Missal*, II.22 gives just two-word incipits for most of the mass forms, and in full the communio, the only form (save for the epistle) identical with the mass that concludes the Digby 36 leaf.

The point of greatest interest for us here remains, then, curiosity as to the liturgical management of double houses where strict separation of sexes was the rule – the churches of such houses were divided longitudinally by a stone wall that ran east to west throughout their entire length – and where also monastic-regime nuns depended for priestly ministrations on canons. The general sense is that where any potential conflict was involved, usages familiar to the canon-priests would prevail.[112] This appears to have been the case even in the key matter of whether the nuns chanted the psalms or merely recited them, probably in a low voice (the respective terms from the *Institutes* are *cantare*, which is forbidden, and *indirecto psallere*, which is mandated); despite the fact that there were commonly several times as many nuns as canons, it seems probable that the men did not have to hear the women singing.[113] Modern-day interest in gender-roles and relationships is not relevant to the present work; nonetheless, the female–male dimension to the worship of the Gilbertines is likely always to be at the center of such attention as a history of the liturgy can devote to them.

[112] At the most obvious point of conflict, between the monastic twelve-lesson and canonical (and secular) nine-lesson form of matins on Sundays and great occasions, the Ordinal refers to all major feasts as being of nine lessons, and this agrees with the grading of the calendar of St John's 239: see Sorrentino, "In houses of nuns," p. 366.

[113] Possible interpretations are discussed in Sorrentino, "Choice Words," pp. 148–55.

9   The non-monastic religious orders: friars

Dominicans

Each of the major orders of friars went through an initial phase of trial and error in seeking definition, clear identification, and regulation. After a generation or so these hallmarks had for the most part been achieved, though questions, often leading to vigorous controversies, remained. It is only after some of these had been settled on the Continent that the various groups appeared in England: Dominicans first, in 1221, Franciscans in 1224, Carmelites in 1241, Austin Friars in 1248. By those dates the notes of papal approval, composition and acceptance of a rule (sometimes more than one), and establishment of a system of continuing centralized governance are discernible for each of these orders; but the regulation of worship tends to come relatively late and, as would be expected, to be an ongoing process. So our task will be to try to sense what would have been the situation during the early years of the presence of each of these groups in England, then to notice the effects of the more or less normative regulations for each group, and finally to get some feel for their adaptations to local circumstances and their inclusions of English saints in their service books.

When the first Dominican friars arrived in England in 1221, the order – *Ordo praedicatorum*, colloquially called Black Friars – had been in existence for less than a decade.[1] Among the principal houses came to be those at Cambridge, Canterbury, Gloucester, King's Langley, London, Northampton, Norwich, Oxford, Winchester, and York. The story of their quick rise to prominence and popularity in England, in circles academic, royal, and merely urban, cannot be gone into here. We need only note that by the mid-thirteenth century there were at least

---

[1] The best summary overview for England is still Knowles, *Religious Orders*, vol. I, chaps. xiii–xiv (pp. 146–70). This is complemented by the lists in *Med. Rel. Houses*, pp. 213–20, and by the rather episodic work of W. A. Hinnebusch in his *The Early English Friars Preachers* (Rome 1951) and his more general book, *The History of the Dominican Order*, 2 vols (Staten Island 1966–73).

two dozen houses in England and Wales, at each of which corporate worship was meant to be carried on, even if kept in strict balance with the demands of study and preaching.

The original Rule, based on that of the Augustinian canons, was not particularly detailed about liturgical matters, but a high degree of liturgical uniformity came to be a concomitant of the tight structure and genuinely international character of the order, above all through regular meetings of Chapters General, at which legislation binding on all houses was enacted.[2] This includes legislation about liturgy, especially through a revision and regularization of Dominican liturgy, the *nova correctio*, executed by Humbert of Romans, then Master General, in 1254–56. This was codified in an authoritative and massive "archetype" volume, to be kept at a stipulated headquarters.[3] It specified fourteen books that were to be used. Some of the nomenclature is unusual enough that the list should be given in full: *ordinarium, martyrologium, collectarium, processionarium, psalterium, breviarium, lectionarium, antiphonarium, graduale, pulpitarium* (out of which certain parts of mass and office were to be sung solemnly at a particular piece of choir furniture, hence the name), *missale conventuale, epistolarium, evangelistarium,* and *missale minorum altarium* (private missal). Of great interest to us is a more or less portable copy of this compendium which seems to have been designed for the Master to take with him when visiting individual priories. This, now BL Add. 23935, lacks the breviary and private missal, apparently on the grounds that the Master would already have possessed them, but contains, in its over 500 folios, all twelve of the other liturgical books.[4] It has been dated at 1260, and forms an irresistible, if somewhat misleading, starting point.[5]

---

[2] There is no synthetic treatment less than half a century old. W. R. Bonniwell, *A History of the Dominican Liturgy* (New York 1944), pp. 1–254, is still useful but covers the whole of Europe, while A. A. King, *Liturgies of the Religious Orders* (London 1955), pp. 325–95, deals with the subject through the 19th cent. and depends heavily on Bonniwell.

[3] Now in the Dominican Archives at Rome, Santa Sabina, MS XIV L 1. Bonniwell, p. 87, provides a facsimile of the contents page, giving the Latin titles.

[4] Of the 579 folios of Add. 23935, fols 3–15 are 14th- and 15th-cent. additions for feasts added after Humbert's time, and 572–79 a 14th-cent. copy of the Dominican *Constitutiones*. The latter addition is printed on pp. 205–53 of G. R. Galbraith, *The Constitution of the Dominican Order 1216–1360* (Manchester 1925), which contains also a detailed description of the MS, pp. 193–202. The "mass ordinary" section of the *Missale conventuale* (fols 480–84) was printed by J. W. Legg in his *Tracts on the Mass*, HBS 27 (1904), pp. 73–94, with notes on pp. 243–46.

[5] Watson, *BL Dated MSS*, no. 292: fol. 74v contains the date 1260, and "alterations made necessary by the Chapters of 1261 and 1262 have been made to the text."

Before Humbert's reforms

"Somewhat misleading" because of course the Dominican friars in England had engaged in liturgical services for some thirty-five years before Humbert's reforms came into effect, and so we must begin by wondering what resources they used in that early period. What service books the order used in its first decades is by no means clear. As taking their rule and pattern originally from the Augustinian canons, the early Friars Preachers would presumably have used, as did the canons and all later Dominicans, books of a secular rather than monastic rite. Notwithstanding, desire for something like a distinctive and uniform Dominican liturgy is evident very early, although details of the various attempts to bring this about are not clearly ascertainable.[6] Particularly vexing is the lack of basic information about the order-wide attempt at revision in 1245 always referred to as that of the Four Friars, because one of the four is known to have been English; but his name, like those of the other three, is lost. Humbert's reform is clearly a watershed, and any sense of the subject that we may acquire for the period before the mid-thirteenth century is certain to be both fragmentary and impressionistic.

The oldest piece of evidence for anything that might be regarded as pre-Humbertian Dominican liturgy in England is probably Bodl. Lat. bibl. e.7. This is a Bible with, after the psalms, a section of masses (fols 199–204) including only one for a saint: Dominic, with another mass for his translation (in 1233, the year before his canonization), added in what Nigel Morgan calls "a nearly contemporary hand." This leads him to date the book to c. 1234–40 because of the extensive illuminations – some sixty-six decorated initials on gold ground – by William de Brailes, an artist known to have worked in Oxford in that period.[7] The small size of the book (165 × 115 mm) suggests that it was designed for the use of someone who expected to be frequently on the move, like a friar, but the sumptuousness of illustration is hard to explain save possibly in terms of a wealthy patron. Morgan notes further that in the fourteenth century the manuscript was "annotated for reading *in refectorio*," which implies possession by a religious house at that date.

---

[6] Neither a breviary supposed to have been used by Dominic himself, now much mutilated and kept as a relic by Dominican nuns at Rome, nor a missal for low mass (BN lat. 8884, datable to 1234–43), nor a noted breviary of which a late copy survives in the archives of the order at Rome, seems to have been regarded as normative. Details are given in Bonniwell, pp. 28–45.

[7] Morgan, *Early Gothic Manuscripts*, I, no. 69. The other books illustrated by de Brailes or his workshop are described at nos. 70–74.

A somewhat similar book, but without sumptuous illustrations, is Fitzwilliam Museum, Cambridge, McClean 16, again a Bible with an abbreviated missal, this time towards the end. It was probably but not quite certainly written in England (a list of texts, apparently for sermons, includes one for Edmund martyr, unlikely to occur anywhere save in England); there are masses for Francis and Dominic, the latter being magnified by inclusion of a proper sequence. The calendar that prefixes the book is probably Dominican; that Peter Martyr is among numerous and otherwise predominantly English saints added to it in a late medieval hand may, like the addition of an office of Elizabeth of Hungary, date the book to before 1254, the year both of those saints are included in the standardized calendar proposed by Humbert. M. R. James's summary observation that "the volume, containing as it does Bible, Kalendar, Missal, Notes for Sermons, and Concordance, would form a very complete equipment for a preaching friar in priests' orders," seems justified.[8]

The Dominican office liturgy

Evidence of Humbert's reform is clear in a thirteenth-century breviary with extensive fourteenth-century additions, now BL Royal 2 A.xi. Again it is a small volume, measuring c. 170 × 120 mm, with 413 folios: clearly the portable *Breviarium* of the fourteen mandated books, as distinct from the combination of psalter, lectionary, and antiphonary necessary for performance of the choir office. Unfortunately, the calendar is not original but rather one of the fourteenth-century elements, and its numerous early additions are in a hand (hands?) difficult to distinguish from the original. The best indication of date may come from the (thirteenth-century) litany of saints, after the psalter and canticles, where among the virgins Martha has been added; she is not in Humbert's calendar, and her insertion into the liturgy of the order was proposed in 1266 and received final approval ten years later.[9] So it is likely that the original part of this breviary was written between 1256 and 1276. It might well repay a monograph-length study.

Perhaps the most interesting section is the sets of lessons for seventeen saints supplied, in a hand later than the original one, on fols 389–413. Though these are written there in a liturgical list, a list here of the ten whose feasts became part of the official Dominican liturgy in the order

---

[8] M. R. James, *Descr. Catalogue McClean Manuscripts* (Cambridge 1912), p. 32.

[9] Bonniwell, p. 199. The name of Margaret, whose inclusion in the litany was approved in 1285, has also been added.

in which they received final approval may enable us to date this section: Edward the Confessor, proposed for inclusion into the Dominican liturgy in 1265 and approved finally two years later; Martha, approved 1276 as noted above; Wenceslaus, 1298; Louis IX, 1301; Ignatius of Antioch, 1302; Alexi(u)s, 1307; Thomas Aquinas, 1326; the Eleven Thousand Virgins, 1331; Servat(i)us, 1332; and Martial, 1336.[10] But two further additions made by the General Chapter in 1355, Adalbert and Procopius, are not found here, which suggests a dating range of 1336–55 for this part of the book. The placing of Martial in the list is a puzzle; styled bishop and confessor, he appears between Servatus (13 May) and Dunstan (19 May; see below), whereas his universally observed day is 30 June. An additional puzzle is the inclusion of Pope Mark (d. 336; 7 October), a saint of exceptional obscurity, placed correctly between Wenceslaus (28 September) and Edward the Confessor (13 October).

The six remaining saints are all British, intercalated in order of feast day with the other twelve: David, Richard, Dunstan, Alban, Translation of Becket, and Winifred.[11] Of these, Dunstan and Alban, each with three lessons, and also Becket's Translation with nine (very brief), are unremarkable. Though never part of the official liturgy of the order, Richard of Chichester (canonized 1262) is doubtless included because he patronized the Black Friars; his confessor and biographer was the Dominican Ralph [of] Bocking (d. 1270), from whose *Vita* the nine lessons are drawn. The two that are surprising are David (nine lessons) and Winifred (three). Inclusion of both in the mid-fourteenth century raises the possibility that the book might have been written for a friar from a Welsh house like Rhuddlan or from Shrewsbury (the center of devotion to Winifred, whose cult is otherwise normally thought of as one of those that increase widely in popularity in the fifteenth century, not the first half of the fourteenth).

The value of this codex is that it provides us with a standard, "Humbertian" Dominican service book adapted for use in England (or Wales). All the distinctive Friars Preachers' feasts are present, in either the thirteenth- or fourteenth-century sections: those for Dominic (two), Peter Martyr, Elizabeth of Hungary, Anniversary of Fathers and Mothers

---

[10] A summary list of the relevant capitular decisions is in Bonniwell, pp. 222–23; a more substantial discussion of additions made by 1326 is L. E. Boyle, "Dominican Lectionaries and Leo of Ostia's *Translatio S. Clementis*," *Archivum Fratrum Praedicatorum* 28 (1958), pp. 362–94, esp. 386–87.

[11] David has been omitted from the list given in G. F. Warner and J. P. Gilson, *Catalogue of the Western Manuscripts in the Old Royal and King's Collections*, 4 vols (London 1921), I.30.

(10 October), *Corona Domini* (4 May), and notably, among those listed above, Wenceslaus, Servatus, and the Eleven Thousand Virgins.

Two later, somewhat complementary books show how standardized the Dominican office liturgy looks after Humbert's work, despite some mid-fourteenth century revisions.[12] Both are collectars. The first, CUL Add. 2770, dates from the mid-fifteenth century and is probably from Dunstable priory. Capitula, in the original hand, for Vincent Ferrer (canonized 1455) and Catherine of Siena (1458), provide a *terminus a quo*. The calendar has Martial at 16 June, after Cyricus (Quiricius) and Julitta. The attention paid to the Eleven Thousand Virgins is intensified by the addition to the calendar of Cordula, one of Ursula's companions, on 22 October, the day after the main feast. More substantial is the appearance in the calendar of Fremund, the obscure ninth-century hermit whose remains were at the important Augustinian priory at Dunstable, near the Dominican house (11 May; the leaf that would have contained collects for days around then is missing).

The second collectar, Fitzwilliam Museum, Cambridge, 3–1967, takes us close to the chronological end of the subject we are pursuing (and is returned to in our final chapter, p. 544). It is dated 1523 and was made at the behest of Robert Miles, prior of King's Langley and also of the English province.[13] Additions to the present calendar (which may not be integral to the book), made probably in the Low Countries in the seventeenth century, are so extensive that they look to be a copy of what might have been the original calendar. Many of the English occasions have been erased, like the Translation of Wulfstan, Botulf, Etheldreda and her Translation, Wulfran, Winifred, Edmund of Abingdon, Hugh of Lincoln, and Edmund the Martyr, but several have survived in the section of collects.

Dominican mass liturgy

There seems to be no missal with which we can compare the Royal 2 A.xi breviary: none, that is, which is both complete and clearly post-Humbertian (certainly not the case with the two abbreviated or select massbook-sections in the Bibles discussed above). In the absence of such a thing, the most useful piece of evidence relating to the mass in

---

[12] Some details of these revisions are given in Bonniwell, pp. 231–35.

[13] There are connections also with Preachers' houses at Worcester and Warwick, and with the short-lived Marian restoration at Smithfield, all noted in the extensive description by P. Giles and F. Wormald, *Descriptive Catalogue of the Additional Illuminated Manuscripts in the Fitzwilliam Museum Acquired between 1895 and 1979* (Cambridge 1982), pp. 533–39.

English Dominican liturgy may be the book, now Worcester Cathedral MS Q.107, called, in accordance with Humbert's terminology, *Evangelistarium*. This is not merely a gospel book, for it contains everything that the (liturgical) deacon needs for performance of his role in a high or conventual mass, including notation for the Exulter and the Christmastide Genealogies and also the various formulas he intones. Although Ker states cautiously "Written in England (?), for Dominican use, s. xiii²," E. S. Dewick, who once owned the book, had earlier suggested a date around 1270.[14] It seems possible to be more precise, for the original sanctorale contains no distinctive saints canonized later than 1253 (Peter Martyr), whereas among the earliest (of four) strata of additions are Antony of Padua, added to the Dominican calendar in 1262, and Edward the Confessor, added 1267. If 1253–62 is the likeliest date-range, the book is exactly contemporary with the Master General's Compendium (as we may term BL Add. 23935) and with the Royal 2 A.xi breviary.

The original hand is possibly, but not conclusively, English.[15] Whether written in England or brought there from, as it might be, northern France, it was quickly supplied with English saints as well as being kept up to date with the addition of the new saints approved by the order's Chapters General, at least through 1355. Saints added to the sanctorale include all of those for whom lessons were supplied in the last two gatherings of the Royal breviary: Ignatius, David, Thomas Aquinas, Richard, Servatus, Dunstan, Martial, Alban, Translation of Becket, Alexis, Martha, Louis, Wenceslaus, Edward Confessor, Eleven Thousand Virgins, and Winifred (Pope Mark is in the original sanctorale). Many of the fifteen English saints for whom collects are supplied in the Royal breviary just before the supplementary offices are also represented among the additions here, but there are some discrepancies. The most notable is the presence of the East Anglian saints Botulf and

---

[14] Dewick described it fully in *Trans. St Paul's Ecclesiological Soc.* 5 (1905), pp. 176–80 and two facsimile plates. Because when it was given to the cathedral library in 1952 it was technically uncatalogued, it fell within Ker's definition of his project in *MMBL* and is treated briefly in IV.675–76; it therefore does not appear in R. M. Thomson's catalogue of the cathedral's MSS (2001). In the second half of the 19th cent. it had been owned by William Morris. It seems still to have been in use in 16th-cent. England, for, as Dewick noted, at the Exultet the words "rege nostro henrico octauo supremo" have been written over the erasure of "beatissimo papa nostro."

[15] Dewick calls attention to a similarity with the hand of BL Egerton 2569, a lectionary written for Mons (Hainault) in 1269 by an English scribe named John of Salisbury; Watson, *BL Dated MSS*, no. 611 and pl. 160. But E. M. Thompson, *An Intro. to Greek and Latin Palaeography* (Oxford 1912), p. 450, states that John "does not write an English hand" (see pl. 187 on p. 452), so even a firm identification would not prove that our book was written in England.

Etheldreda in the Royal but not the Worcester book, where the most notable additions in the latter are Oswald bishop and the Translation of Wulfstan, both pointing unmistakably in the direction of Worcester. The friary there was not established until 1347, and it is logical to suppose that the book, which in its original sanctorale contains not a single English figure save Becket, was a more or less standard Dominican *evangelistarium* taken there soon after its foundation and supplemented with a plethora of appropriate saints.[16]

Reflexes in English society

The best known point about the liturgy of the Friars Preachers in the late fourteenth century is that Richard II is said to have read the divine office in its Dominican form. The basis for this claim is a privilege of Pope Boniface IX in 1395, specifying (in a modern summary) that "the King and all clerics in attendance at Court [are granted] licence to say the Divine Office according to the Dominican use which the Pope learns from the royal petition to be somewhat different from the Roman rite."[17] Although it may seem improbable that the mercurial Richard read anything like the full office in any form, the papal document recognizes a liturgical component to what had long been the case, that royal confessors were overwhelmingly Dominicans. How far back that pattern was established does not seem precisely ascertainable, but it probably extends into the long reign of Henry III.[18] There is even a claim that the Dominican liturgy became that of the king's court under Edward III, but there seems to be no corroboration for this.[19]

To whatever extent the statement about Richard II's observing the office according to the use (*mos*) of the Dominicans is true, what sorts of

[16] A roughly contemporary volume used at mass is Bodl. Rawl. liturg. g. 13, a proser, alias sequentiary, from the late 13th or early 14th cent.: a plain as well as very small (120 x 80 mm) volume, presumably for use by a cantor. Its sanctorale is limited to three feasts of Mary, Augustine, All Saints, Peter Martyr, and Dominic; a later note (fol. 54v) speaks of Albert the Great, who died in 1280 (but was not canonized until 1931).

[17] The summary is that of Bede Jarrett, *The English Dominicans* (New York 1921), p. 140, with reference to the *Bullarium Ordinis Praedicatorum*, ed. T. Ripoll and A. Bremond, 8 vols (Rome 1729–40), II.352. A precis of this is in *Cal. Papal Registers*, V: *1396–1404* (London 1904), p. 67.

[18] Friar William of Darlington seems to be royal confessor around 1260: Knowles, *RO*, I.167.

[19] Made by M.-H. Lavocat in *Liturgia*, ed. R. Aigrain (Paris 1931), p. 861, in the brief section on Dominican liturgy. It may be relevant that in 1356 Edward III brought to fruition a plan originated by his father in 1318, the foundation of a Dominican nunnery – the only one in England – at Dartford, Kent (*Med. Rel. Houses*, p. 285); it was to be subject to the royal foundation of Black Friars at King's Langley, Herts.

books might have been involved? We must probably suppose a number of breviaries along the lines of the Royal 2 A.xi book, and like that book heavily supplemented with English saints. It is unfortunate that no such books seem to be extant from the later middle ages, and especially that the only liturgical book (almost the only book of any sort) that has survived from King's Langley, the great Dominican house founded and richly endowed by Edward II and the first place of Richard II's burial, is the collectar dated 1523, mentioned above.[20]

One distinctive Dominican liturgical practice is said to have had wide popular appeal (aside from preaching, which, as elsewhere in this work, is not considered): the *Salve Regina* procession after compline. As early as the Master Generalship of Jordan of Saxony (1222–37) compline was regarded as the high point of the order's observance of the divine office, probably because of the freedom given to the Black Friars to arrange their days so as to maximize the time available for study. The last hour of the liturgical day was, however, to be attended without fail, and was elaborated by an unusual degree of variability.[21] After the office itself there was, as Humbert's prescriptions spell out, a procession out of the choir and into the nave of the church, while the *Salve Regina* was sung. The mid-thirteenth-century *Vitae Fratrum*, collected by Gerard of Frachet by 1260, speaks of the way people "thronged to our churches" to be present for this procession, but this was presumably in either Italy or France, and evidence for a similar popularity in England is a desideratum.[22] There were by sober estimate as many as eighty friars at the London (Holborn) house in 1243, and ninety in 1305, so the liturgical occasion should have been rather magnificent as well as accessible to a large population.[23]

Some information about the mass-liturgy might be extracted from two still unpublished works by the Dominican Nicholas Trevet (c. 1258–c. 1334). His *De officio missae* survives in at least seven manuscripts, in lengths ranging from about twenty to about thirty folios.[24]

---

[20] The natural presumption that it was well supplied with liturgical books is strengthened by the fact that in 1415 Robert Rede, bishop of Chichester, bequeathed to that house "omnes libros meos preter libros missales et chorales qui sunt de usu Saresburiensi": K. W. Humphreys, ed. *The Friars' Libraries*, CBMLC 1 (1990), p. 198. There is no other information about Langley's library.

[21] This is especially true of the antiphons at the *Nunc dimittis* (that canticle was not part of the monastic office at all): details in Bonniwell, pp. 158–61.

[22] English tr. of the *Vitae Fratrum* by P. Conway and B. Jarrett (London 1924), p. 44; amplified in Hinnebusch, *Early English Friars Preachers*, pp. 220–22.

[23] Galbraith, *Constitution of the Dominican Order*, p. 91 for the 1243 figure, *Med. Rel. Houses*, p. 217 for 1305.

[24] The MSS are listed in Sharpe, *Handlist*, p. 396.

And his Anglo-Norman *Cronycles*, written for Mary "of Woodstock," the fourth daughter of Edward I and Eleanor of Castile, and a rather worldly nun at Amesbury, contains, according to Ruth Dean, "details of the celebration of the Mass, and proper behaviour at it."[25] It is doubtful that much which is distinctively English and/or Dominican would be available there.

On the whole, differentiation between English and Continental Dominican liturgical practice was probably very slight, apart from regional variations in the sanctorale. Further points of particularity among the liturgies of the friars may appear after those of the Franciscans and Carmelites have been surveyed.

Franciscans

By the time the first Franciscan friars (the Order of Friars Minor, also called Grey Friars) arrived in England, 1224, they would have been under not the "Primitive Rule" ascribed to their founder but that of 1223, the so-called *Regula bullata*. Its key liturgical provision is the first sentence of chapter 3, which provided that the ordained member should keep the divine office "secundum ordinem sanctae Romanae ecclesiae excepto psalterio." The *"ordo* of the holy Roman church" referred to here is the breviary that had been developed, most markedly in the pontificate of Innocent III (1198–1216), by the papal Curia – the clerics of which had continued, in keeping with the custom of the canons of St John Lateran (the cathedral of Rome), to use the Romanum version of the psalms; the friars are, more sensibly, to use the by-then standard Gallicanum version, and for this purpose, the sentence concludes, they are to have breviaries different from those of the Curia.[26]

The earliest Minorites in England, whether priests (as very few of them seem to have been) or not, had neither the churches nor the equipment necessary for the celebration of mass, but the clerics among them seem to have had something like breviaries from the beginning. Thomas of Eccleston's classic, if somewhat jumbled, account of the first

---

[25] R. J. Dean, "Nicholas Trevet, Historian," in *Med. Learning and Literature*, Festschr. R. W. Hunt, ed. J. J. G. Alexander and M. T. Gibson (Oxford 1976), pp. 328–52 at 344; list of MSS pp. 351–52.

[26] *Regula*, cap. 3, conveniently available in K. Mirbt, *Quellen zur Geschichte des Papsttums und des römischen Katholizismus*, 6th edn by K. Aland (Tübingen 1967), p. 322. The most commonly cited English translation, that of B. Fahy (*The Writings of St Francis of Assisi* [Chicago 1964], p. 58), indeed renders *ecclesia* as "Curia." Of the position before 1223 J. R. H. Moorman comments "It is unlikely ... that the Primitive Rule can have said anything much about how or where the friars should worship": *A History of the Franciscan Order ... to 1517* (Oxford 1968), p. 16.

quarter-century of Franciscan presence in England contains several references, always in passing, to performance of the office: e.g., three friars sing the office of St Laurence *sollempniter cum nota* at Cambridge in 1225, Brother Walter of Madeley goes to matins at Oxford wearing unauthorized sandals and suffers a nightmare in consequence, the custody (the Franciscan term for the subdivision of a province) of London is marked by "fervor, reverence, and devotion in the Divine Office."[27]

The book out of which the office would have been recited by these early Franciscans is the close adaptation of the curial breviary called the Regula Breviary, after the Rule which sanctions it. There is no trace of it in any surviving manuscript used in England. It, and all questions relating to Franciscan liturgy in the thirteenth century, have been intensively investigated by Stephen J. P. van Dijk, himself a member of the order. His conclusions have been summed up by his necrologist and collaborator, Joan Hazelden Walker: "From 1223–1230 the friars produced a rubricated breviary and missal. They were to attract a wider public beyond the order, but their lack of clarity, universality, system and synthesis had to be corrected by the friar who understood this Roman tradition as well as the needs of his confrères, and indeed of others, north of the Alps."[28] This friar was an Englishman, Haymo of Faversham, and it is his work of revision and regularization that is the watershed for Franciscan liturgy.

Haymo, who, already a priest, joined the order in about 1226, was its fourth General, elected in late 1240. Although he is a figure of considerable importance in its wider history, his significance for us lies in the liturgical work he undertook in the brief years of his generalate (he died early in 1244). First, he provided a new ordinal for the Franciscans to replace the rather confused one of the Roman Curia which was all they had had previously.[29] Secondly, he accomplished, at the request of Innocent IV, a revision of the Roman breviary and missal along lines

---

[27] Thomas of Eccleston, *De adventu Fratrum Minorum in Anglia*, ed. A. G. Little (Manchester 1951), pp. 22, 34, 35 (cap. 3 and 6).

[28] J. H. Walker, obituary and bibliography, in *Archivum Franciscanum Historicum* 64 (1971), pp. 591–97 at 592. Van Dijk (1909–71) most frequently used the initials S. J. P. in his publications, but A(urelianus) or S. A. in some of the earlier ones.

[29] The massive edition of and commentary on Haymo's work is van Dijk's *Sources of the Modern Roman Liturgy: the Ordinals of Haymo of Faversham and related documents 1243–1307*, Studia et Documenta Franciscana 1–2, 2 vols (Leiden 1963). Apparently the edition was originally meant to appear as a Henry Bradshaw Society publication, but a quarrel over editorial policy led to van Dijk's withdrawing everything except the bare bones of the edited texts, which were published, anonymously, as *Ordines of Haymo of Faversham*, HBS 85 (1961). Some help in understanding this is given by Ward, *Pubs HBS*, p. 68. On Haymo see also Rosalind B. Brooke, *Early Franciscan Government* (Cambridge 1959), pp. 195–209, esp. 208–9.

laid out in his new Franciscan ordinal: revisions so successful that they became foundational to what is now known as the Modern Roman Liturgy.[30] There does not seem to be an official prototype copy of Haymo's work for the Franciscans, such as the Dominicans have for that of Humbert of Romans (see p. 312); the most complete copy appears to be that in Mende, B.m. 1, of the early fourteenth century.[31] In addition, it was not for several decades that all pre-Haymonian books ceased to be used, so that it is hard to be certain that the small number of extant thirteenth-century witnesses to Franciscan liturgy in England are all post-Haymonian, though there is none from as early as the 1240s.

Before we look at those witnesses it would be well to remember that Haymo's liturgical experience must originally have been formed in England, presumably in Faversham. His year of birth is not known, nor how long he spent in England before migrating to Paris, where, an academic of considerable reputation, he joined the friars in 1226. The era in which he would have grown up, probably the last quarter of the twelfth century and first quarter of the thirteenth century, is the period during which an early form, at least, of the Sarum rite is being developed (see next chapter), but only as nascent, not accomplished or widespread. It is nonetheless useful to note van Dijk's comment that, the heart of Haymo's liturgical work being the thorough correction of earlier rubrics, the precision of his style in this matter "reflects the higher standards of rubric writing found in England, particularly in the contemporary Sarum books."[32] That there are in fact no such books strictly contemporary does not vitiate the possibilty of English influence on Haymo in this respect.

After the Haymonian reforms were thoroughly assimilated into Franciscan service books – a process that must have taken some time, given the poverty of many of the early houses – the order's liturgy was further settled in the third quarter of the thirteenth century. Some smaller liturgical books envisaged by Haymo were compiled; at the Chapter at Metz in 1254 John of Parma (General 1247–57) issued a detailed set of instructions designed to ensure greater uniformity in the performance of services; and in 1260 his successor (St) Bonaventure ordered that breviaries and missals should be corrected to conform with new typical books (*secundum exemplar verius*) and that there be some changes to the

---

[30] The main subject of the major, and very complicated, book by van Dijk and J. H. Walker, *The Origins of the Modern Roman Liturgy* (London 1960).
[31] Described in great detail by van Dijk, "Some Manuscripts of the Earliest Franciscan Liturgy," *Franciscan Studies* n.s. 14 (1954), pp. 225–64 at 234–47. Part ii is vol. 16 (1956), pp. 60–101.
[32] *Origins of MRL*, p. 305.

calendar.[33] All of the surviving service-book evidence for England was written after 1260, save one missal, to be discussed presently. First we look at two breviaries that exemplify well the features one would expect in early Franciscan books.

Franciscan portable breviaries

Given that the rationale for the breviary in general is portability as well as compendiousness, it seems almost tautologous to speak of "portable breviaries," but some breviaries are much less portable than others. The two early Franciscan breviaries that survive as more than fragments can be called exceptionally portable – probably at some expense of legibility. In CUL Add. 7622 a list of Easter days beginning in 1280 provides a *terminus a quo*. It is a fat but very small book, 570 folios with written space 85 × 65 mm. As will be the case with the missals, to the basic Franciscan calendar have been added numerous English saints. Two of the additions, Translation of Edmund the Martyr on April 29th (after Peter Martyr) and the Dedication of the Friars' Church at Babwell on October 15th, indicate that the book found a home there, just outside the north gate of Bury St Edmunds.[34] As the book is at present constructed, fols 312–50 form a supplement of some nine saints' offices inserted before the sanctorale itself, which begins on fol. 351; included in this supplement are offices for the reception of the Stigmata by Francis and (the lessons only, but the nine of a major feast) for Edmund. The book manifests several peculiarities. Between temporale and calendar the mass ordinal for the temporale is inserted (fols 232–43), but no mass texts. In the psalter each day's material is headed by the matins hymn for that day in Ordinary Time, and for many of the psalms only two or three verses are given, although others are written in full. In the (original) sanctorale proper the nine lessons for Francis's main feast are extremely long (fols 488–505v), most of them with no responsories.

The other early breviary, BL Harley 5037, is either incomplete or oddly constructed. The temporale goes only to the first Sunday after Pentecost (no mention of Trinity Sunday), which would lead us to suppose that it might be the winter part of a two-volume office book; but the sanctorale breaks off, manifestly incomplete, at the Nativity of the

---

[33] The 1254 regulations are printed in van Dijk, *Sources MRL*, II.411–16, those of 1260 on pp. 419–20; see also Brooke, *Early Franciscan Government*, pp. 262–64.

[34] The Minorites finally settled there in 1263, after three decades of tension with the monks of Bury; summarized in *Med. Rel. Houses*, p. 224.

Virgin (September 8th). The first part, including the beginning of the psalter and probably the calendar, is missing; still, although the rubrics are frequently quite faint, discernible words at the beginning of the temporale (fol. 31) make plain what the book is: "Incipit breviarium ordinis fratrum minorum secundum consuetudinem sanctae Romanae ecclesiae." Its "Englishness" is not quite as indisputable as that of the previous book, and there appear to be no hints as to provenance. It is again a very small book, though not as small as some fragments of another thirteenth-century Franciscan breviary (University College, London, Lat. 6, part i), in which most of the letters are about a single millimeter in height – and the pages consequently all but unreadable.[35]

Two early missals

Tiny handwriting also characterizes the two oldest missal-witnesses and raises a large, albeit unanswerable, question about the eyesight of the putative users: how did the early friar-priests manage to read such minuscule script while busy at the altar? This is certainly the case with the oldest of all the Franciscan books we have to consider, a highly portable missal, once owned by a great English student of things Franciscan, A. G. Little, and now Bodl. Lat. liturg. f.26, written between 1255 and 1260.[36] It consists of 157 folios, with a written space c. 125 × 80 mm into which are crammed two columns of 38 lines each. It seems doubtful that a book that small would have been entirely usable by a celebrant at mass, even with some parts of the canon in a larger hand than the rest. In particular, the Palm Sunday passion is marked for solemn singing with the usual + (= Christ), c(antor), s(inagoga) symbols, but the writing is so small that one cannot imagine the book's being used for that purpose. The calendar, which occupies the first six folios, apparently served as a covering for the rest, for the book was folded in half vertically when the book's possessor was travelling.[37] To the

---

[35] Contents summarized in *MMBL*, I.340. Part ii consists of nine folios (19–27) of a Franciscan missal of the same period. Some pages of its written space of c. 115 × 70 mm have 61 lines of writing crammed onto them. Mass forms for the Translation of Anthony (of Padua) were added, as was an office for that feast, to the breviary fragments, in the 14th cent. – which is very likely when the two parts were joined.

[36] A. G. Watson, *Cat. of Dated and Datable MSS c. 435–1600 in Oxford Libraries*, 2 vols (Oxford 1984), no. 551, on the basis of the inclusion of Dominic, introduced 1255, but Bernard, mandated in 1260, is an addition. Linda Voigts has suggested to me that difficulty in reading such texts might have been part of the motivation for friar Roger Bacon (died c. 1292) to undertake his work on optics and be associated with the development of reading glasses.

[37] This is the explanation proffered by van Dijk in his brief description in the catalogue of the 1952 Bodleian exhibition, *Latin Liturgical Manuscripts and Printed Books*, no. 39.

original calendar, clearly Franciscan, have been added, in more than one stage, many English and some further Continental saints. The most noteworthy addition is that of Oswald, bishop, at February 28th and marked *festum patrie*[?], which strongly implies eventual use in the friary at Worcester.[38] The calendar is decorated with miniatures depicting the labors of the months, and the book is far from being a testimony to Franciscan simplicity.

Another eye-strain volume, also probably from the third quarter of the thirteenth century, is a combined Bible-missal, now CUL Hh.1.3. The Vulgate text occupies the first 352 folios; then come immediately proper prefaces and the canon of the mass, followed by temporale, calendar, and sanctorale.[39] The book was certainly made to be used, but again, whether any celebrant could read such tiny writing as is displayed in, notably, the proper prefaces is doubtful. To use it while celebrating the priest would have had to pick up the book at such points and, of necessity holding it open with both hands, peer at it. The beginnings of the temporale and the sanctorale are both written in three columns, but this experiment is given up after one and three folios respectively. The calendar, thoroughly Franciscan, includes also Wilfrid, which suggests use in York.[40]

Some local connections

Three documents, all of the period c. 1280–1320, show Franciscan books being used in, or adapted to, somewhat wider contexts. A putative origin with the Oxford Franciscans has been posited for Bodl. Digby 2, a mostly astronomical miscellany datable to 1282 because of a table of movable feasts.[41] Its calendar is the standard one for the order, with only two distinctive English saints, Edmund Rich and Edmund the Martyr (Becket and Gilbert, also present, are in the standard calendar, but this one contains the Translation of Becket as well). The one possibly unique entry is Laurence O'Toole, archbishop of Dublin 1162–80,

---

[38] Watson's remark that "other feasts [*sc.* besides Oswald's] suggest an origin in Cornwall" is puzzling; Gudwal is among the numerous additions, but, as D. H. Farmer points out, came to have a considerable cult in Worcester (*Oxf. Dict. Saints*, s.n. Gudwal).

[39] Some 367 folios are extant out of an original total of 405; the missing leaves are taken into account in a modern collation pencilled inside the back cover, and only two come from the missal section.

[40] Gilbert of Sempringham is also present, but he formed part of the "Regula calendar" of 1227–30, as printed on the odd-numbered pages of van Dijk and Walker, *Origins*, pp. 425–47.

[41] Watson, *Oxford Dated MSS*, no. 416 (but in neither *MLGB* nor its *Suppl.*); C. H. Starks in *Manuscripts at Oxford: R. W. Hunt memorial exhibition*, ed. A. C. de la Mare and B. C. Barker-Benfield (Oxford 1980), p. 119.

at November 14th; the inclusion also of Patrick may lead us to wonder whether the scribe was perhaps an Irish friar.[42] What else might this kind of individuality betoken?

The second document (Liverpool Cathedral, Radcliffe Collection 27) is a psalter of roughly 1300, with a fairly extensive selection of hymns (fols 141–59v) and an even more extensive selection of masses (fols 159v-87v, including the canon). The calendar occupies the last six folios, and contains all the standard Franciscan saints; but the most obvious of them, including Francis, were erased (not Anthony of Padua, however), probably in the fourteenth century and in connection with the book's having come into the possession of a family called Stone, five of whose obits are entered. One is of Master Richard, "persona Ecclesie de seuenhamton," who died in 1311, having in 1297 been instituted (as Neil Ker noted) at Seavington St Michael in Somerset.[43] The presence of the hymns for Francis and Anthony, as well as the Franciscan character of the litany of saints, show that this is not a secular psalter-*cum*-masses with a friar calendar, and the supposition must be that this book passed, perhaps from the nearby friary at Bridgewater, to its new owner(s), who found it usable for the local parish church.

A possible, or at least eventual, connection with Somerset is also evident in yet another book that strains the eyes: Bodl. Auct. D.5.11, a Bible with epistle and gospel lists as well as a Franciscan calendar with a few English saints. There is a most unusual entry at July 16th, *Canonizatio sancti Francisci*. The pericope lists, called *Pronunctiatio* [*sic*], cover only the most important feasts "per totum annum secundum consuetudinem ecclesie Romane." These lists, the calendar, and a chunk of the dubiously canonical IV Esdras (fols 9–18) occupy just the first 21 folios of the codex, the rest being the Vulgate with its prologues. It is likely that the Bible and not the preliminary matter was the point of appeal that caused one Richard Swann to buy the book "a domino Matheo vicario de Medford" (Mudford, north of Yeovil?) on March 7th, 1475, according to an inscription on fol. 1.[44] Our curiosity would center on how the parson Matthew had come to have this clearly Franciscan book in the first place.

---

[42] Patrick is in only two other (in both cases as later additions) of the 22 Franciscan calendars collated by van Dijk as witnesses to "The Kalendar according to the Use of the Papal Court," *Sources MRL*, II.378.

[43] *MMBL*, III.185–87.

[44] Or possibly Midford, south of Bath, no longer a village but the site of a Gothick folly. Fol. 2 contains a late 16th-cent. inscription in a mixture of French and Latin; the owner then was Leonard Worall Sporall of London.

Franciscan liturgical impact in England

These two cases of Franciscan books coming into the possession of rural parish clergy focus a natural, if unresolvable, question: how widespread was the specifically liturgical influence of the orders of friars? We have noticed (and will notice further) examples of books which are unmistakably Franciscan or Dominican being adapted to reflect cults of English saints. The reverse does not quite seem to be the case; only in a few instances, notably that of Francis, does a major friar-saint become widely present in English secular liturgy. The frequent presence of Dominicans as royal confessors and the possibility that their form of daily office may have been used at the court of Richard II, noted above (page 318), may be the clearest example of friar liturgical influence, but at an extremely limited level of society. The special influence of the Franciscans may be even harder to track precisely: whether their somewhat streamlined liturgy has any impact, by at least the late fifteenth century, on English secular office liturgy, which in general seems to grow in cumbersomeness and complexity (see p. 424). It seems fair to conclude that neither of those orders, despite their intellectual and pastoral impacts on England, became as "English" as did, oddly, the Carmelites, the next object of our attention.

Carmelites

The vexed early history of the Carmelite friars (the full title is the Order of the Brothers of Our Lady of Mount Carmel; colloquially, White Friars) need concern us only to the extent that, by the time they first entered England, in 1241/2, they had come to possess a certain amount of liturgical identity probably somewhat different from that which first characterized them. When in the early thirteenth century there appeared in the West hermits who claimed a corporate existence centering on the traditions of Mount Carmel, they seem already to have had a rule, one supplied by (St) Albert of Vercelli, the Latin Patriarch of Jerusalem, around 1208. This rule stressed their eremitical nature, prescribing common worship only for mass, with the daily office said in the individual cells. Overall, their "rite" (if the word is appropriate for something so undeveloped) may have been little different from that of the Augustinian canons who staffed the Church of the Holy Sepulchre before Saladin's capture of Jerusalem in 1187; that church's Rituale (= ordinal) is contained in Vatican Library, Barberini 659, a copy made probably in the 1230s from an original of around 1160.[45] As long ago as 1912 Benedict Zimmerman, the most eminent Carmelite student of the order's liturgy, noted the extensive influence of the Holy Sepulchre liturgy as reflected in the Barberini 659 ordinal.[46] Certainly the earliest Carmelite calendar was modelled on that of Jerusalem.

Simon Stock and the earliest English Carmelites

Whatever the original nature of the religious who based their identity in some way on Mount Carmel, the order's official recognition, by Gregory IX in 1229, was as mendicant rather than eremitical like, say, the Carthusians. At this point the enigmatic figure of (St) Simon Stock, the Englishman who is the first great hero of the (Western) Carmelites, seems to emerge. The cautious language is necessary because the supposed centrality of his role, as Prior-General of the order elected at a chapter at Aylesford in 1245 (1247?), is known of only through tradition fully developed in the later fourteenth century.[47] Putting aside the most vivid components of that tradition – Simon's earlier hermit-period in a tree trunk (= stock, later supposed to be his surname) and a miraculous Marian vision in 1251 according to which the wearing of the Carmelite scapular guaranteed tremendous spiritual benefits – we note what appears to be both relevant and true: that in 1247 Innocent IV granted additional papal approval, as a result of which two Dominicans, one of them the famous biblical scholar and cardinal Hugh of St Cher, overhauled the governing documents of the Carmelites, the effect of their work being to shift the emphasis of the new order's activities towards study. In short, the first half of the thirteenth century saw the Carmelites change from being a quasi-eremetical group to a

---

[45] Its calendar is printed, by collation with that of Rome, Bibl. Angelica 477 (the famous "Angelica sacramentary"), in Appendix I to F. Wormald's "Liturgical Note" in H. Buchthal, *Miniature Painting in the Latin Kingdom of Jerusalem* (London 1957), pp. 107–21. Another copy of this *Rituale* is at Barletta in Apulia; this "Barletta Codex" is discussed at great length, with an ascription of date around 1240, by C. Kohler in *Revue de l'Orient Latin* 8 (1900–1), pp. 383–500.

[46] Zimmerman's brief section on the Carmelites within the long article on "Rites" in the (old) *Catholic Encyclopedia*, XIII (1912), pp. 72–74, is still the most helpful concise introduction. This is drawn on heavily in the relevant chapter in A. A. King, *Liturgies of the Religious Orders* (London 1955), pp. 235–324 – as usual with this work, a grab-bag of facts, in the aggregate useful but always in need of checking. More extensive (indeed, exhaustive) is P. Kallenberg, *Fontes liturgiae Carmelitanae: Investigatio in decreta, codices et proprium sanctorum* (Rome 1962).

[47] Knowles and Hadcock say severely that "Simon Stock and his reputed achievements must be relegated to the realm of myth" (*Med. Rel. Houses*, p. 232), and *ODCC* states that "he did not (as used to be thought) hold office in 1247" (p. 1503).

tightly-structured, nominally medicant order with a strong academic tinge, in both respects similar to the Dominicans.

The effect of this re-orientation is seen in the English foundations.[48] The earliest, all apparently in 1242, were at remote places suitable for a quasi-eremetical life: Hulne near Alnwick, Burnham Norton in Norfolk, Lossenham and Aylesford, both in Kent. That the founders of at least two of these established their houses on returning from a crusade-type jaunt with Richard of Cornwall (younger son of Henry III) in 1241 further underlines the connection with Palestine.[49] Between 1247 and 1256, however, houses were established at Cambridge, London, Bristol, York, Norwich, and Oxford – the two principal university and four main commercial centers in the kingdom.[50]

The liturgy used by these foundations in their earliest years may in some respects have still approximated that of Jerusalem, but no service books survive by which this could be tested. An enigmatic ordinal is extant in Dublin: Trinity College B.3.8 (194), folios 168–237v, a composite codex, of which folios 165–67 contain other Carmelite documents; the nature of the remaining folios, otherwise totally irrelevant, suggests that the ordinal was written for use in England.[51] It is not precisely datable, but appears to be of the late thirteenth century; two important feasts adopted by the Carmelites in 1306, Corpus Christi and the Conception, are absent here.[52] The only English saints are Becket (a semi-double), Edmund the Martyr, and, most intriguingly, Richard of Chichester, whose canonization in 1262 provides a *terminus a quo*. The first two will remain in the normalization of the order's liturgy in 1312 but not Richard; what it says about the TCD 194 ordinal that he should have been included (at nine lessons but no incipits save that

---

[48] A full discussion is K. Egan, "Medieval Carmelite Houses, England and Wales," *Carmelus* 16 (1969), pp. 142–226; much of the information on the order in *Med. Rel. Houses* is taken from this.

[49] According to A. G. Little, VCH *Kent*, II (1926), p. 201, the Aylesford house was peopled with Carmelites brought from the Holy Land by Richard de Grey, its founder; but of course they may originally have come from the West, even conceivably from England.

[50] Other notable sites during the 13th cent. include Ipswich, Lynn, Newcastle, Northampton, Nottingham, and Stamford: data from *Med. Rel. Houses*, p. 233.

[51] The entire MS is described in M. Colker, *Cat. TCD MSS*, 2 vols (London 1991), I.378–85; the Carmelite part was published by Patrick de Saint-Joseph, *Antiquum Ordinis Carmelitarum Ordinale Saec. XIII* (Tamines 1912–14, from vols II–IV of *Etudes carmelitaines* with consecutive pagination). *MLGB* rejects it for the London Carmelites.

[52] The convenient chronological list of "Fêtes carmelitaines" in V. Leroquais, *Les bréviaires manuscrits des bibls. publiques de France*, 5 vols (Paris 1934), I.cxi, starts only in 1306; for extensive treatment see A. Forcadell, "Ritus Carmelitarum antiquae observantiae," *Eph. Liturg.* 64 (1950), pp. 5–52.

for the collect, which is the standard one) defies ingenuity; there were no Carmelite friaries in either Sussex or Worcestershire, the two areas associated with him, at that time.

Regulating Carmelite worship: an early ordinal and Sibert's revision of 1312

Wherever it was written or meant to be used, that late thirteenth-century ordinal may not have been in effect for long because soon thereafter the work of regulating the liturgy of the Carmelites was taken in hand by Sibert de Beka, Provincial of Lower Germany; in 1312 he produced a new ordinal, the best witness to which seems to be Lambeth Palace MS 193.[53] Reportedly accepted only with reluctance, its differences from the old ordinal seem marked enough to underlie the language of a list of service books at the end of the 1366 library catalogue of Hulne which records, among seven *portiforia*, two signalled as *veteris ordin[ation]is*.[54]

Sibert's ordinal is in many details still congruent with that of the Holy Sepulchre reflected in the Barberini manuscript. Comparison of the calendars implicit in their sanctorales shows a striking degree of coincidence.[55] Saints present in Sibert but missing from the Barberini (= Holy Sepulchre) ordinal are Antony abbot, Patrick, Ambrose, Vitalis, Nicomede, Cyricus and Julitta, Anne, Martha, Eleven Thousand Virgins, Edmund k.m., Linus, Eligius, and Conception of Mary; in addition, Sibert includes Dominic, Louis, Bernard, Francis, and Thomas Becket, all canonized later than the calendar underlying the Barberini codex. Richard has disappeared, and Edmund is the sole English saint besides Becket, while the presence of Patrick (but only to be taken from the common of a confessor) raises the faint possibility that the Lambeth manuscript may have been written in Ireland.

There are also, however, indications of Dominican influence – influence wholly in accord with the increased emphasis on study and preaching among the Carmelites. One instance of this in Sibert's ordinal may be the instruction on fol. 77 that a rubric about the singing of hymns should be inserted "plenario [presumably a large choir breviary] sive pulpitario" *pulpitarium* being a distinctively Dominican

---

[53] Edited by B. Zimmerman, *Ordinaire de l'Ordre de Notre-Dame du Mont-Carmel par Sibert de Beka (vers 1312)*, Bibl. Liturgique 13 (Paris 1910), from this MS.

[54] K. W. Humphreys, ed. *The Friars' Libraries*, CBMLC I (London 1990), pp. 176–77 (list C3).

[55] Zimmerman's edition compares details of the two in a "Table synoptique" (pp. 353–66) and prints calendars extrapolated from their sanctorales on pp. 367–70.

term for a book of chants sung from a specified piece of choir furniture (see p. 312). Another instance may be the inclusion of Martha, who was taken into the Dominican rite in 1276; but her feast among the Carmelites could equally well reflect the heavy presence of Palestinian saints in their tradition.

As with the Dominicans and Franciscans, liturgical uniformity, represented for the Carmelites by Sibert's ordinal, was the ideal. How far from reality this was will become apparent as we look at two important service books of the late fourteenth century.

The later fourteenth century, I: the "Reconstructed Carmelite Missal"

The most celebrated medieval book relating to the order is the famously mutilated manuscript known as the Reconstructed Carmelite Missal (BL Add. 29704–5, with some additional fragments).[56] This was the name given to it by Margaret Rickert who, after many years of study, published her findings in a heavily illustrated monograph in 1952. Her summary description gives a laconic indication of the labor involved: "English Carmelite missal, probably written at Whitefriars, London, before 1391 and illuminated before 1398 by several hands. Latin. Gothic script. 212 paper leaves on which are mounted 1588 vellum fragments consisting of historiated and decorative initials, fragmentary borders and text."[57] The extensiveness and sumptuousness of the illustration would, were the book complete, place it just behind the Sherborne missal and ahead of the Westminster among the great mass books made in England between about 1385 and 1405. Our main concerns being liturgical rather than artistic, we mourn the lack of extensive text – the apparently complete book was cut up, probably to make monograms, by the children (one hopes) of an indulgent former owner – while being grateful for the synopsis of liturgical contents provided in Rickert's monograph.[58]

---

[56] The fragments are organized into six "volumes," distributed among Add. 44892 as well as 29704–5, with a few others in Glasgow, Univ. Lib. BD.19-h.9, no. 1875; this is laid out in the full and recent (1996) description in Scott, *Later Gothic MSS*, no. 2. Another book of cuttings is apparently in a private collection: *MLGB Suppl.*, p. 48.

[57] M. Rickert, *The Reconstructed Carmelite Missal* (Chicago and London 1952), p. 23.

[58] Rickert's synopsis and fuller discussion on pp. 27–44 seem to have behind them the authority of Francis Wormald, who while a staff member at the then British Museum "was assigned ... to supervise and check the reconstruction" (Preface, p. 14); Benedict Zimmerman (note 46 above; died c. 1950?), the dean of Carmelite liturgical studies and himself a White Friar, is also thanked.

All evidence of the temporale from Advent to Easter Eve is missing, and four months of the calendar, placed between temporale and sanctorale. The fragments of the sanctorale actually give textual evidence for only sixteen saints, widely scattered, but enough survives in the way of historiated initials and bits of heading around them for an extensive sanctorale to be extrapolated. This includes thirty-five distinctively Carmelite feasts and at least twenty-one English saints or translations (Becket's main feast would have been in the missing temporale section). Among the latter is the Translation of Richard of Chichester (16 June 1276) as well as his April 3rd feast: so he is back (or perhaps was never missing from English sources not now extant), despite having been omitted by Sibert. A strong London flavor is provided by the presence of Mellitus, Ethelburga, and two feasts for Erkenwald – the placing of whose Translation on November 14th seems to commemorate an occasion of 1148 rather than that of 1326 (on 1 February, a day taken up by Ignatius). There are of course many distinctively Carmelite observances, including the octave of the Annunciation, decreed in 1362; but the absence of three Marian feasts mandated in 1393, Visitation, Presentation, and St Mary "of the Snows," provided Rickert with her *terminus ad quem* for the text.[59]

Several textual points glancingly alluded to by Rickert as illustrating the Carmelite mass rite might well repay more detailed investigation.[60] So might also the key question of donors, in relation to both St Paul's cathedral – the book was written almost certainly in London – and Westminster abbey. The exactly contemporary Westminster missal shares some possibly instructive textual details with the Carmelite book, such as the secret and postcommunion for the fairly rare feast of Mildred, prayers different from those of the St Augustine's missal of the late eleventh century (see p. 113; mentioned here because that abbey claimed to possess her body). Mildred is first included in a calendar of St Paul's in the early thirteenth century, by which time she is also in that of Westminster.[61] The elaborateness of the Carmelite

[59] The date she gave in her monograph was 1391, but 1393 in the 2nd edn of her *Painting in Britain: the Middle Ages*, Pelican History of Art (Harmondsworth 1965), p. 153. This is presumably because of the publication three years earlier of Kallenberg's *Fontes* (note 46 above).

[60] *Reconstructed Carmelite Missal*, pp. 37–43. On p. 37, n. 2 she mentions that "an edition of this Missal was once contemplated by the Henry Bradshaw Society but in view of the many difficulties and uncertainties involved in dealing with so fragmentary a text ... the idea was abandoned."

[61] The St Paul's calendar is in London, Guildhall MS 25512; see A. T. Thacker, "The Cult of Saints at St Paul's in the Middle Ages," in D. Keene et al., eds. *A History of St Paul's Cathedral* (London and New Haven 2004), pp. 113–22, at 117; that of

book's decoration – at least four artists, in three quite different styles, are represented – presupposes wealthy patronage, but no definitive suggestion has emerged.[62]

The later fourteenth century, II: the Cambridge(?) breviary

Contemporary with the reconstructed missal, but happily quite complete, is a breviary-with-festive-missal which belonged to the Carmelites of, probably, Cambridge (now Oxford, University College 9). Its date range seems to be 1375–93, and it is a finely produced book, though nowhere near as sumptuous as the missal was originally.[63] This small, fat book (424 folios, 195 × 125 mm, written space 125 × 75) is interestingly constructed. First comes the temporale of the breviary, then, after five folios of general rubrics as though in an ordinal, the festive – that is, select feasts only – missal, which combines temporale and sanctorale and concludes with proper prefaces and canon. After this the breviary is resumed, with psalter and litany of saints, but there is another interruption for a further missal element consisting of votive masses and masses for the common of saints. Again the breviary continues, with Office of the Dead, sanctorale, and offices for the common. It is hard to work out for whom, or what purpose, a book would have been written which made possible full recitation of the office, with over 180 saints accommodated, but contained masses for only some 39.

Comparison of the sanctorale of the breviary with that from the "reconstructed" missal shows the two to be in large part identical. The noteworthy saints or translations present in the London book but absent in the breviary fall into three groups: first, several of specific importance to London, Alphege, Mellitus, Mildred, Ethelburga, Translation of Edward the Confessor, Translation of Erkenwald; secondly, Edmund archbishop and his Translation, Translation of Richard of Chichester, Hugh; thirdly, three English figures whose absence is entirely puzzling, Botulph, Alban, Etheldreda. Most of these in all three groups are included in the breviary's calendar, which is much fuller than its sanctorale (and possibly not part of the original book; it seems to be a discrete quire, fols 196–201). These additional calendar entries include

---

Westminster, from the famous psalter of that house, BL Roy. 2 A.xxii, is printed in *Westminster Missal*, III.1385–96.

[62] Scott canvasses possibilities at the end of her *Later Gothic MSS* discussion, inconclusively.

[63] J. J. G. Alexander and E. Temple, *Illuminated MSS in Oxford Colleges* ... (Oxford 1985), no. 745: "fine borders and initials." The book is there classified under French MSS, though the authors state, "Made for English use."

a great many English saints, like Wulfstan, Frideswide (two feasts), Chad, Withburga, Wilfrid (two feasts), Fremund, John of Beverley, and, most oddly, on May 31st a "Wlstani ep. & cf." who must be either Walstan of Bawburgh, the Norfolk farm-laborer saint here transformed into a confessor-bishop, or Wul(f)stan of Worcester, whose translation feast, not widely celebrated, was June 7th.[64]

The somewhat antiquarian interest suggested by this list may also help to account for this breviary's possibly unique feature: a feast for the Venerable Bede with nine lessons (fols 326–27; eight of the lessons are proper, the seventh a homily on the gospel for the day). These lessons include a lengthy enumeration of his works, borrowed obviously from Bede's own list at the end of the *Historia Ecclesiastica;* ingenious quotation from the letter of Pope Sergius I (d. 701) to Abbot Ceolfrith of Jarrow supposedy asking for Bede's help; and allusion to the monk Cuthbert's letter giving an eyewitness account of Bede's death.[65] The collect at the end begins "Deus pater omnipotens qui uenerabilem presbiterum tuum Bedam," and is different from that in either the Westminster, Durham (Harley 5289), or Sherborne missals. Most strikingly, Bede is not included in the calendar; this makes it all the more reasonable to suspect that the office for him was composed by a Carmelite at the house to which this book belonged: most likely the friary at Cambridge, a house of considerable intellectual distinction and the headquarters of one of the two *studia generalia* of the order, the other being at Oxford.[66] The latter friary is the source of another witness to awareness of Bede among at least the university-oriented Carmelites, whose hagiography we must now consider.

Carmelite hagiography

Unlike the Dominicans and Franciscans, who were reasonably clear about their founding fathers and other worthies, the Carmelites had many exotic figures in their imaginative and sometimes woolly collection of saints. This comes through plainly in the fifteenth-century calendar and martyrology (now Longleat House MS 16), from the Oxford friary. The calendar, which precedes the martyrology and contains

---

[64] There are also a number of 15th-cent. additions, some English (Oswald bp., Winifred, Kenelm), some Carmelite (Cyril of Jerusalem, Simon of Angers, Lazarus; also Bernard and Francis).

[65] This sentence is taken from my "Bede among the Fathers?" in *Studia Patristica* 28 (1993), pp. 225–29, at 228–29; repr. Pfaff, *LCSSME*, no. X.

[66] Knowles, *RO*, II.144–48, gives examples of Carmelite prominence both intellectually and, in the late 14th cent., politically.

numerous obits of members of the community at Oxford, is extant only from July. For the six months covered it manifests, as had the Cambridge(?) breviary, awareness of both Carmelite and English heritage: Martha, Joachim, Cleophas, and Lazarus on one hand, Kenelm, Winifred, Hugh, et al. on the other (and in large black letters Becket, whose name has not been effaced). There is also a steady awareness of the prominent new feasts: the Visitation with octave, Transfiguration (in the martyrology as well), Name of Jesus, and Presentation of the Virgin (under that styling, rather than the "Oblacio … in templo domini in Ierusalem" of the martyrology entry).[67]

The martyrology is basically that of Usuard, as would be expected, but expanded to contain notices of at least ten English figures besides the two included by Usuard himself, Augustine of Canterbury and Etheldreda. Fairly unremarkable are the notices for Edward Martyr, Dunstan, Alphege, Becket and his Translation, Edmund of Abingdon, and Hugh. But three, all noteworthy, are redolent of Bede. The first is for Bede himself, on May 26th (*vii Kal. Iunii*): "doctoris anglorum sagacissimi. Cuique quanta existunt merita et doctrine fluenta melliflue et bonorum operum exempla testantur." The other two, both on July 7th, are mentioned in his *Historia ecclesiastica*: Haeddi, bishop of Winchester (d. 705), "de quo uenerabilis beda presbiter in gestis anglorum refert quia sepulture eius multe sanitates infirmorum effecte sunt"; then, immediately, "translatio sancte athe[l]burge virginis sororis sancte atheldrithe" (followed by Translation of Becket). Haeddi's death-day is not given in Bede (*HE* V.18) but is established in calendars of Winchester affinity by at least the eleventh century. Bede does specify July 7th for an Ethelburga, the one in question being the daughter of Anna, king of the East Angles, and abbess of Brie, who died in 664 (III.8). To establish the link between Ethelburga and Etheldreda required the Carmelite martyrologist, or his source, to read carefully in Bede, who does not mention the two together, though describing each separately as a daughter of Anna. (It is particularly frustrating not to know whether Bede was included in the calendar, May being missing.)

It would be well worth the effort to trace the source of each of the post-Usuard entries. Here we notice just that for Becket, which is found also in a fourteenth-century martyrology that reflects Exeter use, CCCC 93 (see p. 400). The only other place this notice has been found

---

[67] The calendar in the Cambridge(?) breviary has added to it "Oblacio B.V.M. totum duplex," in the same hand as added the Visitation (Pfaff, *New Liturg. Feasts*, p. 109); the Transfiguration seems an original Carmelite observance, found already in the TCD 194 ordinal.

is in a martyrology of the first half of the fifteenth century, now Bodl. Bodley 731, for which an Oxford origin – like that of the Carmelite book – may be supposed from an entry for the seldom encountered Frideswide (fol. 52).[68]

The electicism of the Carmelite interest in saints is apparent also in a calendar, datable to 1385–87, and thus contemporary with the missal and breviary discussed above and slightly earlier than the martyrology. Now part of a composite codex of unrelated contents (Bodl. Digby 41, fols 59–75v), it lacks January through April. It shows again the characteristically Carmelite combination of saints of the order (e.g., Cyriacus, 4 May, Zacheus, 23 August, Narcissus, 29 October: all are legendary "bishops of Jerusalem") with those of the locality – in this case, perhaps Aylesford, for there is an entry for the rarely found martyr William of nearby Rochester (alias, of Perth), 23 May – and, more widely, of England (like Botulph, Etheldreda [with vigil], Paulinus, Wilfrid, Frideswide).

All Carmelite priories were dedicated to the Virgin Mary. The deep Marian devotion of the order was both reflected and enhanced by the emergence of what comes to be its most characteristic annual observance, one always called *commemoratio* rather than *festum*: that of Our Lady of Mount Carmel on July 16th. It seems to have come about some time between 1376 and 1386, hand-in-glove with development of the Simon Stock legends, in that the Blessed Virgin was thought to have bestowed the wonder-working scapular on him that day.[69] In effect it became a kind of festive commemoration of a papal recognition in 1226 of the order's rule.

An improbable concluding figure: John Bale

The sixteenth-century bibliographer, playwright, and Protestant controversialist John Bale entered the Carmelite friary in 1506, at the age of eleven. Roughly nineteen years later, while prior of the small friary at Burnham Norton in Norfolk, he wrote *de manu propria* a very small book consisting of specifically Carmelite offices and devotions (now CUL Ff.6.28). By 1530 he had left the order and begun to produce the flow of acerbic works that earned him in the seventeenth century

---

[68] The Becket notice is form "d" among the eight collected and discussed in my "Martyrological Notices for Thomas Becket," Pfaff, *LCSSME*, no. VIII, at pp. 3, 7. Bodley 731 was bought by the collector Robert Elyot in 1489.

[69] This is the origin of the popular "scapular devotion," the belief that whoever dies wearing a form of the Carmelite scapular will be saved. It was turned into a formal feast in the 17th and 18th cents.

the nickname of "Bilious Bale"; so this hagiographical compilation of c. 1525 has a particular fascination because of its steadily backward- and inward-looking character.[70] Besides an office "in festo solempnis commemorationis beate Marie specialis carmelitarum patrone" there are *historiae* for Cyril of Jerusalem (construed as an honorary Carmelite), Berthold (first General of the order, died c. 1188), Angelus (another early Carmelite, died as a "martyr" in 1225), Albert (the Patriarch of Jerusalem and Augustinian canon, who drew up the first rule for the hermits of Mt. Carmel; died 1215), and the prophet Elijah (Elias, described as "princeps et fundator ordinis fratrum Carmelitarum").

The apparent vigor that it is natural to infer from this little volume may be misleading (Bale did nothing without vigor, after all); but if the intensity of liturgical and devotional life among the Carmelites was waning in the sixteenth century, there is little sign derivable from the available evidence. In this respect it is regrettable that the most outstanding extant witnesses to the order's liturgy in the middle ages are both of not later than the last quarter of the fourteenth century – the mutilated and now reconstructed missal in London and the breviary-missal likely to have been written originally in Cambridge. When liturgy translates into theology it is relatively easy to track, as also when it transmutes into non-liturgical spirituality; it is much harder with liturgy *simpliciter*, liturgy as practiced by those entrusted with the duty of performing it.

Our impression of the worship of the Carmelites has of necessity been drawn heavily from hagiographical evidence, because (as we have seen elsewhere in this book) that is perhaps the surest way to grasp distinctiveness. And with the major orders of friars their hagiographical distinctiveness was a way of expressing and emphasizing their cherished, sometimes conflicted, corporate identities. That is true of the first three, anyhow, the Dominicans, Franciscans, and Carmelites; what can be said about liturgy for the ostensibly least vivid of the four, the Austin friars, is now to be looked at.

Austin friars

The short name commonly used for the fourth order of the "four orders" of friars frequently referred to in late medieval English sources, Austin

---

[70] He is the author as well of the pioneering effort at British bibliography, the *Index Britanniae Scriptorum*, edited by R. L. Poole and M. Bateson (Oxford 1902), and repr. with intro. by C. Brett and J. P. Carley (Woodbridge 1990).

friars, will be employed here as well, mainly to avoid confusion with Augustinian canons. But the official name, and hence official abbreviation, of the order since its formation, must also be kept in mind: *Ordo Eremitarum Sancti Augustini* (O.E.S.A.). This "order" was, as is well known, originally a conflation of several groups of hermits in central Italy.[71] The conflation took place formally via a bull of Alexander IV in 1256 which united the various groups under a rule deriving from that of Augustine, but twelve years earlier Innocent IV had extended papal recognition to one of the core groups, the hermits of Tuscany, a recognition which included the privilege of using the liturgy of the papal Curia. These hermits, and those of the other groups folded in by the 1256 bull, would therefore have been in the same position liturgically as the Franciscans, whose service books were in the process of transition from the *Regula* books to those reflecting the revising work of Haymo of Faversham (see p. 321).[72]

When therefore the first group of what can be regarded as Austin Friars arrived in England, in 1249, their worship would have presumably have been much like that of the Franciscans, by then well established. The first house was at Clare in Suffolk, established under the auspices of Richard de Clare, the mighty earl of Gloucester, and with the active encouragement of Henry III.[73] But this was a rural location, and the foundation four years later of a house in London by Humphrey de Bohun, earl of Essex, began the pattern which was quickly to become normative, of friaries in important towns rather than in the country. There were roughly a dozen foundations by 1290, another dozen in the next fifty years. Clare and (especially) Bohun patronage remained important.

In 1290 the General Chapter, meeting at Ratisbon, issued a set of *Constitutiones* among which was a mandate that each house have a supply of specified service books.[74] The list resembles in general that drawn up by Humbert of Romans for the Dominicans in 1256 (see p. 312), but there is no mention of breviaries. This implies that

---

[71] D. Gutierrez, *The Augustinians in the Middle Ages 1256–1356* (Villanova, PA 1984), pp. 23–41. This is the first part of the official history of the order; part ii (1983) covers the period 1357–1517.

[72] S. J. P. van Dijk and J. H. Walker, *The Origins of the Modern Roman Liturgy* (London 1960), pp. 399–400. There were actually two stages: the privilege was granted to the Tuscan hermits in 1244 and in the next year "to all hermits living according to the Rule of St Augustine."

[73] F. Roth, *The English Austin Friars 1249–1538*, I: *History*, Cassiciacum 6 (New York 1966), pp. 19–21; vol. II (published earlier, 1961) is devoted to documentary sources.

[74] Roth, I.377–78.

Austin clerics were to have their own, and it is likely that many had personal missals as well.[75] Unfortunately only two or three Austin service books as used in England seem to have survived. The earliest is a psalter of about 1325, now in the Escorial Library (MS Q II 6) and virtually unknown until Lucy Freeman Sandler brought it to light for its very considerable artistic merit.[76] She relates its elaborate illustrations to those of the celebrated Stowe breviary (BL Stowe 12; see p. 423), and it is clearly a high-status book. Its sumptuousness, inclusion of the devotional text of the Joys of the Virgin in French as well as Latin, and several heraldic images of the Bardolf and Bussey families (landholders in Lincolnshire), lead to the suggestion that the manuscript may have belonged to the woman depicted in a Crucifixion miniature which shows an Austin friar at the bottom. Sandler has been able to establish its calendar as being that of the order, as well as its litany. That the latter includes (as well as Becket and Edmund Rich) Edmund the martyr, Etheldreda, and Osyth seems to point to East Anglia, a location consonant with the artistic workshop in which the book was made, most likely in Norwich. In view of the probability that it was owned by the Bardolf woman of the miniature and that the friar shown there was her confessor or chaplain, we can use the book's evidence only to a limited extent.[77]

More useful is an office book (now Vatican Lib., Lat. 11438) which belonged to the London convent, or one of its friars, and which must be dated after 1446.[78] Its calendar includes the Dedication of the London house, June 10th, and a curious note to the effect that the Translation of King Louis should be celebrated on the Tuesday within the octave of the Ascension (not Louis's main feast day, which is August 25th). It is a tiny but thick book, 82 x 55 mm with 383 folios, probably the personal possession of a friar; its cataloguer suggests that the Austin Friar depicted on fol. 1 was most likely its owner. Only the Office of the Dead is provided with notation. As well as a psalter, the book contains

---

[75] Roth points to the clause in the Ratisbon Constitutions that allows friars to use what amounted to a clothing allowance to buy breviaries or missals (I.230, n. 514).

[76] L. F. Sandler, "An Early Fourteenth-Century English Psalter in the Escorial," *Jnl Warburg and Courtauld Institutes* 41 (1978), pp. 65–80; treatment summarized in her *Gothic MSS*, no. 80.

[77] This is all the more true because around the mid-15th cent. the book passed into the hands of the Premonstratensians at West Dereham, Norfolk; there some forty-five additions were made to the calendar, including Osmund, canonized in 1456: Sandler in *JWCI*, p. 67.

[78] The year of the canonization of Nicholas of Tolentino (d. 1305), one of the order's main worthies, who is included. All information about this MS is taken from the description by J. Ruysschaert, *Codices Vaticani Latini 11414–11709* (Rome 1959), pp. 31–34.

capitula and collects for the entire year, but lacks the lessons, responsories, and hymns necessary for performance of the complete office.

Two manuscripts are no basis for describing the liturgy of an entire order, and we must content ourselves with the knowledge that the Austin Friar books are all likely to have been like those of the Roman curial liturgy as revised by Haymo.[79] Some glimpse at what has been lost is provided by the list of books owned by John Erghome, prior of the convent at York in 1385, and included in the remarkable library catalogue of that house.[80] Among the over 220 volumes owned by Erghome was a group of six headed in the list "Libri divini officii." Two, both breviaries (one *completum pro itinere*, the other *completum pro studio*) are marked as having been sold; a diurnal is noted as lost; and two missals (one *completum* and one *manuale*) and a pontifical have been handed over to the sacrist. There is of course no such thing as a mitred friary, and it is noteworthy that Erghome should have possessed, presumably through purchase, a pontifical.

That the impression of the order given by the scanty evidence that survives is of a somewhat grand group is most likely misleading; nonetheless, there are few indications to the contrary.[81] The psalter now in the Escorial belongs to the most sumptuous East Anglian tradition of bookmaking. The York library catalogue of 1372–75 just referred to contained some 646 volumes, including those of Erghome (who clearly possessed, or had access to, considerable funds to indulge his book-buying proclivities) and must have been one of the largest collections in England at the time.[82] The priory at Clare was the burial place of Joan of Acre (second surviving daughter of Edward I and Eleanor of Castile, and widow of a Clare earl of Gloucester) in 1297, as it was of other members of her family; there was some possibility that she

---

[79] Two possible candidates for consideration are ruled out by Sandler's investigations. Bodl. Auct. D.3.2, a Bible with Epistle and Gospel lists and litany of saints, she shows to be of Augustinian Canon, not Friar, use (*Gothic MSS*, no. 13); and Dublin, Royal Irish Acad. s.n., a fragmentary breviary, is almost certainly Italian (*JWCI* article p. 65, see note 76 above).

[80] K. W. Humphreys, ed. *The Friars' Libraries*, CBMLC 1 (1990), pp. 101–2; list A8, nos. 395–400. Humphreys speculates that Erghome probably bought most of his books, especially during some years in Oxford and possibly also when he was in Italy (p. xxx); they are not necessarily English.

[81] The present brief and cursory account cannot even mention the considerable roles Austin Friars played in the theological and political affairs of the second half of the 14th cent., as surveyed in Knowles, *RO*, II.68–71, 118–20, 148–51.

[82] Humphreys, p. xxv, calculates that the 646 volumes contained a total of 2,188 separate works. Still worth consulting is the edition of M. R. James, "The Catalogue of the Library of the Augustinian Friars at York," in *Fasciculus Ioanni Willis Clark dicatus* (Cambridge 1909), pp. 2–96.

might have been put up for canonization.[83] The church of the London house was rebuilt, starting in 1354, largely at the expense of the tenth earl of Hereford, Humphrey de Bohun; its nave was wider than those of Exeter and Winchester cathedrals and almost as long as Canterbury's.[84] On Humphrey's death, childless, in 1361 he left, in an elaborate will, ample funds to enable fifty of the London friars to perform exequies and for each of the fifty to sing thirty masses for his soul within a year of his death.[85] This presupposes that nearly all the friars at the house were at that time priests (there were not more than sixty friars in 1325, the closest date for which we have a number). The observation that their worship must have been much like that of the Franciscans is nearly as much as can be said in summary.

Such a bland generalization may be necessary because of the limitations of evidence, but should not be taken as reinforcing a widespread sense that the Austins somehow lack the vividness of the other three orders. The facts noted in the previous paragraph – one instance each of sumptuous bookmaking, an amazingly extensive library, royal patronage, and a London church next in size only to St Paul's – suggest a more substantial presence, cultural and by extension liturgical, than is consonant with merely bringing up the rear of the file of friars. A final vignette, from towards the end of our story, may be offered as a counterweight. The London chronicler John Stow describes a great procession on St Martin's day (11 November) in 1525, part of which consisted of "the fryars Aystyns with theyr crosse and every fryar a coope … syngynge the letany with faburdyn."[86] Anything like the fifty friars at that house (the number presupposed in Humphrey de Bohun's earlier will), all in copes and singing faburden to the litany of saints, must have been a brave sight – and sound.

[83] Roth, I.260–61. Her daughter, Elizabeth de Burgh, rebuilt the priory as well as founding Clare College in Cambridge.

[84] Roth, I.287–88. The nave survived the Dissolution and was assigned to Protestants from the Low Countries, hence its modern name "Dutch Church." It was destroyed by a bomb in 1940; the replacement is considerably smaller.

[85] On these provisions, and on Humphrey's high-born friar-kinsman William of Monkland (Monklane?), see A. Gwynn, *The English Austin Friars at the Time of Wyclif* (Oxford 1940), pp. 107–13.

[86] John Stow, *Two London Chronicles*, ed. C. L. Kingsford, Camden Soc. 3rd ser. 18 (1910), pp. 1–157, at 11; quoted in Roth II (*Sources*), p. 429.

Excursus: on liturgical books from female religious houses

Had the extant sources permitted this, it would have been desirable to call this Excursus simply, "On liturgy in female religious houses." As things stand, we can only indicate a couple of considerations that apply generally, then provide a brief list of what does survive, and finally look at the one house, Barking, for which several sources are available. Because the sections on the Gilbertines (pp. 303–10) and Bridgettines (pp. 529–39) deal primarily with the female members of those "mixed" religious orders, information given there will not be repeated here.

The most obvious generalization is that those books which survive and can be attributable to a specific female house are overwhelmingly psalters (and *Horae*, excluded from the present work). This is a point that may have a wider application than is immediately obvious. It may say something about the priorities for expenditure in nunneries (the term, if not exactly accurate in all cases, will be used here as an alternative to the bulky "female religious houses" or "houses for women") that it does not seem possible to ascribe a single extant massbook to them. Does this fact suggest that the male celebrants generally brought their own missals – which is scarcely to be supposed – or even that it was not thought appropriate for nunneries to own missals – which is absurd? But it remains the case that, of some thirty manuscript books (or substantial fragments) that can with some confidence be ascribed to English nunneries, not one is a missal. Nor is there even a single breviary: does this allow us to infer that nuns are more likely to have observed their daily offices in choir than male religious, who might more readily have been either travelling, as in the case particularly of friars, or fulfilling other obligations in the monastery or friary, like those of saying masses for the dead or dealing with obedientiary business?

The second generalization is that among those books that survive and are ascribable there is a high percentage of de luxe volumes. This can be viewed in at least two ways. One is that nunneries, especially the markedly aristocratic ones like Amesbury and Shaftesbury, were likely objects of benefactions that sometimes included splendid psalters. Another is that, although nunneries were as thoroughly destroyed as most male houses at the Dissolution, their possessions may have received slightly gentler treatment and/or have in some cases been taken away and preserved by the expelled nuns (there are notable examples of this with the Bridgettines). Though this again seems improbable on anything like a large scale, it is the case that about a quarter of the relevant extant books are today in libraries outside Britain – a vastly greater proportion than with books surviving from male houses.

Because the fundamental trove of information so often cited in these pages, Ker's *Medieval Libraries of Great Britain* plus Watson's *Supplement* of 1987, is organized alphabetically by "library" (which means, in the present case, by religious house), and is concerned only with whether a particular book can be thought to have been owned – not necessarily used – in some way and at some time, by a specific house, its witness to the present subject is, we shall see, sometimes misleading. Here it may be useful to organize such information as we have in a somewhat thematic way.[1]

Surviving books from specific nunneries

The Benedictine nunneries are by far the best represented, though with no more than two or three books each, save for Barking. From WILTON there survive (1) a finely illustrated mid-thirteenth-century psalter, probably made at Salisbury (now London, Royal College of Physicians 409);[2] (2) the fifteenth-century litany, but not the calendar, of a psalter of c. 1265–70 made originally for Dominican use (now Bodl. Rawl. G.23);[3] and (3) a transcription made at Solesmes in the nineteenth century of a fourteenth-century processional, since lost.[4] The latter contains full indications as to the sanctorale, here intercalated with the temporale (no Corpus Christi). As would be expected, Edith and Iwi,

---

[1] There appear to be no lists of books at nunneries in the Corpus of British Medieval Library Catalogues, with the sole exception of a scanty one probably from Wilton, to be discussed presently. On the whole, information included in Ker's *MMBL* IV (1992) was available to Watson for his 1987 *Supplement* to the 1964 *MLGB*.

[2] Morgan, *Early Gothic MSS*, no. 99. He points out discrepancy between litany and calendar, and suggests that the book was possibly "based on a Wilton exemplar but given a Calendar intended for a patron outside the Abbey."

[3] It is not clear how or when the book came to Wilton, but the litany is conclusively that of the nuns there.

[4] G. Benoit-Castelli, "Un Processional anglais du xivème siècle, Le Processional dit 'de Rollington'," *Eph. Liturg.* 75 (1961), pp. 281–326. The transcript is kept at Solesmes Abbey as MS 596.

the main saints of Wilton, are made much of; rather unexpected is the appearance so early of Anne and the Transfiguration.

From nearby WHERWELL less is meaningfully available than would appear from the four books ascribed to it in *MLGB*: three psalters, from three successive centuries, and a twelfth-century calendar now in St Petersburg (once Leningrad).[5] In fact, both the calendar and a slightly later twelfth-century psalter (now St John's College, Cambridge, 68/ C.18) were written at St Albans and adapted for, it appears, Matilda de Bailleul (Balliol), abbess of Wherwell c. 1200. The marginal additions, especially of obits, to the calendar of the psalter give valuable information about Wherwell but little about liturgy there.[6] Another calendar, this one of the fourteenth century, precedes Sarum *Horae* in a composite volume, the second half of which is a thirteenth-century psalter from Wherwell (now Fitzwilliam Museum, Cambridge, McClean 45); the calendar is not that of Wherwell and the litany, which may well be, is exiguous. Finally, an early fourteenth-century psalter (now BL Add. 27866) also contains a Wherwell calendar and litany.

Well known psalters are ascribed to two other aristocratic nunneries, in one case with considerable doubt. Whether AMESBURY was the destined home of the splendidly illustrated mid-thirteenth-century book often called the Amesbury psalter (now All Souls College, Oxford, 6) is controverted; the ascription is rejected in *MLGB*, and Nigel Morgan has explained how the calendar both implies that house and fails to do so.[7] Also somewhat unclear is the extent to which a slightly earlier psalter, c. 1210, is intended for Amesbury (now Bodl. liturg. 407). Amesbury's distinctive saint, Melor, is magnified on his day, October 1st (as in the All Souls volume), but Winchester saints are also emphasized; there is no litany.[8] On surer ground is the ascription to Amesbury of two bifolia of a breviary of around 1300, now at Windsor Castle,

---

[5] Brief description of MS Q.v.I, no. 62, in A. Staerk, *Les manuscrits latins du Ve au XIIIe siècle conservés à la Bibliothèque impériale de Saint-Pétersbourg* (St Petersburg 1910), pp. 274–75; the entries for August are reproduced in full.

[6] The additions are listed, and St John's 68 thoroughly discussed, in R. M. Thomson, *Manuscripts from St Albans Abbey 1066–1235*, 2 vols (Woodbridge 1982), I.56–60, the Leningrad (as he terms it, correctly for that date) calendar on I.37–38, with facsimile of the August page in II, ill. 137.

[7] Morgan, *Early Gothic MSS*, no. 101. He uses as a point of comparison the calendar of a 14th-cent. Book of Hours, CUL Ee.6.16, but the soundness of that ascription is also unclear; the calendar, which displays fanciful elements, is not necessarily integral to the rest of the book.

[8] Morgan, no. 27. The book came into Franciscan hands in the 14th cent., the calendar altered and a hymnal supplied. *MLGB* calls the MS "Liturg. misc. 407"; there is no "misc." in the *fons* name.

Jackson Collection 3.[9] A piece of good fortune is that one of the leaves contains a good deal of the proper liturgy for St Melor.

The ascription of BL Lansdowne 383 to SHAFTESBURY is incontrovertible: the Shaftesbury psalter, safely so denominated, written perhaps in the 1130s and certainly before 1173.[10] The prominence in its calendar and litany of Edward the Martyr (buried there in 979) and of St Ælfgifu (Elgiva; buried there c. 945) secure the place of intended use, wherever the book was actually written. An equally celebrated book, generally known as the Winchester psalter (BL Cott. Nero C.iv), made probably at the cathedral priory there between, at the outside, 1121 and 1161, seems to have been by the mid-thirteenth century at Shaftesbury, the Dedication and other characteristic feasts (but not Elgiva) being entered in the calendar then.[11] How long the book stayed at the nunnery is not clear, nor what influence it may have had on liturgy there; on balance, it cannot be used as a witness for that house. For potential, and fascinating, corroboration of the Shaftesbury calendar through a private book of devotion compiled for its penultimate abbess in the early sixteenth century, see p. 542.[12]

Much less well known is a fine mid-thirteenth-century psalter from the nunnery of St Mary at CARROW, Norwich (now Madrid, Biblioteca Nacional 6422); obits in the calendar, including one of a prioress of Carrow, substantiate the ascription.[13] The calendar has three feasts distinctive to the cathedral at Norwich, Bonitus, Winwaloe, and Taurinus (see p. 205).

A manuscript source of repute not for its illustration but for its musical and literary value is the early sixteenth-century processional

[9] J. Stratford, *Catalogue of the Jackson Collection of MS Fragments in the Royal Library, Windsor Castle* (London 1981), pp. 68–69 and pl. 2 (fol. 4v, the Melor lessons). Four folios of a 14th-cent. breviary are in the collection of C. F. R. de Hamel: *MLGB Suppl.*, p. 1.

[10] Kauffmann, *Romanesque MSS*, no. 48. He points out that this book "has the distinction of being the earliest Western Psalter with historiated initials at the liturgical divisions of the Psalms."

[11] Watson, *BL Dated MSS*, no. 539, dates the addition of the Dedication feast to the late 12th cent., but according to F. Wormald, *The Winchester Psalter* (London 1973), p. 108, that addition, like ten others made to the calendar, is in the same hand as wrote an obit of a knight who died in 1257.

[12] The 15th-cent. psalter (now Lambeth Palace 3285) recorded for that house in *MLGB Suppl.* belonged to Edmund Audley, bishop of Salisbury 1502–24, and was given by him to a niece who was a nun at Shaftesbury: an example of the caution with which the invaluable data in *MLGB* must be used. Similar is the case of a mid-15th-cent. psalter with Hours given by an Oxfordshire(?) knight "ad usum monialium" at Godstow, outside Oxford; now Manchester, Chetham's Library 6717 (*MMBL*, IV.352–53).

[13] Morgan, *Early Gothic MSS*, no. 120 and ills. 108–112. I have not seen this book, and have taken details from his description.

of the nuns of CHESTER, edited under that title by J. W. Legg at the end of the nineteenth century, when it was owned by the Earl of Elles-mere (now San Marino, Huntington Library EL 34 B 7).[14] In Legg's characteristically dry words, "it cannot be said that this book gives us great insight into the rites of the monastery at Chester," and the house itself is obscure. There were thirteen nuns in 1381 and fourteen in 1540, and because the practice seems to have been to process in pairs (certainly with the Bridgettines; see p. 535), we should probably suppose seven such processionals. The rubrics are all in English, and there is a substantial appendix of vernacular prayers and hymns. A notable feature is the identification of one of the stations of the Palm Sunday procession as "Jerusalem," as in "here the priores and other .ij. ladies shall take the prestes & goo in to the cyte of ierusalem and there they shal synge this antym."[15] Rubrics for the washing of altars on Maundy ("Shere") Thursday specify twelve altars, but this seems unlikely in a church the area of which seems to have been 58 by 43 feet.[16]

The only service-book evidence for the thirty-odd houses of Cister-cian nuns is for TARRANT in Dorset, but in both cases in books presented to that house. One contains six months of a late thirteenth-century calendar attached to a mid-fifteenth-century psalter with which it has nothing to do (now Stonyhurst College 9), the other is a psalter of the third quarter of the fifteenth century (now Bodl. Lyell 23). The calen-dar of the latter is certainly Cistercian, but written in the same hand as copied a *passio* of St Margaret divided into nine lessons (and therefore unusable at the nunnery). The calendar in the Stonyhurst manuscript is far from being purely Cistercian; an obit of one Letitia de Kaynes (hence "Keynston," often added to Tarrant) states that she gave the book to which the calendar originally belonged to the nunnery; either the nuns paid no attention to it, or they were not following the Cister-cian rite as discussed above (p. 257).

Another pair of very fine psalters belonged to small houses of August-inian nuns. One, HARROLD in Bedfordshire, had given to it in the early thirteenth century a book apparently written in Kent; the calendar, as Neil Ker observed, is nearly the same as that of Christ Church, Canterbury

---

[14] HBS 18 (1899); not, as Legg acknowledges (p. viii) a full reproduction of the text: all music is omitted, and incipits only of all items as were in the Sarum, York, and West-minster books available in modern editions by 1899.

[15] *Processional of the Nuns of Chester*, p. 5. Legg speculates that this "was perhaps some place higher than the rest from which the anthems were sung" (p. vii).

[16] VCH *Cheshire*, II (1980), pp. 146–50; the measurements were made following excava-tions in the ruins.

just after Becket's death, which is the rough date of the manuscript.[17] The book (formerly Bristol, Baptist College MS Z.c.23, now in a private collection in London) therefore offers little information about the (largely secular) liturgy that the Harrold nuns would have used. No more helpful is a splendidly illustrated mid-thirteenth-century psalter probably from northwestern France, given to the Augustinian nuns at GORING in Oxfordshire (now TCC B.11.5/ 244).

The liturgical books of Barking

It is only from the nuns of Barking, just east of (medieval) London, that enough sources survive for us to get anything like a sense of their worship. Grateful as we are for this, we should note also that the principal source, the Barking ordinal (often referred to in these pages; now University College, Oxford, 169) may be closer to a *unicum* than to anything from which one could extrapolate as to usages in other nunneries. It is certainly unique in having been compiled at a specified date, 1404, by a named person, Sibille Felton, abbess from 1394 to 1414, and clearly a liturgical enthusiast. (Almost as rare is that its modern HBS edition is adorned with notes by another liturgical enthusiast who was also an abbess, Laurentia McLachlan.[18]) Several factors may contribute to the distinctiveness of this document. One is the antiquity of Barking, founded c. 666 by (St) Erkenwald, though re-founded in the days of Dunstan and Edgar, c. 970; it had good warrant for thinking of itself as the oldest female religious house in England. Another is its location in the diocese of London; it shared many of the saints of St Paul's as well as a number of its usages. A third may be its wealth, probably second among English nunneries only to that of Shaftesbury. All three may be reflected in what can be inferred from details in the ordinal: an apparently sumptuous church (of which nothing remains) and a somewhat luxurious attitude towards liturgy.

The best known passage in this work comes after the ordinal proper, in a kind of appendix devoted mostly to specific functions and rights of the abbess: a section headed "Regula cuiusque usus servicium dicendum est." This states that, in order to avoid occasions of discord about

---

[17] *MMBL*, II.189.

[18] J. B. L. Tolhurst, ed., *The Ordinale and Customary of the Benedictine Nuns of Barking Abbey*, 2 vols, HBS 65–66 (1927–28), with consecutive pagination. Dame Laurentia was at the time prioress of Stanbrook abbey (Worcs.), 1925–31, and its abbess from 1931 until her death in 1953. Her notes, pp. 366–90 of vol. II, are full of interesting asides, by no means confined to Barking.

the office and mass such as have happened in the past, it should be understood that the convent has three different elements (*tres modos diversos*) in its worship: "Primo horas suas dicat secundum regulam sancti benedicti. Psalterium suum secundum cursum curie Romane. Missam uero secundum usum ecclesie sancti Pauli Londoniarum."[19] The bearing of those concluding words (which will have to be revisited when we look at the picture at St Paul's cathedral) on the present subject is to remind us that the chaplains to the nuns were secular priests of the diocese of London and could be expected to celebrate mass according to the rite they knew. Nor is it surprising that the office should be observed in its monastic form; but that the version of the psalms used within it should be the thoroughly antiquated, almost arcane, Romanum version is astonishing.[20] It must reflect either an immense, indeed unprecedented, conservatism or an eccentric kind of liturgical antiquarianism. It is generally agreed that the Gallicanum version carries all before it in England by around the turn of the millennium, most likely in the context of the tenth-century monastic revival, of which Barking was a shining product. An implication of the retention of this nearly obsolete psalm-version is that Romanum texts must have been copied into books used at Barking over a span of several centuries – unless the decision to adopt it was very recent, in which case it was all the more eccentric.

It is therefore even more frustrating that none of the other liturgical or para-liturgical books that have a Barking connection contains a text of the psalms against which this statement could be checked. The most directly liturgical is a hymnal (now TCC O.3.54/ 1226) roughly contemporary with the ordinal; but because the ordinal does not always specify the incipits of hymns in the office, it is difficult to compare the two. Many centuries earlier is a gospel lectionary of c. 1000 (now Bodl. Bodley 155) that, while clearly a Barking book, seems to have been copied from an exemplar originating at Landévennec in Brittany.[21] Winwaloe is prominent, with three feasts, but none of the distinctive Barking saints. In the early twelfth century a collection of seven saints' lives was written, either at or for the nunnery; it includes Goscelin's lives of its first abbess, Ethelburga (Erkenwald's sister) and Edith, and

---

[19] *Ordinale*, II.359 (= fol. 219, not 209 as stated by Tolhurst in his preface, p. ix).

[20] Dame Laurentia (II.389) supplies the examples of *Gaudete justi* in place of the Gallicanum *Exultate* at the beginning of psalm 32, and of *Quam amabilia* rather than *Quam dilecta* in that of ps. 83.

[21] Temple, *Anglo-Saxon MSS*, no. 59. Bodl. 155, adorned with two splendid angels, was at Barking by the 12th cent.; the 10th-cent. Breton Gospel list, now Bodl. Auct. D.2.2, was itself given to Exeter by bishop Leofric (p. 130 above).

also lessons for Ethelburga's successor Hildelith (now Cardiff, Public Library MS 1.381, part ii).[22]

Another hint as to a kind of cumulative conservatism at Barking can be inferred from a highly fragmentary calendar of the late fourteenth century (now BL Cotton Otho B.v, part I; parts of four months only) which retains Winwaloe and includes also Bernard of Clairvaux, as well as notices of the deaths of abbesss Isabella de Montacute (or Montague, 1352–58) and of Simon de Montfort in 1265; all four appear in the ordinal also.[23] Possibly a touch of antiquarianism informs these Barking documents in more respects that just the psalm-version used. A glance at the calendar that heads the ordinal shows a disposition to leave no possible sanctorale occasion unobserved. Chaucer's prioress at St Leonard's, Stratford-at-Bow did not, as far as we know, possess a liturgical enthusiasm comparable with that of her exact contemporary abbess Sibille Felton; but it is Sibille and her nuns of Barking who may have been exceptional.[24]

---

[22] *MMBL*, II. 348–49; part i, perhaps joined to ii by Robert Cotton in the 16th cent., is a life of Winwaloe written in the early 13th cent. at Dover Priory.

[23] In the University Library of Bergen are fragments – parts of May and June – of a calendar from a once de luxe MS that may have come from Barking; if not, from the diocese of London; see the images and discussion at that university's "Fragment" website.

[24] The actual prioress at Stratford while the *Canterbury Tales* and (most likely) the Barking ordinal were being written was Mary Suharde, who occupies that office in 1375 and also in 1397: *Heads Rel. Houses*, II.612.

10   Old Sarum: the beginnings of Sarum Use

It is probable that the single best known phrase pertaining to medieval liturgy in England is "Sarum Use." The phrase refers in the first instance to the medieval services at the present Salisbury cathedral, and, more generally, to the totality of rubrics, texts, and saints – eventually, even styles of vesture and certain liturgical colors – supposed to derive from that model. This sounds very neat, and, as it is widely known that that cathedral began to be built in 1225 and was largely finished (save for the spire) in three decades, it is natural to suppose that a new rite was confected for the new building, and even that the articulation of this rite was accomplished by one person: Richard Poore, whose work will be treated mainly in the next chapter.

The actual story turns out to be much more complex, and indeed is by no means perfectly clear at present. It begins in 1075, when, as part of a royal post-Conquest policy of moving centers of dioceses from (more) obscure locations to places that seemed for one reason or another more logical, the headquarters of what had originally been the West Wessex diocese centered for the most part at Sherborne was moved to the hill-fort site usually known today as Old Sarum – the conventional term, retained here so that "Salisbury," if not otherwise qualified, can be reserved for the new city and church, extant from roughly 1225. The 1075 move took place under Her(e)man, who was one of the Lotharingian churchmen favored by Edward the Confessor, and who, after a somewhat stormy time as bishop of Ramsbury fitfully from 1045, became bishop of Sherborne (in combination with Ramsbury) around 1058. By the late summer of 1075 he was attesting as *Seriberiensis episcopus*, but he seems to have been feeble for some time before that; we have no details about whatever nascent cathedral establishment was extant by the time of his death in February of 1078.[1]

---

[1] VCH *Wiltshire*, VI (1962), p. 60; on Hereman in general, see F. Barlow, *The English Church 1000–1066: a Constitutional History*, 2nd edn (London 1979), *passim*, and J. Barrow in *ODNB* 26.786–87.

Putative influences after the move

Three strands may be discerned as possibly influential in the development of worship at Sarum in the earliest decades. The first, if most shadowy, is the monastic. The chapter at Sherborne had been monastic since 993, and after the move a substantial community of monks remained there. Hereman, though himself a secular priest, was strongly drawn to the monastic life, and indeed between 1055 and 1058 tried it at St Bertin. There is, however, little or no evidence that he brought with him to Sarum any monks from Sherborne. The complicated witness of the English additions to the copy of the Roman-German Pontifical, now fragmentarily preserved as BL Cott. Tib. C.i, may reflect conditions at both Sherborne and Sarum, and may well have been brought with him by Hereman; but by its nature, as a book containing episcopal services, it yields no information about worship at his cathedral.[2]

A second strand is that of the prebendal system that seems to have been in effect almost from the outset. The obvious model must have been that of the few genuinely secular cathedral chapters extant in England by around 1075: most obviously, those of Hereford, London, and York.[3] As we know very little indeed about worship in the late eleventh and twelfth centuries at any of those places, this may not appear to be a model at all useful. Yet that within fifteen years of the move from Sherborne the great figure in this part of our story, bishop Osmund (Hereman's successor, 1078–99), had established a full complement of canons like those of the older secular foundations suggests that they must have been looked to as precedents.

A third discernible strand is suggested by the obvious comparison with the move made under bishop Leofric in 1050, when the see center of the Cornish peninsula passed from an originally monastic setting at Crediton to that of a community ostensibly living under the Rule

---

[2] Summary by J. L. Nelson and R. W. Pfaff in Pfaff, ed. *Liturg. Bks. ASE*, pp. 96–97; important discussions in N. R. Ker, "Three Old English Texts in a Salisbury Pontifical," in *The Anglo-Saxons: Studies … to Bruce Dickins*, ed. P. Clemoes (London 1959), pp. 262–79, and in Webber, *Scribes and Scholars, passim*. Its basis is extracts from the Roman-German Pontifical, written in two German hands, but there are extensive additions by some fifteen English scribes, many if not all at Sarum; three of the additions are in Old English. The work may well have continued after Hereman's death, for the prayer "O sempiterne Deus edificator et custos Ierusalem," added in a blank space on fol. 202v, is likely to date from after the beginning of the First Crusade in 1095. The litany of saints beginning of fol. 203 includes only Swithun, Edith, and possibly Augustine of Canterbury among English saints. Contents of the entire MS listed in detail by Hartzell, *Cat. Music*, pp. 250–56.

[3] Lincoln will eventually become the greatest of secular chapters, but the see there had been established only in 1072 (from Dorchester on Thames), so it cannot have been much of a model for Sarum.

of Chrodegang at Exeter (though in that case no monks remained at Crediton, where a collegiate church was later established). Leofric's extensive liturgical program, treated in chapter 4, bears no trace of the monastic, and worship at Exeter must have had much of the character of other, smaller communities whose identities come to be clarified during the twelfth century as that of canons regular, most often of the Augustinian strain (see chapter 8).[4]

Given that the speculative must be the primary mode in thinking about the rite confected for use at the new cathedral at, say, the time of its consecration in 1092, the most concrete analogy may be furnished by the final stage of the Leofric missal. We shall try to use it as the knowable, in Maitland's famous phrase: in this case, to get something of a sense as to the sort of book with which the canons of Sarum in the early twelfth century might have been familiar.

Leofric missal "C" as a possible model

The outstanding extant and clearly non-monastic English massbook dating from earlier than the thirteenth century is the Leofric missal (Bodl. MS Bodley 579), as brought up to date by its "C" component: the material added at Exeter under the bishop of that name, 1050–72. This component is treated more fully in chapter 4 and within the context of Leofric's overall liturgical program; here we shall notice only those few aspects that may assist our effort to "back-read" the earliest Sarum service books we have, dating from the thirteenth century.

To review briefly what has been said earlier: Leofric took an early tenth-century massbook ("A"), augmented by a late tenth-century calendar and a few other additions ("B"), and had it turned into a book which he almost certainly reckoned was suitable for his own use. Some of the additions may be in his own hand, and there is a new *Missa propria pro episcopo*, cast in the first person singular, mentioning the bishop of Exeter in all three prayers, and most likely composed by Leofric himself. A number of his additions are episcopal blessings, although he had a pontifical written for himself as well (see p. 131; bishops of Sarum would have needed the same sorts of materials, at least once the now-fragmentary Cott. Tib. C.i book was no longer adequate, if it ever was). Among other additions made under Leofric were marginal

---

[4] Indeed, Leofric seems to have introduced Chrodegang's Rule at Crediton soon after he became bishop in 1046. There had been a small monastery at Exeter, but when he established his cathedral there he sent its monks to Westminster: *Med. Rel. Houses*, p. 425.

tags indicating lesson- and chant-incipits, elements that a complete missal would have in full. How early there were at Sarum full missals, as distinct from sacramentaries with the presumed associated books, is almost wholly obscure, although it is likely that the proliferation of full missals is to be connected with an increase in the number of side altars and masses said at those altars.

Leofric died in 1072, and his "completed" missal remained at Exeter. We can only speculate as to whether Hereman, or, more likely, Osmund, ever saw the missal or any of the other books that we know were part of Leofric's liturgical program. Massbooks for the new cathedral establishment need not have been furnished with elaborate illustrations like those in Leofric "B"; plainer books, like the New Minster or St Augustine's manuscripts reviewed earlier (chapter 4), would have served, and indeed could have been brought from Sherborne. But because the new chapter was secular, not monastic, a supply of books for use at the office in the first decades at Old Sarum must have been procured afresh. Where those came from, what they were like, and by what means (as well as how quickly) those books were altered and/or replaced towards creating a set of practices that will eventually coalesce into a "use," is beyond even the power of speculation. Although none of the bishops of Sarum compares with Leofric as a liturgical enthusiast, it is worth looking briefly at the episcopates of all three of the great prelates who followed Hereman.

The episcopates of Osmund, Roger, and Jocelin (1078–1184)

Let us postulate that something comparable to Leofric's liturgical regime at Exeter came into existence at Old Sarum in the long twelfth century between the beginning of Osmund's episcopate in 1078 and the conclusion of Jocelin's in 1184.[5] Osmund, Hereman's successor, was a Norman clerk who became a prominent servant of the crown (he may have been the Conqueror's chancellor from about 1070). The critical years of his work at the cathedral, apparently barely begun under Hereman, are almost totally obscure. As Teresa Webber has observed, the documentary sources for the early history of Salisbury cathedral are "completely silent for the period between the granting of permission to move the see in 1075 and the years 1089–91 which saw the formal

---

[5] Jocelin's successor, after a five-year vacancy, was the massively important Hubert Walter (1189–93), but he was so taken up with his secular duties that he is not much of a figure in the present story.

establishment of canons at Salisbury ... . Furthermore, the sources do not permit firm conclusions to be drawn concerning the organization of the canons once they had been formally established at Salisbury, nor the kind of religious life they led."[6] She notes also that the earliest extant mention of canons at the new cathedral, an entry in the complicated document called the Holyrood Chronicle, specifies that in 1089 Osmund established (*constituit*) thirty-six canons.[7] The cathedral was consecrated on April 5th, 1092 (the Monday after Easter week) by Osmund, who then presided over it – there is no evidence in his time for the existence of a dean – until his death in December of 1099.[8]

That is at least a starting point. The ground plan of the original Old Sarum, easily enough ascertainable from the remaining ruins, suggests that the distance from the pulpitum to the semi-circular apse was less than 30 meters, with the width between the piers under 10 meters. After space is subtracted for the high altar, probably seats behind it and possibly steps up to it, the choir area can scarcely have been more than, say, eighteen meters in length.[9] Thus it looks as though provision for the seating of anything like thirty-six "endowed" clergy, not to mention any other clerks or choristers, would be extremely tight, even if there were at least two rows of seating on each side of the central space.[10]

---

[6] Webber, *Scribes and Scholars*, pp. 2–3.

[7] Its entries to 1128 were compiled from English sources, perhaps made in the area of Salisbury: Webber, p. 2, and Antonia Gransden, *Historical Writing in England*, II: *c. 1307 to the Early Sixteenth Century* (Ithaca 1982), p. 82 n. 147.

[8] Not *St* Osmund until 1456, when a campaign for his canonization was finally successful (as one led in the 13th cent. by Richard Poore had not been). The materials gathered for the 15th-cent. campaign are assembled by A. R. Malden, *The Canonization of Saint Osmund...*, Wilts Record Soc. (1901). Much information is available in the semi-popular but substantial pamphlet by W. J. Torrance, *The Story of Saint Osmund ...*, originally published in 1919 but revised and somewhat reduced for the Friends of Salisbury Cathedral, 1978 (before, that is, the discrediting of the *Institutio* in 1985: see note 11 below).

[9] Measurements taken from the amply-sized plan in T. S. R. Boase, *English Art 1100– 1216*, Oxford History of English Art II (Oxford 1953), p. 117. No scale is given in the more complete plans in R. Gem, "The First Romanesque Cathedral at Old Salisbury," in *Medieval Architecture in its Intellectual Context* [Festschrift P. Kidson], ed. E. Fernie and P. Crossley (London 1990), pp. 19–34.

[10] Diana Greenway's observation that "the small size of the cathedral – it was by far the smallest of the cathedrals built in England after the Norman Conquest – suggests that this figure [36] may be too high," *Salisbury 1066–1300*, p. xxii, is balanced by her statement that property given to the canons by Osmund in 1091 was sufficient to support, at the least, twenty-nine. An approach of the sort here undertaken was essayed by W. St. John Hope in an article consequent on the excavations at Old Sarum in 1912–13: "The Sarum Consuetudinary and its relation to the Cathedral Church of Old Sarum," *Archaeologia* 68 (1917), pp. 111–26; the present argument was worked out independently of his.

This was presumably the situation in 1091, the year in which Osmund drew up a rudimentary constitutional document in the form of an impressively attested charter: hence its familiar name, *Carta Osmundi*. It speaks of canons living a "canonical life" (the prebends twice mentioned, whether authentically or in later additions, are not territorial), and of grants being made from offerings at the principal (= high) altar and at other (*ceteri*) altars, though no liturgical information can be inferred from it. From something like the middle of the twelfth century, however, it came to be believed that Osmund had produced a second document, also dated 1091 and known as the *Institutio*, which goes into some detail about the *dignitates et consuetudines* of the church of Sarum; in particular, it is specific about the relative positions of the dean, cantor (later called precentor), chancellor, and treasurer, along with archdeacons and the *reliqui canonici*. In fact, this latter document is a forgery, as was proved by Diana Greenway in 1985. She demonstrated that it began to be compiled c. 1146–60, with additions at the end by the celebrated Richard Poore during his deanship, from 1197 to 1215 (he was later bishop, 1217–28, during the move from Old to New Sarum, and a crucial figure in our story; see p. 366).[11] In fact, we have no more information about Osmund's liturgical arrangements than the small amount that can be inferred from his *Carta*.[12]

We can be only a little less speculative as we move on to consider development of that rite as the establishment became larger, in terms both of space (the marked expansion of the cathedral in the years around 1130) and of personnel (an increase in the number of prebends), not to mention additional endowments.[13] The significance of Osmund's

---

[11] The document is best available, with apparatus, in Greenway's "The false *Institutio* of St Osmund," in *Tradition and Change*, Festschrift for Marjorie Chibnall, ed. Greenway, C. Holdsworth, and J. Sayers (Cambridge 1985), pp. 77–101 at 97–100, the article in which she disproves its authenticity.

[12] The most important MS source for this is the *Registrum Sancti Osmundi*, a composite codex whose contents, put together over a period of decades in the thirteenth and fourteenth centuries, all seemed in the nineteenth century to possess a venerable, and therefore authentic, character; now Trowbridge, Wilts Rec. Off., D/1/1. This is reflected in the title, *Vetus Registrum Sarisberiense*, given to this codex in the Rolls Series edition by W. H. Rich Jones in two volumes, 1883–84, of necessity cited here although highly imperfect.

[13] In addition to the individual sources, to be cited and discussed presently, the two most useful and accurate summaries of relevant information are the introductions by Diana Greenway to *Fasti 1066–1300, IV: Salisbury* (London 1991) and by B. R. Kemp to English Episcopal Acta 18 and 19: *Salisbury 1078–1217* and *1217–1228* (Oxford 1999 and 2000), esp. vol. I, pp. xxxiv–lxi; and Webber, *Scribes and Scholars* is fundamental. Also important is Greenway's "The false *Institutio*," amplified somewhat in a further article, "1091, St Osmund and the Constitution of the Cathedral," in *Medieval Art and Architecture at Salisbury Cathedral*, ed. L. Keen and T. Cocke, BAA Conf. Trans. 17, 1991 (1996), pp. 1–9.

mighty successor Roger, the celebrated power-broker and (reputed) first Justiciar, who ruled the see from 1107 until his death in 1139 (shortly after his falling out with King Stephen and removal from power), is for our purposes mainly architectural. Under Roger the cathedral was substantially expanded, especially in its eastern parts, to such effect that, in R. A. Stalley's assessment, "it is clear that Bishop Roger's choir was a key design in the evolution of a scheme typical of major English churches."[14] The choir was more than doubled in length, an ambulatory path was created around it, and provision was (possibly) made for additional chapels. Impressive processions became feasible. But again, as with Osmund's episcopate, there is little or no evidence as to the actual liturgy used at the cathedral.

There is, however, reason to suspect that during the episcopate of Roger's successor, Jocelin (1142–84), some liturgical revision took place, but when during that long period is not clear; the evidence comes only late in his reign. One of Jocelin's *acta* issued between 1180 and 1184 assigns to a canon named Philip *de sancto Edwardo*, and thereafter to the cathedral, a virgate of land, the proceeds of which were formerly used for the correction of books – the kinds of books are not specified – on condition that the revenues should still be devoted to the same purpose.[15] Is this an indication of a push towards revision and renewal of some liturgical books in the late twelfth century? This speculation is given some plausibility by the account of service books found at the prebendal church of Sonning in Berkshire in 1220; among them was "Unum Missale novum absque epistolis, sine musica et sine gradali, et aliud vetus missale in quo leguntur epistolae, plenum, sine musica" – both in need of binding (*liganda*); with a marginal note "de dono Jordani decani" against the first words.[16] The Jordan referred to was dean c. 1176–c. 1193, and this leads us to ask whether the new missal given by him was a genuinely revised massbook rather than merely a replacement for an older one (which the parish seems still to have had in 1220).[17] To consider that possibility we may need to look over our shoulders, so to speak, at certain elements in extant thirteenth-century sources: a look which, to make sense, will have to be prefaced by a brief

---

[14] "A Twelfth-Century Patron of Architecture: a Study of the Buildings Erected by Roger, Bishop of Salisbury 1102–1139," *Jnl. Brit. Archaeol. Assn.* 3rd ser. 34 (1971), pp. 62–83 at 74.

[15] Printed most recently in Kemp, ed., *Salisbury 1078–1217*, no. 130.

[16] *Vet. Reg. Sarisb.* I.276. This visitation of his prebends by Dean William de Wanda (*recte* Waude) will be discussed in detail in the next chapter.

[17] And is this what is meant by the enigmatic statement in A. A. King, *Liturgies of the Past* (London 1959), p. 300, "Mr Hohler thinks it possible that Salisbury had abandoned its older books in favour of a rehash of Westminster in 1180 or thereabouts"?

explanation (pending further discussion on pp. 412 and 416) of the bearing of three modern editions of Sarum service books on the matter at hand.

The modern editions of the Sarum missal and gradual

The first more or less scholarly edition of an English medieval liturgical text was F. H. Dickinson's *Missale ad usum insignis et praeclarae ecclesiae Sarum*, which appeared in fascicules from the Pitsligo Press at Burntisland, the first in 1861, the last only in 1885.[18] Dickinson's edition was, however, of the printed Sarum missals (forty-seven printings between 1487 and 1534, six more during the Marian reaction), and much of its editorial matter is concerned with variations in structure among these early printings; its helpfulness towards understanding the beginnings of a "Sarum Use" is therefore limited. In the early 1880s Henry Bradshaw broached to J. W. Legg the desirability of an edition based on manuscript books: so states Legg's preface to his 1916 work, *The Sarum Missal, edited from Three Early Manuscripts*. The chief of these manuscripts was the codex now in Manchester (John Rylands Univ. Lib., Lat. 24) but in the years 1899–1901, when Legg was primarily involved with it, still in the possession of the Earl of Crawford, hence its nickname of Crawford Missal (and Legg's *siglum* C, used throughout in the present work). Whatever its precise date – third quarter of the thirteenth century will suffice here (it is discussed at length on p. 394) – it was judged to be somewhat earlier than the other two he used, one at the Arsenal Library in Paris (hence A; MS 135) and one in the University Library at Bologna (his B; MS 2565); A was probably written shortly before, and B shortly after, 1300.[19]

Though earlier by roughly two centuries than the printed editions used by Dickinson, all of these cardinal manuscript witnesses to the Sarum liturgy are markedly later than the putative beginning of the Sarum rite, and even by a generation or two than the move of the canons of Salisbury to the new cathedral in 1225. An additional witness, possibly slightly closer to at least the latter date, is the gradual, now BL Add. 12194, edited by W. H. Frere in fascicules between 1891 and 1894. The title given his work, *Graduale Sarisburiense: a Reproduction in Facsimile of a Manscript of the Thirteenth Century*, lacks the definite article

---

[18] The work had been begun in 1855 (Preface, p. i). His edition is discussed further on p. 416.

[19] Legg also had some access to what is known at the Tiptoft (but to him as the Morris, from its former owner William Morris) missal, now New York, Pierpont Morgan Library M.107, somewhat later than the other three.

of Legg's title (*The Sarum Missal*), and it has not come to be regarded as a more or less definitive text in the way that, helpfully or not, Legg's has.[20] Palaeographically indeterminate beyond rough limits of the middle two quarters of the thirteenth century, the gradual's rubrics may of course antedate the hand(s) in which they are copied; and it may turn out to be that they are the earliest rubrics that we have of the sort that can reasonably be called Sarum.

Frere thought that this manuscript (which we shall call G) was earlier, datable to "after 1203 because it has Machutus and before 1220 because it lacks the Translation of Becket."[21] The former point must be a slip of the pen: Machutus is present at November 15th, but this has nothing to do with 1203, which is rather the year of the canonization of Wulfstan of Worcester: whose absence may or may not be significant. The absence of Becket's Translation may be more decisive (though we must always keep in mind the risk of making definitive judgments on the basis of one or two omissions) as at least suggesting a date for a model of which G might be an early copy.[22]

The situation with the liturgy of the daily office is even less clear (and the salient details must be derived from manuscripts even later than those relating to the mass), and will be taken up when the final form of Sarum Use is discussed. The object of the present review is just to make plain three points, all fairly simple but all frequently overlooked. (1) Dickinson's edition is of Sarum missals in their printed, and therefore latest, stage; so it cannot be taken to represent "Sarum" usage *simpliciter*.[23] (2) Legg's edition, which was published thirty years later than the final fascicule of Dickinson's, is made from three manuscripts which, though (as his title states) "early," do not stand at anything like the beginning of the Sarum tradition. Each of them (C as well as A and B) has behind it other books and influences, themselves traceable only dimly. (3) In the same way, Frere's manuscript gradual

---

[20] Also, the thrust of Frere's extensive preface is avowedly as much musicological as liturgical, as is reasonable given its appearance under the aegis of the Plainsong and Mediaeval Music Society.

[21] Page xxxv. It is hard to imagine what Frere meant here. King, *Liturgies of the Past*, p. 308, points out that the 1203 date must refer to the canonization of Wulfstan of Worcester but then states that the latter feast was adopted at Salisbury "c. 1220": a statement buttressed by neither reference nor, as far as is known, evidence. In fact the MS lacks Wulfstan altogether, though it does contain Machutus (Malo; facsimile, p. 200); so 1203 is unusable as anything like a *terminus a quo*.

[22] It is tempting to try to date G itself before 1220, as Frere wanted to do; but consultation with helpful experts including Diana Greenway, Peter Kidd, and Pamela Robinson, all of whom looked at the hand with me, discourages me from doing so.

[23] It is nonetheless so used in the magnificent textual collations supplied by Legg in vol. III of his edition of the *Westminster Missal*, 1897: which, as is often pointed out in the present work, has led to some serious misunderstandings.

(G) is informative in proportion as one tries to keep in mind both the missal to which it must refer and the model(s) from which it was made. Once more we are faced with the necessity of trying to extrapolate from the knowable to the un-, or at least not yet, known. The most accessible way of doing this may be through some excavations in the sanctorale.

Inferences from the sanctorale: Leonard, Katherine, Wulfram, Aldhelm

In terms of saints' cultus, the period between Osmund's death in 1099 and that of his successor Roger forty years later yields only a scant harvest in the way of "telltale" saints whose inclusion or exclusion can be a marker, albeit not always a conclusive one, towards dating liturgical evidence. Some light may be furnished by looking at forms in the witnesses just reviewed for two figures who become prominent in the first half of the twelfth century. The first is Leonard, whose day is November 6th. In G, which has only the briefest of tags for his feast, that for the collect (the only prayer for which a tag is given, since the celebrant's other prayers are not the business of those using a gradual) begins *Preces nostras*. This agrees with the collect in C and A; but B (the latest of these four witnesses) has a different one, *Maiestati tuae*, and indeed an entirely different set of prayers, although its lesson- and chant-tags are the same as in C and A as well as G. Because the prayer-sets in those three witnesses (C, A, and almost certainly G) are not found elsewhere than in Sarum usage, whereas B's is widespread – used in a variety of monastic settings and at both Hereford and York – it seems reasonable to conclude that C-G-A represent here an "original" Sarum composition.[24] And because Leonard's liturgical popularity in England appears to be sudden and intense after 1106, when Bohemond, the glamorous prince of Antioch, celebrated his release from Muslim captivity by visiting the saint's shrine at Noblac, near Limoges, it seems highly likely that these prayers were put together during Roger's episcopate, 1102–39.[25]

---

[24] The *Maiestati tuae* set (*WM*, III.1606) was also used at Bec in the 13th cent. (*Bec Missal*, p. 211) and by the nuns of Barking (their *Ordinal*, II.331), and is *alia missa* (to a prayer-set drawn from the common) at Fécamp (*Ordinal of ... Fécamp*, ed. D. Chadd, 2 vols, HBS 111–12 (1999–2002), II.614). The C-G-A set reappears at Exeter (*Ordinale Exon.*, I.362), where it might have come from C (see p. 395).

[25] William of Malmesbury, *Gesta Regum Anglorum*, ed. R. A. B. Mynors, R. M. Thomson, and M. Winterbottom, 2 vols, OMT (Oxford 1998–99), sect. 387 (I.692) tells the story of the saint's deliverance. It is not reflected in the wording of the Sarum prayers, which read quite conventionally, although they do not seem to be simply adaptations of familiar Gregorian-Gelasian prayer-sets.

The same thing can probably be said about the prayers for Katherine, another saint newly popular in the twelfth century (25 November), though she had had some earlier recognition. The Sarum prayer-set (here B is no different from the other Sarum witnesses) is apparently used nowhere else in England in the twelfth and thirteenth centuries, when her cult was flourishing.[26] This set may well, then, have been composed by a Sarum cleric, a possibility that points a key question for this chapter: whether from instances of textual independence some sense of self-consciousness can fairly be inferred. Put another way, can we fairly suspect a nascent feeling about a (lower-case) "use of Sarum" decades before the move to the new cathedral?

The case of Wulfrannus, a seventh-century archbishop of Sens, missionary to the Frisians, and latterly monk of St-Wandrille (Fontenelle), is rather more complicated, but may point in the same direction as the previous two. His main feast commemorates his death-day, March 20th 703(?), but in England the 20th is primarily St Cuthbert's day, so a secondary, probably Translation, feast on October 15th is the one in Sarum books. We know that Wulfram (the usual anglicization of his name) was celebrated in England also at Crowland, the first Norman abbot of which, Ingulf (1086–1109), had been a monk of St-Wandrille. The concrete evidence is late, for the only Crowland calendar for which October survives is in a fifteenth-century almanac (Lambeth Palace MS 873), but this contains both his March feast (after Cuthbert's) and the one in October, there marked as *Ordinatio*.[27] Proximity to Crowland must then explain the almost unique dedication of the great parish church at Grantham to Wulfram – a church that was given to Osmund (it is a royal manor in the Domesday Book), and by him to the canons of Sarum in his foundation charter of 1091.[28] It seems likely that awareness of Wulfram at Sarum dates from this gift.

---

[26] In the 14th cent. the Sarum prayers are prescribed in Grandisson's ordinal (*Ordin. Exon.* I.363); at the beginning of the 15th the Barking nuns used the Sarum collect at vespers but one from St Albans (the center of Katherine's cult) at lauds (*Barking Ordinal*, I.344)! On the cult of Katherine in early 12th-cent. England, see Pfaff in *Eadwine Psalter*, pp. 75–76.

[27] The March feast is also in the late 12th-cent. calendar of BL Arundel 230 (Wormald, *Eng. Ben. Kals* II.114); the last four months are missing, but it is probable that the October feast was included also. The Crowland calendar of a psalter of c. 1050 (Bodl. Douce 296), however, knows no such saint; his importation is clearly owing to the connection with St-Wandrille.

[28] It is the last of the numerous churches listed, and the only one not in the western half of England: C. Wordsworth and D. Macleane, eds, *Statutes and Customs of ... Salisbury* (London 1915), p. 20. The document speaks in the plural, "ecclesias de Granham," and there came to be two Sarum prebends in the area, Grantham Australis and Grantham Borealis, probably both by the mid-12th cent.: *Salisbury 1066–1300*, pp. 68–72.

Another, and more direct, connection with St-Wandrille is that the church of Upavon in Wiltshire was held by the abbots of that Norman house, apparently from some time in the twelfth century. This arrangement was strengthened when in the early thirteenth century (in the episcopate of Herbert Poore, who died in 1207) Upavon was constituted as a prebend, held by the same abbots.[29] Wulfrannus appears in the calendars of all three early Sarum missals and the gradual (C, A, B, G), but has proper prayers in the sanctorale only of C; he is "de communi" in the others.[30] Although C's prayers are blandly generic, the movement from common to proper prayers is usually forward in time, and it seems fair to take the agreement of A and G (presence in the calendar but forms from the common of saints) as marking the incorporation of Wulfram's feast at an early stage (the twelfth century?), with the proper prayers in C possibly marking the newly established prebendal status of the abbot. Furthermore, C's calendar contains a revealing detail: after the words "Sancti Wilfranni [*sic*] episcopi et confessoris" (in black) is written, in red, "Sarum ix lec[tiones]," and then, again in black, "iii lec. et t [= Te Deum at the office]." Now, it will be argued in chapter 12 that C is as much an Exeter cathedral as a Sarum book, and certainly the wording just recorded demands attention.[31] It must represent a recognition that the nine-lesson status is a peculiar usage of Sarum quite apart from the fact that the whole missal is presumably, as is stated at the end of the *ordo* of the mass (fol. 155v), "secundum usum Sarum." Corroboration comes from the Legenda drawn up by bishop John Grandisson for Exeter in 1337, where the heading for Wulfrannus's feast reads "quidam faciunt ix lecciones. Set Exonie facimus tres lecciones tantum," and goes on to explain that the three fairly long proper lessons that follow can be divided into six (that is, if nine lessons are being observed; the last three would come from a homily on the day's gospel).[32] It

---

[29] Greenway (ibid., p. xxxii) suggests that this prebend and two others held by Norman abbots were created after the loss of Normandy in 1204. A small dependent cell of St-Wandrille had been established there, probably in the 12th cent. (*Med. Rel. Houses*, p. 93). The Norman abbey held at least five other churches in the diocese of Salisbury.

[30] All three of C's prayers read as though they might have been adapted from the common, but in fact that is true only of the collect.

[31] The only other place where this happens is at Dec. 8th, the Conception, marked "ix lec. Sarum nichil": see p. 405.

[32] Legenda Exon. (= *Ordinale Exon.*, III), pp. 381–82. There is, however, no sign of these in even the very expansive form of the Sarum breviary, the 1531 printed edition published by Procter and Wordsworth in 1879–86; the nine lessons and everything else come from the common of a confessor-bishop (*Sarum Breviary*, III.917). By the late 15th cent. York breviaries contained three fairly short lessons for the feast (*York Breviary*, II.624) and the missals gave incipits for a mass, all drawn from the common.

seems probable that the nine-lesson status is another indication, like the proper prayers in C, of an upgrading of Wulfram's feast, plausibly to be connected with the formal establishment of the prebend. And we may suppose the less dignified, three-lesson status to represent twelfth-century Sarum usage.

A similar pattern may be traceable in the case of Aldhelm. At first glance it would seem to be a foregone conclusion that at Sarum Aldhelm would have a liturgical commemoration with distinctive propers: he was, after all, supposed to have been first bishop (c. 705) of Sherborne, the original site of the West Saxon see. But the matter is not as clear-cut as might be expected. In the earliest Sherborne calendar we have, that in the mid-eleventh-century Red Book of Darley (above, p. 94), Aldhelm appears on his day (May 25th) only second, after Pope Urban, and is in no way distinguished, as are a number of Anglo-Saxon persons in that document.[33] The only pre-twelfth-century book which has a mass for Aldhelm is the Giso sacramentary (which could well postdate the Conquest; see p. 124); here again, in the calendar Aldhelm follows Urban and is not distinguished.[34] Only in the litany of saints in the Salisbury psalter (Salisbury Cathedral MS 150), perhaps originating at Shaftesbury, is Aldhelm truly prominent, being there second (to the usual Silvester) among forty confessors.[35]

As with Wulfram, in A and G the collect is *de communi* (and A has neither secret nor postcommunion). In C alone do proper mass prayers for Aldhelm appear: strikingly, the same set as in the Giso book. There are at least two other sets. One seems to be limited to use at Westminster Abbey, where the feast of Aldhelm's Translation (in 986, by Dunstan) was also kept, at May 5th.[36] The other is of greater interest in the present context. Its collect ("Deus qui inter apostolicos ecclesie doctores sanctum Aldelmum pontificem ... inherere studeamus") is shared by the Sherborne missal of c. 1400 (see p. 236), by Hereford missals, and, most strikingly, by the Kenilworth (Augustinian) missal of the third quarter of the thirteenth century (see p. 294). But each of the three has an independent secret and postcommunion. Sherborne's also occur in the composite missal, BL Add. 11414 (a similar case is cited on p. 502), although the Sarum secret and postcommunion are written in the margin. Sherborne's postcommunion is found as well, with two

---

[33] Wormald, *Eng. Kals*, p. 188.

[34] Ibid., p. 104

[35] Lapidge, *Litanies*, p. 284.

[36] *WM*, II.806. Westminster's collect for May 25th occurs also at Hyde (*Hyde Brev.*, IV, fol. 257), but the feast was not kept at St Albans, and its spread, even among Benedictine houses, seems to have been strictly limited.

slight variants, in B – in the calendar of which, however, Aldhelm finds no place. Once more, this admittedly somewhat wearisome pursuit of textual technicalities yields some indication about Sarum usages in the twelfth century: in this case, that there is a simpler observance (forms for the common, as in A and G) which then gives way to C's proper prayers – here the same as, if not necessarily borrowed from, those in the Giso book.

This rouses curiosity. After the evidence provided by the Giso book (third quarter of eleventh century), there are no discernible proper prayers for roughly two centuries.[37] How, then, might this apparent revival of interest in Aldhelm from the mid-thirteenth century on be explained?[38] Above all, what is suggested by the multiplicity of mass prayers which emerge for this saint? The implication of the fact that C uses the same prayers as Giso is countered by the fact that the Kenilworth book, contemporary with C, has a different set (the collect of which is in use at Sherborne over a century later). The first point would seem to suggest continuity of usage somewhere between Giso's time and that of C, but the second point the opposite, that in the mid-thirteenth century there is felt to be a need for proper mass prayers for the saint. That A and G use only prayers from the common for him seems to make the second possibility the likelier. Further than that we cannot seem to go; there is nothing like the establishment of a prebend (as in the case of Wulfram) to suggest an explanation.

A highly tentative conclusion

Negative evidence points in the same direction as consideration of those four sanctorale occasions: that, taken in combination, the witness

---

[37] It is surprising that in the mid-12th-cent. Sherborne cartulary, BL Add. 46487, Aldhelm is not included among the select occasions for which collects and gospels are given (see p. 176). Nor does there seem to be any information available about the liturgical forms used in the twelfth century at Malmesbury, the center of Aldhelm's cult, despite the fact that William, that abbey's pre-eminent historian, devotes all of book V of his Gesta Pontificum to the saint.

[38] In the section of "Statutes of Worcester III," c. 1240, which its modern editors have termed "Liturgical observances in the diocese of Worc, ?1220–66," the feast of Aldhelm is one of fifteen in the sanctorale for which a ruler of the choir is specified, but is not included in the immediately preceding list of "festa duplicia in ecclesia Salusb," nor in the "festa ferianda" of the diocese of Worcester that immediately follows, containing over forty saints' feasts: C & S 1205–1313, I.323. These are the two dioceses where Aldhelm's cult would be likely to have been the most prominent: Sarum contained both Sherborne and Malmesbury, the latter of which was only a few miles from the diocese of Worcester; and Egwin, third bishop of Worcester, had buried Aldhelm at Malmesbury in 709. At Worcester cathedral Aldhelm had only a commemoration, after Urban: Worcester Antiphonal, p. 33.

of A and G (albeit both clearly of the thirteenth century) often hints at Sarum usages of the twelfth century. Neither contains anything necessarily later than 1173, the year of Becket's canonization: Wulfstan (1203), Becket's Translation and Hugh (both 1220), and Edmund Rich (1247) are all lacking. This fact, which seems to have been overlooked by Frere and those after him who have discussed these sources, makes it plausible that the books from which A and G were copied had been written before 1220 or even possibly before 1203, and therefore that the rubrics in those two witnesses might as logically refer to services at Old as at New Sarum. So it is possible that the *consuetudo Sarum ecclesie* mentioned in a rubric in G and A about the transference of saints' feasts likely to fall during Holy Week could predate the work of Richard Poore, the supposed confector of the Sarum rite, in the early thirteenth century.[39]

Hence this tentative, simple, and indeed obvious conclusion: that there existed a self-conscious Sarum liturgical tradition well before either the new cathedral at Salisbury was begun in 1220 or the "Old" Sarum ordinal was drawn up. When and how that ordinal comes into being is a matter central to the next chapter. There seems to be no intrinsic reason why it is at Sarum, rather than Lincoln or London, that the most highly organized set of liturgical usages developed. (This happens also, to a degree, at York and Hereford, and we shall be tracing those stories presently.) But by the time of the close imitation, indeed almost adoption, of Sarum patterns at Exeter in 1337 (see chapter 12) something approaching a liturgical codification has occurred, one for which the term "Sarum Use" had for some time been widespread. We must next consider by what stages this comes to be the case.

---

[39]   The phrase is also found in C, but B, which here again stands slightly apart from the other witnesses, omits the words entirely in its rendition of the rubric (*SML*, p. 260; *Sarum Gradual*, p. 184). Its placement before the feast of Cuthbert (20 March) in A may reflect an earlier arrangement of rubrics, before Ambrose (4 Apr.) in G and C a later stage.

11 New Sarum and the spread of Sarum Use

The ideal equipment for consideration of the fully developed Sarum mass-rite would be three pairs of manuscript books, a missal and an ordinal: a pair each to represent the circumstances there at roughly the ends of the twelfth, thirteenth, and fourteenth centuries; and then a printed missal of the end of the fifteenth. As should be clear from the previous chapter, the first putative pair simply does not exist. There is neither anything that can be fairly called a Sarum missal surviving from the twelfth century – that is, a massbook of the kind that would have been in use at Old Sarum – nor a separate ordinal from that period. Lacking these, we have had to perform a good deal of rather wearisome extrapolation to get at elements of some sanctorale texts which look to be discernible as "Sarum" peculiarities, though not identified as such. Two hundred or so years later, by the end of the fourteenth century, a high degree of both elaboration and standardization seems to have been reached, and the very full rubrics which reflect what we shall study as the New Ordinal are widely copied into missals. When books with unambiguous titles like *Missale ad usum insignis et praeclarae ecclesiae Sarum* begin to be printed at the end of the fifteenth (the two earliest are 1487 and 1492), the relevant material from ordinals has been thoroughly incorporated into the text of the missal.

The present chapter aims to sketch the outlines of a picture that might be representative of the situation in, say, about 1290. At this point the new cathedral at Salisbury had been completed (except for the spire) for over a generation, and the idea of there being a practice or feast *secundum usum Sarum* was becoming widespread, extending to areas considerably distant from Wiltshire. By that time also a number of major additions to secular English calendars are all in place: the Translations of Edmund Rich (1250), Edward the Confessor (1269, his second translation), Richard of Chichester (1276), and Hugh of Lincoln (1280), as well as the feasts of Francis (canonized 1228) and

Dominic (1234).[1] Not all of these appear in Sarum documents by any means, but they sometimes offer useful dating points.[2] The most useful dating point comes early in the fourteenth century: the year 1319, when the Salisbury Feast of Relics was moved to the Sunday after July 7th, the Translation of Becket. That move is further discussed later (see p. 386); at the moment we need to start a hundred years earlier, when there coincide a crucial moment – the decision to abandon the cathedral at (Old) Sarum and to commence work on a new building at a fresh site – and a remarkable man, Richard Poore.

The work of Richard Poore

One of the most celebrated figures in our story is Richard Poore, widely supposed to have been the confector of the Sarum consuetudinary and possibly of the Sarum ordinal; indeed, the entry in the *Oxford Dictionary of the Christian Church* goes so far as to say that he "probably gave the 'Use of Sarum' its final form."[3] Most likely son of the curial bishop of Winchester Richard of Ilchester, and certainly brother of Herbert, bishop of Salisbury 1194–1217, Richard Poore became dean of (Old) Sarum in the autumn of 1197 and left that position to become bishop of Chichester at the end of 1214. After two years in that diocese he returned to succeed his brother as bishop of Salisbury in May of 1217 and remained there until his translation to Durham in the summer of 1228; he died in 1237.

In terms of the buildings at and for which he exercised his Salisbury offices, the basic chronology seems to be as follows.[4] In the first two or three years of his deanship a decision was apparently made to move the cathedral from the existing hill-top location to the plains (actually, water-meadows) below. But the troubles of John's reign seem to have prevented anything concrete being done about this, and it was only in February of 1217 that the dean and chapter sent to the pope a formal request for permission to make the move. After the papal bull of

---

[1] Corpus Christi, not of course a fixed date, seems to be observed somewhat fitfully until about the second quarter of the fourteenth century; thereafter its presence is nearly invariable.

[2] There comes to be also, though not widely observed, the feast (2 Oct.) of Thomas of Hereford, canonized in 1320. In the 15th cent. a number of figures from the past come into widespread observance, notably David, Chad, John of Beverley, Winifred, and Frideswide, all treated in chapter 13; also, to varying degrees, the important *Nova Festa* of the Visitation, Transfiguration, and Name of Jesus: see Pfaff, *New Liturg. Feasts.*

[3] *ODCC³*, p. 1308.

[4] The most succinct account, largely followed here, is that by Kathleen Edwards in VCH *Wiltshire*, III (1956), pp. 156–210 at 164–66.

authorization was received in 1219, the churchyard was consecrated, a wooden chapel put up, and, on April 28th, 1220, the foundation stones laid. Some formal worship in the new building seems to have begun, or at least been possible, from 1225, when three altars at the east end were consecrated.

If then a Sarum consuetudinary was in fact compiled by Richard Poore "circa 1210" (the date suggested by W. H. Frere in the lengthy introduction to his edition of it, and subsequently widely accepted),[5] the work had to have been done at an extremely difficult time – England was under interdict from 1208 to 1213 – and with reference both to an existing building which he presumably expected would be abandoned and to a building which he hoped would be constructed but for which formal permission had not yet been even requested, let alone granted. Following his two-and-a-half-year stint at Chichester, Richard's return to Salisbury happened a few months after the request had been sent (he cannot have been unaware of it). As a former dean as well as bishop he is likely to have been heavily involved in supervising the new work, along with his successors as dean: Adam (formerly archdeacon of Dorset) 1215–20, and, for the quarter-century 1220–45, William de Waude, who had been precentor from late 1218. (William may turn out to be as notable a figure in our story as Richard.)

Two questions need to be raised at this point: what is this consuetudinary and what is the evidence that Poore is its compiler? Both are addressed in what is probably the most authoritative statement to date on the matter, that of Diana Greenway published in 1991; it is so succinct as to justify being quoted from extensively:

It was almost certainly Richard Poore as dean who completed the composition of the *Institutio* [on this, see p. 355], adding clauses relating to residence, attendance at divine service, and discipline. In 1214, soon after the lifting of the Interdict, Poore and the chapter confirmed a collection of statutes ... known as the *Nova Constitutio*. Around this time, Poore was also engaged in his great summary of Salisbury procedural custom, the *Consuetudinarium*. This compilation, which was both a commentary on and an expansion of the duties of the cathedral staff ... was complementary to the *Ordinale* (the "Old Ordinal"), probably also the work of Poore, which summarized custom in the conduct of the services ... . The *Ordinale* was anterior to the *Consuetudinarium*, in which it is twice mentioned. Together, *Consuetudinarium* and *Ordinale* made up a general guide to the "Use of Sarum."[6]

---

[5] *Use of Sarum*, I.xx; it is astonishing that Frere in offering this date makes no mention either of the interdict nor of the hoped-for move.

[6] *Salisbury 1066–1300*, pp. xxvi–xxvii.

The three stages described in the above statement require separate analysis. The *Nova Constitutio* begins with a dating clause for 7 January 1213/14 and has added to it a set of provisions about vicars dated 15 September 1214 (the latest mention of Richard as dean); its contents are only marginally relevant to our concerns, but there is no reason to doubt Poore's involvement.[7]

With the *Consuetudinarium*, however, his role is by no means as clear. Frere's critical edition (volume I of his *Use of Sarum*, 1898) was made from four manuscripts: (1) the *Vetus Registrum*, which is a composite codex mostly of the thirteenth century (and which he called S; fols 1–20, comprising three quires); (2) two quires of a composite volume known to musicologists as the Dublin troper (CUL Add. 270, fols 3–29; his D), c. 1300, the rest being a basically Sarum troper adapted for use in Dublin; (3) another composite volume, Bodl. Bodley 443, in which fols 138–54 are a partial text, beginning with chapter xii, of the consuetudinary, early fourteenth century (Frere's B); and (4) Frere's base text (his, and henceforth our, H), BL Harley 1001, fols 117–55, also of the early fourteenth century and possessed by the parish church at Risby in Suffolk (as it is apparently also the earliest surviving witness to the Sarum ordinal, it will be treated at length later). There is no (legible) heading to the work in any of these manuscripts save H, which calls it "Liber et ordo de personis et de dignitatibus consuetudinibus et officiis singularum personarum in ecclesia Sarum"; nor does any of these manuscripts contain a dating clause such as that in the *Constitutio*, or any ascription of authorship.

As we have it, the original text of the consuetudinary – leaving aside later additions – looks to have been compiled after 1173 and before 1220: in the lists of double feasts Becket's Deposition must be the fourth of the *quatuor sequentes* after Christmas (otherwise there would be just three; cap. xxi) and is mentioned by name in cap. liv (lvi in S), but his Translation is given as *ex novo* in a group of three feasts that includes Edmund Rich, canonized 1247, in MS H. One possibly significant detail is that in the lengthy list of feasts of three lessons but with invitatory sung by two cantors (cap. xcii) the feast of Vitus and Modestus on June 15th has Crescentia also, coming first in S and third in H. This contrasts with the mass texts we have been consulting (see p. 357), where Crescentia is generally absent: from the gradual (G); from both calendar and sanctorale in the Crawford missal (C); in the calendar

---

[7] Best consulted in the mixed-bag edition *Statutes and Customs of the Cathedral Church of the Blessed Virgin Mary of Salisbury*, by C. Wordsworth and D. Macleane (the latter in a minor capacity only, see p. viii; London 1915), pp. 40–53. The text is printed from the *Vet. Reg.* (see p. 355 above), with reference also to a collection of statutes begun around 1325: Wordsworth's MS E, now Trowbridge, Wilts Record Office D1/1/3.

of the Bologna missal (B), though her name is added in the prayers; and from the sanctorale of the Arsenal missal (A), though present in its calendar.[8] The inconsistency here suggests that the consuetudinary texts of manuscripts H and S reflect a missal older than any we have, and that the extant ones (C, A, B) represent a pruning from an older usage which included all three saints. (The Passion in the early twelfth-century Salisbury passional is of all three saints.)[9] If this older missal tradition antedates Poore's deanship, his responsibility for the consuetudinary can be called into question.

Even if Poore's "authorship" of the consuetudinary is less than perfectly clear, however, the other cardinal document dating from the first twenty-five years or so of the thirteenth century – besides, that is, the consuetudinary, which, as has been seen, cannot be dated exactly – is unquestionably his: the synodal statutes of 1217 to 1219, with additions made during the rest of his episcopate, until his move to Durham in 1228.[10] These statutes, reflecting heavily the Fourth Lateran Council of 1215, are concerned to only a slight extent with matters liturgical; those directly relevant are (by the commonly cited numbering) clauses 57–60 and 65. Clause 57 is the most informative. Although there are some textual differences among the manuscript witnesses, the full form seems to have read, "Item precipimus quod omnes sacerdotes habeant canonem misse secundum consuetudinem Saresbiriensis ecclesie correctum, et ut verba canonis in missa rotunde et distincte dicantur."[11] Clause 65 requires that all parish churches within the diocese should have suitable equipment for the celebration of mass, but of books there are mentioned only those for the office ("libros ad psallendum et legendum"), not missals. Missals are, however, specified in clause 67, which in an effort to ban the alienation of church ornaments provides that priests should write "in missalibus et in aliis libris" a sort of inventory of the books, vestments, and other possessions of the parish.

The visitations of parish churches in 1220

To what extent can these early thirteenth-century *missales* be thought of as *Sarum* missals? This period of Richard Poore's episcopate is also

---

[8] In the Westminster missal the calendar and sanctorale-heading both have Vitus and Modestus only, with Crescentia's name appearing in the mass collect (II.830); but this mass set is totally different from Sarum's, which according to Legg's collations is otherwise used only by Hereford: where, however, her name appears in all three locations (and in each of the mass prayers).

[9] Now Salisbury Cath. 222, formerly Bodl. Fell 1: Webber, *Scribes and Scholars*, p. 156.

[10] *C & S 1205–1313*, I.57–96.

[11] Ibid., p. 79. The heading is something like *De canone*, with some of the MSS or correctors adding phrases like *secundum usum Sarum* and/or *et horis dicendis*.

that of the notable visitation in 1220 of dean William de Waude (in some older transcriptions, "de Wanda") to his prebendal churches at Sonning in Berkshire, assigned to the deanery by 1176 × 1193, and Mere in Wiltshire, probably so assigned by 1139; the former had six chapels belonging to it, the latter three.[12] At Sonning William found some thirteen liturgical books proper, plus two small books, one containing a life of its patron saint Andrew and the other a life of Cyriac, to whom an altar in the church was dedicated. This list will be often referred to elsewhere; for the moment we notice the provision of books relating to the mass:

Unum missale novum absque epistolis, sine musica et sine gradale, et aliud vetus missale in quo leguntur epistole, plenum; – liganda. ... Gradale vetus cum tropario, et ligandum, et aliud novum de dono euisdem Vitalis [the parochial vicar], similiter cum tropario. ... Unus Textus coopertus argento continens Evangelia anni [a gospel lectionary rather than a book of the four gospels]. Unus Troparius per se, in asseribus. Unum Ordinale. Quidam novus liber continens missas privatas.

The inventories of Sonning's chapels are equally informative. Ruscomb, despite being in dilapidated condition, possessed some ten service books, including "Missale vetus, nullius pretii. ... Unum gradale parvum, vetus et nullius pretii, et aliud novum in quaternis, in duobus voluminibus, ligandum, cum tropario imperfecto. Item troparius parvulus, vetus, de dono Thomae, capellani." The chapel at Wokingham also had ten books, one of which was a "missale vetus" and another an "aliud missale vetus, littera Anglica" (what can this mean?), both presumably replaced by the "unum missale cum notula sufficienti" that heads the list. Neither gradual was adequate, one "minus sufficiens" and one "vetus et ligandum." The "antiphonarium cum collectario" was deemed "sufficiens," yet there was also a quaternion "continens lectiones et responsoria de festivitate Omnium Sanctorum" – All Saints being the chapel's dedication. As the list of ornaments that follows the booklist makes plain, this was a well furnished chapel, possessing among other things a processional cross of Limoges work.[13] A similar preponderance of "old" service books seems to have existed at the other chapelries. Hurst (now St Nicholas Hurst) had eight books, three of

[12] *Salisbury 1066–1300*, pp. 7–8; visitations printed in *Vetus Registrum Sarisberiense*, ed. W. H. Rich Jones, Rolls Series, 2 vols (1883–84), I.275–314, 275–86 for Sonning and its chapels.

[13] The building appears to have been similarly impressive. Despite extensive Victorian "restoration," there seems to have been a 13th-cent. arcade of five bays: PBE, *Berkshire* (1966), p. 307. The other churches which were chapels of Sonning have all largely been replaced by later buildings.

them classified as *vetus*: a gradual, a psalter, and a manual. Edburgefeld (now Arborfield), described as *tota ruinosa*, had five "old" books, including a missal, among its eight. Sandhurst, characterized by contrast as "nova et pulchra," had only a "missale vetus sine notula" to use for the celebration of mass, though there was a *sufficiens* gradual.

Another inventory, that of Mere, in the southwestern corner of Wiltshire, yields the valuable fact that its new missal, "novum et sufficiens, cum nota sufficienti," is described in a marginal note as "de dono Adae decani" – that is, given by Richard Poore's successor as dean, 1215 to 1220. That Mere also had in 1220 "unum [missale] vetus cum nota sufficiens" [*sic*, if *sufficiens* is correct and applies to *missale* as a whole and not an error for *sufficienti*, modifying *nota* as with the previous book] suggests that an adequate book was replaced not because it was worn out but because it was during the period of Adam's deanship felt to be outmoded.[14]

The large church at Heytesbury in central Wiltshire had become collegiate, supporting four canonries, around 1165. Although it came to be a decanal prebend only in the period 1271–84, it was also visited in 1220 by Dean William, who found there two missals (not otherwise characterized) and an ordinal, as well as other books, notably "duo breviaria nova" and "duo breviaria vetera."[15] We might from this hazard a guess that in that year Heytesbury church possessed a complete set of up-to-date service books; is it reasonable to extrapolate from this and suppose that what they represent is the "new" use of Sarum? Corroboration of this supposition comes from Dean William's visitation of the chapel at Knook, to which its vicar, also named William, had given what seems to be an entire set of books: gradual with troper, collectar, capitularium, antiphonal with troper, a "breviarium et antiphonarium" apparently still under construction, and finally ".i. canon misse novus."[16]

It is possible, indeed likely, that these two Williams are the same person – that is, that William (de Waude) as dean had visited "his" prebend at Heytesbury, to which, as a collegiate church, that chapel at Knook belonged: of which, in turn, the same William was vicar. The gift of books is otherwise improbably munificent for the vicar of a wooden

[14] *Vet. Reg. Sarisb.*, I.290. Adam also gave vestments to the church and bequeathed some to Sonning.

[15] Ibid., p. 294. The church is described in PBE *Wiltshire*, 2nd edn (1975), p. 266.

[16] Ibid., pp. 295–96. The editor of the Rolls Series printing, W. H. Rich Jones, gives the date of the Knook (*Cnuch*) visitation as "Anno domini mccxxvi," but this seems unlikely because the account comes immediately after the 1220 data for Heytesbury on fol. 41v of the Registrum; the next document (fol. 42), the inventory of Godalming in Surrey (granted to the cathedral along with Heytesbury in the early 12th cent.), is again dated 1220.

chapel to have presented,[17] and the donor is styled *dominus*. (This seems significant in light of the fact that at the inquiry which William, as dean, held in 1222 into the literacy of the clergy attached to Sonning and its dependencies, none of the five chaplains – all of whom turned out to be almost comically ignorant – is so styled.)[18] This hypothesis is congruous with what we glean otherwise about this energetic church-man, deeply involved in liturgical matters as precentor at the cathedral from late 1218 and as dean from September 1220. As the visitations under review – not only of Sonning and Mere and Heytesbury, but also Swallowcliffe and Hill Deverel – took place in the remaining months of that year and into the following March, they would appear to have been assigned a high priority in the agenda of the new dean. We may wonder whether this is because William was, in the course of inspecting the decanal prebends, either attempting to tighten the standard of litur-gical worship among their churches and chapels (i.e., in the spirit of the reforms mandated by Lateran IV) or trying to enforce what would now be called liturgical revision.

That the answer is, almost certainly, both is clear just from the churches appurtenant to Heytesbury. At Horningsham, so badly off that the chaplain who held it at farm conducted services only three times a year (although a list of ornaments found in 1224 suggests that there had once been a considerable liturgical regime), for the celebration of mass there was only one book, apparently pieced together from diverse elements and described as "Missale vetus inordinate compositum continens psalterium et ympnarium," along with an old and unbound gradual; there a general tightening up was clearly called for.[19] On the other hand, Dean William found that already in 1220 Hill Deverel, a further pos-session of Heytesbury, had a "liber ordinalis in novem quaternis"; this stands in contrast to the lack of an *ordinarium* as well as of a *consuetudi-narium* which he noted among the deficiencies at Swallowcliffe.[20]

If, then, at Hill Deverel, one of the obscure chapels of southwest Wilt-shire, there was something called a *liber ordinalis* in nine quires (which suggests a recently written book; this indication is supplied for several books mentioned in the visitation record, and is clearly distinguished

---

[17] *Capella lignea*, the chancel roofed with lead and the rest of the church with shingles, the southern part well covered, the northern in need of repair. Founded in honor of Mary Magdalen, though the present parish church is a small Norman building dedi-cated to St Margaret (PBE *Wiltshire*, p. 282): are these two the same?

[18] *Reg.*, pp. 304–7.

[19] Ibid., p. 313. The overall condition was dreadful; the porch could not be shut, the building open to beasts (*bestiis pervium*) and even pigs (*porcis eversum*).

[20] Ibid., pp. 311, 312.

from *ligandum*, in need of binding), while at another, Swallowcliffe, the lack of such a book as well as of a *consuetudinarium* is deemed a defect, what are we to suppose these books to have been? In 1220 the Sarum *consuetudinarium* is pretty clearly still the document drawn up with reference to the old cathedral, and it is next to impossible to imagine what relevance its detailed prescriptions about the rights, duties, and ceremonial locations of the various dignitaries could have had to worship in what was in effect the small parish church at Swallowcliffe (not the present one, built in 1842). The *ordinale* which it also lacked but which Hill Deverel possessed may, however, have been a different matter – depending on what we can suppose *it* to have been.

The "Old Ordinal" in Frere's *Use of Sarum*

The difficulty of ascertaining the sort of thing meant by *liber ordinalis* in the early 1220s is intensified by the fact that the modern edition of the Sarum ordinal, that of W. H. Frere in 1901, is almost impenetrably difficult to use.[21] The difficulties are twofold. The first is of nomenclature: under the overall title *The Use of Sarum*, Frere called the first volume *The Sarum customs as set forth in the consuetudinary and customary* (1898; discussed above) and the second *The ordinal and tonal* (1901).[22] The distinction between "consuetudinary," discussed earlier in this chapter, and "customary" turns out to be one not of definition, that they are different kinds of documents, but of chronological succession. We noted above (p. 368) that the only heading for his "consuetudinary" among the four manuscripts he used, that in the Risby ordinal, is "Liber et ordo de personis et de dignitatibus consuetudinibus et officiis singularum personarum in ecclesia Sarum." For his "customary" Frere also used four manuscripts – from the heading in one of which, "Incipit custumarium secundum usum Sarum," he apparently adopted the name "customary" – giving two of them the same alphabetical sigla as he had used for (entirely different) consuetudinary manuscripts.[23] The second

---

[21] In vol. II of *The Use of Sarum*; it should nonetheless be emphasized that Frere was a fine scholar to whom the present work is greatly indebted (see p. 10 for further comment on him).

[22] The tonal printed at the end of vol. II, separately paginated in Roman numerals and containing mostly chant incipits on four-line staves, is explained in just a couple of pages in the general introduction. As "its main object is to regulate the antiphonal psalmody and to secure the right connexions between the antiphons and the tones which are allied with them" (p. xxxii), it falls into the vast area of the musicological from which we have had to prescind.

[23] The heading is in his MS "S" for the customary, Salisbury Cathedral 175 (whereas "S" for the consuetudinary is the *Vet. Reg. Sarum*, noted above).

difficulty is that of layout. Frere decided to print the "consuetudinary" and "customary" in parallel columns, even though in numerous places the contents of one are lacking in the other, so that there are many pages of single-column printing. He then gave a double numbering, Roman and Arabic, to the chapters of the consuetudinary, reflecting differences in organization of two of the manuscripts, and Arabic numbers only to the chapters of the customary.[24]

With his printing of the ordinal in the second volume the complication is confounded. In the introduction Frere distinguished a "New Ordinal" from the "Old" by discussing first the New, then announcing that he was for the most part not printing that, "for on investigation it proves to be practically identical with the rubric of the Service-books as printed in the XVIth Century."[25] (This New Ordinal appeared, according to him, only in the late fourteenth century, and is not relevant to the present chapter.) What is printed on pages 1–207 of his second volume as "Ordinale Sarum" is, with very considerable elisions, the Risby ordinal (BL Harley 1001) text – without folio references. In that manuscript folios 1–83 contain the office ordinal, 84–116 that for the mass, and 117–55 the consuetudinary (as discussed above). So in printing the first two sections of this manuscript in his volume II and the third in volume I Frere has split his main witness: one which, though apparently the earliest surviving of its kind, was in any case written in the early fourteenth century, several decades into the story we are trying to trace here, and belonged to a parish church in Suffolk, a long way from Salisbury.[26]

Frere thought that the Old Ordinal, as transmitted in the (later) Risby manuscript, "must be dated *circa* 1270: it contains (p. 117) the Translation of S. Richard (1262 [*sic*]), not Corpus Christi, which was

---

[24] This results in such complexity as that for the chapter covering Easter Monday (I.159), where the numbering of the left-hand column is "lxxviii. (58C, 83 & 58D)" and that on the right hand "28"!

[25] The section of the New that is printed is that leading up to and including the First Sunday in Advent, II.208–33. There is no distinction in the running head for this section, so the reader has to have picked up the explanation on p. x. The MSS of the "New Ordinal" are in fact those used for the "Customary" in vol. I: Oxford, Corpus Christi College 44, Salisbury Cath. 175, BL Harley 2911, and BL Arundel 130, all late 14th to 15th cents.

[26] Risby lies between Bury St Edmunds and Mildenhall. A long-shot link might possibly be Constantine of Mildenhall, bishop's official in the diocese of Salisbury from 1263 to at least 1267 and canon of the cathedral, but as well archdeacon of Sudbury (the archdeaconry in which Risby lay) from 1267, probably also a canon of Wells and perhaps of Exeter: *Salisbury 1066–1300*, p. 119. Another possibility is Constantine's successor as archdeacon in the 1280s, Ralph of York ("II"), canon of Salisbury 1267 and chancellor 1288 until his death in 1309: ibid., pp. 78, 19; he seems to have given at least seven manuscripts to the cathedral.

instituted in 1264 but was adopted somewhat slowly in England."[27] This dating must be roughly correct, even though Richard's Translation was in 1276, not 1262 (which is the year he was canonized), because the *Addiciones* to the ordinal that start on fol. 156, after the consuetudinary ends, begin with a paragraph dated 1278 and ascribed to the succentor. In 1278 this was John (de) Middleton, who held the office from at least 1268 to 1290.[28] These are meant to address the "multi defectus reperiuntur in ordinali Sarum usus": defects of, so to speak, both omission and commission. There are several dozen of these, and it is clear that the process "per strictam examinationem" of which the head-note speaks was detailed and stringent.

One of the omissions rectified in these *Addiciones* stands out because it in fact makes no change at all, and may therefore be signficant. This concerns the feast of Wulfstan, January 19th, for which the "additional" prescription is for a feast of nine lessons, all from the common of a confessor-bishop, save for a proper collect, "Spiritus nobis domine" – which is exactly the same thing as the ordinal proper provides.[29] This suggests that what was being corrected in the 1278 scrutiny was not necessarily the text(s) as in the Risby ordinal, and that the text there may sometimes reflect a later stage of practice than is corrected in the *Addiciones* which are a kind of appendix to it. The case of Wulfstan, canonized only in 1203, may be instructive because his feast is unlikely to have been in the ordinal used at Old Sarum; indeed, it is not found in the manuscript gradual G or its often-agreeing missal A, nor in the Crawford book, completed at the latest by c. 1275, but is in the Bologna missal (B), which was written around 1300 and reflects the wording of the ordinal (and of the *Addicio*).

A curious rubric, present in both the Risby text and (with slight verbal variations) the Crawford missal may shed a further bit of light. It is placed after the mass for Felix, bishop and martyr – that is, as the sanctorale resumes after the Christmastide break between 22 December and 12 January – and before that of Maur (15 January). The subject is the treatment of relatively minor feasts, which normally give way to the commemoration of the Virgin if they fall on a Saturday and to the mass of the Sunday if they fall then. But, the rubric specifies, four feasts of three lessons are to be treated as exceptions: those of John and Paul (26 June), Hippolytus (13 August), Brice (13 November) and,

---

[27] *Use of Sarum*, II.xii.
[28] *US*, II.41. The precentor in 1278 was John (de) Burton, also warden of De Vaux college (p. 15); one wonders why he did not undertake the work ascribed to the succentor.
[29] *US*, II.197, 107.

out of liturgical order, the Eleven Thousand Virgins (21 October; no mention of Ursula). These receive their own mass if falling on a Saturday, and the first three (inexplicably, the Virgins are omitted here) if on a Sunday, unless a new *historia* is to be begun at matins, in which case celebrations of these three shall be put off until the next day.[30] It turns out that in a Lincoln cathedral document datable to 1283/4 the first three of those feasts (not the Virgins) are singled out for special treatment in respect of candles above the altar when their masses are celebrated (see p. 500). It does not seem possible to determine whether the Lincoln provision (which is stated in terms of expenditures that fall to the Treasurer, with no suggestion that this is an innovation) or that incorporated into the Crawford missal is the older; but it is certainly conceivable that we have here an early incorporation, by another important cathedral chapter, of a practice contained in the Sarum Old Ordinal, as confirmed by its appearance in the Crawford book of the 1260s.

It seems probable, then, that the ordinal text represented in the Risby book is *not* that of Poore's Ordinal, which we have seen is likely to have dated from the last years of the regime at Old Sarum, but instead represents practices codified for the new cathedral in the second, or even third, quarter of the thirteenth century. By that time there are several pieces of evidence showing that the (or should we more accurately say, "a"?) Sarum use was being followed in a number of places. Such places are implied by the statement in the office ordinal's section on the Feast of Relics – the original Sarum placement of which at September 15th was becoming increasingly problematic in the later thirteenth century, as liturgical Marian devotion grew – that "Ubi festum reliquiarum hac die non celebratur," the whole service for the day should be that of the Octave of the Virgin's Nativity.[31] There would be no reason to celebrate the Sarum Feast of Relics outside the diocese of Salisbury, so this rubric must mark recognition that the ordinal may be used more widely – though language specific to the cathedral is certainly abundant, as in the provision that the mass of St Sabina (the older, but secondary, feast to the Decollation of John the Baptist on August 29th) should be said *in capitulo*.[32] How early this ordinal, and by extension something, anyhow, of the rite it prescribes, may have come into more general use is the next matter to be taken up.

---

[30]   *US*, II.178; *SML*, p. 238.

[31]   *US*, II.130; repeated in the mass ordinal, p. 187.

[32]   For possible meanings of this disputed phrase see p. 420; at the least, it presupposes a context where there is a chapter house and/or a chapter (of clergy).

The spread of "Sarum" in the mid-thirteenth century

As we have seen, compilation of the Sarum ordinal was supposed by Frere most probably to have been the work of Richard Poore, along with the Sarum consuetudinary, and therefore to date from the first quarter of the thirteenth century; but on the first page of the Introduction to the second volume of his edition of both as *The Use of Sarum* (1898–1901) he allowed that "it is possible in view of the history of Ordinals that it is somewhat earlier in origin." This may indeed be the case, but the line of evidence Frere advanced for this possibility is somewhat shaky. Buttressing his claim that the evolution of the Ordinal was completed by the beginning of the thirteenth century is the notion that the first surviving mention of it is in the Statutes of Bishop Hugh de Nonant of Lichfield (1188–98).[33] But the three leaves in the Lincoln Chapter Muniments which provide the earliest source for this attribution were written in the later fourteenth century and contain mentions of two bishops of the mid-thirteenth; so phrases there like "in ordinali vel in consuetudinario" cannot be regarded as evidence from the late twelfth century.[34]

The earliest clear reference to "Ordinale Sarum" as providing a standard for liturgical practice outside the diocese of Salisbury appears instead to be an order issued in 1223 by Gervase (Iorweth), bishop of St David's, to his cathedral chapter to the effect that "servitium de sancta Maria et servitium pro defunctis fiat secundum Ordinale Ecclesiae Sarum."[35] This probably refers to the ordinal we have been associating with Richard Poore's time as dean at (Old) Sarum, and it suggests some awareness of Sarum as a possible standard. A similar awareness is shown in the inclusion of a list (discussed earlier; see p. 209) of the double feasts in the church of Salisbury which forms part of a kind of brief liturgical memorandum at the end of one of the manuscripts of

---

[33] *US*, I.xxxiv.

[34] *Lincoln Cath. Stats*, II.11–25: this, published in 1897, is cited in Frere's introduction to *The Use of Sarum*, dated Aug. 1898, though he does not mention the date of the leaves in question.

[35] A. W. Haddan and W. Stubbs, *Councils and Documents ...* 3 vols (Oxford 1869–71), I.459, from BL Harley 1249, fol. 2; the editors note austerely that "It does not appear that any other than these two services were to follow the Sarum Use." There are also two references to Sarum customs or usages as being those to be followed in the cathedral at Glasgow as that comes to be established in the third quarter of the twelfth century, but these more likely refer to constitutional than to liturgical arrangements. The references are included in the *omnium gatherum* "Chronological Table shewing the rise and decline of Sarum, Lincoln, and other English Uses" put together by Christopher Wordsworth in his edition, with Henry Bradshaw, of *Lincoln Cath. Stats*, III.824–59, at 831; cf. confirmations of the "Sarum liberties" at Glasgow in 1258–59 on p. 835.

the statutes of Walter de Cantilupe for his diocese of Worcester issued at a synod in 1240 (BL Cott. Claud. A.viii, fols 218v–19; it has to have been written after 1247).[36] The list of Sarum feasts is presented with no explanation or commentary; there follows a section as to when the choir is "ruled" – a mark of an important feast – at Sarum. Both of these almost exactly repeat the wording of chapters xx and xxi, but in reverse order, of the (early fourteenth-century) Risby ordinal. The Worcester document therefore constitutes an important witness to the textual history of the Sarum ordinal. There is, however, no indication that the Sarum lists are meant to be prescriptive; they are followed by a similar list of the *festa ferianda* (i.e., on which no, or little, work is to be done) in the diocese of Worcester, which includes distinctive feasts of Wulfstan and (bishop) Oswald and also the Translation of Becket. A section (89) of Cantilupe's statutes had mandated as of nine lessons (though not *ferianda*) the feasts of Nicholas, Edmund Confessor, Dominic, and Francis. Neither of the latter two becomes a Sarum observance (despite Francis's appearance in the Crawford missal; p. 394). An *ordinale* is among the eight kinds of liturgical books mandated for each church in the diocese at the beginning (section 2) of these statutes, but there is no indication that it is to be that of Sarum.

A generation later, in 1270, the vicar of All Saints church, Bristol, left to it a whole group of service books, including a missal *de usu Sarum* and some sort of ordinal bound up with a gradual, processional, and troper.[37] In 1275 an odd sort of quasi-Augustinian house is founded at Barton on the Isle of Wight for some six clergy whose services are to follow *usum Sarum*, the *ordinale* and *consuetudinarium* being specifically mentioned.[38] As these references indicate, by the third quarter of the thirteenth century there is a clearly understood entity known as *usus Sarum*. Back, then, to the central question: what can we suppose would have been understood by those words?

"Sarum" ordinal and "Sarum" ordinary for the mass

An ordinal is, defined in the simplest possible way, a set of summary indications as to what is said (usually through incipit tags), and to some

---

[36] *C & S 1205–1313*, II.321–24, with C. R. Cheney's discussion of the MS tradition on pp. 294–95.

[37] Wordsworth, "Chronological Table" (note 35), p. 836, citing a charter reproduced in Palaeographical Society, *Fascimiles of MSS*, Second Series, 2 vols (1884–94), pl. 137; I have not seen this myself.

[38] Ibid.; cf. *Reg. Joh. de Pontissara, Ep. Wintoniensis*, ed C. Deedes, 2 vols, CYS 19, 30 (1915–24), I.335–43 at 338–41; there is slight confusion about the original wording as opposed to a later transcription, this register having been published after Wordsworth's "Chronological Table."

extent done, at every occasion throughout the liturgical year, with a certain amount of information as to who is supposed to do it. (Much of the latter information, based on the structure of the cathedral establishment at Sarum as developed by the third quarter of the twelfth century, is contained also in the consuetudinary.) Most of the attention paid to Sarum ordinals in the past has dwelt on whether they testify to the "Old" or "New" Ordinal: about which much remains to be said, but only after the cart has been put behind the horse.[39]

The matter is made more difficult by the fact, already stressed, that no manuscript witness to what can fairly be characterized as a Sarum ordinal dates from earlier than the fourteenth century. This being the case, it may be prudent to turn our attention away from the ordinal for the moment and to ponder the distinction between "old" and "new" missals that appears with some frequency in the visitation records. We recall that there is found at Sonning a new missal, without epistles, music or "gradual" – this seems to mean without notation for the ordinary, especially the proper prefaces, as well as without the chant texts – given by Dean Jordan (in office c. 1176–93), whereas its old missal contained the epistles, which are therefore read from that while the new book is otherwise used. This causes wonder as to what the hurry may have been: why, that is, the dean of (Old) Sarum would have given to one of his chief prebendal churches a book less *plenum* than the one it presumably replaced. The only glaring new saint's feast that would have to have been supplied is Becket's on 29 December (from 1173), which always appears in the temporale and complicates the Christmas octave somewhat; otherwise, a sanctorale of even the early twelfth century would have been adequate. The likeliest supposition would seem to be a considerable development of rubrics: that is, of what cumulatively would go into an ordinal. Such an ordinal could well, with the necessary modifications for buildings less complex than a cathedral, be usable in parish circumstances also.

Instruction as to how the (more or less) unchanging words and gestures of the ordinary of the mass – the similarity between the English words "ordinal" and "ordinary" as employed here is regrettable but unavoidable – are to be used is not included in the ordinal; but putting

---

[39] The intrinsic difficulties of the subject are compounded by the fact that what in English is generally known as the *Pica* or *Pie* has as its full title *Ordinale Sarum sive Directorium Sacerdotum*, as put together by Clement Maydeston and printed by Caxton in 1487: this was edited under that title by C. Wordsworth, HBS 20, 22 (both 1901), and is discussed on p. 427 below. At the beginning of his preface Wordsworth points out that Henry Bradshaw (d. 1886) had wanted to see published an "Ordinale Series," to consist of "the various developments of the Sarum *Ordinale*, from the *Tractatus* of Richard Poore, and the *Ordinale* mentioned therein, if it can now be found, and Maydeston ..." (p. vii). It is that "if it can now be found" that we are still pursuing.

the two together is instructive. A dozen years before his edition of "the" Sarum missal appeared, J. W. Legg published the ordinary "from the oldest Sarum missal known to exist," the Crawford missal (for the circumstances in which he had come to study it, see above, p. 357).[40] As is clear from the ample notes he supplied, his interest there was primarily in comparing this early form with later developments; indeed, the first item in the same volume was his presentation of what he termed "Fourteenth Century Sarum Ordinary, from the Morris Missal" a book of about 1320.[41] So he paid little attention to any light that the (Risby) ordinal published by Frere in 1901 and the Crawford missal's ordinary might shed on each other. We, however, must again immerse ourselves in the depths of textual criticism, here not of prayers but of rubrics and incipit-tags.

For the most part the rubrics of the Crawford ordinary are the same as those in the Risby ordinal, but from such slight differences as there are it is plain that the missal with which the Risby rubrics correspond is of a strain somewhat independent of the three edited or collated by Legg. One example is at the elaborate procession of Rogation Monday. All witnesses specify that it is to be headed by the great banners at the cathedral called *Draco* and *Leo* as well as others, and that there is a certain latitude for choice as to the antiphons and psalms during the procession, depending on local circumstances. In R(isby) these options are limited to "ad pluviam postulandam," "pro serenitate aeris," and "contra mortalitatem," and in this it agrees with the BL Add. 12194 gradual (in our sigla, G: see p. 357) and Arsenal missal (A), whereas the Crawford (C) and Bologna (B) missals continue with forms "contra hostium impugnacionem" and "pro quacumque tribulatione"; but after the offertory at the mass of the day a rubric mentions an optional "sermo ad populum si placuerit" in G, C and R(isby) but not in A or B.

If, then, there is no one set of rubrics common to Legg's three missals and the Risby ordinal, is it possible to regard as what we may call the *Ur*-rubrics any which are identical in G (in which many pages are missing), C, A, and B, and to suspect that they testify to the "original" Sarum ordinal we are pursuing? (This method is not unlike the traditional one used in the study of the Synoptic Gospels, with its century-old search for the *Q(uelle)* supposedly available to Matthew and Luke.)

---

[40] In his volume of *Tracts on the Mass*, HBS 27 (1904), pp. 219–29, with notes on 255–69. Because his 1916 edition of the Crawford book included by collation the Arsenal and Bologna missals, one can see there the slight variants in the ordinary among those three books.

[41] Now New York, Pierpont Morgan Library, M.107 (better known now as the Tiptoft missal); *Tracts*, pp. 1–15 and 233–36, with introduction on xi–xv.

As it has survived, G begins in the middle of the rubric after the collect for the first Sunday of Advent; this first extant rubric deals with the number of collects to be said at mass, and is followed shortly by the rubric about when the Creed is to be said. The one about the collects contains two small variants found in A and B, not in C, while that about the Creed agrees most often with A, sometimes with B, least often with C, and occasionally with none of the three. R(isby) includes in the first rubric three sentences lacking in all the earlier witnesses, and its wording in the second rubric is not identical to any, though closest to C.

Most strikingly, G gives tags for the epistle and gospel for the Saturday after Advent I – an observance of which there is no sign in Legg's missals, all of which confine themselves to indicating pericopes for the Wednesday and Friday only. (The Ember Saturday following Advent III has an elaborate mass, but that is not in question here.) This is in fact a very rare feature, and therefore it is astonishing that R gives pericope tags for the same occasion, followed by a paragraph stating that, because the normal observance for such Saturdays is the mass and office of the Virgin, these lessons may be used on a convenient weekday.[42] (In this pair of tags the epistle that R gives, "Ecce servus meus," is the same as that in G; but R's gospel tag is "Iesus dicebat ad turbas," whereas G's looks to be "Dicebat Iohannes"; the page is muddy here, and in any case the *Iohs* could easily be an error for *Ihs*.) This seems to imply two possibly useful considerations. First, that G's inclusion of these tags may point to a model both quite old and rather out of the way; indeed, there seems nothing to compare it with save the mention in R.[43] Secondly, that the model from which R was directly copied, though as we have seen written no earlier than 1276, also has itself much earlier roots – roots that almost certainly predate the redactions of "Sarum" rubrics seen in C, A, and B.

A further Sarum saint: Cuthburga

In contrast to the putative *Ur*-rubrics we were hoping to uncover a few paragraphs ago is the emergence of a figure who becomes a characteristic Sarum saint, like Wulfram and Aldhelm (discussed on pp. 359–63), but a good deal later – still, of course, with nothing like

---

[42] *Use of Sarum*, II.151; this should be compared with the lengthy paragraphs about the office on that day, II.22–24.

[43] There is a double methodological difficulty here: that G, as a gradual, is not primarily concerned with pericope tags, which are merely tucked in between the noted chants; and that massbooks earlier than G are as likely as not to be sacramentaries, and therefore lacking pericopes entirely.

official canonization. Cuthburga, who is supposed, on the combined authority of the Anglo-Saxon Chronicle and William of Malmesbury, to have been the sister of Ine of Wessex, wife (until they separated) of Aldfrith of Northumbria, and foundress of the double religious house at Wimborne in Dorset, may have died around 725; little further detail is available because, perhaps surprisingly, she is not mentioned by Bede.[44] The house virtually disappeared by the end of the tenth century and was re-founded, most likely in the mid-eleventh, as a small secular college of the sort now called a royal free chapel, eventually possessing a dean, four prebendaries, a sacrist, and some other personnel.[45]

Cuthburga's rather shadowy existence is reflected in the paucity of Anglo-Saxon liturgical interest in her. The only day ever mentioned in conjunction with her is August 31st, which is also that of Aidan of Lindisfarne (whose relics were from the tenth century thought to be at Glastonbury) and of Paulinus of Trier, supporter of Athanasius (not Paulinus of York and Rochester, 10 October); in fact, the day is often vacant in English calendars.[46] There seems, in short, very little evidence for an early cultus. The sole textual piece is a collect in the Wulfstan portiforium (above, p. 129), placed between those for Felix and Adauctus (30 August) and Priscus of Capua (1 September).[47] The name in the heading is spelled with an initial "g," and the prayer begins "Deus qui eximiae castitatis privilegio famulam tuam Guthburgam."

In the Sarum books there is no trace of her feast in either G or A (which often stand in close rubrical relationship), nor originally in C. Only B (the Bologna Sarum missal; the sigla continue as before) contains a mass for her, with tags for the chants and lessons and *oracio de communi* (rather than the one in the Wulfstan book), a phrase meant to cover the other two prayers as well. The chants and lessons indicated are also taken from the common of a virgin-not-martyr. She appears in B's calendar as well, and also in that of A, where she is otherwise ignored, but not in C's. In C, however, there is a note at the foot of the

---

[44] *Anglo-Saxon Chronicle*, ad 718; William of Malmesbury, *Gesta Regum Anglorum*, ed. R. A. B. Mynors, R. M. Thomson, and M. Winterbottom, OMT (Oxford 1998), book I.36.1, cf. Thomson's *Commentary* vol. (1999), p. 335.

[45] P. H. Coulstock, *The Collegiate Church of Wimborne Minster* (Woodbridge 1993), esp. pp. 98–113.

[46] She is present in only three of the pre-1100 calendars edited by F. Wormald: standing alone in BL Cott. Vit. E.xviii, probably from New Minster c. 1060 (but, as he noted, later expunctuated); with Paulinus in CUL Kk.v.32, undetermined West Country affinities; and with both Paulinus and Aidan in CCCC 422, the Sherborne calendar of c. 1061 in the Red Book of Darley; of his post-1100 Benedictine calendars only in a document from Abbotsbury (Dorset) of c. 1300.

[47] *Wulfstan Portiforium*, I.141 (no. 1911).

page in what Legg calls a later hand, "De sancta Cuthburga require in fine libri." Then, at the book's end (on fol. 255v), are written in a hand that supplied marginal notes elsewhere three mass prayers: the collect "Deus qui eximiae castitatis" (as in Wulfstan, but her name beginning with a "c") with a secret and postcommunion of a more general sort, though the latter does contain the saint's name.

The situation may be summarized in this way. Since she is ignored in the body of A, G, and C alike, the earliest notice of her seems to be her inclusion in B (which may be as late as c. 1300), where all her forms are *de communi*. The proper prayers written into the end of C are not simply adaptations of some found elsewhere in the volume, and the fact that the collect dates back to (at least) the late eleventh century shows that they are not original Sarum compositions. They are almost certainly present in C by 1337, because the proper collect is specified in Grandisson's ordinal, issued in that year, for Exeter (where C was by at least 1277; see p. 394); indeed, they could have been added there.[48] But it is the proper prayers, as in C, that appear in the printed missals, so the prayers are not peculiar to Exeter.[49]

All of this complexity compounds the oddity that Cuthburga becomes one of the most distinctive Sarum saints: distinctive in the sense that she appears in no books that are not clearly of Sarum affiliation – not in the secular liturgies ascribed to York and Hereford, nor in the usages of such monastic houses as Westminster, Worcester (despite the fact that she had found a place in Wulfstan's portiforium), or Barking. Noticing how such an intrinsically unimportant figure should have become so securely, if unobtrusively, incorporated into Sarum tradition is a helpful reminder that not everything that goes to make up that "use" is of explicable significance; sometimes it is the insignificant details that will carry the story. (And we still wonder where the prayer in the Wulfstan portiforium may have come from.)

The final point to be made about her is that, rather than having been intrinsic to the tradition, she *becomes* a Sarum saint, most likely at some time in the later thirteenth century, though by paths probably not now traceable. It is tempting to try to connect the appearance of Cuthburga, of importance earlier only at Wimborne, with the very considerable

---

[48] *Ordinale Exon.*, I.356.

[49] *SMD*, col. 890; in the printed breviaries her three lessons and all else come from the common, save for the proper collect: *Sarum Breviary*, III.759. In Grandisson's *Legenda Exon.*, p. 331 there are three proper lessons for her; they begin differently from the *Vita* published by the Bollandists (*BHL*, no. 2034), and close by dating her death at around the impossible year 670. Sherry Reames informs me that there are proper lessons for Cuthburga in the late 15th-cent. Sarum breviary, BL Royal 2 A.xii.

figure of Martin of Pattishall (Pateshull), pluralist and royal justice, who became dean of Wimborne in 1223 and canon of Salisbury two years later.[50] Should this be the case (whether or not the proper prayers would have come from Wimborne), she must be a saint of the new cathedral, so to speak: that is, her incorporation would have been an observance unknown at Old Sarum, the rites at which, at least in the later twelfth century, we have reason to suspect are reflected in the witnesses of manuscripts A and G.

Steps towards a hesitant reconstruction

A tentative reconstruction that takes into account the admittedly sketchy factors laid out in the previous pages might go something like this. (It should be remembered that it is still only the liturgy of the mass that is under discussion; other aspects of the story, including the office, will be considered in chapter 13.) The starting point would be an attempt to grasp the mass liturgy that was established as the chapter of clerics at Old Sarum settled into regular worship. This was, in its outlines, most probably little different from that of other multi-clergy churches in England at the end of the eleventh century. The variable texts would have been predominantly those of the fully developed Gregorian sacramentary (i.e., with the ninth-century Supplement completely integrated and with numerous Gelasian, especially Young Gelasian, texts incorporated). The ordinary would likewise have contained no striking divergences in wording from that used elsewhere throughout the kingdom – or, for that matter, in most of western Europe – and would have been supplied with a minimum of ceremonial rubrics, if any at all. Still less would there have been anything in the way of distinctive rubrics for various occasions throughout the liturgical year, save perhaps for Candlemas, Ash Wednesday, Palm Sunday, and the *Triduum sacrum*: occasions when the influence of a monastic *ordo* is likeliest to have been felt.

By the middle of the twelfth century this pattern seems to have undergone elaboration in two ways. One is through the growth and increasing formalization of the chapter at Old Sarum: the growth reflected in bishop Roger's new choir, the formalization in the self-consciousness about dignities and rank (and consequently about seating) apparent in

---

[50] *Salisbury 1066–1300*, p. 101. He was already a canon of Lincoln, and subsequently archdeacon of Norfolk and dean of St Paul's, all these dignities being held at his death in late 1229. Wimborne was technically exempt from the jurisdiction of the bishop of Salisbury, but that Richard Poore issued an episcopal act in favor of Pershore abbey from there in either 1219 or 1220 shows that it was a place not unfamiliar to him: *English Episcopal Acta 19: Salisbury 1217–1228*, ed. B. R. Kemp (Oxford 2000), no. 341.

the *Institutio* which, as we have seen, must be a product not of Osmund's episcopate but of sixty to a hundred years later. The other kind of elaboration, less clearly discernible, looks to have been a revision of the massbooks used at the cathedral: books marked by more extensive and elaborate rubrics, some of which contained explicit reference to the *mos* (custom) or *usus* of Sarum. Contemporary with these developments is the working out of the full prebendal system, and the consequent spread both of service books and of consciousness of "Sarum Use" outside Salisbury itself. The consuetudinary, in its earliest form, manifests this consciousness clearly.

While the arrangements for mass at the cathedral are likely always have been highly organized, the changes by which those arrangements in parish churches would have been made similarly tidy would have been much slower and much more ragged. This haphazardness is reflected in the reports of decanal visitations of the early thirteenth century, which make plain the rather slapdash nature of the service books in use then. (It should be kept in mind that none of these seems to have survived.)

By 1220, when Dean William de Waude accomplished the most extensive of these visitations, all discussion about "Sarum" service books must have taken place in the context of the construction of the new cathedral, started in April of that year. Worship began there on a limited basis, in the Trinity (alias Lady) Chapel and the adjacent areas, five years later, and as the building progressed towards its completion in 1258 it must have become clear that massbooks from the old cathedral needed to be revised and elaborated. This would have been the case not so much with new feasts to be included – aside from whatever provision had been made earlier for Trinity Sunday, the only truly pressing occasions would have been Becket's deposition feast on December 29th and, after 1220, his Translation feast on July 7th – as with the ceremonial rubrics; for the new building would have offered vastly more scope for the kinds of ceremonies and processions that now come to mind when the term "Sarum Use" is heard.

Response to the opportunities offered by the new building is of course to be connected with the work ascribed to Richard Poore, either as dean or as bishop. Its concrete expression is to be found in his synodal statutes and, somewhat less certainly, in the Sarum ordinal: "less certainly" because of the distance in time and space between Poore (translated to Durham in 1228) and the earliest surviving manuscript, the Risby ordinal from early fourteenth-century Suffolk. Its provisions can be checked against those of the gradual referred to above (G, just possibly written before 1220) and those of what is apparently the oldest extant complete Sarum missal, the Crawford – the testimony of which, however, should not be privileged because of either its sumptuosness or its having been chosen by Legg as the base manuscript of his 1916 edition – complemented by the Arsenal and Bologna books. Comparison of these witnesses enables us to go some way towards discerning what by the time the new building is finished (roughly contemporaneously with the writing of Crawford) is the full round of the year's liturgy. That "full round" is what can fairly be called the Use of Sarum.

Towards the wider spread of Sarum Use

Though we shall now divert our attention from the Sarum tradition narrowly conceived to what may be the most expansive picture of medieval liturgy available to us, that at Exeter, we must close the present chapter by noticing some work of Roger Martival, bishop of Salisbury 1315–30. It was during his reign that the decision (mentioned above) was taken to shift the Sarum Feast of Relics from September 15th to the Sunday after the Translation of Becket. The apparent mechanism by which the decision was made is itself instructive. On October 26th, 1319 Martival had read out in a Salisbury chapter meeting an extremely lengthy and thorough set of statutes for the cathedral – so the account states, though it is doubtful whether the entire thing could have been so read publicly.[51] Little is specifically liturgical (in contrast to the great attention paid to seemly behavior and dress in choir), but cap. xxxviii, headed "De reliquis et veneracionibus sanctorum," is devoted to three specific points concerning the sanctorale: the change in date of the Relics feast, the Deposition feast of Hugh of Lincoln (to be kept with nine lessons and a set of proper mass prayers), and the three hymns (with their tunes) to be used on the feast of Mary Magdalen. Why Hugh's feast, November 17th, is singled out for this kind of treatment is unclear, but may reflect the personal influence of bishop Roger, who had previously been dean of Lincoln (1309–15). Nor is it clear why there should be any dispute over the hymns for the Magdalen, whose feast was scarcely new by 1319.

With the Feast of Relics, however, we get some glimpse of the kinds of factors that resulted in liturgical changes – changes that became incorporated into the practices of Salisbury cathedral, and then became an accepted part of Sarum Use. The clause in the statutes says nothing about a clash with observance of the Octave of the Virgin's Nativity as a reason to move the Relics feast, alluding merely to a "concurrence of

---

[51] Printed, with facing translation in C. Wordsworth and D. Macleane, *Statutes and Customs of the Cath. Church … of Salisbury* (London 1915), pp. 134–275, at 246–49.

festivals" and stressing the undesirabilty of cessation from agricultural labor (*occupacio rerum rusticarum*) on a day in September. The following July 9th Martival sent a "Mandatum ad publicanum statutum pro festo reliquiarum," expanding somewhat on the new date for the feast though still not mentioning the desirability of freeing September 15th entirely for the Octave observance.[52] The mandate was addressed to the subdean, Robert (de) Worth, presumably because the dean from 1311 to 1346 was an absentee, Raymond de Fargis, cardinal deacon of Santa Maria Nova; Worth seems also to have been, at some points, the bishop's chancellor.[53] The document refers to the widespread approbation of the *usus ecclesie nostre* among the uses of other churches, commands that the decision be communicated to parishes throughout the diocese, and points out that the move to a Sunday would not mean an additional holiday for laborers. Although Feasts of Relics are kept at a variety of dates in churches of marked individuality (and in religious houses), we shall see that awareness of the 1319 decision often supplies a kind of litmus test as to the spread of the *usus* of which bishop Roger spoke so proudly.

The story of that spread is both enriched and complicated by the situation at Exeter, most vividly viewed during the episcopate of an even more notable fourteenth-century bishop than Martival, John de Grandisson. Once we have considered the evidence leading up to his reign and that reign (1327–69) itself, we will be in a position to return to the final development of the Sarum Use and to its eventual extension throughout most of southern England.

---

[52] *The Registers of Roger Martival*, ed. C. R. Elrington (et al.), 4 vols in 6, CYS 55, 57–59, 68 (1959–75), II.293–94. It may be material that Martival had from 1298 held the Sarum prebend of Netheravon, a benefice he kept even after becoming dean of Lincoln: see Elrington's notice in *ODNB* 37.29. In 1320 July 9th was a Saturday; so the next day would have been the first opportunity for application of the mandate.

[53] The president of the chapter, in the dean's absence, was formally the chancellor, but Worth, who looks to have been a man of parts, was apparently close to Martival, whose executor he was to become in 1329: *Biog. Reg. Oxf.*, III.2090.

12   Exeter: the fullness of secular liturgy

Although among secular establishments in medieval England it is always Salisbury, the home of the Sarum Use, that occupies center stage, Exeter cathedral is actually the building for which some sense of liturgical life over a period of centuries can be most fully constructed. This is owing primarily, but by no means exclusively, to the ambitious work of two great bishops of the see, Leofric, 1050–72, and John de Grandisson, 1327–69.[1] Leofric's achievement was surveyed at the end of chapter 4, which dealt with the period of the Norman Conquest. There is little, if any, discernible continuity between his liturgical program and that of Grandisson; no part of Leofric's building was extant in the fourteenth century, and whatever influences had been most substantial in the various books that are connected with him were long since submerged in the flood emanating from New Sarum. Nonetheless, a distinct "Exeter" liturgical identity is evident in the program envisaged by Grandisson, an identity of which we can glimpse hints in the episcopates of some of his predecessors.

For there seems to have been, to a perhaps unusual degree, a self-consciousness connected with holding the see of Exeter. This may be seen already in the set of prayers in Leofric missal "C" for a *Missa propria pro episcopo*, most likely composed (as noted earlier) by Leofric himself.[2]

---

[1] The cathedral, diocese, and bishops of Exeter have been well served in a series of publications over the last century and a half, beginning with several works by George Oliver, esp. his *Lives of the Bishops of Exeter and a History of the Cathedral* (Exeter 1861), continuing with F. C. Hingeston-Randolph's editions of the Exeter episcopal registers from 1258 to 1419, 9 vols (London and Exeter 1886–1909), and represented recently by N. Orme, *Exeter Cathedral as it was, 1050–1500* (Exeter 1986), a truly scholarly work of popularization, and by M. Swanton, ed. *Exeter Cathedral: a Celebration* (Exeter 1991), with several brief essays touching on the liturgy and many sumptuous color photographs of MSS. The first two volumes (1909) of J. N. Dalton's edition of the *Exeter Ordinal* (note 36 below) served as the occasion for a review-article by W. H. Frere, "The Use of Exeter," originally in the *Church Quarterly Review* 1911 and repr. in *Walter Howard Frere, a Collection of his Papers*, ed. J. H. Arnold and E. G. P. Wyatt, ACC 35 (1940), pp. 54–71.

[2] *Leofric Missal*, II.52.

The bishop of Exeter is mentioned in all three prayers, with language – like "me famulum tuum .ill. [the name to be supplied] non meis meritis, sed dono tuae gratiae, pontificali cathedra exoniensium sublimasti" – which makes explicit his hope that it will be used by his successors.

Leofric's successors and their legacies: the inventory of 1327

Whether or not this specific hope was fulfilled we do not know; a long interval separates Leofric's books from the highly self-conscious liturgical program of John de Grandisson. For a bit of knowledge about this interval we must have recourse initially to an inventory made in September 1327, just before Grandisson took up his episcopate, of the books, vestments, and other ornaments of the cathedral. The circumstances were not propitious: Grandisson was consecrated twelve months after the lynching in London of his predecesssor, Walter Stapeldon, formerly Treasurer of England as well as bishop of Exeter, in the ugliness that marked the fall of Edward II.[3] This inventory (together with other documents such as a list of Stapeldon's effects and another inventory taken in 1506) sheds useful light on the accretion of liturgical books at the cathedral since Leofric's time.[4]

The information about books in the 1327 document is organized in three ways, apparently with no duplication and with a monetary value assigned to each book.[5] First come patristic authors and two categories (history and law); then bequests from two bishops and two other named persons; finally four other types, *Missalia*, *Antiphonaria*, *Psalteria*, and *Libri divine pagine* (the last group containing also some bequests from specified donors).[6] While the service-book groups will naturally be of the greatest interest to us, a few items from the individual bequests require notice. Among a dozen or so books left by William Warelwast, bishop 1107–37, are listed a homiliary and passional, each in three volumes, a *Legenda sanctorum*, and a pair with intriguing titles, *Communis Liber Sanctorum de Usu Rotomagensi* [Rouen] and *Unus Liber Sanctorum de*

[3] James Berkeley was Stapledon's immediate successor, but was in office only three months before he died in June, 1327.

[4] All of these were printed by Oliver in his *Lives of the Bishops of Exeter*; the 1327 inventory from MS 3671 in the cathedral archives, though this is nowhere stated by Oliver. I am grateful to James Willoughby for clarification of this and related matters.

[5] Any statement about this or any other Exeter inventory is provisional until the CBMLC volume for secular cathedrals, to be edited by Willoughby, appears. The titles are quoted here as from Oliver, pp. 301–10, with his capitalization.

[6] Among the *Libri canonum et legum* is placed a *Martirologium Latinum et Anglicum*, valued at a paltry two shillings (Oliver, *Lives*, p. 304).

eodem Usu, the latter in two volumes. As Warelwast came from about 35 km northwest of Rouen, this statement has a certain credibility.[7] It is, however, hard to see what effect the fact, if true, had on liturgy at the cathedral.

The other bishop of Exeter who is recorded as having left books is the most notable of the twelfth century, Bartholomew, 1161–84. It looks as though he may have tried to counteract the effect of Warelwast's bequest, for the first item of the *Libri Bartholomei* is a *Legenda sanctorum in duobus voluminibus* valued at four pounds.[8] There are also a passional, something (a second passional?) described only as "Liber in octo peciis in uno quarterio [quaternio?], partim de communi et partim de proprio," three further volumes called *legenda* or *breviarium,* two collectars, and a benedictional.[9] In fact, there seems to have been a plethora of Legenda or similar books: after Bartholomew's books come a two-volume "Legenda bona de temporali" left by one "Bratton" (almost certainly the noted jurist Bracton), and two Legendas, one for the temporale (in two volumes) and one for the sanctorale, left by "Alured de Crede."[10]

The next section of the 1327 inventory consists of brief indications (prices only, no donors) for fifteen or so *missalia,* plus "Unum Manuale de usu ignoto" (and, for some reason, a *Summa pauperum*). The missals are particularized as to whether they are notated and if so with or without tropes, whether they contain epistles and gospels, and whether they are *de usu ignoto,* as is the case with one missal (probably what we would term a sacramentary) as well as the manual. Two are called *vetus,* one with notes and one without. Two stand out as valued at three pounds each, one very likely being the Crawford (Sarum) missal: "bonum notatum cum tropariis cum multis ymaginibus subtilibus de auro in canone" (see below). Something seems to have happened to a "missale novum sine Epistolis et Evangeliis de grossa litera," worth two

---

[7] F. Barlow, "William de Warelwast," *ODNB* 57.390.

[8] The only other book on the list valued that high is a two-volume *Moralia in Iob* of Gregory the Great, a work that frequently appears in luxury formats (Oliver, p. 302); these were exceeded only by a "Liber grammaticalis qui dicitur Catholicon" given by Stapeldon and a great portiforium, discussed below, each valued at five pounds.

[9] Three volumes of sermons are listed as well, one of which might be the collection of Bartholomew's own sermons in Bodl. Bodley 449; his preaching activities were notable: A. Morey, *Bartholomew of Exeter* (Cambridge 1937), p. 81.

[10] Henry de Bratton (or Bracton), a man of Devon, held two rectories there and was chancellor of the cathedral 1264–68: P. Brand, *ODNB* 7.395–98. Why this one gift of his should be grouped with Bartholomew's of eighty years earlier is a mystery, as is the identity of Alured de Crede, unless he is the Alured who is thought to have been the first archdeacon of Barnstaple, some time in Warelwast's reign (Oliver, p. 292). Both two-volume Legendas were valued at three pounds.

pounds, for in its place some unspecified person gave "unum Missale cum Epistolis et Evangeliis qua est in magno altari."

The sections on *antiphonaria* (here, chant books in general) and *psalteria* work the same way; each includes books of other types also. Of seven graduals, five contained tropers; there were also two free-standing tropers. Similarly, of four antiphonals two lacked collects, one had collects and a psalter, one contained a hymnal. Included in the *psalteria* section are another *antiphonarium vetus*, two portiforia, a manual, a martyrology with collectar. Six other collectars are listed, five valued only at four shillings each "quia non sunt in usu" and one *novum*, worth a mark (thirteen shillings and four pence). The eight psalters are listed with a variety of detail and prices; one, "de antiqua litera" (as it might be, the BL Harley 863 Leofric psalter; p. 134 above), at only four shillings. Taken together, it looks as though between six and eight of each of the main types of books needed for the daily office were available, but not all of the same age, or consistent with each other: which is only what one would expect with manuscript books in a large and old foundation.

In some ways the most interesting sidelights on the liturgical books at Exeter are those that can be gleaned from the miscellaneous section, *Libri divine pagine*. This ranges from books reckoned to be of little or no value – sixteen "libri Manuales Benedictionales et Capitulares, qui non appreciantur, que non sunt de usu," an "Ordinale de veteri usu" – to those thought to be up to date, some of which must have been quite recently acquired. This would certainly have been the case with the "Historia cum legenda de Corpore et Sanguine Christi" for the feast of Corpus Christi, gradually being adopted between about 1264 and 1320, and the "Legenda in uno quarterno de festo Sancti Gabrielis," which probably dates from the episcopate of Bronescombe, 1258–80 (for this feast, see below). Again, presumably the reason that an *Ordinale* is listed here as bound with a chain is that it represents current usage. The same is probably true of a costly *portiforium magnum* valued at five pounds and chained in the choir *ad deserviendum populo* ("for the use of ordinary people"?), along with a *psalterium bonum*.

Several of the books in a sub-section at the end of the list headed "libri provenientes tempore Thome Thesaurii per personas subscriptas" (Thomas was treasurer 1310–29) are clearly recent gifts, most of them by named donors. A *missale bonum* given by John Wele, precentor in 1317–18, is assigned to the altar of St John; Roger Gosee, who gave a manual, may be the Roger de Ot[t]ery who was chancellor 1309–14; Richard de Brayleigh, subdean 1318–35 gave a book containing the visitation of the sick and Office of the Dead and also a processional;

a *Portiphorium bonum* is the gift of Bartholomew, dean 1311–26; and the inventory ends with a *manuale bonum* given by Richard, now dean, the office he assumed in 1335 (so this copy of the 1327 inventory must date from at least that year). This list supplies a lively picture of the dignitaries of the cathedral competing – or perhaps responding to episcopal pressure – to furnish new books during the reign of Grandisson. We must postpone consideration of that reign, however, until we have looked at a handful of books and developments associated with two of his predecessors from the late thirteenth century, Walter Bronescombe, 1258–80, and Peter Quinil (Quinel, Quivel), 1280–91.

An Exeter/Sarum missal (Exeter Cathedral MS 3510)

A good starting place may be the ostensibly Sarum missal (Exeter Cath. MS 3510) very likely written at Exeter in the time of Bronescombe.[11] The nickname given to this book here, the Exeter/Sarum missal, underscores the fact that it may be the only thirteenth-century Sarum massbook besides the Crawford missal (to be considered next) that can with some confidence be attached to a specific place. The Sarum character of Exeter 3510 is stated both positively – *Festivitas reliquiarum Sarum* at September 15th in the calendar – and negatively, in the marking of at least two feasts, the Conception and Botulf, as *nichil apud Sarum*. In fact, its calendar contains more saints not in other thirteenth-century Sarum calendars than are so indicated; these include Petroc, Pi(e)ran, and Bernard (none of whom ever finds a place in Sarum tradition), and, notably, Richard, whose mass is integral to the sanctorale here. The collect for Richard, canonized in 1262, may offer a useful clue, for it is the one composed, or at least transmitted, by Ralph Bocking, between that year and his death in 1270, and not the one that is found in the later Sarum books (see p. 294). If the 1260s are, then, the earliest decade in which this missal could have been written, there are some indications that its model may have been a good deal older: small details like Dunstan's appearing in the calendar after rather than before Potentiana, the presence of prayers *Ad vesperas* and *Ad fontes* for the weekdays of Easter week,[12] and indeed the format itself, which

---

[11] The suggestion as to Bronescombe's episcopate was made by Ker in his description of the MS, *MMBL*, II.817, based on that bishop's known devotion to Gabriel, prominently evident in this book. A much reduced color reproduction of fol. 67 is in *Exeter Cath.: a Celebration*, p. 133.

[12] These are otherwise in Crawford only, not Arsenal or Bologna or any later Sarum missals.

is closer to that of a sacramentary – besides the mass prayers, tags are provided for the lessons but nothing for the chants – than of a full missal. At least nine sets of additional material, including forms for Corpus Christi and for Gabriel, have been supplied, mostly in the (early?) fourteenth century and often on blank spaces.[13] At the end is an early fourteenth-century list of ornaments in the chapel of St Gabriel, which had been under construction when Bronescombe died in 1280. It is reasonable to suppose that the book was used there in the last decade or so of the thirteenth century; the question is, to what degree it can be employed to look backwards to what may have been the case in earlier decades as well as prospectively towards the liturgical regime established by Grandisson.

In contrast to the well known Crawford book, the Exeter 3510 missal has been little noticed. Lacking as it does the texts of the lessons and signalling a couple of feasts in its calendar as non-Sarum, it is a good candidate to be the tenth of fourteen missals listed in the 1327 inventory as "decimum, absque Epistolis et Evangeliis, de usu ignoto, 10 s." Its greatest hagiographic peculiarity is a feast of *Quinquaginta Oratores*, after Saturninus (29 November) at the end of the sanctorale. This must in some way be connected with the entry in a twelfth-century Exeter martyrology at 17 December, "In oriente apud Eleutheropolim ciuitatem, sanctorum martirum quinquaginta qui sub Sarracenis passi sunt."[14] How these fifty got particularized as "orators" – (pray-ers rather than speak-ers, presumably) – seems an impenetrable puzzle, but the collect and secret both so characterize them (the postcommunion calls them merely martyrs). The space in the manuscript, fol. 144rv, is entirely taken up with these prayers, the following leaves being originally blank; but the sanctorale proper begins back on fol. 71, with Andrew, so this odd feast is not really in sequence, though in the original hand. That it was during the long episcopate of Bronescombe, 1258–80, that this rather obscure book was written is specially noteworthy if, as now appears to be the case, the Crawford missal was also at the cathedral in the same period – by, at the latest, 1277.

---

[13] According to Oliver, *Lives*, p. 224, Bronescombe mandated the Corpus Christi procession some time during the deanery of Roger de Thoriz, 1268–74, but I cannot find this in that bishop's registers, either ed. F. C. Hingeston-Randolph (London 1889) or ed. O. F. Robinson, 3 vols, Canterbury and York Soc. 82, 87, 94 (1995–2003).

[14] From the better, and older, text, Exeter Cath. 3518 (*Exeter Ordinal* [see note 36], IV.28), just as in that of the 14th-cent. CCCC 93, printed by Dalton, *Exeter Ordinal*, II.456. The ultimate source is the martyrology of Florus of Lyon, ed. J. Dubois and G. Rénaud, *Edition pratique de Martyrologes de Bede, de L'Anonyme lyonnais, et de Florus* (Paris 1976), p. 226.

The Crawford Sarum missal: an Exeter book?

This (now Manchester, John Rylands U. L. Lat. 24), the best known of all manuscript Sarum missals because it was taken by J. W. Legg as the base manuscript for his still standard edition of that book, 1916, was discussed also in chapter 10. It demands notice here because of the inscription on the flyleaf, "memoriale Henrici de Ciscestria canonici Exon. prec[ii] lx s." As long ago as 1896 E. M. Thompson had connected this Henry with one of that name who was precentor of the collegiate church at Crediton until 1264.[15] Six years after Legg's edition of the Crawford missal was published, Frances Rose-Troup postulated that this was the same book as (1) the *Unum missale* mentioned in a list of gifts to the cathedral made in 1277 as "De dono Henrici de Cicestre," along with a cope, a hanging pyx for the high altar, and a cup which had by that time been stolen; (2) the missal described in the 1327 inventory as "Bonum notatum cum tropariis cum multis ymaginibus subtilibus de auro in canone, lx s."; and (3) the missal identified in an inventory of 1506 through the *secundo folio* reference, *Induantur.*[16] The book does indeed contain tropes, and has eight full-page illustrations in the section containing the ordinary and canon.[17] The identification can scarcely be in doubt.

What is not perfectly clear, however, is the identity of the memorialized Henry, a matter of some importance. A Henry who is treasurer of Crediton and a canon of Exeter witnesses an episcopal grant in 1242, and in 1249 a canon Henry *de Cirencestre* gets a tenement in Exeter which some fifteen years later he devolves to the Vicars Choral of the cathedral to support an obit for him, kept on June 16th.[18] If these references are to the same Henry (who might well have advanced from being treasurer at Crediton to precentor, as Rose-Troup points out), and if the Crawford missal was indeed his, that it is called in the presentation inscription *Memoriale* suggests that it was given on his death, which must therefore have taken place by 1277 – assuming further that the

---

[15] *Sarum Missal (Legg)*, p. vi.

[16] F. Rose-Troup, "Henry de Cicestria's Missal," *Bull. John Rylands Lib.* 6 (1921–22), pp. 361–64. She points out that her findings came just too late to be included in the James catalogue of the Rylands Latin MSS; given the delay in publication of that catalogue, it is doubtful whether they would have been mentioned in any case: Pfaff, *M. R. James*, p. 278.

[17] Morgan, *Early Gothic MSS*, no. 100.

[18] Evidence as in Rose-Troup, pp. 362–63; on p. 364 is noted a "Henry the Canon" in a document of 1253/4, but Henry was such a common name at the time that this is scarcely conclusive. Further references in *Fasti 1066–1300*, 10: *Exeter* (2005), p. 48; the editor, D. E. Greenway, gives a cautious "Cf." to "Henry de Cicestre, donor of vestments and a hanging ciborium," without mentioning the missal.

missal referred to in that list as given by a Henry *de Cicestre* is the one we are pursuing. Whether the place of origin of this Henry is meant to be Chichester or Cirencester may be material, for in the former case the absence of Richard of Chichester (canonized in 1262) from the missal would be all the more striking if the book were made after that year.[19] Still, it does not seem possible to date the Crawford missal more closely than third quarter of the century, nor, for present purposes, to say more than that it seems to have been available at the cathedral from the last quarter of the thirteenth century on. Unlike the Exeter 3510 book, it shows no signs of Exeter distinctiveness. That it may have contributed to a certain liturgical eclecticism at the cathedral seems a possibility, especially in the light of the next book to be noticed, one that bears clear awareness of variety of *usus*.

From Worcester to Exeter, perhaps by way of Wells

A psalter of around 1225 from Worcester made its way later that same century to Exeter, where it is now Cathedral MS 3508.[20] Its calendar has in the original hand Becket's Translation (1220) and many Worcester distinctivenesses, including the June 7th (1218) dedication of the cathedral and (same day) Translation of Wulfstan, but Francis (canonized 1228) is an early addition. It was, however, used not at the cathedral priory but at St Helen's church; both the dedication of that church and Helena's August 18th feast are in colored capitals, and the highest grading is nine lessons.[21] By the second half of the century it had migrated to Exeter cathedral, where other additions were made to the calendar, notably its Dedication feast at November 21st, Gabriel at March 24th, and the obit of a dean who died in 1252.[22] The book was

---

[19] A Chichester connection later than mere origin cannot altogether be ruled out, for a Henry of Chichester was a canon there in 1267 (and, whether the same man or not) archdeacon of Lewes in the 1270s: *Fasti 1066–1300*, 5: *Chichester*, ed. D. E. Greenway (1996), p. 59.

[20] *MMBL*, II.814. N. Morgan treats what he calls this "rather coarsely decorated book" in "Psalter Illustration for the Diocese of Worcester in the 13th Cent.," in *Medieval Art and Architecture at Worcester Cathedral*, BAA Conf. Trs. 1 (1978), pp. 91–104, at p. 92, with a table comparing certain feasts in Worcester calendars on 100–1. In *Exeter Cath.: a Celebration*, p. 131 is a full-page reproduction of fol. 7v, the calendar for June.

[21] Not the present St Helen's, a modern building in the High Street, now used as the County Record Office. The other saint similarly magnified is Gregory the Great, his Ordination feast being in alternating red and blue capitals; Ker suggested that the book had perhaps been made for use at an altar of St Gregory, but this cannot have been at the cathedral because of the grading system.

[22] The placing of Gabriel's feast on the day before the Annunciation is logical rather than accurate: it was actually kept on the first Monday in Sept. (see p. 402).

still there in 1506, identified in the inventory of that year as *de secunda forma*, so presumably in some sort of use in the choir.

These details are worth mentioning because of the note on fol. 133v, in a blank space before psalm cix, of liturgical practice elsewhere: "De sancta maria in adventu secundum quod canit Salesburiensis ecclesia atque Wellensis ecclesia," with similar language repeated on the verso, plus a further indication of a psalm-usage "quod canit Herfordensis ecclesia." What is being noted is not particularly exciting, but it is striking to encounter such explicit awareness of practices in three dioceses, all of which have secular cathedrals and which, as it happens, lie between Worcester and Exeter. There is a good deal else of interest, such as the copying onto a preliminary quire of indulgences issued in 1317 by "Sanctus Iohannes xxii volens divinum cultum ampliare" (the *sanctus* would certainly have surprised his numerous enemies), and the book might well repay close study. It is mentioned here to show that awareness of a variety of practices may be a factor in the development of even such a powerful liturgical identity as Grandisson's program provides for the chapter at Exeter. Before considering that, however, we have still to look at the work of one more thirteenth-century bishop.

Quinil's work of consolidation

In 1287 Bronescombe's successor, Peter Quinil, issued for Exeter an extensive series of diocesan statutes, one which C. R. Cheney has called "the longest and most ornate" of a number of descendants of the statutes issued for Worcester by its bishop, Walter Cantilupe, in 1240.[23] Quinil's almost exhaustingly thorough series conveys well the optimistic (and sometimes unrealistic) standards that many thirteenth-century bishops attempted to set for their dioceses. There are long sections about the building and repairing of churches and chapels, their dedication, and – of particular interest to us – the ornaments, including books, that they are supposed to have (cap. 12). Another section prescribes that in parish churches the daily office should be reverently observed ("ut secundum formam concilii generalis": what does that mean?) and the psalms not gabbled (cap. 21). Nor should one parish be celebrating a particular feast, especially one that involves cessation of manual labor,

---

[23] Quinil's statutes are printed in *C & S 1205–1313*, II.984–1059, with the MSS and their complicated history discussed by the editor, C. R. Cheney, pp. 982–84; the Worcester 1240 statutes are in I.294–325, and an influential series from Wells, 1258, in I.586–626. On problems of using these, see Cheney, "Statute-making in the English Church in the Thirteenth Century," in his *Medieval Texts and Studies* (Oxford 1973), pp. 138–57, originally published in 1963.

while another (adjacent?) parish is not; so a list of fixed-day feasts of compulsory observance is provided (cap. 23).[24] These include the Conception, which as we have seen is present in the "Exeter/Sarum" (3510) missal but not in the Crawford, both owned by the cathedral well before Quinil's statutes. And the books containing services for these mandated feasts in parish churches are not to be *libri monasteriorum*, even where the churches are appropriated to religious houses; because when they are not *de communi usu* the laity may be led astray (cap. 40).[25]

Two years earlier, when Edward I visited the cathedral, Quinil introduced a devotion that, awkward as it seems, shows the degree of liturgical innovation which that bishop, at any rate, felt to be within his power. This, expressed in a mandate inserted in his register, consisted of a psalm, series of versicles and responses, and two collects (with language like "ut famulus tuus, .N., rex noster, qui tua miseracione suscepit regni gubernacula") to be wedged into the high mass between the Pax and the Agnus Dei; but this may have been intended for only the royal visit, not, as would have been the case with the Corpus Christi procession, as part of the regular liturgy at the cathedral.[26]

It is conceivable that Quinil was also the moving force behind what is often mentioned as a particularly colorful, and apparently unique, piece of liturgical elaboration at Exeter: the ceremony at Christmas matins. This centered on the responsory after the first lesson, and involved a single chorister appearing rather dramatically and, a taper in his left hand, performing a series of demonstrative gestures as he sang "Hodie natus celorum rex de virgine nasci dignatus est"; he was then joined by three choristers on his left and three on the right, thus forming an impromptu chorus of angels singing "Gloria in excelsis deo" (in the office, though it would be sung at mass as well); and at the conclusion of this all seven walked through the choir *morose incedendo* – with downcast eyes, or gloomy expressions, or somber gait, or all three? – and out the west door.[27] The words quoted come from Grandissson's ordinal,

---

[24] As might be expected, there is some interesting variation among the dozen manuscripts, with respect to saints' feasts like those of George, Augustine of Canterbury, Margaret, and Anne.

[25] Cheney points out (*C & S*, p. 1034) that this is a direct echo of cap. 15 of the 1258 Wells statutes, and adds that in the archdeaconry of Totnes in 1342 "books of monastic use were reported in seventeen parish churches" (from G. C. Coulton's printing of the visitation records, *Eng. Hist. Rev.* 26 [1911], pp. 108–24); so the problem was not confined to the diocese of (by 1258) Bath and Wells, where the presence of Glastonbury might easily be overwhelming.

[26] *Reg. Bronescombe, Quivil, etc.*, ed. F. C. Hingeston-Randolph (London 1889), p. 326.

[27] *Exeter Ordinal* (note 36), I.64.

to be discussed presently, but there is reason for wondering whether the practice may predate him. According to Frere, Quinil's 1283 statutes ordered the correction of the Exeter consuetudinary and ordinal and also "the assimilation of the customs in wearing the almuce [amice] to those of the Church of Salisbury; and the Exeter rite stipulates that the boy-angel should be vested, rather unusually, in amice as well as alb."[28] Now, there seems to be no such elaborate bit of ceremony at Salisbury as this rather peculiar Christmas matins practice in either the 1280s or the 1330s, though this cannot be stated definitively without a clear resolution (which cannot be attempted in the present chapter) of the precise pace of development of ceremony at Salisbury, as reflected in the progress from its "Old" to "New" ordinal (p. 414). Whether the custom was introduced at Exeter by Quinil, a native son who spent much of his career there, or by the much more cosmopolitan Grandisson, awareness of a potential Sarum model is always present.

John de Grandisson and his ordinal

How John de Grandisson came to have such a deep interest in matters liturgical we cannot precisely know. A recent biographical notice describes his background as "wealthy, noble, cultivated, and learned," as befits a younger son of a prominent and well connected family.[29] Grandisson was a churchman of the world: educated at Oxford and then at Paris (where one of his teachers was Jacques Fournier, later [1334–42] Pope Benedict XII), sometime chaplain and diplomat for John XXII, made bishop by provision of that pope, consecrated at Avignon. As would have been expected, he was also a notable pluralist, amassing canonries at Wells, York, and Lincoln, plus the archdeaconry of Nottingham. Some idea of his patronage, and his taste, can be gleaned not only from the magnificent nave and western screen front of the cathedral, built substantially during his reign, but also from a small group of ivories that survives in London and Paris and from the orphreys of a chasuble of his.[30] The overall impact of his liturgical

---

[28] Frere, "Use of Exeter," p. 56, citing BL Harley 1027, fols 29–30: "ad similitudinem Sarum ecclesie." Against this possibility is the fact that the presbytery may not have been completed during Quinil's episcopate; the ordinal says only that the boy appears from a place "retro magnum altare."

[29] A. Erskine, "Grandison, John," in *ODNB* 23.266. The spelling "Grandisson" is followed here because it is the form used by F. C. Hingeston-Randolph and by J. N. Dalton in their standard editions of, respectively, his register and his liturgical works; see notes 32, 36, and 57.

[30] Illustrated and discussed in *Age of Chivalry. Art in Plantagenet England*, ed. J. Alexander and P. Binski (London 1987), pp. 463–67, and in *Exeter Cath.: a Celebration*,

work seems summed up in an addition made at the end of the 1277 inventory: the terse list of his gifts begins *Libri chori omnes.*[31]

This must be overstatement. As we have seen, information given in that inventory makes plain that a number of the books were satisfactory at that point, and the gifts of several members of the chapter in the previous fifty years would have ensured that service books were not in short supply when Grandisson was enthroned in his cathedral in August of 1328. Following his consecration as bishop ten months earlier, at Avignon, he had blessed chrism *more Romano*, as he stated to the dean in a message some weeks thereafter. Around the same time, however, he wrote to the bishop of Lausanne, in whose cathedral John Grandisson's uncle Otto, the famous knight and adviser to Edward I, was buried, asking that a search be made among Otto's goods "que pertinent ad capellam, et presertim libros de usu Anglicano," any that were found to be sent back by the bearer of the letter.[32] We wonder what "English use" books might these have been that uncle Otto, during his occasional residences in Britain (mostly in Wales), all before 1307, had collected.[33]

Whatever they may have been, the prime point of reference for his nephew was clearly Sarum. During his first winter in Devon Bishop John sent a request to the archdeacon of Salisbury that, in view of the destruction of Stapeldon's books by the lynch-mob in London, there might be found a "librum pontificalem, antiquum et veracem," within the cloister, one that could be sent to Grandisson so that it could be copied and the "modum Saresburiensis ecclesiae" could be followed "in nostra Exoniensi."[34] And at his initial visitation of the cathedral, six months or so after his enthronement, he had enquired in particular about its ordinal and consuetudinary, "in quibus discrepant ab usu Sarum vel aliarum ecclesiarum" and mandates that such books should be brought to him "ad examinandum, corrigendum, et approbandum."[35]

The result of his "examining, correcting, and approving" activity is his massive ordinal, completed within nine years, by the spring of

pp. 150–54, in both books by Neil Stratford. At least twenty-one books owned by Grandisson are extant: listed in Emden, *Biog. Reg. Univ. Oxf.* II.801, and traceable through the pages of *MMBL* and *MLGB.*

[31] *Ordinale Exon.* [note 36 below], II.549.
[32] *Register of John de Grandisson*, ed. F. C. Hingeston-Randolph, 3 vols (London 1894–99), I.162; 174.
[33] J. R. Maddicott, "Grandson, Sir Otto de," in *ODNB* 23.269.
[34] *Reg. Grandisson* I.214. This is slightly odd; such a request would more logically have gone to his fellow bishop, Roger Martival (1315–30), whose own pontifical survives, Bodl. Rawl. C.400. Neither of the pontificals that Grandisson compiled (and in his will left to his successors: Frere, "Use of Exeter," p. 56) is extant.
[35] *Reg. Grandisson*, I.436.

1337. The title under which the work is commonly cited in its Henry Bradshaw Society edition, *Ordinale Exon.*, covers not only this but also the complementary works which he drew up, a two-volume legenda and a martyrology.[36] The cathedral library contains his own copies, annotated by him, of the Legenda (MSS 3504–5), but no manuscript contemporary with him survives of the ordinal proper; for this the modern editor, J. N. Dalton, used a copy from the second half of the fifteenth century, Cathedral MS 3502, comparing it with a somewhat earlier copy, which also contains the martyrology, CCCC 93.[37]

The ordinal itself is almost overwhelming in its detail. It begins with a statement as proud as it is succinct. "Exoniensis ecclesia, sicut ceteres cathedrales ecclesie, obseruancias proprias et consuetudines habet, tam in dicendo quam in exequendo officio diuino que in scriptis nondum plene fuerunt redacte," and makes no bones about its authoritative nature in being "ab ipsomet [Grandisson] editum, et ab eodem ac decano et capitulo approbatum, et de cetero traditum obseruandum." Nothing seems to be overlooked. The liturgical duties of the different personnel, their behavior in choir, colors of vestments, grading of feasts, the ruling of the choir are all dealt with before the temporale begins. The last section of this preliminary matter, "De custodia librorum," is specially interesting. In order to avoid any "discordia, que auribus abhorrenda totam armonie dulcedinem dissoluit," two books are fixed as standard: "illud ANTIPHONARIUM quod dicitur *GRANSTON* et illud GRADALE antiquum cum PSALTERIIS que idem Johannes episcopus contulit ecclesie, dicuntur ueriora, iuxta que expedit ceteros libros corrigi, et quoad formam antique note Sarum."[38] The prescriptive character of this extends so far as to say that those who have their own books should not presume to sing from them in choir unless first corrected. The notion of privately owned choral books arouses curiosity; even more so, the enigma posed by the words "formam antique note Sarum."

[36] J. N. Dalton, ed. *Ordinale Exon.*, HBS 37–38 (both 1909, and paginated continuously), the ordinal and martyrology; 63 (1926), the legenda; and 79 (1940, posthumously, with G.H. Doble), collations with a better copy of the martyrology, Exeter Cath. 3518 (misprinted on the title page as 3508) and extensive indices (by C. W. Surrey): henceforth in this chapter referred to as *Ordinale*, but in other chapters, for greater clarity, as *Exeter Ordinal*.

[37] Dalton was more a courtier (for many years tutor to two of Queen Victoria's sons, and for forty-seven a canon of Windsor) than a scholar, but in 1917 he published an extensive monograph on the collegiate church at Ottery, endowed by Grandisson (p. 408 below); his antiquarian activities are ignored in the rather dismissive entry in *ODNB* 14.1022–23.

[38] *Ordinale*, I.22; capitals and italics as in edition. Surely the "Granston" antiphonal was the book that had originally belonged to uncle Otto?

In theory it would be possible to reconstruct from the ordinal what we lack in service books proper, an almost complete liturgy of the office as used at Exeter in Grandisson's time: information of a precisely dated and located sort almost without parallel in medieval England. (The separate section about the mass is much briefer.) For present purposes, it must suffice to convey its flavor through a few particularly salient details. At the reading of the genealogy on Christmas Eve all prostrate themselves, kissing the ground, at the words "Jesus Christ is born."[39] The liturgy of the Boy Bishop on Holy Innocents day is spelled out elaborately.[40] On Holy Thursday the Maundy ceremony is to be "ut in GRADALIBUS uel PROCESSIONALIBUS continetur" [I.135]. The Easter Wednesday collect for the procession *Ad fontes* agrees with that in the Crawford missal rather than in Leofric "A" [I.146]. Complications presented by the relatively new feast of Corpus Christi, and especially by observance of the Sunday within its octave, are dealt with squarely: "quia idem festum est mobile et nouum, et antiqua dominica est caput dominicarum estatis," it is provided that, in order to avoid "multa inconueniencia rubricarum antiquarum," the office will always be that of the Sunday after Trinity Sunday, with the middle lessons at matins and *memoriae* at vespers and lauds being for Corpus Christi [I.175]. But – a wonderfully vivid touch – an additional problem is coming up this very year ("anno confeccionis istius ORDINALIS, uidelicet anno domini m ccc xxxvii"), that the feast of St Alban, June 22nd, falls on that Sunday; in which case the saint's feast is to be deferred. So it was in the first half of 1337 that Grandisson promulgated this work of his.

Grandisson's extreme attention to detail is fascinating. This is particularly evident with the minutiae of occurrence and concurrence: e.g., when the Octave of the Assumption (22 August), which gets second as well as first vespers, falls on a Saturday, then there will be no Sunday vespers because first vespers of Bartholomew (24 August), a feast of nine lessons, has to be observed [I.183]. It is apparent also in a concern for accuracy in the headings, as in that which amplifies the title of the feast "In translacione Sancti Swythuni sociorumque eius" with an explanation that, although "alii faciant de communi plurimorum confessorum, Exonie tamen facimus de solo sancto swythuno" because of the

---

[39] *Ordinale*, I.60: "omnes se prosternant deosculantes terram," which suggests that the actions were to be done simultaneously, awkward as that seems.
[40] But can it be correct that the boy bishop is at compline to begin the creed "Credo in unum deum," which would be the Nicene Creed (I.74)?

church at Woodbury, which is dedicated to him (and which had come to be held by the cathedral chapter in 1205).[41] The Exeter diocesan feast of St Sativola (Sidwell), kept on 2 August, bumps that of Pope Stephen, who gets only the middle lessons at matins, and Sativola's *historia* will be read entire, even if on a Sunday [I.245]. The dates of other feasts peculiar to Exeter – Brannoc on 7 January, Keran (Pieran) 5 March, and Petroc 4 June, plus its Feast of Relics (placed at 15 May, actually the Monday after Ascension) and of Dedication 21 November – do not conflict with major or long-established feasts in the same way. The feast most distinctive to the cathedral, that of the archangel Gabriel, is to be kept not on a fixed day but on the first Monday in September; for this office Grandisson provides tags for the elements of a full office, including the little hours.[42]

The *Legenda Exon.*

An ordinal provides only a framework, of course. The services that Grandisson's is meant to regulate would have been contained in the various mass and office books enumerated in the 1277 and 1327 inventories. As far as is known, Grandisson is not responsible directly for any of these save for the massive sets of readings at matins known collectively as the *Legenda Exon.* These survive in two manuscripts in the cathedral library: 3504, the readings for the temporale, and 3505, those for the sanctorale.[43] The initial folio of the first states that the work is "secundum ordinacionem et abreuiacionem Iohannis de Grandissono episcopi," of the second that it was *compilatus* by him; both are annotated in his hand. The modern editor, J. N. Dalton, has pointed out that there is nearly complete correspondence between cues in the ordinal and the readings in the Legenda, and that the biblical readings seem to be more coherently arranged than in the Sarum, York, and Hereford uses. Another focus of the bishop's attention was a series of supplementary readings on many days, after the office of prime but in the chapter house, following the reading of the martyrology; these supplied an opportunity to finish readings that seemed too long for matins or to provide some for saints who came second on a particular day, like Potentiana after Dunstan, or Sabina after the Beheading of John the

---

[41] *Ordinale*, I.240. The matter of Woodbury is noted in M. Lapidge, *The Cult of St Swithun* (Oxford 2003), p. 109.

[42] *Ordinale*, I.186. This office is not among the six listed for Gabriel in A. Hughes, *Late Medieval Liturgical Offices*, I (Toronto 1994), p. 139.

[43] Dalton's edition, *Ordinale Exon.*, III (1926), prints merely references for the biblical lessons and many of the patristic homilies, the latter mostly as in *PL*. Both MSS are described on pp. 1–12; also, more succinctly, in *MMBL*, II.809–10.

Baptist.[44] However the members of the chapter, sometimes undoubtedly drowsy, may have felt about this additional burden of reading, it is the case that the length of the lessons at matins is generally quite moderate.[45]

It is, however, frustrating that the readings for the distinctive Exeter saints mentioned above, Sativola, Brannoc, Keran, and Petroc, are not provided, despite the statement in the summary of contents with which MS 3504 begins that *Tercia pars* (the sanctorale) will conclude with "legenda quorumdam, de quibus fit in ecclesia exoniensi tantum."[46] The unique feast for which lessons are given is that of the archangel Gabriel, which because of the odd way it is dated (first Monday in September, as noted above, rather than a fixed date) appears in the temporale section. They read like an enhancement of Marian devotion, which may help to explain the placement of the feast, between the Octave of Assumption (22 August) and the Nativity (8 September). They seem to date from Bronescombe's time, and according to Dalton are marked by Grandissson for revision.[47]

Grandisson's legacy and Exeter tradition

Although Grandisson was a bishop familiar with the wider world by the time he was enthroned at Exeter on 22 August 1328, there is no indication that he had ever been in his see city previously. Whether or not his possession of canonries at Wells, York, and Lincoln meant that he ever resided at any of those cathedrals, it is clear that it was the usages of Salisbury that bulked large in his mind. As we saw above, less than four months after becoming bishop, at his first visitation of the dean and chapter he ordered correction of certain books, in particular the ordinal and consuetudinary, to ascertain in what respects they differed from the use of Sarum or of other churches (*aliarum ecclesiarum*).[48] What the "other churches" might have been is not stated,

---

[44] *Ordinale*, III.xi–xii.

[45] There are occasional exceptions, in themselves interesting: notably, the nine long lessons (plus supplementary lesson after prime) for the Translation of Becket, pp. 277–80; cf. S. L. Reames, "Reconstructing and Interpreting a Thirteenth-Century Office for the Translation of Thomas Becket," *Speculum* 80 (2005), pp. 118–70, at 131 and 138. The office itself (cues in *Ordinale*, I.239) is not the rhyming office she edits, pp. 164–70.

[46] *Ordinale*, III.13. Instead, MS 3505 ends with three rather long lessons for Wilfrid that should not be there (he is not in the Exeter calendar; Grandisson has written here, "Non dicimus exonie" [p. xiii]) and nine noted lessons from Job for the Office of the Dead.

[47] *Ordinale*, III.xiii. It is unfortunate that Dalton did not print any of Grandisson's annotations.

[48] *Reg. Grandisson*, p. 436; cited in Dalton's preface to *Ordinale*, III.ix.

nor how heavily discrepancies from their usages were to be weighed as compared with those from Sarum. But that he regards Sarum usages as in a sense standard seems clear, from the at least half a dozen places where his ordinal mentions them, and most of all in points where they are not followed.[49]

The most important of these for our purposes is the heading in the Legenda for Ciricus and Julitta (16 June), which notes that "Sarum fiunt hac die translacione sancti ricardi ix lecciones et medie lecciones de eisdem martyribus. Exonie tantum de martiribus" (III.254). As Richard's translation took place in 1276 and the Crawford missal seems to be recorded in the 1277 inventory, it is not surprising that the feast is included in neither its calendar nor its sanctorale.[50] Grandisson's information about this Sarum usage has therefore some source more current than the Crawford missal – that is, something that reflects Sarum practice between 1276 and 1336.

An earlier discrepancy of Exeter usage from Sarum is in the grading of Wulfram, October 15th (actually his translation feast, but his original feast day is March 20th, in England pre-empted by Cuthbert; see p. 360 for more on Wulfram, a significant Sarum saint). In both the sanctorale and the calendar of Grandisson's ordinal the feast is marked as of three lessons at Exeter but nine at Salisbury. In the Legenda the heading is almost embarrassed about this: "quidam faciunt ix lecciones. Set Exonie facimus tres lecciones tantum. Unde lecciones sequentes poterunt diuidi in tres uel in sex, ut patet exterius per signa," the *signa* being paraph marks; and a rubric at the end states that if it is kept with nine lessons, the final three will be an exposition of the gospel reading for the feast (III.381). All of this detail takes on added interest because of the heading in the Crawford missal's calendar, "Sancti Wulfranni episcopi et confessoris. *Sarum ix lec. iii.* lec. et t'[= Te Deum]," the phrase in italics being in red while the rest of the entry is in black. Why, in this supposedly Sarum missal, is it necessary to state that a usage is that of Sarum, while the alternative usage, which is that of the church to which the book is donated, is not given a local habitation? The word *Sarum* appears otherwise only twice in the Crawford calendar: once to mark the Feast of Relics, understandably since it is the Sarum relics that are

---

[49] The only other "use" mentioned is that of Rome, as having six liturgical colors rather than the more usual four, and as prescribing a genuflection at the "Et incarnatus est" clause in the Nicene Creed "more ecclesie Romane" (written over an erasure; *Ordinale*, I.12 and 10 respectively).

[50] Richard's Translation, though not in the ordinal, is included in the later Corpus 93 martyrology, and in its calendar, marked (in a later hand) "Exon nil. set sanctorum Cirici et Iulitte martirum."

(originally) meant; and once, negatively, to state that the Conception of Mary is *Sarum nichil*. That is indeed the case in the sanctorales of the Crawford, Arsenal, and Bologna missals, whereas both calendar and sanctorale of the Grandisson ordinal contain it, as a double feast.[51]

Given that it seems to be the case that Grandisson's work is produced with a tacit understanding that Sarum is standard, two questions follow. First, how completely may this in fact have been the case? The divergences noted in his ordinal concern very small matters indeed, such as the two described above, or that Machutus (15 November) has three lessons at Exeter but nine at Sarum (III.416). Are we to infer from this that there are no divergences of a more substantial sort, and that Exeter usage under Grandisson is to all intents and purposes that of Salisbury? In the absence of more, and more precisely dated, Sarum sources (see p. 365 for further discussion of the problems involved), no definite answer can be given. A point which would seem otherwise decisive is by its nature ruled out. This is whether Exeter followed Sarum's moving, in 1319, the date of the Feast of Relics from September 15th to the Sunday after the Translation of Becket; for that feast at Exeter had, apparently since time immemorial, been kept on the Monday after Ascension, so there was no need to change it when observance of the Octave of Mary's Nativity became the rule and so pre-empted the September date.[52]

The second question involves the extent to which Grandisson expected his provisions to be in effect elsewhere than just in the cathedral. There is certainly some awareness of this: the section on the Feast of Relics ends with a few details about the office on that Monday "ubi non fit de reliquiis," with consequent adjustments for the Tuesday and Wednesday (I.165). For the most part, however, the language is specific to the cathedral. At mass on St Nicholas's day the gradual is to be sung by two *annivelarii*, a species of lower clergy particular to Exeter (I.339). The office of three lessons for Alphege is to be sung near the altar of St Thomas because "in ecclesia Exoniensi dedicatur eciam in honore sancti Alphegi" (I.221). At the masses of Maundy Thursday and Pentecost there are to be seven deacons, seven subdeacons, and three acolytes (I.294).

---

[51] The calendar of Arsenal does include it, at nine lessons; that of Bologna lacks November and December.

[52] Grandisson's ordinal includes information later than 1319: Thomas of Hereford, canonized 1320. Apparently how early Corpus Christi comes to be observed at the cathedral cannot be ascertained; Stapeldon ordered the nuns of Polsloe and Canonsleigh to keep it in Jan. 1320: *Register of Walter de Stapeldon ...*, ed. F. C. Hingeston-Randolph (London and Exeter 1892), pp. 95, 316.

How widely can we then suppose Grandisson's desire for liturgical uniformity – and splendor – penetrated throughout his diocese? Visitations in 1330 and 1331 by commissaries of the dean and chapter to parishes that "belonged" to the cathedral had disclosed a sad picture of the service books in many. "Missale debile, et insufficiens in Canone. Legenda male ligata et non cooperta" at Clyst-Honiton; at Buckerell "Omnes libri sunt male ligati et pro parte consumpti, et fere insufficientes"; at Salcombe Regis, though some of the service books were adequate, there was neither antiphonal nor legenda *per se*, and the manual, ordinal, *capitularium*, collectar, and hymnal were not in the church but were said to be in the house of the (bookish, or wily?) vicar.[53] In both parishes where there were marked deficiencies and those where the books were in general *sufficiens*, could Grandisson reasonably have expected a notable campaign of service-book writing and purchasing? No service book belonging to a parish in his diocese appears in the slim list in *Medieval Libraries of Great Britain*, and by the time there come to be churchwardens' accounts (not, with rare exceptions, until the late fifteenth century) any books immediately reflecting Grandisson's work could be expected to have worn out. Whether there were, in the mid-fourteenth century and later, many churches in Devon and Cornwall where services were consciously conducted *de usu Exonie* must therefore remain in doubt; by that time (at least) Sarum was beginning to seem almost synonymous with south English.

Exeter cathedral and the question of "Use"

The practical necessity of our noting architectural aspects only sketchily is specially vexing in the case of Exeter cathedral, for much of its present, magnificent interior was either finished or in progress during Grandisson's long episcopate. He consecrated its high altar only a year or so after becoming bishop, and by the time of his death in 1369 the famous western screen front was completed; his mortuary chapel is set inside it. The splendor of the building and its fittings, most conspicuously the silver altar with its silver retable, cannot but have been in Grandisson's mind as he compiled his ordinal and legenda, just as the bishop's throne he succeeded to, finished only about 1324 and in grandeur perhaps second only to Durham's, is unlikely to have been conducive to episcopal humility. Veronica Sekules, analyzing this self-conscious splendor, has suggested that, even before the time of Stapeldon (who commissioned the throne), "foundations were perhaps being

---

[53] *Reg. Grandisson*, I.570–75.

laid for a 'cult of bishops' in preparation for the time when one might be canonized"; and relates this further to the absence at Exeter of an important saint or relic: "Lacking a glittering bank of shrines at the high altar, Exeter chose to magnify the authority of the Church and its ministers by an elaborated liturgy, and to surround them in the celebration of its rites with furnishings of equivalent splendor."[54]

Nonetheless, it would be unwise to concentrate too intensively on the nexus between Grandisson's work and the cathedral. His liturgical presence bulks so large as almost to obscure the major question, adumbrated briefly above, of the extent and duration of the influence his work may have had. His will is a vivid record of magnificence.[55] What he leaves to the cathedral in the way of furnishings and equipment, especially vestments, is quite staggering, but the bequests of books are slight: two antiphonals, two graduals, two psalters, and a silver-covered copy of John's Gospel *de antiqua litera*. More substantial, and more important for our purposes, is the legacy of books to his successors; in Hingeston-Randolph's translation,

My pontifical books, the greater and the smaller, which I myself compiled; and three missals, namely one of great value [*preciosum*], noted and containing the sequences, in which is written *In principio*, and this is to remain to my successors; another, new and in good condition, of the same letter, but without notation; and the third a portable one ... . Also the book of the gospels as they are read throughout the year, with covers of silver ... . Also I bequeath to my said successors three portable graduals and one of larger size, for their own use. Also a legend complete, in one volume, belonging to my chamber ... . Also, two books of homilies, for reading in their presence. Also, the larger antiphonary and the psalter, which lie before me in my chapel, together with two other psalters for the clerks.[56]

This may well be the most extensive collection of service books owned by a single person in the whole of our story. (The same is probably true of vestments as well, were they to our immediate purpose.) One

---

[54] V. Sekules, "The Liturgical Furnishings of the Choir of Exeter Cathedral," in *Medieval Art and Architecture at Exeter Cathedral*, ed. F. Kelly, BAA Conf. Trs. 11 (1991), pp. 172–79 at 175, 178.

[55] Printed in *Reg. Grandisson*, III.1549–57, from the only surviving copy, in the register of archbishop (of Canterbury, 1369–74) William Whittlesey at Lambeth Palace; with Eng. tr. by Hingeston-Randolph, pp. 1511–23.

[56] *Reg. Grandisson*, III.1515. The bequests to successors go on to enumerate yet more vestments and other ecclesiastical equipment and, with a grand concluding flourish, "a hundred bullocks and a thousand sheep, if it turn out that I have so many, and a hundred pounds sterling." Other service books go to his great-nephew and co-executor Philip de Beauchamp: the breviary and psalter from the episcopal chapel and a "small and beautiful missal," III.1518.

wonders especially about the missal that struck even Grandisson as *pre-ciosum* and that is specifically to be kept by his successors: can it have been of the magnitude of the greatest mass books of the next generation, those known now as the Westminster missal and Sherborne missal, both of which are connected with named abbots? Indeed, are we lacking *the* "Grandisson missal"?

The main question here is whether the glittering impression we get from the completed cathedral and the completed (as it appears) work of Grandisson is unique to Exeter, or whether if we had similar combinations of a personal liturgical program with a fully accomplished campaign of building and decoration for Lincoln or Wells or London, even York or Hereford (each of which, as having a well recognized "Use," will be treated separately), we would still find Exeter's situation *sui generis*. Even at Salisbury, its building completed, save for the spire, some two generations before Exeter, there is no liturgical intelligence that comes through as vividly and overwhelmingly as does Grandisson's.

The matter of "liturgical" intelligence is pursued here at some length not only because is it so palpable in Grandisson but also because the amplitude of documentation for his reign at Exeter means that we can be less hampered by dead ends, less impaired by blank walls, less often thrown back on speculation and hypothesis, than we have frequently found to be the case. This is nowhere more gratifyingly clear than with the regulations he left for his collegiate foundation at Ottery St Mary.

Ottery St Mary

On 15 December 1337 royal licence was given to Grandisson's new collegiate foundation at Ottery St Mary; within a few weeks its governing document, the *Ordinacio Primaria*, was issued, and elaborately detailed statutes were promulgated at Michaelmas 1339.[57] This sequence means that we can use Grandisson's provision for the new establishment as almost a continuation of his work at the cathedral, but whereas there he was naturally somewhat constrained by the existing fabric, personnel, and customs, at Ottery he could express his liturgical sense *de novo*. There were already two collegiate churches in the diocese, one at Crediton, a somewhat shadowy remant of the community of which Leofric

---

[57] These are all edited, with extensive commentary and photographs, by J. N. Dalton, *The Collegiate Church of Ottery St Mary ...* (Cambridge 1917). He had become drawn to the subject while working on his edition of Grandisson's ordinal (above, note 36), and in some ways the 1917 volume should be seen as amplification of the first two (1909) of the larger work; so it is unfortunate that the de luxe format of the Ottery book makes it rare and difficult of access.

had transferred the greater part to Exeter in 1050 but with usually a respectable quota of twelve to fifteen canons; and one at Glasney (Penrhyn, in Cornwall), founded by Bronescombe in 1265, for up to thirteen clergy and six choristers. There had also been a church at Ottery, which had been given to the canons of Rouen cathedral in 1061. Whatever Norman church had been there had been replaced by a wholly new one, consecrated by Bronescombe in 1259, but this was in turn entirely destroyed to make way for Grandisson's large and splendid church constructed at the center of a group of collegiate buildings.[58]

If the specific provisions for Ottery are, in a sense, those for the cathedral writ large, fresh, and for a church without overt episcopal presence, the point of greatest interest to us must be the way Grandisson casts the overall matter of "use." On this he speaks quite emphatically, in words not easy to translate:

We command that wherever our ordinal or customary or statutes have not dealt with any of the details that may come up during the year, then recourse shall be had to the Sarum ordinal and consuetudinary – provided that everything that *has* been dealt with is scrupulously observed. For, whatever is alleged or said [to the contrary], we do not wish Sarum use every time [*unquam*] to take hold; instead, it should be that of Exeter, or rather, as it might be more accurately put, that proper and special use passed on by us to them [the clergy of Ottery].[59]

It looks as though he is sensitive to an accusation either that the Exeter practices he has codified are just Sarum warmed over or that he wants Sarum to carry all before it. It is frustrating that the identities of those who *allegent uel dicant* are not revealed, but useful to have some corrective to the impression that Grandisson's prescriptions were irresistible. A bit of ugly contemporary slang seems appropriate: Grandisson may have been a liturgical "control-freak," but his instructions cannot always have been followed *ad apicem litterae*.

Two feasts emphasized in his Ottery statutes do seem to have taken permanent root, both of them Marian as befits the dedication of the new establishment. One is St Anne, faintly present in the thirteenth

---

[58] There is a large plan on two unnumbered pages in Dalton, *Ottery*. It is possible that some parts of the mid-13th-cent. church survive in the transepts and exterior choir walls: compare Dalton, pp. 11–12, with PBE, *South Devon* (1952), p. 220.

[59] Item, statuimus quod ubicunque Ordinale, uel Consuetudinarium, uel Statuta nostra non sufficiant forte in multis faciendis per totum annum, quod tunc recurratur ad ordinale et consuetudinarium Sarum, ita tamen, quod semper omnia per nos disposita firmiter obseruentur. Nolumus tamen, quod allegent uel dicant, unquam se usum tenere Sarum; set magis Exonie, uel ut uerius dicant, usum per nos eis traditum proprium et specialem (p. 224).

century (mainly, it seems, around Worcester; see p. 213), at July 26th. The other is the Oblation (more often, Presentation) of the Virgin at November 21st, in this case with something of an earlier existence but in select monastic circles only, and then with a striking revival in the late fourteenth century – after Grandisson's death, so his embracing of it is all the more interesting. His prescriptions for the cathedral mention both feasts, but only in the separate ordinal for the Lady Chapel that comes at the end of the main work: that the mass for Anne's feast is to break in to a rota of Marian-themed votives during the summer, and that there should be *solempnissima missa* on the feast of the Oblation (dated as the day after Edmund the Martyr, but in fact November 21st was the dedication feast of the cathedral: oddly passed over by Grandisson).[60] At Ottery, however, both feasts have a prominent place in the main cycle of observances, and, together with the associated Marian feast of Gabriel (first Monday in September, as at Exeter), are privileged with a forty-day indulgence for attendance at mass on all three occasions.[61]

The passing of the Grandissonian moment

If an antiquarian genie were to make it possible to have complete visual and aural recordings of the liturgy in one place throughout one whole year in medieval England, a good case could be made for settling one's choice on a year in the 1340s at Exeter cathedral (with, if permitted, a side trip to Ottery St Mary). The impetus following publication of Grandisson's ordinal and related works, the continued progress of the nave towards the glorious culmination of the western screen front, the vigor of the bishop (and very likely also of Richard de Brayleigh, sub-dean 1315–35 and dean 1335–53, and, as noted earlier, donor of service books) may well have combined to produce a period of some years of self-consciously "good liturgy." Yet in his visitation of 1354 Grandisson complains of the cathedral's services that (in Frere's summarizing words)

after all his zeal for their improvement these seven and twenty years, they are deteriorating, and will soon be as meanly performed as in a country church. He specifies some of the omissions, makeshifts, and slovenlinesses, traces them to the insufficient number in the choir and the habit of employing the inferior

---

[60] *Ordinale*, I.473–74; on p. 475 Epistle, Alleluia, and Gospel tags are given for both feasts.

[61] Dalton, *Ottery*, p. 144. Further discussion of the Presentation/Oblation feast, and wider context, in Pfaff, *New Liturg. Feasts*, pp. 109–10.

ministers for other tasks when they ought to be at service; and he demands reform in these matters.[62]

Especially given what happened in England between, say, 1347 and 1354 – the first outbreaks of the Black Death and the spate of parliamentary activity that followed – it is not surprising that the rather elitist ethos of the 1337 ordinal seems not to have been maintained for decades thereafter. In any case, by 1391 the Grandissonian regime was at an end; Thomas Brantingham, bishop 1370–94 and Grandisson's successor, induced the chapter to follow the Sarum ordinal in all matters save the local feasts.[63] From then on there is little to distinguish the story at Exeter.

[62] Frere, "Use of Exeter," pp. 69–70; *Reg. Grandisson*, II.1150–51.
[63] Frere, p. 70, citing pp. 10–11 of H. E. Reynolds's edition of the Exeter Chapter Acts, a book unavailable to me.

13   Southern England: final Sarum Use

At some time during the second half of the fourteenth century there appeared a fuller codification of the rubrics according to which services were to be conducted at Salisbury cathedral. A bland word like "appeared" is necessary because we know neither who is responsible for drawing this up nor by what authority (or means) it was promulgated. All that is even remotely clear is that these rubrics are mostly drawn from something called the New Ordinal – the conventional capitals, though possibly misleading, will be retained here – which seems to have been recognized as existing, with wider reference than merely to the cathedral, by the end of the century. The new rubrics are characterized by a great attention to, indeed an apparent fascination with, details of the tiniest sort. It is inevitable that we should attempt to use this New Ordinal as a prime means of understanding both the development of the Sarum rite in its final form and the extension of that rite into most of southern England; but we shall have to do so with caution, above all against being bogged down in too much of that detail.

Frere's *Use of Sarum* again

To begin, we have once again to take a preliminary look at the way the matter has been studied previously: a look that will of necessity recapitulate some of what has been explained in earlier chapters, particularly chapter 11. In the two-volume work entitled *The Use of Sarum* (1898–1901), Walter Howard Frere (on whom, see p. 10) presented documents he termed "consuetudinary," "customary," "ordinal," and "tonal." This work, though foundational to the subject at hand, is by no means easy to use. That subsequent students have taken Frere's presentation as definitive is, if understandable, unfortunate, for it blurs a good deal that requires clarification.

The first two of the four terms listed above represent successive versions of the basic laying out of who does what in the services at the (new) cathedral at Salisbury. The earlier version Frere called

412

"consuetudinary," although that word is not employed in any of the four manuscripts he consulted, his base text being that of the Risby ordinal (BL Harley 1001).[1] For the later version one manuscript (of, again, four) does contain the heading "Custumarium secundum usum Sarum": his justification for calling this later version "customary."[2] But these are in reality two names for the same entity and constitute a chronological distinction rather than a substantial difference. His decision to print them side by side makes both versions difficult to take in, for they are not ordered identically, and many pages have one column blank.[3]

"Consuetudinary" and "customary" being thus presented together in Frere's first volume as "The Sarum Customs," the implication of the subtitle of the second volume, "The Ordinal and Tonal," would seem to be that these two documents somehow form a pair also. This is not at all the case. The tonal is printed as an appendix (with separate, Roman-numeral, pagination) and is dealt with in less than three pages of Frere's introduction.[4] The bulk (pages 1–207) of the second volume, which has no table of contents and no index, is taken up with a printing, though with very considerable omissions and elisions, of the Old Ordinal, primarily as found in the early fourteenth-century Risby manuscript, including the *Addiciones* of 1278 (see below). Then, headed by Frere *Ordinale Sarum* just as the first part had been, comes the initial section of the New Ordinal – ostensibly for the First Sunday in Advent, but as usual containing a good deal of generally applicable material. In his Introduction Frere explains why he has not provided the whole thing: "on investigation it proves to be practically identical with the rubric of the Service-books as printed in the XVIth century and reprinted in our own day."[5] Unlike the first volume, therefore, where the whole "customary" was laid out (albeit often more confusingly

---

[1] As was explained more fully on p. 373, this MS, from the church at Risby in Suffolk, is of the early 14th cent.; it incorporates numerous changes and additions, the latter in a section so marked.

[2] This heading is found in his S, Salisbury Cathedral Lib. 175, end of the 14th cent.

[3] There is also a complicated mis-ordering of sections on pp. 89–91 of vol. I, explained (in a way that itself almost defies understanding) on the Corrigenda page, p. lxxii.

[4] His text, including much music, is taken from three of the four manuscripts of the "customary" – none, as he explains on p. xxxiv, entirely satisfactory. Frere's presentation of the tonal as though it were a kind of afterthought is all the more regrettable because he is a figure of considerable importance in the study of medieval chant.

[5] *Use of Sarum*, II.x–xi. He instances the standard editions often referred to in the present work: Dickinson's *Sarum Missal*, Henderson's *Sarum Processional*, and Procter and Wordsworth's *Sarum Breviary*; offering the useful caution that the printing on which the latter was based, Paris 1531, is deficient in giving the extensive rubrics usually found at the beginning of Advent.

than helpfully) alongside the "consuetudinary" which it succeeded, the second volume gives only a brief extract from the later version, or New Ordinal. This means that, save for the very beginning of the document, one can compare Old and New Ordinals only by using Frere's presentation of the first while scrutinizing the rubrics of the actual service books for the second. This is particularly exasperating because it blurs the fact that the New Ordinal is contained in the same four manuscripts on which he based his edition of the customary – the two, New Ordinal and customary, in effect forming a single work.[6] In fact, we shall come to see that there is no definitive text of the New Ordinal which can be taken as representing what emerged at Salisbury in the later fourteenth century.

Was there a *single* New Ordinal?

When Frere reviewed briefly the history of the Sarum ordinal he distinguished three stages.[7] He pointed out that the text of the Old Ordinal he printed (basically that of the Risby manuscript) shows that "already many alterations have been made, which have changed the Ordinal from what it was at the beginning of the xiiith Century," offering as proof its inclusion of the Translation of Richard of Chichester (misdated at 1262, the year of Richard's canonization; the translation took place in 1276, which actually strengthens Frere's point); many of these alterations are indicated by marginal notes. By 1278 enough seemed to be amiss with the Old Ordinal that, as we have seen (p. 375), the succentor of Salisbury, John Middleton, certified an extensive number of alterations that are headed in the Risby manuscript *Addiciones*. But, as Frere pointed out, these are not all changes to the (Risby) text, for some are already reflected in it.

This suggests that these *Addiciones* may have circulated in more than one form, a suggestion borne out by two witnesses not known to Frere. The first is two bifolia of flyleaves bound with an early twelfth-century copy of spiritual texts by Ephraem Syrus (now BL Royal 5 E.iii). The initial leaf begins, without heading, "Quoniam multa dubia et multi defectus inveniuntur in ordinalibus Sarum usus" (compare Risby's "Quia multi defectus reperiuntur in ordinali Sarum usus"); and although the Royal leaf contains the same authenticating information as Risby, namely that the succentor "per strictam examinationem certificavit" the

---

[6] This becomes clear only when one consults the lists of the contents in the four MSS, I.lvi–lviii.

[7] *Use of Sarum*, II.xii.

document on 8 March 1278, the contents of the bifolia differ enough from Frere's text to make plain that what he printed was *a*, rather than an authoritative, version of these changes. The same is true of another, more substantial, witness, an early fourteenth-century Sarum breviary, later (probably early in the fifteenth century) taken to Scotland, where numerous additions were made; now Edinburgh, University Library 27. Its account starts "Hic subnotantur quidam defectus in omnibus fere ordinalibus ... scrutantur ad instanciam amicorum" (fol. 230), and continues with a rather different format, one more appropriate for the heading used here, *articuli* (rather than *addiciones*): many of the matters covered begin "Quesitum est quale," and some of the responses are couched in the first person plural ("Nos dicimus" and the like). The main points about this *examinatio* of 1278, in whatever form it is transcribed, are that it makes clear (1) that liturgical practice – admittedly, in details of less than the greatest magnitude – was frequently under review at Salisbury; (2) that the results of such reviews were likely to be incorporated piecemeal, and therefore that multiple accounts of the results might exist; (3) that when enough details that had been found wanting had been revised, there may quite logically have been pressure to have drawn up some codification of all of them in a more systematic way. This more systematic way explains, and in substance is, what Frere called the New Ordinal.

How self-consciously, and precisely when, it appears are still matters to be determined. Something called *ordinale Wellwyk* is mentioned in manuscripts used by Frere as containing the New.[8] This must refer to Thomas de Welewick, Precentor of Salisbury 1341–43; and whether or not it constitutes a systematic collection by him of various corrections and emendations, including those in the *Addiciones*, the implication is that this work of the early 1340s is part of what is being replaced by the New Ordinal. Frere noted two framing pieces of circumstantial evidence. The first is the angry Wycliffite comment, in a treatise of about 1370, about (here modernized) "all the study and travail that men have now about Salisbury Use with a multitude of new costly portos [breviaries], antiphoners, grayles [graduals] and all other books."[9] The second is a will of 1389–90 that refers to "a missal of the new use of

---

[8] In a passage which is itself somewhat ambiguous: with respect to when the blessing of salt and water was to take place and the altar aspersed on double feasts, "secundum antiquum ordinale et ordinale Wellwyk": *Use of Sarum*, II.229.

[9] "Of Feigned Contemplative Life ...," in *The English Works of Wyclif, hitherto unprinted*, ed. F. D. Matthew, 2nd rev. edn, Early Eng. Text Soc. o.s. 74 (1902), p. 194; the treatise is now not thought to be by Wyclif. I am grateful to Anne Hudson for help in this matter.

Sarum."[10] These seemed to Frere "to point to the middle of the century as the latest date for the New Ordinal" – or rather, for something thus named, although in reality (as he notes a few pages on) "the MSS. of the New Ordinal themselves vary in fulness; and further there are a certain number of passages in the Ordinal which have not found a place" in the printed editions mentioned above.[11] The simple conclusion to be drawn from all this is that we will look in vain for a single, authoritative text of the New Ordinal; indeed, it seems possible that there may never have been such a thing, only a series of fairly extensive new rubrics collected and transcribed with general, but not complete, consistency. Before attempting to get some sense of a few of these rubrics and trying to match them with reality, we must make ourselves aware of a pitfall comparable to that of chasing *the* New Ordinal: that of supposing that the technology of printing produced *the* Sarum missal, a prime location for these new rubrics.

F. H. Dickinson's edition of the printed Sarum missal(s)

Major ways in which the New Ordinal differs from the Old should be most directly grasped by looking at rubrics of a number of later manuscript Sarum missals alongside those of the printed service books referred to by Frere: but a double methodological difficulty makes this obvious course surprisingly problematic. The first difficulty is that, although a considerable number of fifteenth-century manuscript Sarum missals survive, none is "famous" enough to have been the subject of an intensive study. We cannot use for this purpose celebrated books like the Westminster missal, Sherborne missal, or "reconstructed Carmelite missal" (see p. 331), all connected with regular houses; so a sensible course may be to select as best we can items from a variety of Sarum missals of the required period and in varying states of completeness.

The second procedural difficulty lies with the other half of the field of comparison, that of the printed service books. The "standard" editions – those regularly cited by scholars since their first appearance – by Procter and Wordsworth of the (printed) Sarum breviary and by

---

[10] Quoted in Bradshaw and Wordsworth, *Lincoln Cath. Statutes*, III.841.

[11] *Use of Sarum*, II.xxii, xxv. We would do well to keep in mind a major factor never mentioned by Frere: the massive upheaval within the cathedral that must have attended the heightening of the crossing tower and addition of the spire in the years around 1330 (the dates cannot be exactly determined: see T. Cocke in *Salisbury Cathedral: Perspectives on Architectural History*, Roy. Commn. Hist. Monuments (London 1993), p. 10). William Golding's novel *The Spire* (1964) is a fine analysis of the human cost of such an audacious project.

Dickinson of the (printed) Sarum missal, are notoriously complicated to get around in.[12] The former will be considered later (p. 425); at the moment the object is to understand how Dickinson's edition, which appeared in fascicules over the long period 1861–83, can be most effectively used as showing the final state of the Sarum mass liturgy (its bearing on the study of the early Sarum Use was considered in chapter 10). When Dickinson began his labors, in 1855, there was no workable "modern" edition of any complete English medieval liturgical book. His preface (written probably in 1873) gives three reasons for the undertaking: to throw light on the history of the (Anglican) Book of Common Prayer, to gain insight into "the religious practices of our forefathers," and to provide assistance in making out "the Ritual and Services of the early Church" – the third being singled out as that "which principally guided this effort."[13]

In fact, there turns out to be a fourth emphasis, a comparison of all the (then) known printed editions of the Sarum missal; and it is this that makes the work so difficult to use. For the medium of printing adds two dimensions beyond the obvious one of a major new technology. One is commercial: the early printers competing with each other for customers. The other, not unrelated to the first, is a tension between the thrust of printing in general, which is to produce vastly more uniform texts than is likely with manuscript books, and the desire for "new and improved" versions of whatever is at hand. So Dickinson's observation that "the editions subsequent to A.D. 1500 ... are more full of Rubrics than those before," may refer either to liturgical clarifications and amplifications produced by some, presumably competent, authority, or to a printer's desire to purvey a product superior to those of his competitors.[14] Which dimension accounts for any specific detail (if not both simultaneously) is almost impossible to ascertain in the great majority of cases.

---

[12] It seems ungrateful to complain about works which cost their editors a great deal of labor and which have been so widely used; but it may hearten beginning students who find themselves mired in the complex layouts of both these editions, as also of Frere's *Use of Sarum*, to know that they are not alone. A study of why many scholarly editions of the second half of the 19th cent. seem to be laid out in such complicated ways (and not only in England) would be a useful undertaking.

[13] *SMD*, p. i. Dickinson was a prominent Tractarian layman in Somerset, but no Ritualist; his preface goes on to advocate learning "what we can of the modes of worship of our forefathers ... in the books of this country, rather than from books which contain the traditions of foreign lands."

[14] Dickinson alludes to the *Ordo servandus per sacerdotem in celebratione missae sine cantu et sine ministris* compiled by the papal master of ceremonies Johannes Burchard (Rome 1498) as a possible influence in "the development of Ritual about 1500" (p. x), but this seems improbable as far as England is concerned.

The relevance of this for our present enquiry is that any notion that there was one standard printed Sarum missal must be regarded as a fiction – despite that being the natural inference to be drawn from Legg's using Dickinson's edition as "Sarum" *simpliciter* in his magnificent textual apparatus of 1897 (see p. 358), and also from the obvious comparison with the first Book of Common Prayer, 1549, intended to make possible (and enforce) uniformity of use. The bibliographical information (dates, printers, modern owners) for the fifty-six editions printed between 1487 and 1534 laid out in the last of Dickinson's six prefatory appendices makes it plain that each edition should ideally be regarded as an independent artefact.[15] He decided that there was a meaningful division of all of these into four or five "Classes," and that it would therefore be justified to include a single representative of each class in the textual apparatus. The result is that the witnesses represented are primarily those of editions printed at Venice in 1494, Rouen in 1497, Paris in 1515, Paris in 1526, and apparently London in 1501; the Paris 1526 is taken as more or less the base text.[16] A further, and critical, complication is that two editions of the Sarum gradual were also consulted, though bibliographical details are not supplied for them; this is specially unfortunate because in the apparatus they often form a class by themselves, one which tends to contain fuller rubrics than any of the classes of missals.[17] Information from them, and also from Sarum processionals, of which at least eight editions were printed between 1508 and 1532, has sometimes to be combined with that from the missals if we are to get a full sense of any particular service.[18] All this explains why there is no one book that we sensibly take as *the* Sarum missal, even in printed form as represented by Dickinson's edition. We may, then, find it more helpful to look at some features drawn from a variety of late manuscript missals (and, to a lesser extent, office books) and hope that they will aggregate into something like a coherent sense of the final form of what, by the time of the printed books, is regarded

---

[15] There were seven more editions from 1554 to 1557, during the Marian Reaction.

[16] This summary risks over-simplification of the complicated and often unclear discussion on pp. xvi–xx of Dickinson's preface and the clotted information about size, numbers of leaves, and order of contents in the six appendices with which it closes. My intent here is merely to furnish a guide to what Dickinson provided, not to take account of current information about early printed Sarum books, which is of course much greater, and more accurate, than his.

[17] Dickinson knew of three editions of the Sarum graduals, 1527, 1528, and 1532, all printed in Paris; they are included in his pioneering *List of Printed Service Books, according to the Ancient Uses of the Anglican Church* (London 1850; originally published in *The Ecclesiologist*), p. 9. Pages 15–19 of the same work list printed Sarum missals, in a form in some ways more comprehensible than in his edition of the missal.

[18] Dickinson, *List*, pp. 21–22.

as the Sarum Use – always keeping in mind that the books themselves do not manifest absolute uniformity. The first is a curious rubric about the use of English at two places in the mass liturgy.

The *lingua materna* rubric

One of the most distinctive features of a number of late medieval Sarum missals is the presence, in either or both of two places, of a rubric specifying certain words to be said *lingua materna*. The first is at the procession preceding the principal (in later terminology, high) mass on Sundays and great feasts, as described in the printed processionals as well as in printed, and a number of manuscript, missals. The rubric reads that after the procession has reached the rood figure in the church the priest turns "ad populum et dicat in lingua materna sic": the words that follow being the outline of a bidding prayer – for church and king, archbishops and bishops "et specialiter pro episcopo nostro N. et pro decano vel rectore huius Ecclesiae, scilicet in ecclesiis parrochialibus, et pro terra sancta, pro pace ecclesiae et terrae, et regina et suis liberis. Et cetera more solito."[19] Then, after an exchange of versicles and responses with the choir and a concluding collect, "Item conversus ad populum dicat sacerdos in lingua materna oremus pro animabus N. et N. more solito," after which follows, in Latin, the *De profundis* and associated formulas. This rubric appears as early as the mid-1380s, in the fine missal of William Beauchamp of Bergavenny (now Oxford, Trinity College 8); in one used at Maldon church in Essex (now BL Harley 2787); and, not much later, in those used at Colwich in Staffordshire (now BL Harley 4919) and at St Botolph Aldgate, London (now Oxford, Christ Church 87).[20] It is clearly not a regional variant, and the mention of parish churches shows that it is intended to apply far beyond Salisbury cathedral.

The other *lingua materna* rubric is found in connection with the Sarum Feast of Relics (which, as mentioned earlier, was transferred in 1319 from its previous September 15th date to the Sunday following the Translation of Becket). The language here is that after the procession returns to the church – from where, is not stated – "ibique legantur nomina reliquiarum in lingua materna; et interim abluantur ibi reliquiae,

---

[19] This is the wording as printed in *Sarum Processional*, p. 6 (mainly from the Rouen 1508 edition); cf. *SMD*, c. 37**. In *Use of Sarum*, II.321, the rubric appears somewhat differently, and specifies that in parish churches this devotion comes not after a procession (there might well not be one) but after the Gospel, "ante aliquod altare in ecclesia uel in pulpito ad hoc constituto."

[20] Evidence for dating Trinity Oxford 8 is laid out in Sandler, *Gothic MSS*, no. 144.

choro sequente."[21] This is found in an equally wide range of manuscript missals, such as the St Botolph Aldgate book mentioned above, one having some connection with Oxford (now Oxford, Pembroke College 1, which also contains the bidding prayer rubric), and one that offers a particularly striking case, an early fifteenth-century Sarum missal apparently used at Meath in Ireland (there is a mass for St Finnian, 12 December, ranked as a double feast; now Lambeth Palace 213).[22] This rubric about the washing of relics must come, like that for the bidding prayer during the preliminary devotions, from (some version of) the New Ordinal, a compilation which we may come to think is as noteworthy for its awareness of the extendability of Sarum liturgy as for its sometimes fussy excess of details.

Mass(es) *in capitulo*

Another case of a rubric showing awareness of the spread of the Sarum rite far beyond its original cathedral context is that about the mass *in capitulo*, most often prescribed for the feast of St Sabina on August 29th. This is the secondary (albeit older) feast for that day, the Decollation of John the Baptist being primary; so it makes some sense to provide for an alternative site for her mass. This is specified in the heading for her feast in as early a witness as the Crawford missal (but not in the Arsenal or Bologna books) and is therefore not an innovation of the New Ordinal; but the rubric persists in later missals, including most, but not all, of the printed editions. Precisely what this means puzzled Dickinson, and is still not clear.[23] Whatever it means, it is unlikely to be applicable in parish churches. The basic form of the rubric seems to prescribe that Sabina's mass be said before terce "sicut mos est in ecclesia Sarum," but the scribe of the Colwich (Staffs.) missal was satisfied to write "in capello" (*sic*) as its location. Did priests at churches like Colwich and Maldon (mentioned above) make a mental decision that the rubric was inapplicable to their circumstances? Or did the rubric come to have another, eventually primary, meaning now lost to us?

---

[21] *Sarum Processional*, p. 150; the punctuation is the editor's. This rubric is not in the printed missals.

[22] There it is written twice, in its proper place at fol. 197 and again on fol. 222, at the end of the sanctorale. It is imperfect at the beginning, so, as is the case with many missals, there is no way of telling whether it also had the *lingua materna* rubric for the bidding prayer. The *lingua materna* here would presumably have been Irish.

[23] His 1873(?) preface (*SMD*, p. vii) includes a long note pointing out the improbability that there had been altars in the generally octagonal chapter houses of English secular cathedrals and considering other possibilities, the most plausible of which refers to an alternative name for some side altars.

When is a missal a Sarum missal? (the case of BL Add. 25588)

The two rubrics considered above, relating as they do to the mass as celebrated according to what was understood to be the Use of Sarum, raise the sizeable question of what can fairly be regarded as a Sarum missal. In a book so titled, printed at London in December of 1498, the mass for travellers has the subheading, "de sanctis tribus Regibus Coloniae," and each of the proper prayers contains the names of Jaspar, Melchior, and Baltasar.[24] This mass seems unique to the 1498 among the printed Sarum missals; Dickinson termed it "a very remarkable edition," but without explaining why.[25] One would guess that the (unknown) printer had a missal, or at least mass text, from Cologne, and included this mass as a selling feature – were it not for the fact that the same mass appears in a fifteenth-century manuscript Sarum missal (now BL Add. 25588; fol. 252) from the diocese of Norwich.[26] Its last three leaves, including those containing this mass, are in a different hand from the first part; they may have been written by the Henry Well(y)s who gave the book *huic eccclesie* (unnamed), the dedication feast of which is added to the calendar at June 5th, and who is described as chaplain to the lady Alice Wiche and John Dunstaple.[27] The other contents of these leaves have nothing in common with those in the 1498 printing; so dependence of the manuscript on the printed book for this mass text is highly unlikely.

That is one significant peculiarity of this manuscript missal. Another is the incorporation of a rubric at the feast of the Annunciation, one which shows the added degree of complication characteristic of the late Sarum rite. The thirteenth-century missals had for the most part supplied only a tract after the gradual for this March 25th feast, which almost always falls during Lent, although the Bologna manuscript adds an alleluia and the first four words of a sequence, "Ave mundi spes, Maria" – despite the fact that such forms could normally be used only if Easter fell on March 22nd through 24th (as very rarely happens;

---

[24] *SMD*, c. 891*. This is followed by the collect for a "missa alia, si quis habet devotionem, cum hac oratione, et omnia alia ut supra." This is also in the text of BL Add. 25588, discussed next.

[25] *SMD*, p. xlv; no printer is indicated, and the edition is not included in any of Dickinson's four classes.

[26] Fols 102v–3 are pictured, greatly reduced, in Hughes, *MMMO*, pl. 9, mainly to illustrate incipits for the Gloria in excelsis. The letterpress adds nothing to the brief description in *Cat. Addl. MSS 1854–75*.

[27] So the inscription on fol. 250 reads, very likely in Henry's hand – a different one from that which entered his obit on June 19th, where his donation *huic ecclesie* is noted.

even so, during the Easter octave other feasts would not usually be celebrated). In the later middle ages a feeling seems to have grown that a sequence should be sung despite the season, as is indicated by a rubric in the printed (though not, for the most part, the manuscript) missals instructing that the "Ave mundi" sequence should be used on that day, even if it is in Lent. But the sequence itself is followed by a rubric providing that meanwhile the priest and his ministers "in sedibus iuxta altare privatim dicant tractum sequentem," the text of the old tract then being given.[28] This rubric is reproduced verbatim in Add. 25588 (fol. 174); is this another indication of its eclectic character, or a detail from the New Ordinal's pool?

This missal also witnesses to another characteristic of late medieval mass liturgy in general, the provision of an increased number of votive masses. Here the one "Pro muliere pregnante" has been copied, in a somewhat later hand than the original; at its head are traces of an erased rubric, probably that which describes the hundred days' indulgence granted by (a) pope Celestine in honor of the pregnant sister for whom he composed the mass prayers. This mass commonly appears in printed Sarum missals, but the rubric about the pope only in three (1494, 1497, 1498), and of these the ending of the collect with the words "periculo secura maneat" is only in the 1497 – and in this manuscript missal.[29] If this book really was to be used by a domestic chaplain, the supplying of a prayer for a woman undergoing a difficult pregnancy may have been more a pastoral necessity than a piece of liturgical tinkering.

In the light of these three peculiarities, should we think of Henry Wells's massbook as a Sarum missal, and if so in what sense(s)? If we insist that an English secular missal must be a Sarum or York or Hereford book, then clearly this one is the first. Sarum details, all the more significant because of so little intrinsic importance, are present, such as Sabina's mass being *in capitulo* or that the alleluia on Easter Saturday should be sung by two boys in surplices.[30] Nonetheless, it carries its "Sarum" label rather lightly. Numerous entries in the calendar, some original and some added, are marked *synod.* (= *festa synodalia*), and the dedication of Norwich cathedral is present, in the original hand.[31] This Norwich guise is apparent in a number of Sarum service books, as is

---

[28] *SMD*, c. 727.

[29] This makes it all but impossible that the text of the mass for the Three Kings should have been copied from the 1498 printing, in which it alone appears, but compounds the difficulty of thinking about what model(s) might have been used by the scribe (Henry?) who copied these masses into 25588.

[30] For the latter, *SMD*, c. 379; fol. 121v of Add. 25588.

[31] The fullest indication is for Thomas of Hereford at 2 Oct., marked "Non Sarum set synod. Norwic."

illustrated clearly in a celebrated Stowe breviary, a look at which will lead us also to consider some late Sarum breviaries.

Festa synodalia

For some reason not now apparent, the diocese of Norwich had the most clearly defined group of saints' feasts which were regarded, at least by the fourteenth century, as its peculiar celebrations and which went, to a certain extent anyhow, by the collective name of *festa synodalia*. Other dioceses had such distinctive observances also, as we have seen in the case of Worcester and will go on to survey at York, Hereford, London, and Lincoln. To a slight degree the term was taken up by liturgical scholars around the turn of the nineteenth century, especially Christopher Wordsworth, whose edition of the massive Sarum breviary printed in 1531 will be our next topic. First, though, we should remark this entity – if it was any such thing – as it is alluded to in the notable witness of BL Stowe 12, a sumptuously illustrated, though badly mutilated, breviary summed up in the catalogue of Stowe manuscripts as "of Sarum use adapted to Norwich."

What is meant by this is evident through a few details from the calendar and sanctorale. The main part of the book is datable to a narrow period, 1322–25.[32] In the calendar six saints are marked *non Sarum*: Winwaloe, Felix, Botulf, Anne, Dominic, and Francis. In addition, Thomas of Hereford is included, albeit without a *non Sarum* designation, at October 2nd (his usual feast day, here wrongly called Translation; he had been canonized only in 1320), and Birinus at December 5th is marked "ix lectiones secundum Sarum." There are similar indications in the sanctorale; particularly notable is the assigning of September 15th to the Octave of the Nativity – in, presumably, the diocese of Norwich – while "festum reliquiarum apud Sarum celebratur." (It looks as though news of the 1319 decision to move the Sarum Relics feast to July had not reached the confector of this breviary.) Equally striking is the omission of Hugh of Lincoln, who had been canonized in 1220. Desire not to reflect the great saint of the neighboring diocese of Lincoln seems to balance a self-conscious degree of independence from the usages of Salisbury. As the date of this breviary, the early 1320s, is well before the emergence of the Sarum New Ordinal, so the phenomenon of *festa synodalia* cannot be connected with a fear that Sarum

---

[32] Watson, *BL Dated MSS*, no. 945, explains the dating framework; cf. Sandler, *Gothic MSS*, no. 79. There is added to it a substantial ordinal, fols 358–95, probably written c. 1380–83; not mentioned by Frere, it would be an important witness in any attempt at an edition of the New Ordinal.

books with the new and more exhaustive rubrics will carry all before them. Accounts of Norwich diocesan synods at which the necessary regulations about feasts were made do not seem to be extant. There is plenty of evidence for the continuation of the *festa synodalia* designation (sometimes just as *synod.*) into the fifteenth century, always with reference to the same saints, though not necessarily to them all. Felix and Botulf are the most characteristic, the Breton Winwaloe the most puzzling (Anne becomes a "Sarum saint" by the end of the fourteenth century).

The point at issue here is the balance that seems to have been striven for between adopting wholesale the compendiousness and convenience of the Sarum rubrics and texts and maintaining some variance, in both omission and inclusion, from the standard saints of Sarum tradition. We have in the previous chapter seen this done somewhat successfully at Exeter, where the cathedral chapter was of course secular. In the diocese of Norwich, with its cathedral chapter monastic, the desirability of some sort of liturgical identity separate from that of the monks as well as from Sarum seems to have been at least a bit of a motivating force. The most immediate reflex of this is likely to be found in office books, for the copying of a full office, even one of three lessons, into a breviary is no light matter, whether in "variant" books like the Stowe breviary or in pure(r) Sarum books.

Later Sarum breviaries

Indeed, the tendency towards elaboration of contents and complexity of structure somewhat evident in missals – a tendency apparently both reflected in and a consequence of the New Ordinal for the mass – is greatly intensified with office books.[33] Here Cranmer's famous complaint, that it often took more time to figure out and find what was to be read at any given service than to read the item, is scarcely an exaggeration. How complicated the office books have become by the end of the middle ages is underlined by the fact that the standard modern (albeit well over a century old) scholarly edition of "the" Sarum breviary is almost unbelievably difficult to use, while the two more recent works students most often turn to in pursuit of some clarity are themselves

---

[33] "Office books" is a blanket term that comprises choir breviaries (generally large-format, and noted), noted portable breviaries, portable breviaries *simpliciter* (= not noted), legendaries, and antiphonals (which tend to look like choir breviaries but lack the lessons). A few lesser types of books, like diurnals, are also included. The precise definitions and classifications of all of these falls outside the purpose of the present work.

so clotted that hope is often abandoned soon after they enter.[34] This may be unavoidable; or it may be that an interactive, web-based production, making it possible for the user to bring up various frames simultaneously, might be a way of breaking through the confusion. For our purposes, always primarily historical, it may be thought sufficient to acquire the minimum of necessary historiographical background (from both the late nineteenth and fifteenth centuries), then to look at the commonest structure for later Sarum office books, and finally to attempt to get some flavor of them by sampling a handful of their odder and/or more distinctive contents.

Procter and Wordsworth's *Breviarium ad usum Sarum*

The enthusiasm for "liturgiology" that sprang up in England around the middle of the nineteenth century was no less concerned with the daily office than with the mass. As with missals, the interest was partly bibliographical, partly rubrical. F. H. Dickinson's *List of Printed Service Books*, published in 1850 and mentioned earlier in this chapter, recorded over twenty-five printings of the Sarum breviary between 1493 and 1544 (and almost that many from 1554 to 1557), along with four of the York breviary, one of the Hereford, and one from Aberdeen. As early as 1842–43 Charles Seager published two fascicules of a proposed edition of the Sarum book, but apparently lost interest after his conversion to Roman Catholicism in the latter year.[35] When, thirty or so years later, Francis Procter and Christopher Wordsworth undertook the very considerable task of producing a complete edition, they chose for this purpose the "Great Breviary" printed by Chevallon and Regnault in Paris in 1531.[36] This folio volume contains the lessons at

---

[34] The edition is that of Procter and Wordsworth, 1879–86, discussed more fully below. The modern works are J. B. L. Tolhurst's *Introduction to the English Monastic Breviaries*, HBS 40 (1943; actually vol. VI of his edition of the *Hyde Breviary* (see p. 220) – the fact that it is clearly limited to the monastic office is frequently overlooked by desperate students – and A(ndrew) Hughes's *Medieval Manuscripts for Mass and Office: a Guide to their Organization and Terminology* (Toronto 1982), esp. pp. 50–80 and 160–244, plus a number of greatly reduced facsimile pages, most notably eight folios from the Ranworth antiphonal (see p. 524).

[35] *Portiforii seu Breviarii Sarisburiensis fasciculus primus/secundus* (London 1842–43). Seager became a notable Orientalist.

[36] Procter (1812–1905) was a scholarly country parson who in 1855 published a monument of Anglican liturgical scholarship, his *History of the Book of Common Prayer, with a Rationale of its Offices*; he lived to see the still-standard revision and edition of this, W. H. Frere's (hence the common nickname "Procter and Frere"), published in 1901. For the much younger Wordsworth (1848–1938), see p. 497.

matins at what is often their fullest length, and in that sense, and also in its inclusions of services for the *nova festa* often printed separately, it can be taken to represent the most complete, and most complex, form of the book(s) containing the later Sarum office.[37] Both the completeness and the complexity are amply mirrored in Procter and Wordsworth's edition.

To begin with, the volume issued first, in 1879, reasonably enough contains the psalter and the common of saints, but is called on the title page "Fasciculus II." A short, straightforward introduction of some ten pages is devoted mostly to explaining the constituent parts of the breviary. Column rather than page numbers are used, and there are brief indexes of psalms and of the hymns and sequences found in this fascicule. The second volume to appear, 1882, is called "Fasciculus I" because it contains the matter which came first in the 1531 edition, notably the calendar and proper of time. The general introduction which was promised in the preceding volume is postponed until the final one, but there is an index covering both fascicules I and II. Column numbers are retained, here in Roman numerals – 1,536 of them, so that, for example, the seventh lesson for the twenty-fourth Sunday after Trinity is found on column mccccxliii. The primary matter of the third volume (1886) is the proper of saints (cols 1–1120, now in Arabic numerals), concluding with the *explicit* of the Chevallon-Regnault edition.[38] Finally there are fifteen indexes, sometimes paginated, sometimes columnated, all highly useful once one has mastered the way they are presented.[39] But the chief feature of the third volume is the provision, in place of the earlier-promised general introduction (which "has proved beyond our powers"), of extensive lists of printed editions of Sarum books "from

[37] There were two prior printings of this "Great Breviary," 1496 and 1516, one of a Great Legenda, 1518, and one of the Sarum antiphonal, 1519 (in two vols, only the winter volume being extant). On the *nova festa*, see Pfaff, *New Liturg. Feasts*. Extensive work in progress by S. L. Reames is showing that lessons are sometimes fuller in other Sarum breviaries, including in manuscript, than in the 1531 edition.

[38] This is not quite the end of the text, for there is printed next a critical edition of the brief *Accentuarius* of long and short syllables that appears in more than a dozen printed Sarum missals and breviaries, and two sets of lessons for the Translation of Hugh, taken from MSS in St John's College, Cambridge. The latter are the only part of a proposed selection of *Festa Synodalia* promised in 1879 to be provided; the patience of the Cambridge University Press may have been wearing thin.

[39] For example, the third index, "index generalis in rubricas tertii hujus fasciculi," pp. xlv–xlviii, contains "some of the contributions which we were able to make towards an annotated edition" ("To the Reader," p. xvii), others being in the "Index generalis in priores duo fasciculos breviarii Sarum" of vol. I, cols. mccccxcix–mdxxxvi, where the heading states "Accedunt definitiones quaedam in lingua materna." This contains quite helpful definitions, in English, of such terms as "coucher" and "Deus omnium."

the papers of Henry Bradshaw ... with notes by the editors."[40] These lists (which do not, however, include missals) are among the most substantial remains of the literary work of Bradshaw, who was celebrated for his disinclination to publish almost as much as for his learning and for the influence he had on a younger generation, and reflect his vast bibliographical knowledge.

A fifteenth-century attempt at clarification: Maidstone's *Directorium*

It is not surprising that out of this convoluted mass of material it is difficult to get a coherent idea of how any given Sarum office, or even any one manuscript Sarum breviary, operated. To fault Procter and Wordsworth for this is not entirely fair, for both the daily office and the book(s) containing it had by the fifteenth century swollen to proportions that tended to obscure the basic structure. The structure of the offices themselves remained unchanged, but came to be so encrusted with memorials and substitutions and provisos about occurrence and concurrence that many users found a separate, often annual, guide-volume indispensable. The general name for such a volume was in Latin *directorium*, in English "pica" (sometimes shortened to "pie' or "pye") – as a vernacular word, traced in the *Oxford English Dictionary* to the late fifteenth century and there defined as "A collection of rules ... to show how to deal (under each of 35 possible variations in the date of Easter) with the concurrence of more than one office on the same day, accurately indicating the manner of commemorating, or of putting off till another time, the Saint's days, etc., occurring in the ever-changing seasons of Lent, Easter, Whitsuntide, and the Octave of the Trinity." Because the *OED*'s examples are drawn from printed sources, its citations are the 1487 and 1497 printings of a slightly older work titled *Ordinale Sarum, sive Directorium Sacerdotum: (Liber quem Pica Sarum vulgo vocitat clerus) auctore Clemente Maydeston, sacerdote.* Maydeston (Maidstone) was a Bridgettine monk (for the liturgy of that fifteenth-century order, see p. 529) who, well before before his death in 1456, compiled this laborious directory as, in Simon Walker's succinct words, "a revision of the existing Sarum ordinal which corrected errors and paid particular attention to the liturgical anomalies surrounding the feast of Corpus Christi. A later work, the *Defensorium directorii*, justified at greater length the practice set out in this treatise, and Maidstone also

---

[40] *Sarum Breviary*, III.xli-cxxix; see G. W. Prothero, *A Memoir of Henry Bradshaw* (London 1888), pp. 264–74, and Pfaff, *M.R. James*, pp. 56–8 and 177–78.

contributed to a composite commentary on the rubrics of the Sarum use known, in its printed editions, as the *Crede mihi*."[41] All three of these works were edited around the turn of the twentieth century by Christopher Wordsworth, the two later ones in 1894, just after he had completed his labors on the edition of the Sarum breviary, and the *Directorium* seven years later.[42]

It matters to get the dates of Maidstone's works correct, and to separate their original forms from the early printings, because the *Directorium* came to be regarded, quite unfoundedly, as possessing an almost official character. Indeed, it seems to have been so regarded by Cranmer, whose famous complaint is specifically launched against the "nombre and hardnes of the rules called the pie, and the manyfolde chaunginges of the seruice." The circumstances in which Maidstone compiled his work are those of the 1430s and 1440s: with respect, obviously, not to printed but to manuscript breviaries, books characterized therefore by variety as well as by the shadow of the uniformity implied by the New Ordinal. Consequently, we need next to pass under review a small selection of such breviaries with respect to their shape and to some curious elements.

The shape of later manuscript Sarum breviaries

Such a plethora of Sarum office books survives from the fourteenth and, especially, fifteenth centuries that it will be possible, and probably useful, to consider here only a small fraction. All are large, but in different ways. Their size depends on a number of factors besides the actual dimensions of the page and of its written space: apart from the obvious ones of height of script, amount of music, and illustration, the most substantial are the quantity of rubric and the length of lessons. If the breviary does not cover the entire year its bulk will of course be reduced, and this tendency – to have separate volumes for winter (*pars hiemalis*) and summer (*pars estivalis*) – becomes quite marked, especially with the printed breviaries.[43] The majority of manuscript breviaries are in the one-volume format. An interesting exception is University College, Oxford MS 22, the winter part of a fifteenth-century Sarum

---

[41] S. Walker in *ODNB* 36.163.

[42] In, respectively, *The Tracts of Clement Maydeston, with the Remains of Caxton's Ordinale*, HBS 7 (1894) and, with W. Cooke (who had died in 1894), the *Directorium*, with the full title as given above, 2 vols, HBS 20, 22 (both 1901). Full bibliographical detail for the complicated *Tracts* volume, esp. about the early printed editions, is provided in Ward, *Pubs HBS*, pp. 32–33.

[43] The point of division is not uniform, but the commonest is Advent through Lent, Eastertide through rest of the liturgical year. Breviaries in four volumes, the later Roman Catholic practice, are not encountered.

breviary. This contains an inscription (fol. 338v) stating that according to the will of John Bristowe (possibly the person of that name who was a priest-vicar at the collegiate church of St Stephen, Westminster, in 1463) it is to be passed on to the holder of the stall formerly held by him, and in consequence his soul to be prayed for.[44] This is a very plain book, decorated with only the simplest of red or blue capitals; even so, it runs to 385 folios, with a sanctorale extending only from 30 November to 25 March, and without calendar or psalter – the contents of which would have therefore to be supplied from another book.

Given that each such breviary needs to contain a great deal of material, there tends inevitably to be a trade-off among several of the factors mentioned in the previous paragraph – an added factor, of perhaps the greatest importance to modern students, being that of legibility. Some books are written in such tiny hands that it is barely conceivable that offices of great length and complexity should regularly have been read out of them. This factor exacerbates the problems inherent in the fortuituous nature of manuscript survival in something of the same way as is posed by the existence of de luxe service books: the degree of actual use one can imagine they received. This means that, with few exceptions, it is next to impossible to state exactly what the totality of the Sarum office is for any specific day. Indeed, it is much more sensible to think of the office altogether as possessing four dimensions of decreasing degrees of uniformity: (1) the structure, in which there is no noteworthy degree of variation; (2) the rubrics, which in theory should correspond to what is in the New Ordinal but in practice show considerable degrees of variability; (3) the contents, in terms not only of which saints appear in the sanctorale (and, within that, which have proper offices as distinct from offices drawn, wholly or in large part, from the common of saints) but also of the amount and nature of supplementary material included – elements like votive offices, select masses, and supplementary devotions; and (4) the actual texts, mainly in the lessons for saints' days but to a degree also in the responsories at matins and occasionally even in the capitula at the day hours.[45] In short, anything like a critical edition, in the sense of one which establishes a base text and records variants from it, is with the breviaries that concern us almost a contradiction in terms. As with the mass, we must content ourselves by noticing a few distinctive features in some of the office books.

---

[44] *Biog. Reg. Oxf.*, I.269; this is the likeliest of the five John Bristowes listed there.

[45] Variability in the matins lessons for the sanctorale has been studied several times by S. L. Reames, notably in "*Mouvance* and Interpreation in Late-Medieval Latin: the Legend of St Cecilia in British Breviaries," in *Medieval Literature: Text and Interpretation*, ed. T. W. Machan (Binghamton, NY 1991), pp. 159–89.

Matins in the evening on great summer feasts

An odd rubric, worthy of mention because of its self-consciousness about a matter of no great importance, appears in many late breviaries after first vespers on Trinity Sunday. It specifies that on certain summer-time feasts – Trinity Sunday, Corpus Christi, Nativity of John the Baptist, Peter and Paul, Translation of Becket, and Relics (plus the Patronal and Dedication feasts, if falling in that period) – matins is to be said "hora vesperarum secundum usum Sarisburiensis ecclesiae": that is, at the conclusion of vespers, which at that time of year in southern England would be still in daylight.[46] This "anticipation," to use the later term, of matins would presumably ensure a good night's sleep as those great feasts dawned; but why this should have been regarded as a peculiar feature of Sarum use is inexplicable, as is why this relaxation stops with the Sunday after July 7th (the next occasion of comparable magnitude would have been the Assumption, August 15th). It must be dated to after 1319, when the Feast of Relics was moved to July. The rubric is found in, for example, the sumptuously illustrated breviary, dating from about 1400, owned by Henry Chichele, archbishop of Canterbury 1414–43 (Lambeth Palace 69, fol. 146), and it is pleasant to think of that busy prelate's benefiting from its permissiveness.

The Sarum Lenten litanies

In the second, *Psalterium*, volume of the Procter and Wordsworth edition of the 1531 breviary, after the ordinary of the office come two items: the seven pentitential psalms, with no indication as to their use save an assignment of one of the deadly sins to each, and a litany for use daily during Lent. This litany is invariable in its first part, through the list of apostles, and in its last and largest part, extensive sets of deprecations, petitions, and collects (much of this part was retained by Cranmer in his 1544 English litany); but the selection of saints in the other three categories varies each weekday: twelve to a category, making a total of seventy-two each of martyrs, confessors, and virgins. It would be a useful activity to collate every such list as they are encountered in manuscript office books; here we must just notice the general shape and a small number of variants from the lists as printed in 1531.[47]

---

[46] *Sarum Breviary*, I.mxlvii.
[47] The litanies are in *Sarum Breviary*, II.250–59. A possible model is the kind of treatment offered in M. Lapidge's *Anglo-Saxon Litanies of Saints*, HBS 106 (1991), but none of the forty-six edited there has daily variations, though some of the lists are immensely long.

Most of the saints listed are, as would be expected, from the first
eight centuries or so of Christianity (many of them Frankish), but creative intelligence is discernible in the additions of roughly twenty British
figures. The only one who died after 1000 is Becket, intruded into first
place among Tuesday's martyrs.[48] There is a strong whiff of the tenth-
century monastic revival, especially in its Æthelwoldian-Winchester
strain, among the names: Dunstan, (bishop) Oswald, Æthelwold himself; Etheldreda, Ermenilda, and Sexburga (abbesses of Ely), and also
Edith of Wilton; Swithun and Birinus (both of them connected with
the Old Minster/cathedral at Winchester), Grimbald and Judoc (great
figures at the New Minster/Hyde abbey). Otherwise there are just two
very early figures, Alban and Augustine of Canterbury, three from
the Celtic fringe, Patrick, Winnoc, and Petroc, and three from early
England, Cuthbert, Botulph, and Ald(h)elm. (The last-named may be
of special Sarum interest, as we have seen (p. 362), but not necessarily.) Names surprising by their absence include the martyrs Oswald,
Edmund, Kenelm, and perhaps Ælfheah, possibly Erkenwald among
confessors, Cuthburga and Ethelburga among virgins.

The obvious questions raised by both inclusions and exclusions are
three: who made the decisions; were they made all at one time (and
therefore after 1173, when Becket was canonized) or in stages; and how
were the various saints allocated to specific days – and also (as a matter of speculation) which saints may they have bumped? None of these
questions can be answered here conclusively, but it should be noted that
among the total of 216 saints very few have any place in Sarum, or other
English, liturgies. The original nucleus of the lists looks to be Frankish
(mostly pre-Carolingian), and could have come into England at any
time from the ninth century on. Particularly intriguing among the later
entries are the last three confessors of the week: Leonard (who, as we
have seen, comes to be greatly popular in the early twelfth century;
p. 359), Athanasius, and Oswald of Worcester. Is the inclusion of Athanasius merely a kind of afterthought, and does that of Oswald represent
anything beyond completion of the roster of monastic-reform heroes?

These "Sarum litanies," as they are often called without other
qualification (for example, by James in his catalogues and Ker in the
Medieval Manuscripts in British Libraries volumes), offer an opportunity to assess the balance between the growing uniformity discernible
as a consequence of widespread adoption of something recognized as

---

[48] The intruded character is obvious in the printed lists, where there are thirteen martyrs
for Tuesday; by contrast, in Edinburgh Univ. Lib. 27 (discussed below) Becket's presence has been accommodated by the dropping of Vitus.

"Sarum Use" and points of individuality. Some such points may be purely accidental, but others may suggest something helpful about the places they were used or their users, or furnish a clue as to affinities with other manuscripts. A considerable set of such variances can be seen in the early fourteenth-century Sarum breviary noticed above (p. 415), taken in perhaps the early fifteenth century to Scotland, where numerous additions were made; now Edinburgh, University Library 27. Its "Sarum litanies," in the original hand (fol. 280v), are notable in listing Edmund (of East Anglia; a glaring omission in the 1531 printed list) as first among the martyrs on Saturday, supplying Edmund (Rich) as the twelfth of that day's confessors, and similarly including Milburga (associated with Shropshire, especially Wenlock) as the last of its virgins. There is much other dis- and re-location, but these three details will suffice to show that the litanies in this manuscript reflect a stage datable to between 1247, when Edmund Rich was canonized, and 1319 (the Sarum Feast of Relics is in the calendar here still on September 15th). A pair of variations in another manuscript is perhaps more amusing than instructive. In the early fifteenth-century breviary belonging to Coltishall church in Norfolk (Durham, Univ. Lib. Cosin V.1.3, fol. 338), among Wednesday's confessors Wulfstan appears in place of Wulfran (Wulfram) and Austroberta in place of Ausbert, thus changing that saint's sex as well as name.

A further set of instances that should be noted comes from a breviary, of the later fourteenth century and perhaps from the diocese of Norwich, where after the weekday litanies another list is supplied, as though for Sunday (Liverpool Cathedral, Radcliffe Collection 37, fol. 240). This contains twenty-one each of martyrs and confessors and twenty-two of virgins. Among the martyrs Becket is thirteenth, and the confessors end with Edmund, Richard, and Hugh; but the striking inclusion, perhaps accounting for the "extra" virgin, is Anne, placed first in that category. Anne has been notably absent from the other lists reviewed, and her inclusion here may suggest an up-to-date character about the list in the Liverpool manuscript, though we noticed her, marked *non Sarum*, in the Stowe 12 breviary. Correspondingly, the fact that she never makes the printed lists may imply that the manuscript model(s) for them were not of the most recent vintages.[49] The question raised by

[49] Possible corroboration comes from the 1508 *Processionale ad usum … Sarum*, the printing edited by W. G. Henderson in 1882. In place of the daily Lenten litanies of the breviary it contains litanies for Wednesdays and Fridays throughout Lent, with three saints in each category. In addition to many of the English figures found in the breviary lists, the processional's saints include Kenelm and Oswald among martyrs, Edmund and Richard among confessors, and the distinctively Sarum Cuthburga (see p. 381): *Sarum Processional*, pp. 32–41.

this apparently tiny detail is worth pondering further, especially in the light of the next rubric to be considered, one that takes into account the names given to altars in churches of varied dedications.

"Ubi dedicata est ecclesia in honore ..."

The treatment of first vespers is a perennial irritant among Sarum rubrics. The matter arises particularly when two feasts of some importance fall on adjacent days: does second vespers of the earlier feast take precedence over first vespers of the later one, or vice versa? Four such cases are dealt with by rubrics in the 1531 Great Breviary, those of Anne (26 July, following James on the 25th), the Decollation of John the Baptist (29 August, following Augustine on the 28th), Michaelmas (29 September, preceding Jerome on the 30th), and, as a somewhat different problem, Andrew (30 November, for when the next day is Advent I). At all four the wording is similar but with notable variation. On July 26th first vespers of Anne's feast are to be said "ubi dedicata est ecclesia, vel capella, vel altare in honore eiusdem," with a memorial of James; otherwise, the second vespers of James takes precedence, with memorial of Anne. Similar wording appears for August 28th, when second vespers would be of Augustine except "ubi vero dedicata est ecclesia [no mention of chapel or altar] Decollationis sancti Iohannis Baptistae," and for Jerome, who gets first vespers unless the church is dedicated to Michael. For Andrew, by contrast, there is no first vespers on November 29th if that day has been Advent I, even in a church dedicated to the apostle.[50] Of course a great many England medieval churches were dedicated to Andrew and Michael, so the rubric would be useful there. Many were also dedicated to John the Baptist, though not to his Decollation; so if the wording of the rubric is taken literally, it is in practice meaningless. The case of Anne is rather different, her cult being much more recent in popularity, as has frequently been mentioned in these pages. Roughly thirty pre-Reformation English churches were dedicated to her, but as the rubric specifies that it applies to chapels and altars as well, it might have been of rather wide application.[51]

Now, it is almost certain that Salisbury cathedral never had a chapel or altar dedicated to St Anne, and therefore that this one rubric cannot have arisen because of a particular circumstance there.[52] Furthermore,

---

[50] Respectively, *Sarum Breviary*, III.542, 745, 879, 19.

[51] Thirty is the figure given in F. Arnold-Forster, *Studies in Church Dedications*, 3 vols (London 1899), III.3: a work of pre-scientific character but not yet supplanted.

[52] A slight possibility of a chapel of St Anne over the southeast gateway of the close is discussed, and convincingly dismissed, in C. Wordsworth, *Ceremonies and Processions of the Cathedral Church of Salisbury* (Cambridge 1901), p. 303.

these rubrics commonly appear in manuscript breviaries (sometimes at only three feasts, more often all four) from at least the late fourteenth century on, as in the large choir breviary of that date probably given by a member of the Hyde family to the parish church of Denchworth in Berkshire (Bodl. Lat liturg. b.14). Other instances abound.[53] It seems likely that these rubrics reflect the same mentality as in the New Ordinal, one greatly concerned with minutiae. It is therefore not surprising that much attention is paid also to the classification of feasts.

Classification of feasts

At several places in the documents Frere presented as "The Use of Sarum" the feasts of the liturgical year are listed in accordance with a scheme of classification that must be noticed, but not ossified.[54] The simplest classification, implicit before it becomes explicit, arises from the distinction between (in secular uses) feasts of three and of nine lessons at matins. Ramifications are discernible as early as the late tenth century, but it does not seem to be until roughly the mid-thirteenth that liturgical documents – most often, calendars – regularly witness to another principle of classification, one based on whether antiphons at the office were sung in full before as well as after the psalms and canticles to which they belonged. Such "double" feasts could in turn be divided into greater and lesser (or "simple"), and each of those categories subdivided. Futher principles of classification were occasions on which the Te Deum was sung at matins; those (not necessarily the same by any means) when the Creed was used at mass; those at which the matins invitatory was sung by one, two, three, or even four cantors; those at which an exposition of the gospel for the day is read at matins; and those at which the choir is "ruled" (*cum regimine chori*). Octaves naturally signalled feasts of the greatest importance. (Another obvious principle, that of vesture – how many albs, copes, and the like – is employed mainly in monastic contexts.)

Most of these principles are at work in the final forms of Sarum books, as is easily seen in the modern editions of the printed service books.

[53] References to eight other MS office books are given in my article "Prescription and Reality in the rubrics of Sarum Rite Service Books," in *Intellectual Life in the Middle Ages: Essays pres. to Margaret Gibson*, ed. L. Smith and B. Ward (London 1992), pp. 197–205 at 200 (repr. in Pfaff, *LCSSME*, no XII); a lot of what is said in that piece needs to be revised in the light of later investigations.

[54] Discussions of the subject tend to be rather abstract and to imply a semipiternality and permanence which were rarely the case: for example, Harper, *Forms and Orders*, pp. 53–54, and Hughes, *MMMO*, p. 275.

They come to be deployed only gradually, however, and it is instructive to compare a few easily accessible manuscript service books with the schemes laid out in the Old Ordinal and in the 1278 *Addiciones*. The calendar of the Crawford missal, perhaps of the 1260s (see p. 395), seems to distinguish only feasts of three (with or without Te Deum) and nine lessons, and marks with a cross the twelve occasions that seem to be the greatest feasts. That of the Arsenal book, roughly a generation later (p. 357), gives indications about use of the Creed (sometimes even for feasts of three lessons), and, incidentally, does not agree in all of Crawford's gradings.[55] That in the early fourteenth-century Edinburgh Univ. MS 27 breviary, discussed above, has few gradings in the original hand (many have been added subsequently), but does introduce the term *duplex* for such feasts as the Purification and Annunciation. *Duplex* seems to be the main criterion in the lists contained in the ordinals and the consuetudinary.

A possibly significant detail in the Risby ordinal's text of the 1278 *Addiciones* complicates the already murky picture. This is the provision that "In sexto decretalium uolumus statuimus et precipimus quod festa sanctorum Gregorii, Ambrosii, Augustini et Ieronymi ... pro duplicibus festis solempnizentur."[56] As the "Sext" referred to here, the *Liber sextus decretalium*, was promulgated only in 1298 (by Boniface VIII), this passage cannot have formed part of the proceedings twenty years earlier. (This is another reminder of the trickiness of relying heavily on the Risby manuscript of the early fourteenth century for solid information about the thirteenth.) Furthermore, the notion that Sarum gradings were affected by papal decretals requires scrutiny. In the Edinburgh 27 breviary's calendar only Gregory is marked duplex, while in the composite calendar from the printed missals in Dickinson's edition Augustine is still only ranked at nine lessons with *invitatorium triplex*. And some manuscripts even of the fifteenth century ignore the matter entirely, as is the case with the Salisbury cathedral MS 148, the processional written around 1445, where in its original form the calendar has no double feasts whatever.[57] Considered over a span of centuries – here, roughly

---

[55] Notably, that Dunstan and Aldhelm have nine lessons in Crawford, three (by default) in Arsenal.

[56] *Use of Sarum*, II.206, with footnote reference "Lib. iii, cap. [*recte* titulus] xxii": that is, *Liber sextus decretalium* of *Corpus Iuris Canonici*, ed. E. Friedberg, 2 vols (Leipzig 1881), II.1059.

[57] This is the MS on which Wordsworth based his *Ceremonies and Processions of the Cathedral Church of Salisbury*. All feasts are marked at either three or nine lessons, some of the latter with the invitatory status noted; only the two additions, of the Visitation and the Translation of Osmund (canonized 1456), are marked *maius duplex*, as well as having nine lessons; the third addition, Osmund's Deposition, is marked *principale*.

mid-thirteenth to mid-sixteenth – the subject of grading, even in a Use as supposedly highly refined as that of Sarum, is handled so inconsistently that further instances of complicated variants may be thought not worthy of individual notice. How close the system (if it can be so called) comes to toppling over from its own weight is shown by the next topic to be looked at.

The *Rubrica magna* and its effect

The concern of the New Ordinal with tiny details in the operation of the liturgical year is perhaps most clearly seen in the final office rubric we must look at, the magnificently overblown *Rubrica magna*. A full sixteen columns of the Procter and Wordsworth edition of the 1531 Sarum breviary are taken up with the "Rubrica magna de dominicis et festivitatibus," much the longest of all the Sarum rubrics (indeed, possibly the longest in the whole of medieval liturgy). It is there placed between the offices for the First Sunday after Trinity and the *Historia Regum*, the matins lessons for ordinary days in the early summer. For the most part it aims to sort out potentialities of conflict at vespers between Sundays (or the full Saturday office of the Virgin Mary) and feast days when they are either concurrent or adjacent.[58]

A passage both typical and useful for our purposes is the provision that in years when there are twenty-seven Sundays after Trinity, and consequently when two Sunday masses have to be supplied (there being provision for only twenty-five such Sundays in most missals), one mass should be that for the Sunday within the Octave of the Assumption and the other for the Sunday "infra Octavas Dedicationis Ecclesiae Sarum, ut videlicet si Festum Sancti Hieronymi sit in crastino Octavarum Dedicationis translatum quod fuit anno Domini millesimo .ccc. lxxx–iii." The circumstance envisaged happens only rarely, in those years when Easter falls on the earliest possible date, March 22nd: which was the case in 1383 (the times before and after that being 1136 and 1478). The Dedication Feast for Salisbury was kept on September 30th, a datum which, oddly, was almost never included in calendars.[59] The feast of St Jerome falls on the 30th, which in 1383 was a Wednesday; so apparently in that year it was translated to the first day – October 8th,

---

[58] *Brev. Sar.*, I.mclxxxv–mcc. An attempt to paraphrase some of the more important parts of the rubric is made in Hughes, *MMMO*, pp. 297–300 – largely on the basis of the 1531 Sarum book, but with substantial reference to a 15th-cent. Italian breviary (Chicago, Newberry Library MS 71).

[59] A helpful exception is the calendar of Salisbury Cath. 148 (above, note 57); printed in Wordsworth, *Ceremonies and Processions*, pp. 3–14, and cf. p. xxi.

otherwise free – after the Octave; the mass for the Sunday within the Octave being used on October 4th and that for the Twentieth Sunday after Trinity supplying one of the two that had to be made up before Advent.

This example, almost laughable though its convolution may seem, typifies the amount of detailed thinking that lies behind this Great Rubric. It also supplies, untypically, the helpful specificity of a year, 1383, and this raises the question of the degree to which this rubric evolves over time. The version in the Edinburgh 27 breviary reflects an early fourteenth-century stage. At the other end, that the rubric of the 1531 printed book mentions the Octave of the Visitation as among those always having second vespers probably dates that version of it to after 1481, when Archbishop Bourgchier, ostensibly at the request of Convocation of Canterbury, declared observance of the octave compulsory.[60] So it is reasonable to suppose that this rubric, far from having an absolutely fixed text, grew additional details since its first compilation, but only a critical edition of it as found in a variety of manuscript witnesses could demonstrate this clearly. In its printed form, anyhow, it is at once both plainly keyed to Salisbury cathedral and adaptable for use in other places. Sunday processions are to be those of the saint's day on the feasts of Mary Magdalen, Margaret, Laurence, Martin, and Katherine, to each of whom an altar was dedicated at the cathedral. On the other hand, provision is made for situations "extra chorum Sarum," where there might be a "festum loci" falling at a time that would be awkward, like the Octave of Corpus Christi. In short, the Great Rubric can be taken as in a sense the ultimate expression of late medieval liturgical complexity – with a proliferation of detail that sometimes seems to exist in a self-perpetuating dynamic – and at the same time as showing the comprehensiveness of the later use of Sarum.

New saints' feasts: legislation and implementation

One of the prime manifestations of this comprehensiveness – that is, expansion of the use of the cathedral church of Salisbury to become synonymous with secular liturgy in most of the southern two-thirds of England – is the promotion of feasts for a handful of new (though in fact ancient) saints. With the exception of St Anne, all of them are, if not actually English, capable of being considered as such in the later middle ages: John of Beverley, Chad, Frideswide, Winifred (probably Welsh), David (definitely Welsh), and even, as the patron saint of England, George.

---

[60] The octave is mentioned in col. mxcxv; Pfaff, *New Liturg. Feasts*, p. 47.

More noteworthy than the identity of the saints is the mechanism by which their feasts are pronounced: by mandate of the archbishop of Canterbury. The first such case appears to be in 1383, when Archbishop William Courtenay transmitted a bull of Pope Urban VI's ordering observance of the feast of St Anne (26 July). This is a rather unusual case, in that the impetus for the order may have come from Richard II's queen, Anne of Bohemia, and the wording of the bull is not specific as to the degree of celebration.[61] Although, as has been mentioned again and again (e.g., pp. 213 and 432), St Anne's feast was not common in England before this time, nor was it rare; the papal involvement may be seen as no more than a diplomatic gesture, especially in the light of Urban's need to keep English allegiance during the Great Schism.

Most often the archbishop acted in Convocation, the meeting of representative clergy of his province which increased in frequency and importance from the mid-fourteenth century. There was an initial effort of this sort in 1398, when Roger Walden ("intruded" as archbishop during the exile of Thomas Arundel amidst the partisan struggles that brought about the deposition of Richard the following year) mandated observance throughout his province of the feasts of David, Chad, and Winifred.[62] It is not clear how widely this mandate would have been followed, given Arundel's return to office in 1399; when its substance is re-enacted eighteen years later no mention is made of the earlier pronouncement.

The agent of this re-enactment was Henry Chichele, archbishop from 1414 to 1443. At four of the nineteen sessions of Convocation over which he presided he promulgated decrees about saints' feasts, always with language indicating that they were meant to apply uniformly throughout the province. (In theory this would include the diocese of Hereford, the area in which that use mainly operated; see p. 463 for the situation there.) Such a clear mechanism is of a different dimension than a generalized "spread of Sarum usage," though this fact should

---

[61] D. Wilkins, *Concilia Magnae Britanniae et Hiberniae*, 4 vols (London 1737), III.178. The authority for Queen Anne's initiative seems to be no stronger than a statement in the anonymous Evesham chronicler's *Vita Ricardi Secundi* (ed. G. B. Stow [Philadelphia 1977], p. 134) that she *impetravit* a more solemn celebration of the feast; cf. N. Saul, *Richard II* (New Haven 1997), pp. 324 and 455–56. It may be relevant that St Anne's feast does not appear in the Westminster missal, written in 1383–84 on a commission from the abbot of Westminster (see further p. 227).

[62] Wilkins, III.234–36; a weekly commemoration of Becket, on Tuesdays, is also ordered. The authority for this statement is the register of Edmund Stafford, bishop of Exeter.

not be taken as implying a tension between archbishop and the chapter at Salisbury.[63]

During the late autumn Convocation in 1415, it was mandated that the feast of St George (23 April) should henceforth be kept as a greater double, and that those of David, Chad, and Winifred be observed on, respectively, March 1st and 2nd and November 3rd, all three with nine lessons and the choir "ruled"; and on January 4th (1416) Chichele sent a letter to the bishop of London requesting him to proclaim this.[64] Similarly, a few months later, in the context of the April Convocation, Chichele ordered ("de consensu et prelatorum et cleri hujusmodi," language reminiscent of statutes in parliament) that the feast of John of Beverley be kept, with choir ruled, throughout the province.[65] This was amplified in December in another mandate to the bishop of London, this time linking the saint's cult to the glorious victory at Agincourt on October 25th (1415), which, as well as being the feast of Crispin and Crispinian (the detail of which Shakespeare makes so much), was also that of John's Translation. The wording is useful in its specificity: nine lessons, of which the first three were to be of Crispin and Crispinian *de proprietate*, the next three of the Translation, and the final three an exposition of the gospel reading for plural martyrs; the entire service to be "secundum usum Sarum in talibus fieri."[66]

The magnifying of George's feast should also be seen as part of Henry V's public relations campaign after Agincourt. The singling out of Winifred is harder to explain, though that monarch did make a pilgrimage to her shrine at Holywell in 1416 (as he did to that of John at Beverley four years later). The suggestion that Chichele developed an interest in both Winifred and David when he was bishop of St David's has a certain plausibility but seems improbable.[67] Both David and Chad, successively on the first two days of March, had been long, though fitfully, present

---

[63] Chichele was vicar-general for the bishop of Salisbury from 1397, enjoying also from that year a Sarum prebend and the archdeaconry of Dorset; from 1404 to 1409 he was chancellor of the cathedral, residing there for at least eighteen months: E. F. Jacob, *Henry Chichele* (London 1967), p. 4.

[64] *The Register of Henry Chichele*, ed. E. F. Jacob, 4 vols (Oxford 1943–47), III.6–7.

[65] *Reg. Chichele*, III.14.

[66] *Reg.*, III.28–29. There is a curious dislocation in the lessons in both the printed Sarum (*SB*, III.948) and printed York breviaries (see p. 454), in stating that the translation took place in at York in 1037 under archbishop Ælfric Puttoc and King Edward – who is not king until 1042.

[67] The suggestion is that of D. H. Farmer in *Oxf. Dict. of Saints*, s.n. Winefride. She was not, however, chosen by Chichele around 1441 for depiction in glass on the south side of the chapel at Chichele's foundation, All Souls College, Oxford; in the place where she might have appeared there is Sativola (Sidwell), associated with Exeter: Jacob, *Chichele*, p. 83.

in calendars and sometimes in sanctorales. In the magnificent breviary made, it seems, for Chichele between 1408 and 1414 (now Lambeth Palace MS 69) the calendar includes David, with nine lessons, but he is absent from the sanctorale; there is neither Winifred nor Chad.[68]

The final saint singled out during Chichele's archiepiscopate is Frideswide, for whom it was mandated in 1434 that on October 19th "cum novem leccionibus et aliis que ad hujusmodi festum cum regimine chori secundum usum Sarum pertinent per totam provinciam suam perpetuo celebraretur."[69] This is stated to have been done at the request of the clergy "ob honorem sancte Frideswide alme universitatis Oxon. specialis advocate": a feast, in effect, to please what would now be called a special interest group. Chichele was himself an Oxonian, and his involvement with Oxford was extensive, culminating in his founding of All Souls College in 1438. Its chapel was lavishly equipped with service books, of which fifty-one are mentioned in an early inventory. Of these the only survivor, restored to the college in 1899 and now its MS 302, is an originally fine Sarum missal. Despite later mutilation, there survives in the early March part of the sanctorale an addition to the effect that masses for David and Chad could be found *in fine libri* (now missing, as is the calendar leaf for March and April).[70]

Two aspects of this supposedly compulsory expansion of the sanctorale deserve to be highlighted. The first is the transformation of the use of a particular cathedral – albeit by the early fifteenth century by far the predominant use – into what is in effect a provincial use: though there does not seem to have been any more official mechanism for this than the archiepiscopal mandates described above (and despite the continued existence of the use of Hereford). It is possible, though scarcely capable of proof, that Chichele had the promoting of Sarum use as a conscious goal. In August of 1423, in the context of a metropolitical visitation at Chichester, he came to some sort of agreement with the dean and chapter of its cathedral that their liturgy would be changed (the word *mutacio* is used) into that of Sarum.[71] As next to nothing is known about any distinctiveness in liturgy at Chichester before this time, it is hard to grasp how extensive the changes might have been;

---

[68] N. R(ogers) in *Gothic Art for England 1400–1547*, ed. R. Marks and P. Williamson (London 2003), no. 103, produces convincing evidence that the book was made before Chichele became archbishop; the archiepiscopal arms on fol. 1 "have been added over the border decoration."

[69] *Reg.*, III.256.

[70] *MMBL*, III.586; cf. Jacob, *Chichele*, p. 84.

[71] *Reg.*, III.505: "extitit per dominum et inter decanum ac canonicos predictos de mutacione usus divini servicii in ecclesia illa Cicestren. in usum ecclesie Saresburie … ."

whatever they were, the archbishop apparently sweetened the transition by providing for the canons "certos libros de dicto usu Saresburiensi." Two years later he gave to the prior and monks of the tiny Benedictine house at Abergavenny, who had complained of being out of service books, permission to use the rite of Sarum (including, presumably, its secular office), the necessary service books to be supplied through the generosity of Lady Joan Beauchamp.[72]

The other is the degree to which this apparent push for conformity actually worked. Sometimes Chichele's mandates were followed to the letter. All of the new observances are scrupulously entered in a fourteenth-century Sarum breviary, now Longleat House MS 10, where offices for David and Chad have been added in one fifteenth-century hand and for John of Beverley and Winifred in another (no Frideswide, however).[73] Again, in a large choir breviary (more accurately antiphonal, since there are no lessons; Bodl. Bodley 948) that belonged to the parish church of St Andrew Undershaft, London, all of the feasts mandated by Chichele have been added to the calendar, with the correct gradings (though George has not been upgraded from his original three lessons). This seems to be the case also with a rather splashy missal of the early fifteenth century (BL Arundel 109) belonging to St Lawrence Jewry, London, where additions on the last two leaves include masses for John of Beverley (and his memoria within Crispin and Crispinian) and Winifred as well as Erkenwald and the Translation of Erkenwald: the latter two being adaptations for use in London (see p. 486). A notable example of a book brought rigorously up to date is offered by the sumptuous Sherbrooke missal (Aberystwyth, Nat. Lib. Wales 15536E), originally written early in the fourteenth century. Here masses for each of the "Chicheleian" feasts are added in the margins of their respective pages in the sanctorale.[74]

On the other hand, a glaring instance of non-conformity is presented by the calendar of the Salisbury cathedral processional of c. 1445, where

---

[72] *Reg.*, IV.274. The request had come from the monks, probably because they knew that some Sarum books could be found, but Chichele's acquiescence is couched in more than perfunctory language: "usum illum Sarisburien. famosum et laudabilem ... ."

[73] L. F. Sandler, "An Early Fourteenth-Century English Breviary at Longleat," *Jnl. of Warburg and Courtauld Insts.* 39 (1976), pp. 1–20. The elaborate illustration links it to the Bohun family.

[74] In his full description of the MS, S. C. Cockerell posited a roughly East Anglian origin, on the basis of the extensive illustration: *Descriptive Cat. of Twenty Illum. MSS* [from Henry Yates Thompson collection] (Cambridge 1907), pp. 153–56. The marginal addition of the Translation of Etheldreda, Oct. 17th (probably that of 1252), would seem to strengthen this attribution. Sandler, *Gothic MSS*, no. 65, likens the style to that of the Peterborough Psalter of Hugh of Stukeley, CCCC 53.

the feast of George is graded at three lessons rather than the requisite nine and Frideswide is ignored entirely, as is John of Beverley, though added early.[75] More often the situation is that additions are made to the calendar but nothing more is done to accommodate the new feast. This is the case with the missal used at Closworth church in Somerset, now Bodl. Don. b.6. Here the calendar, almost certainly written after 1456 (canonization of Osmund), has the mandated feasts, in the original hand, but there is no provision of masses for any of them: in effect, lip-service to the archiepiscopal promulgations, but nothing more.

There seems to be only one further case of archiepiscopal command that new feasts be celebrated. This was in 1481, when Archbishop Bourgchier, acting in Convocation, ordered observance of the feasts of Osmund (who had been canonized twenty-five years earlier), Frideswide, and the Translation of Etheldreda, and also, as a double feast and with octave, the Visitation of the Virgin.[76] There is no indication as to why either Frideswide's feast, already mandated in 1434, or that of Etheldreda's Translation should be included along with the genuinely new one of Osmund. As for the Visitation, the diffuse way in which it comes to be observed in England over many decades must be viewed in the context of the related feasts of the Transfiguration and Name of Jesus – occasions frequently lumped together in the later fifteenth and early sixteenth centuries under the simple heading *nova festa* (see further p. 539).

A concluding case study: Hippolytus

This chapter may usefully end with another of the case studies of the kind we have found helpful: ones where the subject, in this instance a saint's feast, is instructive precisely because it is of no great importance. The case is that of Hippolytus, the third-century Roman churchman culted widely (if often confusedly) on August 13th.[77] The printed Sarum missals award him nine lessons in their calendars, and the sanctorales contain a proper mass, the latter with the same forms as in the earlier manuscript missals. In the calendar of the Crawford missal, however, he had been graded at three lessons. This, rather than the

---

[75] Salisbury Cath. 148 (above, note 57). Crispin and Crispinian also have only three lessons, so the Translation of John of Beverley must have been overlooked completely. On the other hand, the feast of the archangel Raphael, apparently borrowed from Exeter, appears on Oct. 5th, with nine lessons.

[76] Wilkins, III.613.

[77] Who this Hippolytus is, or are, is not material here; he is taken in our sources to be a martyr, with companions.

nine lessons of the printed missals, is also the grading in the calendar of the 1531 printed breviary.[78] The treatment of his feast in its sanctorale is almost a *reductio ad absurdum*: there it is treated in two places and ignored in its calendarial sequence. The problem is that by the end of the fifteenth century it had come to fall within the octave of the Name of Jesus (August 7th), as well as that of Laurence (10th), besides having its second vespers potentially conflict with first vespers of the Vigil of the Assumption. The 1531 book therefore provides a summary of the office for Hippolytus while describing the Jesus octave, of which it is the seventh day (as a feast of nine lessons, Hippolytus gets first vespers on its eve, despite that being the sixth day of the octave); then, after the proper lessons for the first six days, there are printed the office forms proper to Hippolytus (notably, antiphons and lessons vii–ix with their responsories), with the reminder that there are also to be *memoriae* for the Holy Name and for Laurence. But we are not then actually at August 13th, for after those proper saint's forms come the lessons for the Sunday within the Jesus octave (after a note that Hippolytus, as a feast of nine lessons, would if falling on a Sunday trump the octave observance); and they are in turn followed by proper lessons for Cyriac (August 8th), Romanus (9th), Tiburtius (11th), and the Octave of Jesus (14th, which is also the feast day of Eusebius, who gets the middle three lessons). The 13th itself is overlooked, and the observant cleric would have to have remembered that for the liturgy appropriate to that day he would have to turn back to, sequentially, the 7th.[79]

This is not the only complexity of that magnitude that could be elucidated. The point of laying this one out is to raise the possibility that efforts to bring about something like Sarum "unformity" – and to ensure the spread of this throughout almost all of the Province of Canterbury – must frequently have foundered under the mass of detail that had accrued through many generations. Taking as successive stages the Old Ordinal (third quarter of the thirteenth century), the increasingly shadowy New Ordinal (maybe mid-fourteenth), Maidstone's original work (most likely 1440s), and the printings of that work and of Sarum service books (from the mid-1480s), we can see that the idea of Sarum uniformity works in a general way only. Even if we were fortunate enough to possess an entire set of service books used at the same time

---

[78] Discrepancy as to whether three or nine lessons should be the norm is found also between the 1487 and 1497 printings of Maidstone's *Directorium Sacerdotum*, in both their calendars and their contents: ed. Wordsworth, I.12 and 179 (in *Sextum B*).

[79] The passages are *Sarum Breviary*, III.639–40, 661–68 – and not 677, which would have been the correct place.

at Salisbury cathedral, we would almost certainly find discrepancies of detail among them.

We may be in danger of falling into the trap of the kind of teleology that we understand is to be avoided (see p. 9). Proceeding with due caution, therefore, it is possible to discern, or at least suspect, a certain casualness about some of the less important, or less exciting, provisions of early sixteenth-century Sarum liturgy. Perhaps it would even be reasonable to posit that, in proportion to the sorts of liturgical vitality that Eamon Duffy's *The Stripping of the Altars* (1992; discussed on p. 552) argues for so energetically and that the vigor of new feasts and of new saints' cults witnesses to also, getting every detail of the liturgical practice of mass and office exactly right came to seem not only extremely difficult but also of less than the first urgency. How likely is it that listening to the reading in English of the names of a church's relics (p. 419), or being present at the vivid, end-of-compline singing of an antiphon of the Virgin (p. 233), may have seemed considerably more compelling than trying to figure out whether the late-afternoon service on August 12th was to be second vespers of the sixth day of the octave of the Name of Jesus or first vespers of Hippolytus?

York Use

What was known in the later middle ages as the Use of York differs in kind from that of Sarum in that it refers to the metropolitical church – York Minster, in common parlance – of the province, whereas Salisbury was just one of fourteen cathedral churches in the province of Canterbury. The province of York was not at all like its southern neighbor. For one thing, it was vastly smaller, in terms both of population and of having only three dioceses: York itself; Carlisle, where a modest Augustinian priory founded around 1123 received cathedral status some ten years later; and Durham, monastic (from 1083), wealthy, powerful, jealous of its dignity and prerogatives.[1] Durham stood also as a bastion, ecclesiastical and otherwise, of English presence in the unclear and often controverted border region with Scotland: expressed in terms of early Anglo-Saxon kingdoms, Durham came to stand for the old north-facing Bernicia, York for the south-facing Deira of which it had always been the center. Not surprisingly, then, some liturgical tension can be discerned between York and Durham; for example, a few secular service books used in the latter diocese follow Sarum rather than York use.

York stands in some tension also with Canterbury. This is reflected obviously in the primacy struggle between the two archbishoprics, a struggle that did not finally end (with Canterbury the victor) until the fourteenth century. More obvious liturgically is York's comparative deficiency in saints. The almost overpowering presence of Durham's Cuthbert in the north came to be balanced, after 1173, by that of Becket at Canterbury; whereas the best York could do was the rather unconvincing (some said, unedifying) figure of archbishop William Fitzherbert,

---

[1] The bishops of Galloway, also known as Whithorn (anciently, *Casa candida*), in Scotland were technically, if disputedly, suffragan to York even after a formal declaration of the structure of the church in Scotland was made in 1192, but after about 1355 this arrangement ceased to have even faint reality.

who died in 1154 but was not canonized until 1226.[2] A third point of contrast is wealth. The area around York had been so impoverished by Viking struggles that from roughly 972 until 1062 the archbishopric of York was held jointly with the rich bishopric of Worcester, and the brutality of the Norman Conquest in the north intensified the misery. It does not seem to have been until the second half of the twelfth century that marked prosperity is discernible, in the reign of Becket's great enemy Roger of Pont l'Evêque, 1154–81.[3]

Despite, or possibly because of, these factors, the strong connection between York Minster and the region of which it has always been the ecclesiastical center has heavily influenced the study of its liturgy and, more widely, of the Use of York in general. The most important collection of York service books is that made by Marmaduke Fothergill, a Yorkshire rector and eventual Nonjuror; many of the books he collected passed to the Minster library on his death in 1731.[4] Wide availability of documents relating to the Minster was made possible by the foundation in 1834 of the Surtees Society, for the publication of unedited manuscripts relating to the area defined in its original statement of purpose as "the Ancient Kingdom of Northumberland" [later amended to read "Northumbria"].[5] It is in this regional context, rather than that of the publication of liturgical texts as such – unlike, that is, the Henry Bradshaw Society, not founded until 1890 – that one of the two the first "modern" editions of an English medieval service book appeared: the York missal, edited by William George Henderson, a Hampshire man who became interested in York books as headmaster of Leeds Grammar School.[6] Similarly, the Society's edition of the York

---

[2] For William, see now C. Norton, *St William of York* (York 2006), esp. ch. v, "Saint William," pp. 149–201. Two of the three great collegiate churches in the diocese also had ties to vivid saints, John of Beverley (who enjoys a great boost in cultus in the 15th cent.; see p. 439) there and Wilfrid at Ripon. The third, Southwell (Nottinghamshire was in the medieval diocese of York) had none.

[3] In the *Cartae baronum* returns of 1166 it appears that, although in comparison with the service of sixty knights owed by the archbishop of Canterbury, York's twenty is a further indication of poverty, archbishop Roger had enfeoffed well over twice that many: D. C. Douglas, ed. *English Historical Documents* II: *1042–1189*, 2nd edn (London 1981), p. 971.

[4] J. Foster, *Alumni Oxonienses 1500–1714* (Oxford 1891), II.521. It is regrettable that there is no entry from him in the *ODNB*.

[5] The leading figure in the early years of the Society was the indefatigable James Raine (1791–1858), who edited seventeen of its first thirty-one volumes. The Yorkshire Archaeological Society began publishing its Record Series only in 1885.

[6] *Missale ad usum insignis ecclesiae Eboracensis*, 2 vols, SS 59–60 (1874). Not a professional scholar in the modern sense, Henderson was an energetic headmaster at Leeds and subsequently Dean of Carlisle (as well as the father of fourteen children, all by one wife). In 1874 he also produced the still-standard edition of the Hereford missal

breviary was undertaken by a local clergyman, Stephen Lawley, who held a family living at Escrick in Yorkshire.[7] (Both these editions will be considered at length presently.)

Little has been done towards the publication of any York books since the edition of the breviary, entirely from printed sources, was completed in 1883. Secondary scholarship has been correspondingly light, and concerned almost wholly with the later middle ages.[8] In a more substantial recent contribution, various dimensions of the Use of York have been drawn out in the context of a reconstruction of a York Requiem mass as it would have been performed in the early sixteenth century.[9] Our purposes require us to try to get some idea as to the liturgical heritage at York before the fourteenth century, when a few extant service books begin to be available. This is most readily done by looking at three bits of early calendarial evidence.

Early York calendars

The earliest witness to a distinctive York calendar seems to be part of a missal now in Manchester (John Rylands Univ. Lib., lat. 186).[10] The textual interest of the book will be considered later in this chapter; for the moment we notice only its calendar. This belongs to a section dating

---

(not in any series), and the following year two further SS volumes: (61) a pontifical owned by Christopher Bainbridge, archbishop of York 1508–14, and (63) the York manual and processional. The first fascicules of F. H. Dickinson's edition of the Sarum missal had appeared in 1861, but the last not until 1883.

[7] S. W. Lawley, ed. *Breviarium secundum usum insignis ecclesie Eboracensis*, 2 vols, SS 71, 75 (1880–83). His father was Lord Wenlock, whose seat was at Escrick Park.

[8] A brief conspectus, "York service books," was drawn up in 1927 by another southerner who had come to live in Yorkshire (at the Community of the Resurrection at Mirfield), the great liturgical scholar W. H. Frere: no. 19 in *York Minster Historical Tracts* (all paginated separately, though published in a single volume), repr. in Frere's *Collected Papers*, ACC 35 (1940), pp. 159–69. The organizer of the tracts was A. Hamilton Thompson, who had also migrated to the north, to become professor at Leeds. The treatment of York in A. A. King, *Liturgies of the Past* (London 1959), pp. 326–47, is helter-skelter but contains some useful information.

[9] P. S. Barnwell, C. Cross, A. Rycraft, ed., *Mass and Parish in Late Medieval England: the Use of York* (Reading 2005). This includes text and translation of the mass, with properly colored rubrics; the text is a composite one, "drawn from several variants in order to create instructions which are readily performable, rather than reflecting any particular manuscript or edition" (p. 146). The reconstructed mass was performed at All Saints Church, York, in 2002.

[10] It came to the library after Mrs Rylands's original benefaction, being purchased from B. Quaritch in 1913, and was therefore not catalogued by M. R. James (who dealt with only the first 183 Latin MSS). The library has a rough typed description by N. R. Ker; this was not included in *MMBL* II because the MS had been noticed in print briefly in a handlist of additions in *Bull John Rylands Lib.* 12 (1928), pp. 581–609. I am grateful to Alexander Rumble for his kind verification of two of the readings noted.

from the second quarter of the thirteenth century, probably not long after 1226, when William of York, entered in the original hand, was canonized. By that time the York Feast of Relics had been set at October 19th, and both it and the expected saints – Wilfrid, John of Beverley, Hilda (but on the odd date of August 25th: see p. 455), Paulinus – are all present. So is the founding abbess of the Yorkshire nunnery at Everingham, Everildis, at July 9th. We note specially one of the most usefully distinctive (in the sense of not being obviously connected with the area) of York saints, Babillus (Babylas) and the Three Boys, January 24th. Even more distinctive (Babillus occasionally appears elsewhere, especially in monastic calendars) is Germanicus, a martyr from Smyrna, January 19th; he seems unique to York. Pelagia, October 8th, is unusual but not unique. The same is true of another figure of desert spirituality, Hilarion, October 21st.

Most of the same saints appear in calendars of two psalters with Yorkshire connections, both dating from around 1260 and both so richly decorated as to have art-historical nicknames. The psalter of Simon de Meopham, the fourteenth-century archbishop of Canterbury (1328–33) who according to a later flyleaf inscription came to own it (now Lambeth Palace, Sion College Arc. L.40.2/L.2), has a calendar clearly of the York diocese.[11] The so-called York psalter (BL Add. 54179) has as well some apparently Augustinian elements in its calendar and also what Nigel Morgan calls "a strong martyrological element."[12]

York statutes and York Use

Identification of certain saints as distinctive to York does not, of course, constitute identifying York Use. The simpler course towards the latter end would be to look only at service books clearly labelled something like *Ad usum Eboracensis*, but, as has been observed, such books are all quite late. Our task first is if possible to ascertain other distinctive

---

[11] Morgan, *Early Gothic MSS*, no. 134; *MMBL*, I.265.

[12] Morgan, no. 133; bequeathed to the (then) British Museum by E. G. Millar (d. 1966), who published bits of it in a Roxburghe Club facsimile in 1952: *A Thirteenth Century York Psalter*. By "martyrological elements" must be meant such exotic figures as Balbina (31 March), Florian (4 May), Valen(ti)s (21 May), and Venantius (11 Oct.); but it also lacks Germanicus (has Wulfstan instead), Babillus, Pelagia, and Hilarion, who do have services in York missals and breviaries. Somewhat later (c. 1290) is the psalter-hours that belonged to the great northern family of Percy, extant now in two parts, of which that containing the calendar was bought for the British Library in 1990 (now Add. MS 70000; the other part remains in private ownership); treated as nos. 11a and b in Sandler, *Gothic MSS*. Sandler relates the Percy calendar in turn to that of the De la Twyere psalter of c. 1305–10 (now New York Public Lib., Spencer 2): her no. 36, noting there a certain mendicant element.

features that justify the term when it comes into widespread usage. It is necessary therefore to notice briefly the building history of the Minster and then to glance at its thirteenth-century statutes. By the last decade of that century the western half of archbishop Roger's building (largely third quarter of the twelfth century) was in the process of being replaced. The great transepts begun around 1220 were finished some forty years later, the chapter house with its amazing unsupported roof completed around 1285, work on the new (and present) nave begun in 1291. The eastern half still consisted largely of archbishop Roger's work: aisled choir, sanctuary, retrochoir, and square east end. (This east end will in turn be replaced by the present one, 1361–1472.) Roger's choir had to be capable of accommodating, in theory, four dignitaries, five archdeacons, and some thirty-two canons.[13] In practice there were generally many fewer, but provision had to be made nonetheless for liturgies of considerable splendor.[14]

The several sets of statutes enacted by the chapter between 1221 and 1294 offer occasional hints as to some of these splendid liturgies, like the dean's celebrations of mass on principal feasts, when it is provided that he was to be assisted by three deacons and three subdeacons.[15] As in other secular cathedrals, liturgical arrangements were primarily the responsibility of the precentor, but the duties were to some degree shared. The chancellor, in addition to preaching *ad populum* sermons on the first Sunday in Advent and Septuagesima Sunday, was to assign the readings (at matins, presumably) on double feasts.[16] The fourth of the *quatuor personae*, the treasurer, had heavy responsibilities in the provision of candles for a whole variety of liturgical occasions – notably, at *tenebrae* during Holy Week, twenty-five *cerceli*, of which four had to weigh a pound each – as well as *stellae* on three occasions when there

---

[13] The church Roger's work replaced was basically that of archbishop Thomas of Bayeux, constructed c. 1075–1100; usefully summarized in E. Gee, "Architectural History until 1290," in *A History of York Minster*, ed. G. E. Aylmer and R. Cant (Oxford 1977), pp. 110–48.

[14] B. Dobson has remarked that from the 13th through the 15th cent. "York Minster was nearly always to be served by fewer residentiary canons than any other cathedral in England": *Hist. of York Minster*, p. 50; cf. his observation that, of eighty-two persons who counted as cathedral "ministers" in one way or another and who showed up at the anniversary of archbishop Bowet's death in 1424, only seven were canons (p. 86). Partly because of the expense of living in the Close, as few as four (occasionally, two) "residentiary" canons actually lived there in the 15th cent. (p. 105).

[15] These "old" York statutes are printed in *Lincoln Cath. Stats*, II. 90–135, here at p. 92. Newer ones date from the 16th cent..

[16] "York Statutes" (as above), p. 96. His duty on double feasts is stated to be "illis qui lecturi sunt lecciones assignare": does this mean that he decides which lessons are to be read, or simply apportions what are already fixed lessons?

seems to have been some sort of dramatic element: one on Christmas night *pro pastoribus*, two on the night of Epiphany "si debeat fieri presentacio trium regum," and an unspecified number for the Boy Bishop ceremony.[17] All the services were to be regulated by a *consuetudinarium* – which, unfortunately, does not seem to be extant. That some such thing existed by at least the fourteenth century is implied by two books from that period.

Witnesses to York Use in the fourteenth century

One of the most explicit instances of such a phrase occurs in a finely decorated psalter (now Bodl. Rawl. G.170) which was written in the early fourteenth century and seems to have passed soon thereafter into the possession of John de Grandisson. Grandisson was bishop of Exeter from 1327 until his death in 1369 and a churchman of avid liturgical interests (as such, he is the hero of chapter 12). A note in a hand that looks very much like his reads "Ista letanie et que sequntur sunt de usu Eboracensi" (fol. 212v) and another, at the end of the Office of the Dead, "De usu Eboracensi et non Sarisburiensi" (fol. 220v).[18] The litany includes such saints as John of Beverley, William of York, Hilarion, and Everildis, all identified above as distinctive to York. The calendar has been somewhat altered in the direction of Sarum usages, through introduction of such figures as Aldhelm (see p. 362 for him as distinctively Sarum) and Edith of Wilton, with later additions like Winifred and Frideswide.

Only a bit later is a missal donated to the parish church of the village of Cuckney in Nottinghamshire (now Oxford, University College 78B). It was given by one William Sheppard at an unspecified date (there is an obit for a Margaret Haverham in 1532). It includes, in both calendar and sanctorale, Germanicus, Babillus and the Three Boys, Pelagia, and the York Feast of Relics; so it is undeniably a "York" book. A few rubrics make plain that adaptations from Minster practice were to be permitted: notably, at the Advent Ember days, when there is a possible conflict with the Vigil of St Thomas, a statement that in smaller (*minoribus*) churches where there was a single chaplain, just the Embertide mass was to be celebrated (with the gospel for the Vigil read separately), whereas *in majori ecclesia* – the Minster – mass was to be sung solemnly

---

[17] Ibid., p. 98. These suggest respectively some sort of Nativity play, Three Kings play, and something that the *Episcopus puerorum* is to find (*inueniet*); the text for the third is corrupt.

[18] An erased inscription on fol. 8 looks to be an obit of Grandisson.

for each occasion, "et similiter alibi ubi habetur copia sacerdotum."[19] Other rubrics replace references to specific cathedral personnel (e.g., *ad nutum succentoris*) with more general language. The sanctorale, which is complete, shows a high degree of concordance with the calendar; indications as to mass forms, mostly to be taken from the common, are supplied for almost every occasion in the latter, even the obscure ones like Germanicus and Pelagia.

York missals and Henderson's edition of them

Henderson seems to have conducted an amazingly throrough search, and his preface describes briefly the seven manuscript missals he came to know of and five printed editions, ranging in date from ?1509 to 1533.[20] Two of the manuscript books have been mentioned already: Rylands lat. 186 (his MS A, which in 1874 he knew as belonging to the Vicar of Leeds) and the University College 78B missal from Cuckney (his C). Of the other four, the most useful to him was (his D) Cambridge, Sidney Sussex 33, definitely from the Minster. Two others are still in its library, MSS XVI.A.9 (his B) and XVI.I.3 (his F); both are markedly imperfect. The remaining two he knew of had strong private connections. Stonyhurst College 3 (his G) was being used at the church in Tatham, Lancashire, in the fifteenth and early sixteenth centuries.[21] The Fitzwilliam missal, written for Richard Fitzwilliam around 1470 (MS 34 in that Museum at Cambridge; Henderson's E), is imposingly illustrated, and was perhaps always in private ownership.[22]

Worthy of notice also are four other York missals, all of the late fourteenth or fifteenth centuries. The earliest, c. 1370 (now Boston Public Library, MS 1576 [f 151]), has seven large illuminated initials and mid-fifteenth-century birth and death notices of the Neville and Gascoigne families; its calendar and sanctorale contain all of the saints

---

[19] *York Missal*, I.8. Exactly the same rubric is in three of the missals noticed in the next section: Henderson's B and C and the one in the Boston Public Library.

[20] By a most unfortunate confusion, the table of sigla on p. vi of vol. I of Henderson's edition fails to match those in his brief descriptions of the MSS on pp. vii–xi. The apparatus in his text is keyed to the correct sigla, which are therefore given here in the interest of clarity.

[21] *MMBL*, IV.372. Its calendar shows it to be a bit earlier than most of the others: most clearly in the omission of the Eleven Thousand Virgins, which becomes a feast of nine lessons, on Oct. 21st, when Hilarion alone is given here.

[22] The printed editions used by Henderson seem, as he said (I.xiii), "to have been made successively, the one from the other, and probably only represent a single MS or, at the outside, two"; even the errors in the first edition remain uncorrected. Where there are some important variants, notably in rubrics at the canon, he prints these in parallel columns, but in general his text is a composite from the manuscripts he knew.

identified above as distinctive to York.[23] The second, written early in the next century, was formerly owned by J. Meade Falkner and is now BL Add. 43380; from at least the mid-sixteenth century it belonged to a family in Westmoreland, where it may always have been used. The third, York Minster Add. 30, is a very large (c. 420 × 290 mm) book written in at least seven hands, very likely for a patron called Ralph, named in the votive-mass prayers on the last leaf; despite its size, it does not seem to have been intended for use at the Minster.[24] Still in private ownership is a book that came to modern light only in 1935, when Francis Eeles described what is clearly a York missal used at a parish church near Preston in Lancashire.[25] It contains a note, possibly around 1530, concerning a donor's gift to the church of "ii westement with a masse boke of Saroume use" – presumably meant to replace this one.

A York gradual in a village church

Noticing the existence of what are clearly York missals but made for use elsewhere than at the Minster leads to a challenging problem, one that is of general application but pointed specifically here by the sole extant York gradual, a manuscript (there appear to survive no printed copies). This, now Bodl. Lat. liturg. b.5, is a book of the mid-fifteenth century that belonged to the parish church of East Drayton in Nottinghamshire. Because of its uniqueness and considerable musical interest, it was studied in some detail by W. H. Frere in 1901, seven years after his edition of the Sarum gradual had been completed.[26] He observed that the book "clearly was designed for a village church, for it takes no account of ordinary week-days, Ember days, or even week-days in Lent." If this is more widely true, it raises interesting questions of both book design and liturgical thinking. Those York missals that seem to have been intended for use outside of the Minster do not share that peculiarity, so at churches in which they were used – like Cuckney

---

[23] Its immediate provenance seems unclear, and it is not noticed in the relevant SMIBI volume. It is likely to repay more detailed study.

[24] *MMBL*, IV.802; Ker/Piper note that one of the sixty-nine sequences, "Celi enarrant," is headed "Sequencia proximo sequens non dicitur in choro Ebor"; and it has the short, "Unus capellanus" rubric noticed above.

[25] F. C. Eeles, "On a Fifteenth-Century York Missal formerly used at Broughton-in-Amounderness, Lancashire," *Chetham Society Miscellany* VI, Chetham Soc. 94 (1935), paginated separately. It was then, and as late as 1987 (*MLGB Suppl.*), owned by the Butler-Bowdon family in Sussex.

[26] W. H. Frere, "The Newly-Found York Gradual," *Jnl of Theol. Studs* 2 (1901), pp. 578–86, repr. in his collected papers, pp. 22–31. Formerly Phillipps MS 2711, it was bought in 1896 by a Nottinghamshire collector and in 1901 by the Bodleian.

in Nottinghamshire and Tatham in Lancashire – there could be, for example, weekday masses in Lent but without music. For a gradual to have been written without such weekdays (and even more, the Ember days, the Saturdays of which have unusually lengthy masses) limits its usability to churches where some, but not extensive, music at mass could be expected. Copying a gradual is a highly labor-intensive activity, and omitting what is not to be used is efficient in terms both of labor and of expense; but it does suggest knowledge of a market for such an abridged book.

The larger question raised by this point requires us to attempt extrapolation: that is, to jump from these scanty details to a sense of some of the decisions underlying the writing of a particular service book. The East Drayton gradual has different, and at times fuller, directions for the Adoration of the Cross on Good Friday than do the missals used for Henderson's edition, both manuscript and printed, as the following detail shows. In the gradual it is two priests who are barefoot as well as the deacons specified in the missals, which in turn specify a role for two vicars (the choral vicars, of whom there would be none in a parish church).[27] Can we extrapolate from this to suppose that there were something like two ordinals at York in the fifteenth century, one copied into books intended for use at the Minster (and perhaps the other collegiate churches of the diocese) and the other copied into books for parish use? If so, what sense would it make to suppose that a church where there were not going to be Lenten weekday or Ember day masses could mount clerical forces of at least two priests and two deacons? Or is it likelier that the rubrics in this part of the York gradual are based on an older ordinal, of which there is no trace in the extant missals?

Some support for the existence of more than one ordinal comes from the York manuals, of which Henderson's edition appeared just the next year after that of the missals.[28] The base text used is that of the first, 1509 edition, printed by Wynkyn de Worde in London, with variants from four MSS. Of the latter, the one most often referred to is dated 1403, owned when Henderson knew it by Sir John Lawson (now Harvard University, Widener MS 1). The York manual contains, somewhat illogically, parts of the Good Friday and Easter Vigil liturgies. The Adoration of the Cross in the former has rubrics similar, though not identical, to those in the gradual. Tellingly, the 1403 manuscript

[27] Frere, "Gradual," p. 29 (of the ACC collection); Henderson, *York Missal*, I.105.

[28] W. G. Henderson, ed. *Manuale et processionale ad usum insignis ecclesiae Eboracensis*, SS 63 (1875). The processional is printed from the first edition, 1530 (the only other was 1555); there seem to be no complete MS processionals.

manual allows for participation by only two priests or deacons rather than requiring a pair of each; and, where the missals have "Interim praelatus, et ministri, et decanus, cum reliquo choro adorent crucem," the manuals eliminate mention of the dean – as is only sensible seeing that they are designed for use by a parish priest.[29] Wynkyn de Worde's multisyllabic title page refers to the book as "quoddam secundum usum matris ecclesiae Eboracensis." On balance it seems fair to assume that York Use books can have more than a single set of rubrics. This putative flexibility is also evident as we turn to a selection of York breviaries to see what light may be extracted from them; though, as is our usual practice, they will be considered somewhat less fully than books used at mass, which tend to be more tractable.

Evidence from York breviaries

Many of the extant York breviaries are in one way or another imperfect, and few (if any) are suitable for use in choir. The distinction that surfaced several times in our discussion of missals, between those intended for use *in majori ecclesia* and those to be used in parish churches, holds here as well. This distinction will not be discernible if we use only the modern edition, for it is basically just a reprint of the probable first edition, printed in Venice in 1493. The Surtees Society editor, Stephen Lawley, does not seem to have been otherwise active as a liturgical scholar, but between 1880 and 1882, when his edition was in progress, he was in regular correspondence with the great student of early liturgical printing, Henry Bradshaw.[30] Lawley's preface is entirely taken up with description of the extant copies of the printed editions.[31] Those from 1526 on contained offices for the *nova festa* of the Visitation – which in 1513 had been mandated by York Convocation for the unusual date of April 2nd – Transfiguration, and Name of Jesus; these are printed as appendices.[32] Unlike Henderson, who had

---

[29] *York Manual*, p. 111; *York Missal*, I.107. The term *prelatus*, often found in York rubrics, could here mean simply the celebrant.

[30] G. W. Prothero, *A Memoir of Henry Bradshaw* (London 1888), pp. 271, 282, 289. It was Bradshaw who supplied the list of editions and known copies of the York breviary, I.xiii, expanded and somewhat corrected in II.xii. There were only three editions after the 1493: 1507, 1526, and 1533 (and possibly one in 1555).

[31] The only mention of manuscripts is the printing, in an appendix to volume II (cols 785–820), of an unofficial office for Richard Rolle of Hampole, the Yorkshire spiritual writer who died in 1349, in the event of his canonization (which never happened). This appendix was entirely the work of Francis Procter, who describes the MSS on pp. x–xi of the preface.

[32] The Transfiguration had been ordered in 1489, the Name of Jesus nine years later; see Pfaff, *New Liturg. Feasts, passim.*

inferred that a single manuscript most likely provided the model for the first printed edition (and thence for the other four) of the York missal, Lawley ignores entirely the question of putative manuscript models; his apparatus consists of noting some points where the later printings differed from that of 1493.

Of the roughly two dozen manuscript York breviaries extant, a handful may be singled out as specially helpful for our purposes. One, of about 1400, is of choir size, c. 440 × 345 mm, and well decorated (now Bodl. Gough liturg. 1, formerly Gough missals 30). It might better be called a choir lectionary, with quite full lessons, especially in the sanctorale. Comparison of those for Jerome in this book and in the printed editions shows the manuscript version to be somewhat fuller; this is true also of those for William of York which, unlike those for Jerome, must be of York origin. This suggests that, at least sometimes, in choir at the Minster the lessons at matins may have been longer than what is available in the printed editions. This seems also to be the case with another book (now Bodl. Laud misc. 84), finely decorated and apparently for use at the Minster, although its dimensions are only half those of the previously considered one. It shows a high degree of correspondence with the sanctorale of the printed breviaries; there are either propers or reference to the common of saints for even calendar figures as obscure as the already noticed Germanicus, Babillus et al., Hilarion, and Pelagia. Hilda has three lessons at her usual York feast of August 25th: a placement itself a puzzle which if solved might hold a key to the development of the York calendar.[33]

An equally large book was used at, if not made for, the church of (Hutton) Rudby in Yorkshire (it is now Durham Univ. Lib. Cosin V.1.2).[34] Its use there may have continued throughout Henrician and Edwardian times, for the calendar contains some twenty obits and other notices,

[33] Hilda seems to have been honored on that day in the earliest York liturgical documents we have, with the lessons for her feast drawn entirely from Bede's *History* (IV.23). The sole evidence for liturgy at Whitby abbey, the later 14th-cent. missal (now Bodl. Rawl. liturg. b.1) used by Legg in his collations, has Hilda at the usual 17 Nov. date, with an octave, but also on 25 Aug., as a *principalis* feast. One would suppose that the August feast was a Translation, but Hilda's relics had supposedly been taken to Glastonbury in the mid-10th. cent. (see *Oxf. Dict. Saints*, "Hilda"). Can there have been, at Whitby and then York (or vice versa?), some confusion or conflation with St Ebbe, abbess of Coldingham and Hilda's exact contemporary – whose feast day, though not widely observed, is Aug. 25th?

[34] Alan Piper most kindly gave me a typescript draft description, revised Feb. 1990, to use alongside the manuscript. His analysis, too lengthy to be reprised here, discerns haste in space planning; at points in the sanctorale: "It seems, from changes of ink and the squashed up appearance of some lections, that they were inserted into inadequate spaces which had been left blank for them."

dating from 1513 to 1553. The volume is now somewhat disordered and seems to lack about half its original contents, but enough survives to give a good idea of an imposing office book, of clear York affiliation, used by a figure as substantial as the parish's rector, Cuthbert Conyers, who (already archdeacon of Carlisle) was inducted into the living in 1513.

A further glimpse into York Use in the countryside is provided by a composite book (now Lambeth Palace Library, Sion College Arc. L.40.2/L.1) analyzed by Neil Ker as a kind of medieval patchwork. To a nucleus which he dates to the fourteenth century were added, in the fifteenth, seventy-one leaves of a similar book, which made for a tolerably complete breviary except for the psalter (with canticles and litany); this is supplied from yet another manuscript. The calendar, in the first added part, has Lovell family obits from 1475 to 1521; they were the dominant family in the Yorkshire village of Skelton, to which the book almost certainly belonged. Not at all a grand book – indeed, when open it is distinctly clumsy, being much wider than it is high –, it shows the York office presented in modest (and therefore probably realistic) circumstances.

The constitutive criteria for York Use

Now that we have looked cursorily at books used at both mass and office, it is time to see whether the distinctivenesses that constitute York Use can be pinned down at all satisfactorily. The threefold approach often employed in the present work, of looking at saints, texts, and rubrics, yields results for York that are, at best, modest. The distinctive saints have been reviewed at sufficient length above: Wilfrid of Ripon, John of Beverley, William of York, Everildis, Hilda (at her odd date) all have special significance in York Use, while the four curious figures of Germanicus, Babillus, Pelagia, and Hilarion are found as a group nowhere save in York books.

It is less easy to identify distinctive rubrics, for the simple reason that the surviving service books contain relatively few: which in turn means that they presuppose an ordinal – or as has been hinted several times, more than one – the lack of which is sorely felt. For the most part there is little variation in the rubrics that do exist. However, Henderson's edition of the missal does print a number of rubrics in the Sidney Sussex 33 manuscript that differ from the conspectus readings of the printed missals.[35] One of these is specially illuminating: it mandates the

---

[35] Henderson says of this manuscript that "the rubrics are very full, and have frequent reference to the Cathedral itself"; noting also, however, that "there are a considerable

attendance at the Minster on St John the Evangelist's day of all parsons (*persone*) and priests (*presbyteri*) of the city "ex antiqua consuetudine ad Ecclesiam Cathedralem"; we wonder how many other such *consuetudines* there were.

Textual distinctivenesses are equally difficult to pin down, with only a few exceptions. The mass prayers for Thomas Becket offer a useful reminder of the difficulty. In what we have seen to be the oldest textual witness to York Use, the original nucleus of the Rylands lat. 186 manuscript, the three original prayers have been erased and in their place have been written the standard collect ("Deus, qui pro cuius ecclesia") and a secret and postcommunion that agree with those in the Whitby missal but with none of the other York manuscript or printed books.[36] In the Sidney Sussex missal the secret and postcommunion agree with those in the Sarum and Hereford books; while the printed York missals and the University College 78B missal have yet another pair. When Ker remarks, then, in his draft description of the Rylands missal that its "thirteenth-century text was much corrected in s. xv to conform with York use," our study leads us to ask which set could fairly be called *the* York mass for Becket.[37]

Adequately full and accurate collations of all variants in the sanctorale, to say nothing of the temporale, would be the work of decades. Here we can look at only one example to glimpse the complexity involved. On Good Friday the Passion is read by a single deacon according to all the missals save the Sidney manuscript, which adds "vel legatur a tribus Presbyteris, si sic ordinatum erit": when, and by whom, would it be so ordered? That manuscript has other directions for Good Friday (e.g., during the *Agios theos* response at the Adoration of the Cross, those in choir kiss the benches(?) three times: *osculantes formulas tribus vicibus*), and in general contains, as Henderson had observed, fuller rubrics, as though the book might have been designed to have been used without an accompanying ordinal.[38]

One matter of book design, apparently unnoticed hitherto, may give the most decisive clue as to continuity of York Use missals. From the

---

number of variations between this and the other manuscript and printed Missals in the Secrets and Post-communions of the Sanctorale, which almost always, but not always, correspond to the Sarum Use" (*York Missal*, I.x). A few other variant rubrics are noticed, esp. for Ash Wednesday.

[36] Compare *York Missal*, I.26–27 with Legg's collations, *WM*, III.1453.

[37] Ker's typescript description (note 10 above) is an obviously hasty and rough draft that does not necessarily represent his final judgment; but the observation is still telling.

[38] This puzzling phrase occurs also in the Exeter ordinal (ed. Dalton, I.323), as the Easter Vigil ends and the mass begins: "omnes genuflectant, osculantes formulas." What is the point of this?

early thirteenth-century part of the Rylands manuscript on, the ordinary and canon are placed just before Pentecost; whereas in many books (including most Sarum) this heavily used section comes between the temporale and sanctorale, and in others (including Hereford) between the Easter Vigil and Easter Day. Even without distinctive saints, rubrics, or texts, it is probable that one could identify a York missal by this peculiarity alone. But that observation does not carry us back even as far as the twelfth century, and for any possible sense of connectedness with the earlier periods we need to look at a part of the mass where variation is not usually to be found.

The canon of the mass at York

A concise, if potentially misleading, synoptic view of the ordinary and canon of the mass at York as compared with Sarum and Hereford was provided as long ago as 1844, in William Maskell's *Ancient Liturgy of the Church of England*.[39] His source for York was a copy of the 1517 edition owned by him (he also owned the 1492 Sarum he used; for Hereford he used a Bodleian copy of the unique 1502 edition). York is shown to have some different preliminary devotions from those of the other two uses, and some ceremonial variations. Symbolic reasons are given as to why there may be one, three, five, or seven mass collects – never more, and never an even number – in a long rubric that, as Maskell observes, runs counter to the general tenor of the York Use, "which is distinguished by the fewness and shortness of its rubrics."[40] One genuine peculiarity is that after the gospel is read the priest says, secretly, "Benedictus qui venit in nomine domini," and then kisses the book. Another is the singing of *Veni creator* (by whom, is not stated) as the celebrant washes his hands. A third requires a threefold signing over the bread and wine before the consecration, to the words "Sit signatum, ordinatum, et sanctificatum hoc sacrificium nostrum."

In the canon itself, at the *Memento, Domine* York adds "atque omnium fidelium Christianorum" to "omnium circumstantium." The most marked particularity here comes in the communion devotions, where

[39] On Maskell and this seminal work of his, see p. 9. Quotations here are from the second edn, 1846. His parallel columns included one for the Use of Bangor, the existence of which he inferred (wrongly) from a manuscript missal he owned that seemed to agree with none of the principal secular uses (p. cliv), and one for the Use of Rome, from the Tridentine missal.

[40] The rubric is longer in *York Missal*, I.169 than the one Maskell prints, and differs slightly in details; both contain an interesting passsage beginning "Secundum autem Romanam ecclesiam," about the formulas for terminating prayers. Some MSS lack this rubric.

York, Sarum, and Hereford all have different prayers and reception formulas. The manuscript York missals show a good deal of variation in the assigning of proper prefaces. One ceremonial detail of wide importance is prescribed in a rubric only in the Sidney missal, that after the consecration of the host the priest should elevate it but not for too long: "elevet eam supra frontem ut possit a populo videri; nec nimis diu teneat elevatum."[41]

There is altogether among the different witnesses a surprising amount of variation in the canon. Two instances bear possible, if faint, light on York Use before the later middle ages. One is the original reading in the Rylands manuscript of "Necnon et illorum quorum hodie sollemnis in conspectu gloriae tuae celebratur triumphans" after the recital of saints' names in the *Communicantes* section. Such a clause does not occur in any of the Gallican, Gregorian, Gelasian, or Milanese witnesses used by Bernard Botte in his critical edition of the Roman canon, and its presence here may reflect some curious variant tradition that cries out for identification; that the words were lined through in the manuscript suggests that the irregularity was recognized, probably as the book was being corrected and supplemented in the fifteenth century.[42]

The other canon-variant that requires our attention occurs in the York Minster XVI.A.9 missal, where at three points names of popes are supplied as having instituted particular features. Between the offertory rite and the proper prefaces this manuscript (Henderson's B) reads "Pelagius papa constituit cantandas novem praefationes," and, after the nine are listed, "Gregorius papa decimam adjecit de S. Andrea apostolo. Quibus etiam Urbanus papa undecimam de sancta Maria addicit." Similarly, between the *Communicantes* and *Hanc igitur* sections a rubric reads 'Eugenius vii instituit. Et cum dicat, parum tangat calicem, dicens," and between the *Quam oblationem* and *Qui pridie* sections, "Alexander papa instituit. Inclinato capite super lintheamina hostiam accipiendo." From at least the time of the early canonist Burchard of Worms (d. 1025) the rule limiting proper prefaces to the nine specified was ascribed to Pelagius II (579–90); the devotion of Gregory the Great to the apostle Andrew was widely known; and apparently

---

[41] *York Missal*, I.186. At this point the considerable missal component in one of the breviaries collected by Fothergill, now York Minster XVI.O.9, has simply "Hic sursum levet corpus ad visionem populi" (*York Missal*, I.187). The printed editions have no elevation of the host but only of the chalice, "usque ad caput," the Sidney missal "usque ad pectus vel ultra caput," and the breviary just mentioned "in altum." Evidently this was a matter about which practices tended to differ.

[42] B. Botte, *Le Canon de la messe romaine: Edition critique* (Louvain 1935), p. 34; *York Missal*, I.184.

Urban II did mandate the Marian preface at the Synod of Piacenza in 1095.[43] So there is a clear historicity about this rubric. Likewise, the ancient historical tradition of the *Liber pontificalis* lies behind ascribing the use of the Words of Institution at mass to the early second-century pope Alexander II. Whatever the "seven" were that pope Eugenius is said to have instituted – they may be either the seven rubrical words that follow, or the seven words "In primis gloriosae et semper virginis Mariae" at the beginning of the *Communicantes* (but those words are rather a long way earlier), or even the seven crosses in two sections that follow (but none is in the *Hanc igitur* section immediately after the rubric) – it seems plausible that his name may be a corruption of Alexander's immediate predecessor, Evaristus, to whom the *Liber pontificalis* assigns the introduction of seven, to be sure: seven deacons as episcopal assistants.[44]

Our purposes do not require knowing the precise sources from which the rubricist whose work is reflected in MS B took his information. The clearly striking thing is that this one missal seems to have rubrics that draw on some sort of liturgical or canonical commentary, a fact which must set this book in a class by itself, even though it is not otherwise as rubrically full or variant as MS D (the Sidney Sussex missal). One admittedly far-fetched possibility has to be raised, if timidly. It is intriguing to note that a Eugenius (III) was pope in 1145–53 (and in that capacity deposed William of York as archbishop) and an Alexander (III) in 1158–81: the point being that the two reigns comprise much of the span of recorded activity for one "Jeremy" of Rouen and York to whom the work widely known as the *Lay Folks Mass Book* is commonly ascribed – a work to which some attention must now be paid.

Towards glimmers about origins, through a vernacular source

In 1879 Thomas Frederick Simmons produced an edition of an untitled vernacular work, giving it the title by which it is always now called: the *Lay Folks Mass Book*.[45] Starting from a reference in Maskell's *Ancient Liturgy*, he became aware of, eventually, six manuscripts of a Middle

---

[43] J. Jungmann, *The Mass of the Roman Rite*, Eng. tr. F. A. Brunner, 2 vols (New York 1951–55), II.120.

[44] *Liber pontificalis*, I.vi (in any edition or translation).

[45] T. F. Simmons, ed. *The Lay Folks Mass Book, or Manner of Hearing Mass*, Early Eng. Text Soc., o.s. 71 (1879, repr. 1968). Although, given its auspices, the thrust of the edition was meant to be primarily philological, Simmons, another learned Yorkshire country parson (rector of Dalton Holme), supplied also a vast section of "Notes and Illustrations" (pp. 155–315) which includes a lot of comments on the mass. He also printed the entire order of mass, with the propers for Trinity Sunday inserted at the

English account in verse, all beginning something like "þo worthyest þing, most of godnesse, / In al þys world, [hit] is þo messe." In two of the versions the author is stated to be a "Dan Jeremy," whose work the anonymous versifier has Englished.[46] No further information is supplied as to who this Jeremy may have been. Simmons claimed that the original language was French, and speculated (or rather, postulated) that the figure in question was the Jeremy (Jeremias) who was a canon of Rouen by 1157 and archdeacon of Cleveland in the diocese of York by 1171.[47]

Simmons then went on to specify five points at which there seem to be similarities between usages described in the *LFMB* and those of the cathedral at Rouen, taking the latter from "the early Rouen missal printed by Martène."[48] Of the dialectical differences in the four English textual strands (matters more germane to concerns of the Early English Text Society, in which this edition appeared, than liturgical minutiae) Simmons was inclined to privilege the northern, as representing a first level of translation from the original French. This, and his identification of Jeremy's York connection, then enabled him to make the jump of supposing that the original (French) text behind the (English) *LFMB* represents primarily adaptation of the contents of the (Rouen-influenced?) original to conform to York Use. Major questions appear at once as to the soundness of these inferences; but if they should be correct – above all, *if* "Jeremy's" putative original is a text of the last third of the twelfth century, and *if* the Englishing was done without serious alteration of the ritual detail of the original – then *LFMB* might help in pointing to an earlier stratum of liturgy at York than the extant service books allow us to reach. These are, however, large "if"s, and the whole chain of reasoning needs to be treated with caution.

It is, though, plausible to suppose that the drastic rebuilding of the Minster under archbishop Roger might have been accompanied by a tightening-up of liturgical life there and, by extension, in the diocese, even the province. Some support for this hypothesis is offered by canon

---

correct places, as from MS B (the one with the "papal" rubrics), with facing-page translation: pp. 90–117. Simmons's title has no MS authority.

[46] Simmons distinguished four textual strands, each represented by a single manuscript, with two further MSS providing various readings. In one of the strands the author is called Jerome.

[47] This identification is seconded by D. Greenway in *Fasti 1066–1300*, VI: *York* (1999), p. 37: "almost certainly author of the original version of the *Lay Folks' Mass Book*." His last occurrence as archdeacon is in 1189. Charter evidence confirms Jeremy's positions but not, of course, his authorship.

[48] This is probably the 1497 or 1499 printing of a Rouen missal, used also by Legg for his collations in *WM* III, as "Rouen."

3 of the Provincial Synod that met in 1195; this orders that, because the *secretum misse* (here meaning the entire canon) is frequently found to be corrupt through either scribal error or the age of the books ("aut scriptorum falsitate aut librorum vetustate"), archdeacons should take care to ensure that in all churches the canon is corrected "ad verum et probatum exemplar."[49] Given that after Roger's death in 1181 there was a ten-year vacancy, and that the person who filled it finally was the disgraceful Geoffrey Plantagenet (bastard son of Henry II and constant thorn in the flesh of Richard I and John), with whom the canons of York were having a blazing row throughout 1194–95, it is not improbable that any such *exemplar* might bear something of Roger's imprint.[50] And, though little is known about Roger's antecedents, the village he came from in Normandy was in the province of Rouen; and one of the canons of the cathedral at Rouen was the Jeremy who became, by 1171, an archdeacon in Roger's diocese – and, if still alive then, would have been one of those to whom the 1195 mandate as to correction of the mass-canon was directed.[51] This is to be sure a thin thread, but one that cannot be wholly ignored. Whatever element of the usages of Rouen may eventually be traced in those of York, at present it does not seem that we can go behind the archiepiscopate of Roger in our quest for the origins of the York Use.

As it is inevitable that the phrase "Sarum Use" brings to mind the Salisbury cathedral basically complete in the 1260s, so "York Use" tends to connote liturgy at the Minster from the 1470s, when the new east end was completed (the building as a whole was consecrated in 1472), until the Reformation changes put an end to the Latin liturgy in England. The vivid impression we have of York Use in its last decades derives not only from the splendor of the Minster but also from the plethora of churches in the city of York (with, especially, their often wondrous glass) and from the magnificence of the daughter minsters at Beverley, Ripon, and Southwell. We are unlikely to get such a vivid sense of the other undoubted secular use in England, that of Hereford; nonetheless, it deserves our careful, and next, attention.

---

[49] *C & S 871–1204*, pt. ii, p. 1048. This was an unique meeting in that it was presided over by an archbishop of Canterbury, Hubert Walter, albeit in his capacity as papal legate.

[50] Hostility reached such a point that the canons threw Chrism blessed by an episcopal supporter of Geoffrey's on a dung heap (see the vivid account by M. Lovatt in *ODNB* 21.764–69).

[51] Jeremy last occurs as archdeacon in 1189, but records during Geoffrey's reign are scanty. Another canon of York in the 1180s and 90s, William de Malapalude, was definitely from Rouen: *Fasti ... York*, p. 54.

Hereford Use

Even more than York, Hereford – its cathedral, the worship practiced there, the "Use" that that pattern of worship came to be called, and the spread of that "Use" – epitomizes a number of the problems we have encountered. The first involves intertwined questions of antiquity and continuity.[52] No other English medieval diocese can claim such a combination of these factors as Hereford: a seventh-century foundation (676, in the Theodoran structuring of the English church) with headquarters always in the same place, no serious disruption by Norse or other invaders, and no change in the type of clergy – at Hereford, always secular – who served the cathedral.[53] Hence it is likely that we may be more than usually curious about liturgy at Hereford in the period before the thirteenth century, when information from distinctive service books begins to be available.

There seems, however, to be no way to trace even a glimmer of the story before the Norman Conquest. The bishop at that time was a Lotharingian, Walter, whose reign lasted from 1061 to 1079 and who was succeeded by another from the same region, Robert de Losinga, until 1095.[54] Robert's brother Gerard may have been the first dean, or functional equivalent thereof, probably before the end of the century.[55] Information about members of what would come to be a conventionally organized chapter (four dignitaries, two archdeacons, roughly twenty-four canons) is for the twelfth century somewhat sketchy, but there is reason to suspect that several were men of some intellectual distinction. This seems clearly to have been the case during the successive episcopates of Robert of Béthune (1131–48), Gilbert Foliot (1148–63), and

[52] The fullest treatment of its story as a whole is now *Hereford Cathedral: a History*, ed. G. Aylmer and J. Tiller (London 2000). Three of its chapters will be adduced subsequently.

[53] The most serious disruption appears to have come in 1055, when Griffith ap Llewelyn's Welsh forces ravaged the city, burnt the early 11th-cent. cathedral, killed many of the clergy, and "captured all the treasures and took them away," according to the C and D versions of the *Anglo-Saxon Chronicle*, ed. D. Whitelock (London 1961), p. 130. The following year the new and warlike bishop, Leofgar, was killed in battle against Griffith, and for the next four years the see of Hereford was held jointly with Worcester by the redoubtable Ealdred.

[54] J. Barrow, "A Lotharingian in Hereford: Bishop Robert's Reorganization of the Church of Hereford 1079–1095," in *Medieval Art, Architecture and Archaeology at Hereford*, ed. D. Whitehead, BAA Conf. Trs. 15 (1995, for 1990), pp. 29–49, has demonstrated that Robert almost certainly came from Liège and may have been in England from as early as c. 1050.

[55] J. Barrow, *Fasti 1066–1300*, VIII: *Hereford* (2002), *passim*; relying heavily on, but qualifying, Z. N. and C. N. L. Brooke, "Hereford Cathedral Dignitaries in the Twelfth Century," *Cbg. Historical Jnl* 8 (1944), pp. 1–21 and 179–85.

Robert de Melun (1163–67).[56] At issue here is the extent to which two mid-twelfth-century manuscripts made for, and still at, Hereford cathedral can be used as precious witnesses to liturgy there before the better documented thirteenth century.[57]

The two are, or at least might have been, complementary volumes capable of being used at the night office: a homiliary (Hereford Cathedral P.viii.7) and a passional or legendary (P.vii.6). They are of similar size and apparently written in the same hand; in both, Rodney Thomson observes that "Run-overs suggest that the scribe was copying column-for-column."[58] What the scribe was copying *from* is of course a key question. The homiliary is basically the Carolingian collection of Paul the Deacon, with some subsequent additions, the latest being two sermons ascribed in the headings to Fulbert of Chartres (d. 1028) and one so ascribed to Anselm of Canterbury but actually by Ralph d'Escures, bishop of Rochester 1108–14 and archbishop of Canterbury 1114–22: this suggests a *terminus a quo* for the scribe's model. This volume contains homilies only for the sanctorale and common of saints, so there must have been at least one further volume for the temporale. There are proper homilies for only a couple of dozen saints, with some curious omissions (Martin most obviously, but also Barnabas, Luke, Simon and Jude); this makes noteworthy the inclusion of homilies for the Seven Brothers, the Translation of Benedict, and, after three for the Decollation of John the Baptist, the *Inventio capitis* of that saint.[59] No English figures are included, nor Gregory the Great.

The passional, however, does bear signs of English ancestry. It is the final volume, covering November 9th through December 31st, of what was apparently a five-volume set. "English" saints present are Edmund

---

[56] This is the period of the brilliant flowering of sculpture in the so-called "Hereford school," seen above all in the parish churches at Shobdon and Kilpeck; specific parallels between figures at Kilpeck and those in Hereford Cath. MS P.iv.3 (Minor Prophets and Gilbert the Universal's Gloss on Lamentations) have often been noted.

[57] These are apparently not included in the gift of the canon Reginald who, according to the Hereford Cathedral martyrology (Bodl. Rawl. B.328) of the mid-14th cent. "contulit Hereford. ecclesie plura volumina, scilicet, psalterium glosatum, epistolas sancti Pauli, unum missale, unum graduale, unum cherubin" (fol. 2). This Reginald was probably the precentor (formerly called "cantor" at Hereford), 1150–63.

[58] R. A. B. Mynors and R. M. Thomson, *Cat. of the MSS of Hereford Cath. Lib.* (Cambridge 1993), pp. 112, 119; the hand is illustrated on pl. 48. I consistently refer to the opinions expressed there as those of Thomson, to whom there fell the entire task of completing, revising, and supplementing the notes and typescripts left by Mynors at his death in 1989. (This is in no way meant to belittle the fundamental contribution of Sir Roger, a close friend of both Thomson's and mine.)

[59] The last has no ascription in its heading and is not identified by Thomson in his otherwise extremely detailed description; it is *BHL Suppl.* 4290d, ed. B. de Gaiffier in his *Recherches d'hagiographie latin*, Subsidia Hagiographca 52 (Brussels 1971).

the Martyr, Birinus, Judoc, Eadburga (of Minster-in-Thanet), and Ecgwine, all at the usual days. In general the saints' days are indicated, but there are two or three notable exceptions. One is John the Almsgiver, who appears in a sequence that runs Ursinus (9 November, with no date), Martin (11 November), Mennas (ditto), John (the life by Leontius of Naples, in 55 chapters!), Paternus (12 November), and Cunibert (ditto). John's usual feast day in the West, albeit not much observed, is January 23rd, but in the East November 12th, so this must be the Eastern day: why, is a considerable puzzle. The second is a most unusual Mary, also without day but placed between Edmund on November 20th and Cecilia on the 22nd. Her *passio* is clearly that of the *Maria ancilla* who is included in the Frankish martyrologies on November 1st; but her placement in this passional, precisely as though her day were the 21st, suggests a confusion with the (largely) Anglo-Saxon feast of the Oblation or Presentation of the Virgin (see p. 92). A similar confusion appears after the entry for Lucia on December 13th: this is followed by what the contemporary table of contents on fol. 1 calls "Passio alterius sancte lucie virginis," although it is in fact that for a martyr Luceia (*sic*) whose usual day is June 25th. These eccentricities seem to indicate that the scribe was working from something like a calendar as well as at least one hagiographical collection; is it reasonable to regard this as anything like an early twelfth-century Hereford calendar? The volume closes with the life of Ecgwin (December 30th) by Dominic of Evesham, who died in 1125; so the terminus for the information in the passional is very close to what we have seen to be that for the homiliary.

The one *passio* noticed by Thomson as marked for nine lessons is that for Chrysogonus, widely if unremarkably observed on November 24th (and sometimes spelled with an initial G).[60] These lessons, indicated in (undatable) pencilled Roman numerals, are quite long; but there is no reason to have marked lessons unless they were going to be used liturgically. By the time of the printed Hereford breviary (1505: to be discussed presently) they have been supplanted by a mere three, all from the common. Wondering when in the intervening three-plus centuries the admittedly not very consequential decision was taken to demote Chrysogonus both in grading, from nine lessons to three, and in specificity, from proper to common lessons may lead us to the next

---

[60] His day is given on fol. 102 as "Quinto kal. Dec.," which is the 27th, but his *passio* is placed between those for Trudo on the 23rd and Catherine on the 25th. A contemporary list of contents at the end of the late 11th-cent. passional for Old Sarum, now Salisbury Cath. 222 (formerly Bodl. Fell 1), includes Chrysogonus between Trudo and Saturninus (29 Nov.), though the text itself breaks off in October: Webber, *Scribes and Scholars*, p. 157, n. 2.

stage in our enquiry: to view evidence from the thirteenth century for something which by that time, if not in the twelfth, has become a self-conscious "Use." This involves a preliminary look at the historiography of the subject.

Modern awareness of Hereford Use

After the mention in Cranmer's famous preface to the 1549 Book of Common Prayer (see p. 497), there seems to have been little consciousness of a distinctive Hereford Use until the mid-nineteenth-century revival of interest in "liturgiology," initially through study of the early printed texts: a study referred to so often in previous chapters that no repetition is needed here. A specific point of departure is offered by William Maskell's printing of parallel texts of the ordinary and canon of the mass according to Sarum, York, Hereford, and Roman (and, in part, what he thought of as Bangor) Uses, in 1844.[61] Some thirty years later W. G. Henderson produced what he called a "reprint of the Hereford Missal ... from the printed edition of 1502 collated with a Manuscript of the fourteenth Century, preserved in the Library of University College, Oxford."[62] The latter, its MS 78A, he thought to have been the only surviving manuscript missal, but there are at least two, probably three, more.[63] The University College missal belonged to the church of St Dubricius at Whitchurch in Monmouthshire, and has some interesting textual variants from the later printed edition.[64] It is clear that Henderson knew also about the noted breviary of c. 1265 which will bulk large in our discussion (Hereford Cathedral P.ix.7), for he collates its calendar (which lacks January and February) with those of the printed and manuscript missal towards establishing a kind of composite Hereford calendar. There is no other editorial matter, save for an appendix which prints, without comment, six brief passages from the surviving Hereford ordinal, BL Harley 2983 (discussed later).

It was primarily on the basis of the information provided by Henderson that Edmund Bishop took up the study of the Hereford liturgy,

---

[61] In his path-breaking *The Ancient Liturgy of the Church of England*; on p. cli of the 2nd edn, 1846, he prints the title page and colophon of the 1502 Rouen edition of the Hereford missal that he used.

[62] *Hereford Missal*, p. iii. Henderson's name appears only at the end of the brief preface, not on the title page. The book was printed in Leeds in 1874, not as part of any series.

[63] Worcester Cath. F.161; BL Add. 39675; and, less clearly, Downside Abbey 48243. These will be considered presently.

[64] Henderson collates those between Advent and Maundy Thursday, pp. v–vi, and also provides a useful list of the eight missing sections, some of them extensive.

publishing in 1894 the first version of an influential article in which he showed that the affinities of Hereford services for Holy Week were much more strongly with Rouen than with Salisbury; but when at the end of his essay he tried to explain why this should have been so, nothing more palpable emerged than the rather feeble suggestion that revitalization of the Hereford cathedral services after the troubles of the disputed succession (Stephen vs. Matilda) in the early 1140s might have been due to bishop Robert of Béthune.[65] The rationale for this was that a fragment of a treatise of John of Avranches which Bishop characterized as "a Rouen ceremonial of the eleventh century" was known in the twelfth century at Llanthony Priory, of which Robert had been abbot before becoming bishop of Hereford.[66] Most of the substantiating detail involves comparing Rouen texts of the fifteenth and seventeenth centuries with Hereford texts of the early sixteenth, and the argument becomes distinctly stretched.

The Rouen "origins" of the Hereford rite having been postulated, albeit with only slim evidence, by such a great figure as Bishop, little further notice was paid to that aspect of the subject. Around the beginning of the twentieth century W. H. Frere turned his attention to Hereford, hoping to produce quickly an edition of the unique 1505 printed breviary (of which Henderson had made a complete but unsatisfactory transcript). But the mid-thirteenth-century noted breviary could not be ignored, nor three other manuscripts which had come to light, most notably a small breviary at Worcester cathedral (its MS Q.86: see p. 473). Associating with himself the Sub-Librarian of Hereford Cathedral, Langton Brown, Frere was able to issue a more complicated product than had originally been envisaged, a three-volume edition, issued by the Henry Bradshaw Society in 1904, 1911, and 1915: nearly 1,300 pages in all, and a work almost as difficult to use as the Procter and Wordsworth edition of the 1531 Sarum breviary, 1879–86 (see p. 425), on which Frere's largely depends.[67] The outcome was the

---

[65] Edmund Bishop, "Holy Week Rites of Sarum, Hereford, and Rouen Compared," first published in vol. I (1894) of the *Transactions of the Society of St Osmund*, but always cited from his collected essays, *Liturgica Historica* (Oxford 1918), pp. 276–300, where there are several bracketed alterations.

[66] The relevance of this is weakened by the fact that this MS, now BL Roy. 8 D.viii, belonged to Lanthony secunda, founded in 1136, the Gloucestershire cell of L(l)anthony prima in Mons., which was the house of which Robert had been prior from (probably) the early 1120s until 1131: *Heads Rel. Houses*, I.172. Furthermore, the fragment in question, less than a page (fol. 132v), is concerned with the canonical hours, not the mass.

[67] A "guiding principle" of his edition is stated to be "that the text itself should not be printed in full, but that where the Breviary agreed with the Sarum use, reference should be made to the reprint of the Sarum Breviary": *Hereford Brev.*, I.vi.

text of the 1505 printed edition, with variants from the manuscripts in footnotes, rather than, as might have been hoped, an edition of the thirteenth-century manuscript breviary with *comparanda*.

Although the edition itself is something of a disappointment, Frere's extensive introduction to the third volume, aiming to provide "a brief comparison of the three chief English medieval secular breviaries," is in fact a highly useful survey of the secular office as a whole.[68] But, still ignoring the matter of origins entirely, he takes the later medieval Hereford rite as a given – a position which we now see was taken already in the thirteenth century.

Consuetudo Herefordensis *in the thirteenth century*

We have noticed Edmund Bishop's somewhat unsubstantiated opinion that the origin of the Hereford rite as distinctive may have lain in the episcopate of Robert of Béthune, bishop 1131–48, who (he thought) imported what was basically the rite used at Rouen. Whatever element of truth there may be in that view, more than a hundred years later something identified as the *consuetudo Herefordensis* is, as such, exported to the Continent, to a church in Savoy founded by a Savoyard bishop who ruled the diocese of Hereford from 1240 to 1268.

The somewhat improbable story works out in this way. It appears to be the case that during the period from about 1230 to 1270 a confluence of developments produced both a considerable set of changes in the liturgy at Hereford and a self-consciousness about it. Obvious elements would seem to be awareness of what was going on at Salisbury at the time (see pp. 364 and 385); relations, most likely in the form of tension, between the Hereford clergy and their bishop; and the presence in the chapter of one or more members energetically interested in the liturgy. Possible figures of this sort include Ralph of Maidstone, dean 1231 to 1234 and bishop from the latter year until 1239, when he resigned his see to become a Franciscan friar; Stephen of Thornbury, Ralph's successor as dean from 1234 until at least 1241, possibly 1247; Robert of Ewerby, precentor by late 1233 until probably the early 1240s; and, though less plausibly, Giles of Avenbury, dean from October 1247 until he resigned in unhappy circumstances and became treasurer.[69] Of these, Ralph (whose career is somewhat reminiscent of that

---

[68] *Hereford Brev.*, III.vii–lxi. His treatment of the other two uses is based on the Procter and Wordsworth edition of the Sarum and the Surtees Society edition of the York books.

[69] Barrow, *Fasti, passim*. It is possible that Giles regained the deanery for a few months, or years, in and after 1276.

of his older contemporary Richard Poore, dean and, after a two-year interval, bishop at Salisbury), seems the likeliest candidate. He emerges in the years between 1215 and 1223 as treasurer of Lichfield, archdeacon of Shropshire (in the diocese of Hereford) and then of Chester (in Coventry and Lichfield), master at the University of Paris in the late 1220s and subsequently at Oxford, where he is Chancellor by mid-1231; so he is vastly experienced when he becomes dean of Hereford later in that year and bishop three years later.[70]

But there is no direct evidence for his involvement with liturgical change, and it was instead during the long episcopate of Ralph's successor that both the earliest surviving book clearly of "Hereford Use" was written (see next section) and the earliest extant reference to that Use was made – the latter by, indeed, that successor, Peter of Aigueblanche, bishop 1240–68.[71] It is hard not to connect the two things. By 1267 bishop Peter, laying down statutes for the collegiate church of St Catherine that he founded in his native region of Savoy (diocese of Maurienne), refers twice to the Hereford *consuetudo*: "Omnia vero officia ecclesiae in matutinis, missis, et in omnibus aliis horis fiant secundum consuetudinem herefordensis ecclesiae ut in libris ordinatum invenietur."[72] Even the legends of the saints in the daily office (like those in the passional discussed above) were to be those of Hereford: "legenda tam de sanctis quam ferialibus per totum annum secundum eandem consuetudinem herefordensis ecclesiae legetur."

Bishop Peter's apparent attachment to Hereford ways seems surprising, given that his main activities in England were either in the promotion of Henry III's cause against baronial opposition or in defending himself from attacks by his irascible royal patron. Furthermore, he was seldom in England after 1256 and apparently not at all after 1265; nor, according to Matthew Paris, did he speak any English.[73] Deeply unpopular with the Hereford clergy, he secured the deanery for a nephew, John, and at least five other of the disliked Savoyards ("Burgundians") got

---

[70] Barrow, pp. 6 and 11, citing *Biog. Reg. Oxf.* At Lichfield in the time of Hugh Nonant, bishop 1188–98, there had been some imitating of constitutional arrangements at Salisbury, and what Frere calls "extensive borrowing from Sarum on the liturgical side" under bishop Hugh de Patishull, 1239–41: *Use of Sarum*, I.xxxiii–xxxv.

[71] Peter had been brought to England in 1240 by William of Savoy, Queen Eleanor's uncle. F. M. Powicke has called him the "most detested of bishops in Henry III's reign": *King Henry III and the Lord Edward*, 2 vols (Oxford 1947), I.264.

[72] Quoted from F. Mugnier, *Les Savoyards en Angleterre au XIIIe siècle* (Paris and Chambéry 1891) in *Lincoln Cath. Stats*, II.41–42.

[73] T. F. Tout in (old) *DNB* 15 (1895), pp. 946–51. A more balanced view is taken by N. Yates, "Bishop Peter de Aquablanca (1240–1268): a Reconsideration," *Jnl Eccles. Hist.* 22 (1971), pp. 303–17; cf. N. Vincent in *ODNB* 1.475–78.

preferments in the diocese. So to posit anything like the emergence of a self-conscious Hereford Use to Pierre d'Aigueblanche himself would seem to stretch credulity. If, as Julia Barrow asserts, "It was during Peter's pontificate that the cathedral liturgy was overhauled, and a full set of cathedral statutes drawn up," this is unlikely to have been because of harmony between bishop and chapter.[74] But the statutes do seem to have been codified between 1246 and Peter's death in 1268, and Barrow may be right that those and the Hereford breviary, to which we now turn, show between them "a new spirit of institutional confidence within the cathedral."[75]

Clearer light: the thirteenth-century breviary

Whatever the dynamics between bishop Peter and the chapter, it is during the years when he was largely absent from Hereford that the noted breviary still at the cathedral (P.ix.7) was made.[76] This, which seems to be the fullest English secular breviary of any use that survives from the thirteenth century, has several advantages for our study: it is virtually complete; it can be dated within a seven-year period, 1262–68;[77] and, though not edited *in extenso*, it has been collated (with the printed 1505 Rouen edition) in the Henry Bradshaw Society edition discussed above. Its contents can also be compared with those of the two books, noticed earlier, made almost certainly at and for Hereford cathedral in the third quarter of the twelfth century (the homiliary and the passional, both covering the saints of late autumn), as well as with the ordinal to be discussed below.[78]

---

[74] J. Barrow, "Athelstan to Aigueblanche, 1056–1268," in *Hereford Cathedral: a History* (note 52 above), pp. 21–47 at 45–46. A papal confirmation of privileges after a dispute with Peter marks a victory for the Hereford chapter in 1245: E. Crosby, *Bishop and Chapter in Twelfth-Century England* (Cambridge 1994), p. 289; W. H. Bliss and J. A. Twemlow, eds., *Calendar of Entries in the Papal Registers ..., Papal Letters*, 18 vols (London 1893–), I.222

[75] Barrow (as above), p. 47. The printing of these in *Lincoln Cath. Stats.*, II.36–89, is mainly from a MS of c. 1400, BL Roy. 2 A.x. Of special note is the injunction that those who take part in the choir office should within a year and a day know by heart (*corde tenus*) psalter, antiphonal, and hymnal, "ne per defectum ipsorum ecclesia suo seruicio defraudetur" (p. 80).

[76] Described by Frere in his Introduction to the HBS edition, vol. III (1915), pp. lv–lxi; the text is furnished by collation (siglum H) with that of the 1505 printed book. See also Mynors and Thomson, *Cat.*, pp. 124–25 and pl. 51, and the numerous references in *Hereford Cathedral*, esp. pp. 369–74, with ills. on p. 372 and colored pl. IVa.

[77] This precision of dating is made possible by the obits, written in the original hand (see below): Mynors and Thomson, p. 125; though Frere (III.lx) uses the same evidence to calculate the date-span as 1254–58.

[78] As, for example, in the fact (already mentioned) that in the passional Chrysogonus's *passio* (27 Nov.) has been marked in pencil for nine lessons, whereas it is a feast of

At least two facts about this breviary raise the suspicion that it represents a reworking of the (office) liturgy at Hereford in the thirteenth century – again, conceivably influenced by what was going on at Salisbury at the time.[79] The first is that there is a marked change in the structure of the common of saints between the twelfth-century homiliary and this mid-thirteenth-century breviary. The homiliary has just seven categories: plural apostles, one martyr, several martyrs, one confessor, one bishop-confessor, several confessors, and one virgin.[80] The breviary has no fewer than twelve, six of them divided into sub-categories of three and nine lessons: one evangelist (needed only for Mark and Luke), plural apostles, one martyr (ix lect., iii lect.), one martyr pontiff (here *pontifex*, not *episcopus*), many martyrs (ix, iii), one confessor pontiff (ix, iii), one confessor not pontiff or abbot (ix, iii), one abbot, several confessors, one virgin martyr (ix, iii), one virgin not martyr (ix, iii), several virgins.

The second fact is that, although complete in its contents, the book is structured rather differently from the way breviaries come to be most often arranged (calendar, psalter, temporale, etc.). Here the temporale comes first, then calendar, with psalter following that. Furthermore, the psalter is not "liturgical" but simply gives the psalms in numerical order; this means that some sort of additional text, at the least an *ordo*, would be necessary to make the book practically usable. Two other points suggest that this may have been more a reference-source than a book for daily use. First, the single scribe who wrote it (in what Thomson calls "one expert English rotunda bookhand") has copied into the calendar some two dozen obits, mostly of cathedral dignitaries, which implies that the book had a kind of official character as a volume of record.[81] Secondly, between the temporale and the calendar come four folios (179–82) giving directions that the tunes of hymns

three lessons in the calendars of both the Hereford manuscript and Rouen printed breviaries, and in the sanctorale in neither.

[79] An additional, inconclusive fact is that its initial folio, codicologically a singleton, is a leaf from an early 12th-cent. antiphonal, the contents being antiphons and responds from the octave of Pentecost until early August. Frere thought these to be "according to some other use" (*Heref. Brev.*, III.lvi), but it is entirely possible that they represent the office liturgy at Hereford – not necessarily the same thing as "Hereford Use" – at the period of writing. Differences in wording between that leaf and the later Hereford texts are slight but noticeable.

[80] There should be a category for several virgins as well, but not so. "One apostle" is scarcely needed because each of the apostles save Matthias and Bartholomew has a proper homily in the sanctorale, as do Philip and James; the plural apostles can apply only to Simon and Jude.

[81] Printed Mynors and Thomson, *Cat.*, pp. 124–25, and Frere, *Heref. Brev.*, III.lviii–ix. A few more may have been added by the same (original) scribe. Further obits, including two dated 1417 and 1446, are irrelevant to the present discussion.

should be sung according to Hereford custom and in a particular way ("consuetudinem Herefordensis ecclesie in hunc modum"): this may imply some degree of novelty, or at least individuality, an aspect of the self-consciousness of what can reasonably be called Hereford Use. Thus it seems possible that this manuscript may represent a codifying of the office at Hereford.[82]

Such a self-contained office book would scarcely have been needed in choir at the cathedral, where the constituent volumes would have been available. By at least the late fifteenth century it was no longer there, having apparently been taken to the parish church at Mordiford (about four miles southeast), the dedication of which has been added to the calendar. Thomson has noted "signs of heavy use," but there is no way of telling at what time it was used most heavily. Twelve new feasts have been added to the calendar as well, and the office of Corpus Christi. The likeliest guess would seem to be that the book came to be owned by a canon of the cathedral whose prebendal estate included the village of Mordiford (not itself a prebend).

Further evidence for liturgy at Hereford in the late thirteenth century is provided by the one surviving ordinal (now BL Harley 2983).[83] As it stands it is something of a muddle; its compilation is analyzed by Frere as follows.[84] The first 46 folios represent an addition, albeit at the beginning of the book, to an original nucleus which dealt with the breviary (fols 47–82; Frere's O²): this is definitely an addition, in that fol. 1 picks up where 82v had left off and completes the section on the office (fols 1–21; O¹). The same hand then supplies material for processions and the mass (fols 21–46; O³). Working backwards, Frere asserts that O³ "clearly belongs to the cathedral," as is proved by ceremonial directions for Holy Week which "could apply only to that building" and to its personnel; that O¹ is "of a piece with O³," and therefore written for the cathedral as well; and that O² is "an incomplete copy of the Ordinal of Hereford, probably written for the Cathedral at the end of the thirteenth century" and taken over by the supplementing scribe some years later.[85]

---

[82] Also, perhaps, in terms of music. The *venitarium* and tonary at the end of the codex (fols 360v–64v) are really reference features for the planning of the office chants and are unlikely to have been used in performance of the offices themselves, even if the book was in the possession of the precentor.

[83] Six snippets had been printed by Henderson as an appendix to his *Hereford Missal* edn., pp. 459–61.

[84] *Heref. Brev.*, III.lxii–lxvii.

[85] Frere's editorial treatment is almost as complicated as the book itself. All the text relating to the office (O¹ and O²) is collated with the breviary texts in vols I and II of his edition; in addition, the complete texts of O¹ and O² for the first two days in Advent have been printed in full (III.39–63). Then the text of O³ dealing with the

At one point in the ordinal there is evidence of a desire for simultaneous liturgical participation by all of the principal *personae* of the
diocese. The original section, O², specifies that at matins on the first
Sunday of Advent the verses of the great first responsory *Aspiciens a
longe* are to be said respectively by "duo maiores, scilicet episcopus et
diaconus si interfuerint," by the two archdeacons (Hereford and Ludlow), and by the treasurer and chancellor (the precentor is excused, as
co-ordinating all of this); but in the continuation and revision implied
by O¹ this is changed to "due persone maiores ..., alie due persone pro-
pinquiores in dignitate ... [et] duo de senioribus canonicis," as though
it had been realized that the presence of all six dignitaries at the same
service was improbable.[86]

That is clear enough evidence that the ordinal is in the first instance
drawn up to regulate worship at the cathedral. But the rubricist O¹ is
equally aware that a wider audience is to be provided for. Still in the section on Advent I (when, coming as it does at the beginning of the temporale, there is always likely to be the greatest concentration of rubrics) we
are told that towards the end of prime the martyrology is to be read "in
ecclesiis ubi habetur martilogium," while in churches "ubi non legitur
martilogium" the service continues with no such interruption.[87]

Fourteenth-century changes

The two manuscript witnesses to the Hereford office in the fourteenth century are a composite breviary and a collectar that survives
in a highly defective form. The breviary, now Worcester Cathedral MS
Q.86, is made up of a late thirteenth-century psalter (like the Hereford
cathedral manuscript, with the psalms in numerical rather than liturgical order), with material of the second half of the fourteenth century
on either side: temporale and calendar before, sanctorale and common
of saints after.[88] The footnote collations in Frere's edition show how

---

mass and with its processions is printed for Advent I (III.65–67) and collated with
Henderson's edition of the missal for the rest (III.68–81). Finally, a summary table of
contents (O¹ and O² in parallel columns) is supplied in the Introduction, III.lxiv–lxvi;
the information provided as to saints included in O¹ is quite incomplete.

[86] *Heref. Brev.*, III.47; the text of the breviary itself then follows the revision as in O¹.

[87] *Heref. Brev.*, III.54. Similarly, the text of the Hereford cathedral breviary provides
three collects to be said at compline "in ecclesiis vero ubi congregatio fratrum et soro-
rum habetur": I.94. By the time of the surviving missals there is a rubric at the end of
the Maundy Thursday rite that mentions the washing of the altars "in aliis ecclesiis
parochialibus et cappellis per totam diocesim": *Heref. Missal*, p. 90.

[88] R. M. Thomson's description (*Cat. Worc. Cath. MSS*, 2001, pp. 178–79) adds a good
deal to that of Frere, *Heref. Brev.*, III.lxi–ii, who collates the text as MS W and prints
the calendar (II.xiff.).

extensive the differences are, specially in the lessons, between this and the witnesses on either side of it chronologically, the thirteenth-century breviary and the early printed edition.

Such differences in lessons do not necessarily account for the very large range of variation in the collectar (Balliol College, Oxford, MS 321), of apparently about the same period as the Worcester Q.86 breviary. Though now mutilated (it lacks about a quarter of its putative contents), the collectar was originally, as Frere described it, "a fine, practical book, written in specially large writing, such as is usual in books of this class, which were intended for the Dean or other senior person present."[89] In several places it disagrees with the manuscript and printed breviaries, most markedly in the sanctorale, where something like 10 per cent of the collects are divergent. This includes the prayers for at least one major occasion, the Conception, and for a whole raft of "English," and therefore possibly informative, saints such as Milburga (not in the breviaries at all), Oswald of Worcester, David, Botulph, Swithun, Grimbald, Kenelm, Osyth, Paulinus, and Wilfrid; also for many saints of distinctly secondary importance like Firmin or Nicasius. Overall, there is such a lot of divergence from either the Hereford Cathedral P.ix.7 or the Worcester Cathedral Q.86 breviaries that no one officiating at daily offices according to those books could use this collectar.

What then might have been its purpose, and what may this say about the integrity of what is usually thought of as a uniform "use"? Frere notes three mentions of *addiciones* in the rubrics of the printed edition, all ascribed to bishop John Trillek (1344–61), in two cases alongside the term *usus modernus*. The points at issue are so minor that it is hard to believe that they represent the entirety of a systematic overhaul. Nonetheless, it is plausible that, as Frere suggests, something analogous to the "New Ordinal" at Salisbury was drawn up at Hereford, either in Trillek's time or, less probably, in that of bishop Hugh Trefnant (1389–1404).[90] Certainty is impossible to attain, because the necessary fullness of rubric is available only in the 1505 printed edition, while the late thirteenth-century ordinal manuscript is often garbled.

[89] *Heref. Brev.*, III.lxvii. The text is provided by collation, only divergent material being noted, III.1–36. The initials, not noticed by Frere, take up from two to five lines in alternate red, purple, and green, and the ordinary letters of the "specially large writing" he mentions are 6–9 mm high: a size easily read if the book is held by an acolyte.

[90] *Heref. Brev.*, III.xlvi. There had been a great enhancement of worship in the Lady Chapel in 1330, when a benefaction was diverted to endow a staff of ten choral vicars: a possible result being, according to John Harper, "a significant development in musical celebration ... especially in the Lady mass": "Music and Liturgy, 1300–1600," in *Hereford Cathedral: a History*, pp. 375–97 at 384.

The distinctiveness of Hereford Use

Nonetheless, from the evidence available by roughly the beginning of the fourteenth century something can be said about the distinctiveness of the Hereford Use. There are two obvious "Hereford" saints, one from the Anglo-Saxon period and one from the later middle ages. The former, Ethelbert the Martyr, King of the East Angles, was anciently venerated in far-off Hereford, perhaps from not long after his death in 794; by at least the late tenth century his name had been added to Mary's as dedicatee of the cathedral.[91] The ordinal specifies frequent *memoriae* for him, and a mid-fourteenth-century manuscript missal (BL Add. 39675, considered further below) had added to it in the fifteenth century a mass to pray that the relics of St Ethelbert might be discovered.[92] The latter, Thomas (of) Cantilupe was the stormy-petrel bishop of Hereford from 1275 until his death in 1282 in Italy, where, having been excommunicated by archbishop Pecham, he had gone to seek papal absolution. After some of his body parts had been returned to Hereford there was material for an unofficial translation in 1287, but his official canonization did not occur until 1320.[93] Ethelbert's feast day was May 20th, Thomas's October 2nd, with his official Translation (in 1348) on the 25th.

Another saint whose presence is mildly distinctive, though shared with Exeter, is the fifth-century Cornish hermit Pi(e)ran, present as early as the ordinal just discussed; but he never rates more than a commemoration on his day, March 5th.[94] Also shared with, or rather borrowed from, Exeter, is the feast of the archangel Raphael, introduced at Hereford in 1445 by Thomas Spofford, bishop 1422–48. With unusual precision, Spofford specifies not only the day, October 5th, but also that the office and mass were to be those used at Exeter – where his predecessor at Hereford (1417–20), Edmund Lacy, went as bishop (1420–55) and was a great promoter of Raphael's cult.[95] October 5th was not a

---

[91] S. Keynes, "Diocese and Cathedral before 1056," in *Hereford Cath.*, p. 10.

[92] Before passing to the BL the missal belonged to the liturgiologist E. S. Dewick, who maintained that this mass (of which he prints the prayers) shows that the missal was most likely a Hereford cathedral book: *Trans. St Paul's Ecclesiol. Soc.* 4 (1900), p. 236.

[93] Of the various essays in Meryl Jancey, ed. *St Thomas Cantilupe Bishop of Hereford: Essays in his Honour* (Hereford 1982), see esp. Philip Barrett, "A Saint in the Calendar: the Effect of the Canonization of St Thomas Cantilupe on the Liturgy," pp. 153–57.

[94] N. Orme, ed. *Nicholas Roscarrock's Lives of the Saints: Cornwall and Devon*, Devon and Cornwall Rec. Soc. n.s. 35 (1992), pp. 166–67.

[95] The innovation was sweetened by Lacy's sumptuous gift of "a set of high mass vestments and three copes of red velvet, with orfreys of gold and red cloth, together with coverings and frontlets of cloth worked with falcons, for the high altar and its two

convenient day liturgically at Hereford, for it impeded celebration of the octave of St Thomas Cantilupe; one wonders why Spofford, who seems to have been a pious Benedictine with a special devotion to St Anne, was willing to interrupt this distinctive Hereford celebration with the notably prolix services for Raphael.[96]

Other points concerning saints have to do primarily with the gradings of their feasts.[97] In a number of cases the Worcester Q.86 breviary has nine lessons where the somewhat earlier Hereford P.ix.7 book had specified only three: in late April and May alone, Mark, Philip and James, Invention of the Cross, John at the Latin Gate, Ethelbert and his octave. This kind of inflation in the status of feasts is a well known phenomenon of the later middle ages; the calendars of the early printed breviaries (including the 1505 Hereford) are clotted with nine-lesson occasions (this makes all the more noteworthy the demotion of Chrysogonus to three lessons, as noticed above).[98]

To identify distinctive saints is relatively easy. To pin down distinctive texts is much harder, because to do so requires comparison with a confidence-inspiring body of other texts comparable in age and circumstance – not to mention, of older texts from which those at hand may (or may not) have been derived. Too much variation, however, complicates the quest hopelessly. This is specially true of the office, which is so complex in itself (as witness the variations just noted in matins-

---

collateral altars, the whole exceeding the value of 200 marks ...": G. Oliver, *Lives of the Bishops of Exeter* (Exeter 1861), p. 103.

[96] Possibly the Raphael office came to be regarded as optional: in the 1505 breviary (*Heref. Brev.*, II.354) the three brief lessons for the fourth day of Thomas's octave are followed by a rubric, "Vel si placet totum servitium de sancto raphele [*sic*] in modum qui sequitur cum memoria de sancto thoma." Spofford's devotion to St Anne is apparent in glass now part of the heavily-restored east window at Ross-on-Wye, where he is depicted kneeling before her. Richard Marks notes that Spofford "was formerly represented with her in lost windows at Catterick in North Yorkshire and Ludlow," *Stained Glass in England during the Middle Ages* (London 1993), p. 16.

[97] Frere provides a useful, if typically hard to navigate, table of the calendar variations in the Add. 39675, Univ. 78A, and 1502 printed missals and the Heref. P.ix.7, Worcester Q.86, and 1505 printed breviaries in *Hereford Brev.*, III.253–63.

[98] A sheer peculiarity is that at some time in the mid-14th cent. (between the date of the ordinal for mass [O³] and that of the surviving missals) Saints John (Chrysostom) and Julian (of LeMans), bishops, begin to appear, and together: an unlikely pair, apparently grouped only because of the day they share, Jan. 27th. There is a further peculiarity on that day: some witnesses add a *memoria* for Paula, the late 4th-cent. Roman matron and friend of St Jerome; she appears in calendars of the printed missal but not the printed breviary, of the manuscript Univ. Coll. Oxf. 78A missal but not the Worcester Q.86 breviary (the January page of the Hereford P.ix.7 breviary is missing). This must be significant, but I cannot imagine why. The Univ. 78A missal that, as noted above, came to belong to the church of St Dubricius (Dyfrig) at Whitchurch in Monmouthshire has a mass for Dubricius at Nov. 14th, but the cult seems to have been confined to that church.

lessons within the Hereford P.ix.7, Worcester Q.86, and 1505 printed versions) that evidence inferred from it has to be so heavily qualified as to become of doubtful use. Even with the much simpler mass texts, the "Hereford" witnesses do not always speak with one voice. It was noted above that the University College, Oxford MS 78A missal shows considerable textual variation from the unique 1502 printed edition. This is true also of the other manuscript missals, beginning with what is perhaps the earliest one extant (now BL Add. 39675; the book with the mass in hope of finding Ethelbert's relics, mentioned above), which seems to date from before 1348.[99] As the BL catalogue description notes, "The text differs considerably from that of the printed edition, most of the sequences being omitted, and many of the secrets, post-communions, etc. being different." Particularly interesting here is the mass set for Leonard, where the collect and secret of the printed missal have been erased and those of the predominant Sarum set written instead (fol. 157).[100] Another point of independence is its supplying of a tract for Oswald of Worcester (28 February), "Ecce vir prudens qui edificavit domum" (fol. 180v), whereas he has only a *memoria* in the printed missal.

Supplementary witness comes from two other manuscript missals, both of the fifteenth century. Downside Abbey MS 28243 is summarized by Ker as "a missal for use in Herefordshire."[101] In contents this is really a "select" missal, with six combined temporale and sanctorale feasts before the canon (which lacks music) and nineteen after it, followed by a large number of votive masses. It provides numerous sequences (especially for saints) where the printed missal indicates either none or one from the common.[102] Its size, 130 × 85 mm, suggests that it may have been designed for travel; its rather fine decoration, that the intended traveller was a priest of some distinction, at least financially. It is improbable that it would have been useful, or used, at the cathedral.

By contrast, the other manuscript missal, now Worcester Cathedral F.161, does indeed seem to be a cathedral book, though cautiously described by Rodney Thomson only as "made for a major church within

---

[99] The Translation of Thomas of Hereford in that year is a later addition to the calendar.

[100] It should be kept in mind that the readings given as H(ereford) in Legg's 1897 *WM* III apparatus are those of Henderson's edition of the 1502 printed missal.

[101] *MMBL*, II.455–58. Actually, the diocese of Hereford included south Shropshire and a few parishes elsewhere.

[102] Examples are David, Margaret, James, and Leonard; the sequence for the Translation of Thomas of Hereford is *Magnae lucem*, as on his Deposition, rather than the printed missal's *Novi plausus incrementum*.

the diocese of Hereford."[103] It is hard to believe that that church is not the cathedral. In both size and decoration this is an expensive volume. For our purposes its chief value lies in the unusually extensive rubrics, which seem to match those of the printed missal so completely that both appear likely to represent something like the Hereford ordinal of at least the fifteenth century. An extremely long preface, "Qui invisibili patris," at the blessing of the font on Easter Eve is also identical in both.

These rubrics, above all for the *Triduum sacrum*, are a feature also of the one surviving Hereford gradual, dating probably from the late fourteenth century, now BL Harley 3965.[104] In a number of instances it has fuller rubrics than the missals; for example, it is explicit about the three Easter Vigil litanies, the first to be sung by five boys, the second by five deacons, and the third (after the sanctification of the font) by three clerics "of the third form" (fol. 34). Overall, it deserves close study from a rubrical as well as musical point of view.

End of Hereford Use or end of the middle ages?

It seems likely that the Hereford Use continued to be followed, in the limited area to which it had always been confined, until it was suppressed in favor of Sarum by the decree of 1543 that supposedly put an end to diversity of (Latin) worship in the province of Canterbury. The dynamics of religious change in England in the 1530s and 1540s can form no part of the present work. In the early sixteenth century the fact that two printers of Rouen, Jean Richard and Inghelbert Haghe, thought it worth the effort and expense to produce editions of, respectively, the Hereford missal in 1502 and breviary in 1505 suggests some vitality. That there was only a single edition of each implies, however, that the market was not large.[105] As in most such cases, we cannot with confidence point to the specific manuscript exemplars from which these printed editions were made. So it is not possible, for example, to ascertain whether the somewhat expansive contents of the printed missal originated in a late manuscript book that has not survived, or whether commercial considerations are the primary cause. Features of this expansiveness include (1) a considerable section of preliminaries – *Cautelae missae*, exhaustive

[103] R. M. Thomson, *Cat. Worc. Cath. MSS*, p. 110.

[104] It belonged eventually to St Peter's church in Hereford ("Egloys seunt peder her-ifordd," fol. 140), and is so assigned in *MLGB*; but the rubrical content shows it to be almost certainly a cathedral book.

[105] The breviary was dedicated to, and apparently in some sense sponsored by, Lady Margaret Beaufort, mother of the then king, Henry VII (see p. 549) why, is not clear.

rules about collects, the texts of farsed kyries and their assignments to specific occasions – between the calendar and the missal contents proper; (2) occasional historical notes, like the statement that the Exultet and the paschal candle are "juxta institutionem beati Zozimi papae," with the points of symbolism duly explained; and (3) the canonical interpolation of a constitution of Pecham's about the baptism of children born around Easter.[106]

In the same way, the ingenious complexity of arrangement in the printed breviary – there are seven sections, which can be bound in a variety of ways – suggests awareness that potential customers might find some freedom of choice in the matter an attractive feature.[107] Whether its fullness of rubrical direction, greater than that of the extant manuscripts, is in effect an early sixteenth-century publisher's decision or reflects a very full manuscript exemplar which we do not possess must again be left an open question.[108] Presumably all the rubrics, as well as text, of the exemplar were included; otherwise it is hard to imagine how there survived the distinctly odd rubric that at compline on Holy Saturday canons and clerics should gather in surplices, "et sic erunt in albis tam in feriis quam in festis usque ad matutinas sancti hieronimi, que erunt in crastino sancti michaelis."[109] Immediately after that compline the printed breviary contains an elaborate ceremony around the Easter Sepulchre, one of which there is no notice in the extant manuscripts. This, comparable in dramatic impact to the famous *Quem queritis* ceremony of the tenth-century *Regularis Concordia* (see p. 78), must count as a major feature of the Paschal liturgy at the cathedral; but there is no evidence for it before (and beyond) the 1505 edition of the breviary. Is it therefore better considered a meaningful feature of the Hereford Use or an innovation observed only in the last half-century or so of liturgical life there?

Enough has been said to show that what we can assert with confidence about the Hereford Use is, on the present state of knowledge, even more

---

[106] Respectively, *Heref. Missal*, pp. xxxiii-xliii, 105, 112. The wording of the last is virtually identical with that of the Council of Reading, 1279 (*C & S 1205–1313*, II.836).

[107] Frere, *Heref. Brev.*, I.viii, enumerates the contents of each section and explains that they could be printed as either one or two volumes and arranged in several possible orders; that followed in the HBS edition is "merely a matter of convenience in printing."

[108] It is easy to overlook Frere's explanation, on the same page, that he has marked rubrical passages peculiar to the 1505 printed edition "by enclosing them between a single and a double asterisk."

[109] *Heref. Brev.*, I.323; second vespers of Michael (Sept. 29th) runs up against matins of Jerome (30th), with only compline between them liturgically; but why this should be offered as the model for Holy Saturday passes understanding.

problematic than with Sarum. Degrees of variation among the relatively small pool of sources are so extensive that positive statements almost always have to be qualified. Even the relatively simple points that seem to particularize liturgy at Hereford can only rarely be traced earlier than the mid-thirteenth century. The contrast between this lack of certainty and the venerable antiquity of the diocese expressed through the almost unbroken centuries of worship at the cathedral – features of Hereford that were noticed at the beginning of this chapter – is glaring. The record of what liturgy was like there c. 1500 is clearly not the whole story; but it appears that much of the earlier part of that story is yet to be uncovered.

London (St Paul's) "Use"

On October 25th, 1414, Richard Clifford, bishop of London (1407–21) sent a mandate to the dean and chapter of his cathedral to the effect that as of the following December 1st the Use of St Paul's ("Antiquuum Usum Sancti Pauli vulgariter nuncupatum") was to be replaced by that of Sarum, with the proviso that some sixteen feasts distinctive to St Paul's in either observance or grading should be retained. If asked what beyond those feasts the "ancient Use of St Paul's" consisted of we can still reply only as its librarian and diligent archival mole, W. Sparrow Simpson, did as long ago as 1892, upon discovering and printing the document: "I fear that this is a question which cannot now be answered."[110] Our challenge at the moment is to try to ascertain whether it ever could have been.

That no one seems to know precisely what it was that was "abolished" in 1414 is probably inevitable, given the striking lack of relevant service books in sufficient quantity and variety to make possible some systematic reconstruction. This makes the distinctivenesses for which we are accustomed to look, of texts, rubrics, and saints, exceptionally difficult. An additional factor may be implied by the usual name for what was abolished in 1414: the Use of St Paul's rather than that of London, though the latter term is to be sure sometimes employed also. The relationship between the cathedral church and those of its populous diocese, which included Middlesex and Essex and parts of Hertfordshire as well as the (medieval) city, may have been somewhat clouded by,

---

[110] W. S. Simpson, "A Mandate of Bishop Clifford," *Proc. Soc. Antiquaries of London,* 2nd ser. 14 (1891–93), pp. 118–28. The mandate was not preserved in Clifford's register, and the document containing it came to light only in the 1880s (though ecclesiastical historians such as Dugdale may have seen it much earlier).

among other factors, the large number of religious houses throughout the area.

Other than its abolition in 1414, the only somewhat well known fact about the Use of St Paul's is that ten years earlier the nuns of Barking Abbey were supposedly worshipping at mass according to it (see p. 348 Near the conclusion of the ordinal and customary of the nuns there, promulgated in 1404 at the initiative of their abbess, Sibille Felton, a "Regula cuiusque usus servicium dicendum est" states that to avoid altercations and discord "tres modos diversos" were to be followed: the hours according to the Rule of Benedict, the psalter in the (very old-fashioned) Romanum version, and mass "secundum usum ecclesie sancti Pauli Londoniarum."[111] This is interesting but not very helpful. In the Notes to the modern edition Dame Laurentia McLachlan called this "a tantalizing statement, for the old Use of St Paul's is not preserved in a single manuscript, so there is no basis for collation," and cautioned that it would be rash to accept the mass inferrable from the Barking document as being that of St Paul's. So the Barking prescription takes us little further, if at all; we must rely mainly on booklists, visitation records, and a few calendars – and on some splendid recent work.[112]

Backwards, towards a possible twelfth-century ordinal?

What might be termed the pre-history of the Use we are searching for goes back to at least some time in the tenth century, when a "Rule of St Paul's" – an adaptation of the *Institutio Canonicorum* of Amalarius of Metz – seems to have been adopted. Specific liturgical prescription does not form part of that document, however, and in any case how long it remained influential is not clear; it may have been included in its only surviving source, a collection of cathedral statutes c. 1300, for antiquarian reasons.[113]

---

[111] *Barking Ordinal*, ed. J. B. L. Tolhurst (with notes by L. Maclachlan), 2 vols, HBS 65–66 (1927), II.359.

[112] The massive collaborative volume, *St Paul's: the Cathedral Church of London 604–2004*, ed. D. Keene, A. Burns, and A. Saint (New Haven and London 2004) is now a valuable resource, above all for the chapter by Alan Thacker, "The Cult of Saints and the Liturgy" (pp. 113–22). I am grateful to him for a copy of his chapter in pre-publication form; my conclusions, worked out largely independently, agree almost entirely with his. A highly accessible account of the medieval history and constitution of the cathedral is C. N. L. Brooke's "The Earliest Times to 1485," in *A History of St Paul's Cathedral*, ed. W. R. Matthews and W. M. Atkins (London 1966), pp. 1–99. On all matters relating to the cathedral's principal cult figure, see E. G. Whatley, *The Saint of London: the Life and Miracles of Erkenwald* (Binghamton, NY 1989).

[113] It appears to survive only in the register of dean Ralph Baldock (1294–1304); printed in W. S. Simpson, ed. *Registrum Statutorum et Consuetudinum Ecclesiae Cathedralis Sancti Pauli Londiniensis* (London 1873), pp. 38–43.

Our search begins to be fruitful only in the later twelfth century, in the deanship of the talented historian and ecclesiastic Ralph de Diceto (probably from Diss in Norfolk), from 1180 to around 1200.[114] Towards the beginning of his tenure he and two canons, Henry of Northampton and Robert de Clifford, undertook the first known survey of the lands and churches that in some sense "belonged" to the chapter. Returns from that survey have not survived, but a good deal can be inferred from three thirteenth-century inventories of books in the cathedral treasury, studied by Neil Ker some forty years ago.[115] These inventories, set in motion by another energetic dean, Henry of Cornhill, 1243–54, list large numbers of service books – all save a handful of the 123 items in the 1245/55 list are, in the broadest sense, books pertaining to the liturgy – and include many details as to original ownership as well as condition. Analysis of some of these, though of necessity a somewhat gritty procedure, may yield an important clue.

Throughout the lists several names are mentioned, of members of the chapter or of bishops, either in the genitive case ("Passionale Roberti de Clifford") or as *quod dicitur/fuit* ("Missale quod dicitur H. de Norhamton"; "Capitularium et collectarium ... quod fuit Radulfi de Diceto Decani"). According to Ker, such phrases, no less than the unambiguous *de dono*, imply gift; if so, it looks to have been something of a custom that members of the chapter would give service books, sometimes to particular altars or for specific purposes. One of the most lavish donors was the Henry of Northampton mentioned above; his name is associated with a capitulary-collectar, a breviary with noted antiphonary, two missals, an epistolary, a possible sanctorale-antiphonary ("liber sanctorum cum antiphonario"), and, the 1295 list adds, three gospel books (*textus*, the third with Epistles also). Henry was prebendary of Cantlers (Kentish Town) between at least 1174 and 1191; he also founded a hospital and witnessed several episcopal charters, especially those of Gilbert Foliot (bishop of London 1163–87), whose clerk he may have been before becoming a canon.[116]

---

[114] Ralph was prominent in the diocese as archdeacon of Middlesex from 1153. His *Opera historica* were edited by W. Stubbs, RS 68 (1876); relics and books that he left to the cathedral are listed on pp. lxx–lxxi.

[115] The earliest, made in 1245 (ed. W. S. Simpson in *Archaeologia* 50.ii [1887], pp. 464–500), breaks off after the first 35 books; these entries were recopied in a second, 1255, list, along with information about nearly 100 more; and the 1255 list was itself repeated and brought up to date with some 130 new items: ed. N. R. Ker, "Books at St Paul's Cathedral before 1313," in his *Books, Collectors and Libraries*, ed. A. G. Watson (London 1985), pp. 209–42; first published in *Studies in London History Presented to Philip Edmund Jones*, ed. A. Hollaender and W. Kellaway (London 1969), pp. 41–72.

[116] A. Morey and C. N. L. Brooke, *Gilbert Foliot and his Letters* (Cambridge 1965), p. 282.

In the 1255 list the books are roughly grouped by type. One such group is specially noteworthy, that of seven missals (nos. 42–48), all apparently fine books in one way or another. The third and fifth were given by Henry of Northampton, and the fourth (seemingly the least grand of the group: "Missale parvum sine nota") by bishop Gilbert Foliot. The donor of the first was Robert de Clifford, the other surveyor of parishes, along with Henry, in Diceto's deanship; Robert, who had been at Hereford as canon and, like Henry, was clerk to Foliot when the latter was bishop there, moved to London, presumably at the behest of his patron, around 1171.[117] The sixth (no. 47), which has no donor ascribed, is described as "vetus sed de bona littera," and as having an alteration that catches our attention: "in quo ponitur novus canon de parva littera." Thus equipped, it is assigned to the important prebendal church at Chiswick, where it is duly recorded in an inventory of goods in 1252 as a "missale bonum et sufficiens" sent from the treasury at St Paul's.[118]

The final missal in this group of seven, "Missale quod dicitur Alberici," takes us to the enigmatic but possibly central figure of Alberic – whoever he is. In the 1245/55 inventory he is mentioned in connection with, besides this missal, a gradual (no. 71) and an antiphonal in two volumes (nos. 54–55). The latter book is described in a particularly intriguing way: "in duobus voluminibus in quorum quolibet premittitur kalendarium inmixto ordinali in uno et cum tonale, et sunt quasi unius voluminis." Are we to understand by this that at the beginning of the first volume is a calendar expanded to provide a kind of rudimentary ordinal, with a tonal concluding the second volume?[119] Further enlightenment, or obfuscation, comes in the 1295 inventory which describes a *liber ordinarius* owned by dean Henry of Cornhill as being *secundum Albericum*, albeit "per eundem [Henry, presumably] in aliquo emendatur."[120] This Alberic is most probably the canon who occurs first in 1148/9 and last in 1162, and the one who is often identified as the "Third Vatican Mythographer."[121]

---

[117] Ibid., pp. 270, 285.

[118] "Books at St Paul's," p. 221, n. 47.

[119] The next three items are also antiphonals: no. 56 from Robert de Clifford "in quo similiter kalendarium cum tonali"; no. 57 from Ralph "de sancto Benedicto" (unidentified) "in quo premittitur kalendarium, sine ordinali"; no. 58, the smallest, prefixed by a hymnary, not a calendar. These four, the compiler notes, were often in the choir – presumably in contrast to the next two, connected respectively with bishops William of St-Mère Eglise (1199–1221) and Roger Niger (1229–41). The final antiphonal in the group was given by the parson (*persona*) of Beauchamp; the reason for this is not stated.

[120] "Books at St Paul's," p. 234, no. 123.

[121] A canon Alberic was prebendary of Wenlocksbarn: *Fasti 1066–1300*, I: *London*, p. 86. Sharpe, *Handlist*, no. 82, is not convinced about the ascription of authorship to

These various hints combine to suggest a codification of liturgy at St Paul's in either the third or fourth quarter of the twelfth century. If it were not for the references to Alberic, one would suppose that the 1180s – the decade during which Ralph de Diceto, Henry of Northampton, Robert de Clifford, and also (until his death in 1187) Gilbert Foliot were all active – would be the likeliest time. Perhaps the obstacle posed by Alberic's dates is more ostensible than real. The "last appearance" year of 1162 is merely his final appearance as a witness in a (surviving) charter; as Sir Richard Southern has pointed out, "we do not know when he died."[122]

By the middle of the thirteenth century, when the 1245/55 inventories were being compiled, a clearer view emerges. On a visitation of some of the cathedral's dependent churches in 1252, Henry of Cornhill, the dean who emended to some extent the "liber ordinarius ... secundum Albericum," noted that one of several problems with the service books at Furneaux Pelham was that its rather jumbled breviary had a section of proper saints' services that was "nec London nec Sarum ordinem."[123] Furthermore, it is during Henry's deanship that we find clear mentions of the Use of London or of St Paul's: in the 1255 list, an antiphonary given by "T," archdeacon of Essex, is criticized as being not entirely of that use, "non tamen per omnia de usu ecclesie beati Pauli."[124] Moreover, such an ordinal is clearly implied by one of the clauses in the synodal statutes of the bishop during Henry's deanship, Fulk Basset (1245–59), ordering that the canon of the mass should be emended "according to the use of London" and that the "ordo London. ecclesie" be followed in both the night and day offices.[125] This suggests an extensive body of prescriptions such as would be contained in an ordinal.

All this leads us to wonder whether Henry of Cornhill, whose vigor is known to have been expressed in the cathedral statutes produced during his reign, may have had a hand also in constructing a discrete

him, and suggests a later date of "fl. 1200" for the Mythographer. Is it conceivable that the St Paul's figure meant is instead Alard de Burnham, dean c. 1200–16, some combination of "Al" and "b" having been mis-expanded to yield Alberic?

[122] R. W. Southern, "The English Origins of the 'Miracles of the Virgin'," Med. and Ren. Studies 4 (1958), pp. 176–216 at 202. The author of the first French translation of the collection, William Adgar (early 12th cent.), states that the copy from which he worked had been owned by a "mestre albri."

[123] "Visitations of Churches belonging to St Paul's Cathedral 1249–1252," ed. W. S. Simpson, Camden Miscellany IX, Camden Soc. n.s. 53 (1895), p. 19.

[124] "Book at St Paul's," p. 227, no. 65. This is likely to have been Thomas de Fauconberg, Treasurer 1228–66, rather than his predecessor, Theobald de Valognes, 1221–(last occ.) 1225.

[125] C & S 1205–1313, I.649. There are, among the 115 clauses, several other mentions of "Usus sancti Pauli London" or "Usus ecclesie London": e.g., pp. 645, 650, 657.

liturgical use for the cathedral, or at least in revising and systematizing what had come down, perhaps under the name of Alberic, from the previous century.[126] If so, the situation would parallel closely what we have come to suspect about Salisbury (p. 364): the drawing up of an ordinal in the late twelfth century and its reworking forty years or so later, possibly with the new cathedral in prospect. The great difference is that we have no text to work with, nothing for a modern-day Frere (should one exist) to edit.

The St Paul's saints

Were an ordinal extant, it might have allowed us to infer rubrics and, since ordinals often specify incipits of liturgical forms, to be able to identify texts of some prayers and chants. In its absence, we are forced to concentrate on the saints who seem to be distinctive to the "Use of St Paul's" or "London Use." Getting at these distinctive saints involves excavating and sifting among several calendars – as well as keeping in mind that they are less than ideal sources of evidence, here used heavily only because of the absence of whole service books. Four range in date from the third quarter of the twelfth to the middle of the thirteenth century. These are calendars in (1) a combined psalter and *Horae* made in England probably around 1170, later at Sens (now BN lat. 10433);[127] (2) a "rental" of London churches compiled fairly soon after 1220 (now London, Guildhall 25512); (3) a psalter made in the 1220s apparently for the Augustinian nuns at either Clerkenwell or Halliwell (now TCC B.11.4/423) and (4) two leaves from a service book of an indeterminable kind used in the church of Writtle in Essex, with the oldest of its three calendar-layers perhaps dating from just before 1220 (now Liverpool Cathedral, Radcliffe Collection 51; of this only four months, May through August, survive).[128] Of these, only (2) looks to be in any sense proper to the cathedral, and it is a financial rather than a liturgical document.

---

[126] At the visitation of Heybridge, where several of the service books were deemed worthless, two psalters were found, one old and one "bonum novum ex dono domini Gosselini in presencia domini Decanis": the pointed mention of the presence of Dean Henry is perhaps worthy of note (Simpson, *Visitations 1249–52*, p. 11).

[127] Becket's 29 Dec. feast has been added. By the 14th cent. the book was at the abbey of Saint-Pierre-de-Vif in the diocese of Sens. I have not seen the MS; Alan Thacker has kindly supplied some details not available in published descriptions.

[128] The detached leaves are printed and discussed by F. C. Eeles, "Part of the Kalendar of a XIIIth-Century Service Book once in the Church of Writtle," *Trans. Essex Archaeol. Soc.* 25 (1955), pp. 68–79; cf. Ker, *MMBL*, III.212. The month of April in the rental calendar is reproduced in color in *St Paul's* (2004), p. 116. On the TCC book see Morgan, *Early Gothic MSS*, no. 51; possibly relevant also is his no. 37, BL Lansdowne 420, another psalter of the 1220s.

Although these four witnesses do not agree in every detail, they let us discern two groups of saints' feasts that can be regarded as distinctive. In the first group are the obvious figures peculiar to London: Erkenwald (its principal saint; d. 693) on April 30th, with Translation feast November 14th (1148), Mellitus (first bishop) April 24th, and Ethelburga of Barking (abbess, and Erkenwald's sister) October 11th. Probably to be included here also is Osith of Chich October 7th (possibly two saints, the other sometimes remembered on June 3rd), one of whose arms was supposed to have effected a miraculous healing for bishop Richard of Belmeis I (1108–27).[129]

The other group, disparate but far more interesting, includes John of Beverley on May 7th, Ethelbert (the martyred king of East Anglia) on May 20th, the Translation of Andrew as well as Nicholas on May 9th, Grimbald on July 8th, the "apostle" Silas on July 13th, Genesius (either of Arles or of Rome) August 25th, and Antoninus (probably the one of Pamiers in southern France rather than Apamea in Syria) on September 2nd. All of these do not appear in any one calendar, and each can be found in calendars from elsewhere (though Silas is extremely rare), but that each is present in most of these sources is distinctly striking; nor are they "Sarum saints." John of Beverley, Ethelbert, the Translation of Andrew and Nicholas, Grimbald, and Antoninus are in place in the BN 10433 calendar, contemporary with the episcopate of Foliot at London, 1163–87. A possible explanation for the appearance, first in the Liverpool 51 fragment, of Silas (probably not related to his colleagueship with the apostle Paul, otherwise Timothy should be important as well), may involve a curious link with Grimbald, whose presence is usually connected with the New Minster (later Hyde Abbey) at Winchester. Here, though, the connection may be that Grimbald was born at Thérouanne (near St Omer), the church of which claimed to possess Silas's body, and that a bishop of Thérouanne had performed Gilbert Foliot's somewhat controversial consecration as bishop of Hereford in 1148.[130] Foliot's influence might also explain the presence of Ethelbert the martyr, to whom (along with the Virgin Mary) the cathedral at Hereford was dedicated. Antoninus may be connected with an appurtenant church of St Antholin (probably the same name) from the early twelfth century. The presence of Genesius, also in the Liverpool fragment and subsequently, seems a total mystery.

---

[129] Details in Thacker, "The Cult of Saints," p. 117; the same page reproduces the indulgence granted by the bishop to all who venerated the relic.
[130] Morey and Brooke, *Gilbert Foliot*, p. 97.

All of these unusual saints' days are still present in the calendar of the late fourteenth-century compilation called the "Greater Statutes."[131] We find there also St Radegund (Clovis's wife), for whom there had been a chantry altar in the cathedral from the 1190s, and Oswald king and martyr, whose altar was in the crypt.[132] Explanations of a similar sort might explain the otherwise puzzling presences of Genesius and (also in the Liverpool fragment), Helen(a), Constantine's mother, at August 18th. We would not expect such saints, specific to the topography of the cathedral, to be widely culted outside it, though Oswald seems to have been.

This is apparent in two sets of injunctions from the thirteenth century that reflect episcopal efforts to establish some uniformity throughout London with respect to the more important saints' days. Between 1229 and 1241, the years of Roger Niger's episcopate, statutes issued for the archdeaconry of London provided, among other matters, a list of the feasts to be celebrated *per civitatem*.[133] They include, among those noticed above, Mellitus, Erkenwald, Ethelbert the martyr, Oswald the martyr, Osith, Ethelburga, and the Translation of Erkenwald, but none of the more exotic figures who had figured in the calendars just reviewed. When Roger's successor, Fulk Basset, issued a massive set of statutes for his diocese some time during his episcopate (1244–59), some eighteen clauses (of 115 in all) set down rules to take away the scandalous *diversitas* indulged in by rectors of certain churches as to observance of major saints' feasts. Those to be observed uniformly are laid out month by month and in several categories, based mainly on the degrees of work to be allowed (for example, on St Matthias' day *omnes operationes* are forbidden except *opera pietatis*). Further lists follow, again organized by categories of work (such as *opera carucarum* or *opera rusticana*) prohibited or allowed. In neither set of lists do distinctive saints of cathedral topography appear (save, again, Oswald); we find only Erkenwald, Mellitus, and Ethelbert the martyr (plus the St Paul's dedication feast on October 1st), with the feasts of Osith and Ethelburga mandated only for the Essex rural deaneries in which were their principal shrines, Tendring and Barking respectively.[134]

---

[131] W. S. Simpson, ed. *Documents illustrating the History of S. Paul's Cathedral*, Camden Soc. n.s. 26 (1880), pp. 61–73; save for John of Beverley, there supplanted by the Octave of Erkenwald.

[132] Thacker, "The Cult of Saints," p. 118.

[133] *C & S 1205–1313*, I.329. Further provisions deal with such matters as processions and the consecration of Chrism, and seem to reflect concern about chaplains flocking into London (to be chantry priests?) and bringing with them a diversity of practices.

[134] Ibid., pp. 653–56 (the lists; Fulk's statutes as a whole, with prefatory editorial note, take up pp. 632–58).

All this careful regulation is in effect glossed by a clause in a sort of appendix promulgated in, apparently, 1268, ordering that *libri* (here, service books; the rest of the clause is about vestments and altar linens) should be "de usu ecclesie London., quod in civitate et diocesi diligenter observetur."[135] The relationship between the putative St Paul's Use and liturgy in the many churches, conventual and parochial, of greater London will be considered presently, particularly with regard to some of the unusual saints noticed above. First, though, we need to look at two further bursts of episcopal vigor that between them span the fourteenth century.

Episcopal tightening: Baldock and Braybrooke

Ralph (de) Baldock's ecclesiastical life centered on St Paul's for over thirty-five years. He was archdeacon of Middlesex by 1278, elected dean in 1294, and chosen as bishop in February of 1304 (though not consecrated for almost two years). During his deanship he oversaw a collection of the cathedral's *Statuta et consuetudines* which the latest biographical notice calls "unparalleled among medieval English cathedral codes for its comprehensiveness and logical arrangement."[136] As with other documents of this kind, bits of liturgical information are scattered throughout these statutes (for example, forms for the election and installation of a new dean and the dean's distinctive duties during the divine office). There is also a frustrating lack of specificity as to the date at which each of the many provisions came into effect; as we saw earlier in this chapter, the (?)tenth-century "Regula canonica ecclesie London." is included here (and survives apparently nowhere else). So it cannot be assumed that every section included reflects actual practice at St Paul's c. 1300, still less that each was introduced *de novo* by Baldock.

Nonetheless, it is reasonable to suppose that on the whole the provisions do represent the way the cathedral worship was, or was meant to be, organized. In the sections concerning grades of feasts, divided into five "dignities," the latest datable feast is the Translation of Becket, in those of the second class; unfortunately, feasts in the fourth and fifth classes are not enumerated, so we cannot know whether either Edmund of Canterbury or Richard of Chichester (canonized in 1250 and 1262

---

[135] Ibid., p. 657. The textual history of these statutes is somewhat complicated; as the editor, C. R. Cheney, explains on p. 633, this appendix (cl. 108–15) is found only in BL Royal 7 A.ix, fol. 83, of c. 1300.

[136] H. A. Tipping, revised by M. C. Buck, in *ODNB* 3.438. Baldock's Statutes are printed as parts I–V in the jumbled collection by W. S. Simpson, *Registrum Statutorum* (note 113 above), pp. 9–79.

respectively) was among them. Corpus Christi is not mentioned. Much of the third part (of five) of the statutes reads like an ordinal, sometimes including information so basic that one would scarcely suppose it was worth mentioning: for example, that in the invitatory at matins, "Venite, adoremus, regem martirum dominum," the word "martyr" should be replaced by "apostle" or "confessor" as necessary.[137] If all of the instructions here about bowing, the ringing of bells, the reading of lessons, and the like add up to the substance of what the Use of St Paul's was, our search for it would seem to be complete; but, as no distinctive texts are included (the few incipit tags are all of common formulas like the Te Deum), such an inference seems either rash or meaningless. A certain interest attaches to learning that, for example, during Sunday matins three boys of the first form (*gradus*) are to read the first three lesssons and two of the second form the next two, while the sixth is always read by the canon hebdomadary or his vicar (or, another clause reads, on double feasts, by the chancellor);[138] but that interest lies perhaps more in the glimpse we get into Baldock's mind than in the details themselves.

Baldock's mind may also be glimpsed at work on a kind of psalter manuscript that seems to have been written originally in the last quarter of the twelfth century and in the area of Worcester (now St Paul's Cathedral MS 1). It is an odd book indeed, and the story to be drawn from it is highly complicated.[139] Here it must suffice to notice that it seems to have come into the diocese of London around the middle of the thirteenth century; Erkenwald, Francis, Elizabeth of Hungary (canonized 1235), and Edmund of Canterbury are added to its calendar, but not Clare (canonized 1255), although she is added to the litany of saints. Somehow the book came into the possession of (Ralph) Baldock, who had obits entered for three members of his family and two benefactors, and who subsequently left the book to his cathedral.[140] While in his ownership he, or a contemporary, engaged in what may fairly be called liturgical doodling at various places throughout it: a less vandalistic performance than it might seem, for the tinkering

---

[137] Simpson, *Registrum statutorum*, p. 55.
[138] Ibid., pp. 50–51, where also (cap. 42) is the nice detail that on the feast of All Saints the eighth lesson, *de virginibus*, is to be read by a boy, whereas it normally falls to a priest (*sacerdos aliquis*, cap. 40).
[139] For a full discussion see my article "Bishop Baldock's Book, St Paul's Cathedral, and the Use of Sarum," in Pfaff, *LCSSME*, no. XI. My initial studies of the book, in the early 1990s, were much aided by the cathedral's librarian, J. Joseph Wisdom.
[140] Along with, as far as is known, all his other books: listed in *Biog. Reg. Oxf.*, III.2147–49. The 126 books are characterized as *libri scolastici*, and none seems to be a service book as such.

reflects the eccentricity of the original book, which seems to be a kind of proto-breviary, offering the sort of template- or "sample-" week for the office that we have noticed in two other manuscripts (see pp. 135 and 170). In a number of respects the office presented in the original book cannot have been used in any liturgical week.[141] The doodlings – not really systematic corrections – entered around 1300 may have been made with an eye to tinkering with the office at St Paul's, or perhaps to comparing what seems to have been the Sarum office at this time. And it may be relevant that when in 1297 Baldock conducted a visitation of parishes belonging to the cathedral chapter, nine of the twenty churches visited possessed an "Ordinale de usu S. Pauli," and three had an "Ordinale de usu Sarum."[142] So it seems conceivable that the doodlings in this enigmatic book reflect an attempt on his part to make more precise the practice in his cathedral church, an attempt which would be quite congruous with the masses of tiny details in his statutes.

Baldock appears to have been, both as dean and as bishop, a man of initiative and resolution. On his death he left to the cathedral not only his books but also funds for completion of the "New Work," including an elongated Lady Chapel, completed in the 1320s. His liturgical activity, insofar as we can get a sense of it, is reasonably summed up by the modern locution "pro-active." In contrast is the somewhat rearguard approach of the bishop of London at the end of the fourteenth century, Robert Braybrooke (1382–1404). He appears in our story as trying to restore a somewhat deteriorating situation: he complained of too few prebendal canons in residence, regularized the position of the minor canons by instituting a formal college for them, and in 1386 claimed to have been scandalized by the casualness with which the feasts of the cathedral's great saints Paul and Erkenwald were observed. As remedy for the latter, he ordered careful observance of the Conversion and (June 30th) Commemoration of Paul and of the Deposition and Translation of Erkenwald. Curiously, he specifies that the service for Erkenwald (for which feast, is not stated) should be "de communi unius Confessoris et Pontificis," with three proper mass collects, the text of which follows.[143] It is hard to believe that no proper forms for Erkenwald had existed before this time; the saint's shrine had become very grand already by

---

[141] For example, the office of vespers on Monday is suddenly interrupted by forms for the little hours, and the lessons for the Sunday are wildly eccentric, while Saturday's are totally disconnected from those for the other weekdays.

[142] W. S. Simpson, ed. *Visitations of Churches belonging to St Paul's Cathedral in 1297 and in 1458*, Camden Soc. n.s. 55 (1895), p. lii.

[143] Simpson, *Registrum*, pp. 393–95.

the middle of the thirteenth century, and after a fresh translation in 1326 a new shrine in the north arcade was even grander.[144] That Braybrooke found it necessary to provide mass prayers for his cathedral's second patron saint may be taken as an indication of how much we still do not, and probably cannot, know about liturgy there.

Yet the prayers cannot have been unknown before that time, for they appear in the Westminster, alias Lytlington, missal, completed in 1385 (see p. 227) – apparently identical with those in Braybrooke's register, even to one rare wording. Both in Sparrow Simpson's 1875 printing from that register (itself still unpublished), and in the missal the postcommunion prayer begins "Sacri corporis domini nostri repleti libamine et precioso sanguine debriati." Simpson tried to correct the last word to *inebriati*, but *debriati* is an attested, if uncommon, word in medieval Latin. He had not the capability of using Legg's edition (of this part, in 1893). Nor does Legg, in his textual apparatus published four years later, say anything about St Paul's usage, but rather remarks that the Westminster mass seems "almost particular" to that house; he then prints the only other set he had encountered, that of the Sherborne missal (only a few years later than the Westminster; p. 236). This is truly puzzling. Erkenwald is resolutely avoided in the Sarum tradition, and his appearance at Sherborne is likelier to be a result of his reputation as a monastic founder (Barking and Chertsey) than of any connection between that Dorset house and London.[145] With the Westminster mass the situation appears to be the other way round. How far may it have been the case that the royal monastery in the western suburbs would share cultic preoccupations of the city's cathedral church? And, by extension, what might be the picture with the other regular churches in the area of London?

St Paul's Use and the churches of London

Though it is not surprising that St Erkenwald's main feast should be observed at Westminster abbey, it is striking that the calendar of its famous missal, exactly contemporary with the St Paul's "Greater Statutes," contains not only him, Mellitus, and Ethelburga, each graded at three lessons, but also Antoninus (with three), and Genesius (with the last four on August 25th, the first eight being devoted to Audoen: but of

---

144 The drawing of the new shrine made by Wenceslas Hollar for Dugdale's *History of St Paul's Cathedral* (1658) is reproduced in *St Paul's* (2004), p. 120.

145 Erkenwald is present in the Sherborne-based calendar of the Red Book of Darley (CCCC 422; see p. 94), c. 1060.

course there survives no book in which these lessons were contained). It is unlikely that the influence could have gone from abbey to cathedral – typical monastic emphases, like a high grade for Benedict, are not apparent in the St Paul's documents – and the appearance of these two distinctly odd saints suggests at least a reverent nod at Westminster to St Paul's usage.

Barking was obviously a different matter, since the nuns there made such a point of retaining the St Paul's Use at mass. The calendar of their ordinal includes, as well as the obvious Erkenwald-Mellitus-Ethelburga-Osith group, most of the more unlikely feasts that seemed distinctive – John of Beverley, Translation of Andrew as well as Nicholas, Grimbald, Silas (the latter squeezed in on July 13th after Barking's dedication feast and Mildred), and Radegund (after Hippolytus on August 13th). Only Genesius and Antoninus are totally absent. All of those in the calendar are represented as well in the sanctorale, at least with a *memoria* and, as is true of ordinals in general, with only a minimum of tags. However, in laying out the April 30th feast of Erkenwald and the subsequent oct-ave this ordinal does yield the valuable information that the lessons, at least during the octave, are taken from the *historia* of one confessor rather than being proper. This is surprising, because at Erkenwald's other monastic foundation, Chertsey abbey (in Surrey, and therefore in the medieval diocese of Winchester) proper lessons are taken from the collection of the saint's miracles made around 1140 by Arcoid, a canon (and nephew of bishop Gilbert "the Universal," 1128–34); these appear in the fragmented Chertsey breviary of the first quarter of the four-teenth century (this part being Bodl. Lat. liturg. e.39).[146]

For the rest of the religious houses in London there is no evidence either way.[147] No service books appear to survive for the Augustinian priories at Aldgate (Holy Trinity) or Smithfield (St Bartholomew); Cis-tercian abbey of St Mary of Graces; Dominican convent (Blackfriars); Franciscan convent (Greyfriars); Crutched (Holy Cross) Friars con-vent; Hospital of St John of Jerusalem, Clerkenwell; the Temple; the nunneries of St Helen, Bishopsgate, St Mary de Fonte, Clerkenwell, St John the Baptist, Holywell (Shoreditch), St Leonard, Stratford-at-Bow, or the (Franciscan) Minories; any of the many hospitals; or the some-times shadowy secular colleges (of which may be noted especially

---

[146] Three other parts are in the Bodleian, Lat. liturg. d.42, e.6, and e.37, and a fourth in California, Univ. of San Francisco MS BX 2033.A2 (this contains the last fifty psalms, most of the canticles, and the litany). See further Whatley, *The Saint of Lon-don*, esp. p. 67.

[147] Except possibly for the TCC B.11.4 psalter noticed above as possibly from Clerken-well or Halliwell.

St Martin le Grand and the Guildhall College). Fortunately, there is a little more evidence concerning parish churches, though it is all inconclusive.[148]

Of four extant manuscript missals that were almost certainly used in London parish churches, the oldest is a book of, apparently, the late fourteenth century, now CUL Dd.1.15. Its calendar is missing and also many other leaves, some of which might have been instructive as to its date and provenance. The rubrics are for the most part those of Sarum books. On fol. 106, at the foot of the canon page, an inscription requests prayers for Hugh Wyche, knight, and William Holt, mercer; and a different but contemporary hand adds the words "Sanctae Margaretae de Lothbury." On the end flyleaf an extract from a will of 1373 leaving certain annuities to St Margaret's tends to confirm use of the book there. A minuscule straw to be grasped may be the provision that on the Vigil of Christmas the epistle lesson is "troped," with the biblical text sung by one clerk and the "farsing" (*farsuta*) by another, the distinction being signalled on the page by the use of red ink for the text and black for the farse.[149] This does not seem to be a usual Sarum practice; may it have been one borrowed from St Paul's? Or was the book, which is very large (440 × 300 mm) and has good initials at major feasts, written without regard to the diocese in which it was to be used? (Erkenwald is absent from the sanctorale, which is written in a slightly different, and probably later, hand, with the feast of St Anne being a notable feature.)

The only other parish church-owned missal that may pre-date the "suppression" of the St Paul's Use in 1414 is one, again predominantly of the Sarum type, used at St Botolph Aldgate (now Christ Church, Oxford MS 87) that seems to have been written at the beginning of the fifteenth century. The calendar includes both the parish church's dedication feast on May 20th and Botulf's main feast on June 17th; but there is no mass for him in the sanctorale, which probably means that a custom-written calendar was affixed to a stock, if rather fine, missal;[150] but the calendar itself appears to contain no indication of awareness that the church where the book was to be used is in the diocese of

---

148 A striking bit of negative evidence is that of 128 dedications of London churches, mostly from the 11th and 12th centuries, none is to one of the distinctive St Paul's saints save perhaps one to St Helen: statistics compiled by Caroline Barron, who has very kindly shared them with me in advance of publication.

149 D. Hiley, *Western Plainchant: a Handbook* (Oxford 1993), p. 237, cites an example from Limoges.

150 J. J. G. Alexander and E. Temple, *Illuminated MSS in the Oxford Colleges* (Oxford 1985), no. 406: "fine penwork initials."

London, nor that its mother church is St Paul's; the mandates of bishop Fulk in the 1250s seem not even a memory.

In books written after 1414 a tiny amount of perfunctory "Londonizing" can be discerned. This is evident in a bifolium adddded to probably the best known of the few service books that can be associated with London parish churches: the lavishly decorated Sarum missal (now BL Arundel 109) which was given to St Lawrence Jewry in 1446 by William Melreth, alderman and sheriff; his donation is celebrated in a verse colophon of seven roughly rhyming Latin couplets, which appears under a splendid miniature of the Trinity worshipped by the donor (fol. 262v). An additional bifolium, inserted after the donation page, contains, in a hand contemporary with the rest of the book, as well as masses for John of Beverley, the Visitation (with Octave), Crispin and Crispinian, Winifred (all mandated by Convocation of Canterbury, the Visitation Octave only in 1481; p. 437 above) and for the two feasts of Erkenwald, Deposition and Translation.

A similarly perfunctory degree of "Londonization" is clearly evident in the sumptuous two-volume mass lectionary given in 1508 to the church of St Mary Aldermanbury by Stephen Jenyns, formerly Master of the Merchant Taylors company, in the year that he was Mayor (now BL Royal 2 B.xii, xiii). Only the most important feasts of the temporale and sanctorale are covered, and among the roughly thirty occasions in the latter we find Erkenwald – but with a note to consult the common of saints for his lessons, whereas all the other feasts (save for Edward the Confessor, whose presence may be a nod to Westminster) have proper lessons.

By 1508, of course, no one could remember the abandonment in 1414 of whatever had once been understood by the words "Use of St Paul's." Secular liturgy in London would in common memory "always" have been that of Sarum, with mentions of Erkenwald and perhaps one or two other distinctive saints. The last manuscript witness to be looked at provides a clue, if only a tiny one, towards another direction – a clue for once of a textual sort. Over thirty years ago Neil Ker noticed, in describing a fine missal that belonged to the church of St Botolph without Aldersgate (London, Guildhall MS 515) that after the normal sequence of Sarum votive masses there were five of a somewhat unusual sort; and that in one, *Pro congregatione*, the collect was similar to that for the same mass in the Westminster missal of c. 1385.[151] Now, a mass *pro congregatione* makes no particular sense in a secular book, and indeed does not seem to appear in Sarum missals at all; so its inclusion here may

[151] *MMBL*, I.74.

alert us to the possibility that some influence from the monastic houses of London (including the greatest of them all, in its western suburb) may have seeped into the secular liturgies at which we've been looking.

What Clifford ended

The scanty evidence from parish churches in and around London suggests that the process of making the liturgies used in them approximate to those of Sarum was extensively under way well before the decree of 1414. One possible explanation is that service books according to anything like a Use of London had not been written for some time even in the fourteenth century; it should be remembered that we have not a scrap of textual evidence for such books. At the cathedral itself it is conceivable that no fresh ordinal had been compiled since perhaps the late thirteenth century. (It might be relevant here to recall what was noticed in chapter 11, that the main contents of the Sarum New Ordinal appear to have been incorporated in the later missals and breviaries of that Use.) And these possibilities lead us to wonder whether, after a burst of the episcopal and decanal bossiness that is apparent in the thirteenth century, widely elsewhere as well as in London, the "Use of London" itself had come to be not much more than a matter of observing at the cathedral the feasts of the distinctive St Paul's saints.

Certainly Clifford, a politically ambitious and careerist prelate with no antecedent ties to the diocese before he became its bishop, does not seem to have been pronouncing summary execution on something of great vitality. Five of the sixteen feasts that he specifies as the only exceptions to the Sarum Use which is otherwise to prevail are the obvious ones: Erkenwald (two), Mellitus, Osith, Ethelburga. Three others are unsurprising: Ethelbert of Kent (the supposed royal founder), Ethelbert of East Anglia and Hereford (the martyr), and Radegund; but the latter has only a *memoria*, the main feast on August 13th being that of Hippolytus, who is also on the list (exactly as at Barking). Among the rest, why Laurence, whose August 10th feast is always important, should be included here is a mystery, as is the appearance of Helena eight days later; the trio of Oswald (of Worcester), David, and Chad, on the three successive days 28 February to 2 March, appear not to correspond to any discernible earlier emphases, either. Nor has anything led us to suspect that the feast of Bede (27 May) would complete the list, however gratifying to students of history that may be.

In sum, although a good deal of liturgical vitality can be sensed in the region of greater London in the later middle ages, there seems no strong reason to suggest that it was centered at St Paul's. The complicated history of the medieval building, culminating in its destruction in the 1662 Fire of London and the construction of its succcessor under the direction of Christopher Wren, makes it unusually difficult to say anything about liturgy there. Perhaps the fact that, to our knowledge, no London printer (of whom there were several by c. 1500) put out a service book that claimed to be particular to that cathedral provides an adequate, if negative, conclusion to this inconclusive story.

There is, however, a brief coda. In the middle decades of the sixteenth century Thomas Batemanson, a quondam minor canon and chantry priest at the cathedral and then, from 1556 to 1558, vicar of Kensington, copied into what may have been a priest's manual of the previous century some nineteen collects. That book does not survive, but in 1782 the antiquary William Cole transcribed the prayers, and his transcription (now BL Add. 5810, fols 198–202) was in turn published by Simpson.[152] There are collects for twelve of the sixteen feasts singled out by Clifford for retention in 1414: none for Erkenwald's two feasts, which were in the original manuscript, nor for Laurence (which would scarcely have been necessary) or for the rather confused August 13th combination of Radegund and Hippolytus. The remaining collects copied by Batemanson are for Osmund, Winifred, and the Translations of John of Beverley, Etheldreda, and Frideswide – precisely the feasts mandated by archbishops of Canterbury in the fifteenth century (see pp. 439–42). Whether Batemanson made his copies as an act of nostalgic piety (he had lost his chantry income when all such foundations were dissolved in 1547) or in the course of resuming the Latin liturgy in the reign of Mary Tudor depends on precisely when he was writing. We cannot know that, but it seems reasonable to assume that for him the material he was copying *was* the Use of London.

Usages at Lincoln and (faintly) Wells

"Lincoln Use" may be a chimera – hence the double inverted commas – but the presumption of its existence is widespread enough that the subject cannot simply be ignored. For one thing, the magnificence of Lincoln is in several respects commanding. Its cathedral establishment became the largest in England, with at the fullest five dignitaries (including, from 1145, a subdean), eight archdeacons, and fifty-six prebendaries. The building, often called Lincoln Minster, in which their worship was

---

[152] Simpson, *Docs ill. Hist. St. Paul's*, pp. 35–40, with prefatory explanation on pp. xxi–xxii. The 15th-cent. MS was supposed to have been at Emmanuel College, Cambridge in the late 18th cent., but no trace of it has been found.

conducted, largely complete (after a complicated history) by 1280, was, and remains, extraordinarily splendid. The diocese was also the largest in England, very likely in medieval Europe; and several of its medieval bishops were figures of great note, most obviously Hugh (1186–1200, canonized 1220) and Robert Grosseteste (1235–53). As for the "Use," if nothing else, the mention in Cranmer's famous preface to the 1549 Book of Common Prayer, that some followed "Salsbury use, some Herford use, some the use of Bangor, some of Yorke, and some of Lincolne," would compel notice. And, as a matter of historiography, the assiduous efforts of Henry Bradshaw and Christopher Wordsworth (both of whom have often appeared in these pages) resulted in a publication so extensive that it seemed by implication to establish Lincoln as, so to speak, *the* medieval cathedral of reference constitutionally, just as Salisbury appeared to be liturgically.

In 1879 Bradshaw started to work on an edition of the *Liber niger*, one of the nine volumes of statutes or customs then in the Muniment Room at Lincoln Cathedral. This one, begun in the early fourteenth century, was itself a complicated mish-mash of regulations and chapter legislation which would have required a lot of editorial deftness to present in a comprehensible way. After Bradshaw's death in early 1886, the work was taken up by Wordsworth, whose father (also Christopher) had been bishop of Lincoln from 1869 to 1885. The result of this rather accidental collaboration was the publication of *Statutes of Lincoln Cathedral ... with illustrative documents*, in three volumes, 1892–97.[153] Like the earlier collaboration of Wordsworth (the younger, not the bishop) with Francis Procter in producing their edition of the 1531 Sarum breviary in three volumes, 1879–86, this one is organized and presented in a markedly muddled way. The "illustrative documents" turn out to include, as well as much post-medieval Lincoln material, chunks of the medieval statutes and customs of the cathedrals at Lichfield, Hereford, and York, and even those drawn up for the cathedral of the then new (1877) diocese of Truro. Here we need to notice only what bears directly on liturgical practice at Lincoln – most importantly, its earliest major element, a consuetudinary apparently dating from the earlier

---

[153] Which are called two volumes, "vol. II" being broken into parts i (pp. ccxc + 1–160) and ii (pp. xxvi + 161–957). Theoretically, as the title pages read, the *Statutes* are "arranged" by Bradshaw and "edited" by Wordsworth; the latter's preface, pp. v–viii, makes plain how the published work came about. In 1898, the year after the final vol. of *Statutes* appeared, Wordsworth published a "semi-popular" work, *Notes on Mediæval Services in England, with an Index of Lincoln Ceremonies*, which is a (mostly) alphabetical collection of bits and pieces, often fascinating, from a wide range of sources covering several cathedrals but primarily centered on Lincoln.

part (c. 1260?) of the episcopate of Richard Gravesend, 1258–79, to be discussed presently. But the story cannot begin there; rather, we must go briefly back to the end of the eleventh century, when the center of what had become (owing to various Norse depredations of the previous two centuries) a vast diocese, encompassing most of nine counties from Lincolnshire to Oxfordshire, was moved from Dorchester-on-Thames to Lincoln.

Lincoln origins

The decision was taken initially in May 1072, with papal approval following shortly thereafter.[154] The first bishop, Remigius, named to the see of Dorchester in 1067, had been a monk of Fécamp, but it seems to have been clear from the beginning that the establishment at Lincoln was to be secular, not monastic like the slightly later one at Norwich (see p. 203). The closer comparison is with Old Sarum after the move there in 1075. There must have been some legacy from the church at Dorchester, but we know next to nothing about that. A more prominent legacy is likely to have come from the minster churches with which the area included in the diocese of Lincoln abounded, churches of the magnitude of Stow or Brixworth. Again, however, little can be ascertained about what that legacy might have been, save possibly cults of Guthlac, Botulf, and Ives – all, however, having monastic associations with, respectively, Crowland, (mainly) Ely, and Ramsey. Of directly monastic influence, whether from such English houses as those or from Fécamp, there is little trace at Lincoln. In the late twelfth century Gerald of Wales claimed that Remigius, "constituta ecclesia et juxta ritum Rothomagensis ecclesiae stabiliter collocata," established prebends for twenty-one canons.[155] Whatever Gerald understood by the "rite of Rouen," to a large extent Lincoln seems to have been a liturgical *tabula rasa*, about which most of what can be said arises from well attested traditions concerning the cathedral chapter.

The most substantial of these traditions is that in the last quarter of the eleventh century there emerged at Lincoln, as almost simultaneously

---

[154] Succinct details in D. Greenway, *Fasti 1066–1300*, III: *Lincoln* (1977), p. ix.

[155] In Gerald's *Vita S. Remigii*, cap. iv, *Opera* VII, ed. J. M. Dimock, RS 21 (1877), p. 19: information called by Greenway "not wholly reliable" (p. xiv). The claim was repeated by canon John de Schalby in the early 14th cent.: ibid., p. 194. The rite of Rouen could have been transmitted through the *De officiis ecclesiasticis* of John of Avranches, written in the 1060s. That putative influence, and problems of dealing with it, are discussed in the section on Hereford above, p. 467; cf. *Lincoln Cath. Stats*, I.76–79.

at Sarum and York and also to a considerable extent at London, a body of canons (supported by individual prebends) with, at their head, a dean and (usually) three other dignitaries.[156] Each of these other three places is discussed elsewhere in this volume; at them, as at Lincoln, we tend to know anything of their early liturgical life through information about their constitutions rather than through service books. The growth of the chapter at Lincoln is reflected by precious information in the surviving volume of its two-volume Great Bible (now Lincoln Cathedral MS 1), a list of forty-three members of the chapter in the 1130s together with the incipit of the psalm(s) that each was to say daily – the accrued recitations ensuring that the entire Psalter would be recited each day.[157] In 1214 envoys from the nascent cathedral establishment in Moray came to Lincoln to learn how its chapter was structured; the information they received was full constitutionally but said nothing about liturgy.[158] The oldest information we have about that is the small amount that can be extracted from the consuetudinary of c. 1260 (albeit entered in the *Liber niger* a century or more later, so the possibility of textual corruption cannot be ruled out).

The Lincoln consuetudinary and the (non-existent) ordinal

This consuetudinary, though for our purposes somewhat disappointing, is noteworthy as containing one of (apparently) only two surviving references to a "Use of Lincoln" (the other, a phrase in a missal, will be considered later). The context is unremarkable, almost casual: that no canon should celebrate at the high altar "secundum usum lincoln[iensis, presumably]," unless he has attended matins earlier that day.[159] The entire document has a great deal of detail about such matters as who says which parts of the daily office, rules for the ringing of bells, and the curious and charmingly irreverent custom of issuing invitations to dine at the canons' common table during the singing of the *Te deum*.[160] There is also a fair amount concerning ceremonial, but relatively little about

---

[156] The position is summarized by R. M. T. Hill and C. N. L. Brooke in the opening chapter of *A History of York Minster*, ed. G. E. Aylmer and R. Cant (Oxford 1977), pp. 1–43 at 26–27.

[157] The list is published in *Lincoln Cath. Stats*, III.789–92, with corrections in *Fasti*, pp. 152–53; a second list, c. 1187, shows further growth of some twelve canons (*Fasti*, pp. 162–64).

[158] Explained and summarized by Bradshaw in *Stats*, I.40–42.

[159] *Stats*, I.384 (within pp. 364–96, the consuetudinary).

[160] *Stats*, I.372. Such invitations would be highly prized by minor canons, choristers, and others in choir who were not canons. The procedure for inviting "ministers of the altar" (including a *sacrista laicus*) is on p. 378.

anything that would have made practice at Lincoln verbally distinct from what was being said or sung in other great churches. For example, much is said about personnel and usages (above all, bells) at various classes of feasts, but what these feasts were is not specified. The reason is that the regulations in the consuetudinary presuppose an ordinal, which is indeed referred to ("in aliis que secuntur tangit ordinale et ideo non est plus hic tractandum") but which does not survive – as would be necessary to give us anything like a full picture of that "usus Lincoln" reference, which is on the same page.[161]

If indeed this consuetudinary dates, at least in substance, from the time of Gravesend, the circumstances it witnesses to must reflect the present choir ("St Hugh's Choir," finished about 1200), transepts, and nave. The degree to which the glorious Angel Choir, under construction during Gravesend's entire episcopate, is also reflected is not clear; he died about ten months before the translation of St Hugh into that shrine space on October 6th, 1280. The annual commemoration of that, perforce not mentioned in this consuetudinary, became the feast most distinctive to Lincoln – and rarely found elsewhere, whereas Hugh's November 17th deposition feast came, albeit with no great speed, to be widely observed throughout England by roughly the mid-fourteenth century.[162]

A few further points of distinctiveness, less obvious than the Translation of Hugh, can be garnered, mostly from documents subsequent to the consuetudinary. The first, a set of regulations dealing with the duties of the treasurer and datable to 1283/4, yields what may be a quite decisive point, one that arises, as we have seen often to be the case, from an apparently tiny rubrical detail. In a section about the particular feasts on which special candles above the altar were to be provided we find, grouped, those of John and Paul (26 June), Hippolytus (13 August), and Brice (13 November).[163] We have encountered this grouping of apparently unrelated feasts before, in our consideration of the Sarum "Old Ordinal" (p. 375), and we noted that there a fourth was added, the Eleven Thousand Virgins (21 October). The point of the Sarum

[161] *Stats*, I.384. This ordinal is referred to at least five other times in the consuetudinary.

[162] The uncertain spread of the feast is demonstrated by the three "early" Sarum MS missals edited by Legg: the earliest (Crawford) gives the proper mass prayers in a muddled marginal note alongside the forms for Anianus (also 17 Nov.), while the slightly later Bologna missal states that the mass comes from the common of saints, and the Arsenal missal ignores the feast entirely. The feast on Oct. 6th in most Sarum books is generally that of Faith (Fides).

[163] *Stats*, I.289. For this candle-provision these three feasts are grouped with the octaves of Martin, Agnes ("*Agnes secundo*"), and John the Baptist.

rubric, however, was that, unlike other feasts of three lessons, those specified were given their own masses even if they fell on a Saturday (when normally the commemoration of the Virgin Mary would take precedence); and the same was to happen for the first three if they fell on Sunday in most circumstances.[164] Why the Eleven Thousand Virgins were not included in the Sunday provision at Sarum is obscure; whatever the reason for that, the somewhat improbable grouping of the other three is exactly as in the Lincoln document – which, concerning as it does candles above the altar, clearly implies the celebration of mass. The point here is that the singling out of these three feasts implies either that the Lincoln and Salisbury ordinals had a common ancestor or that one borrowed from the other. Further, that the Virgins are not in the Lincoln provision about candles suggests that that feast was an addition, or afterthought, to the Sarum rubric about Saturday masses, and therefore that the Lincoln version is the original one. The grouping of John and Paul, Hippolytus, and Brice is repeated in the statutes of Bishop William Alnwick (1436–49) – still without the Virgins.[165]

But the putative sanctorale at Lincoln differs often from that of Sarum. What we have seen to be three peculiarly distinctive Sarum saints – Aldhelm, Cuthburga, Wulfrannus – find no mention in the pages of the *Liber niger*. Instead there is Pelagia, on whose feast day (8 October) certain distributions of offerings are made and the celebrant at mass gets the considerable sum of six shillings and eight pence, according to a section of the *Liber niger* apparently to be dated 1321/2.[166] We have encountered her in connection with the Use of York, where she seems to form part of a group along with Babillus, Germanicus, and Hilarion. None of the other three appears at Lincoln, so it looks as though the line of transmission for a cult of Pelagia may not have been the same as for York; whatever the case, it was certainly not through Sarum.

These few indications of what might have been distinctive about the sanctorale at Lincoln may be compared with Evidence Rolls – a kind of memorandum-summary of the actual liturgical observance of each day during the year in question – that survive for 1471/2 (save for the months of June through September, months for which a similar roll of 1435 is

---

[164] The Crawford Sarum missal, exactly contemporary with Gravesend's reign at Lincoln, has the full form of the rubric, including the provision about Sunday (*SML*, p. 238), which the early 14th-cent. Risby ordinal MS lacks (*Use of Sarum*, II.178).

[165] In the *Novum Registrum*, as in *Stats*, III.305; and, in a slightly different context (as having bells rung during the *Te Deum*; cf. I.388) in the copy of Lincoln customs made for Matthew Parker when he was dean there, 1552–54 (III.571; for Parker's involvement, p. 565).

[166] *Stats*, I.337.

extant).[167] There the feasts of John-and-Paul and of Pelagia have been swallowed by octaves (of John the Baptist and Translation of Hugh respectively), and Brice seems to have disappeared also, but Hippolytus is still observed. Two other feasts call for attention, however. One is the Translation of Andrew (9 May), a puzzling occasion in that on the fairly rare occasions when it does appear it is most often combined with the Translation of Nicholas (which did take place on that day in 1087). In the 1471/2 list it is ranked as a double, with no mention of Nicholas. Furthermore, it was added to the list of Lincoln *festa ferianda* (i.e., abstention from work, and with a double allowance of wine for the sacristan) in 1527.[168] What can explain this curious prominence? A second curiosity is the persistence of the Ordination of Gregory feast on September 3rd. We have seen (p. 115) that it had a certain popularity early, largely in monastic circles. Its appearance in the 1472 rota of feasts at Lincoln is rare witness to secular observance.[169] Again, an explanation remains to be sought. Neither this feast nor the Translation of Andrew is found in Sarum usage.

The scanty service-book evidence for Lincoln "Use"

Trying to complement these bits of witness from documents about liturgy at Lincoln with evidence from surviving service books contributes little of substance. That the Translation of Hugh is included in the "rogue" Sarum missal often mentioned earlier (BL Add. 11414) was almost the only reason for supposing it to witness to anything like a Lincoln Use. The appearance in that book of Botulf (June 17th) might be something of an indication, but is by no means conclusive; an indication to the contrary is that the feast on May 9th in that missal is the Translation of Nicholas rather than, as noticed above, that of Andrew. The same two feasts, Botulf and the Translation of Hugh, appear in the calendar of a magnificently illustrated psalter of the third quarter of the fifteenth century (now Corpus Christi College, Oxford, MS 18); but

---

[167] The oddly named "Rotuli de *Re* et *Ve*" (*Stats*, III.811–23).

[168] *Stats*, III.546. It is the only feast so added in 1527, and to a month, May, that already had a cluster of three such days, Philip and James (1st), Invention of the Cross (3rd), and John at the Latin Gate (6th). Cf. p. 569, where it reappears on the list of thirty-two double feasts compiled for Parker (n. 165).

[169] The mass prayers cited in Legg's 1897 apparatus are from Westminster, Canterbury St Augustine's, Durham, St Albans, Abingdon, and Sherborne. What can have been the source for the forms used at Lincoln? The only other secular mention I am aware of is the inclusion of that feast in the calendar (but not sanctorale) of the Arsenal missal, one of its several archaic notes.

it is a highly imaginative, and sometimes stupid, document, and adds nothing to our quest.[170]

The distinction between a discrete Use (perhaps signalled more clearly by employing the capital initial) of Lincoln and books made for use in that vast diocese is easy to blur. Two manuscripts now in unusual repositories in the Midlands illustrate this. One is a late fifteenth-century Sarum missal (now Rugby School MS Add. 3) which contains the mass for the Translation of Hugh; it was used by a priest named William in a chapel, probably in Northamptonshire, as late as 1525, according to an inscription in the ordinary-and-canon section.[171] The other is a partial mid-fifteenth-century Sarum missal, also with the Translation of Hugh (now Spalding, Gentlemen's Society MS M.J.11). Both include a sequence, "Spirat odor renovatus," that according to Ker appears nowhere else.[172] That these are both definitely Sarum missals seems to make it impossible to argue that appearance of Hugh's Translation feast, especially with this unique sequence, is by itself proof of the existence of a Lincoln Use.

A more convincing case may be based on a fragment of three leaves from a fifteenth(?)-century missal, now bound into a miscellany of a dozen treatises (Bodl. Tanner 4); for it has both the other surviving manuscript mention of a Use of Lincoln (besides that in the consuetudinary) and some unusual readings. The leaves contain masses for the first three weeks of Advent, and in a rubric after the sequence on Advent I comes the phrase that has been characterized as the strongest evidence for the existence of what we are currently pursuing: "Et sciendum est quod in omnibus festis novem lectionum et in quibus chorus regi debet, sicut post Pascha, secundum usum Lincoln cantari debet sequentia nisi a Septuagesima usque ad Pascha."[173] W. G. Henderson

---

[170] Among the oddities are both Eastern and Western feast days for Helena (21 May and 18 Aug.) and a virgin Sophia (15 May); among the stupidities, a confessor-bishop Augustine on 28 Feb. (Oswald?), Guthlac turned into a bishop, and 1 Aug. blank. In the litany "Ethmund" (Rich) and Thomas (of Hereford?) are second and third among the thirty-eight confessors, with Swithun last and Hugh nowhere; nor is Becket among the twenty-two martyrs.

[171] *MMBL*, IV.228–29. Ker mentions that there is a description in the School Library, but it does not seem to be there now.

[172] *MMBL*, IV.353–54. He remarks that a typescript description by Christopher Hohler is kept with the MS, and that the sequence is printed, from the Spalding MS, in R. M. Woolley, *St Hugh of Lincoln* (London 1927), p. 201.

[173] The fragment is printed in its entirety by W. G. Henderson in an appendix to his Surtees Soc. edn of the *York Missal* (above, p. 451), II.343–48. S. J. P. van Dijk calls the leaves "practically the only remains of what once was the use of the diocese of Lincoln": *Latin Liturgical MSS and Printed Books*, Bodl. exhibition cat. (1952), no. 30.

(on whom, see p. 446), introducing the rather fortuitous printing of these leaves in his edition of the York missal, provided a table comparing epistles, gospels, one Alleluia, and one sequence from them with the Sarum, York, and Hereford forms. This showed that, out of the eleven forms analyzed, there were eight variations between the Tanner 4 missal leaves and the printed Sarum missals as edited by Dickinson; also six divergences from York and eight from Hereford.[174] Most of the variations occur in the readings for the Wednesday and Friday masses, where there is a notable amount of instability (as there is also among missals in general, as to which provide different pericopes for weekday masses, or indeed any such masses at all). Three cases, all of weekday Epistles, seem to be unique; Legg's 1897 apparatus shows no parallel among any of his witnesses.[175]

While the evidence of this fragment cannot be dismissed out of hand – it is, after all, the only combination of any text with the term *usus Lincoln.* – it scarcely seems extensive, or conclusive, enough to justify the statement made in a recent history of the cathedral:

Unfortunately, very little can yet be written of the distinctive features of the particular liturgical Use observed at Lincoln, since little surviving material has yet been identified. Nevertheless, a thirteenth-century consuetudinary and a fragment of a fifteenth-century missal without music are enough to show that the ceremony and rite of Lincoln Use, while highly complex and elaborate, was no mere variant of the Uses of Salisbury or York, but was of independent character and origin.[176]

That is certainly possible. It seems equally possible, however, that reification of a Lincoln Use has resulted from a combination of four factors: (1) occurrences, from the thirteenth century on, of the word *usus* followed by the name of a cathedral city (e.g., Wells, Lincoln, London); (2) the existence of printed service books from 1483 to 1555 with title pages that read "secundum usum ecclesiae Sarum *or* Ebor. *or* Heref."; (3) Cranmer's 1549 Preface, often alluded to in these pages; and (4) investigations made in the second half of the nineteenth century into the three clearly once-extant Uses, Sarum, York, and Hereford. Whether there should similarly be posited a Lincoln Use does not perhaps matter much. The dignitaries and canons of Lincoln must have

---

[174] *York Missal*, II.x.

[175] The other apparently unique case, a prose for Advent III that begins "Precamur nostras, Deus, animas," reads like a misplaced collect, and appears, headed "Prosa ad Sequentia *Ostende* minor," as the 49th of 90 York *Prosae* printed by Henderson in *YM*, II.303.

[176] R. Bowers, "Music and Worship to 1640," in *A History of Lincoln Minster*, ed. D. Owen (Cambridge 1994), pp. 47–76 at 48.

had quantities of service books out of which they conducted services "their way." That next to nothing of these books has survived induces pause as well as frustration, as does the scantiness of any evidence for spread of "their way," whatever it was, throughout that vast diocese. May it not have been the case that its very vastness militated against widespread circulation of books like the ones available to the canons, so that the apparently much more readily available Sarum books came to be used in large parts of it almost by default?

Wells cathedral

The light that the complicated history of Wells as a cathedral church can shed on our story is largely refractive; Salisbury seems to be the model as early as, and to the extent that, we can derive any concrete information about its liturgy. A natural starting place might seem to be the massbook generally ascribed to Giso, bishop of Wells 1061–88, often referred to in earlier chapters (BL Cott. Vit. A.xviii), but it is in fact only doubtfully relevant; as was suggested above (p. 126), the book might well have migrated to Evesham following Giso's death. After the see center was moved to Bath abbey around 1090, organized ecclesiastical life at Wells seems to have fallen into something like abeyance until the vigorous bishop Robert of Lewes (1136–66) reframed it, apparently on the model of Sarum, at the beginning of his episcopate.[177] Whether the borrowing extended from the structural to the specifically liturgical we can only guess. In any case, the church for which borrowings from Sarum were implemented was almost completely replaced by one begun at the impetus of Robert's successor, Reginald Fitz Jocelin (1174–91). This building, consecrated in 1239, is (with later additions) the present glorious cathedral, but it did not receive full cathedral status until some time in the 1230s, when papal permission was obtained to establish a two-cathedral regime, Bath continuing to function in that way.[178]

  Although Reginald was a grand curial prelate, he seems also to have been a conscientious diocesan bishop; this makes it probably relevant that he was the son of Jocelin de Bohun, bishop of Sarum 1142–84. As

---

[177] The charter establishing the new structure probably dates originally from 1136, which means that any Sarum arrangements being imitated are those in effect under bishop Roger of that diocese (see p. 356), and implies that Robert must have taken counsel immediately on his election. A likely source for such counsel is Henry of Blois, abbot of Glastonbury since 1126 and Robert's patron.

[178] The matter is even more complicated than that, for bishop Savaric (1191–1205) wangled a move from Bath to Glastonbury in 1197; so Jocelin (1206–42) was technically bishop of Bath and Glastonbury, and it is only from his successors on that the see has been officially Bath and Wells.

we have seen (p. 364), it is highly possible that the "original" Sarum ordinal dates from that prelate's reign. So even if Sarum usages had not been imported under bishop Robert along with its constitutional arrangements, there seems a strong likelihood that they would have been present at Wells by the end of Reginald's episcopate.

No document survives, however, to witness to whatever liturgical arrangements came to be in place at the new, eventually cathedral, church.[179] The hero of the story of its regaining of cathedral status was a native son of Wells, Jocelin, who became bishop in 1206, just as King John's troubles with the papacy began to peak. In 1241, a year before Jocelin's long episcopate ended, new cathedral statutes included a provision mandating a revision of the ordinal.[180] However complete this revision was, it seemed unsatisfactory to the next generation, for in 1273 an energetic dean, Edward de la Knoll, led the chapter in producing a new set of statutes "in which the Ordinal is again corrected to prevent confusion and irreverence."[181] This revision notwithstanding, yet another was ordered under dean Haselshaw as part of the extensive statutes of 1298: two committees were to be established, one of *discreti* to revise the ordinal and martyrology, the other of vicars choral for the antiphonary and gradual.[182] But, tantalizingly, we lack any details as to the resulting recommendations.

Whatever those details may have been, this revision antedated the great building program of c. 1310–45 by which the east end of the cathedral was renewed and extended, the result being a new Lady Chapel, a reconstructed choir, and the architecturally sublime retrochoir connecting the two. The liturgical implications of this have been studied by Arnold Klukas, who suggests that "a change in the liturgical programme used by the Chapter" was the precipitating factor in the rebuilding.[183] The ordinal that resulted from the 1298 mandate is, he

---

[179] Many of the Wells documents are collected in its *Liber Ruber*, a miscellaneous collection written, apparently, c. 1400, now in the Cathedral Archives; a number are summarized in C. W. Church, *Chapters in the Early History of the Church of Wells A.D. 1136–1333* (London 1894).

[180] Church, p. 233, citing *Liber Ruber* ii, fol. 17; not printed in *C & S*.

[181] Church, p. 275, citing *Liber Ruber* ii, fol. 3. Another set of statutes, those promulgated for the entire diocese in 1258 or -59 by bishop William of Bitton I (1248–64; Jocelin's successor but one), speaks in passing of the duty of archdeacons to ensure that in every church they visit there may be "canon misse secundum quod est in ecclesia Wellensi correctus," but the language is highly conventional, with verbal parallels to statutes of York as well as Salisbury; the ultimate point of reference is Lateran IV: *C & S 1205–1313*, I.613, with textual discussion on pp. 586–88.

[182] Church, pp. 345–48, citing *Liber Ruber* i, fol. 215 and ii, fol. 219.

[183] A. W. Klukas, "The *Liber Ruber* and the Rebuilding of the East End at Wells," in *Medieval Art and Architecture at Wells and Glastonbury*, BAA Conf. Trs. IV, for 1978

contends, substantially the document included in the *Liber Ruber* (itself, however, written roughly a century later) as *Antiqua Statuta de officiis cuiuslibet persone ecclesie cathedralis Welln*.: the text of which "shows the almost complete dependence of the Wells manuscript upon the Sarum use."[184] By "the Sarum use" he means here primarily the consuetudinary, which of course requires extensive adaptation. Whether such differences in language as there are between the Sarum consuetudinary and the Wells *Statuta* are significant enough to require the positing of an intermediary manuscript (or even a common ancestor?) are questions of such a conjectural nature that they cannot usefully be addressed; what is adequately clear is that the numerous processions called for in the *Liber Ruber* are vastly better accommodated in the extended and remodelled east end at Wells than they would have been before the drastic architectural changes, and that such details as can be ascertained about them show them to be strikingly like those at (new) Salisbury.

Included in the *Liber Ruber* is an elaborate directory of the colors of vestments to be used on various occasions at Wells, in two sections: one for feasts of the temporale, the other for the sanctorale, listed by month but without dates.[185] The latter section gives an idea of the calendar in use at Wells, which again agrees largely with Sarum but with some points of independence. Notable among these are the presence of the Leo whose feast was on April 11th (see p. 153), Translation of Andrew (the patron saint; May 9th, apparently without Nicholas), Decuman (August 30th), and a puzzling Gabriel on September 4th(?);[186] also the exclusion of Germanus of Paris at May 28th (the July 31st Germanus of Auxerre is present). That Congar, along with the hermit Decuman the main local Somerset saint, is omitted at November 27th is odd. The colors themselves (a topic which the present work has had almost entirely to avoid) seem noteworthy mainly in the frequency with which

---

(1981), pp. 30–35 at 30. This was before D. Greenway demonstrated in 1985 that the so-called *Institutio Osmundi* cannot have been the work of that eponymous bishop (see p. 355); Klukas had accepted the traditional ascription.

[184] Klukas, p. 31. The *Antiqua Statuta*, in addition to being found in the *Liber Ruber*, were copied in a Laudian context in 1634, and this transcript, now Lambeth Palace MS 729, was in turn printed by H. E. Reynolds, *Wells Cathedral: its Foundation, Constitutional History, and Statutes* (n.p. [Leeds] 1881), pp. 55–68.

[185] Printed in Reynolds, *Wells Cathedral*, pp. 95–96, 101–3.

[186] The Bologna Sarum missal has in its calendar a "Sancti Gabrielis archangeli" on Sept. 6th, with, further to the right on the page, "memoria de sancto Zakaria," the whole line written in the hand that has supplied many obits of members of the Mowbray family (*SML*, p. 517). The day works out to be the octave of the Decollation of John the Baptist – with which, of course, the Gabriel–Zechariah story has nothing to do! Gabriel's presence in the Wells list needs further thought.

yellow and green together, as distinct from either color by itself, are specified – for doctors of the church, but also for the English figures of Dunstan, Augustine of Canterbury, Edmund of Abingdon, and Hugh of Lincoln, as well as for a few other major saints like Mary Magdalen and Martin. This must have been particularly striking in the new choir, the surviving glass of which is unusual in the predominance of yellow and green.

Information from this list can be compared with that in a free-standing calendar datable (from its Easter tables) to 1463 and clearly reflecting Wells usages; now BL Add. 6059.[187] It includes the July 16th Translation and December 4th Deposition of Osmund (canonized 1456; here marked as *Sarum*), as well as John of Beverley and Winifred, but not the new feasts of (at least) the Visitation and Transfiguration so often found in calendars by then. The Wells Feast of Relics is on October 14th, the cathedral's dedication on the 23rd of that month; on the latter day Romanus (of Rouen) is given as the Sarum feast. Another, seemingly inexplicable, Romanus appears at 17 June and graded at nine lessons; he does not appear to be any of the numerous Romanus-Ronan-Rumon possibilities of a Celtic fringe sort. The nine lessons awarded to Petroc (June 4th) are noted as a peculiarity of Wells. Another is the reduction of Machutus to three lessons, though the nine of Sarum are duly recorded. It is surprising that Congar is graded at only three and that Decuman is missing. By contrast, Egwin on December 30th is graded at nine lessons "at Wells," as the entry reads, which is a notably high grade for a saint who does not usually appear in English secular uses. That this calendar marks its few divergences from that of Salisbury again underlines the extent to which Sarum usages are regarded as being the norm, for Wells and, by the mid-fifteenth century, increasingly throughout southern England.

It is perhaps not surprising that so little survives in the way of concrete evidence for liturgical services at Wells (and no service books at all); possibly relevant is that Somerset tended to be a heavily Puritan area in the troubles of the seventeenth century. The contrast between

---

[187] It has an unusual format: saints on the verso, computus on the recto of each opening; March and April are missing. Noticed by J. A. Robinson in the discursive essay on "Somerset Medieval Calendars" prefacing his edition of a calendar of Muchelney abbey in *Muchelney Memoranda*, Somerset Rec. Soc. 42 (1929; also printed separately), pp. 4–6 and 22–24 (of the separate pagination). In Elizabethan times the calendar had belonged to the great Cecil family, hence Robinson's calling it grandly "calendarium Cecilianum."

the beauty of the cathedral and the dearth of information as to what its medieval liturgy was like is nonetheless glaring.

Liturgy in parish churches

Consideration of liturgy as practiced in English medieval parish churches is unavoidably bound up with the coming into being of such churches themselves. Scholarly work in recent decades has shown how complex this subject is (see above, p. 63, on the problem posed by minster churches). While it is easy enough to distinguish a parish church from a cathedral or large monastic establishment, such a distinction becomes blurred, sometimes to the point of unrecognizability, in the case of several kinds of small establishments which have as common identity only that they are meant to be served by several clergy rather than by a single priest. It is no easy matter to define what is meaningfully to be understood by the phrase "parish church" in liturgical terms. Several definitions are possible, depending largely on the criteria used. For our purposes, a rule-of-thumb principle will have to suffice: a parish church is one that serves a community defined more by locality (e.g., "the church at Burford" [Oxfordshire]) than by adherence to a rule (Tewkesbury abbey) or a set of statutes (Salisbury cathedral). Such a common-sense approach enables us to specify as parish churches buildings as elaborate as Tideswell in Derbyshire or St Mary Redcliffe in Bristol and as humble as Escomb in County Durham or Inglesham in Wiltshire (to mention four well known cases). By contrast Ottery St Mary in Devon (Grandisson's splendid foundation: p. 408 above), Sherborne abbey in Dorset (where the nave functioned as the parish church), and Southwell Minster in Nottinghamshire (made a cathedral in 1884, but in the middle ages a collegiate foundation, albeit the sole church in the town) are not usefully to be so regarded.[188]

A further complication arises from the fact that numerous parish churches were "prebendal": that is, churches of villages which formed all or parts of a specific prebend in a large (secular) collegiate church, whether of cathedral status or not. In such cases one must factor in the

---

[188] This leaves in a grey area of unclarity some small collegiate churches like Penkridge in Staffordshire or Howden in Yorkshire, whether royal (what would later be termed "royal free" chapels) or founded by a secular patron. In some cases they function indistinguishably from parish churches; in others, they swell the number of small religious houses of obscure origin which at some (probably early) point in their existence adopted a rule, most often that of Augustine, thus falling under the broad umbrella of canons regular (see chapter 8).

degree to which the resources of the mother church are brought to bear in a parish setting. For example, is an elaborate gradual belonging to a prebendal parish in Wiltshire evidence for sumptuous liturgy there or for the preferences and resources of the canon of Salisbury whose church it "was"?[189]

Virtually no service-book evidence for the subject exists before the thirteenth century, and even from that period – the parochial structure of England being by then clearly articulated – there is not much. Inevitably, consideration of liturgy in English parish churches in the middle ages is skewed towards the fourteenth and fifteenth centuries: a skewing that can lead imperceptibly to the kind of implied teleology discussed, and warned against, in the Introduction (see p. 9). This means that, although it would be unrealistic not to devote the largest amount of attention to where the most extensive amount of evidence lies, which is in later medieval service books that can be clearly identified as belonging to a specific parish, we must be constantly aware that the subject is not distinctively a late medieval one, like, say, the proliferation of chantry chapels. Because so few service books connected with parish churches survive from before the fourteenth century, it may be useful to begin by reviewing a few of the lists of books prescribed for parishes in episcopal statutes or inventoried in visitations (some of these lists have been dealt with more extensively in earlier chapters, especially pp. 369–73).

Booklists and visitation returns

A well known starting point here is a mid-eleventh-century Old English list of treasures (madmas) at Sherburn-in-Elmet.[190] This records, in the following order, two gospel books, one Aspiciens (sic: an antiphonal), one Ad te levavi (sic: a gradual), two epistle books, one massbook, one hymnal, and one psalter, along with various furnishings. The liturgy of the mass is adequately provided for between the massbook (almost certainly a sacramentary rather than a plenary missal), gradual, and a pair each of epistle and gospel books, each one possibly covering a half year. Whether the daily office could be performed depends on how full the

---

[189] The case in point is Great Bedwyn, Wilts, discussed below, p. 515.
[190] Printed by M. Lapidge, "Surviving Booklists from Anglo-Saxon England," *Learning and Literature in Anglo-Saxon England*, Festschrift Peter Clemoes, ed. Lapidge and H. Gneuss (Cambridge 1985), repr. in *Anglo-Saxon Manuscripts: Basic Readings*, ed. M. P. Richards (New York 1994), pp. 87–167, at 122–23; and by A. J. Robertson, *Anglo-Saxon Charters* (Cambridge 1939), p. 248. Lapidge's treatment covers the books only, Robertson's the furnishings as well.

Aspiciens and psalter were; if the former contained collects and lessons and the latter included canticles and litany, this was possible, otherwise not. The furnishings include one chalice and one paten, two crosses (*rodan*; no information as to portability or material is supplied), two chasubles (?: *mæssereaf*), three copes (?: *mæssehakelan*), two cloths (*ouerbrædels*, presumably for the altar), four hand-bells, six hanging bells: an adequate provision, certainly, for a single priest. But question as to whether this collection of books and goods is in some way exceptional is raised by the fact that is has been entered on one of three bifolia added to the celebrated York gospels (York Minster, MS 1), along with a survey of lands at Sherburn and some devotional material.[191] Here questions of nomenclature and status complicate the matter: it seems likely that Sherburn was a minster church.[192] If any of these books was used in the late Norman church of All Saints which survives there it would clearly be evidence for parochial liturgy, but taken as a whole they may represent a richer supply than most eleventh-century parish churches would have possessed. And there is little (indeed, apparently nothing) comparable for the rest of that century or even for the twelfth.

From the thirteenth century on there is a good deal more such evidence. Several canonical documents – diocesan statutes, episcopal instructions, and the like – prescribe the liturgical books that parishes ought to possess. These tend to read as though copied from a standard list. This is the case with the constitution of Walter de Cantilupe, bishop of Worcester, in 1240, that among the equipment parish churches in his diocese should have are "missale, breviarium, antiphonarium, gradale, troparium, manuale, psalterium, [et] ordinale."[193] Slightly fuller are the comparable requirements laid down by Peter Quinil (or Quivil), bishop of Exeter, in 1287; here are listed, after hangings and vestments, "missale bonum, gradale, troperium, manuale bonum, legenda, antiphonarium, psalterium, ordinale, venitarium, ympnarium, collectarium."[194] His statutes distinguish carefully between the equipment for worship that parish churches are expected to have and what is needed "in maioribus ecclesiis": twice, or even three times, as much ("duplicentur vel triplicentur"); and one wonders why the manual should be singled out as needing to be *bonum* as well as the missal.

---

[191] Ker, *CMCAS*, no. 402; facsimile edn by J. J. G. Alexander et al., *The York Gospels*, Roxburghe Club (London 1987).

[192] It is marked with a query in the index-list compiled by J. Blair at the end of *Minsters and Parish Churches: the Local Church in Transition 950–1200*, ed. Blair, Oxf. Univ. Comm. for Archaeology, Monograph 17 (Oxford 1988), p. 211.

[193] *C & S 1205–1313*, I.296.

[194] *C & S 1205–1313*, II.1005–6. One of the twelve MSS adds *capitularium*.

Such prescriptions can be counsels of perfection, or at least of aspiration, and the picture they offer has to be balanced by looking at such evidence as survives for service books that parish churches actually owned. We have already noticed (p. 370 above) the lists of liturgical books inventoried in 1220 by William de Waude, dean of Salisbury, in the course of a decanal visitation to his prebendal churches. We may remind ourselves of the situation in just two of these churches. Sonning in Berkshire was quite well supplied for mass, with two missals (the older but not the newer one *plenum*, both in need of binding), two graduals, a troper, a silver-covered gospel lectionary, an ordinal, and what must be a select missal ("quidam novus liber continens missas privatas"). Similar, slightly smaller, collections were noted at the four chapelries of Sonning, which was a large and apparently grand parish, suitable for a decanal prebend. Another church visited by de Waude was that at Heytesbury, which had become collegiate around 1165. Here the difficulty of distinguishing a parochial from a small collegiate church – it had four canons – is obvious: the two missals and two old plus two new breviaries he found there might have been just adequate to a multi-clergy establishment of that size, but it would seem as likely that the church was in fact served by a single priest.

Records from later in the thirteenth century include an account of the service books at another kind of small collegiate establishment, the royal free chapel at Bosham (Sussex), a church complicated in status because its nave was the parish church and also because episcopal jurisdiction was controverted between the bishop of Chichester, the diocesan, and the bishop of Exeter, the patron and, in theory, the dean of the college.[195] A report to bishop Quinil in 1281–82 mentions a new gradual, two psalters, a legendary, a manual, but both a "missale novum de usu Sarum" and an antiphonal are marked *deficit*.[196] (See page 484 for some comparable information about London churches.)

Similarly, the collegiate church of All Saints, Derby seems to have functioned like a well endowed parish church, having six or seven prebendaries but supposedly subject to the dean of Lincoln.[197] An

---

[195] J. H. Denton, *English Royal Free Chapels 1100–1300* (Manchester 1970), pp. 44–47.

[196] *Reg. Bronescombe and Quivil*, ed. F. C. Hingeston-Randolph (Exeter 1889), p. 316. A collectar and capitulary are also mentioned as *item*, after "deficit unum antiphonarium."

[197] Although destroyed, save for an early 16th-cent. tower, in the 18th cent. and replaced by a fine Gibbs building, which is the predecessor of what is now the cathedral church (since 1927) of All Saints, Derby. For the somewhat controverted medieval history, see VCH *Derbyshire* II (1907), pp. 87–92, heavily dependent on J. C. Cox and W. St. J. Hope, eds., *The Chronicles of the Collegiate or Free Church of All Saints, Derby* (London 1881).

inventory taken there in 1466 gives a sober sense of the service books available to a clerical staff of that size (there were, at least in theory, to be seven vicars, one for each prebendary). There are listed only two missals and one each of gospel books and collectars; two manuals, three "greles" ("grails": graduals), four processionals (one for each pair of clerics, a fairly standard provision), and eight "antiphonars" – in all, adequate, if rather bare-bones, equipment for mass and office and for pastoral liturgies (the two manuals).[198] The wording of the final item, two ordinals, "on gudde the oder of smalle valore," suggests that there was a more or less up to date ordinal and an obsolete one. The Derby list is curiously reminiscent of that of Sherburn-in-Elmet, some four centuries earlier.

Books that parish clergy used: thirteenth and fourteenth centuries

None of these books, from Bosham, Derby, or elsewhere, survives, but we may usefully keep them in mind as we survey some of the lamentably small number that are extant, all later than the twelfth century. Between sixty and seventy extant liturgical books can be assigned with some confidence to specific parishes.[199] Evidence for such ascriptions comes in the great majority of cases from the fifteenth century. Of course it must be remembered that evidence of ownership is not necessarily evidence of use; a church could have been left an out of date book, say, or one designed for monastic use, and marks of the new ownership supplied – most often, through the date of its dedication feast being entered in the calendar – without the book's ever being used in worship at the new location. Nonetheless, in most cases ownership implies at least some degree of use.

Among the small number of relevant books that survive from the thirteenth century, only a few will detain us here.[200] A couple of others have been discussed already, notably a missal used at Hanley Castle, Worcestershire in, but possibly not until, the fifteenth century (CUL

---

198 The list is edited and discussed by H. Bradshaw, who appears so often in these pages, in an Appendix to *Chronicles of All Saints*, pp. 87–92.

199 As listed in the "Books formerly owned by parish churches and chapels" appendix in Ker's *Medieval Libraries of Great Britain* (1964) and Watson's *Supplement* (1987).

200 Excluded from this discussion is a calendar of s. xiii/xiv in BL Harley 273 which contains the dedication of St Lawrence, Ludlow; it is in French, part of a volume containing a psalter, bestiary, and other material all in that language (therefore not a liturgical book). The calendar shows a special interest in Frideswide; Athanasius is rendered as *Anestas*!

Kk.2.6) that seems to have Augustinian affinities.[201] A breviary which appears to have been used in the Worcestershire village church of St Michael at Rochford (Bodl. Bodley 547) is treated in some detail, as an Augustinian book, by Timothy Morris in his 1999 thesis, but he has ignored entirely the evidence of parochial use.[202] Though there are clear signs of Augustinian origin, both textual and calendarial, it seems improbable that this breviary was ever used in a religious house. For one thing, there is a glaring contrast between the calendar and the sanctorale; the former contains over four dozen entries ignored in the latter, which however has two saints (Eusebius and Rufus) not contained in the calendar. Furthermore, the vast majority of entries in the sanctorale (which contains no English saint at all) are provided with only a proper collect. Either the priest who used the book relied on the common of saints very heavily or, as may be suspected, gave somewhat short shrift to the majority of the saints. In several places the *preces in itinere* have been altered to include the name of Michael (fol. 137v), and there are a number of obits in the calendar, including one of a vicar of Rochford who died in 1262.

This question posed above – how likely it is that indication of parish church ownership can be taken as evidence for liturgical use in that church – is given point by a thirteenth-century martyrology with "dedicacio ecclesie Bathewyk" entered at 16 October (now Cambridge, Jesus Coll. Q.B.14 [31]), the Bathwick in question being almost certainly now an eastern suburb of Bath (no church survives). The particular interest of this book lies in the numerous entries added in the margins. These include groups of saints specially important in Kent (for example, Adrian abbot, Laurence archbishop, Edburga, Ermenilda), in the West Country (Wulsin of Sherborne, Branwalator of Milton Abbey, Egwin of Evesham), and in lowland Scotland (Vigean [= Fechin], Kentigern, Finian of Clonard), as well as of the four Englishmen canonized between 1163 and 1203 (Edward the Confessor, Becket, Gilbert of Sempringham, Wulfstan of Worcester). It is puzzling that the York Feast of Relics should be added (19 October); a marginal addition of Augustine of Hippo, 28 August, describing him as "sancti patris nostri," suggests that the book may at one point have been in Augustinian hands – possibly in a Yorkshire house? On the one hand, it seems that the possessor(s) of this book clearly had an interest in expanding its contents to keep it

---

[201] P. 280; see p. 395 for the early 13th-cent. psalter from St Helen's church, Worcester, but at Exeter cathedral later in that century (now it MS 3508).

[202] T. M. Morris, "The Augustinian Use of Oseney Abbey," 2 vols (unpublished Oxford D.Phil. thesis, 1999), I.120–22 (discussed above, p. 274).

to some extent up to date, and had a wide-ranging awareness of local saints; on the other, it is hard to envisage a parish priest of Bathwick engaged in anything like the liturgical reading of the martyrology that is prescribed in the regulations of conventual and cathedral churches. Was this book for him merely an interesting thing to have around?

Another kind of problem is presented by a Sarum antiphonal of c. 1300 long at the parish church of All Saints in Springfield, now a northern suburb of Chelmsford in Essex. The book was hidden, probably in the mid-sixteenth century, in the roof of the church and discovered there in 1867. Henry Bradshaw secured it for Cambridge (now CUL Add. 2602) and published a brief description of it, remarking that "I have never seen a book of the kind anything like so perfect."[203] In its original state the book was, in Susan Rankin's words, "copied from a pure Sarum exemplar, and includes no added non-Sarum liturgy for local use." There are no clues as to how it got to Springfield. What was added later, obits and the like, shows that it was there in the 1420s, but not necessarily earlier, though the book was certainly used hard somewhere and there are numerous marginal additions. That Erkenwald is among the fifteenth-century additions to the calendar suggests that it was only then that the antiphonal reached Springfield (at that time in the diocese of London). Other additions show that it was being consulted as late as 1456, the year of the canonization of Osmund.

Another chant book presenting comparable problems is a gradual belonging, at least by the mid-fifteenth century, to the prebendal church of Great (sometimes called West) Bedwyn in Wiltshire (now CUL Add. 8333). When the book was bought for its present home in 1982 the dealer's catalogue described it as "the oldest known manuscript of the Sarum rite," suggesting the second quarter of the thirteenth century as a date. Certainly the feasts of its original sanctorale are conservative; there is no trace of any new feast of the thirteenth century, Translation of Becket, Wulfstan, Richard of Chichester, Edmund Rich, Hugh; nor of Corpus Christi in the temporale. Sarum custom is twice mentioned, and the rubrics generally agree with those of the earliest Sarum missals. It may be that the book was designed for use in the cathedral and was seconded to Great Bedwyn by one of the holders of the prebend when the absence of so many saints' feasts became glaring. A possible prebendary-donor of this sort is Thomas de Wickhampton

---

[203] Published first in the *Trans. Essex Archaeol. Soc.* in 1873 and reprinted, with an illustration, in n.s. 18 (1925–28), pp. 224–27. Subsequently discussed by Susan Rankin as no. 18 in *Cambridge Music in MSS*, ed. I. Fenlon (Cambridge 1982), pp. 62–66, with reproduction of fol. 168; and by Jayne Ringrose, who has kindly supplied me with her typescript description of 1994.

(or *de Grano*), who was archdeacon of Salisbury from at least 1275 to around 1307 and was most likely related to Robert of Wickhampton, dean of the cathedral from around 1259 to 1274, when he was consecrated bishop of the diocese (died 1284).[204] Attestation for its presence at Bedwyn consists of an inscription in a fifteenth-century hand on fol. 1. As with the book considered just above, then, it is shaky to regard this one as evidence for worship in a parish church, even though it (eventually) belonged to one.

We are on somewhat firmer ground with a few fourteenth-century Sarum missals that belonged to parish churches; four illuminate points of some general interest.[205] The first such point is again best posed as a question: did books originally intended for a grand church often end up being seconded to parish churches? This is raised by a large missal (400 × 265 mm; now Bodl. Lat. liturg. b.4) to the calendar of which the dedication of the church of St Peter, Northampton, has been added at May 29th. It looks to be of the later part of the century, but the (Sarum) Feast of Relics, both in the calendar and in the sanctorale, is still on September 15th, the date that was abandoned in 1319. The Bodleian *Summary Catalogue* posits that the book "was written for some large church or cathedral"; a reasonable supposition is that it was given to this parish church as a somewhat out of date cast-off.[206] Among the numerous additions to the calendar are the moveable feasts of Pentecost, written very faintly at June 13th, and Corpus Christi, after John the Baptist on June 24th. The only feasible year in which these dates corresponded to reality is 1451; although that is shaky evidence for dating, it is hard to imagine for what other reason the entries should have been made.

Two other additions are quite astonishing. One is a note at October 25th (Crispin and Crispinian): "Medie lectiones de Frontone" – Fronto, bishop of Périgueux in the mid-fourth century. As we saw earlier (p. 439), in December 1416 Archbishop Chichele mandated the three middle lessons on that day to be those of the Translation of John of Beverley. While it is not possible to date this addition to the missal's calendar as having been written before or after 1416, it almost exceeds coincidence that there should be two "middle-lesson" observances on the same, rather obscure, day. The other addition is even odder: at November 21st, "Sancti regenarii ... martyris looke att his seruys in

---

[204] *Salisbury 1066–1300*, pp. 47, 33, 11, 5.
[205] A Hereford missal (Oxford, Univ. Coll. 78A from Whitchurch, Mons.) and two York missals (Oxford, Univ. Coll., 78B, from Norton-Cuckney, Notts, and Stonyhurst College 3, used at Tatham, Lancs.) are discussed in the chapters on those Uses.
[206] *Bodleian Summary Cat.*, VI (1924), p. 187.

the olde masse boke. ix lectiones." Ragener (Regenhere) is distinctive, indeed unique, not just to Northampton but to St Peter's church there, for it was under the floor of that church that in the mid-eleventh century a body was found (in miraculous circumstances, needless to say), identified by a convenient scroll as that of a nephew of the East Anglian martyr-king Edmund.[207] The story appears first in the *Sanctilogium* of John of Tynemouth, rearranged alphabetically by John Capgrave into the *Nova legenda Angliae*. Presumably the nine lessons referred to in the calendar-addition would have been drawn from this; but they would of course have appeared in a breviary, not a missal – and in any case the book's sanctorale is defective from October 28th on. The point here is the freedom which the fifteenth-century user, presumably the parish priest, felt to add entries, one highly eccentric and the other determinedly local, without any sort of official sanction. If, on November 21st, he celebrated a mass in honor of St Ragener, did anyone notice?

A second general point has to do with how much variation, or even independence, from the Sarum norm, a book for parochial use is likely to have. This is illustrated by a mid-fourteenth-century missal into which the dedication of the church at Shepton Beauchamp in Somerset (now Liverpool Cathedral, Radcliffe Collection 29) has been added on February 7th. In several places its ordinary of the mass differs from either the fourteenth-century ordinary published by Legg (from the Morris/Tiptoft missal) or that of the printed Sarum missals as edited by Dickinson.[208] These variants are in both rubrics and texts of the priest's preliminary and vesting prayers (the latter of which come, eccentrically, after the Nicene Creed), and they suggest a model that arouses (unsatisfied) curiosity. The canon was apparently rewritten about 1400, so it is not possible to ascertain whether variants continue into the original canon. In the sanctorale the Feast of Relics is placed in July (the "modern," post-1319 location) and rubricated "In festo reliquiarum saluberiensis ecclesie," so there is no question that this is meant to be understood as a Sarum missal. This makes all the more striking the lack of uniformity in what one would have thought the most stable element in the mass.

A third general problem, the extent to which a grand service book donated to a parish church by a prosperous patron, and which has very likely survived because of its splendor, could actually have been used in

---

[207] The story is told succinctly in H. Farmer, *Oxf. Dict. Saints*, s.n. Ragener; the 2nd edn, 1987, refers to a missal in the Bodleian, without specification, but it is in fact this book.

[208] J. W. Legg, ed. *Tracts on the Mass*, HBS 27 (1904), item i. The fact of variation is noted by Ker in his description in *MMBL* III, but no details are given.

a parish setting, is raised by the sumptuousness of two further missals. The well known Lapworth missal (Oxford, Corpus Christi College 394) is particularly useful here because we have for it precise information as to the date it was completed, who gave it to what church, and when: 20 December 1398, Sir Thomas Assheby to Lapworth church (Warwickshire), by at the latest 1418.[209] Its decoration, particularly its full-page crucifixion miniature, has received considerable attention from art historians and seems to be by an artist whose work can be traced in a series of other high-status manuscripts.[210] There seems nothing specially distinctive about the contents save the omission of Corpus Christi (quite astonishing for a book of the very end of the fourteenth century) and in the calendar a *memoria* at October 1st of Mellor, the patron saint of the aristocratic nunnery at Amesbury. Again we notice, as with the St Peter's, Northampton book, the factor of size: the Lapworth book measures some 425 × 275 mm. A missal nearly eighteen inches in height is not easy for the celebrant to use; it almost certainly necessitates a good deal of neck movement, and flipping from one section to another will not be easy, whether the book lies on a pillow or on some sort of stand.[211]

Another fine missal, now Bodl. Don. b. 5, illustrates a further point, that some books apparently belonged to two parish churches.[212] The book seems to have been made around 1380, and at that time or soon thereafter the dedication of the church of St Mary at Adderbury (Oxfordshire) was entered into the calendar at December 1st. There is no indication as to a donor, nor as to how by the mid-fifteenth century it has migrated to Berkshire, to the church of Buckland, the dedication of which is entered on July 4th, with a note added around that time on November 20th: "the day of the frary chirche."[213] The building

---

[209] It is included, with a specially full description, in *MMBL* III because it somehow escaped being catalogued by H. O. Coxe in his 1852 conspectus of Oxford college MSS.

[210] Scott, *Later Gothic MSS*, no. 6; she points out that it is not certain that the book was made for donation to the church, though a now erased calendar entry at 18 July was read by ultra-violet light, c. 1931, as "Dedication of the Lapworth church."

[211] Modern altar missals tend to be around eleven inches (280 mm) in height; a book half again as tall, and proportionately broader, is harder to keep one's place in, even on a well designed printed page. With a manuscript book much depends on the size and legibility of the writing, of course.

[212] It was given to the Bodleian in 1933 in memory of J. Meade Falkner, who had owned it; it is therefore too late to have been included in the *Summary Cat.*, and the typed description in van Dijk's *Handlist* seems still to be the fullest treatment of it. It is again very large, 320 × 290 mm.

[213] Bonshommes friars, established at Edington (Wilts.) in 1358, held the rectory and advowson of Buckland: VCH *Berkshire*. IV (1924), p. 460.

history of Adderbury church suggests something of its importance. The church was held since the early eleventh century by the bishops of Winchester, one of whom presumably paid for its enlargement in the early fourteenth century. In 1381 the great William of Wykeham gave the patronage to New College, Oxford (founded by him two years earlier), at the expense of which the present chancel was built in 1408–19.[214] Curiosity naturally arises as to whether there is some connection between this book and William of Wykeham's new foundation. At least eight leaves are missing, mostly in the section that would have contained the canon (probably with a full-page crucifixion like the Lapworth book) and Easter, so how fully decorated it was is not now clear, but from what survives of borders and historiated initials it seems to have been fairly elaborate.[215] The calendar is somewhat fuller than the sanctorale in ways that may be suggestive; it includes Anne, Francis, and Frideswide (the patron saint of Oxford), all of whom are lacking from the proper of saints, although in late July (fol. 271) there is a marginal note, "Festum sancte Anne matris marie require in fine libri" – where her propers were presumably supplied, though that section of the book is now missing. The lengthy provision of chant-intonations and noted proses (fols 355–99, where the current contents end) would have made possible extensive musical celebration; but again there is the practical problem posed by the book's size, and in any case it cannot be supposed that the celebrant was meant to be singing the proses from the altar himself. Overall, this can scarcely be regarded as a typical book written for use in a parish church; indeed, we may wonder whether it was not intended in the first instance for New College itself, though why it later showed up at Buckland remains a mystery. In order to find a plainer book possessed by a parish with no particular pedigree, we may need to look for candidates within the very numerous surviving missals of fifteenth-century date.

Fifteenth-century books less than sumptuous

Of several possibilities, one of the most helpful for our purposes is a mid-fifteenth-century Sarum missal putatively used at Gawsworth in Cheshire (in the medieval diocese of Lichfield; Bodl. Barlow 1). This is

---

[214] J. Sherwood and N. Pevsner, PBE *Oxfordshire* (1974), pp. 413–15. The screen has been compared with that in the Lady Chapel at Winchester cathedral and was probably made by Winchester workmen.

[215] O. Pächt and J. J. G. Alexander, *Illuminated MSS in the Bodleian Library, Oxford*, III (Oxford 1973), no. 668; pl. lxv reproduces fol. 7, exorcism at blessing of salt and water.

not a particularly beautiful or ostentatious book, though the removal of at least seven leaves hints that there may have been more decoration than now appears. Two successive rectors had long tenures, George Baguley 1470–97 and Randle Fitton 1497–1536; the calendar contains obits of both, as of other members of the Fitton family.[216] As is often the case, the calendar is much fuller than the sanctorale. The former includes as original entries Frideswide, David, Chad, Erasmus (at 4 June, marked *non Sarum*), Translation of Frideswide, and Osmund, none of whom is mentioned in the original sanctorale; the feast of the Visitation, however, appears in both. At the end masses have been added for Antony abbot, David, Chad, and the Five Wounds. The sequence for the latter is the extremely rare "Plangat Syon salvatorem."[217] It would be most instructive to know how this sequence came to the notice of the scribe (the rector?) who copied it.

This rather workaday book contrasts usefully with a large early fifteenth-century missal probably used at Strensham in Worcestershire (Bodl. Rawl. liturg. c.3), another large volume (368 × 252 mm), which has fine borders and colored initials on a gold background: a suitable book to have been given by the local gentry family the Russells, the obit of at least one of whose members, Robert (d. 13 July 1433) – possibly the donor? – is entered in the calendar.[218] Someone with a strong Franciscan interest made four additions there: Francis and his octave (October 4th and 11th), Translation of Clare (October 2nd [1260]), and the extremely obscure Elzear of Sabrano (September 27th).[219] The dedication of the church at Deerhurst (Glos., eight or so miles down river from Strensham) has been added at December 10th, but there are sixteenth-century entries about members of the Carsy family, who had intermarried with the Russells, so it looks as though the book remained

---

[216] Four members of the same family were given monuments there between 1608 and 1643: N. Pevsner and E. Hubbard, PBE *Cheshire* (1971), pp. 222–23.

[217] Pfaff, *New Liturg. Feasts*, p. 89. The sequence is found otherwise only in BL Add. 24198, an Irish Augustinian select missal with some later additions for St Thomas's church in Dublin. It includes the wonderfully garbled stanza, "Virgo, mater Christi Iesu, / Scribitur in threnis vau, / Iod, heth, teth, lamed, tau. /Moysi pentatico."

[218] Brasses of what may be his grandfather and father, Robert and John respectively, are on the chancel floor; the former (d. 1390) is illustrated in N. Pevsner, PBE *Worcestershire* (1968), p. 274.

[219] Of whom the Benedictines of Ramsgate say, "Married to St Delphina of Glandèves, he was the perfect type of Christian gentleman. According to an old tradition both he and his wife were Franciscan tertiaries. His wife was present at his canonization in 1369": *The Book of Saints*, 4th edn (London 1947), p. 198. The same hand has added Evaristus, pope (d. c. 108) at Oct. 27th; this seems distinctively Franciscan also, appearing as early as the *Regula* calendar of 1227–30: S. J. P. van Dijk and J. H. Walker, *The Origins of the Modern Roman Liturgy* (London 1960), p. 442.

at Strensham. Also added are masses for four newly popular feasts or occasions, the Five Wounds, Holy Name, Visitation, and "pro pestilentia vel morte."[220]

Another book instructive for present purposes is a select missal of the early fifteenth century given to the church – technically, a chapel of the parish of Beddington – at Wallington in Surrey by 1423 (now Rugby School, MS Bloxham 1009).[221] The phenomenon of the select missal, which we have encountered in other contexts, is specially curious in a parochial setting. The temporale includes only eighteen occasions, from Advent I through Corpus Christi, and the sanctorale only twenty. There is no common of saints, nor any "template" masses for the vast majority of Sundays in the year; so it is hard to figure out why, or how, the book would have seen anything like regular use. Yet one blank space has been filled in with the mass "ad delendum febres [sic]" and another with the mass "pro mortalitate evitanda," while on twelve fresh leaves at the end are written forms for four further masses popular in the fifteenth century ("pro remissione omnium peccatorum," St Gregory's Trental, Five Wounds, and Name of Jesus).[222] Clearly the book was kept in continuous use; but what precise purpose can it have served? What else was used for Ash Wednesday, and the entire Lenten season, and Maundy Thursday, and second through fifth Sundays after Easter, and all the Sundays after Trinity, not to mention important feast days like the Nativity of the Virgin?

Books for the office in parish churches: Penwortham, Wollaton, Ranworth

So far we have looked at mass books of the fourteenth and fifteenth centuries that seem to have been used at churches in nine counties, all in the province of Canterbury. Despite the suspicion that those which have survived have done so predominantly because of their sumptuousness, particularly of illustration, and consequently that our sense of the subject may be distorted, we are able to get something of an idea of variety within an overall sameness. (This is all within the general penumbra of Sarum books; different kinds of variety may be discerned with the York and Hereford books.) When we turn to books used for

---

[220] Pfaff, *New Liturg. Feasts*, pp. 55, 67.
[221] A lengthy inscription on fol. 1v records the dedication of the high altar at Wallington in that year: *MMBL*, IV.224.
[222] Also, the calendar has had Deposition of Osmund added at 4 Dec., and a totally puzzling Elburga at 23 Jan.

the daily office in parish church settings, anything like a coherent picture becomes even more difficult to make out. It may of course be the case that it is those office books which there is no reason to assign to any particular parish church that would be the most informative; but speculation seems dubious without specificity. Three books obviously demand attention.

The first is the Penwortham breviary (now BL Add. 52359), so called from a memorandum on fol. 500v stating that one Thomas Harwode, "chaplain"' presented it to the parish church of Penwortham in Lancashire in 1486, with instructions that, in Derek Turner's words, "it was to be kept carefully by the churchwardens, who were to deliver it to the curate of the church for the celebration of mattins and vespers."[223] The gift was of a book close to two hundred years old (c. 1300), a Sarum breviary predating the 1319 changes (see p. 386), handsomely illustrated with fourteen historiated initials and with coats of arms of five noble families, and decorated in a style which is generally thought to be East Anglian. Furthermore, as Turner has pointed out, the original litany of saints seems to be Augustinian-Victorine, while in the mid-fourteenth century two unusual feasts of St Anthony, his Translation and Invention, were added to the calendar as well as his deposition feast, 17 January. The book is extensively noted, and is of high importance in that respect. Our present concern, however, is its putative use at Penwortham from 1486 on.

At Penwortham, now a suburb of Preston, there was a small priory cell of Evesham abbey, which seems to have had the patronage of the parish church. There seem never to have been more than a prior and two monks, and the abbey was reponsible for provision of a chaplain for the parish church.[224] Was Thomas Harwode that chaplain, leaving to the parish a book he had used during his tenure there? The monks at the priory would have to have used the monastic rite, if they said the office there at all. In this definitely secular, Sarum book – in general Sarum seems to have been used in Lancashire rather than the more proximate York as might have been expected – the sanctorale is very full, occupying fols 285–466, the common of saints proportionately

---

[223] D. H. Turner, "The Penwortham Breviary," *British Museum Quarterly* 28 (1964), pp. 85–88.

[224] Two monks in c. 1330, 1381, and 1417: *Med. Rel. Houses,* p. 73; VCH *Lancashire,* II (1908), pp. 104–6. VCH *Lancs.* VI (1911), p. 54, states that "There was no endowed chantry at Penwortham, but there seem, nevertheless, to have been three or four resident priests before the Reformation," with reference to a 1548 visitation list.

shorter (466–501).[225] This runs somewhat counter to the dimensions of the book, which at 225 × 145 mm is clearly capable of being portable. Whatever materials for recitation of the office had been there before, the donor seems to have thought this fat, portable book an improvement.[226]

If the Penwortham breviary is small as noted office books go, its antithesis in dimension is an antiphonal (alternatively termed, as in *MMBL*, "a massive noted Sarum breviary without lections") belonging to the church of St Leonard in the Nottinghamshire village of Wollaton.[227] It measures a gigantic 590 × 400 mm and ran originally to 413 folios, of which 410 survive. The book was made under the patronage of a Nottinghamshire knight, Sir Thomas Chaworth of Wiverton, and his second wife Isabella, a wealthy heiress. It is possible that it was intended for his chapel at Wiverton Hall; there does not seem to have been a parish church in the village. After Sir Thomas died in 1458/9 the book was bought by the executors of the late rector of Wollaton, William Husse (d. 1460), for use in that church: "pro diuino seruicio ibidem celebrando."[228] Janet Backhouse ascribes the making of the book to East Anglia or the northeast Midlands, about 1430, and points out that "it must have been intended for use on a lectern ... from which the musical notation would have been visible to several singers simultaneously."[229] Whatever church the patron had in mind when he commissioned the book, therefore, its size and the fact that it makes sense only if several singers are performing the office did not deter Husse's executors from

---

[225] Although it looks as though fols 357–72 should follow 488, which would make the common slightly longer.

[226] It is curious that a printed Sarum missal (Rouen 1508) owned by the same church also survives, Bodl. Vet.E.1.c.45: *MLGB*, p. 222. Lancashire Recusant piety seems a likely explanation.

[227] *MMBL*, IV.667–68. Kept, on loan from St Leonard's church, Wollaton, at Nottingham University, Hallward Library, as MS 250 (I have not studied it there). Wollaton is now swallowed up in the Nottingham conurbation; Wiverton is a few miles east. A. duB. Hill, "The Wollaton Antiphonal," *Trans. Thoroton Soc. of Nottinghamshire* 36 (1932), pp. 42–50, wondered if the book might have been intended as a gift to the chapel of St Lawrence de Wyverton, to which Sir Thomas's mother had left a vestment and money c. 1400 (p. 49).

[228] Sir Thomas's will leaves to his son William a number of service books including "the lesce Antiphonere of iiii"; it is almost inconceivable that if the Wollaton book was one of the three others it should have been in no way distinguished in this very lengthy and detailed document, published in *Testamenta Eboracensia* II, SS 30 (1855), pp. 220–29, esp. 227.

[229] These facts are laid out succinctly by Backhouse in the catalogue *Gothic: Art for England 1400–1547*, ed. R. Marks and P. Williamson (London 2003), no. 312, with facing full-page color reproduction of fol. 133, the Easter page, full of ostentatious heraldry.

having bought it, presumably in accordance with his wishes, to be used in his not otherwise remarkable church. That it was so used is shown by three additions: of the office of John of Bridlington (d. 1379, canonized 1401), of *Variaciones* on the eight chant-modes, and of what *MMBL* calls "fifteen memoranda in English, naming, for the most part, shrines and dates (Sundays and festivals, at which collections were taken up?)." These shrines include one at Knaresborough, the site of a nascent cult of the hermit Robert (died around 1218), which is consonant with the additions to the calendar of William of York and Wilfrid as well as John of Bridlington. There were fitful claims that Nottinghamshire was properly in the province of York, and it seems likely that one or more of Husse's successors was of that mind, though the original book is unmistakably of Sarum tradition.[230]

Enigmatic though it now is, the Wollaton antiphonal is not the only grand choir book of that type used in a parish church. A much better known book, the Ranworth antiphonal, was used in at least the sixteenth century at the parish church of Ranworth in Norfolk, and to this day kept mostly there.[231] At 525 x 380 mm it is not much smaller than the Wollaton book (590 x 400); like it, the Ranworth book was acquired by bequest, in this case from one William Cobbe in 1478. According to D. J. King "the likelihood is that it was a standard workshop production with a basic Norwich diocesan calendar," and he suggests that it may have been made at the Premonstratensian priory at Langley, which held the patronage of Ranworth church.[232]

Even if there could have been an adequate scriptorium at Langley (there seem to have been between thirteen and eighteen canons in the later fifteenth century), it is hard to believe that such an elaborate book would have been written there simply on speculation. In this case, that the office for St Helena, to whom the church at Ranworth was dedicated, is written integrally on the last three leaves of the book and in the original hand would seem to indicate that that was the original destination – unlike the situation at Wollaton. The predominantly Sarum calendar, no doubt part of the "stock" original, looks to have been written after 1457, for the Deposition and Translation feasts

---

[230] This is clearest in the placement of the Feast of Relics, for which there is a major decorated border, between John the Baptist and the Assumption: that is, at the (later) Sarum July date.

[231] In some winter months it is moved to the Castle Museum, Norwich. Brief description in *MMBL*, IV.194–95; Hughes, *MMMO*, frontispiece and ills. 22a–h, has much reduced facsimiles of fols. 1 and 52v-60; he describes it as "a rubricated antiphonal which also often gives the complete texts of some non-musical items" (p. 343).

[232] D. J. King in *Medieval Art in East Anglia 1300–1520*, ed. P. Lasko and N. J. Morgan (Norwich 1973), no. 69.

of Osmund are original (as is the quite amazing entry at May 24th, "Sancta Iohanne [sic] uxor Cuze": the follower of Jesus and wife of Chusa, Herod's steward, first mentioned in Luke 8.3).[233]

More precise dating may be possible. Helen has been added to the calendar (August 18th), along with the Transfiguration and Name of Jesus, which suggests that the book came to be destined for Ranworth between the time that calendar page (fol. 138v) and the office for Helen (fols 281–83v) were written. At November 27th there is an unusual entry, in red, *Adventus domini*, followed by the name of Linus (whose feast day is normally the 26th). The 27th is the earliest date on which Advent I can fall, and occurs on that day before 1478 (when the book is mentioned in Cobbe's will) only in 1457, the year of Osmund's translation, and 1468. Since that translation did not take place until July, the former of these years seems improbably early, and 1468 appears to be a reasonably firm date.[234]

The question that again arises here is the degree to which possession – in this case the book seems clearly to have been intended for the parish church where it ends up – implies use. Here there are at least two indications. One is the restoration of references to Becket and the pope (though this could simply have been a matter of devotion rather than a prescription for use). The other is the survival at Ranworth of a splendid fifteenth-century cantor's desk, which Charles Tracy, in the catalogue of the 2003 Late Gothic exhibition, suggests "may have been designed for use on a pulpitum or rood-loft ... likely to have been of local manufacture."[235] It is a two-level, swivelling piece of equipment, which means that two books can rest on it simultaneously (and makes it difficult to think of any likely liturgical use from a rood-loft). The sloping face of one of the desks is large enough (560 × 440 mm) to hold the antiphonal, and it is tempting to speculate that the lectern might have been commissioned for that purpose, with perhaps an office lectionary intended for the other side.

---

[233] This is noteworthy in that the "Holy Kindred" of Jesus are depicted on the celebrated screen at Ranworth, including Mary Salome and Mary Cleophas: Eamon Duffy, *The Stripping of the Altars* (London and New Haven 1992), p. 181 and pl. 74; and Joanna is linked with Mary the mother of James (= Mary Salome) and Mary Magdalen in Luke 24.10 as the first witnesses to the resurrection. May 24th is Joanna's date in some early martyrologies, esp. that of Usuard (J. Dubois, ed. *Le Martyrologe d'Usuard*, Subsidia hagiographica 40 (Brussels 1965), p. 234), and thence to the *Martyrologium Romanum* of 1584.

[234] Although a similar kind of dating argument, from books that locate Easter on March 27th, is quite invalid – that being a commonly used conceit, symbolically attractive because it places the feast of the Annunciation on Good Friday – in the Ranworth case, there is no discernible reason for highlighting the occurrence of I Advent on a particular day.

[235] *Gothic: Art for England 1400–1547*, no. 272; there dated "early 15th century."

Less splendid (and more instructive?) service-book evidence

It should be emphasized that the three books just considered, like many of those noticed earlier, are grand books, important enough in their illustration to have attracted the attention of art historians. We may conclude this chapter by looking at two more modest manuscripts which share, as well as absence of fine decoration, somewhat confused contents. The first is a mid-fifteenth-century missal used at the church at Esh in County Durham (now Ushaw, St Cuthbert's College 5).[236] It was a chapel of the collegiate church at nearby Lanchester, the dean of which from about 1460 to 1490 was John Rudde. He spent a number of years at Oxford (B.C.L. 1459), during which it is possible that he may have had made for himself this book; in any case it is a liturgical oddity, containing variable contents that are mostly Sarum (with some feasts that may reflect the diocese of Lincoln, in which Oxford lay) but with the canon being of York use.[237] As it happens, that combination reflects the oddity of the statutes at Lanchester by which bishop Antony Bek of Durham, who turned the parish church into a collegiate establishment in 1284, permitted either the York or the Sarum rite to be used. Precisely when Rudde gave this missal to Esh church is not clear; the inscription recording his donation is written after his death, probably in the same hand which added forms for Oswin, John of Beverley, and the Translation of Nicholas. Just after this an early sixteenth-century hand has inserted in the margin a memorandum about four fields of land asigned to the church for the provision of lights. Ian Doyle suggests interestingly that Rudde's donation "was presumably to replace an earlier worn-out copy, more likely of York use." One wonders to what extent the parishioners of Esh noticed the change.

The final book to be considered here is among the most enlightening pieces of evidence for the subject we are pursuing: the Lavington manual (Bodl. Lat liturg. f.25).[238] Although the single term that best characterizes it is "manual," it is in fact a composite volume put together, probably by a fifteenth-century parish priest in the village of West Lavington

---

[236] A. I. Doyle, "Two Medieval Service-Books from the Parish of Lanchester," *Trans. of Archit. and Archaeol. Soc. of Durham and Northumberland*, n.s. 6 (1982), pp. 19–22, both expanding on and condensing the discursive treatment of E. Stephens, "A Note on the Esh Missal," *Ushaw Magazine* 49 (1939), pp. 153–57; 50 (1940), pp. 39–48 and 118–21; and 57 (1947), p. 44. The church at Esh has disappeared.

[237] Doyle characterizes the book as "altogether an expensive professional product, not however of the bulk or script (the traditional gothic text-hand) which was customary for the main altar missal of a church or chapel, so perhaps a personal possession."

[238] I have laid out the story of how it was discovered and of the often amusing interplay of expert scholarly opinion brought to bear on it in "The Lavington Manual and its Students," *Bodleian Library Record* 17.i (2000), pp. 10–23.

in Wiltshire, from bits of three books. The first fifty-nine folios come from an early fourteenth-century manual and are straightforward in contents: baptism, marriage, visitation of the sick, various liturgies for the dead, some votive masses, and the beginning of the canon. To supply the rest of that essential component the compiler found and reused the canon, together with some additional votive masses, from a missal of the thirteenth century (precisely when in that century became a subject of scholarly debate in the early twentieth; probably third quarter). The remaining contents – other manual offices – were supplied by a gathering of twelve leaves probably written in the late fifteenth century, at the time the book was put together in its present, hotchpotch form. The resulting book, as ungainly as it was thoroughly utilitarian, attracted no collector when its rites were no longer in use. Instead, it was somehow buried, perhaps hidden in the hope of being recovered if the old liturgy ever came back into use, in the chancel wall of the church: from which it seems to have fallen out – why or how is not clear – and into the hands of the curate in the mid-nineteenth century or somewhat earlier. Its discovery, and the study subsequently devoted to it, provide us with a picture of parochial liturgy at West Lavington driven primarily by the services the priest needed rather than by the existence of a polished, often sumptuously decorated, mass or office book.

Two fields largely unploughed

The West Lavington story is an unusually satisfying one, involving as it does aspects of the archaeological and personal as well as strictly liturgical. Those aspects may serve as a reminder of two further kinds of sources that must remain mostly unmined here. First, the fabric of every one of the surviving medieval parish churches throughout England offers potential witness. The most cursory look at the fifty-odd volumes of Nikolaus Pevsner's staggering "Buildings of England" series (see p. 26) shows how great both the opportunities and the obstacles are: on one hand, a vast quantity of sedilia, piscinas, squints, remains of medieval altars, and all the other apparatus that so excited nineteenth-century students of ecclesiology; on the other, the almost universal post-medieval alterations and (often especially vexing) restorations, some of the latter so cunning as to lead astray even Pevsner and his associates. Among other aspects of architectural evidence that might bear on the subject at hand are the length and shape of chancels, the placement of the main altar and of any subsidiary altars and chapels, and the existence of rood screens deep enough to accommodate performers in liturgies on special occasions like Christmas or Palm Sunday. To do anything like justice to this mass of evidence, much of it difficult to interpret, would require a volume the size of the present one. A good deal of literature has long been available on the purely architectural side; and Carol Davidson Cragoe's doctoral thesis on parish churches in the early thirteenth century has focused attention on their liturgical functions.[239] Further investigation is needed to extend the subject into the later thirteenth century and beyond.

Similarly unmined must be the bulk of the more personal kinds of written evidence, again overwhelmingly from the later middle ages: letters of the Paston, Stonor, and Cely families, the revelations to Julian of Norwich and from Margery Kempe, the vast trove of vernacular literature from the late fourteenth century on. Above all, there is the evidence of wills, like the notable one of Sir Thomas Chaworth about the Wollaton antiphonal, cited above. A systematic trawl of the large number of surviving wills would yield a certain amount of information about devotional wishes of the testators which may in turn have driven the production of service books. This is most obvious if the commonly encountered specifications of enormous numbers of masses for the souls of testators and/or of those they wish to benefit are meant to be taken anything like literally, for each mass requires at least a priest, an altar, and a missal. The serious problem thus raised about the provision of an adequate number of service books is one of the tantalizing questions that will have to be posed (only to be left unanswered) in our final chapter.

---

[239] C. F. Davidson (now Davidson Cragoe), "Written in Stone: Architecture, Liturgy, and the Laity in English Parish Churches, c. 1125–c. 1250" (Birkbeck College, Univ. of London, 1998).

15   Towards the end of the story

For the hundred years or so with which this book must conclude there is a vast amount of material, more than can be taken in and used effectively. The difficulty is one of selection: the opposite of that with the earliest periods, where we had to squeeze the few available sources for every possible drop of inference. Despite, or perhaps because of, this plethora of material, the ground is potentially tricky here. In general, any mention of the close, or end, of the middle ages conjures what in conventional periodization comes "next," *the* (note the definite article) Reformation. The difficulty here is not partisanship – happily, no longer the bugbear of dispassionate investigation – but the implicit teleology of which we have been steadily aware (often mentioned, from p. 9 on). Even recognizing the temptation, we may find it hard when talking about liturgy in the late fifteenth and early sixteenth centuries to avoid attitudes expressed in metaphorical language like "autumn" and "tiredness" – and, these days, even harder to avoid those that suggest "freshness" and "vitality." The cogency of the argument for each pair of nouns will be examined briefly at the end of this chapter; we need to begin it by going back earlier in the fifteenth century, to the founding of a new religious order in England, the Bridgettines.

The Bridgettines

The religious establishment with the simplest, and at the same time most paradoxical, character in our story is that of the *Ordo sanctissimi Salvatoris*, usually known as Bridgettines, whose English presence began in 1415 at the instigation of king Henry V.[1] "Simplest," because there was to be only one house in England for this double order, nuns

---

[1] The fullest modern account of the Bridgettines in England is A. J. Collins's introduction to his edition of *The Bridgettine Breviary of Sion Abbey*, HBS 96 (1969), pp. i–liii. A succinct presentation of the basic facts is offered by Vincent Gillespie in his edition, *Syon Abbey*, CBMLC 9 (2001; with *The Libraries of the Carthusians*, ed. A. I. Doyle), pp. xxix–lxv. The Charterhouse at Sheen (Surrey) had been established in 1414, also

and brothers, which had been founded by Bridget of Sweden, who died in 1373 and was canonized eighteen years later.[2] That house was originally at Twickenham in Middlesex, but was moved in 1431 to a somewhat more favorable site nearby, called Syon. It remained there until its dissolution in 1539, and continued thereafter on the Continent (with a brief return to England during the reign of Mary Tudor) until the nineteenth century; eventually the nuns – there were no longer brothers – settled at South Brent in Devon, where a house survives to this day.[3]

"Most paradoxical" because although the order was (and remains) thoroughly international, the house in Middlesex seems to have devoted itself to what would now be called acculturation: from the outset it adopted the Sarum rite for mass and the office used by the brothers (the sisters' office will be treated presently); it incorporated an early and high degree of the vernacular in the rubrics of its service books; and members of the order engaged in a great deal of literary activity, much of it in English. Their literary productivity is not part of our business here, but the "Englishness" of their liturgy very much is, particularly because it has such a relatively tidy temporal beginning.

What we are trying to assess, then, is the place in our story of a late medieval liturgy of a mixed sort, regular (though not monastic) in theory but largely secular in execution. An added peculiarity is that the female Bridgettines seem to have outnumbered the males greatly, a preponderance possibly reflected in the fact that there survive at least five processionals and at least twice that many books for the daily office, but nothing at all for the mass. The church is supposed to have been extremely large, but precise dimensions do not seem to be extant; those of some of the monastic buildings may be reflected in the ground plan of the present Syon House. Such a picture as we can get of Bridgettine liturgy must come primarily from the extant service books.

Bridgettine liturgical books

The order's formal inauguration in England came one year after the bishop of London's mandate that the whole of his diocese, which included Middlesex, was to adopt Sarum Use (see p. 480). Bridgettine

(see p. 480)

---

on Henry's initiative; its income in 1535 was £800, the highest among the Carthusians in England (*Med. Rel. Houses*, p. 133), but less than half of Syon's £1731.

[2] More than one English house was apparently projected, but no other was founded; the somewhat muddy early history is discussed in Knowles, *RO*, II.175–82.

[3] Details of the course of their movements are given in VCH *Middlesex*, I (1969), pp. 182–91. The considerable collection of pre-1850 books belonging to the abbey is now kept in the Exeter University Library, but this does not include the eight medieval MSS, which are still at South Brent and are described in *MMBL*, IV.335–49.

custom was basically to follow diocesan use, so it would have been Sarum patterns that would have been followed for mass and for the brothers' office: from, that is, about 1420, when, a sufficient number of religious having been gathered and the *Addiciones* – the adaptations of St Bridget's basic Rule which had to be made for each house – settled, we can suppose the complete round of corporate worship to have begun. The full community was supposed to contain sixty sisters and twenty-five brothers, of whom thirteen were to be priests (there were to be, in theory anyhow, thirteen altars in the conventual church). The numbers reported for Twickenham in 1428 of forty-one sisters to fourteen brothers (eight ordained, six lay), though not quite reaching the ideal complement, amount to a considerable worshipping community.[4] By that time, the gathering of a suitable quantity of Sarum missals cannot have been difficult, and they could presumably be used almost without alteration. Office books, however, presented a more complicated problem, in two respects.

The first complication was that the sisters used not the office of the diocese in which the house lay but a more distinctive office. This latter survives in at least three extant breviaries, one of which, Magdalene College, Cambridge F.4.11, is happily available in a modern edition.[5] This, called a diurnal by M. R. James in his catalogue of the college's manuscripts, is instead the full daily office for Bridgettine sisters: in this case, sisters who read English easily, for all the rubrics are in the vernacular. As the book was almost certainly written in the 1420s, this astonishing fact implies that any Swedish sisters who had come from the mother house at Vadstena had either gone home, died, or learned English. The distinctive practice in this women's office is, as the rubric puts it, that "the sayd seruyce is principali departed in vii hool stories which stories the sustres of the said ordir shal vnchaungebli syng eueri weke through the Zere except certen festes and tymes hereaftir expressed." These "stories" (*historiae*, in Latin books), laid out in three lessons a day throughout the week, consist of the meat of St Bridget's revelation as told to her spiritual director, Alfonso da Vadaterra, and arranged liturgically by one Petrus Olavi.[6] The rationale for this practice is contained in the "Prolog that the deuout fadir alfons some tyme bishop

---

[4] The other numbers recorded in *Med. Rel. Houses*, p. 202, are for Syon in 1539: at least fifty-six women and seventeen men.

[5] That of Collins, 1969 (note 1 above). It omits the psalter, canticles, and litany (fols 109–219), the latter being specially regrettable. After the Dissolution the book came into the possession of the minor 16th-cent. poet Barnaby Go(o)che and then of his son Barnaby, Master of Magdalene 1604–26.

[6] Two people of identical name figure in this story; Collins, *Bridg. Brev.*, p. xviii, attempts to untangle them. Their precise identity is not material here.

in the kingdome of spayne and aftir hermitt made to the excellence of the blessid virgyn mari indited and geue to saynt birgitt by the angel of god": the *Sermo angelicus* that was Bridget's warrant, so to speak, of extraordinary holiness and that constitutes the daily "stories."[7] As that prologue implies, the content of these lessons is almost wholly Marian.

The other complicating factor in the Bridgettine office has to do with the ritual arrangement of the building. The details prescribed by St Bridget were to be followed in all churches of the order; to the exent that they were (some variation was inevitable), a kind of two-storey interior was envisaged. In A. J. Collins's summary,

The choir of the sisters, mainly a wooden structure, was raised high above the centre of the nave; it apparently occupied the second and third (of the five) bays and was supported by their six pillars which pierced its floor. The sisters would seem to have entered the church from their convent through a door in the upper part of the north wall, whence they reached the choir by crossing a bridge over the north aisle. There was no other access. Eastwards from the choir they looked upon the Lady-altar, at which a priest-brother celebrated for them the daily Mary-Mass. ... Westward from their choir the sisters looked down upon the High-altar, placed at the east end of the choir of the brothers. Their choir, almost square in plan, probably projected from the western extremity of the church. ... [In the upper choir] the sisters said the Hours of this Breviary and their part of the Mary-Mass; they also saw the ceremonies performed at the High-altar and could hear the brothers as they chanted in their stalls.[8]

That the women's office should be sung at a different time and in a different place from that of the men was awkward but not unique (a similar arrangement obtained among the Gilbertines; see p. 310). What is unique here is the character of this Bridgettine office: in effect, a largely invariable votive office of Marian devotion which for this order constituted the women's daily non-eucharistic worship. There were no concerted readings from Scripture or from the Fathers, no lives of saints; very little variation, save for some twenty-five principal feasts, but even then the lessons at matins did not change.[9]

Other copies of the sisters' breviary survive, notably in Magdalene College, Cambridge F.4.12 and Bodl. Auct. D.4.7. The former is close to being a duplicate of its shelf-mate, F.4.11, but has the rubrics in Latin and some additional matter. It appears to be somewhat later than

---

[7] Collins, *Bridg. Brev.*, pp. 134–37.

[8] Ibid., pp. xiii–xiv.

[9] The feasts are listed ibid., p. 117: five of Mary, three of Bridget, and otherwise from the sanctorale only John the Baptist, Peter and Paul, Anne, Peter's Chains, Augustine, and Michael.

the F.4.11 book, and it has the look of a "showing copy" about it; the obits of both Henry V and Thomas Fishburn, first confessor-general (the male, spiritual head of the house; he died in 1427) are supplied in purple and red, whereas Bridget's three feasts (*Natale*, Translation, Canonization) are in red alone.[10] The Bodleian book is also a handsome volume, close to being uniform with the F.4.12, Latin rubrics and all. It has also two extensive additions to the calendar, of both Continental and English names. Among the former are Helena of Auxerre (22 May); Antony of Padua (13 June); George and Aurelius, martyrs of Cordoba (27 July); Amandus, first bishop of Strasbourg (26 October); Gentianus, Fulcianus, and Victoricus, also early Gaulish figures (11 December); among the latter, Hilda (at the unusual date of 20 April); Fremund (11 May, relics at Dunstable); and, in a different hand from other additions, the extremely rare Godric of Finchale (21 May). A comparable but rougher book is Bodl. Rawl. C.781; despite being less elegant, it had good borders and initials, many of which have been cut out. Of greater interest is its perhaps literally complementary volume, University College Oxford 25, which if put together with the Rawlinson book makes up just about the contents of Auct. D.4.7. The Univ. 25 book was apparently compiled by Elizabeth Yate, one of the sisters at the Dissolution, who with several of her colleagues continued religious life privately, in the first instance at her father's house, taking with her this book (and, presumably, the Rawlinson manuscript); on fol. 4 she wrote, "This book perteyneth to me Elysabeth Yate." Its nucleus is a Sarum psalter, with calendar and canticles, printed by Francis Byrckmans at Paris in 1522; the distinctive Bridgettine contents are then added by (her?) hand, including a litany of saints close to, but not quite identical with, that of Magdalene F.4.11.[11]

In contrast to these plural witnesses to the sisters' office, apparently the sole extant manuscript of a breviary used by the brothers is BL Royal 2 A.xiv. It antedates by a quarter century or so the establishment of the order in England, and is simply a Sarum breviary with commemorations of Bridget and forms for the saints' cults mandated in 1415–16

---

[10] They are, respectively, 23 July, 28 May, and 7 Oct.; the F.4.12 calendar also has, at 5 Aug., "Hac die reuelata fuit b. Birgitte regula S. Saluatoris."

[11] The most unusual entries in these litanies are Joachim (husband of St Anne) and Joseph (always called *custos Mariae*). All of the MSS mentioned above are described summarily by Collins, pp. xlii–l, including a choir lectionary, now Syon Abbey MS 6 (which I have not seen). Specially frustrating is the survival of only seven leaves of a folio breviary (415 × 265 mm) with some music, now CUL Add. 7634, bought in 1964. C. de Hamel, *Syon Abbey: the Library of the English Bridgettines* (Roxburghe Club 1991), p. 138, suggests that it is "probably the copy given to the Abbey by John, Duke of Bedford (Henry V's brother) in 1426."

added. The lessons are often a good deal shorter than those in the 1531 printed edition presented by Procter and Wordsworth (see p. 425), but the shortening cannot be ascribed to the Bridgettines; the book came into their hands that way. It has been prepared for heavy use: at least twenty-two sewn-through tags are evident.

Two psalters may provide further light. Brasenose College, Oxford 16 is a well illustrated early fifteenth-century Sarum psalter which either lacked a calendar or had its calendar removed; late in the century an extensive, and sometimes highly imaginative, calendar was supplied (almost, but not quite, a saint for each day), preceded by a Bridgettine litany and collects. The litany-and-collects, calendar, and original psalter are each of different dimensions; the point of curiosity is whether they were put together with a view to use, presumably by someone of that order, or simply out of late medieval antiquarian interest. A similarly imaginative calendar, this time apparently original to the manuscript, appears in an early(?) fifteenth-century English psalter (now Edinburgh University Library 59); its litany is unfortunately missing. It cannot be proved that the book remained in Bridgettine possession into the mid-sixteenth century, but the addition around then of a number of extraordinarily rare saints, mostly female, suggests this: figures like Marciana of Mauretania (9 January), Theodosia of Tyre (2 April), Agape, Chonia, and Irene (3 April), and a Sophia (15 May, without her sister Quirilla); what is probably Henry of Uppsala (19 January) is the clinching name.[12] Its litany of saints would probably have been like the one added to a composite psalter (now Lambeth Palace 535) with a Dominican calendar, itself with no English traces, or like the almost identical one in the Brasenose manuscript.[13]

Five Bridgettine processionals survive. The oldest is apparently one that was long the property of the Bristol Baptist College (MS Z.d.40), but since 1991 CUL Add. 8885.[14] They are all closely related, one scribe

---

[12] This last is read incorrectly as "Herry[?]" in C. Borland's catalogue of the Edinburgh Univ. Lib. MSS (1909), p. 107. She gives only a sampling of the many striking entries, and this calendar could repay systematic study, especially in view of its provenance: as she states, "According to an inscription on the fly-leaf, the MS was presented to the Library by the graduates of the year 1636" – as a kind of Laudian gesture?

[13] The book is now too tightly bound to allow collation, but the hand changes on fol. 262, where the litany begins. As the M.R. James catalogue points out, a final collect is in the feminine gender (*famulam tuam*), which makes ownership by a Bridgettine nun likely.

[14] Ker's description in *MMBL*, II.194–95 is under Bristol; it was reprinted, together with C. de Hamel's for the 1991 Sotheby sale catalogue, in J. Hogg, "An early sixteenth century book of devotions from Syon Abbey," in *Studies in St Birgitta and the Bridgettine Order*, Analecta Cartusiana 35:19/2 (Salzburg 1993), pp. 249–53.

working on parts of Syon Abbey 1, St John's College, Cambridge 139, and possibly St John's College, Oxford 167, another on parts of the Syon book and that formerly at Bristol.[15] The marked importance of processions in the nuns' liturgical life is reflected in the detailed provisions in their Rule (with the "Additions" for England), as summed up by Christopher de Hamel: "The whole convent of sisters in pairs, side by side, the abbess and the prioress together and the chantress and sub-chantress together, but all the others in pairs in the order of their profession. Presumably they would share manuscripts, one between two."[16] Three of these processionals contain pairs of names of nuns, most of whom have been identified; two lived past the middle of the sixteenth century.

Some possibly instructive confusion is discernible in the selection and arrangement of saints in the litanies for Rogation days, in the four days' worth of litanies of saints contained in these manuscripts after the forms for the Dedication feast.[17] These are not identical with the Sarum Lenten litanies for each of the six weekdays (p. 430 above), though they seem to work in roughly the same way, with between twelve and fifteen saints in each of the four main categories (the apostles remaining constant). For instance, the lists in the St John's College, Oxford processional have Osmund last among the confessors on all four days.[18] Among British figures, Becket, Kenelm, and Oswald each appear on two days. Slips add four names encountered in other Bridgettine documents, those of Joachim and Joseph (always among confessors) and of Katherine (Bridget's daughter and successor as abbess; d. 1381) and Elizabeth (probably the mother of John the Baptist). There are plenty of English names among the confessors and virgins, and it is clear that this is basically a list compiled in England, not Sweden. The rubrics are in the vernacular in the Magdalene F.4.11 breviary, whereas those in Syon Abbey 1 are in Latin.

---

15 Syon Abbey 1 is presented in photocopied facsimile by Hogg in *Spiritualität Heute und Gestern*, Anal. Cartus. 35:19/11 (1991), pp. 45–299. The fifth processional is owned by the Duke of Northumberland, Alnwick Castle, MS 505a.

16 De Hamel, *Syon Abbey*, pp. 85–87.

17 Apparently it seemed convenient to combine the Greater Litany, fixed on Apr. 25th, with the variable Rogationtide Monday through Wednesday litanies, which occur on the three days prior to Ascension Day.

18 Fols 81v-83v. R. Hanna, *Descr. Cat. of the Western Med. MSS of St John's College, Oxford* (Oxford 2002), pp. 232–34. In *New Liturg. Feasts*, pp. 29 and 57, I stupidly misdated the book to the episcopate of John Kempe, bishop of London 1421–25, on the strength of a privilege from him on fol. 100v; this, which appears in the other processionals also, clearly calls him *bone memorie*, which implies a date after his death in 1454.

Bridgettine liturgical bookishness

As was stated earlier, the extensive literary activity of the Bridgettines in England can form no part of our investigations, not even the fascinating phenomenon of the translation of the *Sermo Angelicus*, which forms the nucleus of the sisters' office, into English as *The Myroure of oure Ladye*.[19] We do, however, need to notice two collections among the 1,465 entries in the *Registrum* of the brothers' library at Syon made in the first quarter of the sixteenth century (now CCCC 141), splendidly accessible in the Corpus of British Medieval Library Catalogues series; the main scribe was Thomas Betson, who was one of the four deacons of the house and died in 1516.[20] The volume listed by Betson as M.14 contains thirty-three items (in a book of 124 folios, the contents mostly patristic), of which the twenty-eighth was described as "Instituta quedam diuini officii a Sarum aliena cum eorum mistica significatione." How whatever aspects (*instituta quedam*) of the Bridgettine office that differed from the Sarum could occupy some twenty-five folios (82–107), even with fairly wordy mystical significance, rouses strong curiosity in itself. And this curiosity is much intensified by the fact that the book (not extant, of course) is ascribed to one who had practiced Sarum liturgy and who was also, it seems, a bibliophile: John Bracebridge, whose name is next to no fewer than 112 volumes in this list, and who was a master at the cathedral school at Lincoln and a vicar choral there until 1420, when he seems to have entered the house at Twickenham as among its first recruits.[21] The entry provides tantalizing evidence of an attempt to think systematically about the distinctivenesses of Bridgettine liturgy.

Some such distinctive bits and pieces look to be recorded in the very next entry (M.15; no name attached) in this massive *Registrum*. Of the sixteen items enumerated in this entry, about half bear on liturgical observance. They include a "Longa litania cum suffragiis sequentibus" (long indeed: fols 26 to 58!); a *historia* for Joachim and one for Joseph – two figures we have seen added to Bridgettine litanies – and also one for the prophet Elisha; masses for the Visitation, "in commemoracione

---

[19] Edited by J. H. Blunt, Early English Text Soc., extra series 19 (1873); a new edition, by Ann M. Hutchinson, is awaited.

[20] Gillespie, *Syon Abbey*, pp. 1–438, as "SS 1." There is also a supplementary index made by Betson, pp. 505–66.

[21] Gillespie, *Syon Abbey*, p. 570, notes that Bracebridge "appears to have been the only graduate among the brethren at the election of the second confessor-general in 1428," and points out that although the thirty-first item, "Quoddam Registrum de libris," might represent an early listing of books at Syon, "it is more likely to be a list of Bracebridge's own substantial collection of books" (p. 221).

omnium festorum gloriose virginis Marie," and "in commemoracione omnium festorum domini nostri Jesu Christi et de vita eius"; a mass for Elisha (*Heliseus*); a *vita* of the Three Kings of Cologne (again immensely long: fols 108–87), followed by their *historia*, perhaps a boiling down of the *vita* for possible liturgical use (fols 187–207); and "many devout prayers" on the Name of Jesus and on Mary, the latter ending with the Bridgettine Marian devotion of the "Fifteen Oes."[22] We have noticed a mass of the Three Kings in a late medieval Sarum missal (see p. 421), but a mass for Elisha seems almost exotic in its rarity. A similar touch of the exotic is heavily evident in the English adaptation of the Syon martyrology produced by one of its brothers some thirteen years before the Dissolution.

Whitford's *Martiloge* (1526)

Among the most notable literary figures connected with Syon is Richard Whitford (or Whytford), who had enjoyed extensive education and experience before entering the house in, probably, 1511.[23] In 1526 there appeared from the press of Wynkyn de Worde at Westminster a volume compiled by Whitford and titled *The Martiloge in Englysshe after the Use of the churche of Salisbury and as it is redde in Syon, with addicyons*.[24] The constituent parts of that title are true in descending proportion. The work is certainly a martyrology and clearly in (not very eloquent) English. Whether it is based on *the* Sarum martyrology cannot now be ascertained, because no such single entity exists, though texts of that sort are extant. And if its being rooted in *the* martyrology as read at Salisbury cathedral in the early sixteenth century is doubtful, that the Latin original behind Whitford's work was the one read at Syon is still more questionable, for there is much that is palpably ridiculous (despite the fact that he was at one point supposed to have been friendly with Erasmus). Finally, the "Additions" are a totally private compilation, not to be confused with the adaptations of Bridget's Rule made for England.

---

[22] Gillespie, ibid., suggests that the Three Kings material was John of Hildesheim's *Historia trium regum*, printed in Cologne in 1477. Among the items noted two entries later, M.17, is a *Vita trium Regum Colonie in anglicis* [*sic*].

[23] See the good account of his literary work by J. T. Rhodes, *ODNB* 58.714–15. Rhodes is much more positive about Whitford's learning and English style than was E. S. Dewick (see next note). Whitford's name is associated, presumably as donor, with twenty-four entries in the Syon Registrum; see Gillespie's note, *Syon Abbey*, pp. 591–92.

[24] Edited under that title by F. Procter and E. S. Dewick, HBS 3 (1893); STC 17532. Apparently the former was mainly responsible for the transcript, the latter for the quite important Introduction, in the course of which he is rather scathing about Whitford's Latinity and sloppiness as a translator.

Nonetheless, Whitford's work supplies for our purposes a sense of Bridgettine hagiography at its most luxuriant. Particularly because the sisters' breviary has no proper sanctorale beyond the special forms for each of the six select feasts (plus those of Bridget and Mary), it is tempting to think of them as austere in their observances of saints' days. Strictly interpreted, the sisters' office liturgy does seem to be more spare in this respect that that of any religious body we have reviewed. If what they heard in the daily chapter-house reading of the martyrology is anything like what Whitford cobbled together, however, a very different impression emerges. A Latin Bridgettine martyrology, now BL Add. 22285, survives; but whether by, at any rate, the end of the first quarter of the sixteenth century the nuns and brothers were hearing that daily reading in the Latin or in the vernacular version is not clear; and it seems sensible to suspect the latter as likelier.

The "Englishness" of the English Bridgettines

From their inception under the patronage of the self-consciously nationalistic monarch Henry V, the Bridgettines at Twickenham/Syon were understood to be more English than international. This understanding was formalized by a bull of pope Martin V, *Mare Anglicanum*, issued in 1425, recognizing the independence of the English house.[25]

We have noticed in an earlier chapter the work of the Bridgettine brother Clement Maidstone (or Maydeston; see p. 427) who some time before his death in 1456 compiled the original versions of two works: first, the *Ordinale Sarum, sive Directorium sacerdotum*, better known as the Sarum *Pica*, or *Pie*, laboriously detailed lists laying out the complexities of occurrence and concurrence according to forty-two possible schemata (six for each of the seven days of the week); and, somewhat later, the *Defensorium directorii*, a kind of *apologia* for the previous work. Precisely when these two (and another rubrical compilation called *Crede michi*) were put together is not known, but it was after he became a Bridgettine around 1430, having earlier belonged to the house at nearby Hounslow of the obscure, quasi-fraternal Trinitarians. The popularity of his major works was so great that widespread circulation of the printed versions of 1487 and thereafter have made them seem more reflective of the turn of the fifteenth century than of its middle

---

[25] Consequently the new customary of the brothers of the orders, composed at the mother house of Vadstena in the mid-15th cent., did not apply to those of Syon: S. Risberg, ed. *Liber usuum fratrum monasterii Vadstenensis*, Acta Universitatis Stockholmiensis, Studia Latina Stockholmiensia 50 (2003), esp. p. 19.

third. The point here is that the scholar who appears to be the ranking authority on the Sarum liturgy at that time is not a secular cleric, let alone a canon of Salisbury, but a Bridgettine brother who himself uses the Sarum rite – and clearly finds it fascinating. In the prologue to the *Directorium* Maidstone makes plain his religious affiliation, stating that he works to the praise and glory of the Blessed Virgin Mary, St Joseph her spouse, and Blessed Bridget, "in cuius religione professor indignus existo"; emphasizing at the same time that he is explicating the ordinal of Sarum, which he is bound to follow and of which he is indeed *studiosus relator* (or perhaps even *zelator*).[26]

In their different ways, Maidstone and Whitford witness to the salient character of Bridgettine liturgy alluded to earlier: the predominance of the English secular strand over the international religious. To recapitulate: its male office (and mass, celebrated solely by males) is that of Sarum, with only the three feasts of Bridget as notable additions; its female office, while totally distinctive and not at all English in content, is presented in service books with vernacular rubrics and with, at its core, an account of the foundress's vision and of the *historiae* that relate it – both translated into English. Had the religious houses of England not been dissolved in 1536–39, and had vernacular translations of the Latin office, and even mass, become widespread, it is hard to believe that the Bridgettines would not have been in the forefront of those welcoming the change.

The *Nova festa* and para-liturgical "feasts"

One characteristic of liturgy in England by the early sixteenth century is a strong interest in a series of new feasts or of devotions approximating the character of feasts. All have in common that they are not feasts of saints, like those mandated by Chichele in 1415 (p. 439 above), but of a biblical and/or devotional sort. The vagaries and complexities of their coming to be observed were traced in a book, now nearly forty years old, by the present author, and will not be rehearsed here.[27] The principal ones of these are the Transfiguration, which came to be celebrated

---

26 *Ordinale Sarum sive Directorium sacerdotum*, ed. C. Wordsworth (from transcription by W. Cooke), 2 vols, HBS 20 and 22 (both 1901), I.24. The main text followed is the printing of Richard Pynson, London 1497, somewhat revised by a Cambridge Master of Arts, W. Clerke; this edition has *relator*; but printings of 1487 and 1488 read *zelator*. An edition from MSS, of which there is a preliminary list in Wordsworth's, I.xviii, would be welcome.

27 My *New Liturgical Feasts in Later Medieval England* (Oxford 1970), often referred to in the previous pages. So much material has come to be available that a proper new edition would threaten to be twice the size of the original book.

on August 6th; the Visitation, on July 2nd; and the Name of Jesus, on August 7th. The Visitation was officially promulgated in 1481, but had been observed to a considerable extent for some decades before that. Likewise, a papal bull of 1457 had supposedly prescribed observance of the Transfiguration, but that feast has an even stronger "pre-history" than the Visitation, and the bull does not seem to have been particularly decisive in England. The Holy Name has as its nucleus a votive mass, the popularity of which seems to have spawned, so to speak, a feast with elaborate hymns and office texts. This popularity, rather than any papal involvement, led to official recognition by the Convocations of Canterbury in 1488 and of York the following year.

To these three widely popular feasts should be added four or five that had varying degrees of acceptance. Two were Marian. One, the Compassion of the Virgin, looks in England to originate as both a votive mass and a votive office, but no feast day seems ever to have been fixed; some time in Passiontide would have been logical. The affective theme of the Virgin's sorrow at the suffering and death of her son, expressed in painting and sculpture in the subject called *Pietà*, leads to this mass sometimes being called *de Pietate*, from the opening words of its collect, "Pietatem tuam." How the vital factor of printing both reflects and contributes to the popularity of a devotion possibly on its way to becoming a feast is demonstrated by the venture of William Caxton in printing an office "Commemoracio lamentacionis sive compassionis beate Marie" to be celebrated the Friday before Passion Sunday. There was apparently just a single edition (1490), of which only one copy survives; and the devotion did not become a feast.

Contrasting in both antiquity and specificity of date is the feast mostly known in the later middle ages as the Presentation of the Virgin and observed on November 21st. It is in fact the same, in occasion and date, as what was called, apparently from the early eleventh century, the Oblation of the Virgin. This was present in England – and may indeed have originated there, or possibly in Ireland – in a few monastic contexts, and its spasmodic subsequent appearances have been noticed often in these pages (for example, in the Sherborne missal; see p. 240). Its late medieval popularity, and distinctive name, can probably be traced to the persuasiveness of a returning Crusader, Philippe de Mézières, who in 1372 convinced both Charles V of France and Pope Gregory XI to embrace the feast, for which he had composed a mass and office. These are included in many late medieval Sarum missals and breviaries, though there continued something of an older tradition among regular clergy of simply adapting forms for the Virgin's Nativity – not illogically, since the feast commemorates the ancient apocryphal story, from the *Protevangelium* or *Book of James*, of Mary's being presented (or offered, *oblacio*), as a three-year-old child, for service of the Temple by her parents.

Two other of these observances reflect the intense devotion widespread in the later middle ages to the sufferings of Christ: the Five Wounds, like the Name of Jesus in origin a votive mass, and the Crown of Thorns (or *Corona Domini*). The former never came to be associated with a precise day nor, in England, to have a proper office; in the strict sense it is never a feast, only a votive mass. But this mass of the Wounds, probably imported from the Continent, enjoyed great popularity in England – popularity enhanced by a rubric that incorporates the legend of a pope's being miraculously healed by the merits of this mass and therefore issuing a generous indulgence for its celebration.

The reception of the Crown of Thorns at Paris by Louis IX in 1239 seems to have been the impetus for a feast centering on that devotional object. The feast was taken up by, in particular, the Dominicans, and was observed sometimes on August 11th but more often on May 4th. How such a feast emerges – a verb useful more than once in thinking about the present subject – is shown by a psalter with votive masses that belonged to Oliver Whetenal, who was vicar of Besthorpe in Norfolk from 1445 to 1469 (now Bodl. Don. d.85). One of the votive masses added in a different hand from that of the orginal book is headed "In festo corone domini," with a separate Alleluia specified for the period after Ascension Day, so a date in May is likely (fol. 103v; though nothing has been added to the calendar).

One further instance – it can hardly be characterized as even an "incipient" feast – centered on a very old story of the Ritual Murder sort, a tale, supposedly set in Beirut and given the authority of Athanasius's name, which was apparently offered in aid of the Iconodule cause at the Second Council of Nicaea in 787: the tortured object being in this case not a person but an image, most often called the *Iconia Domini*. Unlike the previous two, the emergence here as anything like a feast springs not from a more or less votive mass but from a lengthy office, found in Sarum breviaries printed in 1495, 1516, and 1531.[28] A mass seems to have come into existence by the early sixteenth century also. When it appears it, like the office, tends to be placed at November 9th, very likely through confusion or conflation with the date assigned to the dedication

---

[28] I have been trying for many years to sort out the complexities of the liturgical observance of this "feast," as distinct from the Ritual Murder aspect to which it bears witness and about which there is a large literature centering on the anti-Semitism to which the story contributed markedly.

of the (old) Lateran basilica, originally called something like "Basilica Salvatoris." This is reflected in the heading "Festum Salvatoris" sometimes encountered – another instance of a feast starting to appear from liturgical haze, one that was here many centuries a-building.

Sanctoral luxuriance: Elizabeth Shelford's book of liturgical devotions

The fascination with liturgical and para-liturgical feasts suggested by the preceding paragraphs is well illustrated by a devotional book (now Fitzwilliam Museum, Cambridge, 2–1957) of some 132 folios which was written in, probably, the first decade of the sixteenth century for Elizabeth Shelford, perhaps to mark her election in 1505 as abbess at her nunnery of Shaftesbury.[29] It contains an elaborate calendar, forms for prime throughout the year, the so-called "Capitular office" (reading of the martyrology and a portion of the Rule of Benedict, plus devotional accretions), Hours of the Virgin and (to a limited extent) of the Cross, *memoriae* to various saints, the Penitential Psalms and litany, Votive Office of the Virgin, Office of the Dead, and a lengthy *ordo* for the commendation of souls. So it is misleading to call this simply Hours of the Virgin, as the modern catalogue does. Rather, we may take it as indicating, at least in part, some of Dame Elizabeth's varied liturgical proclivities.

These are most evident in the calendar, which though a highly personal document may provide also rare information about feasts possibly observed at Shaftesbury – information otherwise confined largely to the celebrated Shaftesbury psalter of the third quarter of the twelfth century (BL Lansdowne 383; p. 345 above). Although, as we have often reminded ourselves, appearance in a calendar by no means guarantees liturgical celebration, Dame Elizabeth's calendar looks as though it may reflect actual usage as well as enthusiasm. Here we find entered the Transfiguration, *Festivitas corone domini* (4 May), *Miracula sancte Crucis* (9 November: the *Iconia domini* feast), and the Visitation as *triplex* (the highest grade), as is also the Oblation of the Virgin, under that wording rather than Presentation.[30] Striking as well are the

---

[29] The extensive treatment in F. Wormald and P. M. Giles, ed., *A Descriptive Catalogue of the Additional Illuminated Manuscripts in the Fitzwilliam Museum Acquired between 1895 and 1979 (excluding the McClean Collection)* (Cambridge 1982), pp. 516–22, includes many but by no means all of the details noted below. A partial edition of the MS would be very welcome.

[30] Had I known this MS when writing *New Liturgical Feasts* I would have highlighted it as perhaps the most vivid example of the popularity of the liturgical phenomenon of these *nova festa*.

numbers of translation feasts and also those of twelve lessons (often with octaves). The former include, as well as the Translation of Edward the Martyr (Shaftesbury's principal saint, having been buried there in 980), those of Mary Magdalene (19 March), Nicholas (20 April), Audoen (5 May), Bartholomew (13 June), Richard (16 June), Becket (7 July), Swithun (15 July), Osmund (16 July), Æthelwold (12 August), and Edith (3 November). Many of these are marked as being of twelve lessons, but so are numerous other and surprising feasts, such as Mary of Egypt (2 April), Alphege (19 April), Aldhelm (25 May), Grimbald (8 July), Martha (29 July), Gabriel the Archangel (2 September: a borrowing from Exeter?), Ethelburga (12 October), Savinian and Potentian (19 October), Austreberta (20 October), and Osmund (4 December).[31] There is also a sprinkling of hard-to-account-for nuns: Modwenna (mainly culted at Burton-on-Trent, here at the unusual day of 9 July), Elfleda (of Glastonbury, 23 October, not the better known Northumbrian saint of that name), Edburga of Winchester (misspelled as "Coburga," 15 June), as well as the less surprising Edith (as a *triplex*; she has also a Translation feast), Osith, and Cuthburga. Possibly unique in an English calendar is Aurea, after Francis on 4 October (in red, with eight lessons; she is supposed to have been a Syrian religious who became abbess at St Martial in Paris in the early sixth century).

Local notables are not neglected. Besides Edward the Martyr, Shaftesbury's "own" saints were Elgiva (Ælfgifu) and "Brithelm." The former, the queen-wife of Edmund of Wessex, was regarded after her death in 944 as a second or co-foundress of the nunnery; she has two feast days, 18 May and 18 August, in the calendar. In the section on the commendation of souls, she is coupled, as receiving an "anniversary" celebration, with Brithelm (correctly, Beorhthelm), probably a West Saxon bishop around the time the house was founded.[32] The rubric there mentions, without specifying, his feast day, and refers to his tomb as the goal of a procession.

---

[31] Calling especially for investigation are Savinian (elsewhere spelled Sabinian) and Potentian, early martyr-bishops of Sens, whose feast day is usually Dec. 31st. F. G. Holweck, *A Biographical Dictionary of the Saints* (St Louis and London 1924), p. 877, states that at Sens itself the date was Oct. 18th, and the 19th at Chartres. Savinian and Potentian are fourth and fifth among martyrs in the litany of the Lansdowne 383 psalter, so interest in them at Shaftesbury must go back to at least the mid-12th cent. A miracle was recorded around Sens in 1068: *BHL Suppl.*, no. 7437m; might that have been the impetus?

[32] The suggested identification is John Blair's, "A Handlist of Anglo-Saxon Saints," in *Local Saints and Local Churches in the Early Medieval West*, ed. A. Thacker and R. Sharpe (Oxford 2002), pp. 494–565, at 516. There seems to have been no bishop of Sherborne of that name, and the likeliest candidate is the Beorhthelm who was bishop of Wells 956–73.

It seems worth rehearsing all of this detail because, taken in the aggregate, it suggests a woman who was something of a liturgical *connoisseuse*, having her book tailored to reflect her interests as well as perhaps supplement the office books of the house. When she died the codex came somehow into the possession of the rector of the parish church in Shaftesbury – what, we wonder, did he make of it? – and was bought back from him by a nun of the abbey, Alice Champeneys, for the not inconsiderable sum of ten shillings (there are twelve good decorative initials, though the book is not sumptuous). Alice was pensioned in 1539 and still alive in 1553; the king's instructions have been followed in the matter of erasing the word *papa* and Becket's name.

Elizabeth Shelford's book is an outstanding example of what might be called sanctoral luxuriance. Whether this luxuriance tips a notional balance, so that sanctorale occasions threaten to predominate in the liturgical year, may be considered an open question.[33] "Predominate" suggests a value judgment of the kind we are trying to avoid; unquestionably, however, there are a great many such occasions here, and it is hard not to characterize some of them as distinctly exotic.

The collectar-plus of Robert Miles, OP

A comparably instructive book is the collectar written for the prior of King's Langley, Robert Miles, in 1523 (now Fitzwilliam Museum, Cambridge, 3–1967). It remained in Dominican possession through at least the seventeenth century, mostly on the Continent, and there are dozens of additions to the calendar.[34] The sections containing capitula and collects have also been much added to, but it is possible to get close enough to the original contents to gain a sense of the balance between English elements and the traditions of the order, a matter broached in the treatment of Dominican liturgy (where the book was noticed briefly on p. 316 A continuing Dominican feature is the presence of Adalbert, the martyred bishop of Prague and "Apostle of the Slavs," at April 23rd or 24th. It is an original entry among the collects, as are the Thomas Aquinas, the Crown of Thorns, and the Eleven Thousand

---

[33] There is a detailed discussion of this problem in my article, "Telling Liturgical Times in the Middle Ages," in *Procession, Performance, Liturgy, and Ritual*, ed. N. van Deusen (Ottawa 2007), pp. 43–64 at 57–61.

[34] The careful description in Wormald and Giles, *Fitzwilliam Additional MSS*, pp. 533–39, lists all the additions, but some claimed as "Continental, 17th cent." seem in fact to be either original entries or English additions of the 16th. In the 1964 edition of *MLGB* it belonged to Blackfriars at Oxford and is listed, with a query, for King's Langley.

Virgins, but there are also English figures such as Botulph, Cuthbert, Dunstan, Richard, and Winifred.

Miles was a man of education and, one would guess, sophistication: a Cambridge Doctor of Theology (1520) and from 1525 Prior Provincial of the English Dominicans.[35] The final items in the book are lengthy sections on communicating the sick, last rites, and the burial "in nostro cimeterio" (presumably, that at King's Langley) of an *extraneus*, someone to whom the community would be wise to afford the privilege ("si talis fuerit qui a conventu suscipi debeat"). His successor as prior of that prominent friary (on which, see p. 319), Richard Ingworth, occurs in that office in 1530 and seven years later becomes bishop of Dover and one of Thomas Cromwell's henchmen in the campaign against religious houses. Miles's book seems to have gone to the friaries at Worcester and then Warwick and shows up again in 1557 at the Dominican house re-established for a short time at London (Smithfield). It may have been something of a curiosity by then, for it is likely to have been one of the last service books (as distinct from books of liturgical devotions) to have been hand-written in England. By 1523 the vast majority of new production was in printed form.

Printed service books

The field of early printed books has been investigated in such minute and sophisticated ways that it is not easy to avoid being bogged down in facts which, generally fascinating in themselves, are peripheral to our purposes here. Two pitfalls in particular are to be circumambulated. The first is the disproportionate weight attached to the idea of incunabula. Whether a Latin service book was printed before or after 1501 makes no difference to us, save that those printed before that date have on the whole been studied more intensively than the later ones. The second is the problem that, paradoxically, is presented by the marvellous tools known to students by their initials, STC and EEBO.[36]

---

[35] A. B. Emden, *Biog. Reg. Univ. Oxf. 1501–1540* (Oxford 1974), p. 397.
[36] STC (or ESTC) refers to A. W. Pollard and G. R. Redgrave, *A Short-Title Catalogue of Books Printed in England, Scotland, and Ireland and of English Books Printed Abroad 1475–1640*, 2nd edn rev. and enlarged by W. A. Jackson, F. S. Ferguson, and K. F. Pantzer (London 1976–91). Early English Books Online (EEBO) is an electronic resource produced by Chadwyck-Healey which (so the website claims) "contains digital facsimile page images of virtually every work printed in England, Ireland, Scotland, Wales and British North America and works in English printed elsewhere from 1473–1700." The final clause means that Latin liturgical books printed on the Continent for use in England are not included, a serious limitation for study of the present subject.

Although, employed together, they enable one to look at images of all the pages of most of the books of interest to us, a frustrating amount falls under their net: most pointedly, perhaps, the 1531 folio Sarum breviary printed in Paris by Claude Chevallon and taken as the basis of that "modern" edition by Procter and Wordsworth so often referred to in the present work. In short, the tools of "bibliography" in its literal sense may be of only limited use to us; we need to look at the subject with other concerns in mind than the technicalities of printing and printers. As might be expected, the overwhelming majority of printed service books is for secular rather than religious use.

The compilations of data by earlier students are almost entirely concerned with printed books for secular Uses. These compilations go back to the list put together by Francis Henry Dickinson in 1850 (see p. 425) – still the only compendium of information about printed editions of all the types of service books (as he classified them) of the three clearly identifiable English "Uses." The information contained there was much elaborated in his pioneering edition of the (printed) Sarum missal, presented in five detailed if somewhat confusing appendices.[37] The much more extensive, indeed discursive, lists of printed Sarum service books in any way related to the daily office that were compiled by Henry Bradshaw in the mid-1880s, published as an appendix to the final volume of the Procter and Wordsworth edition, by definition omit all those related to the mass and anything pertaining to York or Hereford. Editors of the service books of those Uses have for the most part provided lists of the printings of the books in question; these are discussed in the relevant chapters above. All these undertakings tried to include indications of ownership and/or location, but much has changed in this respect in the course of the last century and a half.

Armed with the benefits of all this previous labor, and aware of some of its negative aspects, we may find both some simple observations and some unanswerable questions proposing themselves. The first of the former is that both of the earliest service books to be printed for use in England date are not, as we might expect, missals, but Sarum breviaries: a quarto printed probably in Cologne in 1475 (only fragments survive, in four different locations) and a complete octavo-size volume printed in Venice in 1483.[38] Not until 1486, and at Basel, was a Sarum

---

[37] The edition (on this, see p. 416) appeared in fascicles from 1861 to 1883; the preface was supposedly put in type in 1873, so these appendices, which are there explained, pre-date most of the major reference works on bibliography.

[38] The 1483 breviary was stolen from the CUL and ended up as the property of the Irish-French collector Justin MacCarthy Reagh ("Count MacCarthy," 1744–1811);

missal printed, by Michael Wenssler; but for what English bookseller is not known. The oddity here is that a breviary is a much more complicated book to set in type than a missal; so there must have been some sense of a market or need for a complete printed book for the daily office before there was a comparable sense for the mass.

The next thing to notice is the attention paid by early printers to marketability. This is clear from the very first liturgical book printed in England, and by the first English printer, William Caxton: a printing of the *Ordinale Sarum* – so-called, in fact the "Pie" of Clement Maydeston (see p. 427) – in 1477. The previous year Caxton had brought the press he had been operating in Bruges for four or five years to England and based himself near Westminster abbey. The 1477 *Ordinale* was marketed with the aid of an "Advertisement" in English, emphasizing its special convenience for those whose churches were dedicated to the Virgin Mary and who therefore did not have to factor in a weekly commemoration for the dedicatee saint as well as those for her and Becket.[39] This eye to what would sell is evident also in three *libelli* produced by Caxton which reflected popularity of the *nova festa*: *Festum visitationis beatae Mariae uirginis* possibly as early as 1481, *Commemoracio lamentacionis Mariae* in 1490, and *Festum transfiguracionis Iesu Christi* probably in 1491.[40] Similarly, the Sarum missal printed for him in Paris by Guillaume Maynal in 1487 had the English portions of the marriage rite left blank, to be filled in by hand – presumably to avoid Francophone garbling – upon arrival in England. (The same French printer produced a *Legenda secundum usum Sarum*, also in 1487, almost, but not quite certainly, for Caxton.)

We should note also that for quite a long time Continental, not English, printers produced the great majority of service books for all three secular uses. All five editions of the York missal (1509, 1516, 1517, 1530, 1533) were printed in either Rouen or Paris, the two or three York breviaries (1493, 1526, possibly 1530) in Venice or Paris, and both the sole Hereford missal (1502) and sole Hereford breviary (1505) in Rouen. Of the roughly thirty-three editions of the Sarum breviary between 1475 and 1541 only two were printed in England: a folio of 1506 by Wynkyn

---

after his death it was sold to the Bibliothèque Nationale: E. G. Duff, *Fifteenth Century English Books* (Oxford 1917), no. 61.

[39] Facsimile of an excerpt in N. F. Blake, *Caxton: England's First Publisher* (London 1975), p. 42.

[40] Only a few leaves survive of the *Festum visitationis*; the others range from 10 to 32 leaves. In 1493, the year after Caxton's death, his successor Richard Pynson published a *Festum nominis Iesu*, thus completing the forms for the most popular *nova festa*; this was repeated in 1497, slightly smaller.

de Worde (only fragments survive) and a folio two years later, on vellum, by Richard Pynson.[41] The situation was much the same with Sarum missals: besides the 1487 book printed in Paris for Caxton, mentioned above, and a 1498 printing commissioned by de Worde at Westminster, only four were printed in England, all by Pynson and all folios: in 1500 (at the expense of archbishop Morton, apparently for Henry VII), 1504 (on vellum, perhaps for Morton himself), 1512, and 1520.[42] The splendor of Pynson's productions and the lack of other English printings of the missal suggest that the Continental copies may have been cheaper. Indeed, the canon section of his 1500 folio is in manuscript, with decoration as elaborate as the finest of books entirely written by hand.[43]

An obvious question is whether this Continental predominance was a function more of English technological backwardness or of a sense on the part of English printers that the market for liturgica was less great than for other kinds of books. It is striking that, as H. S. Bennett observed, with the exception of Caxton and possibly one or two obscure figures, "all the printers at work [in England] until 1513 appear to have come from abroad"; and he goes on to point out that "Not less than 60% of all breviaries, books of hours (or primers), manuals, misssals, etc. printed by 1557 came from overseas presses, despite the restrictions on the importation of books printed abroad from time to time."[44] Students of the earliest printing in England tend to stress, as G. D. Painter has put it, "the inability of English printers to rise to the required magnificence of type-founts and woodcut decoration, and to meet the exceptional technical demands of high-quality red-printing, music printing, and beauty of setting" that characterized the best missals.[45] Continental printers

[41] In 1541 and 1543–44 there appeared editions of "King Harry's Breviary," omitting the name of the pope and making other changes; these (respectively a tiny 16mo and an octavo, both in two vols) were printed at London by Grafton and Whitchurch. They properly form part of the Reformation story.

[42] Noteworthy also is the Sarum missal printed by Ulrich Gering with B. Rembolt of Strasbourg c. 1498 and given by Humphrey de la Pole to Gonville Hall, Cambridge, for use in its chapel: now Gonville and Caius College, Incun. 86. (I owe knowledge, and a sight, of this to David Abulafia.)

[43] Illustrated in D. McKitterick, Print, Manuscript and the Search for Order, 1450–1830 (Cambridge 2003), figs. 4 (beginning of the canon) and 5 (end of MS and beginning of printed sections): from the copy in Trinity College, Cambridge, VI.18.21. The canon page on the Bodleian copy (Auct. I Q.infra), from which the EEBO reproduction is taken [STC 16173], is not nearly as elaborately decorated, and the T[e igitur] initial has not been filled in. Two other copies are extant.

[44] H. S. Bennett, English Books and Readers 1475 to 1557, 2nd edn (Cambridge 1969), pp. 30 and 66. Various levels of restrictions, for example in 1515, 1523, and 1529, culminated in an Act of Parliament in 1534 effectively shutting down the foreign element in the English book trade.

[45] G. D. Painter (with D. E. Rhodes and H. M. Nixon), "Two Missals Printed for Wynkyn de Worde," British Library Journal 2 (1976), pp. 159–71 at 159.

seem to have perceived a demand, and frequently used a woodcut of St George and the Dragon at the beginning, or occasionally the end, of Sarum missals.[46]

Service books for Lady Margaret Beaufort

The aspect of splendor – what would be called in the manuscript world high-status books – must to some degree have warred with the factor of producing multiple copies that is one of the salient advantages of printing. The Pynson Sarum missals mentioned above are clearly at the high-status end of the range. We wonder next what the case would have been when large numbers of service books were required at close to the same time. The outstanding case here is that of Lady Margaret Beaufort, mother of Henry VII and a formidable intellectual figure in her own right. In addition to furnishing books for a chapel at Westminster Abbey that was regarded as "hers" and for a domestic chapel at her principal residence at Colleyweston (Lincolnshire), she had a hand in the provision of service books for her magnificent foundation of Christ's College in Cambridge. Her activities in this respect have been studied by Susan Powell, mostly through the archives at St John's College, the other foundation Lady Margaret projected (but did not live to see established in 1511, two years after her death).[47]

An inventory of her "domestic" chapel records, among numerous service books, eight antiphonals (one valued at eight pounds) and seventeen processionals. These figures seem roughly congruous with the chapel personnel, a dean and sub-dean, twelve chaplains, twelve "gentlemen" (presumably singing-men), and ten children.[48] No antiphonals were printed in or for England until 1519–20 (the sole edition), nor any processionals until 1508, so all of those books in her chapel must have been manuscripts. Some at least of the twenty mass books recorded in the same inventory must, however, have been printed. She gave to her chapel at Westminster "ii new messe bookes in prynt velym," and the loose quires noted in the inventory are the *libelli*, mentioned earlier, of offices of the Compassion (alias Lamentation), Transfiguration,

[46] Y.-C. Wang, "The Image of St George and the Dragon," *The Library*, 7th ser. 5 (2004), pp. 370–401 at 394–97. Ten of thirty-five Sarum missals printed abroad from 1497 to 1534 had such images at the beginning, three at the end; at least six printers used the same image.

[47] S. Powell, "Lady Margaret Beaufort and her Books," *The Library*, 6th ser. 20 (1998), pp. 197–240, esp. 204–13.

[48] Powell, p. 205, n. 48, taken from F. Kisby, "The Early-Tudor Royal Household Chapel 1485–1547," unpublished Univ. of London doctoral thesis, 1996. The figures are for 1508.

Visitation, and Holy Name – the last being apparently the most intense focus of her devotional life.[49] In the years 1505–8 there were purchased for the chapel at Christ's not only "some masbokes printed in velime" but also six antiphonals and two graduals, chant-books that, again, must have been in manuscript.[50] One further connection between Lady Margaret and printed liturgical books is her sponsorship of the sole edition of the Hereford breviary (see above, p. 478), that printed by Inghelbert Haghe at Rouen in 1505. A wordy dedication by Haghe mentions specifically her initiative, but hints nothing as to why this project might have been of special interest to her.

Service books for the religious orders

Different sorts of questions have to be asked about books for use in religious houses. Here the presumption has been, in James Clark's words, "that monastic books and book-collections had fallen into neglect" by the middle of the fifteenth century; he contends, however, that "this approach overlooks a significant body of evidence that suggests that the monastic order did develop a special interest in the new technology."[51] That may be true in general, but whether this interest manifested itself in the production and purchase of printed liturgical books remains to be determined.

An instructive case is that of William More, prior of Worcester 1518–36. A list of some eighty-four items giving details of books bought by him includes at least half a dozen liturgical books in manuscript and three "masse boks of print."[52] The first of the latter cost three shillings and four pence, the other two being four shillings and two pence for the pair; very likely they were, as the modern editor suggests, Sarum missals. By contrast, the "new masbok beying at Jesus awter" that More had made in 1519 cost him over six pounds, including flourishing and gilting, and a "new great grayle [gradual] beyng before the prior in

---

[49] Powell, pp. 208–11, summarizes evidence for how intense this was and provides an important supplement to my treatment of the subject in *New Liturgical Feasts*. There was also apparently an office (?) for the 6th-cent. hermit St Nectan (ibid., p. 205); is this in some way a remembrance of Lady Margaret's husband, Edmund Tudor (d. 1456), the father of Henry VII?

[50] Powell, p. 237; the three antiphonals bought in 1507 cost a total of £18 and must again have been rather fine books.

[51] J. G. Clark, "Print and Pre-Reformation Religious: the Benedictines and the Press, c. 1470–c. 1550," in *The Uses of Script and Print, 1300–1700*, ed. J. Crick and A. Walsham (Cambridge 2004), pp. 71–92 at 74.

[52] Edited by R. Sharpe in *English Benedictine Libraries: the Shorter Catalogues*, CBMLC 4 (1996), pp. 664–74, at 664, 666, 667.

the quyre" a bit more. No costs are given for the four other books, so they may not have been greatly expensive, in contrast to the "ii claspes of selver and gylt to the priors masboke in his chappell at Worceter," for which he paid six shillings and eight pence. He also made a point of redeeming "a litle portuos [portiforium]" left by a predecessor at Rome, and then had it bound and furnished with silver-gilt clasps at a total cost of nineteen shillings. It looks as though to More the printed books may have been an inexpensive modern curiosity, whereas he expected to pay substantial amounts for the writing and preservation of books for actual liturgical use.

At Durham the dozens of numerous surviving printed books include none of a directly liturgical sort.[53] Nor does there seem to be any-thing liturgical among the numerous extant printed books ascribed to a great range of religious houses, with a few enigmatic exceptions. We noticed above (p. 269) the existence at the London Charterhouse of a Carthusian breviary most likely printed in Venice in 1491, as well as a psalter and a book of exequies, both of which may have been printed as well. We know, too, that in 1528 John Scolar, who had recently moved from Oxford to Abingdon, printed an office book "ad usum nigrorum monachorum Abendonie."[54] Similarly, a Dutch printer named John Herford set up shop in the town of St Albans and in (prob-ably) 1535 printed there, among other books, a breviary for the abbey. There seems to survive only one copy of the St Albans book, now BL C.110.a.27, and as it is very small, c. 80 × 130 mm, it is unlikely to have been useful in choir. Around the time it was printed there were some forty-eight monks at the abbey, with more at Oxford.[55] It would seem to have made better sense if such a tiny book had been written by hand and several dozen identical choir books printed, but there is no evidence that this was done. The calendar, unmistakably that of St Albans, has been brought up to date; "Obitus Henrici septimi regis" [1509] appears at May 11th. The Visitation has an octave, the Trans-figuration is *in cappis*, and the Name of Jesus is a *festum principalis*. At the same time, there are old and/or odd occasions: in September

---

[53] Conveniently laid out by A. G. Watson in the 1987 *Supplement* to *MLGB*, pp. 16–34. The closest thing is a two-volume homiliary printed at Cologne around 1475, now Durham Cath., Inc. 13a, b.

[54] Two copies seem to survive: one in Emmanuel College, Cambridge, a *pars hiemalis* (I am grateful to Susan Rankin for confirming this) and a fragmentary one in Exeter College, Oxford. The latter (now bound with a 1554 paraphrase of Cantica Canti-corum) is apparently not a breviary proper but, as a colophon states, a psalter with hymns. The psalms, canticles, and most of the litany are lacking, and perhaps much more. (STC 15792, but neither copy has been filmed in EEBO.)

[55] *Med. Rel. Houses*, p. 71.

alone, the Ordination of Gregory (3rd), an Octave for the Decollation of John the Baptist (5th, with eight lessons), Ninian (16th, also with eight lessons). The sanctorale matches the calendar quite well, with the lessons tending to be short and many drawn from the common of saints. The number and complexity of sanctorale occasions is reflected by the fact that the *Rubrica de festis concurrentibus* with which the book ends is fifteen pages long.[56] Why, and in how many copies, this book was printed, a bare four years before St Albans and all the other major monasteries were dissolved, is a mystery.

The end of the story

As, in the light of the evidence considered above, we try – as we proposed to do at the beginning of this chapter – to weigh the validity of words like "autumn" and "tiredness" on the one hand, "freshness" and "vitality" on the other, we have to take some account of an historiographical climate epitomized, if not indeed created, by a single book: Eamon Duffy's *The Stripping of the Altars*, first published in 1992.[57] It vigorously champions a view of the worshipping life of English people c. 1450–1550 as characterized by an intense and widespread emotional and intellectual investment. This view has been questioned in some quarters, but to what extent criticism of his main thesis is valid is not an urgent concern for us.[58] Rather, we need to remind ourselves of three things. (1) Duffy has widened the field of enquiry about matters liturgical by drawing heavily on such written sources as churchwardens' accounts, wills, and gild records, and on the physical fabric of churches, particularly in East Anglia. (2) His primary concern is really with *sentiment religieuse*, above all when expressed liturgically, and his view of liturgical expression is broader than that of the present work, especially in his extensive use of Books of Hours and other manuals of private

---

[56] On the verso of the last page is a woodcut of a saint(?) with a cross in his right hand and a stick or staff in the left: who is this meant to be?

[57] The second edition, 2005, has a lengthy preface reviewing the response to the original edition and clarifying somewhat the book's stance (the body of the book is unchanged from the first edition). It should ideally be read together with Duffy's subsequent *The Voices of Morebath: Reformation and Rebellion in an English Village* (New Haven and London 2001), in effect an extended case study based on a remote Exmoor parish.

[58] The most pointed objection is that raised by D. Aers in his review article, "Altars of Power; Reflections on *The Stripping of the Altars*," *Literature and History*, 3rd ser. 3 (1994), pp. 90–105: that Duffy's almost total ignoring of Lollardy distorts the picture he seeks to paint. The present work also has almost no mention of Lollardy, an undeniably important phenomenon with, as near as I can tell, little immediate relevance in the area of liturgical history.

devotion.[59] And (3) his focus is steadily on parish churches, which from our admittedly austere standpoint of relying primarily on surviving service books yield less than cathedrals and the churches of religious of various kinds, monks, canons, and friars.

Given this range of sources, attitude to what counts as liturgical evidence, and privileging of parochial circumstances, Duffy's position is closely, if selectively, argued – and hard to dispute. The present chapter has in no sense meant to be in dialogue with, still less a refutation of, *The Stripping of the Altars*, nor of any of the recent studies, many of them exploiting the kinds of sources he has emphasized, that have tended to reinforce his view, at least as far as parish churches are concerned.[60]

Switching our attention to the liturgical life of those in religious houses, we have observed a number of cases where vitality seems palpable. These range throughout the orders. Alongside the liturgical miscellany written for the abbess of Shaftesbury around 1505 and the collectar-plus for a Dominican prior datable to 1523, both discussed earlier in this chapter, here are four reminders. First, the Carthusian from London who in 1510 took to the Charterhouse at Mount Grace a supply of new service books including at least one "conteynynge certeyn masses," doubtless those for the *Nova festa* (p. 539). Next, the partial breviary compiled by the Bridgettine nun Elizabeth Yate, building it around a printed Sarum psalter of 1522 (p. 533). Third, the book of Carmelite offices hand-written by John Bale around 1525 when he was still a friar of that order, though he was soon to become a vitriolic ultra-Protestant (p. 336). Fourth, the putative (at least) market that made it worth a printer's time and effort to set in type breviaries for Abingdon in 1528 and St Albans as late as 1535. The sense one gets from such examples is markedly contrary to that of the "bare ruined quires" in the remains at Rievaulx or Glastonbury or Bury St Edmunds. The monks can scarcely have supposed that their choirs would soon be bare, as at Abingdon, or ruinous, as at St Albans.[61]

---

[59] As is explained on p. xiv, I have largely avoided using the genre (*Horae*, primers, and the like), regarding them as at best para-liturgical: one of several matters on which he and I have differed over years of friendship.

[60] See in particular K. L. French, *The People of the Parish. Community Life in a Late Medieval Diocese* [Bath and Wells] (Philadelphia 2001), esp. ch. 6, "Liturgical Celebrations and the Cult of the Saints in Place." A similar approach, stressing ordinary parishioners in a particular locality, is M. Harvey, *Lay Religious Life in Late Medieval Durham* (Woodbridge 2006).

[61] Though at St Albans the main structure survived, narrowly, as the town's principal parish church, and from 1877 as the cathedral church of a new diocese.

The picture with cathedral and collegiate churches is a more blurred one, probably for two somewhat contradictory reasons. The first is that for roughly half the cathedrals the dissolution of the religious houses in 1535–39 meant a marked break structurally as well as liturgically; the result was that at Canterbury, Rochester, Winchester, Bath, Worcester, Ely, Norwich, Coventry, and Durham, the communities of monks (and the Augustinian canons at Carlisle) were transmuted into (much smaller) chapters of deans and canons.[62] There were, to be sure, much reduced liturgical obligations in terms both of the number and duration of the services that comprised the daily office and of the numbers of masses.[63] Acknowledging how much less, in quantitative terms, liturgical worship there was in England in 1575 from that offered in 1525 can easily lead to a feeling that the sum of such worship had become so burdensome by the former date – which by the seasonal metaphor would be something like the "December" of the middle ages – that it was ready to topple of its own weight. The numerous liturgical changes on the Continent, including those mandated at the Council of Trent, may lend substance to this feeling.

On the other hand – the second reason – the founding between 1438 and 1555 of numerous colleges at Oxford (seven) and Cambridge (also seven) meant in effect an infusion of new collegiate churches, like Lady Margaret Beaufort's Cambridge foundations of Christ's and St John's, noticed above; Magdalen College, Oxford, with a choral tradition unbroken almost from its establishment in 1458; and, perhaps most vivid, King's College, Cambridge, its chapel going up by fits and starts over a period of some six decades. In one dimension in particular – ironically, the one steadily ignored here – the musical, so much evidence from these foundations (and outside the universities as well, like the collegiate church at Tattershall in Lincolnshire, founded in 1439) has been uncovered and recorded in the past half century or so as to give an impression of tremendous vitality.

The story of the dissolution of the religious houses, and more pointedly of the suppression of the Latin liturgy in England and its replacement by the English liturgy of the Book of Common Prayer in 1549, is ground that cannot be gone over here. Calling our final chapter

---

[62] Also, for the ten years 1540–50, Westminster, as the cathedral of a short-lived diocese of that name.

[63] This would have been true also of the nine secular cathedrals (London, Chichester, Salisbury, Exeter, Wells [with Bath], Hereford, Lichfield [with Coventry], Lincoln, and York), which, though undergoing liturgical change, remained constitutionally steady.

"Towards the End of the Story" is meant simply to underline the fact that, as our subject of study had a discrete beginning at the close of the sixth century, so it has an end in the second quarter of the sixteenth century. The relationship between this story and the story of the vast religious and cultural changes in England from the 1530s on is an absorbing one – but not to the purpose of this book.

Index of Manuscripts

Aberystwyth, National Library of Wales
15536E: 441
Alnwick Castle 505a: 535n

Berlin, Deutsche Staatsbibliothek
Hamilton 553: 53n
Lat. 105 (Phillipps sacramentary): 42,
57n
Blackburn, Museum and Art Gallery
091.21195: 267n
Bologna, Bibl. univ. 2565 (Bologna
missal): 153n, 168, 357–63 *passim*,
369, 375, 380–86 *passim*, 405, 421,
500n, 507n
Boston, Public Library 1576 (f 151):
451–52
Bristol
Baptist College
Z.c.23 (formerly, now privately
owned): 104n, 347
Z.d.40: see Cambridge University
Library Add. 8885
Public Library
2: 290n
12: 260n
Bury St Edmunds, West Suffolk Record
Office E 5/9/408.7: 194n

Cambrai, Bibliothèque municipale
162–63: 155
164 (Hadrianum Gregorian
sacramentary): 57n
Cambridge
Corpus Christi College
9: 161n, 212, 222n
41: 66
44: 92n
53: 441n
93: 335, 393n, 400, 404n
141: 536–37
146 (Samson pontifical): 122

173: 103n
191: 130n
201: 67n
265 (Ælfric's letter): 86
270 (St Augustine's missal): 93,
113–17, 118, 122, 149, 154, 161,
162, 163, 185–86, 283
286: 37
367: 174n
391 (Wulfstan portiforium): 121,
126–29, 134, 136, 150, 161n,
163n, 175, 212, 214, 214n, 226–27,
382, 383
422 (Red Book of Darley): 94–96,
176, 178n, 362, 382n, 491n
465 (Norwich customary): 203–8
470: 206
473 (Corpus Winchester troper): 85
Emmanuel College 252: 276n
Fitzwilliam Museum
2-1957: 542–44
3-1967: 316, 544–45
34: 451
369 (Lewes breviary-missal): 244,
245–46
McClean 16: 314
McClean 45: 344
Gonville and Caius College 732/771:
267
Jesus College
A.12 (12): 267
Q.B.14 (31): 514
Q.G.7 (55): 302–3
King's College 31: 164, 247
Magdalene College
F.4.11: 531–32, 533, 535
F.4.12: 532–33
Pembroke College
120: 195n
226: 308–9
Peterhouse College 276: 270n

Index of Saints

This is an index of persons who have feasts in one or more witnesses, or who are included in calendars and litanies. Some names not in their original forms have been normalized into what seems the commonest English usage; e.g., Albert the Great, not Albertus Magnus; Brice, not Britius; Etheldreda, not Ætheldrytha or Æthelthryth. Ælfheah/Alphege (and variants) is a special case, here usually given the Old English spelling in contexts before the Conquest. Minor differences in spelling (like Maccabees/Machabees, Osith/Osyth) are ignored. The main feasts relating to Christ and the Virgin Mary are also included.

General Index

Place names and historical characters are indexed only for pages at which there is substantive discussion (liturgical commemorations are in the separate Index of Saints). Modern scholars mentioned in the text are included, as are those named in the footnotes if there is analytical or qualitative comment as distinct from mere bibliographical reference. Medieval persons widely known as "of somewhere," like Francis of Assisi or Richard of Chichester, are generally indexed under their given names; nonetheless, clear surnames take precedence even if they once designated places of origin: John (de) Grandisson under Grandisson, Henry Chichele under Chichele. The prepositions "de" and "of" are ignored in alphabetization; "ch." = "[parish] church." Specific designations (abbot, bishop, etc.) are provided only when there is otherwise likely to be confusion or unclarity.